George Grote, Alexander Bain

The Minor Works of George Grote

With Critical Remarks on His Intellectual Character, Writings, and Speeches

George Grote, Alexander Bain

The Minor Works of George Grote
With Critical Remarks on His Intellectual Character, Writings, and Speeches

ISBN/EAN: 9783742857156

Manufactured in Europe, USA, Canada, Australia, Japa

Cover: Foto ©Andreas Hilbeck / pixelio.de

Manufactured and distributed by brebook publishing software
(www.brebook.com)

George Grote, Alexander Bain

The Minor Works of George Grote

THE

MINOR WORKS

OF

GEORGE GROTE.

WITH

CRITICAL REMARKS ON HIS INTELLECTUAL CHARACTER,
WRITINGS, AND SPEECHES,

By ALEXANDER BAIN.

PREFACE.

In the present volume are brought together the most important of Mr. Grote's minor writings. The subjects are very varied; in all of them the composition is highly wrought; and the scholarly and philosophical essays are for the most part treated in a popular manner.

The earliest work of the author given at full is the 'Essentials of Parliamentary Reform.' It came out at the commencement of his public and parliamentary career, and sets forth in a systematic shape his theory of Representative Government. Since the date of its publication this country has passed through forty years of unexampled political excitement and discussion; nevertheless, from the thoroughness of the author's grasp of political principles, the freshness and vigour of his illustration, and, not least, the high moral tone pervading the whole, the work is neither antiquated nor commonplace. In particular, his mode of supporting the doctrine that makes property the basis of the franchise, so far from being hackneyed by repetition, has lain unused on occasions when it might have been employed with effect.

The short paper on Hobbes is a notice of the first

and second volumes of Sir William Molesworth's luxurious and complete edition of Hobbes's writings. An interesting account of the circumstances that led Molesworth to undertake the edition, at a considerable outlay, is given by Mrs. Grote ('Life,' p. 128). The notice is exceedingly characteristic of its author, and reproduces some of his most deep-seated convictions, and most frequent topics of conversation.

The article on Grecian Legends, published in 1843, was preparatory to the first part of the 'History of Greece,' which deals with Legendary Greece ; going over the ground of the sixteenth and seventeenth chapters of the work. It is not bereft of its interest by the more expanded handling in those chapters. One of the examples given of a myth created in our own times, has been reckoned a felicitous contribution to the author's general theory.

The article on Boeckh's 'Metrology,' published in 1844, in the *Classical Museum*, is a careful and elaborate estimate of the evidence remaining to us respecting Ancient Measures, Weights, and Money. The interest of the discussion is not confined to the scholar. By means of the usages relative to the standards of measure, weight, and money coinage, the general reader will obtain glimpses of ancient life, while ample proofs are afforded of the Eastern origin of this part of Greek and Roman civilisation.

The 'Presidential Address to the City of London Scientific Institution,' and the 'Address on delivering the prizes at University College,' are deliberately composed, and express the speaker's sentiments as to the aims of young men preparing themselves for the work of life. The pursuit of knowledge, both as a means, and for its own sake, is strongly put forward in combination with a high ideal of self-reliance and patriotic citizenship.

The Review of Sir George Lewis's work, on the 'Credibility of Early Roman History,' is both an interesting summary of the work, and a close criticism of its positions. Concurring with the author in his standard of historical evidence, and in his reprobation of the long-prevalent looseness of historical statements, Mr. Grote points out instances where he thinks Lewis's scepticism is carried too far. The reader will be gratified to see the agreements and the differences of these two great authorities, as to the historical value of the earliest Roman records.

The article (originally published as a pamphlet) on Plato's Doctrine respecting the Rotation of the Earth, is throughout polemical, and on that ground alone shows the author to advantage. The point in dispute is—Whether Plato maintained the Rotation of the Earth about its axis, in opposition to the then received view of its being stationary. To have anticipated the greatest of astronomical discoveries would have been immensely to his honour. The question apparently involves the meaning of a Greek word; but it really turns upon a very different consideration, namely, whether Plato could hold two doctrines inconsistent with each other—the revolution of the starry sphere and the revolution of the earth. Plato, in a fanciful manner of his own, maintained both doctrines, and did not feel the inconsistency; and, Mr. Grote, so far from being shocked or astonished at the circumstance as his opponents appear to be, characteristically regards it as a very frequent situation of the human mind. The discussion brings out some curious specimens of ancient modes of thinking.

The 'Review of John Stuart Mill's Examination of Sir William Hamilton's Philosophy' is a studied production, and takes a wide scope. It is prefaced by a warm eulogium on the elder Mill, which has a permanent biographical value. Before entering upon the Examination of Hamilton, Mr. Grote surveys the other works of its author—the 'Logic,' the 'Political Economy,' and the 'Liberty'; and avows his own obligations more particularly to the 'Logic.' The review of the work on Hamilton lucidly discusses the chief topic in debate, and is distinguished among other points for pronouncing a more favourable opinion upon Hamilton on the whole than that expressed by Mill as the result of his critical examination.

The Papers on Philosophy are printed from the author's MSS. The principal topic handled in them is the great question of Metaphysics—the Perception of the External World, on which Mr. Grote had long and intently meditated, but without having published his conclusions. There is also a criticism written shortly before his death on some parts of M. Taine's work, 'De l'Intelligence,' chiefly with reference to another favourite subject—the primary truths of science. .

The Introduction contains abstracts of the Essay on Mackintosh, the Review of 'Mitford's Greece,' and the Speeches in Parliament—the six Ballot Speeches being given by themselves—followed by a critical survey of the 'History of Greece,' the 'Plato,' and the 'Aristotle'; and ends with a notice of Mr. Grote's later public career, particularly in his connection with the University of London.

A. B.

LONDON, *October*, 1873.

TABLE OF CONTENTS.

INTELLECTUAL CHARACTER AND WRITINGS

OF

GEORGE GROTE.

———◦◦◦———

CHAPTER I.

WRITINGS FROM 1820 TO 1830.

MR. GROTE's literary career may be said to have commenced with a pamphlet on Parliamentary Reform, which, as has been stated in his biography, he composed by the bedside of his wife, in 1821. This first essay in the field of political science was prompted by an impatience of the plausible fallacies put forth by a writer in the 'Edinburgh Review,' No. LXI., in an article afterwards ascribed on good grounds to Sir James Mackintosh.

In that article, Mackintosh is strongly in favour of Reform, and throughout displays much liberality of tone. He is, however, especially averse to Universal Suffrage and to the Ballot; and propounds a scheme for representing classes equally, although the numbers composing the classes might be very unequal.

Grote's reply is scathing. We detect in his theory of politics, now for the first time promulgated, strong marks of Mill's famous article on Government; we see also that he had already matured his conviction as to the ballot. There is, moreover, in the article, a highly sustained Rhetoric,

b

which may well have been nourished by Burke's Speeches, but was probably his own ideal of effective composition, the result of continued intimacy with the best literary productions ancient and modern. His subsequent style plainly shows that he considered this first attempt as too figurative. In the ballot speeches his style was much less rhetorical, and more effective. The present pamphlet also contains many sentences obscurely worded; while his later style was remarkably clear.

At the outset of the pamphlet, he regards the 'Edinburgh Review' as evincing a rooted hostility to any effective Parliamentary Reform, and accounts for this by its connexion with the great aristocratical Whig party. Section I. is entitled 'General Principles of the Reformers.' It begins by applying to political science Bacon's exposure of the low condition of the sciences generally, the test being their fruits or practical workings. Bacon's remedy, namely, to sift and verify fundamental principles, if applied to political philosophy, would consist in enquiring what experience teaches concerning the laws of human action. Now, the amplest observation attests that the conduct of every individual will be determined by his interest. This is true not merely of individual, but also of conjoined action. If a hundred individuals possess the privilege of passing and executing the laws for a large country, they will to a certainty appropriate the wealth and services of the inhabitants just as far as they are permitted. A governing company, therefore, must be constructed on such a scale that the majority of its members shall profit as little as possible by misgovernment. For that end, there are two requisites: First, the numbers must be considerable, so that the share of each individual may be low. Secondly, the relative situation of the members must be so arranged, that if they combine for sinister purposes, the benefits of misrule may be distributed equally. The first precaution would be nugatory without the second; had there been a slave suffrage at Athens, the masters would still have been the sole gainers; the slaves would have had no share. Again, as any large number is unfit for the exercise of deliberative power, the ruling company must be divided into two classes — periodical electors, and elected legislators ; an enlarged numerical qualification can belong only to electors. But this enlargement is nugatory, unless the suffrage of each person is emancipated from control : which is possible only by *a system of secret delivery*. Moreover, as a Legislative share in the privileges of government is more valuable than an Elective share, this difference must be reduced by *frequency of election*.

How do these principles apply to the British Constitution ? If the slightest credit is due to the incessant and flaming proclamations of the Whigs, the majority of the ruling company, as at present constituted, draw a decided benefit from misgovernment. In 1793, Earl Grey presented to Parliament a petition in which it was asserted, and evidence tendered in proof, that a majority of the Commons was returned by seventy-one peers and ninety-one commoners. This is a sufficient explanation of the abuses denounced by the Whigs. What is the remedy ? The advocates of Reform, in demanding an extended number of electors, do not urge the absolute necessity of making the suffrage universal : they do, however, maintain secret suffrage to be a vital requisite.

Section II. is ' Modes of Attack employed by the Enemies of Parliamentary Reform.' The just mode of attack is to propose alternative means for attaining the end. One means proposed is the scheme of a disinterested ministry, in other words, a Whig ministry.

The Whigs, it is pretended, will reject the benefits of misgovernment, and be content with their share, in common with the rest of the people, of a cheap system. But now, he asks, Upon what do these splendid pretensions rest ? On nothing but the speeches and promises of the Whigs themselves. The track of lofty and flattering promise has long been known as conducting to power, and many are the knaves that walk therein. Yet farther, when we hear that there are citizens who may be securely entrusted with the licence of inflicting evil, of course, for such persons, crime can have no attractions, and laws are needless and inoperative. Does then our penal code except the Whigs from its sanctions? Not only so, but such men ought to be above the ordinary self-interested motives of payment for services. Do then the salaries of the Administration of 1806 remain untouched in the Exchequer? If not, this alone places them on the level of ordinary life. It is not meant by such remarks to make any special censure upon the Whigs. But were they to claim an immunity from all penal laws whatsoever, the boon would be trifling as compared with the pretensions to power. If there were no law to deter them from crime, voluntary associations would arise and probably restrain their licence; while no exemption from private law could lay at their feet a spoil so secure and alluring, and, at the same time, so compatible with an untarnished fame as the posts that they aspire to.

The next mode of argument for evading Reform is to set up the check of public opinion. Conceding, in the first instance, that public opinion is successful in defeating extravagance on the part of the administration, would it give a decided interest in good government? It is at best a check, and not a spur. However efficacious pronounced opinion might be in keeping off new taxes, it would inspire no zeal for reduction of present burdens. The motive is a powerful one, but will it never be misled or disunited by official pretence or stratagem? A government can easily alarm people into unnecessary wars, and so provide for a useless squad of dependents. The popular sentiment would probably become highly distempered by the poisonous matter that an interested body could infuse. The concession, however, now made in favour of the influence of public opinion is too much. The machinery of the social system, in the construction of laws, attests the impotence of the bridle of opinion. Unless the penal code can be turned into a useless scroll, it follows that from no one crime are we sufficiently guaranteed by the avenging murmurs and by the uplifted arm of the public. Far less would public opinion maintain a vigilant censorship on an evil-intentioned government. As a preventive of private enormities—a rape or a murder—public opinion acts with the greatest advantage: no corrupt associations distort our sentiments, no expectations of profit from connivance can dull the horror of the act; the sympathy is kindled by the concentration of the suffering; the act itself is distinct and conspicuous; the character of the deed is flagrant; the criminal is a marked man; and, finally, public opinion has an ally in the injured party or those connected with him. Now, mark the deductions to be made from all these counts, when the same check is intended to subdue the sinister interest of a government. Experience attests our indulgence and even admiration of robbery and murder when on a grand scale; our feelings are averted from the injustice and desolation of a war to partake in the triumph of the general, and extol the terrific power that has done the work. The majesty of power that veils from our eyes its flagrant enormities completely white-washes the more insignificant minutiæ of oppression; not to speak of the hopes of place and profit to individuals. The extortion of a politic government, may impose but a trifling privation on each member of the community; the evil may be enormous in the sum, but it appeals rather to cool reflection than to our excited sensibilities. Again, the acts are of a kind very difficult to detect; how can public opinion keep steadily in view the nice boundary between necessary and unnecessary taxation? Farther, the body to be acted on is numerous, and forms the most opulent, powerful and best instructed class in the community. Their mutual interest creates a train of peculiar feeling, and a perverted standard of conduct, rendering them insensible to reproach, at least until it swells to the loudest pitch. Mere languid disapprobation is insufficient; the feeling must be kindled into animosity and menace, and England stimulated into a clamorous effervescence, from the Thames to the Tay. During this time, the partisans of the government intersect the popular sentiment in all directions; perplex and disturb its unison, counterwork its effect on the timid and the indifferent, by impeaching the designs of its adversaries, and by setting up, on their own side, a still louder cry of impiety and rebellion. If reduced to yield, they find means by adroit concessions to retain part of their ground: and as opinion cannot long keep its lofty pitch, if the government can hold on for a limited period, the threats of the public will quickly subside. Even, if the public opinion should thwart any pernicious measures, it inflicts no punishment, and impresses no motive for the future. Again, as abuses seldom press signally on one individual, or on a small knot of persons, they do not draw forth a leader; so that public opinion is left to organise itself in desultory detachments. To all which we must add, that as laws are made because an injured person would inflict excessive punishment on his enemy, an incensed people triumphing in a successful insurrection cannot be expected to impose a stricter rein on their resentment. The impotence of the check is proved by the amplest testimony, seeing that it is the one check that springs up everywhere. Yet when we unrol the great mass of mankind, how striking and irresistible are the proofs of its incompetency! That it is an insufficient check upon the present governing class in England, we are informed by the most satisfactory evidence. The Whig members of Parliament expatiate upon the defiance of the popular sentiments by the Ministry; and the Ministers, while confessing that the many are against them, declare that the sound, the rational part of the community, those alone *known to the Constitution* are in their favour. Others maintain that the people are too ignorant to detect misgovernment. The remedy is—let them see only the good; present to men of ability no hope of reward from misrule.

The author now considers the Reviewer's plan for a

Representation of Classes. The proposal is to examine the variety of local and professional interests composing the general interest, and to give to each of these suitable representatives. In order to consider the effect of this plan, the author takes a simple case: let a community consist of three classes—lawyers, landholders, merchants—each returning a member to make a governing body. What will be the course of this triumvirate? Each deputy is devoted to his class, but he can do nothing singly; but if he combine with another, the concurrence of the third is of no importance, and his interest is disregarded. That equal protection to all classes, which the theory supposes, is in practice unattainable. The interests of no class can be protected unless they can return a majority of the governing body. All that one class can do is to combine with other classes, merging what interest it has in opposition to these, and standing up only for what the united classes have in common; and if a majority is formed, that common interest will be secured. The ancient Roman class-system was in the Reviewer's model; and the two wealthiest of the six classes were able to outvote all the rest, while these included an overwhelming majority of the people.

The second half of the pamphlet takes account of the Reviewer's Objections to a thorough Parliamentary Reform. And first, his objections to Universal Suffrage. The Reviewer supposes Ireland to be an independent state, with four-fifths of the population Catholics, and a government elected by universal suffrage; where, in that case, would the Protestants be? The author retorts, where would they be on the class system? As the whole island is composed of Protestants and Catholics, under every possible system one or other sect must have the majority, and must dominate the other. The Reviewer seems fully aware that universal suffrage would entail a neglect of the interests of the few; he omits to remark that the return of a majority by the few would produce the same inattention to the interests of the many. When the rivalry in the state is merely as to the possession of good things, there will be a partial renunciation of interest, so as to appease the discordance; but an unconquerable antipathy like that between Protestants and Catholics, blacks and whites, is irremediable.

In the case between the many and the few, it may be undeniably proved that a majority chosen by the many will pursue the interest that the many have in common with the few. This position the author explains at length. The most interesting and original part of the argument is where he deals with the common allegation that the many would not respect *property*. He points out the insidious attempt to restrict this word to the large proprietors. Strictly speaking, the poorest labourer has property, for which he needs the full protection of the law; and the laws for protecting large properties must equally protect the small. Mr. Grote, as we shall see, on subsequent occasions reverts to this fallacy. (See on this point, p. 53 *et seq.*)

A considerable portion of the pamphlet is occupied with the Reviewer's attack on the Ballot. The line of attack is rather strange. The Reviewer thinks it a fallacy that the value of popular elections depends on the *exercise of a deliberate judgment* by the electors; the real value is in diffusing *publio spirit*. The author deals with this in his most vigorous style, shewing that it essentially consists in assigning to the general public the very worst part that they can play—the part of mobs. It is the result of the existing state of things, that the bulk of the community have interfered in national affairs by a display of physical force; and reasoners have thereby been led to consider collective agency as an essential requisite of their political life. But the display of physical force should no more enter into politics than into mutual protection against lawlessness. The Reviewer still farther urges the loss of excitement and heat through secret voting,—the lifelessness and want of motive to go to the poll; the virtues of the community do not arise from secret meditation, and do not flourish in solitude. The replies are sufficiently telling; and although the author's illustration, every time he touches this question is fresh and racy, I shall defer the specimens of his handling until I come to the speeches in Parliament.

The vigour of the pamphlet furnished a new weapon to the friends of Reform. The 'Examiner' styled it "a very able and a very seasonable pamphlet," and regarded the defence of the Ballot as the most comprehensive and useful part of the work; adding that "Reformers have paid too little attention to this excellent plan for curbing .the sinister and immoral exercise of bribery and intimidation on the part of the great."

We may see that Mr. Grote's studies in politics, theoretical and practical, were now well advanced. He had thoroughly imbibed the method and views of James Mill, which he developed by resources peculiar to himself.

On the 25th of April, 1822, Lord John Russell moved in the House of Commons, " That the present state of the representation of the people in Parliament requires the most serious consideration of this House." A long debate ensued, in which Mr. Canning delivered an elaborate oration. The motion was rejected by 269 to 164.

Mr. Canning's speech drew out from Mr. Grote a letter published in the 'Morning Chronicle,' full of his usual argumentative power and vigour of language. We need not reproduce it in full, but one or two extracts will be useful in showing the author's intensity of feeling on Reform. The introduction is to this effect:—

"That Mr. Canning's eloquence should prove triumphant in an assembly, so large a portion of which is 'self-elected' (to use the unanswered and unanswerable phrase of Lord John Russell), can excite no surprise whatever. His task is indeed an easy one on the floor of St. Stephen's. Would he but condescend to essay his powers on the other side of the question, would he persuade gentlemen to surrender close, privileged, and hereditary seats, accompanied with a lucrative expenditure of 22,000,000*l.* per annum, and as much or as little to do as they please; and to descend into the character of industrious, economical, and responsible legislators—this indeed would be an aim worthy of the rhetorician. And I much question whether even Mr. Canning's eloquence, if exerted on this side, would produce quite so many cheers, and such frequent laughter, as it seems to do at present.

" To appreciate duly the extent of this gentleman's oratory, let us remove it from the circle of sympathising and confidential critics among whom it was delivered, and measure its effect upon the larger public without. Will his speech impel their minds in the proportion of 269 to 164, as it has already won the House of Commons? Let us review its contents briefly, with reference to that public for whose benefit the debate is *imagined* to have taken place."

The essence of the speech, he states, as consisting of three arguments. The first is " Reformers do not agree in their proposals: Ergo, there ought to be no reform." The second is " A Reform in the Parliament would depress and extinguish the Crown." The writer remarks—

" This is an unqualified avowal, that monarchical government is highly injurious to the people. For such a declaration, I or any one else, anybody except Mr. Canning or Mr. F. Robinson, would be prosecuted. ' Any Legislature,' says the former, ' really elected by the people, responsible to them, and therefore promoting solely and exclusively the public good, would abrogate the Royal Prerogative. The latter, therefore, is irreconcileably at variance with the public happiness and interests.' Such is the view entertained by Mr. Canning, and by the Parliament who second Mr. Canning, of the genuine value of Monarchical Government. A more severe condemnation of the Throne cannot be pronounced, than this assertion, that an assembly aiming at the public happiness would never retain it."

" Next comes an argument cogent indeed, but not easily

referable to any known rules of logic :—'The present constitution is the one under which Mr. Canning was born, and
which therefore ought on no account to be changed.'   When
an infant of celebrity is born, we are commonly flattered
with the hopes of some striking improvement which he is to
accomplish—a reproduction of the golden age or of the
Saturnian system of government.   But Mr. Canning's god-
fathers and godmother appear to have vowed in his name,
that the world should be bound fast exactly in the position
which it held when that gentleman first saw the light."

Canning's fourth argument—"that it is not a good thing
that the House of Commons should be so constituted as to
coincide with the sentiments of the people "—is dealt with
us we should expect.   The concluding paragraph is—

" Having thus anatomised the chief part of Mr. Canning's
speech, I may venture to predict that it will not divide the
nation in the proportion of 269 to 164.   But this will be only
a fresh demonstration of that general incapacity of the
British race, which Mr. Canning so pointedly notices—from the
melancholy effects of which we are providentially extricated
by possessing a Legislature wise by blood and by inheritance."

––––––––––––––

Among some essays, preserved in MSS. of the date 1822,
there is a short paper wherein Mr. Grote refutes the alleged
hostility of the bulk of the people to property, as inferred
from occasional popular injustices.   He meets the charge by
several arguments.   In the first place, he remarks, while so
much stress is laid on the individual rich man whom the
people have despoiled, no notice is taken of the many rich
whom they have left untouched.   Secondly, in order to
predict the behaviour of any man or body of men, we must
consider what their permanent interest points to.   Thirdly,
if it were admitted "that because the people have committed occasional violations of property, therefore the people
are hostile to property," the same might be equally affirmed
of every other form of government.   We ought to compute

the instances of spoliation, under governments responsible to the people, and those under governments of one, or a few, in order to decide the question with perfect accuracy. But as this proceeding is impracticable, there remains one other method, namely, to apply the maxim "that every man will pursue his own interest," under which it will appear that the bulk of the people have a most essential interest in strengthening the motives to the accumulation of capital, because upon that depends the demand for labour. It is the very poorest that have the strongest interest in promoting accumulation. On the other hand, a monarch or an aristocracy, or both allied, have an interest directly at variance with the public happiness. They have an interest in plundering and degrading the community to the deepest extent, and in forcing the subjects to toil in their behalf; this being the mode by which they will reap the largest harvest of wealth and power. Lastly, an attack of the people upon the property of an individual rich man no more proves that the people are hostile to the laws of property, than their attack upon his life would prove that they were inimical to the laws protecting life. In both instances, they may be misled to make a particular exception, but this does nót prove them insensible to the value of the laws of property and life, or to the importance of adhering to them on other occasions.

In the 'Westminster Review,' for April, 1826, appeared the celebrated article on Mitford's 'History of Greece.' It already evinces both the extent of his minute research and the decision of his views on Grecian politics. Whilst his democratic sympathies were engendered by the studies pursued in preparation for the History, his controversial faculty was aroused by the misstatements of this widely-read Historian; Mitford being at this period in possession of the educational field, as well in the universities as in family circles.

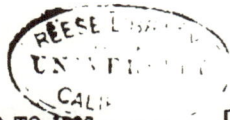

The introduction to the article is a clear and condensed statement of the chain of cause and effect in the evolution of the Grecian mind. First of all was the subdivision of the Grecian population into a great number of distinct city-communities. The smallness of these communities brought the whole of the members into intimate fellowship and personal communication of views upon the public situation. In such a state of things, a hereditary chief, or mere head of a clan, could not hold his ground; and the collective government of the state superseded personal government. The executive function was much better administered, being under the eye of the whole community. Moreover, everything in the condition of the Greeks favoured publicity of life, and interest in affairs. The desire of applause acquired extraordinary ascendency: and in this motive lay the stimulus to individual excellence in whatever accomplishments the public held in esteem. The extinction of the hereditary chiefs threw open the supreme power of the state to rivalry and competition; and, when the circumstances excluded the agency of mere force, the grand and foremost engine was the power of persuasion, particularly as applied to assembled multitudes. The materials of persuasive address consisted of all manner of facts, analogies, and reasonings, bearing on the eligibility of any public measures; involving a strong interest in contemporaneous critical history, the first specimen of which we owe to Thucydides. When these various mental acquisitions were sought as means of ascendency, esteem was conferred on the man that could teach them. Numerous instructors arose, in Rhetoric chiefly and avowedly, but indirectly in all the branches of knowledge then existing; and the success of those instructors in money and in fame was very great. But the teaching of the persuasive art led the way to the philosophy of the mind; and it was amidst the intellectual excitement of ancient Greece that this master-science had its beginning. The field for the observation of human beings was no less ample than interesting: the variety of laws and institutions, the number of social experiments so to speak, the contentions of parties, the criticism of public men, the diversities of individual excellence, in oratory, in poetry, in war, in legislation, stimulated critical enquiry into the causes of success. Superior men arose, with the aptitude for system and science; by these the special experiences were converted into general rules; and there thus gradually emerged the sciences of rhetoric, politics, ethics, and logic.

Another influence was derived from the religious festivals and gatherings. To these we apply the inadequate word *games;* the real term was *contests* (ἄγωνες). The appetite for glory was greatly fostered at such gatherings; while the chief attention was given to gymnastic exercises; but the garland was also bestowed for music and poetry.

"Considering the Grecian institutions as having brought into operation these incentives to individual excellence, they will appear without a parallel in the history of humanity; and judging by the same standard, too, it is abundantly certain that democracies were by far the best among all the Grecian governments; nor will it be too much to affirm, that had it not been for democracy, and that approximation to democracy which a numerous and open aristocracy presents, this wonderful precocity of intellectual development among the Greeks would have been impracticable, and that people would have been now forgotten amidst so many others who have marched only with the average pace of human improvement. Publicity and constant discussion of all matters relating to the general interest—accessibility of the public esteem, which could not be thoroughly monopolised by any predominant few—intense demand for those great political qualities which are fitted to command the respect and assent of the general community — encouragement to eloquence, and to all those acquirements which eloquence presupposes, as well as to that system of instruction and mental philosophy which follows in its train—all these characteristics were to be found in the democracies more completely than in any other Grecian governments, and these, as we have above shown, were the great stimulating causes of Grecian eminence. Where a state was under the close government of one or of a few, circumstances were highly unfavourable to the develop-ment of individual superiority; the ruling powers not only held out no encouragement to it, but even interfered to sup-press and banish it by force as a rival to their own monopoly."

It was never Mr. Grote's custom to advance positions of this nature without supporting them by facts: and his ex-posure of Mitford gives him an opportunity of unfolding his resources. I shall select only one point, because of its paramount interest, and because it is one of Grote's charac-teristic points of political doctrine.

After giving a series of facts to set forth the atrocities of ancient oligarchy, he adds a testimony of tremendous and indisputable force. This is the oath (apparently the sena-torial oath) cited by Aristotle as formally sworn among some of the ancient oligarchies, containing these words—"*I will be evil-minded towards the people, and will bring upon them by my counsel whatever mischief I can.*" The philosopher's own remark is not less significant: his suggestion to the oligarchs being—"Let them misgovern if they choose; but let them at least employ some decent pretences to delude the people into a belief of the contrary." But for our ex-perience of the irresistible effect of the habit of submission among men, we might wonder that any government thus affected towards its subjects could be suffered to exist a single month.. Yet the subversion of the oligarchies almost always arose, not so much from popular resistance as from dissensions among the leading men themselves; there being always room for aspiring nobles to acquire popularity by appearing to act as protectors of the oppressed many. Thus were formed two aristocratic parties—denominated by Mitford the party of the poor, and the party of the rich; appellations employed both by Plato and by Aristotle, but yet involving an important mistake. The party called the "party of the poor," ought to be called the community minus the rich. Rich and not-rich are the proper terms for bisecting the community. The classification into rich and poor is a fallacy, the source of many most erroneous political reasonings. Thus, according to Aristotle, Oligarchy has a place when the wealthy few possess the government, and employ their power for their own ends, not for the public good; Democracy is when the poor many, possessing the powers of government, use these powers for their own interest, not the public interest. The philosopher seems to imagine that if the wealthy as a class possess no distinct privileges, the government is necessarily in the hands of the poor, and that the poor have an interest contrary to the public interest. Now the word " poor " is here used in a double sense: it signifies at one time the whole community excepting the rich; and at another time the destitute poor. Only in this last sense can the poor ever be said to have an interest distinct from the public interest; the whole community excluding the rich has obviously the same interest as the whole community including the rich. As not more than one man in a hundred can be called rich, ninety-nine hundredths of the community are poor ; and the interest of ninety-nine hundredths of the community must always be the same as the interest of the whole community.

There can be little doubt that the persistent denunciations of Grecian democracy, of which Mitford's book is a notable sample, were kept up for the sake of their application to modern instances; and Mr. Grote, by his vindication of Athens, has powerfully counterworked one of.the machinations for retarding the growth of popular government in the present day. He is, however, fully alive to the weaknesses and defects of the old democracies, just as he is sensible of many defects in the popular constitutions of our own time ; but, " taking these defects at the utmost, and comparing the Grecian democracies with any other form of government, either existing in ancient times, or projected by the ancient philosophers, we have no hesitation in pronouncing them decidedly and unquestionably superior. That the securities they provided for good government were lamentably deficient, we fully admit; but the oligarchies and monarchies afforded no securities at all." The complaint made against these democracies, by Xenophon and Aristotle, was not that they missed their own end, but that they aimed at, and to a certain degree attained, the happiness of all the free citizens, minus the rich, to the prejudice of the separate interests of the rich.

His replies to Mitford's other charges,—that the popular assemblies were fickle in their decisions; that the democracies were unstable and torn with dissensions; that, in them rich men were unduly taxed (as by the *liturgies* at Athens); that unjust accusations were prevalent; that re-division of the lands was a favourite measure of democracy,—are overwhelming from the array of counter facts to every one.

The latter half of the article is occupied with exposing the gross perversions in Mitford's narrative of transactions. This we need not exemplify; for although the calumnies against democracy have a permanent vitality, the historical blunders of such writers as Mitford are dead and decomposed. It is not often that the mild temper of Mr. Grote permitted of sarcasm, so we may quote this sentence from the criticism of Mitford's inaccuracies respecting the early proceedings of Philip of Macedon:—" Ancient writers have left us lamentably in the dark respecting many most important parts of ancient history; but we ought not to be severe upon them for their want of minuteness in describing plans which were never concerted, and treaties which were never entered into."

The article concludes thus:—"It is sufficiently obvious that the historian who can thus deviate from his authorities in recounting specific facts, is still less to be relied upon for accuracy in any general views, where the result arising from a comparison of several different authorities, not separately assignable, is to be laid before the reader. If partiality can discolour the former, it will prevent any approximation to truth in the latter. And should Grecian history ever be re-written with care and fidelity, we venture to predict that

c

Mr. Mitford's reputation, for these as well as for other desirable qualities, will be prodigiously lowered. That it should have remained so long exalted, is a striking proof how much more apparent than real is the attention paid to Greek literature in this country; and how much that attention, where it is sincere and real, is confined to the technicalities of the language, or the intricacies of its metres, instead of being employed to unfold the mechanism of society, and to bring to view the numerous illustrations which Grecian phenomena afford, of the principles of human nature. It is not surprising, indeed, that the general views of Mr. Mitford should be eminently agreeable to the reigning interests in England; nor that instructors devoted to those interests should carefully discourage all those mental qualities which might enable their pupils to look into evidence for themselves, and to deduce just inferences from the Greek authors who are put into their hands. But though such instructors cannot be prevented from teaching superficially, they may at least be deprived of the credit of teaching otherwise than superficially; and few works would more effectually conduce to this end than a good history of Greece." *

* It ought to be mentioned, in recording the literary labours of Mr. Grote during this decade, that he bestowed much time upon some MSS. of Jeremy Bentham's, which the venerable sage entreated his young disciple to put into a readable form.

The pile of materials being carefully digested and arranged by George Grote, he produced in 1822 a small octavo volume, with the following title : "Analysis of the Influence of Natural Religion on the Temporal Happiness of Mankind, by Philip Beauchamp."

The MS. was handed to Mr. Place, who employed Richard Carlile to print the tract; the reason being that Carlile was lying in Dorchester gaol, and thus safe from farther prosecution. At that period the London booksellers were afraid of having anything to do with writings wherein Religion was in question. The original papers, in Bentham's handwriting, became the property of Mrs. George Grote under the Author's will, and are still extant, as well as the letter to G. Grote which accompanied the packet.

CHAPTER II.

SPEECHES ON THE BALLOT.

ON the 25th of April, 1833, Mr. Grote made his first motion in favour of the Ballot.

At the outset of his speech he quotes Lord John Russell's expression in originally proposing the Reform Bill:—" So constituting this House, as that it should enjoy, and command, and deserve, the confidence of the people." He calls on the House now to review the mode of taking votes upon the same simple, precise, and momentous principle. The Reform Bill has given a numerous and intelligent community, say a million of voters. What would have been said if there had been a clause in the bill dividing that constituency into two classes—one class free, the other subject voters? What if the bill had numbered all the tenants on a great man's estate, and all occupiers of houses under him, as so many lip-voters, necessary, indeed, as mechanical instruments for transmitting his will to the hustings, but legally incapable of expressing any determination but his? But it is not by law alone that the freedom of voting is subverted; natural causes may work the same thing. One half of the present constituency are unable to call their votes their own. No doubt there are some splendid examples of political virtue—men who give an honest vote and incur the consequent hazard; but the larger number stifle the voice of conscience, and give way before an overruling destiny. The public mischief thus arising is that the House does not command the confidence of the people; the elective system is a failure and a nullity; for the only characteristic distinguishing it from a vain mummery is the genuine suffrage of each qualified voter. The private mischiefs are the solemn falsehoods at the poll, the sense of self-abasement at being

c 2

the instrument of another's will, the political apathy and recklessness, the thousand angry feelings everywhere accompanying private terrorism. Now, whatever be the sources of this evil, the condition of its agency is publicity of votes. The Ballot may not put an end to all persecution for political sentiments, but it will put an end to compulsory and insincere voting. In France, during the last ten years, the Ballot proved the single guarantee against an overwhelming government ascendency.

Under the Ballot individual bribery could have no place; collective bribery would be hazardous and difficult. But for one vote perverted by bribery, twenty are perverted by intimidation.

He next deals with the objections to secrecy, as tending to mendacity and promise-breaking. Now it is true that a tenant voting by Ballot *may* thus break his promise, but why should you suppose that he *will* do so? There is only one answer; the promise has been given contrary to his genuine and conscientious feeling. Preferring A in his conscience, the elector has beencon strained to promise that he will vote for B; such a promise involves the necessity of lying one way or the other; either to his country, if he keeps the promise, or to his superior, if he breaks it. But what falsehood can be worse than a dishonest vote at the poll? If a juror who gives a dishonest verdict, or a witness who deposes an untruth, sins in poisoning the fountains of justice, the electoral trust-breaker sins scarcely less in poisoning the fountains of legislation. The opponents of the Ballot talk as if the only falsehood a voter can tell is the breaking faith with one who has extorted from him a dishonest promise. There is another and greater wrong, the breaking faith with the public. What this House should recognise is the superior obligation of the public trust to the private pledge. The promise is bad enough; the act would be far worse. All that can be said against the Ballot is, that it enables these compulsory and immoral promises to be violated with impunity; thus getting rid of the more noxious of the two lies.

But this is not the fair way of looking at the effect of the secret vote. The compulsory and dishonest promises, whence the lying proceeds, will seldom be exacted. To tie a man down to a hateful pledge, when you cannot ascertain whether he keeps it, is a fruitless affront; tending to rouse the galling ideas of coercion, without attaining a real hold over the conduct.

Even now, is there no promise-breaking under the open vote? Does it not eternally happen that a dependent is compelled by his superior to break a promise already voluntarily made to another?

Speaking in a whisper is not synonymous with lying; much less is speaking aloud synonymous with openness of heart and truth-telling. There are cases where secrecy conduces to fraud; there are cases where it is the only sure road to truth. When a witness deposes to facts, it is essential that his testimony should be public; but when you wish a man's private unbiassed judgment, you will be nearer your end by making his communication strictly confidential. This last is the situation of an elector at the poll.

He then proceeds to another favourite objection. The elective franchise, it is said, is a trust; every elector is responsible for the way that he exercises it; publicity is a necessary consequence, for the sake of the non-electors. He admits that there would be great weight in the argument, if the objector could show that open voting was either a benefit or a security to the non-electors. He thinks he can prove that the reverse is the fact. He assumes that the electoral trust means this, namely, that an elector shall deliver his genuine and conscientious opinion at the poll, whether it agrees or disagrees with that of other people. Now this can be obtained only by his own free will; no extremity of force can wring it from him. The open vote cannot convert a single voter from dishonesty to honesty; but it makes thousands of honest voters dishonest against their inclinations. Every voter becomes controllable by one or a few private masters, who exercise over his comfort a paramount influence. Under the mask of responsibility to the public, you fasten round his neck the base and dismal chain of private dependence. Moreover, is it really contended that non-voters are competent to exercise control or supervision over the voters? The only reason for setting them aside as non-voters, is their presumed incapacity of judging on political subjects. When the non-electors do intermeddle it is as ardent partisans, and in a manner purely mischievous. Dictation by a private individual, the *vultus instantis tyranni,* and dictation by an assembled crowd, the *civium ardor prava jubentium,* end in the same deplorable result—spurious and insincere voting.

If the voters are sufficiently numerous, and well-distributed, so as to have collectively the same interests as the community, they can have no wish except to choose honestly; and this is the only ground on which the recent extension of the constituency can be vindicated. If responsibility had to be relied upon, as the guarantee for honest voting, any extension of the constituency would have been absurd and injurious; a small constituency is far more pointedly responsible than a numerous one; every step in enlarging the electoral body, is a step in diminution of the responsibility of each individual elector. Nay, upon this principle, the single-headed constituency of Old Sarum would have been the best in the whole kingdom.

Another argument is that the influence of rich men over voters is a very salutary thing, and that the Ballot is mischievous as tending to abridge it.

" How much influence over voters ought a rich man to have? As much as he can purchase? No, certainly—for even the present law forbids all idea of his purchasing any influence. Not as much as he can purchase, but as much as he deserves, and as much as unconstrained freemen are willing to pay him. Amongst unconstrained freemen, the man of recognised superiority will be sure to acquire spontaneous esteem and deference; these are his just deserts, and they come to him unbidden and unbespoken. But they will come to him multiplied tenfold, if along with such intrinsic excellencies, he possesses the extrinsic recommendations of birth and fortune—if he be recommended to the attention of his neighbours by the conspicuous blazon of established opulence and station—and if he be thus furnished with the means of giving ample range and effect to an enlightened beneficence. This is the meed which awaits men of birth and station, if they do but employ their faculties industriously and to the proper ends. Poorer men may, doubtless, attain it also; but with them the ascent is toilsome, the obstructions numerous, and the success at best uncertain : to the rich man the path is certain and easy—the willing public meet him half way, and joyfully hail the gradual opening of his virtues. He is the man to whom they delight to pay homage ; and their idolatrous fancy forestalls and exaggerates his real merits.

" This, Sir, is, in my opinion, the legitimate influence of wealth and station; to serve as the passport, the ally, and the handmaid, of superior worth and talent. This influence is as gentle and kindly as it is lasting and infallible ; it is self-created and self-preserving ; and it is, moreover, twice blest, for it blesses as well the few who exercise it, as the many over whom it is exercised."

But it is the curse and misery of our species that the great and wealthy choose to govern by mere dint of wealth and station, unallied with those beneficent ingredients. Wealth, in any hands, carries with it the power of befriending one man, and injuring another ; it can extort the votes that the possessor has not virtue enough to earn. This is the illegitimate influence of wealth and station—when it supersedes and disenthrones the diviner qualities of the man and the hero. Under open voting, the influence of wealth is alike in every hand ; nay, the worse a man is, the more effectively he will employ the bad weapons. The Ballot decomposes the mixture of good and evil, with the exactness of a chemical agent. The man that employs wealth and station as they ought to be employed will not lose a particle of influence; his standard is planted in the interior of men's bosoms; his ascendency is as sure and as operative in the dark as in the light. And what would be the harm, if that coarser and baser influence, which cannot subsist without coercive force, were suppressed and extirpated altogether? The question was started by Berkeley, "Whether an un-educated gentry are not the greatest of all natural evils?" The counter part of the proposition is no less true—That a gentry well-educated and of enlarged sympathies, are among the foremost of national blessings. The most effectual way of preserving that blessing will be to render the vote of an elector inaccessible to all coercion, and attainable only by such as have gained his genuine esteem. This is the only prize that can stimulate the listlessness, or soften the natural pride, of one whose wealth places him above the equal communion of his fellow-men; and by rendering the suffrage secret, you lock this precious prize in a casket, which can neither be stolen by fraud, nor ravished by tyranny; you reserve it in the inmost sanctuary, as a free-will offering to ascertained merit, and as a stimulus to all noble aspirations.

In the peroration, he says:—"If ever there was a case in which the address to your reason was vehemently and powerfully seconded by the appeal to your feelings, that case is the emancipation of honest voters—the making peace between a man's duty and his worldly cares—the rescue of political morality from the snares which now beset it, and from the storms which now lay it prostrate. You are called upon to protect the rights, and to defend the integrity, of the electoral conscience; to shield the innocent from perse-cution at the hands of the guilty; to guard the common-wealth against innumerable breaches of trust, committed by the reluctant hands of well-meaning citizens. You are called upon to bridle the tyranny of those who violate, by the same blow, their duty to their neighbour and their duty to their country. You are called upon to encourage the formation of an electoral conscience in those bosoms where it has as yet had no existence ; and to cure that recklessness and immorality with which unprincipled voters now prostitute their franchise, in order to conciliate custom or promotion. Above all, you are called upon to make this House, what it professes and purports to be, a real emanation from the pure and freespoken choice of the electors ; an assembly of men commanding the genuine esteem and confidence of the people, and consisting of persons, the fittest which the nation affords, for executing the true end and aim of government. When all these vast interests, collective and individual, are at stake in this one measure, am I not justified in demanding from you not merely a cold and passive attention, but an earnest sympathy and solicitude ? "

The motion was vigorously supported, in a short speech, by Dr. Lushington. Mr. Cobbett replied to the objections founded on the American use of the Ballot. Daniel O'Connell made a short and telling speech, which brought up Sir Robert Peel, who dwelt upon the apathy and dead languor that would take place if canvassing were put an end to; the impossibility of preserving secrecy; the evil of making the House more democratic than it is. It was merely absurd to say that a man with ten thousand a year should not have more influence over the Legislature of the country than a man of ten pounds a year. He thought universal suffrage more plausible than vote by Ballot. There were arguments in favour of extending the franchise to women, to which it was no easy matter to find any logical answer: other and more important duties were intrusted to women ; women were allowed to hold property, to vote on many occasions in virtue of that property—nay, a woman might inherit the Throne, and perform all the functions of the first office of the State. The electoral system had not had a fair trial ; and members would be better employed in reading the report of the Poor-Law Commissioners, and considering some remedies for the evils there depicted.

The vote was—Ayes, 106; Noes, 211; Pairs, 26.

The second occasion of bringing on the motion was on the 3rd of June, 1835. He had the advantage of being able to appeal to the recent election as furnishing abundant instances of gross intimidation, and by the help of these, and by varying his illustrations, he contrived to impart a degree of freshness that was not apparent in any of the speeches in reply.

He began by assuming that in conferring upon any man the title and functions of an elector, you really intend to invest him with a substantive and independent character. The contrary would imply, that Parliament, while pretending to bestow a vote upon him, designs, in fact, to bestow underhand a second vote upon somebody else. If the law intends to play this trick with voters, the sooner it is proclaimed the better. The secret voter may give a wrong judgment, but at all events his vote is his own determination. Publicity of the suffrage enables intermeddlers from without to work on the hopes and fears of individual electors. Referring to the recent election, he observed that the newspapers of every party abounded with complaints of undue influence; so familiar was it, that it seemed the ordinary course of nature in the electioneering world. Sometimes a landlord generally notified to his tenants that he did not mean to interfere with their votes; but this edict of manumission would appear both preposterous and insulting, if the pre-existing dependence had not been felt. The voters seem to be considered as lawful prize and prey, *mutum ac turpe pecus*, belonging of right to that party which can drag them with the greatest violence. It is but too evident that the efforts of the imperative classes of society to subjugate the will of the humbler voters are nowise likely to be suspended or relaxed for the future. He next criticised a bill brought in by the member for Shaftesbury (Mr. Poulter), for making intimidation penal, and concluded with a reply to the stock of objections to the Ballot (its being un-English; causing promises to be broken; withdrawing responsibility from the voter; reducing the influence of the wealthy.)

Lord Howick insisted that the machinery of the Ballot was impracticable. Lord John Russell saw no hope of improvement, except in the better dispositions of the men of property themselves. Lord Stanley was at much pains to show that the Grey cabinet when they carried the Reform Bill, had come under a pledge to go no farther. Sir Robert Peel spoke at some length, but with no originality.

Division, 146 for, to 319 against.

The following year (1836) on the 23rd of June, instead of a motion declaratory of the principle of the Ballot, Mr. Grote brought in a bill containing the provisions and machinery for secret voting.

It would be superfluous, he remarks, to insist upon what all constitutional writers admit, that the primary condition of representative government is the efficient operation of the elective principle. It is therefore no waste of time to consider the question of freedom or purity of election. What are the facts at present? So notorious are the evils and abuses that they are come to be treated as light and familiar. In introducing the Reform Act, Lord Grey proclaimed that nomination of members of Parliament should cease to exist. It is time to fulfil this beneficent pledge. The reality and prevalence of election abuses can now be made to rest on the testimony of Committees of the House, which have brought out a body of dark and infamous details, showing the springs and working of what we extol and sanctify under the name of representation. All parties make loud complaints of intimidation. Much is made, in the Irish elections, of intimidation by the people and the priests, but still more frequent is the dictation of landlords and agents, and of the rich in general. Irish abuses are only English abuses on a gigantic scale. The clergy of the Church of England have not been behindhand in their zeal at the critical moment of an election; the Vice-Chancellor of the University of Cambridge dismissed his gardener for refusing to vote for the present member for that town. But the nation in its collective majesty has a paramount title to the free and independent suffrage of each separate elector. It is time for the House to interpose a remedy when the distempers of our electoral system have been proclaimed by its own authority. Have gentlemen made up their minds to see this leprosy cleave to us and to our posterity for ever? The remedy is secret voting. It trenches on no existing rights. Voting by Ballot is unfettered and unbiassed voting; when Cicero, in speaking of the Ballot at Rome, calls it *Tabellæ, vindex tacitæ libertatis* —the upholder of silent liberty—he says what is emphatically true.

He next goes on to reply to objections. It is said, that however an elector may vote, people will guess or suspect how he has voted. Why so? Because his sentiments are known, and he has no motive to depart from them. There is an eternal and indissoluble alliance between secrecy and freedom. Gentlemen make intimidation by the mob an object of abhorrence; they may abolish it by a measure that protects from all modes of intimidation at once. The much-extolled responsibility of the elector is either a phantom or a mask for the precise mischief of intimidation. The publicity of the votes of members of Parliament rests on three distinct grounds, all absent in the case of the electors. The smallness of their number gives them an interest of their own, apart from, and often hostile to, the community; the same smallness enables the public to watch their conduct; lastly, the speciality and continuity of their functions also enable the public to judge whether they discharge their duties. But, on the other hand, how idle to talk of the responsibility of seven or eight hundred thousand persons. Lord John Russell had said the Ballot would remove the electors from good and improving influences. But what are the good influences that can operate upon a man apart from his own conscience and conviction? The good influences will really be expanded and fostered. The specific agency of the Ballot is against intimidation; its effect is not so conclusive, but will still be powerful against bribery. There may be a corrupt agreement in a small constituency; but this proves only that small constituencies are faulty. Surely it is a noble object to watch over and cherish the honest and untainted portion of the constituency. As to the breaking of promises, the first purpose of a representation is to collect the real sense of the qualified voters; the duty towards a private party is a secondary object. Yet the Ballot does not command any man to break his promise; it merely enjoins him to perform the act of voting without a witness. Promise-breaking in this situation is the proof that the voter has been constrained. To tell the intimidator —because you have compelled a voter to promise against his will, therefore you have acquired a good title to compel him to vote,—is to guarantee the last stage of tyranny out of respect to the first. Then as to the influence of property, there is only one influence that will be withdrawn—the power of rewarding or punishing electors according to their vote. Does the House recognise in any one citizen of this community—a peer or commoner, titled or untitled—a legitimate authority to reward or punish electors for their votes?

Leader seconded the motion in a speech of some length, and Charles Villiers spoke with his wonted ability in the course of the debate. None of the Whig or Tory leaders spoke.

The House divided—Ayes 88; Noes 139.

On the 8th of March, 1837, the motion was next brought forward, also in the shape of a bill; but the speech abstained from the explanation of the machinery in detail. I select a few of the points.

It is not enough to say that secret voting disengages you altogether from the disorderly tumult and vexatious obstruction inseparable from the pronouncing of a candidate's name at the hustings, and from the continuous proclamation of the varying state of the poll. The main purpose is to procure

froe, sincere, and independent voting. This ought to secure
for it the consent of all parties; for how can any man repudiate the principle of general freedom of votes, without
assuming to himself a despotism little less monstrous than
the ancient inquisition in matters of religion? Free agency
is the very soul of voting. Such is the English constitution
in theory at least. Listen to Blackstone, and you will be
beguiled into the belief that every man's vote is his own
vote; descend into the committee-room, and you will find
that the canvassers of election rack their ingenuity to discover, not modes of persuasion, but modes either of com-
pulsion or of seduction. It was acknowledged by the present
Prime Minister only last year, that the great evil of the day
is that every one thinks he has a right to employ his influence
over another.

In an article in the 'Edinburgh Review' against the Ballot
(written by Lord Brougham), the extent of intimidation at
elections is described in language which it is impossible to
surpass. On this point the reports of the committees of this
House afford materials enough for the most insatiable appetite. Wherever any man possesses the means of inflicting
injury on another, or withholding benefits, the power is used
for electioneering purposes. As to exclusive dealing, the
Tory organs are preaching it openly as a matter of political
obligation. For all this, no one else has suggested any
remedy. The Ballot will be an act of emancipation for all
dependent voters. Some gentlemen tell us that while averse
to theoretical or organic reforms, they burn with zeal for the
removal of all proved abuses. Let them peruse the report
of the Intimidation Committee, and they will find a harvest
of proved abuses, rank, and pining for the sickle. Whence
is it that election abuses in all their grossness and variety,
at least three parts out of four, take their origin? It is
from the struggles of extraneous tyranny to grasp the vote
of the voter. Now the surest mode of warfare against crime
is to disappoint the criminal of his expected booty. Instead
of secrecy being dishonourable, it is used in every private

association, and its introduction is only treading in the beaten path of sound and practical legislation. Objectors, putting aside freedom of election as a light and worthless consideration, reproach the Ballot with multiplying false promises and false declarations. What then? Is there to be no privacy anywhere because falsehoods may be made and remain undiscovered? The secrecy of the post opens a door to falsehood; yet if there be any act of despotism that excites peculiar abhorrence it is the breaking the seal of private letters. Persecutors of every class may well be angry with the Ballot; it enables the voter to do his duty without baring his bosom to the assault of private malice. The victims of religious oppression in all ages have carried on their worship secretly, and no historian has ever dared to revile them. Is it an unpardonable sin, under the pressure of penalties, to combine outward conformity with secret dissent? Secrecy is the refuge of the weak against the strong. Publicity enables the political prosecutor to combine with the hundred arms of Briareus, the hundred eyes of Argus. If the Ballot makes hypocrites, open voting makes hypocrites, at least as many in number and much more in kind. Under the Ballot influence will be futile: when the process of intimidation is forbidden to be consummated, it will not be begun. Then, as to bribery. A voter accustomed to take bribes will feel that his market is struck from under him when he is directed to vote in secrecy. In ensuring ignorance of the poll, it prevents the candidate from knowing how many votes he must buy to secure his majority. Next, as to the argument from responsibility. You cannot make the elector responsible for voting ill; for where is the standard? Among Tories, to vote ill is to vote for a Whig or a Radical, and conversely. As to the multitude that have no votes, why are they excluded? What arguments should we hear in reply to a motion for universal suffrage? But if these men are to coerce the voters, admit then at once they are the superior party of the two. If the non-electors acted generally on the invitation given to them, we should have universal suffrage

practically, but brought about by the most violent and un-
warrantable means. The unrepresented classes have nothing
to lose and much to gain, from placing every qualified voter
in circumstances for an honest and conscientious use of his
franchise; it concerns them that the poorer voters should not
be subservient to the richer; that the franchise should be
kept at least as wide as at present. At one time the Ballot
is assailed because it will extinguish the influence of wealth;
at another time because it will extinguish the influence of
disfranchised poverty. If you insist that the elector shall
be responsible to the people at large, you are bound to protect him against the tyranny of the great man in his neighbourhood. Coercion and counter-coercion are assumed to be
the essential and tutelary forces which keep the electors in
their proper orbit. It often happens that the pressure from
two opposing quarters is so violent that the elector knows
not which he ought to obey.

The concluding sentences are:—" I feel that in advocating
the Ballot, I am upholding nothing less than the sacred right
of free judgment and free utterance in political matters. I
am treading in the steps of those illustrious men who have
rescued the individual conscience from its trammels, and
vindicated its liberty and inviolability in matters of religion.
I am striving to baffle the guilty efforts of that spirit of
persecution which still harasses the political world, and still
defiles the sincerity and solemnity of the elective franchise.
If, Sir, you can break the sword of the persecutor, and assure
freedom of election, without the aid of the Ballot, proceed to
the task without delay, for never was there a case of more
pressing necessity. But when it is notorious that this cannot be done, and when the alternative of the Ballot is ready
within your reach, I beseech you to consider whether you
can, with a safe conscience, license and perpetuate the countless mischiefs of an unprotected suffrage."

The debate was short, and the opposition was somewhat
milder in tone than in former years.

The House divided—Ayes, 155; Noes, 267; Pairs, 5.

The motion was renewed in the recently elected Parliament of 1838 (16th of February); and the mover availed himself of the experience at the elections.

If it were proposed to cut down the present number of seven hundred thousand qualified electors to four hundred thousand, the attempt would be resisted alike by those who desired to adhere to the present franchise, and those who desired to enlarge it. Yet open voting is a practical disfranchisement to hundreds and thousands of electors. Many decline to exercise the franchise at all : and with regard to those who do vote, what is the difference between taking away the vote and taking away the voter's liberty of voting as he inwardly prefers ? There is little difference of opinion as to the main purposes of a representative government; it is to get a House of Commons possessing the confidence of the people ; for this we go through the harassing and costly business of a general election. Does the practical working conform to this ? The evidence shows that the existing system is not a representative system. Many votes are given, of all shades of party, that express the genuine sentiments of the electors; with respect to a large proportion, the reverse is the truth. The innumerable discourses of candidates on the hustings during the late election, the daily criminations and recriminations of all the newspapers —Whig, Tory, and Radical—all certify the virulence of the evil. He quoted a number of individual testimonies—Lord Palmerston at Tiverton, the Whig and Tory versions of the election in the West Riding of Yorkshire, and others. The number of ejectments, notices to quit, changes of dealing and dismissals of employment, if it could be collected, would be large and remarkable ; and as one punishment inflicted corresponds to a thousand persons deterred, these acts are but a small proportion of the cases of undue interference. In many cases, the franchise is hated as a burden. An election sheds a disastrous twilight over all the relations of social life,—tyranny, ruin for conscientious behaviour, success of unprincipled compliance, suspension of inter-

d

course, factitious riot and disorder. If no protection be allowed, the franchise must fall into the same degeneracy and disgrace as the old system before 1831. Lord John Russell had expressed his strong sense of the "terrible position" of the landlords, and rather than that it should continue, he would adopt the Ballot. Since then, there have been two general elections, and the terrible position is unaffected. If the supporters of the Reform Act wish to reap the good they have sown, they must adopt the inexpugnable safeguard of the secret vote. As knowledge is power, absence of knowledge is absence of power. It is in vain to reason with the intimidator, to cajole him, to cry shame upon him, to hold out legal penalties. Intimidation is too gentlemanlike and fashionable to be subdued by such leaden weapons. It is the inmate of courts and manor-houses: the cherished companion of lordly bosoms: all the pride of wealth and rank, and all the fierceness of political bigotry conspire to uphold it; the clergyman who discourses eloquently in the pulpit on charity and forgiveness of enemies, neither enjoins nor manifests any such dispositions during a contested election ; even ladies of high fashion are not ashamed to direct with their own delicate hands, the instant discontinuance of a tradesman who has dared to vote for the shocking Radical. Under the Ballot those who now dictate votes by means of servile and selfish fears must resort to other methods of guidance : if they disdain to substitute persuasion for control, they will be left, as they ought to be, to impotent and unavailing complaints. Some persons maintain, that secret voting will be inoperative unless canvassing is also prohibited. The word "canvassing" is equivocal; it includes something that is harmless and even indispensable, and much that is revolting and odious. Under the Ballot, you would have a committee and a canvass; to consult the prevailing sentiment, to communicate information, to rectify mistakes, and to convince, as well as might be, such as are adverse. Beyond these limits begins the odious part of the practice. In no scene on the face of the earth are the harassing and ungenerous arts of enforcing constrained compliance more skilfully practised than at an English election. Then as to violation of promises. What is the behaviour of a country gentleman when the Tory canvassers tell him that Farmer So-and So, his tenant, has promised his vote to the Radical candidate? To hear the arguments against the Ballot, one would think an election by open voting was a school of probity and veracity. Instead of that, the promise of a dependent voter is respected just so far as it coincides with the will and dictates of his superior. The promises now broken are precisely the best class of promises. The elector is under a paramount obligation, from which no act of his own can discharge him, to give his vote according to his own conscientious preference. A promise to vote contrary to his own judgment, is a premeditated breach of solemn public duty. If there be in human affairs an unlawful covenant, that is one of the deepest dye; wrong in the man who gives the pledge, wrong in the highest degree, and altogether without excuse or extenuation, in the man who extorts it. The responsibility of the elector is an abuse of terms. It is seduction and intimidation under another name.

The debate that followed was well sustained. The motion was seconded by Mr. Ward, in an effective speech. Mr. James referred to a time some years ago, when he presented a petition in favour of the Ballot, which was received with shouts of laughter. Lytton Bulwer spoke in favour of the motion. Lord John Russell replied at some length. It was on this occasion that Sir Robert Peel made his principal speech on the subject; merely the old topics more elaborately worded. He treated the position of the elector and of the member of Parliament as the same; he declared that the best institutions had their abuses; the abuses in elections were greatly exaggerated; secret voting is at variance with the institutions, usages, and feelings of the people, and with free discussion; then, there will be no secrecy with the Ballot; on the day of election, the doubtful voter will be asked to stay away; the voter will as a rule keep his promise, or else blab to his wife or somebody, who will tell the agent; there may be great political outbursts, when the public are so unreasonably prejudiced, that they need enlightened control; the Ballot has not worked well in other countries, nor did it in Rome; it will have to be followed by universal suffrage.

The Division stood—Ayes, 200; Noes, 317.

The sixth and last time the motion was made, was on the 18th of June, 1839. The speech introducing it was less than a column of the newspaper report. Apologising for iteration, he said his historical experience had taught him that it was not the introduction of novel arguments which political truth depended upon for its success, but in having the proper arguments frequently brought forward and considered. It was not fruitfulness of invention that enabled the advocates of Catholic emancipation to carry their point: the novelty of every argument had been exhausted long before the final triumph. Even though they meant the Reform Act to be final, did they mean also to embalm its deformities? As the evils were fully admitted, why did not some one propose a remedy different from the Ballot? He could not understand the objection of its being too democratic a measure, unless the objectors held that democratical opinions prevailed amongst the majority of the electors throughout the country, and that the Ballot would enable them to vote more freely in favour of their opinions. The measure was indispensable to any state of the franchise—household, educational, or universal. He did not envy the feelings of any gentleman, who, after having witnessed a contested election, did not feel for the hardships to which many persons were exposed, and who did not wish that some measure of protection should be extended to them. The undue interference with the exercise of the suffrage was not consistent with the perfect freedom of the country; the Ballot was the only antidote against the taint which poisoned the life-blood of the representative system. It might be rejected, but it would not be rejected long.

The debate was enlivened by the brilliancy of Macaulay in support of the motion. He began with a long apology for open questions, as the Ballot was now made in the cabinet. He admitted that the Ballot would take from the voter some good, while it destroyed many bad motives. There was a time when he hoped that the evil of intimidation would yield to the force of public opinion and the progress of intelligence; he had, however, been compelled to relinquish that view. The evil had increased within the last seven years—within the last three years; and he attributed the increase in some measure to the Reform Bill. In saying so, he was only charging the Reform Bill with what accompanied every measure of improvement; the Reformation in the Church, and the Revolution both gave rise to new evils. The Reform Bill had extended the suffrage to thousands who were open to intimidation; and better be elected for Old Sarum than owe a seat to fear-extorted votes. All tyranny was bad, but the worst kind of tyranny was that which used the machinery of freedom. Intimidation was corruption in its worst and most loathsome form—it was corruption stripped of every blandishment and grace—of every savour-. ing of hospitable bounty and good humour. He was opposed to the reconstruction of the Reform Bill, but to make that Bill effectual they should not allow nomination to remain in an altered and more odious form. Lord John Russell made a laboured reply to Macaulay, and was himself severely handled by Sheil. Sir James Graham went into the vexed historical question, often brought up in the Ballot debates, as to what was the understanding of the original framers of the Reform Bill on the subject of the Ballot. Sir Robert Peel in a short speech lectured the cabinet on their doctrine of open questions.

On a division, the Ayes were 216; Noes, 333.

CHAPTER III.

MISCELLANEOUS SPEECHES.

1833.

MR. GROTE's maiden speech was delivered on the 22nd of February, in support of a motion to refer to the committee then sitting on Municipal Corporations, a petition from the Merchant Tailors' Company of the City of London. It had been denied that the City Companies were corporations in the same sense as the municipal corporations. Mr. Grote contended that as they were not companies in the commercial sense of the term, and as they passed regulations for particular trades, they exercised powers belonging properly to a municipal corporation.

More important was the occasion of his next speech, five days later, in opposition to the Irish Coercion Bill. In spite of his respect for the quarter whence the measure came, he could not approve of it. It contained some wise and tutelary provisions; but as a whole it would not answer its end. He could not speak of it but as a most revolting measure. He had listened patiently to the catalogue of enormities detailed by the noble lord (Althorp). This was nothing new to him; the Irish had ever been a lawless people, a fact not sufficiently dwelt upon. They (the legislature) should strengthen the hands of justice under the existing tribunals. The proposed courts-martial would not be impartial courts; and their mistakes would be on the side, not of mercy, but of severity. These courts-martial were held responsible only to higher courts-martial, which was no guarantee, for the condemnation of one military man by another would be prevented by the *esprit de corps* among officers. He objected to the Bill on two distinct grounds. The first was subjecting Ireland to the government of military tribunals; the next was the prohibition of public meetings, and the right to petition. "He was sure that they had not arrived yet at the period when the relations between the governors and the governed in that country were so pure, and so free from suspicion, as to enable the people to dispense with all the bulwarks of the constitution." There were abundance of grievances yet to redress in that country of long standing, and it would be wise as well as delicate in the Government to pause before they shut the door against all the public complaints from the people of Ireland.

On the following day he presented a petition from a number of persons called Separatists, who sought to be exempted, like the Quakers, from taking oaths. (This was afterwards done by Act 3 & 4 Will. IV., c. 82.)

On the 7th of March he presented a petition from Norwich, stating that the return of Lord Stormont and Sir James Scarlett had been effected by means of bribery and corruption, and praying that a Parliamentary Commission might be sent down, fully and fairly to enquire into and expose the system. He supported the prayer of the petition; but the Solicitor-General objected to it as irregular.

On the 13th he presented a petition from Marylebone against the Irish Coercion Bill, and gave his cordial support to the prayer of the petition.

On the 31st of May, he spoke on Lord Althorp's resolutions for a renewal of the Bank Charter. He concurred generally in the resolutions; but, on the 1st of July, in the debate on the second resolution, which made the promissory notes of the Bank of England a legal tender (although always payable in gold at the Bank itself, or any of its branches), he avowed an entire change of opinion, on the ground that in the poor districts there would not be an adequate supply of specie; there would, in fact, be a commission charged for gold over what would be demanded for notes. The clause would also hinder small depositors—men who had their thirty or forty pounds—from carrying gold to the country bank. He had a farther distrust of the measure from its being adopted and praised by gentlemen who held certain opinions on the question of the currency, sincerely enough, he had no doubt, but in his view injurious if adopted.

Lord Althorp followed, and declared that he had himself been much influenced by Mr. Grote's former opinions, given in evidence before the Committee on the Bank Charter, and could not concur in his new views. Mr. Clay thought that the manly and noble conduct of the honourable member for London, in thus frankly avowing what he now considered to be an error of opinion, was above all praise; and, instead of detracting from his character for talent and judgment, would only increase his deservedly high reputation. On Lord Althorp's fourth resolution, fixing the allowance to the Bank of England for managing the public debt, Mr. Clay moved an amendment in favour of reduction. Mr. Grote spoke in favour of another amendment for postponing the resolution, and making further investigation before fixing the allowance, which he did not think too great.

On the 19th of June, on the resumption of a debate on the claims of English subjects on the Danish Government, he presented a petition from claimants in the City of London; and contended that the case was one of great injustice.

On the 21st, in Committee on the Church Temporalities (Ireland) Bill, on clause 147 (application of monies arising from sale of perpetuities) being read, Mr. Secretary Stanley proposed the omission of the clause. A very excited debate followed. O'Connell indulged in his bitterest taunts. Dr. Lushington said he had never heard a discussion in which the decency of parliamentary language, or the courtesy of public life had been so much departed from. The question in dispute was the alienation of Church property to secular purposes. The clause involved this alienation in a small degree. At the same time the Government got out of the difficulty by maintaining that the funds alluded to were not Church property. Still, the clause was now surrendered. Mr. Grote spoke shortly, but with more than his accustomed

point and terseness. He did entertain an objection to the
Bill in the first instance, because it "did not, in his opinion,
go the length that people expected it would go towards
rectifying that great ecclesiastical enormity of Europe—the
Irish Church." Still, knowing the difficulties the ministers
would have to contend with in getting it passed, he felt
anxious to support it; but when he found that, defective as
it was, it was to be robbed of one of its chiefest members, he
felt bound to oppose the withdrawal of the clause. The
supposition was that the withdrawal had a view to what
might happen in the Lords; but what worse could the Lords
do than send the Bill back, and then they might consider
the omission of the clause. His advice to ministers was,
instead of offering a few crumbs of reform to the people, and
afterwards endeavouring to pare down even those few, to give
such measures as they might think just and necessary, without any reference to what might be the conduct of another
assembly.

Lord John Russell "confessed he turned with gratification
from the frothy declamation which had so lavishly been
bestowed on the subject, to the calm, and as usual, rational
arguments which had been addressed to the House by the
honourable member for London." The gist of his speech
was to avoid a contest with the Lords until there was a question of still greater importance to contend for; "he was of
opinion that this country could not stand a revolution once
a-year."

On the 2nd of July he presented a petition from the
merchants of London, trading with Oporto, complaining of
the losses undergone by them in the struggle existing for the
last ten months in Portugal.

On the 30th Mr. Roebuck moved that the House would,
with the smallest delay possible, consider the means of
establishing a system of national education. Mr. Grote
seconded the motion, in the belief that two things were perfectly true; the first, that the present system of education
was defective: the other, that the defects could not be

remedied without the assistance of Government. He referred
in terms of great commendation to Cousin's book on 'Education in France.'

On the 7th of August, on the third reading of the Customs'
Duties Bill, after commenting on the enormous duty on cur-
rants—14s. 4d. per cwt.—he moved its reduction to 28s.; the
motion was defeated by a small majority.

On the 9th, on a clause in the Renewal of the Bank
Charter, continuing the renewal for ten years, he urged that
seven years would be a sufficiently long period.

On the 10th he recommended that the variations in the
Bank circulation should be published weekly in the *Gazette*.

1834.

The opening days of this session were troubled with the
discussion of a charge made against Mr. Sheil, that while
voting against the Irish Coercion Bill of last session, he had
privately expressed himself to the effect, that Ministers ought
to press the Bill, and that it is impossible to live in Ireland
without it. An extraordinary personal altercation took place
between Lord Althorp and Mr. Sheil; and they were both
ordered into the custody of the Serjeant-at-arms until they
gave assurances that they would take no steps outside the
House. Mr. O'Connell moved the appointment of a Committee of Privileges to investigate the charge, which was
carried by a large majority. Mr. Grote was made chairman
of the committee. On the 12th of February he rose in the
House to move, by request of the committee, that Mr.
O'Connell's name be now added to the committee; he having,
in his motion, declined to name himself. After some stick-
ling, the motion was agreed to. On the 14th Mr. Grote
brought up the report of the committee, which was a complete vindication of Mr. Sheil's character.

On the 20th of February he presented a petition from the
parishioners of Allhallows, Lombard Street, disapproving of

the conduct of the Dean and Chapter of Canterbury, in preferring to the incumbency of the parish a non-resident; and
took the opportunity of making some remarks on the necessity of an early measure of Church Reform.   In a speech
palliating the appointment, Sir R. Inglis acknowledged the
calm and temperate manner in which Mr. Grote had discussed
what persons, not of his temper and discretion, would have
made an occasion to provoke other sentiments than he had
roused.

On the 18th of March he took part in a debate on the
Tea Duties.

On the 14th of April, in Committee of Supply, he objected
strongly to the amount of the vote for the Consular Department, and also to the discrepancies of the salaries.   The following day, on a vote of £20,000 for education, he was of
opinion that the Government ought to extend the vote.

On the 30th he opposed the second reading of Sir A.
Agnew's Bill for the Observance of the Sabbath.   He considered it nothing more or less than a sentence of imprisonment upon the working classes of society upon the Sabbath.
" Religion to be effective must be spontaneous and sincere."

On the 9th of May, Lord Althorp moved the second
reading of the Poor Laws Amendment Bill.   Mr. Grote was
an active supporter of the measure in all its stages.   In the
debate on the second reading, he spoke with intense fervour
on the necessity of the change.   He had perused with deliberate attention all the Reports of the Commission of
Inquiry.   Even the vast and abusive expenditure under the
present law was as dust in the balance compared with the
evil effect on the character and comfort of the labouring
classes.   He was aware of the great jealousy expressed at
the powers to be vested in the Commissioners; but the
question was, did the urgency of the case require them?
His concluding sentences are :—" Entertaining a strong and
decided opinion on this subject, I have done my best to
persuade the House to read this Bill a second time.   I know
that I have done this at no small risk of favour and popu-

larity to myself; for I understand that a petition was this day presented from my own constituents, directed strongly against the passing of this Bill. Sir, it is not without the deepest regret and concern that I find myself opposed to constituents to whom I am attached by every tie, and to whom I owe the honourable station which I now occupy. But so strong is my conviction of the absolute necessity of some large remedial measure as an antidote to the overwhelming evil of pauperism—so firm is my belief of the necessity of some central supervising agency to secure the fulfilment of any salutary provisions which the legislature may prescribe—so strong is my conviction on these cardinal points, that if it were to cost me the certain sacrifice of my seat, I should feel bound to tell my constituents that I dissented from them, and that I would do my best to promote the attainment of this necessary, and, in the main, valuable remedy. In doing so, I should feel with pain that I had decided contrary to the opinion of my constituents; but I should also feel, that I had decided in unison with the best interests of my country."

In Committee, he spoke frequently on the details. He opposed the concession of the Government to limit the appointment of the Commissioners to five years. On the bastardy clauses he complained that Lord Althorp was making concessions to the public feeling rather than to reason or argument.

On the 27th of May, Mr. Ward brought forward his motion for reducing the revenues of the Irish Church. Mr. Grote was to second the motion. Those who sought to identify the two Churches of England and Ireland would degrade the one church without elevating the other. There was only one case in Europe where the temporalities of the established church went, not to a majority, but to a small minority of the people, and that was Ireland. In France, under the bigoted reign of Charles X., the cost of religious worship to the State was less than one shilling a head; in Ireland it was one pound ten shillings a head. Some contended

that the State had no right to touch the property of the
Irish Church, or to apply it to other than religious purposes.
This might be maintained by a Roman-Catholic, but every
Protestant must be aware that in the progress of the Reformation church property had been diverted to' other purposes.   If the legislature attempted to continue the Irish
Church in its present magnitude, the legislature would share
in its. unpopularity ; it was considered a grievance upheld
only by the irresistible influence of English connexion.
When the advocates of the repeal of the Union put forward
the evils of the Irish Church establishment, no man replied.

Although this speech was composed and appears in
Hansard, it was not delivered (see " Life," p. 90.)

On the 8th of July, he supported Mr. Ward's motion for
taking authentic lists of the divisions of the House.   The
motion was carried ; and from that time commenced the
recording of the names of those that vote in the divisions.

On the 25th, on the Order of the Day for the House to
resolve itself into a Committee of Ways and Means, Mr.
Goulburn made an attack upon the Government for increasing offices, by Commissions and otherwise, and particularly
instanced an office held by Macaulay.   Mr. Grote defended
the expenditure upon Commissions of Inquiry, but with
regard to the salary given to Mr. Macaulay, with all his
admiration for that excellent and most gifted individual, he
could not but consider it extravagant.

1835.

Sir Robert Peel was now in office, and the opening of the
Session was marked by an animated debate.   In the Commons
an Amendment on the Address was moved by Lord Morpeth,
strongly expressing the desirableness of prosecuting measures
of reform, and condemning the recent dissolution of Parliament.   Mr. Pemberton replied to the very vigorous attack
of Lord Morpeth.   Mr. Ewart spoke for the amendment.

Mr. Richards made an apology for ministers, on the ground that the late Government itself was not giving satisfaction to reformers; among other illustrations, he quoted their reception of the Ballot. Mr. Grote then rose. He said his reform principles conducted him to very different conclusions from the member who had just sat down. As a reformer, he could not consent to look for a ministry in the ranks of the party over the most hostile to reform. If his present vote would have the effect of displacing the present Government, that would be an additional reason for giving it. Lord Grey's administration had been slow in making reforms, but that could not be said of Lord Melbourne's, seeing it had not been allowed that fair trial for which the advocates of the present Government were so clamorous. Great public excitement had been created, which could be allayed only by the assurance, contained in the Amendment, that the cause of reform was not to suffer. The Royal Speech, if it had come from a ministry he confided in, would not have given him satisfaction, but coming from a ministry in which he had no confidence at all, was still more objectionable. Its defects would have justified a still stronger amendment. He could not forget their acts previous to 1830. The Government of Lord Grey was the first that had openly approved of and acted on the principles of Reform; it did not come up to his wishes; but however slow, it would never stand still. The mover of the address had spoken of a morbid desire for change; what he found was an ardent wish for improving our institutions. Whoever asserted that there was anything incompatible with law and government was guilty of a calumny upon the body of the people. Reformers had been taunted with want of unanimity, but they had quite enough of sense and reflection to pursue the stream of Reform peaceably and calmly, without even allowing the impediments that they might meet with to force them out of their channel, or to make them fret and foam with vexation. He thought the defence of the ministry by a reference to the King's prerogative, would soon lead the prerogative itself to be questioned.

The Amendment was carried by 309 to 302.

On the 10th of March, in a debate on the Malt Duties, Sir James Graham had made allusion to a change of ministry, and said "they had been told of, or rather threatened with, a Grote and Warburton Administration." Mr. Grote rose in consequence. He said a friend "had been pleased to connect his name with a possible ministry: he, however, regretted such a fancy had ever been started, inasmuch as such a situation was as much above his ambition, as it would be foreign to his taste, his pursuits, and his interests." Moreover, on the present question, he dissented from the very persons that were to be coupled with him in the supposed ministry. He objected to the repeal of the Malt Duties, and considered Sir Robert Peel's arguments to be unanswerable, and rejoiced that he had dispersed so many of the agricultural fallacies so often put forth in the House.

The following night, Sir George Grey moved for a Committee to enquire into the most effectual method to put a stop to bribery at elections. Mr. Grote expressed himself willing to go into the Committee with the fullest disposition to consider any remedy that might be proposed, apart from the Ballot, and trusted that if they were unsuccessful, they would follow the example of the member for Edinburgh, and get over their former scruples and objections to the Ballot. The Committee was appointed.

On the 18th, Sir John Campbell moved the second reading of the Imprisonment for Debt Bill. The Bill abolished imprisonment, except in the cases of fraud. Mr. Grote said the Bill was recommended both by policy and by humanity: and he was more convinced of this by the speech (hostile) of the President of the Board of Trade than by any other reasoning on the subject. He was better pleased that his views should be sustained by the failure of his opponent's arguments, than by the success of his own.

On the 27th of May, Mr. Shaw presented several petitions expressing, in somewhat violent language, alarm and dismay at the proposed measure respecting the Irish Church.

Various members commented upon the language of the petitions. Mr. Grote would make only one observation on the subject. Much had often been said as to the ferocious language of the Radicals and the working classes: but no petition coming from these ever abounded in such calumnious assertions, and imputation of the worst motives as the petition now coming from the Conservatives of South Lancashire, and likewise the petition from Durham. It was right that the same character should be applied to violent language, whether it came from the ultra-Pious or the ultra-Radical.

On the 15th of June, the Municipal Corporation Bill was unanimously read a second time. Mr. Grote, commenting upon a speech of Lord Stanley's, objected to the large number of councillors allowed by the Bill; and advocated the removability of charitable trustees, and also of the recorder. He also protested against a proposal for retaining the franchise of the freemen. Both on this occasion, and afterwards in Committee, he opposed the qualification of a three years' occupancy.

On the 26th of June, he presented a petition from Great Yarmouth, praying for the Ballot, in consequence of the drunkenness, riot and corruption at the last election there. He should have wished the petition referred to a Select Committee, but he was personally overcharged with Committee business, and could not attend to it.

On the 1st of July, in Committee on the Municipal Corporation Bill, on clause 23, providing that one-third of the Town Councils should go out of office annually, an amendment was moved by Mr. Charles Buller, to the effect that the whole be elected annually. Mr. Grote supported the principle of annual election, and from the experience of the City of London, refuted the objection that it would cause a continual influx of new and inexperienced men. The same evening he moved, in a short speech, the introduction of the Ballot at Municipal Elections; but did not press the motion to a vote.

On the 31st of August, there came on for consideration the Lords' Amendments to the Municipal Corporations Bill. Considerable public excitement had been aroused by these amendments. Lord John Russell stated what points the Government would, and what they would not, surrender. Sir Robert Peel followed and assisted in compromising the differences. Mr. Hume objected to the amount of the concessions. Mr. Grote still more emphatically. Whatever he might think of the proceedings of the House of Lords in other respects, he was bound to acknowledge that they had resolutely adhered to their independent character; and it would not be amiss if the Commons would do the same. It would ill become the dignity of that House—the assembled representatives of the people of England—to yield important principles merely for the purpose of conciliating the other House of Parliament. When the people of England were fully and justly represented in that House, there ought to be no other power in the State which should be able to stand against them. He complained that Lord John Russell, in one or two of his concessions, had gone the length of vindicating the Lords' amendments on their merits. He would rather wait for a better Bill than barter away the best principles of the measure for the purpose of getting the immediate consent of the other House.

Both on that occasion and next night, he objected strongly to the test of pecuniary qualification, which Lord John Russell agreed to retain with a modification suggested by Sir Robert Peel. He had come down to the House with the full intention of dividing upon this question, but had been induced, in consequence of the observations he had heard, to alter his purpose. Still he was anxious to give his reasons, namely, his repugnance to the principle of qualification, and his sense that the concession was too great. He thought the tone of the present debate was calculated to have no other effect than to give the Lords a power of legislating over this House, and to make the country believe that this House would not stand by any great principle which it had endeavoured to establish. He could not see what the country had gained by the Reform Bill, which had in a great degree put an end to the system of filling the House with nominees of the Lords, if the other House was to exercise its power in another way, by enabling minorities of the Commons to triumph over decided majorities of the representatives of the people.

1836.

On the 20th of April, a keen discussion arose as to members of the House voting on Private Bills wherein they had a pecuniary interest. Mr. Grote agreed in the principle, but did not see how it could be fully carried out. The inference that he would draw was that Committees of that House were not fit tribunals for deciding private business.

The same night, in presenting a petition from sixty merchants of the City of London, complaining of the ill effects, on our commerce with Turkey, of the overbearing interference of Russia,—he deprecated any course that would involve this country in a war with Russia. It had of late become the custom to use very unmeasured language as to the aggressions of Russia, respecting which, whatever opinion he might entertain as a private individual, he considered unwise and impolitic when expressed in the House.

On the 22nd, a motion was made to inculpate Mr. O'Connell for his share in making a corrupt bargain at the Carlow election, notwithstanding that a Select Committee had sat upon the transaction and given in a Report in an opposite sense. It was a purely party move. Mr. Grote stood upon the decision of the Committee, as being cool and impartial, whereas the present motion had the character of political hostility to O'Connell. It was somewhat remarkable that hon. gentlemen opposite, who were now so anxious to preserve the purity of election, had taken a very different course last year when the York and Great Yarmouth cases were under discussion. The House on that occasion was content with pronouncing a slight censure on the parties implicated; but if the hon. members on that (the Ministerial) side of the House had insisted on dragging those men up again, would it not have been denounced as an act of the grossest partiality, emanating from a low spiteful feeling of personal hostility?

On the 29th, he presented a petition for the equalisation of the duty on East and West India sugars; and thought that they were called by every reason of justice, fairness and policy to abolish the discriminating duty in favour of the West Indies.

On the 9th of June, the House had to consider the Lords' Amendments to the Municipal Corporations (Ireland) Bill; the debate lasting two nights. Lord John Russell, on the part of the Government, took a more decided tone on this occasion than in the case of the English bill; but yet proposed certain concessions. Mr. Grote spoke as usual shortly, but with increased emphasis on the hostile attitude of the Lords. He would have preferred that the Lords' Amendments should have been at once rejected, unless they had found any one that they could in their consciences approve. If ever there was a Bill, on which the House should look to its own dignity, it was the one now before them, for it had been dealt with by the other House in a manner in which no Bill had ever before been treated. The representatives of the people might have been spared the pain of making concessions to those who had declined, he might almost say exultingly declined, to make anything like concessions to them. He did not wish to speak lightly of a collision between the two Houses of Parliament; but let the collision come when it might, it never would arise on a more noble or a more natural object than the present. The fact that they must meet with the same spirit of opposition from their Lordships on all important measures, rendered him less solicitous than he might otherwise have been for the settlement of the difference between the two Houses on this particular subject. When he saw the House of Commons perpetually considering upon all measures of reform, not how much they ought in justice to give, but how much the Lords would be disposed to grant, he thought that the time was come when they ought to inform their constituents of that melancholy truth, and let them decide whether they would be governed on the principles avowed by the House of Lords, or on those acted on by the House of Commons.

On the 16th of July, in Committee on the Stamp Duties Bill, he strongly trusted the time would soon arrive when the Chancellor of the Exchequer would propose the abolition of the penny duty, and thereby remove every obstacle to the diffusion of knowledge throughout the country.

On the 25th the Established Church Bill was read a third time. In the debate Mr. Grote protested against the allowances to the bishops. The very lowest salary granted by the bill he held sufficient for the Archbishop of Canterbury, instead of 15,000*l.* a year as proposed. Why, was it possible to conceive any set of duties which could be more easily or tranquilly performed, or which were more exempt from all those difficulties that required labour, assiduity and talent to surmount them, than those allotted to the Archbishop of Canterbury? It was impossible not to draw a comparison between those incomes and the miserable stipends of the working clergy. It was said 100*l.* or 150*l.* a year was enough for a curate, yet the Archbishop of Canterbury was not in anywise the superior of the humbler individuals so remunerated.

1837.

In April this year came up the Canada Resolutions, on which Mr. Grote spoke repeatedly in opposition to the Government. His first and longest speech was on the 21st, in answer to Sir Robert Peel's criticism of Mr. Roebuck's proposal that the Upper House of Assembly should be merely advisers to the governor and not a co-ordinate branch of the legislature. He considered that the exercise of a veto upon the popular assembly by such a council as was proposed was infinitely more obnoxious than the veto of the governor, who had the prestige of a representative of the power and majesty of the king. On the bringing up of the Report of the Resolutions on the 28th, he declared his continued regret at the decision of the House regarding them.

On the 10th of May he supported a bill for abolishing the qualification arising out of the payment of rates and taxes, required by the Reform Act for borough, but not for county voters.

On the 22nd, in Committee on the Bill for abolishing the Punishment of Death in the Burning or Destroying Buildings and Ships, he urged that if the punishment of death was to be retained, it would be better that it should be inflicted in private, as public executions were never attended with beneficial results.

The death of the king having led to a dissolution of Parliament on the 17th of July, the Houses reassembled on the 15th of November. On the 20th was moved the address to the Queen's Speech. On that night, and on the following, Lord John Russell gave answers to the complaints made by the advanced liberals, that the Government was backward in measures of further reform. Mr. Grote gave the noble lord credit for his candour, but could not award him any higher commendation. He complained that the noble lord had regarded the Ballot as inseparable from the two other questions of extension of the suffrage and repeal of the Septennial Act. He was favourable to the two last measures, but would bring forward the Ballot on its own independent merits. If such arguments as were now used by the noble lord had been allowed to prevail on a former occasion, the Reform Bill itself would never have passed. He felt deeply sorry for the declarations just made by the noble lord; they would produce a greater and much more painful sensation than the Duke of Wellington's celebrated declaration against the Reform Bill.

On the 4th of December, on going into Committee upon
the Municipal Officers' Declaration Bill, framed for the relief
of Quakers and Moravians, Mr. Grote moved that the bill
be extended to all classes of Her Majesty's subjects. The
extension was meant for the Jews. The amendment was
lost by a majority of 16.

On the 13th of December, in a speech of great delicacy
and tact, he took exception to a proposal for granting an
addition of 8000*l.* a year to the income of the Duchess of
Kent. He was one of those who took the strongest view of
the duty of economising the public money. He often, therefore, felt bound to resist the claims made on the public purse
by those in the middle station, and in that more humble
than it. He could not take that course with satisfaction to
his own feelings and conscience, unless he was prepared to
exercise the same scrutinising investigation into the claims
of those who filled an exalted station.

On the 15th the Civil List had to be voted. Mr. Hume
moved the reduction of the vote to Her Majesty (385,000*l.*)
by 50,000*l.* Mr. Grote would most willingly support everything that could add not only to the comfort and elegance,
but also to the dignity and splendour of the Sovereign; yet
he was of opinion that the best friends to the respectability
of the Crown were those who were most anxious that it should
not appear in the light of an odious and unnecessary burden
on the shoulders of the people.

On the 19th he made a motion to remove from the Civil
List the sum allotted to pensions. He argued against those
pensions in a speech of some length. His objections were
that no adequate public advantage accrued from the fund;
that it involved a double and conflicting reference to the
reward of merit and the relief of distress; that in this last
application it was in contradiction to the strict principle
involved in the Poor Law Amendment Act; and that it was
a means of patronage to the Government of the day.

On the 22nd, a debate was brought in by Mr. Leader on
the affairs of Canada, now in a state of rebellion. Mr. Grote

traced the present calamities to last year's resolutions: he
would not have these resolutions on his conscience for anything that could be offered him. He regretted to find the
confidence prevailing on both sides of the House, that the
expression of a strong opinion from a large majority in
the British Parliament, was alone necessary to put down at
once all idea of resistance in the minds of the people of
Canada. Many had said that there was no analogy between
the present state of Canada and that of the provinces of the
United States in 1774. He contended that the grievances
in both cases were the same, the principal being the right of
the British Government to take the people's money. He
had listened with surprise to the member for Newark
(Mr. Gladstone) when he said it was not a mere speculative
grievance, or grievance of principle, but a series of protracted oppressions, which had led the United States of
America to shake off the yoke of Britain. That statement
was entirely inaccurate. The British Legislature had assumed
over Canada, as it had done over the United States, a right
of control, which however the noble lord (Lord John Russell)
might regard it, he was sure would have been considered by
the Lord Russell of former days, and by Algernon Sydney,
as equal to a sentence of slavery.

1838.

Canada was the first subject of this session.

On the 16th of January, Lord John Russell moved an
Address to the Queen, expressing regret at the Canadian rebellion, and assuring Her Majesty "that while this House is
ever ready to afford relief to real grievances, we are fully
determined to support the efforts of Her Majesty for the suppression of revolt and the restoration of tranquillity."

Mr. Grote used very strong language in disapproving of
the Government for the absence of all conciliating measures,
while bent upon the employment of force to suppress the

rebellion. He unfavourably criticised the whole policy of the Home Government in the treatment of the colony. He could see no benefit from severity and coercion, whilst it must produce the great evil of continuing in the minds of the inhabitants a feeling of despair that justice would be done to their country.

Next day, he presented and supported a petition from Mr. Roebuck, praying that he might be heard at the bar in the defence of the House of Assembly of Lower Canada, and in opposition to the measure of "impolicy and injustice" which Government meant to introduce with regard to that country. The petition was ordered to be printed.

On the 22nd, he formally proposed "that John Arthur Roebuck, Esq., be heard at the bar of the House, as the agent of the Assembly of Lower Canada, against the Canada Bill, on the second reading thereof." As the Bill meant to suspend the constitution of the colony, which was, in fact, a suspension of the House of Assembly, it was a matter of justice to give the agent of that body an opportunity of defending the body at the bar of the House.

Mr. Gladstone followed, and while agreeing that it would be most desirable to hear Mr. Roebuck, protested against recognising him as "the agent of the House of Assembly."

After speeches by Lord John Russell, Lord Stanley, and others, on the technical form of the proposal, the House decided in favour of hearing Roebuck. Accordingly, on the Order of the Day for the second reading of the Lower Canada Government Bill, he advanced to the bar, and addressed the House. On his retiring, the debate commenced on a motion that the House go into committee on the Bill. On the second night of the debate (23rd of January) Mr. Grote spoke. He concurred in the propriety of sending out Lord Durham as Governor of Canada; and he could also express his satisfaction at the announcement of the intention of the Government to exercise clemency towards those who had been engaged in the late revolt. He complained, however, that the chances of Lord Durham's success were very much spoiled by the suspension of the Assembly. He had before expressed an opinion, which was not very favourably received in the House, but which he, nevertheless, sincerely entertained, that a separation between the colony and the mother-country was the most desirable thing that could happen, both for the mother-country and for the colony. Already there was the commencement of a feeling of sympathy between the Canadas and the people of the United States. If they would have colonial possessions such as Canada, they had this difficult problem to solve—they had to maintain the supremacy of this country, and at the same time to give satisfaction to the Canadian people. It was usual to make severe remarks on the speeches of what is called the Radical party in the House (of Commons), and to speak contemptuously of the smallness of their numbers, although he was rather surprised, if the Radical party were really so small and contemptible, that honourable members should find so much in their speeches worthy of comment; but he must say, that of the speeches in the House that were likely to alienate the feelings of the colonists, it was not those that spoke for them, but those that spoke against them, which were more likely to produce such a result.

On the 29th, there was a debate on the third reading of the Canada Bill. Mr. Grote spoke with the same emphasis as before. He saw in the Bill no remedy proposed for any of the evils that now constituted the grievances of the Canadians, while he saw in it one great grievance added to those already existing, of which, even those that had hitherto abstained from taking part in these matters must feel the burden. The representation of the people in Canada would now be a name and a shadow. In answer to the allegation that the constitution had become unworkable, he blamed the Executive Government for not using its prerogative in the appointment of members such as would be acceptable to the majority of the people. They might foresee the difficulties of suspending an existing constitution, when they heard the proposition of a supporter of the Government to saddle the colony with an

Established Church. The same reasons that led him to wish to improve the representative institutions in this country, which imperfectly and unfaithfully represented the people, induced him to be strenuous in preserving the Canadian Assembly, which really did represent the people. He doubted and mistrusted the power of the Government to restore the Assembly, and he did not feel confident that they wished it; the more so, when he observed that the Government had to conciliate Sir Robert Peel, and to obtain his support, in whatever new constitution might be given to Canada.

On the 25th of April Mr. Serjeant Talfourd moved the second reading of his Copyright Bill, which was to extend the term of copyright to sixty years. Mr. Grote opposed the measure as replete with mischief to the public, doubtful in its pecuniary results as to the authors themselves, and calculated to rob those authors of what, he was persuaded, they set a greater value upon than any pecuniary gain—a wide and enduring circle of literary and intrinsic admiration.

On the 19th of July, on a proposition of Lord John Russell for an additional advance of money to the relief of the owners of compositions for tithes in Ireland, he offered his strenuous resistance, confessing, however, that after the surrender of the appropriation clause, he had ceased to take any interest in the Tithe Bill. At the same time, when he found that a large sum of money was to be paid out of the pockets of the people of England, he was bound to declare that no proposition had ever been submitted to the House since he became a member to which he felt a more unqualified opposition. Lord John Russell replied in the usual strain, that the Government could not, in their circumstances, with the hostility they encountered both in the Commons and in the Lords, do more than they had done.

On the 26th, the Irish Tithe Bill was read a third time. The debate was stormy. Mr. Grote excelled himself in the energy of his denunciation of the measure. The Bill would only raise increased odium to the existing constitution of the Irish Church. Now he had been as unreserved as any man in the expression of his abhorrence of the monstrous principle, and the equally monstrous effects of that establishment, but he would not for that reason support a Bill which he conscientiously objected to. If any settlement of the Irish Church question were proposed, founded on just principles, and likely to be final, he would not object to a grant for closing a wound that had so long been bleeding.

On the 15th of August, on the Order of the Day for the third reading of the Canada Government Declaratory and Indemnity Bill, he declared his satisfaction at being one of the inconsiderable minority that had opposed the Act for the temporary government of Lower Canada, out of which had arisen the necessity for this Bill. He could not reconcile the Bill with the encomiums passed by its supporters on Lord Durham; if the noble lord deserved those encomiums, that Bill was not necessary; and if he had been guilty of illegal acts, the encomiums could not be right.

1839.

Parliament was opened on the 5th of February, but Mr. Grote's name does not appear in the debates, till the 5th of March. On that day he supports Mr. Milner Gibson, in urging Lord Palmerston to counteract the Russian influence that had been brought to bear on Sweden against making Slito a free port.

On the 12th of March, Mr. Villiers brought on a motion on the Corn Laws, which led to a five nights' debate. On the second night, Mr. Grote supported the motion in a speech occupying ten pages of *Hansard*. His characteristics as a debater—the mastery and handling of facts, the argumentative vigour and point, the telling retort of the allegations on the other side—are fully displayed on this occasion. But in a subject so completely thrashed out, it is not advisable to occupy space with an analysis of the speech.

On the 19th, there was a debate, introduced by Lord Sandon, on the French blockade of the Mexican ports. Mr. Grote took part, and after unfavourably criticising the French proceeding, he found fault with Lord Palmerston for the tardiness of his interference.

On the 21st, Mr. Hume made a motion in favour of Household Suffrage, and prefaced it by an elaborate speech. Lord John Russell followed Mr. Hume, and was followed by Mr. Grote. The noble lord, he said, had dwelt very much on the mischiefs of the future changes, and the danger of unsettling the principles of the Reform Act; and he must say that the noble lord had borrowed many of his observations from the speeches made by the opponents of his own Bill in 1831 and 1832. He did not think the noble lord would carry the public with him by simply telling them that they had got the Reform Bill, and must be content to take it for better or for worse. He could not consent to treat the Reform Act as a kind of canon of Scripture, which was to have nothing added and nothing taken away. He saw no valid reason for withholding the elective suffrage from any man, unless it could be proved, or a strong presumption could be raised, that he was unfit to exercise it; that was the view of representative government in every nation that possessed one. The householders under £10 were men labouring assiduously every day, discharging faithfully all the obligations of private life, having the greatest possible interest in the inviolability of the laws that ensured the stability of property and secured the earnings of industry. Instead of having the interest imputed to them by the noble lord of defrauding the public creditor, the working classes would lend no approbation or acceptance to a measure so injurious to themselves.

On the 15th of April, in consequence of Lord Roden's motion carried in the House of Lords to appoint a Select Committee to enquire into the state of Ireland, Lord John Russell, in a very long speech, asked the House to express approval of the Irish administration of the Government.

On the third night of the debate that followed, Mr. Grote spoke shortly. He said that if the question now at issue were simply the conduct of the Irish executive under the Marquis of Normanby, he should have no hesitation in giving his vote in favour of the resolution. He must, however, guard himself against being supposed to go beyond the letter of the resolution, or to express confidence in Lord Melbourne's Government generally. The Irish executive administration is in truth almost the only remnant of Liberalism which now distinguishes ministers from the gentlemen opposite; and for this reason it has been most abundantly attacked. What is the doctrine of finality so often preached from the Treasury bench, but the Conservative principle announced in all its plenitude and in all its vigour? For the first time in modern English history, we have neither a Liberal Ministry nor a Liberal Opposition.

On the 3rd of May, Lord John Russell moved that the House go into Committee on the Jamaica Bill, by which it was proposed to suspend for a time the Legislative Assembly. Mr. Grote, as might have been expected, strongly opposed the Bill, both on the score of justice and on the score of wisdom. The smallness of the ministerial majority (5), led to the resignation of Ministers, and to Sir Robert Peel's attempt to form a Government, which was frustrated by the Queen's refusing to part with her ladies of the bedchamber.

On the 8th of July, Mr. Hume moved for a Committee on the whole history and constitution of the Bank of England. Mr. Grote approved of an enquiry, but considered it too wide in its scope to be undertaken at so late a period of the session.

1840.

During this session, Mr. Grote spoke but seldom.

On the 1st of April, he took part in the three days' debate

on the Corn Laws, raised on a motion by Mr. Charles Villiers.

On the 15th of May, in the debate on the Budget, he urged the removal of the stamp duty on policies of marine insurance.

The only other speech was with reference to a motion by Lord Althorp (10th of March) for a Committee to enquire into the effects produced by the note-issuing banking establishments. Mr. Grote was favourable to the appointment of the Committee, and mentioned the points that he thought it should take up, and also those that he thought it should avoid.

1841.

In the debate on the Address, on the 26th of January, Mr. Grote made a noted speech on the Syrian question. He could not forget that we have been exerting our force against persons with whom we have not the slenderest grounds of quarrel: neither Mehemet Ali nor his supporters, nor any other person in Syria, has done the least injury to English men or to English interests: nay, we have been gainers by the government of the Pasha in Syria. We are told the expedition was undertaken for maintaining the integrity of the Ottoman empire, under a treaty of July, 1839. Setting aside the French opposition to the treaty, and our dangers arising therefrom, he disputed the wisdom of the guarantee. He asked whether we have fully viewed the extent of the consequences of this guarantee. It was often said that we should interfere in Turkey, to prevent Russia from interfering. If the only method of excluding the Emperor Nicholas from Constantinople is to keep constantly ahead of him in devoted offers to the Sultan, our chance is but slender. The real security is the direct terror of our arms. But as to our Syrian expedition, Russia is herself the grand projector of the enterprise. We are consulting the very party whom we suspect of entertaining thievish designs as to the best means of locking up and preserving our treasure. We have been hurried to the verge of an European war. The rupture between England and France is a signal calamity for both. The initial cause of so fatal a change— the tropical point from which the sun of peace began to avert his cheering rays from the latitude of Europe, is to be found in the treaty of last July, and in our Syrian expedition which followed it. The Foreign Secretary has cured, or professes to have cured, a distemper in the extremities of the Continent; but the medicine has driven the distemper into the heart and vitals. If the noble lord has accomplished a new settlement of the Ottoman empire, he has at the same time forcibly abrogated a pre-existing settlement, to which he himself had assented. That we should undertake to maintain the integrity of the Ottoman empire, both against foreign invaders and against itself and its own internal causes of disruption, he must record his deliberate protest, as well as against our recent embodiment of the principle in the Syrian expedition. If, in respect to our internal affairs, we are destined to obtain no farther progress; if the cold shadows of finality have at length closed in around us, and intercepted all visions of a brighter future ; if the glowing hopes once associated with a Reform Ministry and the reformed Parliament have perished like an exploded bubble,—at least in regard to our foreign affairs, let us preserve from shipwreck that which is the first of all blessings and necessities ; that which was bequeathed to us by the ante-Reform Ministry and the unreformed Parliament —I mean peace and accord with the leading nations of Europe, but especially with our nearest and greatest neighbour, France.

On the 15th of March, he strongly supported a motion by Lord John Russell, for a loan to the colony of South Australia, to rescue it from pressing financial difficulties. He had been one of the original supporters of the plan for forming the colony, and although he had no pecuniary interest in it, he considered, in opposition to many members, that the colony had not been a failure.

In the discussions connected with the Poor Law Amendment Bill, Mr. Grote took an active part. He uniformly defended the principles of the Bill, and supported its most stringent provisions; in Committee he suggested a number of amendments. In replying to Mr. Duncombe's attacks on the Commissioners, he remarked, that he had supported the Bill of 1834, in opposition to his own constituency; but he had now the satisfaction of knowing that in the City of London the law was favourably regarded by the great body of the ratepayers.

On the 25th of March (and again on the 22nd of April) he brought forward a series of resolutions relative to New South Wales. The resolutions were grounded on the complaint that our Government had thrown upon the colony the whole burden of the gaols and police, rendered necessary for the convicts sent out from this country, and had appropriated for that purpose the money arising from the land and emigration fund. He proposed that the charge should be in some way apportioned between the colony and the mother-country. A considerable debate ensued, but the motion was negatived by 54 to 10.

His final effort in Parliament was in the great Sugar Duties debate on the 11th of May of this year. He put forth all his argumentative power on this occasion. At the commencement he descanted on Free Trade generally, and forcibly urged the mischiefs of protection in corn; the alternate hot and cold fits of the corn-trade must be regarded by every one as a serious evil. Applying himself to the Sugar question, he took up the protectionist's favourite argument from the encouragement of slavery, and turned it over on every side. His own abhorrence of slavery is expressed in terms of unmistakeable sincerity; while he exposes all the subterfuges of protection in claiming to discourage the slave-labour of Brazil and Cuba. As regards our home population, he did not wish to draw pictures of distress, or to move the

feelings of the House by describing the circumstances of those whose condition is the least comfortable. He never thought that a just or deliberate judgment upon any controverted question could be promoted by such a mode of treating it. It was enough for his argument to state the plain matter of fact, that there are millions of persons in these realms to whom the difference in the price of sugar is most sensibly felt in their morning and evening meals.

CHAPTER IV.

'THE HISTORY OF GREECE.'

THE actual composition of the 'History of Greece'—such as it appeared in a published form in 1846—was commenced in 1842.

The preparation for the work may be shortly summed up thus:—

First, in the reading, re-reading, and cogitation of the original sources and authorities, together with the study of the commentators, critics, and interpreters of the facts. For many years had he pondered the authors of classical Greece; his interest not being limited to historical narrative, but extending to the literature for its own sake, and still more to the philosophy for its own sake. His desire from the beginning was to realise not merely the events, but also the manners, habits, modes of life, and institutions, private as well as public. On all these matters he had already composed methodical and, as far as possible, exhaustive sketches.

He had also systematically gone through a wide course of reading of the manners, habits, customs, institutions, and peculiarities of all other recorded nations, especially at the earlier stages of civilization. In his commonplace books and references he had a very great collection of such facts, and the 'History' itself is strewn with illustrative allusions from that source. Of late years, still greater attention has been paid to this region of historical wealth; and the available material has been considerably augmented; while novel inferences have been drawn from the experience thus brought to view.

Mr. Grote possessed that essential quality of a historian—

the historical or narrative interest. In school days he
devoured novels; in later life the place of these was taken
by histories and biographies relating to every nation and
time. He felt and avowed the still more peculiar interest in
the process of growth or evolution, whether in political institutions, in literature, or in philosophy and science. The
historical taste was thus with him a very wide and mixed
susceptibility, and his narrative compositions became corre-
spondingly varied in their interest.

His earnest devotion to mental science, in all departments — psychology, ethics, metaphysics, and logic — had
no small share in the characteristic excellencies of his
historical compositions. Very few metaphysicians have
become historians on the great scale; the most conspicuous
examples are Hume and James Mill. To these authors
has always been attributed, among other merits, a peculiar
subtlety in the dissection of motives and the exhibition
of character. Metaphysical superiority is the cause (or,
at all events, the evidence) of one great quality of the
historian—the *analytic* aptitude or faculty. Science and
analysis are nearly convertible terms. The chain of cause
and effect in phenomena or events is enveloped and en-
tangled in a mass of irrelevant or unconcerned accompaniments. The scientific explanation of a fact is the separating
of the essential from the casual antecedents; an effort very
severe and uncongenial to the untutored mind, being an-
tagonistic to our habits and to many of our strongest
feelings, which are mainly gratified by facts in the lump or
the undissected concrete. There is a favourite rhetorical
comparison of history to the course of a noble river; the
poet exhibits the river in the scenic grandeur of its totality;
but if we wish to explain scientifically its different aspects—
the volume of its waters, the speed of its current, its sedi-
ment, its saline constituents, and its temperature—we must
perform an operation repugnant to the natural mind; we
must resolve the imposing aggregate into the abstractions
of magnitude, gravity, force, solubility, and make a like

f 2

analysis of the rocks and soil in its bed and on its banks. This analysis is not indeed the consummation of scientific discovery, but it is the indispensable preparation; the deeper, the correcter the analysis, the greater the chances of a profound and just explanation of the phenomena.   The philosophical historian of the French Revolution .has to disentangle, in the antecedent history and condition of France, the productive from the unproductive circumstances —performing a conjoint operation of analysis and proof, for which, apart from other qualifications, few historians have had the requisite scientific steadiness.   Moreover, the final terms of a historical analysis are facts and laws of the human mind; in these, therefore, all historical explanation must centre; and he that adds, to the ample experience of an observing man of the world, the precise handling of the psychologist, must be, of all others, the best fitted for the highest part of the historian's duties.

Had Mr. Grote written only the ‘History,’ a lengthened discourse might have been required to show that he was in no mean degree an accomplished and original psychologist and logician.   The proofs might have been conclusively drawn from the ‘History,’ but they would have been mostly inferential and indirect.   In regard to psychology, or the science of mind strictly viewed, we could point to his studies on the influence of the feelings in matters of truth and false-hood, which studies gave the master-key to the legendary or mythical ingredients of the Grecian story.   The corruption of the intellect by the emotions and passions was one of his earliest and most strongly iterated themes.

Under logic proper we should naturally have to advert to his theory and standard of evidence, which was up to the severest demands of historical accuracy.   This high standard, however, had various determining motives.   He notices, in the preface, the growing strictness of historians in their exaction of evidence, and quotes individual instances. Special to himself was a severe regard to truth, as opposed alike to the false and to the vague.   There can be nothing deserving of the name of truth without preciseness in the use of leading terms, and this condition is never lost sight of in Grote's writings. His early logical training bore this fruit; and at a later period he entered with avidity into the principles and methods of inductive evidence as elaborated in the 'Logic' of John Stuart Mill.

His career as an English politician and member of Parliament, during a great democratic struggle, was necessarily of the greatest value for understanding the free governments of antiquity. This has often been remarked upon as a point in his favour when compared with the erudite German professors, who had never "learned from personal experience the nature of a popular deliberative body." Such experience, however, would have availed but little, had it been unaccompanied with intense popular sympathies. The democracies of Greece had commended themselves to his ardent feelings for human improvement; they were not always what he could have wished, though greatly in advance of anything that the world had seen before them, and of the greater number of the polities that came after them. Athens—

> the eye of Greece,
> Mother of arts and eloquence—
> Was the democracy by pre-eminence,

the object of his special interest and affection. He found (he used to say) many admirers of Athens, but no one possessed with a strong philo-Athenian sentiment. He avowed himself, at the outset of his work, as the historian of Grecian freedom; the plan, as stated in his own words, was to "exhaust the free life of collective Hellas."

For the ancient world and ancient modes of thinking, in some of their contrasts with the modern, he had a strong predilection; and hence he turned Grecian studies to their proper end of correcting the one-sidedness of our prevailing notions and usages. This he esteemed the great recommendation of classical culture, and the motive for its being retained in general education. More especially did he

regard the ancient ethics as an essential supplement of our
modern views; but, unfortunately, we are precluded from
knowing, except in a general way, to what extent and on
what points.

A rapid survey of the leading features of the 'History'
will enable us to note its characteristic merits, as settled by
the judgment of competent critics, while alluding at the
same time to the points whereon opinions are still divergent.

As to the general effect, perhaps the most emphatic
testimony was given by Mr. Mill, in these words :—" Though
the statement has the air of an exaggeration, yet, after much
study of Mr. Grote's book, we do not hesitate to assert, that
there is hardly a fact of importance in Grecian history which
was perfectly understood before his re-examination of it."

The opening of the 'History' is marked by the peculiar
mode of dealing with legendary Greece. The author had
already published an article giving his views as to the origin
of the Legends; that paper is reprinted in the present
volume, as containing illustrations not wholly superseded by
the fuller handling in the first volume of the 'History.' I
summarise his later positions, nearly in his own words :—

Having regard to the standard of evidence recognised for
modern events, " I begin the real history of Greece with the
first recorded Olympiad, or 776 B.C. To such as are accustomed to the habits once universal, and still not uncommon,
in investigating the ancient world, I may appear to be
striking off one thousand years from the scroll of history;
but to those whose canon of evidence is derived from Mr.
Hallam, M. Sismondi, or any other historian of modern
events, I am well assured that I shall appear lax and
credulous rather than exigent or sceptical. For the truth
is, that historical records, properly so called, do not begin
until long after this date; nor will any man, who candidly
considers the extreme paucity of attested facts for the centuries after 776 B.C., be astonished to learn that the state of
Greece " for seven or more centuries previous "cannot be
described upon anything like decent evidence."

" The times which I thus set apart from the region of
history are discernible only through a different atmosphere
—that of epic poetry and legend. To confound together
these disparate matters is, in my judgment, essentially unphilosophical.   I describe the earlier times by themselves,
as conceived by the faith and feeling of the first Greeks, and
known only through their legends, without presuming to
measure how much or how little of historical matter these
legends may contain.   If the reader blame me for not assisting him to determine this—if he ask me why I do not
undraw the curtain and disclose the picture, I reply in the
words of the painter Zeuxis, when the same question was
addressed to him on exhibiting his master-piece of imitative
art—' The curtain *is* the picture.'   What we now read as
poetry and legend was once accredited history, and the only
genuine history which the first Greeks could conceive or
relish of their past time; the curtain conceals nothing
behind, and cannot by any ingenuity be withdrawn.   I
undertake only to show it as it stands, not to efface, still less
to re-paint, it.

" Three-fourths of the two volumes now presented to the
public are destined to elucidate this age of historical faith,
as distinguished from the later age of historical reason: to
exhibit its basis in the human mind—an omnipresent religious and personal interpretation of nature; to illustrate it
by comparison with the like mental habit in early modern
Europe; to show its immense abundance and variety of
narrative matter, with little care for consistency between one
story and another: lastly, to set forth the causes which over-
grew and partially supplanted the old epical sentiment and
introduced, in the room of the literal faith, a variety of
compromises and interpretations."

The author's peculiarity lay in illustrating the origination
of tradition, whether with or without foundation of fact, in
the emotional tendencies of the mind.   By no one had this
mental operation been hitherto made fully apparent; since
his exposition, it has become a received doctrine of human

nature. "The influence of imagination and feeling is not
confined simply to the process of retouching, transferring, or
magnifying narratives originally founded on fact; it will
often create new narratives of its own, without any such
preliminary basis." Whenever any body of sentiment is
widely prevalent, all incidents in conformity with that sentiment are eagerly believed. If real incidents are not at
hand, their place will be supplied by impressive fictions;
the perfect harmony of such fictions with the general feeling
stands in place of testimony; and to question them is to
incur obloquy. In the innumerable religious legends—
deriving their origin not from facts misreported, but from
pious feelings pervading the society—not merely the incidents, but often even the personages, are unreal; the generating sentiment being conspicuously discernible, and providing its own matter as well as its own form.

We have now the word "Myth" or mythus, to express
not a mere fiction, falsification, or untruth, but a narrative
shaped to suit a strong sentiment or feeling, and believed
in solely through the influence of that feeling.

In accordance with this view, the Historian occupies his
first volume with detailing the chief legendary tales and
narratives of Greece, first as regards the gods, and next as
regards heroes and men: following a systematic order so as
to connect each locality with its own legends. The two concluding chapters are devoted to the discussion of the Grecian
myths. The one chapter takes them up as understood,
felt, and interpreted by the Greeks themselves, and traces
the altered state of the Grecian mind respecting them, from
the unflinching credence of the early Greeks to the alteration of view following the influence of extended commerce
and the development of physical science, together with the
advanced ethical standard of later times. The subject is
illustrated by the author's usual thoroughness and exhaustive
learning, and the chapter, when read for the first time, is
one to leave an indelible impression. The concluding chapter
is "The Grecian Mythical View Compared with that of

Modern Europe." The author hero pursues the illustration through the Middle Ages, adverting to the Legends of the Saints, the Romances of Chivalry, the Teutonic and Scandinavian Epic, and our early English history.

Taken in their proper character, the Grecian myths constitute an important chapter in the history of the Grecian mind, and of the human race. The faith of the Greeks in their historical narratives is as much subjective and peculiar as their faith in their religion; the two are intimately conjoined, and cannot be separated without violence. Gods, heroes and men, religion and patriotism, matters divine, heroic, and human—were all woven together into one indivisible web, in which the threads of truth and reality, whatever they might originally have been, were not intended to be, and were not in fact, distinguishable.

To realise to himself, and to bring before the reader, the religious feelings of the Greek mind at its different stages was regarded by Mr. Grote as an indispensable portion of his duty as a historian. He never loses an opportunity for this end; and his success has been admitted. The work has been done once for all.

On one point, however, subsequent inquirers have not coincided with him. He maintained, with emphasis, that we could not go back beyond the legends as they stand. "The legendary age had its antecedent causes and determining conditions, but of these we know nothing, and we are compelled to assume it as a primary fact for the purpose of following out its subsequent changes. To conceive absolute beginning or origin is beyond the reach of our faculties; we can neither apprehend nor verify anything beyond progress, or development, or decay—change from one set of circumstances to another, operated by some definite combination of physical or moral laws. In the case of the Greeks, the legendary age, as the earliest in any way known to us, must be taken as the initial state from which this series of changes commences." This view is remarkably characteristic of the author's thorough appreciation of, and acquiescence in, the limitation of the human faculties. In resignation to the inevitable, at all points, he had effectually schooled himself; and the triumph of his discipline is best seen in matters of knowledge.

The despair of ascending beyond the recorded legends has not been shared by all inquirers. Comparative philology has been invoked to show the connection between the Greek legends and the Hindu mythology; the names and functions of the deities have been found to be strikingly allied.

Again, the very incidents of legendary narrative are shown in various instances to be of wide-spread occurrence over different countries, pointing to some remote common origin.

Moreover, the attempt had often been made to assign a speculative origin to the polytheistic creed, in accordance with known laws and tendencies of the human mind. Comte's three stages have become familiar to the public mind, and were well known to Mr. Grote. An interesting statement of the theoretical development of religious belief up to the point of the Grecian legends was given in Mr. Mill's review of the first and second volumes of the 'History.' Since then, minute attention to the records of primitive societies has greatly advanced these speculations. Within the last few years the writings of Sir John Lubbock, Tylor, and M'Lennan have thrown new light upon the stages antecedent to the Greeks.

Had these works appeared before Mr. Grote wrote the early chapters, he would have studied them most carefully, and have extracted from them whatever satisfied his judgment as bearing on the anterior stages of religious belief. He was, however, slow to admit the sufficiency of the evidence for such theories : and at the time when he wrote there was nothing that he could rely upon for carrying him back beyond the stage of the legends.

One great advantage has been gained from his taking up this position, namely, perfect impartiality in representing the facts as they are actually recorded. It is true that, even when he had a theory to support, he was scrupulous to a degree in his statement of facts : yet, our satisfaction is here unalloyed by the possibility of suspicion. Consequently, the comparative mythologists and speculators can accept his rendering of Grecian facts as authentic data, of equal value with the original records; while his empirical generalities meet the other theorisers half way.

I cannot help referring to one singular and undesigned coincidence between one of his generalities and a theory derived from a totally different region of facts. He remarks in the worship of the Greeks a concurrence of three things in the objects of worship, whether gods, demi-gods, or heroes—the tribal name, the deity worshipped, and the fact of descent: all this is conjoined in the "eponymos" of each tribe. The Herakleids, besides bearing the name, deified Herakles, and called themselves his descendants. Now Mr. M'Lennan has generalised the same coincidence under the name "totemism," derived from the word "totem," among the American Indians, absurdly rendered "medicine" by the early travellers. He shows that the "totem," which may be various in kind, but draws largely from the lower animals, is the tribal name, the ancestor, and the object of worship: and "totemism," in the shape of animal worship more particularly, is traced by him as a phenomenon of wide-spread occurrence, and comprising a very large department of the religious worship of early nations.

In the twentieth chapter of his work, Mr. Grote endeavours to derive from the Homeric poems an account of the state of society in legendary Greece. The attempt had been often made ; still, in the author's treatment there is considerable freshness and many new suggestions. The triple political institution—*basileus* (king), *boulë* (senate), *agora* (assembly)—he minutely examines, as the precursor of the democracies of later Greece. One of the favourite extracts of the reviewers is that passage where he traces to the infancy of the nation "the employment of public speaking as the standing engine of government and the proximate cause of obedience." He also takes great pains to illustrate the character of the moral sentiment in the ages depicted by Homer. The keynote is struck thus :— " There is no sense of obligation, then, existing between man and man, as such, and very little between each man and the community of which he is a member ; such sentiments are neither operative in the real world nor present to the imaginations of the poets." Personal feelings either towards the gods, the king, or some near and known individual fill the whole of a man's bosom.

While copiously illustrating, by citations from the histories of early society, the features and peculiarities of the Homeric Greeks, he still refrains from speculating on the anterior stages; and the remark already made, as to his veraciousness of rendering, is equally applicable here. In this department, too, much has been done to elucidate the condition of primitive man, but hitherto the researches have not sufficed to assign a situation immediately preceding that given in the Homeric poems.

In a chapter on the internal structure of the Iliad and Odyssey, he maintains that, while the Odyssey possesses a unity throughout, the Iliad bears traces of the combination of two separate poems, one an Achilleid, having for its subject the wrath of Achilles, the other (Books 2–7 and 10) an addition converting the Achilleid into an Iliad. The evidence is drawn from the internal structure of the poem, a kind of evidence that he himself always held to be extremely precarious. He accordingly treated his view as having merely a probability superior to any other. No part of the history, however, was more frequently dissented from by critics; but though he perused all the hostile criticisms, he saw no sufficient reason for giving up his case.

The entire compass of the Homeric field has been more recently surveyed by Mr. Gladstone, in an exceedingly careful and elaborate disquisition, entitled 'Studies on Homer and the Homeric Age.' He devotes one volume to the ethnology of the Greek races; another to the religion and morals of the Homeric age; in a third, he inquires into the polities, or political constitutions, compares the Trojans and Greeks, discusses the geography of the Odyssey, and expatiates on the artistic merits of Homer. On various points he comes into collision with Mr. Grote. He takes very high ground as to the historical value of Homer, maintaining that in regard to the religion, history, ethnology, polity, and life at large, his poems stand far above any later traditions; that of all the ages that have passed since Homer, not one has produced a more acute, accurate, and comprehensive observer; and that he alone was imbued from head to foot with the spirit and the associations of the heroic time. He thinks that a great error has been committed in not distinguishing Homer by a broad line from all the other sources of legendary narrative—namely, Hesiod, the tragedians and the minor Greek poets, the scattered notices of the historians, the antiquarian writers near the Christian era, and the scholiasts. He considers that Mr. Grote's treatment of the legends has countenanced this error, and he opens up for consideration the question whether the personality of Agamemnon and Achilles has no better root in history than that of Pelasgus, of Prometheus, or of Hellen; and whether all these are no more than equal in credit to Ceres, Bacchus, or Apollo.

While Mr. Grote regards as hopeless any inquiry into the ante-Hellenic Pelasgians, Mr. Gladstone undertakes to show, from Homer, that two distinct races appear on the stage, a superior and an inferior; the superior were the Hellenes, represented by the Greeks, the besiegers of Troy; the inferior, the Pelasgi, represented by the Trojans. The Hellenes culminated in Attica, the Pelasgians in Arcadia. The two races had distinctive aptitudes, and the Greek mind in its highest development combined the two.

Mr. Gladstone's account of the religion consists in a minute examination of all the deities introduced by Homer. Starting from the idea that the Homeric theology is a corruption or defacement of the primitive Scriptural traditions, he shows by what downward steps the true and pure idea of God became transformed into the imperfect deities of Homer. He distinguishes what he considers the traditive from the inventive element of the theogony. In passing from the theology to the morals, he replies with some warmth to Mr. Grote's remark that the Greek terms for good and evil (ἀγαθός, ἐσθλός and κακός) originally meant power, and not worth; that the ethical meaning hardly appears until the discussions raised by Sokrates and prosecuted by his disciples. "I ask permission to protest against whatever savours of the idea that any Socrates whatever was the patentee of that sentiment of right and wrong, which is the most precious part of the patrimony of mankind. The movement of Greek morality with the lapse of time was chiefly downward, and not upward." The discordance of the two authorities is here fundamental and incurable.

On the politics, or political constitutions, Mr. Gladstone re-examines Mr. Grote's view of the three great constituents —king, senate, assembly, or agora. Most interesting, perhaps, is his minute discussion of the standing of the agora, or assembled freemen. Mr. Grote, interpreting the picture of the assembly in the second Iliad, regarded the people as having no status whatever but to listen and obey. Mr. Gladstone, already for a quarter of a century experienced in the workings of assemblies, brings to bear many subtle and powerful arguments to show that the assembly had considerable influence on the decisions of the monarch, although he fully admits the force of Mr. Grote's remark that there is no record of the taking of a vote. Among other indications he refers to the cheers of the people as a proof of their power; for in every tolerably-regulated assembly the giving of applause distinguishes the body itself from mere strangers or spectators; it being a truth common to every age that such applause constitutes a share in the business and contributes to the decision.

Mr. Gladstone combats at length Mr. Grote's theory of

the double structure of the Iliad, resenting especially the
suggestion of the possibility of double authorship. His
reasonings are very subtle, and many of them are of a kind
that might not be generally convincing; yet the discussion
is highly stimulating, opening up varied aspects of the poem
and starting new problems.

Legendary Greece together with the Homeric poems occupy
the first volume of the 'History' and nearly one half of the
second. The author now changes the designation to—" Part
II.—HISTORICAL GREECE "—under which all his subsequent
chapters are numbered. Not content with indicating his
sense of the broad distinction between the legendary and
the historical times by this very emphatic mode of shaping
the titles, he performs the somewhat violent operation of
transposing the Geography of Greece from its natural place
at the outset of the work to the beginning of Part II.
He was aware of the awkwardness of the arrangement,
and admitted that the legends, in common with the historical facts, were susceptible of elucidation from the geography, but did not consider the artifice too much for
marking the chasm between the legendary and the historical
domain.

The geographical sketch is careful and highly interesting;
it might have been advantageously enlarged; the bearings
of the geographical facts on the character, institutions,
and history of the Greeks are by no means exhausted.
An often-quoted passage, on the effect of the configuration of
the Grecian territory on the political system and the intellectual development, is remarkable for the author's caution
in not crediting physical influences with more than their
legitimate worth. For explaining the many-sided superiority
of Greece to the rest of the world, we must postulate, in
the first instance, an inherent superiority of race. The
scattered branches of the human family being, from whatever causes, most unequally, as well as most variously,
gifted in their natural organisation, some one people must
be at the top. A favourable surrounding converts the small

primitive inequality into a divergence of careers so great as to seem wholly incompatible with a common origin.

I quote the following summary from Mr. Mill:—

" In the six concluding chapters of the second volume Mr. Grote comprises the sum of what is known respecting the early condition of those Grecian states which have properly no history prior to the Persian invasion, and brings down the history of the Peloponnesian Greeks to the age of Crœsus and Pisistratus. The fragmentary nature of the information, and the conscientious integrity of the author, who scruples to supply the deficiency of certified facts by theory and conjecture, render these chapters, with one exception, somewhat meagre. The exception is the chapter treating of the legislation of Lycurgus, the earliest Grecian event of first-rate historical importance."

The chapter on the " Laws and Discipline of Lycurgus at Sparta " has a twofold interest. The main subject is the origin and character of that extraordinary system of public discipline which forms the point of departure of the action of Sparta in the vicissitudes of the Grecian story. The one-sided Spartan culture, with its astonishing results, was a favourite subject with the Greek philosophers; and it will descend through all time as a unique manifestation of humanity. Mr. Grote has applied his analysing power to the phenomenon, and we can scarcely hope ever to extract from the materials a more thorough account than he has given us.

The other point in the chapter is the examination of the evidence for one important item in the alleged reforms of Lycurgus—the equal division of the lands. Intrinsically this is not incredible, considering what Lycurgus really effected; but being unmentioned by all the authors that were alive while the institutions of Sparta were still in force, and appearing for the first time in Plutarch, the evidence for it must be held as defective. After exhaustively reviewing all the earlier authorities, Mr. Grote comes to inquire how the allegation could have sprung up in the age of Plutarch; and here he is rewarded by a most felicitous application of his theory of the generation of the mythus. To all previous historians such a statement as Plutarch's seemed necessarily to contain some truth : to him the origin suggested itself apart from any vestige whatsoever of underlying fact. It was fiction from first to last— "tho expression of some large idea and sentiment, so powerful in its action on men's minds at a given time as to induce them to make a place for it among the realities of the past." A situation actually occurred in the times of Agis III. (about 250 B.C.) when men's imaginations were heated to the proper pitch for fabricating a legend. The missing link is thus supplied, and the Lycurgian division of the lands of Sparta has taken its place among mythical creations.

The second instalment of the 'History'—volumes three and four—appeared in 1847. Two more volumes followed in 1849. The critique in the *Edinburgh Review* on these four volumes was by Sir George Cornewall Lewis.

The third volume opens with a chapter entitled, "The Age of the Grecian Despots," one of the author's best contributions to political philosophy, as well as to Grecian history. It records the gradual change from the primitive political constitution of Homer—King, Council, and Assembly—to the advent of Democracy. The early stages are obscure. The Homeric king, strong in his divine right and personal ascendency, appears to have been superseded by his council, as an oligarchy, who acted in a body for legislative purposes, while one of their number, by rotation or otherwise, headed the executive. It was out of these oligarchies that there came forth, between 650 and 500 B.C., the class of rulers termed *Despots*, who got possession of the supreme power in various ways, but exercised it without check or control, and often with such tyrannous excesses that their name became odious in Greece. While in some states, as Sparta, the ancient hereditary king was maintained, his authority being withdrawn and himself superseded, except as a venerable relic, by more modern creations, in the greater part of Greece the kingship disappeared.

g

This whole chapter is full of interesting political reflections as to the historical changes in the institution of monarchy. The remarks on the British Constitution as it would have appeared to Aristotle, are highly suggestive and curious.

Two chapters are devoted to the early history of Athens; the first recounting its political constitution and history (so far as ascertainable) before Solon; the second embracing the legislation of Solon. On this last subject the author bestows especial attention. The reforms of Solon were called forth by great internal dissension, produced by the misery of the poorer population. This misery seemed to have been greatly owing to the workings of the law of debtor and creditor, to which Solon applied the relief of the sponge, with a palliation to the creditor by debasing the money standard.

Mr. Grote is in his element in the exposition and vindication of these strong measures, and gives us a valuable episode on the prejudices entertained in antiquity against lending money at interest. Reviewing at length the various changes made by Solon, he corrects the confusion that afterwards prevailed between these and the institutions of subsequent legislators. Solon, indeed, laid the foundations of Athenian democracy; yet his institutions were not democratical, but oligarchical. The concluding eulogy on the legislator himself is highly illustrative of the author's own type of human nobleness. "He (Solon) represents the best tendencies of his age, combined with much that is personally excellent; the thirst for enlarged knowledge and observation, not less potent in old age than in youth; the conception of regularised popular institutions, departing sensibly from the type and spirit of the governments around him, and calculated to found a new character in the Athenian people; a genuine and reflecting sympathy with the mass of the poor, anxious not merely to rescue them from the oppressions of the rich, but also to create in them habits of self-relying industry; lastly, during his temporary possession of a power altogether arbitrary, not merely an absence of all selfish ambition, but a rare discretion in seizing the mean between conflicting exigencies."

Before the death of Solon occurred the usurpation of the despot Pisistratus, which Solon vainly but courageously resisted. The narrative of his reign is interrupted for many chapters by a survey of the Asiatic Greeks (Ionic, Æolic, and Dorian) and the natives of Asia Minor, with whom the Greeks became connected. A chapter is devoted to the Lydians, Medes, Cimmerians, Scythians; one to the Phœnicians, one to the Egyptians, one to the growth of Carthage. The author exhausts all available sources in rendering complete his account of these various nations, not merely for their intrinsic historical interest, but for their influence on the Greek mind and history; this being very notable in the case of Egypt. Then comes Grecian colonisation in the westward direction—Italy, Sicily, and Gaul: the Sicilian settlements being more peculiarly momentous in the succeeding events, while celebrity attached to some of the cities of the Italian Greeks. In his review, Sir G. C. Lewis remarks that "Greek colonisation is discussed with remarkable success." Other chapters take up the Akarnanians, Epirots, Illyrians, Macedonians, Pœonians, Thracians, and Greek colonies in Thrace. The survey is completed by a chapter on Kyrene, Barka, and Hesperides.

A short but interesting chapter (xxviii.) deals with the Pan-Hellenic Festivals — Olympic, Pythian, Nemean, and Isthmian; investigating their origin, character, and effect on the Greek mind. These are severally brought before the reader in their most striking and picturesque details.

The Lyric Poetry is next passed in review; from which, singularly enough, there is an insensible transition to the constellation of Wise Men (usually called Seven), the beginners of Greek Philosophy. In continuation of these is the commencement of Greek prose. The same chapter embraces the rise of Grecian art.

A chapter on the Government of Peisistratus and his sons at Athens contains the episode of Harmodius and Aristogeiton, on which the author's commentaries are fresh and interesting, and contain an additional application of his law of the growth of legend.

The expulsion of the Peisistratus family is the signal for the next great advance in democracy, under Cleisthenes. Mr. Grote has the merit of clearing up this great revolution, and of teaching its unspeakable importance to the future of Athens. Among the institutions ascribed to Cleisthenes is the ostracism, which is for the first time rationally explained as a great constitutional sedative, at a period when the State could not afford the presence of restless intriguers. It was a mild substitute for impeachment; and Sir George Lewis thinks that had it existed in England, in the time of Charles I., it might have got rid of Strafford and Laud without the necessity of sending them to the block.

The historian's concluding reflections on the reforms of Cleisthenes stir the heart like the sound of a trumpet. Never weary of the theme of human liberty, he re-touches it on each occasion with fresh and glowing colours. What Herodotus puts in the front rank of the advantages of democracy—"its most splendid name and promise"—is no mere rhetoric, but a real power, the source of all the exploits that have conferred immortal renown on the Athenian name.

Four chapters contain the events preparatory to the great Persian struggle, and bring it down to Marathon, "the narrative of which cannot be read, for the hundredth time, without deep emotion." The rise of the Persian empire, under its founder Cyrus; the succession of Cambyses and of Darius; the Ionic revolt and its suppression by Darius; the invasion of the mainland of Greece, with a special view to be avenged on Athens; the encounter at Marathon—all belong to the purely narrative work of the historian. After an interruption, to be noticed presently, he continues, in five chapters more, the invasion of Xerxes, which led to the immortal conflicts at Thermopylæ, Artemisium, Salamis, Platæa, and Mycale. "Marathon and, for the most part,

Salamis and Mycale are the work of Athens; Thermopylæ, and to a great extent Platæa, of Sparta. By the courage, intelligence, and moral superiority in contending against overwhelming numbers which the Greeks exhibited at this great crisis, they have earned the imperishable gratitude of all civilised nations." (G. C. Lewis.)

We ought not to pass the chapter on Marathon without some reference to the concluding portion, which is occupied in dealing with the charges made against the Athenians for their ill-treatment of Miltiades after his great services. The vindication is in Mr. Grote's very best manner. Extenuating nothing, he shows that the conduct of Miltiades that led to his punishment was reprehensible in the extreme, that his past services were fairly taken into account, in the only admissible way, to wit, in mitigation of the penalty. It was from no fickleness in the people that they turned against him; they had been most lavish in their gratitude after the great victory, and their change of mind was due to an adequate cause. It was a weakness in the Greeks to be too much carried away by their impulses of gratitude for distinguished services. With this fitted in, often to fatal results, another weakness (perhaps having the same root in the mind) which Mr. Grote deploringly signalises. "There is no feature," he says, "that more largely pervades the impressible Grecian character than a liability to be intoxicated and demoralised by success; there was no fault from which so few eminent Greeks were free; there was hardly any danger against which it was at once so necessary and so difficult for the Grecian governments to take security, especially the democracies, where the manifestations of enthusiasm were always the loudest."

In a chapter (xxxvii.) introduced during the panic of the Persians after the defeat of Marathon, he takes occasion to notice the great Ionic philosopher, Thales, and his successors; and recounts at full the views, character, and political position of Pythagoras in the colony of Italian Greeks at Croton, in Italy. This is the author's first contribution to the rise and progress of Greek philosophy, which he included in his original plan of the 'History of Greece.'

The conclusion of the Persian repulse is followed by a chapter on Sicily, whose history is resumed with the brazen-bull despot, Phalaris of Agrigentum, and continued through a series of despots in the different cities, to the establishment of popular governments throughout the island.

Returning to Athens, the historian enters on a new phase of his undertaking—the growth of the Athenian empire, as a consequence of the Persian war. I shall here again borrow, unfortunately for the last time, the summary expressions of Sir George Lewis:—" The imperial rule of Athens was, as Mr. Grote has shown, exercised, on the whole, with moderation. There were no very unusual obligations imposed on the subject state; and so long as it was quiet, and submitted patiently to its condition of dependence, it had little to complain of. But the loss of independence was a bitter privation to the Greek freeman, and hence the dominion of Athens rested ultimately on force or fear. Her own orators and statesmen accordingly always represent her as standing in the same relation to her dependent cities as a despot to his individual subjects; and openly proclaim the necessity of using towards them the terrible maxims of Greek despotism. Hence, revolt was summarily punished, as in the memorable case of Mitylene; while, on the other hand, the proceedings of Brasidas, in Thrace, show that much persuasion and cajolery, backed by the presence of a Lacedemonian army, might be necessary in order to induce an Athenian dependent city to throw off its allegiance."

" The history of these subject-allies of Athens—of the transition from a voluntary *hegemony* or headship, to a compulsive imperial rule—has never been so well written, or half so well explained, as by Mr. Grote."

One of the model chapters of the 'History' is (chapter xlvi.) the account of the changes in the Athenian constitution under Pericles; the final development of the democracy, as it stood during all the remainder of Athenian freedom. The

central fact of the change was the instituting of the Dikas-
teries, whereby the judicial power was finally separated from
the executive. Mr. Grote reviews in an exhaustive way the
momentous bearings of this change, and shows that every
feature in the new system had a significance entirely overlooked in the usual rough-and-ready criticism of Athenian
institutions under the guidance of the comic poets. He
makes the happiest use of our modern trial by jury in the
elucidation of these Athenian courts, and strikingly remarks,
especially with reference to the large number of the dikasts
(several hundreds in one court), that there was at that time
no other conceivable mode of bringing to justice rich and
powerful criminals.

The mighty drama—the Peloponnesian War—occupies
nearly three volumes of the original issue (vi., vii., viii.) The
story is related with all the author's narrative power; his
sympathies are deeply engaged throughout the memorable
vicissitudes of those twenty-nine years. The splendid bursts
and temporary triumphs of the doomed heroine irradiate the
deepening gloom.

In the course of this war, Mr. Grote has introduced many
of his novel points of view, as regards both characters and
incidents. As might be supposed, his estimate of Pericles is
lofty, it is also in the details peculiarly his own. "Pericles,"
he remarks, "is not to be treated as the author of the
Athenian character; he found it with its very marked
positive characteristics and susceptibilities, among which
those that he chiefly brought out and improved were the
best." He repressed the lust of conquest and regularised
the democratic movement; and, most of all, did he favour
the pacific and intellectual development—rhetoric, poetry,
arts, philosophical research, and recreative variety. Agriculture, trade, the means of defence, were all enormously
advanced during his time; and he is identified with the
clothing of Athens in her imperial mantle of architectural
decoration. His love of philosophy, and his studies under the
philosopher Anaxagoras, are carefully quoted in his favour.

Of the characters that have to be drawn in the narrative of the struggle, the most trenchant, and yet irresistibly just, is the sketch of Nikias, the principal cause of the ruin of Athens. The contrast between Pericles and Nikias could have come from no other hand. The mistaken confidence in a man of even mediocrity, from the lustre of his religious professions and practice, and the extreme decorum of his private life, coupled with pecuniary liberality and incorruptibility, shows the Athenian public to be not so far removed from human nature in our own time. Sydney Smith's picture of Perceval is a historical parallel.

Cleon, the leather-seller, is extricated from the hands of both Aristophanes and Thucydides. Our historian's warm admiration for the greatest historical authority of the ancient world does not prevent him from discerning the occasions when bias crept into his narrative, and one of these is the picture of Cleon. The leather-seller had his faults, and expiated with his life the weakness of his judgment in military affairs. He had the qualities that in all countries of free debate go to make a great opposition speaker; but the charges of Thucydides, amplified by Aristophanes, are treated by Mr. Grote as inconsistent with themselves and contrary to evidence. Moreover, there were critical moments when Cleon, in Mr. Grote's opinion, did eminent public service.

Alcibiades necessarily occupied a large share of attention during these trying events. He contributed more than any other man to plunge the Athenians into the disastrous expedition to Syracuse; and more than any man, after Nicias, to turn that adventure into ruin, and the consequences of it into still greater ruin. Yet, he was never once defeated either by land or by sea; in new situations he was never wanting. On the whole we shall find few men in whom eminent capacities for action and command are so thoroughly marred by an assemblage of bad moral qualities as in Alcibiades.

In a remarkable eulogy on the Spartan Callicratidas, Mr. Grote does honour to an enemy of Athens, on the high grounds of his moral superiority to his age and nation, as shown in declaring that, so long as he was in command, not a single free Greek should be reduced to slavery if he could prevent it. The grandeur and sublimity of this proceeding was without a parallel in Grecian history. But Mr. Grote is careful to guard his admiration, for the allies would make the reasonable remark—" If *we* should come to be Conon's prisoners, he will not treat *us* in this manner." " *Reciprocity* is essential to moral observances, public or private, and doubtless Callicratidas felt a well-grounded confidence, that two or three auspicious examples would sensibly modify the future practice on both sides. But some one must begin by setting such examples, and the man who does begin, *having a position that gives reasonable chance that others will follow*, is a hero."

One of the most extraordinary incidents in Athenian history was the mutilation of the Hermæ, or half-statues of the god Hermes, which stood in vast numbers in all parts of Athens. One night all these statues were mutilated and defaced by unknown hands. The profanation excited a ferment of feeling, which historians have usually treated as exaggerated and absurd. Mr. Grote corrects this notion, by his juster appreciation of the religious sentiments of the Greeks. He had given notice, in the preface to his first volume, that this incident would be a testing case of a historian's "entering into the way in which the Greeks connected their stability and security with the domiciliation of the gods in the soil ; " and his own handling has amply complied with the test.

Equally happy and convincing is the explanation given of one of the melancholy acts of the Athenian public, the condemnation of the ten generals after the battle of Arginusæ, a victory to Athens deplorable from the loss of Callicratidas. Mr. Grote reviews the case in all its particulars, as if he were the judge in a supreme court of appeal. He shows that the accusation against the generals was proceeding in due form, and might have been decided with perfect justice, but for the occurrence of a grand family solemnity of the Ionic race, the Apaturia (our Christmas in an intensified form), during which the empty places made in the family circles by the recent battle, led to excited reflection on the culpable neglect of the generals to perform the obsequies to the slain. The trial was resumed under this excitement. The formalities provided by the constitution for securing a fair trial were violently set aside (Socrates alone of the presiding officials daring to withstand the current), and the generals were condemned. "It was an act of violent injustice and illegality, deeply dishonouring the men that passed it and the Athenian character generally." It was long and bitterly repented. Much as the subject had been discussed, Mr. Grote was the first to perceive in the incidents of an Athenian Christmas, an adequate explanation of the vindictive proceeding.

Another remarkable event in the war is the setting up of the oligarchy of the Four Hundred. This is the subject of a thrilling narrative, and also furnishes additional illustrations of the Athenian democracy; and, not least, of the extraordinary respect for constitutional forms, which was the *rule*, while the fatality just mentioned was the exception, in the best times of Athens.

The naval fight at Ægospotami ended the twenty-nine years' combat between Athens and Sparta. Athens was ruined. The Spartan conqueror is master of the city, destroys its material defences, sets up the oligarchy known as the Thirty Tyrants, whose wholesale executions did not suffice to uphold it. The democracy is again restored. With deep satisfaction the historian depicts their lenity towards the usurpers—both the Four Hundred and the Thirty —as contrasted with the cruelties they had suffered at the hands of the oligarchs. The respect to the rights of property was an equally honourable distinction of the democratic rule.

Our author leads us to the end of the restless career of Alcibiades, and then indulges in a pause, which, however, is only to enter on a campaign in another field. Chapter lxvii. is entitled, "The Drama, Rhetoric and Dialectic, *the Sophists :*" the real interest of the chapter being concentrated in the last head. A most offensive odour had been imparted to these men; and the grounds of it are now challenged for the first time. The charges are gone over point for point, and confronted with a broadside of destructive facts, for ever silencing the calumniators of the unfortunate Sophists. The present chapter is generally considered to have done the work: but, we shall not see the last, nor the most curious part of the case, till we come to the "Aristotle."

The succeeding chapter is equally exciting in its originality—the account of Socrates. The author found here a vent to discharge his very strongest impulses—the love of free inquiry, the reprobation of the tyranny of sentiment in the human mind, the delight in the self-acting judgment of the individual; and he followed out the opening with his usual energy. In the story of Socrates he does justice to the sublimity and the pathos of the circumstances attending the trial, and measures out strict justice to the Athenian people, who were on their trial no less than Socrates. But his greatest interest centred in the Socratic cross-questioning, an unparalleled phenomenon in the history of thought. I well remember his conversation in the heat of composing this chapter; his astonishment at the invention of such a weapon, and his belief that if it could be resumed in any shape, it might still have an extraordinary potency in quickening independent thought.

These two chapters on the Sophists and Socrates closed the eighth volume. A critic in the *Times* gave utterance to the opinion that the work was now virtually closed; as if the remaining narrative could furnish no equal displays of the author's originality, or impart no new surprise. There might be a momentary plausibility in the supposition; yet the subsequent volumes did not confirm the critic's judgment.

The ninth volume opened with three long chapters on the famous expedition of the Ten Thousand Greeks. The author carefully recounts every turn of this memorable expedition, which did not effect its purpose, but yet taught the contemporary world the impotence of the Persian land force, while possessing an undying interest as a display of Athenian qualities and accomplishments. It "exemplifies the discipline, the endurance, the power of self-action and adaptation, *the susceptibility of influence from speech and discussion*, the combination of the reflecting obedience of citizens with the mechanical regularity of soldiers, which confer such immortal distinction on the Hellenic character." Now it was the Athenian democracy, and its allied institutions, of which not the least important was the schooling of the rhetors and sophists, which raised men able to sway the minds of others by speech, and educated the mass of citizens to listen to reasons and follow prudential guidance. This fact was never shown to better advantage than in the difficulties of that remarkable expedition, and in the way that they were met and overcome by the oratory of Xenophon; the persuasiveness of which essentially consisted in a series of appeals to the self-regarding forethought of the audience. The Spartans were undoubtedly great on the field; yet the salvation of the Cyreian force was chiefly due to qualities that were not Spartan but Athenian.

The author avows his strong engrossment and interest in the proceedings of these mercenaries. In a private letter at the time, to Sir George Lewis, he describes himself as at work on the 'Anabasis,' and "finds the day too short."

The Lacedemonian empire, in its brief tenure of power, falls next to be described. Greece now saw the merits of the Athenian supremacy in a new light. The Spartan tyranny was too hot to last, and it soon met with a crushing reverse, under the Thebans and Epaminondas. The recital of this great Nemesis is a cheering and brilliant ray after the deep gloom of Syracuse and Ægospotami. In regard to the illustrious Theban, Mr. Grote cannot add to, or take from, the admiration of all succeeding times; but his portraiture, as usual, contains fresh and characteristic touches.

As in the case of Solon and Pericles, we are told that Epaminondas, in addition to all the education of an accomplished Theban citizen, sought with eagerness the conversation of the philosophers within his reach, and came under the influence of two that had been companions of Socrates. In this way, he both enlarged his intellectual grasp and, like Pericles, emancipated himself from that superstitious dread of signs and omens that had enslaved so many Grecian commanders. His eloquence was effective even against the best Athenian opponents. The combination of such great capacity with a modest and unambitious disposition was a rare exception to the prevailing forwardness and self-esteem of Greeks generally. Nor was he less remarkable for the gentleness of his political antipathies, the repugnance to harsh treatment of conquered enemies, and the refusal to mingle in intestine bloodshed.

The prowess of Epaminondas left the Spartans helpless, and enabled Athens to regain a certain measure of her old ascendency. Nineteen chapters, occupying the bulk of two volumes, are devoted to the bringing about of this mighty result. But the historian, in a few significant sentences, strikes the delighted reader with a cold shudder of apprehension and foreboding. The recovery of the Chersonese by Athens, which was the moment of her maximum of returning greatness, almost exactly coincided with the revolt among her principal allies, named the Social War, and with the accession of Philip of Macedon.

" At the opening of my ninth volume, after the surrender of Athens, Greece was under the Spartan empire. Its numerous independent city-communities were more completely regimented under one chief than they had ever been before, Athens and Thebes being both numbered among the followers of Sparta.

" But the conflicts recounted in these volumes (during an interval of forty-four years—404-3 B.C. to 360-59 B.C.) have wrought the melancholy change of leaving Greece more disunited, and more destitute of presiding Hellenic authority, than she had been at any time since the Persian invasion. Thebes, Sparta, and Athens had all been engaged in weakening each other; in which, unhappily, each has been more successful than in strengthening herself. The maritime power of Athens is now indeed considerable, and may be called very great, if compared with the state of degradation to which she had been brought in 403 B.C. But it will presently be seen how unsubstantial is the foundation of her authority, and how fearfully she has fallen off from that imperial feeling and energy which ennobled her ancestors under the advice of Pericles.

" It is under these circumstances, so untoward for defence, that the aggressor from Macedonia arises."

The historian now turns to Sicily, unmentioned since the Syracusan catastrophe. The first of the Sicilian chapters brings the Carthaginians on the stage, and recounts the fall of the Gelonian dynasty and the rise of the elder Dionysius. Another chapter is devoted to this noted personage, whose career is a model of the "Despot's progress." A third chapter completes his terrible reign of thirty-eight years. All the power of Carthage was arrayed against him, but he had an effective ally in the pestilence. At the moment of his death, Dionysius boasted of having left his dominion " fastened by chains of adamant, " sustained by a large body of mercenaries, well trained and well paid, by impregnable fortifications in the islet of Ortygia, by four hundred ships of war, by immense magazines of arms and military stores, and by established intimidation over the minds of the Syracusans. He was succeeded by his elder son Dionysius the younger; but a far higher part in the government was taken by Dion, brother-in-law of the elder Dionysius. An entirely new and unique interest attaches to the joint careers of these two men. The philosopher Plato had gained an ascendency over the mind of Dion, and was pressed by him to take a part in re-organising the government of Syracuse. Three different visits did the philosopher pay to Syracuse, one abrupt and unsatisfactory, in the time of the elder despot; a second and third, with better omens, in the time of the younger. On this intimacy between Plato and Dion Mr. Grote dwells at some length, regretting the impracticable temper and views of the philosopher, as throwing away the chance of an interesting experiment in politics. The two masters—king and minister—became alienated; Dion is banished, lives at Athens, his property being first allowed him and then withheld. He collects a small armament, invades and raises Sicily against the despot; plays a really noble part for a time, and shows intellectual and moral qualities worthy of the pupil of a lofty philosophy. He gains the day, is master of Syracuse, but collapses into ignominious blundering, instead of achieving an illustrious name as the liberator of Sicily. Accordingly, the work has to be done over again. A man of higher mould, one of the upper ten of Grecian commanders, is sent from Corinth to the Syracusans in their distress. This is Timoleon, whose home life at Corinth was already remarkable for the act of killing his own brother who had made himself despot. Mr. Grote does not fail to turn this preliminary incident to the edification of us moderns, in whom he remarks the sentiment of family covers a larger proportion of the field of morality, as compared with obligations towards country, than it did in ancient times.

The hazardous enterprise succeeds through Timoleon's bravery, his skilful plans, his quickness of movement, coupled with extraordinary good fortune. He speedily gains possession of Syracuse. He could have easily and even plausibly become despot; instead of which he determines at once to pull down the nest of all the previous despotisms—the stronghold of Ortygia. Very soon he has to meet a vast Carthaginian armament, which he utterly defeats with inferior numbers. He clears Sicily of enemies and despots. Finally, he lays down his power at Syracuse, spending his life in retirement, and acting only as an adviser in emergencies. Epaminondas had been his model, and, if he could not be said to improve upon that original, he varied the noble type.

Having done due honour to the Sicilian hero, the history now reverts to Athens. The dreary tale of ineffectual resistance to the onward tread of the Macedonian conquerors is still relieved by flashes of heroism and genius.

After all that Athens had suffered, and after the disunion among the Grecian states, the new hazards from a great military neighbour like Philip of Macedon were serious indeed. The spirit of Athens was yet equal to ordinary efforts, and there came forward one man who, as an orator, political leader, and diplomatist, has had no superior, if he ever had an equal. But the ability of Demosthenes at home was unsupported by any corresponding generalship in the field. The presence now of Epaminondas in Greece might have nipped Macedonian conquest in the bud. The Athenian general Iphicrates had displayed powers equal to the occasion, but, owing to a personal quarrel in the beginning of the Social War, he and Timotheus, another general of ability, were lost to Athens. The agency of corruption was extensively employed by Philip: he could always gain partisans in every popular assembly in Greece—one of the unavoidable weaknesses of popular government. The Athenians were cursed with a new incubus, different from Nikias, but not less fatal—the incorruptible and plain-spoken Phokion. Mr. Grote takes the measure of Phokion's deserts, and credits him with a large share of the ruined fortunes of his country. Athens became at last demoralised as regarded one of her capital virtues: her citizens had contracted a growing reluctance to personal military service. Many adventurers were now to be bought, like the Ten Thousand Greeks, and to these mercenaries unavoidable operations were mainly entrusted; but they also involved expense. "The energy of the Periklean Athenian of 431 B.C. had been crushed in the disasters closing the Peloponnesian war, and had never again revived. The Demosthenic Athenian of 360 B.C. had, as it were, grown old. Pugnacity, Pan-Hellenic championship, and the love of enterprise, had died within him. He was a quiet, home-keeping, refined citizen, attached to the democratic constitution, and executing with cheerful pride his ordinary city duties under it; but immersed in industrial or professional pursuits, in domestic comforts, in the impressive manifestations of the public religion, in the atmosphere of discussion and thought, intellectual as well as political. To renounce all this for foreign and continued military service, he considered as a hardship not to be endured, except under the pressure of danger near and immediate." It was the glory of Demosthenes to struggle all his life against this declension of public spirit, and to be able to whip it up to occasional efforts; it was the merit of Phocion to pander to it and indulge it, to furnish it with justification and excuse, when wrought upon by his younger rival.

The disastrous and disgraceful betrayal of the Phokians in 346 B.C., one of the bad turning-points in the contest with Philip, and the silence of Demosthenes at the opportune moment, are severely commented on, and yet too well accounted for, by our historian. I cite this, as one of many instances, with a view to show how far he was from glossing the real weaknesses of the Athenian democracy, and also to prepare the way for a closing remark as to his handling of Athens throughout.

I attribute to the thoroughly scientific and logical cast of Grote's mind, in conjunction with his wide knowledge of political facts, the novelty and the soundness of his views as to the governments of Greece, whether democratical or otherwise. There were many floating allegations as to the workings of these governments, some of them sober although inadequate, others wholly uncertified by evidence and biassed by partisanship. By careful scrutiny of the authorities, he ascertained, so far as possible, what was true and what was false; how far the aspersions of the democracies and the praise of despots and oligarchs was well founded. This was a matter of historical evidence. But, as I remarked at the outset, there followed a second and more difficult operation—a truly scientific, analytic, and logical procedure

h

—to assign the proper causes of effects that were proved to have taken place. Here a historian is constantly misled, in the same manner as the everyday politician, by mere coincidences, which he is tempted to pronounce cause and effect. While many persons professing to be educated are disposed to resolve all the peculiar differences between American and English habits into the difference in the form of government of the two countries, it will seem very natural to attribute all the faults and misfortunes of Athens to her democracy alone. It is the province of a scientific or logical discipline to raise the student above this level, and teach him by what arts mere coincidences can be eliminated and genuine causation established. The Baconian method of varying the circumstances, improved upon in the experimental philosophy of the last two centuries, has to be applied to historical events, and has to be accommodated to the peculiarities of the case. When people say democracy did so and so, oligarchy so and so, the logician asks, among other things, has the alleged effect of democracy been always present in democracies, and always absent from the other forms of government? This is not conclusive of the point, but it is enough to dissipate a host of silly assertions. Then again, in political cause and effect, there must always be shown some *natural tendency*, growing out of the laws of the human mind, in an alleged cause to produce the alleged consequences; this is to follow out what is called the deductive method in logic.

Half of the twelfth and concluding volume is occupied with the conquests of Alexander the Great, first in Greece, and next in Asia. " Apart from the transcendent merits of Alexander as a soldier and a general, some authors give him credit for grand and beneficent views on the subject of imperial government, and for intentions highly favourable to the improvement of mankind." Mr. Grote sees "no ground for adopting this opinion. As far as we can venture to anticipate what would have been Alexander's future, we see nothing in prospect except years of ever-repeated aggression and conquest, not to be concluded until he had traversed and subjugated all the inhabited globe. The acquisition of universal dominion was the master passion of his soul." He could have consolidated nothing. His best administrative device was the imitation of the Persian satrapies, with Macedonians as his instruments. He was neither Macedonian nor Greek in sentiment. The substitute for nationality of feeling was an exorbitant self-estimation inflamed by success into the belief of divine parentage, which entitled him to treat all mankind as subjects under the common sceptre to be wielded by himself. Hellenic in genius, he was Oriental in purpose.

At the close of the narrative of Alexander's career, the reader will find a careful estimate of the civilising influence of Greece upon Asia, following on Alexander's conquests, through the immediate agency of his successors. Hellenism, properly so called, never passed over into Asia. All that did pass was a faint and partial resemblance of it, carrying the superficial marks of the original. A great number of individual Greeks found employment in the service, military and civil, of the Greco-Asiatic kings. Important social and political consequences turned upon the diffusion of the language, but the Hellenised Asiatic was still a foreigner, with Grecian speech, exterior varnish, and superficial manifestations. The world, as a whole, was a loser by the disappearance of the genuine article and the substitution of this spurious product.

After the narrative of Alexander's exploits, two chapters close the account of Grecian affairs at home. Stirring passages bestrew these chapters, and the author's characteristic handling crops out on notable occasions: not the least remarkable, perhaps, is the scene of Phocion's condemnation. But the end draws near. Demosthenes is sacrificed. Athens passes under an oligarchy; she is a political nullity. The countrymen of Aristeides and Pericles have fallen into degrading servility and suppliant king-worship. "An historian accustomed to the Grecian world as described by

Herodotus, Thucydides, and Xenophon, feels that the life
has departed from his subject, and, with sadness and
humiliation, brings his narrative to a close." A chapter on
the Sicilian and Italian Greeks ends the eventful narrative.

The style of the 'History' has had a full share of
criticism. Great merits have been conceded to it, while
certain defects have been taken notice of. The author's
character admits of being illustrated by the peculiarities of
his language. Endowed with a great verbal memory, passing
his life in the company and conversation of cultivated and
refined society, well-read in English literature, he could
not but attain a full command of the best English diction.
His taste and resources were still farther improved by his
familiarity with the choice literature of five other languages,
Greek, Latin, French, German, Italian. He keenly appreciated the *belles-lettres ;* they constituted part of his pleasures
all through life.

It does not seem that he imitated, in his early compositions, any one model. He contracted his own ideal of
effective composition, which was, first of all, to be thoroughly
intelligible ; next, to be forcible and pointed ; and, lastly, to
be elegant and refined. He had a few mannerisms, but no
affectation.

His vocabulary inclined to an excess of classical words,
by which he gained superior precision and occasional terseness. He coined a good many words from Latin and Greek,
such as autonomy, hegemony, gens, phratry, dikastery, hop-
lite, demus, most of which are admitted as necessities,
while several have been deemed superfluous. His compounds
with "self" are characteristically numerous : self-agency,
self-sufficing, self-acting, self-judging, &c.

Of the figures of Rhetoric, he freely indulged in similes
and metaphors, of which he had a good command. His only
other figurative device was the manipulation of abstract
nouns and adjectives for brevity :—as "a standing protest
against forward affirmation," "dilatory tactics," "mature
divine efficiency," "the negative vein." The bolder figures

—epigram, hyperbole, interrogation, climax, are scarcely ever used. He has one notable epigram for the myth— "a past that never was present." Antithesis, or pointed balance, so abundant in Macaulay, is entirely wanting.

His sentences are generally simple and intelligible in arrangement; sometimes periodic, but more commonly loose. They are tolerably, but not studiously, various in plan ; and long and short are freely intermingled. Their flow is easy and unaffected.

Of the expository qualities of style, precision and perspicuity took precedence. Extreme simplicity, or the being intelligible to the lowest capacity through the employment of homely and familiar phrases, was not aimed at.

As regards the emotional qualities, he could, on occasions, command strength and pathos alike, and both impart their charm to the 'History.' Humour he never sought to attain. His touches of high poetic elegance, if not numerous, are sometimes exquisite in quality.

The chief complaint against the style generally is that it is not continuously artistic ; and this must be admitted. The remark is also made that, in the distribution of the materials, the author allows the discussions, authorities, and quotations, to hang like a weight on the narrative ; that he has both repetitions and dislocations. To all which the reply is, that his mind was occupied, in the first instance, with other objects than the making of a work of art :—the getting at truth by laboriously sifting insufficient materials, the elucidation of political principles, the inculcation of ethical and political lessons. There is a limit to the capacity of the greatest mind. Had he bestowed an additional quarter of a year on every volume, with an eye to the form and language solely, he might have improved the 'History' as a composition ; but it is doubtful whether this would have been the most useful occupation of his time. It was not his habit to re-write his works ; he did so readily, if he discovered anything defective in the matter or in the general arrangement ; but as regarded mere expression, he was satisfied with the revision of the manuscript and the careful correcting of the proofs.

The greatest virtue of a writer undoubtedly is to rise to the occasion, and this can fearlessly be predicated of Mr. Grote.

In October 1847 appeared the Letters on Switzerland, printed first in the *Spectator* and afterwards in a small 8vo. volume. In August of that year Mr. Grote made an excursion to Switzerland, in order to observe, close at hand, the nearest modern analogue of the Grecian republics. His visit coincided with the crisis of the Swiss revolution. I quote from the Preface his own account of the purpose of the visit :—

"The inhabitants of the twenty-two cantons of Switzerland are interesting on every ground to the general intelligent public of Europe. But to one whose studies lie in the contemplation and interpretation of historical phenomena, they are especially instructive—partly from the many specialities and differences of race, language, religion, civilization, wealth, habits, &c., which distinguish one part of the population from another, comprising, between the Rhine and the Alps, a miniature of all Europe, and exhibiting the fifteenth century in immediate juxtaposition with the nineteenth —partly from the free and unrepressed action of the people, which brings out such distinctive attributes in full relief and contrast. To myself in particular they present an additional ground of interest from a certain political analogy (nowhere else to be found in Europe) with those who prominently occupy my thoughts, and on whose history I am still engaged—the ancient Greeks.

"In listening not only to the debates in the Diet, but also to the violent expressions of opposite sentiment manifested throughout the country during the present summer, I felt a strong impulse to understand how such dispositions had arisen; to construe the present in its just aspect as a sequel to the past: and to comprehend that past itself in conjunction with the feelings which properly belong to it, not under the influence of feelings belonging to the present. The actual condition, and reasonable promise, of Swiss federal politics were different in 1841 and 1844, and have become again materially different in 1847. We have to study each period partly in itself, partly with reference to that which preceded it, and out of which it grew.

"A man must have little experience of historical phenomena to suppose that in any violent political contention all the right is likely to lie on one side and all the wrong on the other. I have not disguised my conviction that both the Swiss parties have committed wrong; nor is my statement likely to give satisfaction to either of them: to show the prolific power of wrong deeds in generating their like, is, in my judgment one of the most important lessons of history."

The Letters may be fairly regarded as a masterly unravelling of Swiss politics, in which the author traces the chain of events from the first inflammatory incident—the election of Dr. Strauss to a chair in the University of Zurich—and shows that the moving power throughout was the aggressive action of the Roman Catholic Church. The work will remain as an interesting chapter on Swiss history, and as one of the many narratives illustrating the disturbance of civil politics by the cry of "Religion in danger." The writer holds the scales with the hand of Justice herself, showing at what points both parties overstepped the bounds of political morality. His dread of foreign intervention, and his strong condemnation and distrust of M. Guizot, are very expressive of his way of looking at foreign politics. The familiar spectacle of the great Powers overbearing the small was to him a source of unmitigated repugnance.

CHAPTER V.

WORK ON PLATO.

In May 1865, nine years after the completion of the 'History of Greece,' appeared 'Plato and the other Companions of Socrates.'

The Preface puts the reader at once into possession of the author's leading aims and peculiarities. His point of departure, in rendering an account of the Platonic Philosophy, is Socrates himself. Connected with him is the large intermixture of the *negative* vein in Plato's 'Dialogues,' which the author for the first time brings into the foreground. The setting forth of the negative side of all doctrines—the arguments against as well as the arguments for—he considers as not merely a distinction of these two philosophers, but as an essential of philosophy itself. Discussion, polemic, dissent, are the marks whereby the habits of the philosopher are distinguished from the unreasoned acquiescence of the multitude in the traditional and prevalent beliefs. It was, moreover, a trait of Socrates, maintained in one half of the Platonic Dialogues, to terminate a discussion in a purely negative result, to unsettle without settling. It was a farther following up of the same peculiarity in Plato to start different, and even opposing, views in his different compositions, and to leave behind him inconsistencies never reconciled. The perception of these inconsistencies has led critics either to force them into harmony by subtle considerations, or to make a choice among the Dialogues, accepting some as the real Platonic compositions and rejecting the others as spurious. Mr. Grote, on the contrary, recognises such inconsistencies as facts, and as very interesting facts, of

the philosophical character of his author. Once more, the career of Plato shows two stages, the first marked by the confessed ignorance and philosophical negative of Socrates; the last, with the peremptory, dictatorial, affirmative of Lycurgus.

The Preface closes with the following reflections:—"The philosophy of the fourth century B.C. is peculiarly valuable and interesting, not merely from its intrinsic speculative worth—from the originality and grandeur of its two principal heroes—from its coincidence with the full display of dramatic, rhetorical, artistic genius—but also from a fourth reason not unimportant—because it is purely Hellenic; preceding the development of Alexandria and the amalgamation of Oriental views of thought with the inspirations of the Academy or the Lyceum. The Orontes and the Jordan had not yet begun to flow westward and to impart their own colour to the waters of Attica and Latium. Not merely the real world, but also the ideal world, present to the minds of Plato and Aristotle, were purely Hellenic. Even during the century immediately following, this had ceased to be fully true in respect to the philosophers of Athens; and it became less and less true with each succeeding century. New foreign centres of rhetoric and literature—Asiatic and Alexandrian Hellenism—were fostered into importance by regal encouragement. Plato and Aristotle are thus the special representatives of genuine Hellenic philosophy. The remarkable intellectual ascendency acquired by them in their own day, and maintained over succeeding centuries, was one main reason why the Hellenic vein was enabled so long to maintain itself, though in impoverished condition, against adverse influences from the East, ever increasing in force. Plato and Aristotle outlasted all their Pagan successors—successors at once less purely Hellenic and less highly gifted. And when Saint Jerome, near 750 years after the decease of Plato, commemorated with triumph the victory of unlettered Christians over the accomplishments and genius of Paganism, he illustrated the magnitude of the victory by singling out

Plato and Aristotle as the representatives of vanquished philosophy."

It has been a very common remark that Mr. Grote, from his peculiar turn of mind and his doctrinal views, was not the most qualified person to comment upon Plato, while he would be quite in his element with Aristotle. The remark is somewhat infelicitous and misplaced; the semblance of foundation for it being both insignificant and unreal. The interest and admiration felt by him for the Platonic writings as a whole could not be surpassed by anyone, although he differed from many as to the nature of Plato's merits. Far from being unpoetical in his own tastes, he was all his life a lover of poetry; he could have said with Plato, "I myself might have become a tragic poet." He relished the dramatic beauties of the 'Dialogues,' and emulated in his own style the happy illustrative similes of his author. But the rack could not have extorted from him the admission that poetry is truth, that emotion is evidence. For imagination working in its own sphere, and also as lending itself to the elucidation and adornment of the results of the scientific reason, he had the greatest respect; for imagination taking the place of reason he had no respect, whether in Plato, in Aristotle, or in any other man.

The work begins with an exhaustive review of early Greek Philosophy, from Thales to Democritus. A second chapter contains an interesting commentary on the position and points of view of these primitive thinkers, and prepares the way for the next stage of Grecian thought, by the remark that common to them all was the absence of Dialectic, or systematic negative criticism. The inventor of dialectic, we are told by Aristotle, was Zeno; and his extant philosophy and method are described by Mr. Grote with a detail corresponding to his sense of the momentous nature of the innovation. The opening of the negative vein imparts from this time forward a new character to Grecian philosophy—a character never present in the most advanced Oriental speculation. The positive and negative forces, emanating from different aptitudes of the human mind, are, henceforth, both of them actively developed, and in strenuous antithesis to each other. It is not enough to propound a theory in obscure, oracular metaphors and half-intelligible aphorisms, like Heracleitus, or in verse, more or less impressive, like Parmenides or Empedocles. Every theory must be sustained by proofs, guarded against objections, defended against imputations of inconsistency, compared with other rival theories. From this quarter we have to approach both Socrates and Plato.

The life of Plato is next reviewed. In making the most of the scanty notices preserved, Mr. Grote is careful to place before the reader the political surrounding of the period from his nineteenth to his twenty-fifth year (409–403), a period of extraordinary disaster for Athens, and involving, among other things, the severest strain upon all able-bodied citizens for military service. Philosophical study must have been very much restricted; moreover, as Plato entertained at first a political ambition, he would not think of philosophy until he failed in that object. His studious life, when it began, had no marked interruption but the episode of his Sicilian visits. He was the founder of the earliest establishment for philosophical teaching—a building with grounds, lecture-room, and library. This was the Academy.

In chapter iv. the author considers the Platonic Canon. Both ancients and moderns were at one as to the real works of Plato, down to the end of the last century. During the present century, the genuineness of many of the alleged works has been called in question: in consequence of which, Mr. Grote examines at length the external evidence for the received canon, which evidence he regards as peculiarly strong, being far above what we possess for the works of Demosthenes, Euripides, Aristophanes, Isocrates, or Lysias. The great point in the argument is the perpetuation of the Academy, with its library, up to the date of the foundation of the Alexandrine Collection, which collection would acquire a well-guaranteed set of the genuine Platonic writings; while our present canon rests on the authority of that collection and its librarians.

In a separate chapter, Mr. Grote considers the grounds of the recent objections to the time-honoured canon. The new turn was given by Schleiermacher, who began by assuming as fundamental postulates—first, a systematic unity of scheme and purpose, running through all the Dialogues; secondly, an intentional order, with a view to this scheme. Upon these two assumptions he classifies the Dialogues, rejecting some that do not fall within the scheme. He is followed by other critics, who, without agreeing altogether in his assumptions, are yet more sweeping in their rejections. Against all these critics Mr. Grote produces reasons that seem irresistible. The different theories laid down respecting the general and systematic purposes of Plato, he regards as uncertified and gratuitous; the "internal reasons" are only another phrase for expressing each critic's opinion respecting Plato as a philosopher and a writer.

"Considering that Plato's period of philosophical composition extended over fifty years, and that the circumstances of his life are most imperfectly known to us, it is surely hazardous to limit the range of his varieties on the faith of a critical repugnance, not merely subjective and fallible, but withal entirely of modern growth: to assume, as basis of reasoning, the admiration raised by a few of the first dialogues—and then to argue that no composition inferior to this admired type, or unlike to it in doctrine or handling, can possibly be the work of Plato. 'The Minos, Theagês, Epistolæ, Epinomis, &c, are unworthy of Plato: nothing so inferior in excellence can have been composed by him. No dialogue can be admitted as genuine which contradicts another dialogue, or which advocates any low or incorrect or un-Platonic doctrine. No dialogue can pass which is adverse to the general purpose of Plato as an improver of morality and a teacher of the doctrine of Ideas.' On such grounds as these we are called upon to reject various dialogues; and there is nothing upon which, generally speaking, so much stress is laid as upon inferior excellence. For my part, I cannot recognise any of them as sufficient grounds of exception. I have no difficulty in believing not merely that Plato (like Aristophanes) produced many successive novelties— ' not at all similar one to the other, and all clever '—but also that among these novelties there were inferior dialogues as well as superior: that in different dialogues he worked out different, even contradictory, points of view—and among them some which critics declare to be low and objectionable; that we have among his works unfinished fragments and abandoned sketches, published without order, and perhaps only after his death."

Mr. Jowett's remarks on this perplexed theme are as follows:—

"I cannot agree with Mr. Grote in admitting as genuine all the writings commonly attributed to Plato in antiquity, any more than with Schaarschmidt and some other German critics, who reject nearly half of them. . . . . On the other hand, Mr. Grote trusts mainly to the Alexandrian canon. But I hardly think that we are justified in attributing much weight to the authority of the Alexandrian librarians in an age when there was no regular publication of books and every temptation to forge them, and in which the writings of a school were naturally attributed to the founder of the school. And even without intentional fraud there was an inclination to believe rather than to inquire. Would Mr. Grote accept as genuine all the writings which he finds in the lists of learned ancients attributed to Hippocrates, to Xenophon, to Aristotle? The Alexandrian canon of the Platonic writings is deprived of credit by the admission of the ' Epistles,' which are not only unworthy of Plato, but in several places plagiarised from him and flagrantly at variance with historical fact."

To the query of Mr. Jowett, " Would Mr. Grote accept as genuine all the writings attributed to Hippocrates," &c., an answer was given in anticipation, grounded on the special preservation of the Platonic writings in the library of the Academy, no similar advantage belonging to the other writers.

Mr. Jowett rejects, not without hesitation, Lesser Hippias,

First Alcibiades, and Menexenus. He considers it right, however, to give them a place in his work. He is thus substantially at one with Mr. Grote on the Dialogues, but not on the Epistles, whose genuineness is supported by Mr. Grote, both in the 'History' and in the 'Plato,' by arguments of no small cogency, which we should like to see Mr. Jowett answer in detail. Bentley, the crusher of spurious Epistles, allowed the Epistles of Plato': his extraordinary learning did not enable him to detect in them "flagrant violations of historical fact." Subsequent scholars, while denying their genuineness, allow them to be the work of early and well-informed authors. The seventh epistle especially is, by Boeckh, considered genuine, and by Ueberweg, the work of a well-informed contemporary. Cicero, Plutarch, Aristeides, &c., all attest facts on the authority of these Epistles. The chief objections to them by critics generally are founded on their being unworthy of Plato. Mr. Grote does not think himself competent to determine à priori what the style of Plato's letters may have been; he has no difficulty in believing that Plato may have expressed himself with as much mysticism and obscurity as we now read in the second and seventh epistles: he is not surprised at the allusions to details which critics who look upon him altogether as a spiritual person, disallow as mean and unworthy.

It is curiously remarked by Ueberweg that Mr. Grote's "accepting as genuine all the dialogues accredited by Thrasyllus has caused him to lose sight of *the essential unity present in Plato's thought and works, and to admit in its stead a multifariousness abounding in change and contradiction.*" The real fact is, Mr. Grote is not blinded by his acceptance of the canon of Thrasyllus. He sees no possibility of gaining the "unity" by any number of rejections; he has followed the upholders of unity through all their clashing experiments, and found only confusion and contradiction.

The regaining of unity and consistency in Plato's writings, by rejecting a sufficient number of dialogues, involves an entirely new theory of the tactics of a forger of writings, namely, that he should contradict all the leading doctrines of the author imitated. Now, although it is one of the usual marks of a spurious writing to contain inconsistencies unfelt by the writer, but detected by well-informed critics, it is surely not the practice of any forger to make such open and vital contradictions as those existing between the supposed spurious and the real dialogues of Plato. How should a forger of epistles of Paul expect to succeed by maintaining a series of doctrines in marked opposition to all the characteristic views of the apostle? There is but one conceivable situation suitable to this policy: namely, where there was a wish to gain the weight of a great name to certain views special to the forger, and where all external circumstances were so far favourable to the reception of the forgery as to outweigh the internal discordance.

In chapter vi., entitled "Platonic Compositions Generally," Mr. Grote gives his views as to the method of Plato. Although on isolated points others have agreed with him, yet the general strain of the criticisms on Plato's plan and purpose has the character of novelty. The first impression produced by the Platonic writings is their exceeding variety; no one epithet can describe them all. Some critics in antiquity described Plato as essentially a searcher or inquirer, and as never reaching any certain result. This is going too far; he is sceptical in some dialogues, dogmatical in others. Again, Aristotle characterised his style of writing as something between poetry and prose, and declared that the doctrine of Ideas obtained all its plausibility from metaphors. This is also true to a certain extent; many of the dialogues possess a degree of poetic exuberance condemned as excessive by contemporary and subsequent critics, who had before them, for comparison, the most finished compositions of Greece. Moreover, the power of his dramatic situations would have carried away the prizes at the Dionysiac festivals, if he had followed the drama as a profession. But these poetic attributes are not found in all the Dialogues. Plato was sceptic, dogmatist, religious mystic, and inquisitor, mathematician, philosopher, poet (erotic as well as satirical), rhetor, artist, all in one—or at least, all in turn,— throughout the fifty years of his philosophical life. So much appears in his published Dialogues. But he was a lecturer besides, and of his lectures we have no record, excepting only a tantalizing observation of Aristotle. The only occasions where he lays aside the pen of "Imaginary Conversations" and speaks in his own person, are in the much repudiated Epistles, from which Mr. Grote brings before us some singular views as to the mode of communicating knowledge. He peculiarly disclaims written compositions, and regards oral communications and debate, coupled with intense meditation apart, as the only effective mode of intellectual illumination. Also his standard of mastery of any subject was that the learner shall be able to endure from others, and himself apply to others, a Socratic elenchus, or cross-examination as to all the difficulties.

In classifying the Dialogues, our author starts from one of the divisions given by Thrasyllus—the two-fold division of Dialogues of Search and Dialogues of Exposition, setting aside the Apology of Socrates and the Menexenus as compositions apart. Deviating from Thrasyllus in the detailed enumeration, he gives nineteen Dialogues of Search and fourteen of Exposition. The most elaborate example of Search is Theætetus. Among Expository dialogues, Timæus is a marked example, being devoid of all negative criticism. Many are not purely of either character.

Mr. Grote's strong point, as is already apparent, lies in his rendering of the Search Dialogues. This is a species of composition now rare and strange: modern readers do not understand what is meant by publishing an inquiry without any result—a story without an end. To settle a question and finish with it—to get rid of the debate, as if it were a troublesome temporary necessity—is not what Plato desires; the torpedo shock of conscious ignorance is what he, after Socrates, aims at imparting. He tells us himself that he is a searcher, and has not made up his own mind;

critics generally will not believe him ; Mr. Grote does. Most historians of ancient philosophy fail to realise, because themselves disliking, the process of mere negation. They would tolerate it in small doses, and as an aid to affirmation; requiring that, when you deprive a man of one affirmative solution, you must ,be prepared at once with another. " Le Roi est Mort; Vive le Roi!" the dogmatic throne must never be empty. The claims of the objector must be satisfied before the affirmer can be held solvent.

For the mere evoking of literary charm, Plato was attached to the polemic form. He feels a strong interest in the process of enquiry, in the debate *per se;* and he presumes the like interest in his readers. He has no wish to shorten the process; he claims it as the privilege of philosophical discussion that the speakers are not tied to time by the Klepsydra. And he really succeeded in inspiring readers with something of his own interest in the dialectical process. The charm imparted by him to the process of philosophising is one main cause of the preservation of his writings from the terrible shipwreck that has overtaken so much of the abundant contemporary literature.

But the most important consideration, in Mr. Grote's view, still remains. It is the special ground assigned by Socrates for his negative procedure, namely, that chronic and deep-seated malady of the human mind, the false persuasion of knowledge. To this state Socrates applied his Elenchus, making people explain what they meant by Justice, Temperance, Courage, Law, and other familiar terms. The answers elicited were simple expressions of the ordinary prevalent belief in matters wherein each community possesses established dogmas, laws, customs, sentiments, fashions, points of view belonging to itself; many of them diametrically opposed to what is accepted in other communities. There can be no philosophy unless these consecrated opinions are to be freely canvassed and disturbed. Philosophy is thus the proclaimed enemy of orthodoxy; the philosopher, by the

i

law of his being, is a dissenter. Accordingly the indictment against Socrates ran thus: "Socrates commits crime, inasmuch as he does not believe in the gods in whom the city believes, but introduces new religious beliefs." Nomos (Law and Custom) King of All (to borrow the phrase cited by Herodotus from Pindar) exercises plenary power, spiritual as well as temporal, over individual minds; moulding the emotions as well as the intellect according to the local type; determining everyone's sentiments, belief, and predispositions to believe; fashioning thought, speech, and points of view, no less than action; yet reigning under the appearance of habitual self-suggested tendency. Never before did King Nomos meet with such an adversary as Socrates.

In these very decided views as to the Platonic position in the Dialogues of Search, Mr. Grote has as yet very little following. Mr. Jowett, alluding to the Gorgias, one of the Dialogues emphasised by our author as putting forward the right of dissent or private judgment, regards this mode of stating the question as really opposed both to the spirit of Plato and of ancient philosophy generally; so far from advocating toleration or free thought, Plato (in the Laws) has laid himself open to the charge of intolerance; no speculations had as yet arisen respecting the liberty of prophesying.

Now, it must be distinctly allowed that Mr. Grote, being himself an ardent apostle of free enquiry, is naturally predisposed to find allies among the greatest of mankind. He may, therefore, somewhat overstrain the amount of support lent to individual freedom by Socrates and Plato. Yet his case is far stronger than Mr. Jowett would lead us to suppose. As regards Socrates, it is seemingly irresistible. In Plato it does not rest on the Gorgias alone. There, indeed, does Mr. Grote find the remarkable expression put into the mouth of Socrates: "You, Polus, bring against me the authority of the multitude, as well as of the most eminent citizens, all upholding your view. But I, one man standing here alone, do *not* agree with you." In the Phædon, also, Socrates is made to give a dying testimony to the freedom of debate:

" If I appear to you to affirm anything truly, attend to me; but, if not, oppose me with all your powers of reasoning." A very emphatic passage to the same effect occurs in the Politicus, the chief spokesmen being made to complain of the interdict maintained against adverse criticism of the legal and consecrated doctrines.

Mr. Grote admits the change that had come over Plato when he wrote the Laws. Instead of adducing it, however, to neutralise the animated protests in favour of liberty in the Gorgias and the Phædon, so as to show that Plato, taken as a whole, was indifferent in the matter, he deplores it as the most repulsive feature of Plato's senility.

After all, Mr. Jowett cannot be far off from Mr. Grote's views, when he allows himself to represent Plato " as asserting the duty of the one wise and true man to dissent from the folly and falsehood of the many."

Occasions necessarily arise for adverting to Plato's treatment of the Sophists, on which modern historians of philosophy have bettered the instruction. The author repeats, that the charges made against the Sophists (as well as the Megarics), namely corrupting youth, perverting truth and morality, by making the worse appear the better reason, subverting established beliefs,—were all urged against Plato himself by his contemporaries, and indeed against all the philosophers indiscriminately. They are outbursts of feeling natural to the practical, orthodox citizen, who represents the common sense of the time and place; declaring his antipathy to those speculative, freethinking innovations of theory, which challenge the prescriptive maxims of traditional custom by a theoretical standard. In point of fact, the persons commonly called Sophists did far less violence to the orthodox sentiments than either Socrates or Plato. Indeed Plato's dislike to the Sophists was part and parcel of his dislike to the general multitude of Athenians. In the Republic, he says emphatically, that the Sophists teach nothing but the opinions of the multitude, and call these wisdom.

Mr. Jowett so far agrees with Mr. Grote that the Sophists

did not, as so generally alleged, corrupt the youth; the
Athenian youth were no more corrupted in the time of
Demosthenes than in the time of Pericles. He puts the
question, however,—"Would an Athenian, as Mr. Grote
supposes, in the fifth century before Christ, have included
Socrates and Plato, as well as Gorgias and Protagoras, under
the specific class of Sophists?" and answers "No." "The
man of genius, the great original thinker, the disinterested
seeker after truth, the master of repartee whom no one ever
defeated in an argument, was separated, even in the mind of
the vulgar Athenian, by an 'interval which no geometry can
express,' from the balancer of sentences, the interpreter and
reciter of the poets, the divider of the meanings of words,
the teacher of rhetoric, the professor of morals and manners."
Now, there was one marked peculiarity of the Sophists: they
received regular pay; Socrates and Plato merely accepted
presents. But in the eyes of both Socrates and Plato,
teaching for pay was exceedingly discreditable; we are not
told to what length the Athenian public shared in this antipathy. As to any of the other points mentioned, it is exceedingly difficult to discover why the vulgar Athenian should
set up Socrates and Plato as immeasurably superior to the
general body of teachers, called Sophists. Mr. Grote thinks
highly of the Athenians, but he utterly refuses to accredit
them with a fine sense of what distinguished the true philosopher from the eloquent repeater of commonplace.

It is in the present work that Mr. Grote has found opportunities of unfolding a number of his own philosophical views.
He has indicated his tenets in some of the highest questions
of Psychology, Logic, Ethics, and Metaphysics. I shall here
briefly sketch his leading positions as a philosophical
thinker.

In adhering to experience as the sole fountain of legitimate belief, and to utility, as the sole criterion of what is
morally right, he was thorough-going and consistent. He
disclaimed the criterion of Intuition or Instinct in both
spheres; and, incidentally in commenting on Plato and on

Aristotle, has argued with no little force in favour of his own side. He embraced with eagerness several of the most important aspects of the great law or doctrine of Relativity, respecting which many sagacious glimpses appear in ancient philosophy. Mr. Jowett speaks too lightly of the import of this doctrine, when he calls it a truism of the present time. No doubt it is well enough recognised in a few familiar applications such as pleasures and pains, fine art, and some aspects of knowledge; but I doubt if in its full compass, any great number of persons would either understand it or tolerate all its legitimate consequences. Yet it is one of those cardinal doctrines that must be true universally, or not at all.

It is in the exposition of Aristotle's Categories that the author takes note of Relativity as the essential fact of all Knowledge or Cognition. Every fact or quality exists only with reference to some other fact or quality, as its correlative or opposite—light, dark: cold, hot; up, down; wise, foolish. This is the most fundamental of all the aspects of the doctrine.

A more restricted but exceedingly momentous aspect is largely dwelt on by Mr. Grote; the correlation of subject and object in perception; the mutual implication of the percipient mind with the thing perceived—the *percipiens* and the *perceptum*. His mode of handling this antithesis in connection with the Berkeleian idealism is most fully shown in one of the essays in the present volume (p. 332).

The mode of Relativity most forcibly stated in the 'Plato,' is the relativity of truth or belief to the affirming or believing subject. This is dwelt upon in the commentary on THEÆ-TETUS, as the most probable rendering of the Protagorean dictum — *homo mensura*, "man is a measure to himself." As he understands the doctrine, Mr. Grote is thoroughly at one with Protagoras, although the view was impugned by both Plato and Aristotle. He attributes no small importance to the doctrine; it being, in his opinion, the philosophical formula of the right of private judgment, as opposed to the assumed infallibility of some one man or body of men.

In this grand *chef-d'œuvre* of Plato, Mr. Grote's philosophical handling everywhere appears to full advantage, and the student will find a rewarding exercise in comparing him with the other commentators on the dialogue.

His opposition to the *à priori* philosophy is stated in the discussion on the meanings of Cause, in the Phædon. Following Hume and Brown, he understands "by causes nothing more than phenomenal antecedents constant and unconditional, ascertainable by experience and induction."

In connexion with the Protagoras, the Gorgias, and the Republic he sets forth certain ethical points of view that he lays great stress upon. In Protagoras, Plato affirms the doctrine that good and evil are identical with pleasurable and painful, and that virtue is an affair of measurement and computation. Mr. Grote, in like manner, holds that there is no intelligible standard of reference for application of the terms good and evil, except the tendency to produce happiness or misery; if this standard be rejected, ethical debate ceases to be a matter of rational discussion, and becomes only an enunciation of the different sentiments, authoritative and self-justifying, that are prevalent in each community. An important qualification, however, has been omitted by Plato. His measurement omits to take account of man as a member of society, and to value the pleasures and pains of others. This is one of the defects of Plato's ethical theory. In Gorgias he takes a totally different view of virtue—the preservation of a high tone of mental health. Vice he treats as a kind of disease, and the eradication of this taint or disease is what the virtuous man must aim at. Mr. Grote tries to give a meaning to what lies under this high-flown metaphor; remarking how our being is divided between the transient impressions made upon us, and a certain permanent element, namely, the established character, habits, dispositions, intellectual requirements—the accumulated mental capital of the past life. This permanent element must be kept in good condition; we must not for the sake of present and transitory pleasure impair the general stock of pleasurable accumulations. Still, the permanent itself derives all its substance and value from the regard to pleasures and the avoidance of pains.

In the first book of the Republic, which is occupied with a stirring polemic on the nature of justice, Plato, in opposition to the received opinions of mankind, declares that justice is a good thing in itself, without regard to the consequences. This is the first statement of the doctrine, afterwards insisted on by the Stoics, and repeated in modern ethics, that virtue is all-sufficient to the happiness of the virtuous agent, whatever be his fate in other respects. As a counter thesis, Mr. Grote strikingly illustrates the essential *reciprocity* of virtuous conduct—one of the many phases of the Law of Relativity. Plato has endeavoured to accredit a fiction misrepresenting the constant phenomena and standing conditions of social life. Among these conditions, reciprocity of services is fundamental. Each individual has both duties and rights : each is required to be just to others : others are required to be just to him. The rights and obligations of any one towards the rest are inseparably correlated ; without this the terms " right " and " obligation " are . void of meaning.

In Plato we have the first faint indications of what is now called *Teleology*, or a science of Ends, as distinct from the sciences of the Order of Nature. Aristotle was more explicit; he being the first to shape the practical sciences of ethics, politics, and rhetoric, into whose definition there entered a statement of the End. Mr. Grote, at an early period of his studies, worked out this conception of the practical sciences, and I believe instigated Mr. Mill to compose that striking chapter, added to the second edition of his Logic, entitled ' The Logic of Practice.'

CHAPTER VI.

WORK ON ARISTOTLE.

MR. GROTE began the 'Aristotle' in his seventy-first year. His preparatory studies had been ample, including a life-long acquaintance with most of the Aristotelian treatises. All his accumulated knowledge on ancient Greece as a whole, and his persistent devotion to philosophy in its modern as well as its ancient phases, could be now brought to bear on his concluding and most laborious task.

That his unremitted exertions for six years at an advanced age should terminate in a fragment only, is matter of lasting regret, but not of astonishment. The difficulties of the subject are great; and his mode of dealing with it, combining lucid interpretation with critical comparison, could cost nothing less than a protracted effort. Ten years of his prime would have scarcely sufficed to complete the projected survey of Aristotle and his contemporaries, as a parallel to Plato.

The two volumes that have been published are mainly occupied with the logical treatises of the great philosopher. Prefixed to the account of these are two chapters—one on the life of Aristotle, the other on the Canon.

The extant notices of Aristotle's career are very unsatisfactory. The facts are few, and many of them doubtful from conflicting testimonies. The biographer's task is chiefly made up of the sifting of authorities, and the comparing of the statements with the history of the time as otherwise known.

The opening paragraph deserves to be quoted, as a bird's-eye view of the situation of philosophy in the Aristotelian age:—

"In my preceding work, 'Plato and the Other Companions of Sokrates,' I described a band of philosophers differing much from each other, but all emanating from Sokrates as common intellectual progenitor; all manifesting themselves wholly or principally in the composition of dialogues; and all living in an atmosphere of Hellenic freedom, as yet untroubled by any overruling imperial ascendency from without. From that band, among whom Plato is *facile princeps*, I now proceed to another, among whom the like pre-eminence belongs to Aristotle. This second band knew the Sokratic stimulus only as a historical tradition; they gradually passed, first from the Sokratic or Platonic dialogue —dramatic, colloquial, cross-examining—to the Aristotelian dialogue, semi-dramatic, rhetorical, counter-expository; and next to formal theorising, ingenious solution and divination of special problems, historical criticism and abundant collections of detailed facts: moreover, they were witnesses of the extinction of freedom in Hellas, and of the rise of the Macedonian kingdom out of comparative nullity to the highest pinnacle of supremacy and mastership. Under the successors of Alexander, this extraneous supremacy, intermeddling and dictatorial, not only overruled the political movements of the Greeks, but also influenced powerfully the position and working of their philosophers; and would have become at once equally intermeddling even earlier, under Alexander himself, had not his whole time and personal energy been absorbed by insatiable thirst for Eastern conquests, ending with an untimely death."

Among the most interesting aspects of the philosopher's life are those opened up by Mr. Grote, through the contemporary history. While attending the school of Plato, he contracted intimacy with a fellow-pupil, Hermeias, a man of great ability and energy, who became despot of two little towns in Asia Minor, Atarneus and Assos (opposite the island of Lesbos). In consequence of a hurt when a child,

he was known to be a eunuch, and had become the slave of
the prior despot of Atarneus. On Plato's death, Aristotle
left Athens and accepted an invitation to reside with
Hermeias, during which residence he married Pythias, the
despot's niece. The happy intimacy was put an end to by
the treachery of the Persian general in command of the
neighbouring region, who decoyed Hermeias into his grasp
and sent him up to the Persian king, by whom he was put to
death. Aristotle's deep grief is permanently recorded in a
hymn or pæan composed to the memory of his friend. The
Persians took possession of the towns of Hermeias, and
Aristotle went to Mitylene. His next recorded movement is
to the Macedonian court, as tutor to the youthful Alexander;
an appointment partly owing (we may suppose) to his
father's having been Philip's court physician, and partly to
his own already acquired reputation for philosophy. His
residence at Pella, the Macedonian capital, and his instructions to Alexander, continued, with occasional interruptions,
till Alexander's accession to the throne in 336 B.C. In the
year following, which saw the completion of the preparations
for invading Persia, he went to Athens, and opened a new
school of philosophy, as a rival to the Academy, still kept
up by the successors to Plato; in that school he spent the
remaining thirteen years of his life. Apart from his philo-
sophic teaching and pursuits, he had by no means an easy
time. He was under Macedonian patronage; he was still
consulted by Alexander, and maintained a constant correspondence with Antipater, Alexander's deputy or viceroy
in the government of Macedonia and its dependencies. He
was thus in a position of antagonism to the sentiments of
the majority of the Athenian public.

" It will thus appear, that though all the preserved
writings of Aristotle are imbued with a thoroughly independent spirit of theorising contemplation and lettered
industry, uncorrupted by any servility or political bias—yet
his position during the twelve years between 335–323 B.C.
inevitably presented him to the Athenians as the Mace-

donising philosopher, parallel with Phokion as the Macedon-
ising politician, and in pointed antithesis to Xenokrates at
the Academy, who was attached to the democratical constitution, and refused kingly presents. Besides that enmity
which he was sure to incur, as an acute and self-thinking
philosopher, from theology and the other anti-philosophical
veins in the minds of ordinary men, Aristotle thus became
the object of unfriendly sentiment from many Athenian
patriots, who considered the school of Plato generally as
hostile to popular liberty, and who had before them examples
of individual Platonists, ruling their respective cities with a
sceptre forcibly usurped."

The death of Alexander at Babylon, in June 323 B.C.,
came upon the world with a shock: and gave hopes of
deliverance to enslaved Greece. There was an anti-Mace-
donian rising at Athens; Phocion and the other Macedonian
leaders went for safety to Antipater; and Aristotle's enemies
thought the moment opportune for an onslaught on him.
Following the Socratic precedent, the chief priest of the
Eleusinian temple entered against him an indictment for
impiety. The grounds of the indictment were peculiar;
consisting mainly of the Hymn to Hermeias, and the inscription on a statue to Hermeias at Delphi. To this
was added the citation of certain heretical doctrines from
his published writings, of which the chief seems to have
been a declaration against the efficacy of prayers and sacrifices. On this curious indictment Mr. Grote remarks that
the hymn or pæan in honour of Hermeias would be more
offensive to the feelings of an ordinary Athenian than any
philosophical dogma extracted from the cautious prose compositions of Aristotle. Such hymns had been previously
composed in honour of individual Greeks by Pindar and
others; the same lofty and exaggerated comparison to
deities had been indulged in: yet the searching eye of
the historian of Greece discloses a difference. Hermeias
was a compound of three enormities—a eunuch, a slave, and
a despot. He was not a despot pure and simple, but a

eunuch-despot, beginning from a slave; while there was no redeeming public exploit that would have softened the harshness of the combination. A groundwork of political antipathy, overlaid by such a charge, gave Aristotle small chance at that moment; he bowed to the storm, which he knew could not last, retired from Athens, and would have soon returned, but for his death. A sentence of his composed defence is preserved, wherein he rebuts the charge of deifying Hermeias (ranking him in the ode with Herakles, and others) by alleging that he had notoriously erected a tomb, and performed funeral ceremonies to him as a mortal. Mr. Grote remarks, that this did not meet the case: the Athenians would not have felt the logical inconsistency of the two proceedings; what they felt was the worthlessness of Hermeias, to whom he rendered these great honours, whether as divinity or as human being. The solemn measure and character of a pæan was disgraced by being applied to so vile a person.

Mr. Grote has farther supplied illustrative comments on the position of Aristotle with reference to the rival schools, namely, of Isocrates and of Plato; and gives what evidence remains of his feelings towards his rivals, on which bitter reflections were common.

The second chapter is entitled the 'Aristotelian Canon.' The problem of what are Aristotle's genuine writings has far greater complication than attends the Platonic canon; and Mr. Grote exhausts his learning and acumen in the attempt to unravel it. We shall not follow him in this research, but shall advert only to his concluding dissertation on the exact meaning of the renowned distinction between Esoteric and Exoteric doctrine. The basis of explanation of these words, as occurring in Aristotle's own writings, is exceedingly narrow. The word 'Exoteric' occurs in eight passages of the extant works (taking in the Eudemian Ethics, which is disputed by some critics); seven of these are indecisive; but reasoning from the eighth, Mr. Grote thinks that the word means *dialectical debate* as contrasted with *demonstration*; a fundamental distinction with Aristotle. This is very different from the common acceptation of the two contrasting terms—exoteric and esoteric. According to Mr. Grote, the 'esoteric' is the essence of science or philosophy itself, in its deductive, demonstrative, or syllogistic march; the 'exoteric' is something lying outside of this, extrinsic, but yet a valuable province in itself, the province of the probable, the disputable, where there is no proper demonstration, but a series of arguments *pro* and *con.* The Organon or Methodised Ratiocination of Aristotle, fell under corresponding heads, the one (Demonstrative) represented by the Analytica, the other (Dialectic) by the Topica.

Of the prodigious total of works composed by Aristotle, the larger number have perished. There still remain about forty treatises, of authenticity not open to any reasonable suspicion, attesting the grandeur of his intelligence, in respect of speculative force, positive and negative, systematizing patience, comprehensive curiosity as to matters of fact, and diversified applications of detail. In the order of study most generally agreed upon, the first place is given to the collection of treatises called the ORGANON, six in number:—The Categories; De Interpretatione or Dè Enunciatione; Analytica Priora; Analytica Posteriora; Topica; De Sophisticis Elenchis. The last, although a short treatise, is very important; it forms naturally a part of the Topica; so that, in fact, there are five distinct treatises: each having a well-marked subject.

Mr. Grote's greatest originality as an expositor appears in his account of the first treatise — CATEGORIÆ, the Categories. It corresponds to the logical department of *Terms,* although the best known logicians have discarded Aristotle's treatment, and have usually given in some detached chapter a List of the Categories without connecting explanation, often accompanied with an insinuation that the subject does not belong to Logic. Nevertheless, the nature of Terms, and their various distinctions, have their beginning in the book of the Categories. Aristotle was the first to distinguish

terms as *Equivocal* and *Univocal*, and to regard predication
or the proposition as made up of terms.

The Ten Categories or Predicaments are a comprehensive
classification of all things that enter into a proposition,
either as Subject or as Predicate. They are:—" 1. *Essence*
or *Substance;* such as, man, horse. 2. *How much* or *Quantity;* such as, two cubits long, three cubits long. 3. *What
manner of* or *Quality*; such as, white, erudite. 4. *Ad aliquid*
—*To something* or *Relation*; such as, double, half, greater.
5. *Where;* such as, in the market-place, in the Lykeium.
6. *When;* such as, yesterday, last year. 7. *In what posture;*
such as, he stands up, he is sitting down. 8. *To have;* such
as, to be shod, 'to be armed. 9. *Activity;* such as, he is
cutting, he is burning. 10. *Passivity;* such as, he is being
cut, he is being burned."

" In this enumeration, Aristotle takes his departure, not
from any results of prior research, but from common speech;
and from the dialectic, frequent in his time, which debated
about matters of common life and talk, about received and
current opinions. We may presume him to have studied and
compared a variety of current propositions, so as to discover
the different relations in which subjects and predicates did
stand or could stand to each other; also the various questions which might be put respecting any given subject, with
the answers suitable to be returned. "

The chief stress of Aristotle's exposition rests upon the first
four categories—*Substance, Quantity, Quality, Relation;* as
to the six last—*Where, When, Posture, Having, Activity,
Passivity,* he says little upon any of them; upon some
nothing at all.

The cardinal explanation of the whole scheme turns upon
the First Category—SUBSTANCE or ESSENCE. From the
prevailing signification of this term, as the most extreme and
attenuated of all abstractions, we are unprepared for the
meaning given to it by Aristotle, namely, the *Concrete
Individual.* The First *Ens* or First Essence—that which is
Ens in the fullest sense—is the *individual* concrete person or

thing in nature ; Sokrates, Bukephalus, this man, that horse, that oak-tree, &c. This First *Ens* is indispensable as Subject or *Substratum* for all the other Categories, and even for predication generally. It is a subject only ; it never appears as a predicate of anything else.

Having defined in this fashion substance or First Essence, by which he placed himself in diametrical opposition to Plato's Ideas, Aristotle states what he means by a Second Essence, namely the species that a thing belongs to; Sokrates First Essence; man or animal—Species or Second Essence. Here in reality, he is going on another tack, mixing up with the categories a different set of distinctions; these terms, however,—First and Second Essences, are of vital moment in the Aristotelian philosophy. The proper antithesis to SUBSTANCE is seen in the remaining nine Categories— *Quantity, Quality,* &c, which are predicates for clothing the First Essence, or Individual. An individual man, horse, building, possesses *Quantity* in various ways ; also *Quality* as white, living, costly. Aristotle discusses and classifies the modes of Quantity, as shown in the mathematical sciences, and in the adjectives of degree little, much, &c.

He then proceeds to *Relation*, and gets out of his depth, not seeing that relation instead of being a property co-ordinate with Quantity, Quality, and the rest, is at the foundation of the whole, as Mr. Grote amply shows. The ancient philosophers had far-seeing glimpses into the principle of Relativity, but usually broke down at some point or other, and landed themselves in confusion and even contradiction ; and the present attempt of Aristotle is a signal example.

In seeking a clue to what was in the mind of Aristotle when he drew up this very imperfect classification of things entering into either the Subject or the Predicate of propositions, Mr. Grote points out the last as the most suggestive. Every one is astonished, after surveying the sweeping generalities—*Quantity, Quality,* and *Relation*, to come down to *Posture* (sitting, lying), *Having* (possessing shoes or arms); for while the higher, and grander attributes, include everything in their sweep, the last can apply only to some human being or animal. We infer from this that Aristotle had in his mind chiefly some individual man, and put all the different questions that could be answered respecting that individual.

The caprice in choosing the number *Ten*, was the remains in Aristotle's mind of the fascination for particular numbers, which so largely affected the Pythagoreans, and after them, Plato. The number might easily have been extended, or it might have been contracted, as it was by the Stoics, who recognised only Four: while Plotinus and Galen each made out Five.

" He was, as far as we can see, original in taking as the point of departure for his theory, the individual man, horse, or other perceivable object; in laying down this Concrete Particular with all its outfit of details, as the type of *Ens* proper, complete and primary; and in arranging into classes the various secondary modes of *Ens* according to their different relations to the primary type and the mode in which they contributed to make up its completeness. He thus stood opposed to the Pythagoreans and Platonists, who took their departure from the Universal, as the type of full and true Entity; while he also dissented from Demokritus, who recognised no true *Ens* except the underlying, imperceptible, eternal atoms and vacuum. Moreover, Aristotle seems to have been the first to draw up a logical analysis of Entity in its widest sense, as distinguished from that metaphysical analysis which we read in his other works; the two not being contradictory, but distinct and leading to different purposes. Both in the one and in the other, his principal controversy seems to have been with the Platonists, who disregarded both individual objects and accidental attributes; dwelling upon Universals, Genera, and Species, as the only real *Entia* capable of being known."

The second treatise of the Organon is called DE INTERPRETATIONE, the doctrine of the Proposition. This, with the

' Analytica Priora,' is the source of the theory of Propositions in modern Logic. Denial or negative affirmation was in a very confused state in the philosophies prior to Aristotle ; and although his terminology is not in all respects fully developed, he made the great step of distinguishing the Quantity of Propositions—as Universal or Particular, from which followed the two modes of denial, Contrary and Contradictory. The Maxim or Law of Contradiction was a part of this theory, which Mr. Grote attributes exclusively to Aristotle, in opposition to Sir W. Hamilton's attempt to trace it up to Plato.

A considerable portion of the treatise is devoted to the so-called MODAL Propositions—the Possible and the Necessary—and rings all the changes growing out of their opposites. Much dissension has taken place among logicians as to these modals. Mr. Grote shows that they have a place in Logic, but have not been satisfactorily dealt with by Aristotle, being a very serious clog in his handling, both of the proposition and the syllogism.

Next follows the ANALYTICA PRIORA containing the theory of the syllogism. This great artificial construction is claimed by Aristotle, as exclusively his own, and there is no reason to contest his claim. He had no model to proceed upon except geometry, which had already in his time been cast into its present form, although not with Euclid's system. By examining a vast number of examples of reasoning or arguments, he had detected the uniform presence of two primary propositions, related to each other, and to the proposition to be proved, in certain definite ways. He provided technical language for expressing the constituent propositions and terms, and found out nearly all the modes of relationship of the premises that would give true conclusions. He prepared the way for the mutual resolution of argumentative forms (called reduction) by laying down the laws of the Conversion of Propositions, although his attempts to prove these laws are a manifest failure. He

k

characterised Figure by the position of the Middle Term, and worked out by trial all the valid moods in the Three Figures (the Fourth was a later addition). He was the first to employ alphabetical letters to abbreviate the statement of propositional forms, having seen something of the same sort in geometry. He set great store upon the superiority of the First Figure, as the only one wherein we can prove the Universal Affirmative,—the great aim of scientific research. His exposition is not always satisfactory, and is greatly encumbered by the introduction of Modal Propositions. He exemplifies the dialectical applications of the syllogism, still farther carried out in the treatise called *Topica* : and handles various forms of fallacy.

Mr. Grote is always careful to remark Aristotle's admission that the *principia* or premises of demonstration are furnished by experience and induction, each separate science contributing its own quota; astronomical observation and experience furnishing the basis of astronomical laws, and so on. This was one of his marked points of opposition to Plato. Nevertheless, he was very far from steady in his hold of induction. In the second book of 'Analytica Priora,' occurs his attempt to give induction the form of syllogism, which Mr. Grote fully shows to be utterly fallacious, although renewed by most formal logicians down to Whately. It was the distinguishing glory of John Stuart Mill to show the relation of Induction to Deduction, and Mr. Grote zealously adopted his explanation. Aristotle, as Mr. Grote points out, was not wedded exclusively to the deductive formalities. In his numerous treatises on other subjects, scarcely any allusion is made to the syllogism, nor to its rules as laid down in the 'Analytica.' He held that the deductive process was only the last half of the process of inference, and presupposed a foregone induction. It was the deductive portion that he himself analysed, and if any one had performed a similar analysis of the other half, we may fairly believe that he would have welcomed it, as filling up a gap in the complete theory of reasoning.

Various leading points of Aristotelian doctrine, occurring in the 'Analytica Priora,' are elucidated in Mr. Grote's commentary. The antithesis of *notior nobis*, and *notior naturâ*, is strongly insisted on in many of Aristotle's writings. Here it is expounded by the contrast between example or induction, and deduction. The distinction is intelligible enough, but the phraseology is somewhat strained and figurative, and is not employed in modern philosophy.

The 'Analytica Priora' is intended to give the complete theory of the syllogism, or deductive reasoning. There are two great applications of the syllogism—*demonstration* and *dialectic*—processes fundamentally contrasted by Aristotle. To the first, demonstration, he devotes a treatise called 'Analytica Posteriora;' to the second a still larger treatise, the 'Topica.'

The POSTERIOR ANALYTICS—ostensibly devoted to demonstrative or scientific truth, and the processes implicated in demonstration—is somewhat miscellaneous in its character; it contains a good deal of foreign matter, although all of interest in the Aristotelian philosophy.

Mr. Grote takes pains, at the outset of his commentary on this treatise, to illustrate the distinction between science and dialectic. Science or demonstration meant with Aristotle, as with us, the region of knowledge laid out by special inquirers after careful examination; it is confined to a small number of subjects; it has recognised *principia*, or first principles to start from; these principles are universally and essentially true, and admitted by all; they are obtained from the induction of particulars. On the other hand, dialectic is common sense or opinion, the knowledge of general society; it extends to all manner of subjects; its principles are the received opinions of the community, or the dicta of individuals of more or less weight; these are at best but probable. Both departments agree in coming under the scope of the syllogism.

It was a feature of Aristotle's business-like sagacity or

practical good sense, always to be aware of the comparative degree of certainty attainable in different subjects. There were two extremes—the exact sciences of demonstration, and the utterly loose and undigested opinions of the multitude upon complicated and difficult topics; between these two extremes lay a middle region, represented by his various miscellaneous treatises on topics theoretical and practical.

For demonstration he takes the best illustrative type, Geometry. The learner of a demonstrative science must possess certain *præcognita*, in the shape of definitions and axioms, on which the teacher is to proceed. But then arises the Platonic paradox: learning is an impossible act; for either you know a thing already, or you don't know it; if you don't know it, how can you go in search of a thing that you are wholly ignorant of? Aristotle shows the way out of this puzzle by distinguishing between imperfect and perfect knowledge. He then deals with a different class of objectors, persons that failed to see the cardinal property of demonstration; one set maintaining the possibility of demonstrating backward *ad infinitum;* the other contending for the legitimacy of reasoning in a circle.

Again, in demonstration, the principles must be necessary or essential, and not concomitant or accidental (this is not the case.) He next contends, very properly, that the *principia* should be of the very highest universality, not inferior or derivative principles, which of course are themselves demonstrable. Further, in demonstration, the conclusion must follow *necessarily* from the premises. Again, the premises must be appropriate to the matter in hand. Moreover, the process of demonstration, although requiring universal propositions, neither requires nor countenances the Platonic theory of ideas—universal substances beyond and apart from particulars. Once more, the grand fundamental maxim of contradiction, appealed to in demonstrating by *reductio ad absurdum,* is not enunciated in any special science, but is a point of contact or communion of all the sciences; it belongs to the First Philosophy, and is not to be made the

subject of scrutiny by the geometer or other specialist as
such. In dialectical disputation, the questions and answers
should always be kept within the limits of the science; hence
it is futile to discuss geometry with persons that are not
geometers.

Mr. Grote follows this treatise through its numerous windings and repetitions, and succeeds in making plain the
author's drift, even when he is crude and inconsistent.
There is some confusion of thought in applying the syllogistic designation, the middle term, to intermediate links in
physical cause and effect, and the celebrated four causes are
brought in to explain the meanings of knowledge. Generally
speaking Aristotle has a good grasp of the main conditions
of demonstration: he is less steady, but still very knowing,
in the niceties of definition. From our present logical point
of view we can see distinctly what he is aiming at, and where
he misses: and the interest of the work consists in tracing
the struggles of an original mind.

The concluding chapter of the treatise discusses the mental
origin of the *principia* of demonstration themselves. Mr.
Grote gives a careful rendering of Aristotle's view of this
disputed problem, showing that he cannot be ranked with
intuitionists, inasmuch as he held these first principles to be
acquired; still he regarded the inductive process as cul-
minating in the infallible Noûs, or theorising intelligence.

The TOPICA is a very remarkable treatise. It is the
working out of an artificial scheme for conducting dialectical
debates, in which Aristotle exhausts all the resources of his
logical subtleties. In this, as in the syllogism itself, he
claims entire originality. He found teachers of contentious
dialogue, as well as of rhetoric, but they knew nothing of
the theory of their art; he compares them to a teacher
of shoe-making that should merely show his pupils ready-
made shoes.

Long and elaborate as this treatise is, Mr. Grote follows
it through all the details, and leaves a very fresh and vivid

impression of Aristotle's genius for fine distinctions and technical abstractions.

The first book is preparatory. It repeats the contrast between demonstration and dialectic, showing in particular the foundation of dialectic in common opinions instead of scientific principles. But not content with drawing the real distinction between the demonstrative and the dialectical syllogism, Aristotle makes a farther distinction between dialectic and *eristic*, on which Mr. Grote remarks that he is here carried away by his fixed determination to damage the Sophists—a purpose manifested at intervals throughout the treatise, and involving him in frequent inconsistencies.

The Aristotelian name for the first principles in dialectic debate is *endoxa*, meaning opinions more or less authoritative, being fortified by a certain amount of prevailing belief or acceptance, and therefore possessing a certain presumption in their favour. These *endoxa* are opposed to *adoxa*, propositions wanting in authority, of which the extreme variety is named *paradoxa*, which have the predominant authority of opinion against them. We have naturalised this last class in our word *paradox*; we ought also to have *endox* and *adox*, the *endox* especially is necessary to the understanding of the present treatise. "The essential feature of the *endoxon* is, that it has acquired a certain amount of recognition among the mass of opinions and beliefs floating and carrying authority at the actual time and place. When Josephus distinguished himself as a disputant in the schools of Jerusalem on points of law and custom, his arguments must have been chiefly borrowed from the *endoxa* or prevalent opinions of the time and place; but these must have differed widely from the *endoxa* found and argued upon by the contemporaries of Aristotle at Athens.

"It is within the wide field of floating opinions that dialectical debate and rhetorical pleading are carried on. Dialectic supposes a questioner or assailant, and a respondent or defendant. The respondent selects and proclaims a problem or thesis, which he undertakes to maintain; the

assailant puts to him successive questions, with the view of
obtaining concessions which may serve as premisses for a
counter-syllogism, of which the conclusion is contradictory
or contrary to the thesis itself, or to some other antecedent
premiss which the respondent has already conceded. It is
the business of the respondent to avoid making any answers
which may serve as premisses for such a counter-syllogism.
If he succeeds in this, so as not to become implicated in any
contradiction with himself, he has baffled his assailant, and
gained the victory. There are, however, certain rules and
conditions, binding on both parties, under which the debate
must be carried on. It is the purpose of the Topica to indicate these rules; and, in accordance therewith, to advise
both parties as to the effective conduct of their respective
cases—as to the best thrusts and the best mode of parrying.
The assailant is supplied with a classified catalogue of materials for questions, and with indications of the weak points
which he is to look out for in any new subject which may
turn up for debate. He is further instructed how to shape,
marshal, and disguise his questions, in such a way that the
respondent may least be able to foresee their ultimate
bearing. The respondent, on his side, is told what he ought
to look forward to and guard against. Such is the scope of
the present treatise; the entire process being considered in
the large and comprehensive spirit customary with Aristotle,
and distributed according to the Aristotelian terminology
and classification."

The debate is valuable, first, as a stimulating mental exercise; next, as facilitating our intercourse with the multitude, whose opinions we should know and be able to modify;
lastly, in the scrutiny of the principles of science proper.
The first head is substantially the Platonic view of the Dialogues of Search. The second is characteristic of Aristotle,
who was careful to collect the current opinions of the multitude on all matters.

He is also careful to lay out the class of problems suitable
for debate; they must neither be what all persons believe,

nor what no one believes; there must be doubts and difficulties, and yet the premises needed for their solution must
not be far-fetched or recondite.

The plan of the treatise follows that fourfold division of
propositions, known as the predicables, which, in later times,
were enumerated as five. Looking to the nature of a proposition, as made up of two things—subject and predicate,
the ordinary case should be that the subject means one
thing, the predicate another; "generalship needs long experience;" "generalship" means one property, "needs long
experience" means another; and the coupling of the two is
a piece of information or communicated knowledge. Now
the proposition appears in its full character, when the two
meanings are wholly unconnected by nature, so that we should
never by considering one arrive at the other; of such kind
are propositions as to the original locality of minerals, plants,
or animals; for by looking at a mineral specimen we have no
means of telling where it came from. To this extreme dis-
connection of subject and predicate Aristotle gave the name
concomitant predication; it represents the proposition in its
highest reality as imparting knowledge.

Another case is where subject and predicate are distinct in
meaning, but yet so far involved in one another, that by a
full study of the subject, one might discover or discern the
predicate. Such are the propositions as to geometrical
figures. In a triangle the sum of two sides is greater than
the third. Now a triangle means a three-sided figure, and
that is all; the fact that the combined length of two sides
exceeds the third side is a distinct fact, but yet it is implicated in, or grows out of, the essential nature of the triangle,
the three-sided property. For this new mode of predication
Aristotle invented a term translated *proprium* or property;
and the distinction reflects honour on his subtlety. Concomitant and property are thus the two modes of real predication. But this is not all. People are very often ignorant
of the meaning of the subject itself, or if not wholly ignorant,
they may be imperfectly cognizant of its exact and full

meaning. Hence many propositions are framed, not to unite a subject and a predicate as distinct facts, but to declare the meaning of a subject: "a triangle is a three-sided figure," "generalship is the art of commanding of an army"—are propositions of this nature. Here is an entirely new mode of predication, it has the form and not the reality of a proposition. Some other name must be found for this third situation; we call it now *definition*, verbal predication, essential predication.

This threefold distinction in the forms of predication is most important; it was made by Aristotle, and constitutes the predicables. But for the third mode he used two designations—definition and genus; the later logicians perplexed the matter still more by using three heads, genus, species, difference; their reason, probably, being that definition was explained by Aristotle as *per genus et differentiam*—stating first the genus of a thing and next its specific difference.

It is obvious to us now that the verification of these three modes of predication proceeds by quite different routes. In the totally disconnected propositions—those of circumstance or accident, the proof (in the last resort) must be observation of fact; in the *propria*, observation may be brought in, but is not essential; a skilful inference from the meaning of the subject evolves the predicate. In the third kind, we have not to deal with truth or falsehood, but with conformity between particulars and a general statement.

Aristotle was very far from discerning fully the exact nature or conditions of each of these three modes of predication; yet he had marvellously shrewd glimpses of their respective characteristics.

Farther: each of the predicables must fall under one or other of his Ten Categories, which gives enlarged scope for multiplying distinctions. Occasionally Aristotle makes this reference to some of the categories, but to no good purpose; the categories themselves are too roughly laid out for any pregnant application.

Aristotle's acuteness discovered another circumstance in

connection with the debating of true and false, namely, that the question often turned upon an *identity*; whereupon, as usual, he takes to dividing the modes or kinds of identity— identity (1) *numero*, (2) *specie*, (3) *genere*. This also survived in the schools as he gave it.

Finally: "What helps are available to give to the dialectician a ready and abundant command of syllogisms? Four distinct helps may be named: (1) he must make a large collection of propositions; (2) he must study and discriminate the different senses in which the terms of these propositions are used; (3) he must detect and note differences; (4) he must investigate resemblances."

This is bravely sketched; but the filling up disappoints us. The first and second helps are fairly discussed; the two last—to our present apprehension, the most vital and fundamental facts of knowledge—are merely made the ground of some remarks upon classification and induction. Aristotle saw that induction, syllogism, and definition, were all processes of resemblance; and he brought under the same head, as an *endoxon*, that what happens in any one of a string of similar cases, will happen in the rest.

The meaning of *topos* (which gives the title *Topica*), in Latin *locus*, is a place where may be found arguments or modes of arguing, suited to each purpose or occasion—*sedes argumentorum*. A short exemplification of Aristotle's copious detail of *Loci*, will show his meaning. Beginning with those theses where the predicate of the proposition to be impugned is Concomitant or Accident—the real proposition in the strictest sense—he enumerates no less than thirty-seven distinct *loci*, or argumentative points of view regarding it. Most of them suggest modes of assailing the thesis; but there are also occasional intimations to the respondent in the debate, how he may best guard himself. Of the thirty-seven Mr. Grote recounts twenty-two, remarking, that "there are some items repetitions of each other, or at least not easily distinguishable"—a serious derogation from Aristotle's logical acuteness.

The first *locus* is highly to the purpose. The supposition and pretension is that the proposition is one of Concomitance. Let the assailant, therefore, look and see whether in point of fact it does not fall under some of the other predicables; whether the predicate may not be of the genus, essence, or definition of the subject itself; the very common mistake of confounding a real with a verbal proposition. If the proposition, White is a colour, be given as a Concomitant, it can be impugned and shown to be an affirmation of the genus of the subject, for "white" is a species under the genus "colour." By showing this, an opponent may gain a dialectical victory.

The second *locus* goes to the truth or falsehood of a universal proposition, affirmative or negative, and declares the real basis or proof of a universal, namely, the truth of the particulars. This is of course the foundation of all inductive proof. Out of this arises at once the policy of an assailant or objector—review the particulars, and if any of them is untrue, the proposition is broken down. Or, instead of reviewing the ultimate particulars which might be endless or impossible—take them in genera and species, or sub-propositions; inasmuch as the higher generalities are frequently an aggregate of inferior, having a smaller compass; "all bodies gravitate" (highest universal): solids gravitate, liquids gravitate, airs gravitate (sub-propositions). Aristotle's own example is a favourite doctrine of his, belonging to the Relativity of Knowledge.—The cognition of opposites is one; and he divides Opposites into the several species, *Relata*, and *Correlata*, Contraries, Contradictories, and opposites respecting *Habitus* and *Privatio*.

Instead of dealing with this *locus* as merely one out of thirty-seven, Aristotle should have made it the head and front of the whole dialectic of Concomitant Affirmation. The proof or disproof of a universal, by examination of particulars, is the alpha and omega of science, proof, or certainty in knowledge.

His third *locus* is also fundamental, but it should have been first—to define the terms used both in the subject and in the predicate. Not a step should be taken with any proposition till its terms are defined. Moreover, definition is a branch of logic by itself, and in the sequel, Aristotle has a vast number of *loci* bearing upon definition, this being one of his predicables or divisions, so that he need not have introduced the process, except by reference, among the *loci* of concomitance.

A fourth *locus*, both for assailant and for respondent, is to discriminate the cases where the authority of the multitude is conclusive from those where it is not; a rather trying operation, although exceedingly to the purpose. This should have been done once or for all by philosophers like Aristotle himself; there should have been provided a set of canons of authority, to be applied by the disputants whom the present treatise addresses.

Aristotle gives more than one suggestion as to cases where the terms of a universal thesis have a double or triple sense. This should come under definition; for the carrying out of the process of defining discloses double meanings and equivocation. When there is an equivocation, a wary disputant can make use of it against an unwary opponent. Consent is obtained to the proposition under one meaning of a term, and then extorted for the other meaning.

The refutation of a universal, by quoting contradictory particulars, unavoidably comes up again and again, and ought to have been consecutive and systematic. Thus, if a predicate is a generic quality, as in "the soul is *moved*," some of the specific modes must be applicable—some known variety of motion, as increase, destruction, generation, &c. If none of the recognised modes of motion apply to the soul, then the thesis is refuted.

A very pertinent *locus* is, look to the antecedents and consequents of the thesis—what things it assumes, and what will follow from it; if any of these can be disproved, the thesis fails. This is repeated, without material difference, in a subsequent *locus*.

A *locus* belonging to the tactics or management of a

debate (called by Aristotle a *sophistical* procedure) is to transfer the debate to some point where we happen to be more at home.

It may be advantageous in attacking the thesis, to construe the terms in their strict etymological sense, rather than according to usage. This is merely a repetition of the *loci* bearing upon equivocation or double meanings of words,

The predicate may belong to its subject either necessarily or usually, or by pure hazard. Here Aristotle forgets the nature of concomitance, which is to exclude *necessary* connexions ; or else he repeats his first *locus*.

The thesis may have predicate and subject exactly synonymous, so that the same thing will be affirmed as an accident of itself. Grows also out of attention to the meaning of the terms, or definition.

A number of *loci* bear upon the nature of *opposita,* according to Aristotle's classification of them, which he handled dexterously, and for the most part soundly.

Very properly, he has a *locus* for reasoning by analogy, although imperfectly appreciating the nature and limitations of the process.

He had also a considerable mastery of the argument from concomitant variations, or the proof from more or less ; out of which he extracts a highly serviceable *locus.*

An argument described by Aristotle as *ex adjuncto,* is something like what we now call the method of difference. " If the subject, prior to adjunction of the attribute, be not white or good, and if the adjunction of the attribute makes it white or good, then you may argue that the adjunct itself must be white or good."

The foregoing selection contains the leading points of the second book of the 'Topica,' perhaps the most remarkable book of the ten, when we consider that it sets forth, in a crude condition, the principal canons of inductive logic. These statements cannot be called germs, for they never germinated; inductive logic was developed from other sources; they are rather crumbs and crudities, examples of the numerous great truths that Aristotle touched in his speculative course.

The third book carries out the same predicable, viz., accident or concomitant, to the practical department of good or evil, *expetenda* and *fugienda;* the question being, of two or more distinct subjects which is the better or more desirable. This is really an abuse of the forms of logic, which Aristotle is guilty of in the Ethics also, to suppose that they could be applied with any advantage to determining good and evil. There are doubtless certain formal maxims and criteria that may be laid down in this department, but the logical technicalities, accident, proprium, genus, species, are much better away from all that class of discussions.

That such topics should be frequent in the dialectical debating at Athens was inevitable. They came closest home to every bosom. And as Aristotle himself was intensely practical, and the author of the best treatises in antiquity on ethics and on politics, he could bring his sagacity to bear upon the modes of comparing different ends of pursuit. Accordingly he here casts into the form of *loci* for debate a number of his views and theories. For example :—" Of two good subjects compared, that is better and more desirable which is the more lasting, or which is preferred by the wise and good man, or by the professional artist in his own craft, or by right law, or by the multitude, all or most of them. That is absolutely or simply better and more desirable, which is declared to be such by the better cognition ; that is better to any individual which is better by his own cognition." A thing is more desirable when good on its own account than when good by accident. What is good to all and at all times is better than what is good only for a special occasion or individual ; to be in good health is better than to be cut for the stone. What is good by nature, as justice, is better than what is good by artifice or acquisition, as the just individual, whose character must have been acquired. Good in the primary and more exalted elements of any subject, is more desirable than good belonging to the derivative, secondary,

and less exalted; health, which resides in the fundamental
constituents of the body (wet, dry, hot, cold) is better than
strength or beauty, residing in the hues and muscles.   An
end is superior to the means.   These are a few out of a
prolix enumeration of *loci* for good and evil; they are given
in the common forms of ethical disquisition, but in the latter
portion of the book the language of formal logic is made to
apply to this class of questions.

For example.   He supposes the thesis to be propounded
to be a particular proposition.   In that case we can apply
the logical rule that the universal proves the particular,
affirmative or negative.   So the *loci* from opposites can be
applied to particulars of the present class.   It is a *locus* of
contraries, if all pleasure is good, then all pain is evil; hence
if some pleasure is good, some pain is evil.   Again, there is
an argument, *à fortiori*, thus: if some capacity is a less
good than science, while yet some capacity is good, then
some science is good.   A debater may propound a thesis
with the assumption that, if true or false in any one case, it
shall be accepted as true or false universally (if the human soul
is immortal, all other souls are immortal).   This is evidently
to extend the particular into an universal, and the respondent
must try to prove the negative in some particular case.

Those and other cases where the forms of logic are applied,
might have been introduced into the previous book.   The
criteria special to a practical question are not brought forward at all: the propositions are treated purely in the
logical aspect.

The fourth book of the Topica is occupied with the predicable "genus."   It is really an excursus upon the relations
of genus and species, of which Aristotle had an adequate
mastery.   Simple as the relationship is, it might be very
readily blundered, especially in abstruse instances, so that
many debates would arise upon the referring of a species to
its proper genus.   Suppose A is declared to be genus of B;
if now there be any members of B that cannot come under
genus A, then B is not species of A, that is, A is not genus

of B. Again, the species has all the attributes of the genus and something more; if, then, an alleged species has not all the generic qualities, it is not a species of that genus. Farther, the same species cannot be in two distinct genera, unless either one of the two be subordinate to the other, or both are comprehended under some common higher genus [not always then]. Thus the thesis may declare that justice is science; now justice is in the distinct genus "virtue"; but as both science and virtue can be referred to one and the same higher genus, the thesis "justice is science" is not open to refutation.

As usual, he makes this predicate run the gauntlet of his contraries, but does not clearly extricate the situations that he creates. He supposes cases where the species has some contrary, but the genus has not, and *vice versâ*; sickness in general (he says) has for its contrary health in general, but particular species of sickness, as fever, gout, &c., have no contrary. In all this part, he goes astray from defective views of contrariety and correlation. Altogether, his handling of genus is historically curious, but uninstructive to the modern reader.

The fifth book, devoted to "proprium" as a predicable, is not satisfactory. It was a great stroke of subtlety to chalk out this predicable, but his hold of it is very loose. His refinements and distinctions violate the true nature of the proprium, and he admits irrelevant matter without knowing it. He distinguishes a proprium *semper* from a proprium occasional; it is the proprium *semper* of a god to be immortal; it is the proprium sometimes of a man to be walking in the market place. Now while it is a nice point to determine whether immortality be the essence (definition) of a god or the proprium; the modern logician would regard "walking in the market place" as accident or concomitant of a man, although the power or capability of walking would be regarded as proprium. Among things of doubtful relevance is the prescription that the proprium should be better known than the subject whereof it is predicated; the suitable place for this remark is under definition, where also it is given. There is farther a *locus* or caution against equivocal terms, which applies alike to every mode of predication. A proprium may be impeached, in debate, if it belongs to other subjects equally with the one that you attach it to. Perhaps the correctest observation respecting the proprium, as expressly defined by himself is this:—To set out the proprium well, the predicate ought to reciprocate and ought to be co-extensive with the subject, but it ought not to affirm the essence thereof, as "man is an animal by nature gentle," where the predicate is co-extensive with the subject and yet does not declare the essence.

The *loci* regarding proprium are numerous and prolix, and the repetitions and inconsistencies have incurred strictures from the commentators. He does not fail to ring the changes in his *opposita ;* he introduces his *locus* of more and less, and brings in the still more abstruse distinctions of his philosophy, as his favourite *esse* and *fieri.*

The sixth book, the predicable of "definition," is a grand effort of logical manipulation. The author shows his usual minuteness of distinction, and copiousness of enumeration, with the same faults of confusion and irrelevance. Mr. Grote follows him through thirty-six different *loci* bearing on the matter or substance of definition, while there are others bearing on the expression. From a few examples, the reader can imagine the general drift of the book as rendered by Mr. Grote.

In debates respecting definition, the attack or defence may turn upon one or other of five points;—the alleged definition may not apply to the subject at all; a genus may have been given (defining being *per genus et differentiam*) but not the right genus; the definition may include extraneous matter; it may not declare the essence; it may be good in substance but badly expressed or set out. The three first points belong to the previous books, the two remaining are the subject-matter of the present book. Of these two, one relates to the substance of definition, the other to the form or expression. The last is taken first.

l

Bad expression may appear in two ways; there may be indistinctness; and there may be redundancy. *Indistinctness* may arise from equivocal terms; from the misuse of metaphors; from employing terms that are far-fetched or little known (exemplified from Plato); from not making clear the *contrary* of the defining quality; lastly, when the defining marks are insufficient to make known the thing meant (a criterion which Aristotle's own definitions often lamentably fail to satisfy). *Redundancy* arises if the terms include other things besides the object defined (this error is not well described by "redundancy"); and if the same attribute be predicated twice over.

Much more numerous, as well as more interesting, are the *loci* bearing on the substance of the definition. As in the other predicables, Aristotle puts his best foot foremost; his first *loci* generally touch the fundamental conceptions of the subject. He starts with the sweeping requirement that the matter of the definition must be *prius* and *notius* as compared with the definiend. One of his favourite distinctions is between things more known absolutely, or *by nature*, and things more known *to us;* by *nature*, the point is better known than the line, the line than the surface, the surface than the solid; to us, the solid is best known; we begin by conceiving the concrete solid; and afterwards attain to the abstractions—surface, line, point. Too plainly, a. definer may commit many sins against such an abstruse requirement as this; and hence the scope for an acute opponent fitted out from the Aristotelian armoury. A second *locus* impugns a definition that does not mention the genus; a third is aimed at insufficiency of enumeration—there being three or four facts, and only one mentioned. The genus may be properly given, while there are faults in giving the differentiæ. A definition may be exclusively negative, *e. g.,* a line is length without breadth. If the subject be relative, so must the differentiæ. If the subject admits of More and Less, the definition must say so. When a *relatum* has to be defined, the true correlate must be given. As usual, all modes of opposition furnish *loci.* The terms of a definition must not conjoin incompatible facts; white has been defined, colour mingled with fire; now colour is incorporeal, and cannot be mingled with fire which is corporeal. It is a mistake to define a subject by what is its highest excellence, a rhetor is one that omits nothing that can be plausibly said for a cause. You may not be able to attack a definition as a whole, but may successfully impugn some of its parts. Moreover, you may take an adroit advantage of obscurity or intelligibility, by clearing it up so as to suit your own purpose.

The seventh book continues the theses on definition, and enters upon the important collateral question of identity or sameness, already discriminated by Aristotle with sameness *numero,* and sameness *specie* or *genere.* His close observation of the field of logical proof could not but disclose to him this property, just as he obtained an insight into the fact of relativity; but he necessarily failed to put both facts into their position as the fundamentals of all cognition.

The predicables are now finished, and the eighth book brings us back to the kind of general considerations advanced in the first. What is the order of procedure most suitable; first, for the questioner or assailant; next, for the respondent or defender? This order is different for the dialectician and for the man of science or philosopher. Aristotle classifies the different purposes of the debate, and claims originality in so doing, as well as in prescribing rules for each kind separately. He administers counsel to both partners in the conduct of the debate; he indicates the mode of approaching it by preparatory questions; these fall under the four heads—induction of particulars, maintaining the dignity of the discourse, concealment, and the imparting of clearness. What he has to say about induction has already been noted; of dignity he says little; the arts of concealment are detailed at great length, and include deception of manner as well as masking of operations; for clearness he prescribes the use of familiar examples taken from well-known poets like Homer.

He instructs the respondent separately, and with considerable minuteness, although, in point of fact, the equipment for both partners must be very much the same. Towards the close of the book the dialectic shades off into the syllogistic logic, with which it is more or less implicated, the logical fallacies being also dialectical fallacies. In the present book he treats of *petitio principii*, and *petitio contrariorum* as occurring in dialectic. His concluding remarks consist of sound advice for exercise and practice in debate.

The ninth and last book of the 'Topica' illustrates the remark just made as to the interlacing of logic and dialectic. So thoroughly has this been regarded as a logical treatise, that it has been adopted as a constituent part of the syllogistic or scholastic logic, and is the classical dissertation on fallacies slavishly retained in its minutest details to our own time. None of the other books of the 'Topica' have found a place in our modern education; the scheme of the predicables has been borrowed from it, but without Aristotle's copious elucidations and applications of them.

Although Mr. Grote's analysis of the *Sophistici elenchi* will be found to contain fresh points of view, even to those that have studied the 'Fallacies' in 'Whately' or any other work on the scholastic model, we shall do no more than call attention to the chapter as concluding the author's vindication of the Sophists.

It never occurred to any one before Mr. Grote to remark on the extraordinary liberty taken by Aristotle with the so-called Sophists, when he used their name to designate the entire body of fallacies, or intellectual errors and weaknesses, which it was the object of a logical discipline to provide against and correct. "Fallacy," he said, "thy name is Sophist." If there had been one special mode of error indulged in by the Sophists as a class, or in any way identified with their vocation, as when philosophers are styled theoretical, or when politicians are said to take low views of human nature, there might have been a show of propriety in calling such error by their name. The disparaging word

" empiric" was first given by Hippocrates to the medical
men of his own time, because they did not combine general
views or theories with their practice.   But to gather together
every known species of error, to compile a treatise professedly
exhaustive of the violations of sound reasoning, and to name
the whole after the Sophists, as if they alone were guilty of
such transgressions, and the rest of the world were infallible,
was a proceeding equally strange and reprehensible.

Aristotle adopted Plato's dislike of the Sophists.   One
might perhaps suppose that they had better reasons for
thinking badly of the class than Mr. Grote has for dissenting
from their concurrent view on such a matter.   But the inconsistencies of both philosophers in maintaining their ill
opinion of these men are enough to rouse suspicion.

The Sophist, according to Aristotle, is one who makes
money by a show of wisdom without the reality.   The
ostensible purpose of the present treatise, judging from its
title, is to expose the bad arts and unsound arguments of
this personage; the actual contents of the treatise must be
regarded as, for the time, an admirable classification of
logical fallacies, executed at no small cost of time and
labour.

The Sophistical Elenchus or refutation, being a delusive
semblance imposing on ordinary men, cannot be understood
without the theory of Elenchus in general; and this theory
cannot be understood without the entire theory of the syllogism, of which the Elenchus is one variety.   We must know
the conditions of a good and valid syllogism before we can
study the tests of a valid elenchus, which last must be known
as a preparation for the pseudo-elenchus—the sophistical,
invalid, or sham—refutation.

There are four species of debate: (1) didactic, (2) dialectic,
(3) peirastic, (4) eristic or sophistic.   Between the two first,
Mr. Grote remarks, there is a real antithesis, much dwelt
upon by Aristotle; but the peirastic and the eristic are mere
aspects or varieties of dialectic.   Dialectic is essentially
gymnastic and peirastic; gymnastic in reference to the two

debaters, and peirastic in reference to the arguments and doctrines made use of. Victory is the aim of the disputants in every case, but the arts employed may be honest and creditable, exemplifying the worthy debate. If, however, the assailing champion, bent upon victory at all cost, has recourse to dishonest interrogative tricks, or the defensive champion to perverse and obstructive negations, beyond the prescribed boundary, the debate is called by Aristotle *eristic* or *contentious*, from the undue predominance of the controversial spirit and purpose; also *sophistic*, from the fact that there existed (as he asserts) a class or profession of persons called Sophists, who regularly studied and practised these culpable manœuvres, first with a view to reputation, and ultimately with a view to pecuniary profit, being pretenders to knowledge and wisdom without any justifying reality.

It must be apparent that no man, not even Aristotle himself, could consistently carry out this distinction. In the first place, it is altogether irrelevant to the scope of logic, which considers the value of arguments and not their purpose. In the next place, the line between the worthy and the unworthy disputant is impossible to draw. Mr. Grote's concluding observations on Aristotle's false position in this whole matter are irresistible and yet mild :—

" I think it a mistake on the part of Aristotle to treat the fallacies incidental to the human intellect as if they were mere traps laid by Sophists and litigants; and as if they would never show themselves, assuming dialectical debate to be conducted entirely with a view to its legitimate purposes of testing a thesis and following out argumentative consequences. It is true that, if there are infirmities incidental to the human intellect, a dishonest disputant will be likely to take advantage of them. So far it may be well to note his presence. But the dishonest disputant does not originate these infirmities; he finds them already existing, and manifested undesignedly not merely in dialectical debate, but even in ordinary discourse. It is the business of those

who theorize on the intellectual processes to specify and
discriminate the fallacies as liabilities to intellectual error
among mankind in general, honest or dishonest, with a view
to precaution against their recurrence, or correction, if they
do occur; not to present them as inventions of a class of professional cheats, or as tares sown by the enemy in a field
where the natural growth could be nothing but pure wheat.

"In point of fact the actual classification of fallacies given
by Aristotle is far sounder than his announcement would lead
us to expect. Though he entitles them sophistical refutations, describing them as intentionally cultivated and exclusively practised by professional Sophists for gain, or by
unprincipled litigants for victory, yet he recognises them as
often very difficult of detection, and as an essential portion
of the theory of dialectic generally. The various general
heads under which he distributes them are each characterised
by intellectual or logical marks."

The Topica completes the Organon or logical treatises of
Aristotle. It was Mr. Grote's intention to add here a chapter
of his own on the modern logic as compared with the
Aristotelian; but the time already consumed upon a single
department of his author warned him that he must proceed
to other subjects. Next to the Organon came the META-,
PHYSICS. Of this department he takes a very enlarged
view.

To attain supreme and commanding generalities has been
the aim of great thinkers in all ages. The first Greek
philosophers were distinguished by their search after some
all-embracing unity; they thought to comprehend the
Universe under a single idea. In Aristotle's time the
plurality of the sciences was recognised; the mathematical,
the physical, and the biological departments were separately
sketched, while the mental department was seen to be distinct and unique. Nevertheless, it was felt by Aristotle that
there must still be a central or master science, some common
ground where all the departments come together, as one in

the many.   By the search after such a science the philosopher was distinguished from the specialist.

For the construction of this first philosophy, as he called it, Aristotle laid hold of the logical maxim called the principle of contradiction, and took much pains to expound it, and to vindicate it against some of his predecessors who seemed to deny it.   He took a very just view of the nature of this maxim; he regarded it as common to all reasoning, in every department, and as in itself indemonstrable.   In addition to the purely logical law of contradiction, he embraced, as suitable for his first philosophy, his four causes, the distinction between potential and actual, and the abstractions form, matter, and privation, which play a great part in his philosophy.

The treatises termed (by an accident) Metaphysica are occupied with the numerous discussions raised upon these points, and with criticisms upon the views of the preceding philosophers respecting them.   Since, however, the Physica, although nominally the special department treating of the physical phenomena of the universe—motion, force, &c., is really expounded in the strain of the Metaphysica, Mr. Grote couples the two, and entitles his account of them 'Physica and Metaphysica'.   Unfortunately he has executed only one chapter of this design, which, however, taken along with a free translation of the six leading books of the Metaphysica, will convey to the reader a very distinct view of the Aristotelian handling of the highest abstractions of philosophy. These treatises are the classical authority for the opinions of the early Greek philosophers, and in that view alone must always be resorted to by the student of the history of philosophy, and Mr. Grote has done much to satisfy the desire of the English reader for this information.

Mr. Grote had formerly prepared an account of the very difficult treatise on the Soul (DE ANIMA).   Although not so full as he might have made it, had he come upon the subject in regular course, and with time and strength at his com-

mand, it embraces all the leading and difficult points of
Aristotle's Psychology. While working on this treatise, he
repeatedly stated that he had gained new insight into the
fundamental positions of the Aristotelian philosophy. More
particularly he was led to see that one pervading conception
of Aristotle's mind was the notion of the Celestial Body—a
mixture of science and emotion—which was to him both a
philosophy and a theology. His vital distinction of Form
and Matter was invoked to express the relation of Soul
and Body. The Soul was "Form"; and the grand region of
Form, in the Universe, is the Celestial Body—the vast, deep,
circular, perceivable mass circumscribing the Kosmos, and en-
closing, in and around its centre, Earth with the three other
elements (Water, Air, Fire), tenanted by substances generated and perishable. This celestial body is the abode of
Divinity, including many divine beings who take part in
its eternal rotations — the Sun, Moon, Stars, and other
gods. Every Soul (there being a hierarchy of souls from the
Plant upwards), every Form that animates the matter of a
living being, derives from this celestial region its vitalising
influence.

This doctrine of the divine body, as the source of Soul, is
not stated in the 'De Animâ,' but imported from other
treatises, to supply gaps in the information; and the application is a novelty. It is carried out still farther into the
vexed question of Aristotle's opinions as to the highest
human soul—the Nous, or thinking principle, divided into
two functions, receptive (*Intellectus Patiens*) and constructive
or theorising (*Intellectus Agens*). Of the two, the last —
Intellectus Agens—is the more venerable; it is pure intellectual energy, unmixed, unimpressible from without, and
separable from all animal body. It is more especially identified with the celestial substance, and is eternal and immortal. But this immortality is not conferred on *individuals*,
or on the theorising Nous as it exists in Socrates, Plato, or
any other man: the individualities of these men perish with
the body. Such is Mr. Grote's rendering of Aristotle's

obscure indications on this subject. Other interpreters suppose that the doctrine of a personal or individual immortality can be inferred from certain passages. Sir A. Grant puts stress upon the remark,—" It is uncertain whether the soul be not the actuality of the body in the same way as *the sailor is the actuality of his boat*," from which the inference might be, although it is not drawn by Aristotle, that the sailor could, at the end of his voyage, step out of his boat. Of one thing we may be tolerably confident, that Aristotle would not pronounce a decided opinion against so venerated a doctrine as our continued existence after death ; although he makes very little of it as a motive, in the Ethics.

There are included in the work, several polemical discussions as to Aristotle's doctrines respecting UNIVERSALS and the mental origin of FIRST PRINCIPLES. The paper on Universals brings out the contrast of Plato and Aristotle on Universals, shown chiefly from the Categories, wherein the Platonic ideas are met by the Aristotelian doctrine of Substance, in the First Category, as being constituted by a particular or concrete individual, of which the universals were predicable. The "Hoc Aliquid" is the only complete "Ens" or substance, and the Universal exists along with it, as a predicate, but is nothing in itself apart.

As regards the mental origin of our knowledge of First Principles, or Axioms, this is the question debated in modern times under the designation Intuitions as opposed to Experience. The supporters of intuitive or innate ideas, or common sense, have often claimed Aristotle as on their side, and Sir W. Hamilton in particular, has produced an array of thirteen citations to that effect. Mr. Grote examines all these citations, and shows that in only one of them does Aristotle appear as the champion of authoritative common sense. The other twelve citations, he maintains either to have no bearing upon the point, or to indicate the very reverse ; and he charges Hamilton in regard to many of them, with mistaking or misrepresenting Aristotle's meaning.

In a separate dissertation, he gathers together the statements of Aristotle respecting first, the authority of common sense; and secondly, the origin, in the mind, of the axioms or *principia* of science. The result arrived at on the first head, is that common sense is an inferior authority, as compared with science. The second head involves a difficult psychological enquiry, that Aristotle was very imperfectly qualified to resolve. He evidently inclines to the inductive origin of first principles. In the Analytica, he states that axioms are derived by induction, from particulars of sense, and are apprehended or approved by the Nous or intellect; which leaves an undecided margin between the two origins —*à posteriori* and *à priori*: and it is not possible to extract a definite settlement of the question from his conflicting modes of representation.

It has been made a complaint against Mr. Grote, and is the principal objection taken against his work, that while rebutting Hamilton's appropriation of Aristotle to the modern sect of intuitionists, he is himself guilty of the like offence in forcing his author to speak in the language of the *à posteriori* school, to which he was attached. I think the charge misapprehends Mr. Grote's way of looking at the great philosophers of the past. It was certainly agreeable to find Plato or Aristotle holding his own favourite opinions (more especially on ethical subjects); but he studied and admired their writings altogether irrespective of this consideration. Moreover, he would not have been flattered by their adhesion to his views, in the absence of valid reasons; his idea of philosophy was emphatically Ferrier's "reasoned truth." He never looked to Aristotle to confirm his own opinions; and would not have considered himself a gainer by forcing a coincidence of view out of precarious and vacillating statements. At the same time, seeing that authority is one of the strongholds of the belief in innate ideas (being homogeneous with the doctrine itself), he considered it worth his while to show that Aristotle could not be fairly enrolled among the "testimonies" for that creed.

In Mr. Grote's exposition of the Aristotelian doctrines there is nothing more characteristic than the stress he lays upon Substance as equivalent to the Individual Concrete, basing on the opposition in which the first of the Categories is made to stand to all the rest. Objection has been taken to this interpretation on the ground that the treatise Categoriæ is of doubtful authenticity, if not certainly spurious. The answer is twofold. In the first place, Mr. Grote did by no means overlook the question of the authenticity of the Categoriæ, as is clear from his note in Vol. i. p. 80, where he says that he is not convinced by the arguments that have been urged against the treatise. And, secondly, the same note claims that in any case the treatise should be considered, because the doctrine of the Categories is indisputably Aristotelian. As touching the nature of Substance this is so true that from others of the works never suspected, there is no difficulty in establishing the identification with the Individual Concrete, or at least in arguing as strongly as Mr. Grote argues for it.

Complaint has also been made by the critics that the discussion on the Canon in Chap. ii. is inadequate to the subject, all questions as to the received works being waved aside with the general remark that about forty treatises remain of authenticity not open to any reasonable suspicion. The objection is in so far well founded that there is room for much remark both as to the genuineness of some of the printed works and as to the form and exact constitution of others. Mr. Grote, however, in p. 59 gives it plainly to be understood that at the particular places he meant to discuss such matters, adding that he should not be able to fall back, as for Plato, upon a single authoritative catalogue of the works. Besides, it remains uncertain whether he did not intend to devote a part of the treatise of three chapters left in the MS. between his second chapter and the chapter on the Categoriæ to farther consideration of the Canon in general. With the opinion that he certainly had of the authenticity of the chief works, he might well be anxious, at his time of

life, to postpone external discussions till he had worked out
his exposition of the works themselves.

The frequently-expressed regret that Mr. Grote had not
undertaken the Politics and the Ethics is natural and just.
With respect to the Politics, it was not merely that he had
been long conversant with both the theory and the practice
of politics, and without bias except towards the interests of
the people as a whole: there was a still deeper reason for the
regret. Aristotle's leaning as a theorist in politics must
have been qualified by his own position in Athens, the
greatest of existing democracies. He was "semi-Macedo-
nian in his sympathies. He had no attachment to Hellas
as an organised system, autonomous, self-acting, with an
Hellenic city as president." He had no love for the
democratical constitution as such, and probably contemplated with satisfaction its approaching extinction. Yet
our present knowledge assures us that but for the democratical system of Greece, philosophy would never have
reached the point that it did in his person; no despotism
would have been so tolerant of philosophers as was the
Athenian people.

Now the Politics of Aristotle was written under circumstances rendering it scarcely possible to do justice to democracy. He professes to be an impartial critic of all political
systems, and probably is so to a very considerable degree;
but he wants to be carefully tracked by some one thoroughly
conversant (as far as a modern can be) with the workings of
the Greek governments. No man has yet appeared so competent for this task as Mr. Grote; with the utmost respect
and tenderness towards Aristotle himself, he combined an
exact view of his political situation, and all the attainable
knowledge of the political facts of Grecian history. He had
occasion to challenge Aristotle's estimate of Nikias, as completely belied by the facts before us. And there might have
been still more to say on his political theories—his search
after the phantom of a golden mean in political constitutions
that could always be a tyrant's plea against the popular prin-

ciple, which alone had been identified (as Mr. Grote believed) with the superiority of Greece, and whose extinction by Aristotle's patrons had permanently depressed the condition of the world, both politically and intellectually.   ·

As regards the Ethics, there can be no doubt that Mr. Grote's handling of Aristotle's doctrines would have been unique. Those doctrines he regarded as not only a great advance upon Socrates and Plato, but as in various respects superior to some of our modern conceptions. His leanings as an ethical theorist are shown in the 'Plato,' both with reference to Plato himself and in the delineation of the Cyrenaics and Cynics; while the present work contains brief though expressive notices of Epicurus and the Stoics. But the work of Aristotle, so minute in its detail of points respecting virtues, conduct, and happiness, would have afforded numerous openings for fresh remarks on the questions that come home to every one.

Many have asked why he might not have postponed, or contracted, the Logic, so as to secure the Politics and the Ethics. To reply that he followed a natural order of the works would not be the whole explanation. The fact must be told, that, while he had no small interest in ethics and politics, he had a fascination for logic and metaphysics. He was one—

"That unto logic haddë long y-go."

CHAPTER VII.

LATER PUBLIC LIFE.

MR. GROTE was one of the original founders of the London University, afterwards called University College, and was an active member of Council from the commencement, in 1827, up to the year 1831. He entered with zeal into the scheme, as proposing to impart an education that should be at once extensive and unsectarian. He again joined the Council in 1849, and from that time till his death took a leading part in the administration of the College. In 1860 he became Treasurer; and on the death of Lord Brougham, in 1868, he was elected President.

His was one of seven names added by the Crown, on the 19th of March, 1850, to the Senate of the University of London, the others being Lords Monteagle and Overstone, Sir James Graham, Thomas B. Macaulay, Sir George Cornewall Lewis, and Henry Hallam. From the date of his appointment he gave unremitting attention to the business of the Senate, entering into every question that arose, and taking a lead in the most critical decisions of the University during the twenty-one years of his connexion with it. The first subject of great importance that came up after Mr. Grote's appointment was the admission of the Graduates to a position in the government of the University. On the 26th of February, 1850, there was laid before the Senate a declaration and statement, signed by 361 Graduates, desiring that the Graduates might be admitted into the corporate body. This was the commencement of a protracted agitation and struggle, terminated, in 1858, by the issue of a new Charter, conceding what had been fought for. Mr. Grote cordially supported the claims of the Graduates. His aid in this cause was warmly acknowledged in a resolution of the Annual Committee of Convocation passed shortly after his death.

On the 1st of February, 1854, a memorial was presented to the Senate, signed by eleven persons (including Sir Rowland Hill and his three brothers, and Mr. William Ellis), in favour of throwing open the degrees of the University to all classes, irrespective of the manner or place of their education. On the 5th of April was presented another petition to the same effect, more numerously signed. No notice appears to have been taken of these applications. On the 19th of November, 1856, the Senate admitted the London Working Men's College among the affiliated colleges of the University. Mr. Grote opposed this step, on the ground that so long as the University required attendance on classes, a line should be drawn between those who could give up their whole time to study and those that spent their day in industrial avocations. He had been hitherto favourable to the combining of certified class instruction with examinations as requisites to the degrees. The admission of the Working Men's College (carried chiefly by members of Senate opposed to the restricting of the degrees to students in the affiliated colleges) shook his faith in the value of the class certificates. About the same time it became known to the Senate that certificates were granted by some of the affiliated colleges on mere nominal studentship. This completed the conviction in Mr. Grote's mind that the degrees should be thrown open, and granted on the exclusive test of examinations. Accordingly, when the subject came up in connexion with the Draft Charter, by which the Graduates were to be admitted, he supported the insertion of a clause for abrogating the original constitution as to affiliated colleges; which clause was carried in the Senate by a large majority. Many remonstrances followed this decision, especially from the affiliated colleges. The Senate entrusted to Mr. Grote and Mr. Warburton the drawing up a report on these remonstrances, which was presented to the Senate on the 22nd of July, 1857. This report was Mr. Grote's composition, and contains an exhaustive discussion of the arguments of the remonstrants.

On the 8th of July, 1857, while the Draft Charter was under discussion, a memorial was laid before the Senate, signed by twenty-four men of science, Fellows of the Royal Society, suggesting the institution of degrees and honours for proficiency in mathematical and physical science. On the 14th of April, 1858, the Senate appointed a Committee to consider the propriety of establishing degrees in science; of this Committee Mr. Grote was a member, along with the Chancellor, Mr. Warburton, Sir James Clark, Dr. Arnott, Mr. Faraday, Mr. Brande, Mr. Walker, and Mr. Hopkins. The Committee held a series of meetings, and examined the memorialists individually as to their views and wishes, and afterwards drew up a report in favour of the principle of degrees in science. Being reappointed by the Senate to prepare a definite scheme, the Committee agreed that there should be a Bachelor's Degree, which should rest on a broad and comprehensive basis of scientific acquirement, and a Doctor's Degree for eminence in special branches. A draft-scheme for the several Degrees was, at the Committee's request, prepared by Dr. Arnott. It was very much owing to Mr. Grote's advocacy that the Moral Sciences were retained in the programme, several members of the Committee being disposed to limit the subject of examination to the Physical and Natural-History Sciences. On the 7th of July, the Senate, with one dissentient voice, adopted the report. The degrees were instituted accordingly. The other universities are slowly entering upon a similar course.

On the 27th of February, 1862, he succeeded Sir John Lefevre as Vice-Chancellor.

It was a singular testimony to the largeness of his views, that Mr. Grote's life-long classical studies and associations left him free to appreciate fully the great importance of science in education. In point of fact, however, he combined with his own erudite pursuits an intense avidity for the phy-

sical sciences, along with the metaphysical, and they formed
a considerable portion of his reading to the last. He uniformly resisted all proposals to limit the study of logic and
moral philosophy, or to lower its position in the degrees
where it had obtained a place; and, generally, he was an
advocate for the breadth of culture maintained in the Matriculation and Degree Examinations, as contrasted with the
restricted number of subjects required for the Oxford and
Cambridge degrees.

Another subject that he lost no opportunity of pressing
was the Education of Women. The Senate had been advised
that, under the terms of the original charter of the University,
women were inadmissible to the examinations, and when
Miss Elizabeth Garrett, in 1862, applied to be admitted as a
candidate for matriculation, the application was refused by a
majority of seven to six.

At a subsequent meeting of the senate a memorial was
presented from Mr. Newson Garrett and others, in favour of
procuring such an alteration of the charter as would extend
to women the privileges of the University. This memorial
was taken into consideration on the 7th of May, and Mr.
Grote moved :—

"That the senate will endeavour, as far as their powers
reach, to obtain a modification of the charter, rendering
female students admissible to the degrees and honours of the
University of London, on the same conditions of examination
as male students, but not rendering them admissible to
become Members of Convocation."

The motion was lost by the casting vote of the Chancellor.

Mr. Grote's speech on the occasion, as preserved in his
own handwriting, was to the following effect :—

"I am glad that the senate, by the vote which they have
passed at an earlier period of this meeting, have agreed to
maintain the matriculation examination as it now stands,
with its full curriculum and requirements. In my conception the first duty of the senate is to keep up a high standard
of liberal education, and make their certificates and degrees

attainable only by a large and comprehensive range of study. Subject to this primary condition, their second duty is to throw open their examinations to all who have gone through the prescribed studies, and who are prepared to give proof of their having done so with diligence and efficacy.

"My present motion is consequent upon Mr. Garrett's letter, which stands on the minutes of this day, wherein he intimates that his daughter, Miss Elizabeth Garrett, has gone through the studies which give her a prospect of passing the matriculation examination of the University of London, and his hope that the technical legal objection, which now excludes her as well as other women from the examination, may be removed by a modification of the charter. The senate will recollect that the application of Miss Garrett came before us at a former meeting, and that doubts were then entertained by various persons whether the legal interpretation of our charter did exclude women from our examinations. Since then all doubt has been terminated by the opinion of the Attorney-General (taken, not by us, but by those who desire to obtain admission). He pronounces that such is the legal interpretation, and that females are at present inadmissible.

"Though I accept this as the unquestionable legal interpretation, I think that Mr. Garrett is perfectly right in calling it technical. It is altogether at variance with the spirit of the charter, as expressed in the large words of the second clause: 'Her Majesty deems it to be the duty of her royal office, for the advancement of religion and morality and the promotion of useful knowledge, to hold forth to all classes and denominations of her faithful subjects, without any distinction whatsoever, an encouragement for pursuing a regular and liberal course of education.' After reading these words, I say, which express the most unequivocal totality, and forbid the introducing of any distinction whatsoever, no one would imagine that the first step would be to take a distinction so important and so far reaching, that it strikes off one half of Her Majesty's faithful subjects, and those, too, all the members of her own sex. The motion which I am now about to make is in full conformity with the spirit and with the ordinary meaning of those most comprehensive phrases. It goes only to make the legal interpretation of the charter harmonise with its spirit.

"It is known to every one, however occasionally overlooked, that the cultivators of literature and science, though the majority of them are men, include also in their ranks a minority of women. Among this minority of women, some have rendered essential service to science and to all who seek for scientific instruction. The great French astronomer Laplace acquired imperishable renown by the profound and original researches of his 'Mécanique Céleste'; but an English lady, Mrs. Somerville, rendered a service, though inferior, not less real, by doing what few men were competent to do, by adapting that work to English readers in her book called the 'Mechanism of the Heavens'; and she rendered a still greater service by her better-known works—'The Connection of the Physical Sciences,' and 'Physical Geography'—to which works a large circle of readers, males as well as females, have been greatly indebted for instruction. The fact thus stands upon record, and is undeniable, that there exists a female minority who cultivate literature and science, and that some of the members of that minority have entitled themselves to take rank along with the most eminent men, even in the most abstruse and difficult branches of science.

"Such being the case, I maintain that when an university is constituted, as ours is, for the express purpose of encouraging a high measure of scientific and literary studies, the plainest principles of justice require that we should take the literary and scientific world as it is and deal equally with both sexes; that we should acknowledge the female minority as well as the male majority: and that, after having determined proper conditions of examination, we should admit individuals of the sex of Mrs. Somerville to be examined, as well as individuals of the sex of Laplace. The *onus probandi* lies on those who contend that the female minority should be excluded from our examinations, and none but members of our own sex admitted, and a masculine type, and that to admit women to the studies suitable for men would be confounding a distinction important to uphold. Gentlemen who hold this opinion have undoubtedly a full right to judge for themselves on the type of female education, and I am quite aware that a very respectable portion of the community judge as they do about it. But *I* dissent from them: I hold the opposite opinion; and another portion of the community, equally respectable, hold the opinion along with me. I believe that the studies included in our curriculum are improving and beneficial in their effect upon the minds of women, where women are disposed and able to appropriate them, as well as upon the minds of men. Now those females who hold the same views as I do on feminine education, and their fathers or guardians, are powerfully interested in the admission of women to our examinations; but those who adopt the same opinion as Lord Overstone have really no interest in the question at all. Whether the University is open or closed to women, these females will pursue their own educational march in a different direction, without being affected by our regulations. They have a full right to do this; but they have no right to make their own opinions upon female education binding on all, whether assentient or dissentient; they have no *locus standi* entitling them to insist on closing the doors of our University against all those other females who approve and desire to pursue the studies which it prescribes.

"I make no pretensions to exalt my own opinion on female education, and that of those who agree with me, as a type of orthodoxy, but neither can I admit the right of any other person to stigmatise it as heresy.

"Mr. Garrett says to us:—'My daughter is devoting herself to those studies which your charter declares to be laudable and to deserve encouragement; she has qualified herself by diligent application to fulfil the requirements of your matriculation curriculum. I ask you to allow her proficiency to be tested at your examinations, and to give her a certificate if she can answer the questions satisfactorily; she, as well as myself, considers that the certificate will be an honour and credit to her, and an advantage to her future plans of life.' Now to this request on the part of Mr. and Miss Garrett the senate are called upon to reply:—' We cannot admit Miss Garrett to be examined. We consider our studies as laudable and deserving encouragement only for men; we consider them not laudable, and we intend to discountenance them, in women. We cannot grant any academical honours and advantages which will tend to encourage what is a bad and wrong type of education for women.'

"This is the answer which the senate are called upon to make in declining to admit Miss Garrett, and I maintain that it is an answer which the senate is not warranted in returning. The senate, in making such an answer, and in enforcing an exclusion justified by it, would be usurping a right of determining by authority a point which Mr. Garrett and his daughter have full discretion to determine for themselves.

"I contend that every female (assisted in the cases of those *in statu pupillari* by parent or guardian) has a right to choose for herself among the various types of education, which of them will best suit her own aptitudes, tastes, or plans of life. The choice will of course be different under different circumstances. One woman may prefer a highly ornamental education, exuberant in accomplishments; another may study the full perfection of domestic management and housewivery; a third may take to modern languages; a fourth may address herself to science and the severe departments of literature: and, lastly, others may blend all these different matters in every conceivable proportion. All these varieties will co-exist; I lay down no uniform rule, nor do I imagine that any one rule can be laid down. My argument is that the choice between them all lies with the female

herself; and that if, among the various types, she prefers
that which coincides with our curriculum, we ought to be
the last persons to discountenance or discredit her for doing
so. It is enough for me to show that our type is one among
many admissible types of feminine education ; one which any
woman may choose, if she feels in herself a vocation for it,
and a capacity of going through the study and application
which it involves.

"If gentlemen will look at the question fairly and impar-
tially, I think they will see that the objections in detail
against admitting females to our examinations are not less
untenable than the objections on principle. Our University
would come to consist of graduates and matriculated students,
in majority male, in minority female. How it can be less
respectable in any one's eyes from this conjunction of female
names with male names in our printed calendar, I am at a
loss to understand. In my eyes it would be more respectable, because I should feel that we had done our best to
recompense and to encourage intellectual power, combined
with steady application, wheresoever and in whomsoever it
was to be found. The only case in which I see the possibility
of inconvenience from a minority of females is in the mem-
bership of Convocation. That case I expressly except in the
words of my motion. The functions of Convocation are conducted by public meeting and public debate. I see no
advantage to women in assigning to them a share in those
debates, nor do I anticipate that they would themselves wish
it. The great recompense and privilege to them is that
which they will share with male graduates—authentic record
of their proficiency, upon proof given of diligent and successful study.

" It is well known to all that, as matters now stand, a large
proportion of the business of teaching in this country is performed by women: moreover, no small proportion of current
and periodical literature is also furnished by women. Whoever goes to the great reading-room at the British Museum,
as I do very frequently, will see there every day of the week

a considerable number of females among the various readers
who avail themselves of the privilege of visiting that large
stock of books. He will farther see these females in the reading-
room engaged not simply in reading, but in writing: employed
with manuscript and copy-book, and surrounded by books of
reference, which plainly indicate that they are occupied with
some literary work. Now, seeing that this literary work
and this teaching work is at present actually performed by
females, it will undoubtedly be better performed by instructed
females than by the uninstructed. To open for females, as
our examinations would do, a test for distinguishing the most
instructed from the least instructed, would be a benefit alike
to them and to the public. To the superior and the best
qualified teachers, who look to that profession as their means
of living and their ground of personal importance, we should
be rendering one of the most valuable services which could
be rendered. We should enable them to distinguish themselves, by an honourable and unequivocal characteristic, from
the number of other women who, as it is but too well known,
undertake the duty of teaching without any intellectual
preparation for it, often simply through pecuniary misfortunes in their families, which throw upon them the unexpected necessity of living by their own exertions. Our
certificate would afford to them an improved chance of
obtaining that preference which they deserve for a professional appointment in their own line; and we should furnish
to those, with whom the appointment is vested, the best
evidence of intellectual fitness which can guide their choice.

" The conviction has spread much, and is spreading more,
among both sexes, that women must be taught much more
than they have been, to earn for themselves and by their
own efforts an honourable and independent living. There is
a larger proportion of women now than formerly who are
dissatisfied with a life of mere dependence, without any
active purposes or prospects. To throw open to them the
field of professional competition more largely than is now
done appears to me most desirable as well as most equitable;

but it is an essential preliminary to success in any line that habits of steady, accurate application should be formed at an early period of life. Wherever a female has that genuine aspiration to attain an independent and self-maintaining position, which in my judgement is a virtue alike in both sexes, the prospect of access to our examinations and certificates will tend to stimulate that diligent and serious application in early life which is now wanting, because it goes untested and unrewarded. Complaints of the general inaccuracy of women's minds are sufficiently frequent to have reached every one. Let those women who are superior to this very frequent infirmity, and who are prepared to prove themselves superior, have the opportunity of doing so by admission to our examinations.

"An objection will probably be taken against me from the other side. It may be said that if females were admitted, few would come, and scarcely any one would pass, because our examinations are too severe. I might reply by saying, that, assuming none to come, we should stand only as we are now, with the advantage of having abolished a harsh and unfair exclusion. The fact, if it be a fact, is no valid objection against my proposition. I am prepared to admit that at first very few females will come. It cannot be otherwise: for our examinations cannot be approached by persons of either sex without careful and special preparation. But I do not believe that this will last long. How many will come, no one can know until the experiment is tried. We are sure that the females will always be a minority as compared to the numbers of our sex. But they will be a distinguished and valuable minority who have proved their worth, their superiority, and their title to confidence by diligent application, and by the fact of having attained, under disadvantages of education, an amount of proficiency which even persons of our sex, with far greater advantages, have to work hard for.

"I will now submit my motion as it stands here to the decision of the senate. Our present exclusion, on the simple ground of sex, appears to me unfair and objectionable, and I trust that the senate will weigh attentively and dispassionately the strong reasons which exist for abolishing it."

On the death of Henry Hallam, in 1859, Mr. Grote became a Trustee of the British Museum, and, as in the case of University College and the University of London, he gave unfailing attendance on the meetings of the trustees, and sat on the most laborious committees. In 1864 he was also elected a trustee of the Hunterian Museum.

Mr. Grote's published writings, coupled with the record of his life and work, reveal the lineaments of a great character, the intellectual and the moral ingredients supporting each other. In his public career, and in his wide literary research, a clear, powerful, and originating intellect was guided by the purest aims and the most scrupulous arts. With scholarly resources of language, his rhetoric is the servant of truth. At all points merging his own self-importance, he takes account of all opposing considerations, and does justice to every rival. The reverse of sanguine as to human progress, he yet laboured for every good cause that satisfied his mind, —science, education, and the self-acting judgment of the individual. Differing in many points from the prevailing opinions of the time, he avoided giving needless offence, and co-operated with men of all shades of doctrine, political and religious. In the depths of his character there was a fund of sympathy, generosity, and self-denial rarely equalled among men; on the exterior, his courtesy, affability, and delicate consideration of the feelings of others were indelibly impressed upon every beholder; yet this amiability of demeanour was never used to mislead, and in no case relaxed his determination for what he thought right. Punctual and exact in his engagements, he inspired a degree of confidence and respect which acted most beneficially on all the institutions and trusts that he took a share in administering; and his loss to them was a positive calamity.

ESSENTIALS

OF

PARLIAMENTARY REFORM.

1831.

PREFACE.

THE extraordinary advance of the public mind, on the subject of Parliamentary Reform, within the last two or three years, is such as the most careless observer cannot overlook or dispute. Even the warmest friends of the existing system of representation are among the first to confess and to lament this ominous change; and those who recorded their disapprobation of the system, at a time when its deformities were less acknowledged, may congratulate themselves that their efforts, aided by recent events, have not been thrown away.

To any one who examines the signs of the times, there will appear a remarkable analogy between the present period and that which in France preceded the first French Revolution. The supreme power—the source of all the painful restraints and burdens imposed upon society—has lost its hold on our moral feelings, and is becoming worn out and discredited. From ancient habit, and from the imperious necessity of one known standard of action, men still pay their taxes and obey the commands of the Legislature; and they have done so from the Revolution of 1688 to the last few years, without ever seriously asking themselves what title that Legislature possessed to their confidence. The mere name of Parliament has sufficed to strike them with awe: a body of English gentlemen, variable under certain conditions, and bearing the same denomination as those assemblies which fought the battles of the people against the Stuart princes, has always been and still is sitting at Westminster; and the mass of the people, as it commonly

B 2

happens, have been slow to perceive that the relations of that assembly towards them are the very reverse of what they were in the seventeenth century. A partial community of interest between the House of Commons and the people, prior to 1688, was created, not by the mode of their election, but by common fear of the Crown: and so soon as the alliance — equally profitable to both parties — between the House of Commons and the Crown, was organized, the divorce of the former from the people was an immediate and inevitable result. But no glaring evidence of such a divorce appeared on the face of affairs: on the contrary, the attention of intelligent observers was called more to the improvement in the administration of the Crown, than to the deterioration in the character of the House. Nor can we wonder at the general inattention to this latter fact, when we recollect that the formalities of election remained unaltered:—that the great and wealthy, and all the talented dependents on greatness and wealth, had the strongest interest in upholding the degenerated assembly, and in continuing to cry up the blessings of securities against the Crown, when the Crown, as a separate enemy, had ceased to be formidable; and farther, that the English Government during the last century was really both good and free, in comparison with even the best of those on the Continent.

During the last forty years two circumstances have been simultaneously operating to sharpen the insight of the English people into the real character of their Constitution — diffusion of knowledge, and increase of burdens. The number of those who read and talk politics has been prodigiously multiplied: newspapers, though their circulation is studiously restricted by a pernicious tax, are now numbered among the aliments of life by the population of every considerable town; and an extensive class of independent thinkers, unconnected with the leading strugglers for power, and refusing to be regimented either as Whig or Tory, has grown up all around. While political knowledge and feelings were monopolised by a small knot of gentlemen, the whole of their narrow circle, whatever might be their dissensions amongst themselves, had a separate and exclusive interest as against the whole community, and their debates were shaped accordingly. But the circle has now been so enlarged, as no longer to have any interest at variance with the whole community; and the tone of political discussion, instead of being purely personal and factious, has consisted, to a great degree, of principle and philosophy, making their way by slow degrees against established corruptions and ancient prejudice. Whoever has watched the proceedings in Parliament during the last ten years, on the subjects of Law Reform and Commercial Reform, must have seen ample evidence of this truth.

But, even if the intelligence of the English people had continued unexcited and stationary, it is scarcely possible that such taxation as ours could have been permanently endured without impairing their good will towards the Government which imposed it. The amount of money drawn from the nation and expended by the English Government, since the year 1793, is something which defies all power of conjecture, and which we can scarcely believe even when the Parliamentary returns are summed up before our eyes. No conqueror ever wrung from vanquished and despised aliens so severe a tribute as the English Aristocracy have extorted from their subjects and fellow-countrymen. During the war, men paid without murmuring, on the assurance that such exorbitant demands would only be temporary, and that peace would bring with it relief and abundance: during the first years of peace, promises of retrenchment in progress operated to appease their discontent; but when year after year passes, and the amount of taxation is still found most weighty and distressing, the sufferers become painfully disappointed and clamorous. Even the most patient and reverential men begin to inquire into the system which bears upon them so heavily, and to look with an invidious eye on the receivers of the public money. They judge of the tree by its fruits: their painful sense of the effects is transferred to the cause. They listen with attention to criticisms on the Constitution, and a new light beams within them, when the character, the interest, and the working, of the House of Commons, as at present constructed, are made evident. Nothing short of impenetrable stupidity could make the English people continue to trust a House to which they owe such immoderate burdens, and from which they have at length ceased to expect relief.

These two causes taken together—diffusion of knowledge, and unrelenting taxation—sufficiently explain the growing discredit of that system which passed current with the thinking men of the last century. Taken as it now stands in public opinion, the English Government seems approaching to the condition of the old despotism of France, prior to the Revolution of 1789. Its anomalies, its abuses, its want of system and coherence throughout, its immoral and corruptive effects upon the whole community—are becoming too palpable and revolting to make it suffice as an engine of taxation. The men of wit and eloquence, like Mr. Canning, who undertook to deck out all these hideous deformities—*arcem facere ex cloacâ*—have passed away, and few new orators venture to risk their reputation on the same dangerous ground. We may even congratulate ourselves on possessing a Ministry whose disapprobation of the existing system has been unequivocally proclaimed. At such a juncture, therefore, there is every reason to expect that the perilous consequences of keeping up the disgraced machinery will be duly appreciated, and that some attempts to amend it will no longer be postponed.

But whether such attempts will be sincere or deceptive—judicious or mistaken—comprehensive or superficial—is a point by no means equally certain. It is nevertheless of incalculable consequence. For, if the real defects of the existing representation are not accurately conceived—if the general principles, from whence alone these defects arise, are not laid bare and kept in mind—we run much risk of having some new delusion palmed upon us, equally objectionable in substance with the present, whereby misgovernment may be rendered, for another half century, decorous and endurable. The workings of the sinister interest may be reproduced under another name, and with a slight variation in the external forms, unless the public are taught to recognise and detect the seeds of evil in an untried scheme, before its bitter fruits shall have been actually tasted.

There is much reason to fear that the amendments contemplated by the Whig Ministry will be of this insufficient description—that they will apply themselves rather to clear away the obnoxious symptoms of a rotten system, than to redress the real source of mischief. The various speeches of Whig Reformers within the last ten years, and the doctrines broached in the great Party Review, display so errroneous a conception of the real vices of our representative system, and so decided an aversion to the only effectual remedies, that gentlemen of that school can scarcely be expected to recommend any such Reform as will really impart a new heart and spirit to the Sovereign Council. It will be something, indeed, to obtain even a partial Reform; and when we reflect on the opposition which the Boroughholders are likely to offer, a Ministry may deserve our thanks for accomplishing something widely removed from perfection. But it is of the last importance that the public should accept such a Reform only for what it is worth—that they should not mistake it for the whole improvement requisite—and that they should continue to withhold their confidence from the Parliament until it be so elected as to afford them full and adequate securities for good government.

It is to assist in guarding against this error that the present pamphlet is composed. Assuming that some Reform is admitted to be necessary, I am anxious to place in relief the leading features which are essential to its efficacy—to expose those mis-statements of its real end, and those sophisms as to the means, whereby half might be passed upon us for the whole, or changes of name and form for

newly acquired securities—and to signalize, especially, some
of the fallacies which I think most likely to mislead a
Whig Ministry.   In the year 1821, I published a pamphlet
entitled 'Statement of the Question of Parliamentary
Reform,' in refutation of an article in No. 61 of the 'Edinburgh Review.' That article, ostensibly a review of Mr.
Bentham's work on Radical Reform, contained an elaborate
exposition of the Reviewer's ideas on the subject of Parliamentary Reform, and an earnest and deliberate recommendation of the theory of representation by classes, as the
best security for a good Parliament. Some of the remarks
which I then offered, in reply to that Reviewer, appear to
me suitable to the present juncture, and I shall embody the
substance of them in the following pages.

PARLIAMENTARY REFORM.

When a people first awake to a strong feeling of discontent against Institutions of long standing, their indignation will seldom be directed in due proportion against all the objectionable parts. Accident brings to their view some one of the many ramifications of evil in a glaring manner, and at an opportune moment: while others, no less mischievous in themselves, either are not obtruded so indecently on the public, or find it otherwise occupied, and thus escape notice. This disproportionate and partial perception not only has the effect of retarding the proper outcry against unobserved abuses, but tends farther to keep out of view those great principles which connect one abuse with another, and which form the common source of all of them. Where the evil is thus imperfectly conceived, the remedies demanded are likely to be equally incomplete and superficial.

Something of this sort is discernible in the clamours raised against the Representative System. Men fasten upon some special incongruity or abomination, as if the removal of it were the grand object to be effected by a Reform. Manchester, Leeds, and Birmingham, are great cities, important enough to have their interests protected by Representatives of their own : Old Sarum, Gatton, and Weobly are insignificant hamlets, yet their interests are better protected than those of the three greatest manufacturing cities in England. As long as the argument for Reform is thus put, its opponents meet it satisfactorily, by showing that, if the suffrage were transferred from the three hamlets to the three cities above-mentioned, all things else remaining unchanged, the residents in the latter would be neither better nor worse protected than they are at present. In like manner some persons exclaim against the open bribery at the Liverpool election, or against the severity of the Duke of Newcastle in expelling his tenants at Newark, and are anxious that such transactions should bo prevented in future. But here, too, it is easy to reply, that little would be gained by tying men down to bribe in secret, and with some degree of coyness and ceremony. Nor is it without reason that the Duke of Newcastle complains of having been held up as a single and unique tyrant, while other landlords are accomplishing the same end with greater certainty and good fortune.

Such abuses are indeed indefensible; but they ought to be attacked, not as vicious excrescences on a system sound in the main, but as symptoms, rather gross and magnified, of widespread internal corruption. The system of representation should be surveyed, conceived, and criticised, as a whole: the purposes which it ought to answer should bo compared with its actual workings; and it should be accounted a blessing or an injury according as the one of these coincides with or departs from the other. No Reform can be treated as complete which does not render the Representative Body on the whole an efficient and trustworthy instrument of good government.

That which the people require at the hands of their Government is, protection for their persons, their earnings, and their inheritances: good, accessible, cheap, and speedy justice, for settling private disputes, and for bringing offenders to punishment: together with an adequate public force, for ensuring execution of the laws, and for keeping off external enemies. No less sacred is the duty, though

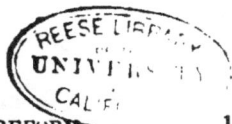

reserved for unborn statesmen to fulfil, of ensuring to the poorer classes universally the largest attainable amount of instruction; I would add, of protecting them against indigence, were I not persuaded that well directed instruction would implant in them the habit of regulating their own numbers, and thus of maintaining wages, by their own prudence, at the proper level. To pay for all these services, adequate taxes—not insignificant in amount, even under the best management—must, of course, be levied.

All this may be summed up in a few comprehensive words: but, in reality, it comprises an unceasing series of laborious acts and painful supervision, sufficient to weary the zeal and fret the temper of benevolence itself: it calls for complete devotion of time, on the part of some of the ablest heads in the community: nor has the man ever yet existed, who could continue engaged in such employments without wishing to leave them half-performed. The nature of the case forbids that free competition, which ensures steady perseverance in the most repulsive private professions: for every public servant is necessarily a temporary monopolist. On the other hand, if there be this temptation to elude the obligations incident to office, there is a motive yet more unconquerable to multiply demands for taxes: to create pretences for palliating unlimited expenditure; and to acquire ascendency, or gratify liberality, at the expense of the public purse.

To counteract, as much as may be, such overwhelming temptations, a feeling of anxious responsibility must be kept up in the minds of Government functionaries; and the romancers of the last age, complimenting the House of Commons at the expense of King, Peers, and subordinates, were pleased to assign that House as the body through whom responsibility was to be ensured. Not that Members of Parliament were supposed to be endued with any inborn virtue greater than that of gentlemen in office whom it was their business to watch: but their aptitude was affirmed to be derived from their being elected periodically by the people. Election by the people, real or supposed, was the ultimate source of security.

The framers of this seducing picture, misled by common parlance and tradition, overlooked the fact that elections by the people were a pure fiction: that the persons who elected formed only a fraction of the people; and that to this electoral fraction, in the last resort, all the security was to be traced. According as the majority of the electors had interests identified with or opposed to the people, would be the security for good government arising from election. If the former, then security would be real and efficacious: if the latter, then not only would there be no real security to the people, but the pretended security would be a source of great separate evil, inasmuch as the House of Commons would be under the same temptations to neglect and abuse their trust as the functionaries whom they were assumed to control. To take precautions against King, Peers, and Public Officers in general, is sufficiently difficult: but if the House of Commons and the electors be also interested in mis-government, the very idea and possibility of precaution becomes extinct; and the phalanx against the people is multiplied, strengthened, and rendered more irresistible than it could be by any other contrivance imaginable.

If the electors form only a small fraction of the people, they and the persons whom they choose must inevitably have a greater interest in conniving at misgovernment and sharing in its benefits, than in the obnoxious task which a rigid duty towards the people would impose upon them. A small fraction, set apart and vested with power, may at particular emergencies act in behalf of the people against some common enemy: as the old French Parliaments occasionally resisted the enormities of the court; but their uniform tendency, here and elsewhere, now and in ancient times, has been directly opposite. It is fruitless to search for any peculiar set of men, exempted by peculiar virtue, or by station in society, from this predominant disposition. Individuals, superior to these and even to greater temptations, may doubtless be accidentally found: but if our earth were blest with any such celestial breed, elections and electors would be superfluous altogether. Government officers might on that supposition be trusted to perform their duties without any control, or a King and Peers to control them without any Commons. It really implies an insult both to King and to Peers to suppose that they can derive any accession of virtue from Commons chosen by a narrow electoral fraction, and thus under the same misleading influences as themselves. Whoever is of this opinion, must imagine the King and the Peers to be worse than ordinary men: a supposition which the true theories of Government do not by any means countenance.

The great question, therefore, with regard to the electoral body, will always be, are they few or many? Do they form a large or a small proportion of the people? If many in name and appearance, are they all so protected that each elector counts for a separate and independent unit? Unless such questions can be satisfactorily answered, the whole process of election will certainly be useless, and, probably, worse than useless; productive by its own working of much separate and peculiar evil.

How they are to be answered in England, Lord Grey in vain warned the country by his memorable Petition of 1793. The truth then proclaimed, is now better known and less disputed. Less than 200 families, partly Peers, partly Commoners, return the majority of the Lower House. Of the remaining minority, a large proportion owe their return to money or local influence—to electors who vote from hope of gain or from fear of loss: and the handful which remains, chosen by a few electoral bodies under very peculiar circumstances, serve only to show what the House might be if the whole system were amended.

When this wonderful paucity of the real, determining, electors is thus made out to us, we see at once that the Constitution is now and long has been only an oligarchy governing under certain forms and ceremonies. So long as

it retains this character, no improvement is to be hoped for.
So long as the House of Commons is chosen by a small
fraction of the community, the community will derive from
its existence no security which they would not have enjoyed
equally well without it, from King and Peers only. Paucity
of the real electors is the grand, the specific evil: multiplication of the real electors, until they cease to have a
separate interest from the community, must be the vital,
the effectual remedy. Nothing short of this can regenerate
the body chosen. It is useless to substitute one small body
in place of another, under pretence of picking out rich or
enlightened individuals: it is useless to render the small
body a trifle larger, until they become *pauci*, instead of
pauciores or *paucissimi:* it is equally useless to prescribe new
forms, or to invent new fictions, by way of giving respectability to their proceedings. Let other circumstances be as
they may, if the electors remain a narrow minority, elections
will be in the last result just what they are now: and the
tree, deriving nutriment from the same pernicious soil—
radice in Tartara tendens—will still continue to bear its
bitter and poisonous fruits.

Among those doctrines, which divert the public eye from
the real vices of our representation, there is none more
current or more easily received than that of founding the
Representative System on property—of making *property the
basis of the elective franchise.* The sense put upon these
words, indeed, is neither uniform nor well-defined: but all
the fluctuations in their meaning appear reducible to
two leading distinctions, which I propose successively to
examine.

Some persons, when they affirm that property is the only
suitable basis for representation, seem to intend that every
man should be vested with an elective power proportioned to
his fortune—that the weight of each in determining the
members to be chosen should be measured by the amount of
property which he possesses. Because (they maintain), the
richer a man is, the greater the stake which he has in the

country—the greater his interest in the preservation and augmentation of its wealth and power. If this principle were openly followed out, without equivocation or disguise, we should see the votes of men graduated and valued: there would be voters of one star, two stars, three stars, and so on, as there are in the lists of East India Proprietors: and perhaps Sir Richard Arkwright, and Mr. Alexander Baring, by virtue of the countless stars which would stand opposite to their names, might be deemed qualified to return a member between them.

But the reasoning, on which any such preference to great proprietors is founded, is altogether untenable and fallacious. Not only is it untrue that they have a greater interest than small proprietors, or non-proprietors, in good government, but it may be clearly shown that they have much less. Among all the obligations which a good government ought to discharge towards a body of citizens, there is none of which the omission will not be far more painfully felt by the small than by the great proprietor. Suppose the course of justice to be dilatory, expensive, or corrupt. By all these circumstances the small proprietor is ruinously aggrieved: the course of his industry is interrupted or cut off: that constant aggregation of petty savings, without which he cannot leave his family in the condition occupied by himself, is rendered impossible; and if he escapes loss or fraud in his own person, he is sure to be called on to rescue less fortunate friends or kinsmen. The great proprietor, on the other hand, is far less exposed to injury from such sources : he is embarrassed by no daily calling: his wealth attracts around him a host of private dependants, who conspire to protect him against the world without, and enable him almost to dispense with the shield of law : while he acquires a power, frightful indeed to society, but profitable to himself, of dealing out unredressed outrage to others. The state of society throughout Europe during the middle ages amply attests that which is here stated : and if the administration of our law were to recede from what it is now to what it was three or four centuries ago, the blow to the middling and the poor would be inconceivably severe, while the great proprietors would gain in one way as much as they lost in the other.

Take, again, the economy of the public revenue. It is the small, not the great, proprietor, whose interest in this desirable object is most powerful. For though the latter pays a larger positive sum in the shape of taxes, yet any given proportion of a large income subtracts much less from the enjoyments of the possessor than the same proportion of a small one: and, what is more important still, whenever excessive taxes are raised, it is the great proprietor who stands the best chance of determining the parties to be benefited by them. High taxation is to the rest of the community pure, uncompensated, sacrifice: to the great proprietor it is sacrifice on the one side, with the prospect of patronage on the other. In no case is he injured by this description of misgovernment so much as the small proprietor: frequently, he proves a considerable gainer by it.

But if the great proprietor is less interested than the small in the performance of the obvious duties of government, still more is this true with regard to the remote and exalted obligations. What member of the community has so little to gain by diffusing instruction among the poor, as a very rich man? He sees and hears less of them than any one else: and as he is always able to pay for the services of the choice few among them, his comfort is scarcely at all affected by the good or bad character of the mass. With respect, again, to the moral effect of the government—to its influence, so prodigious either to good or to evil on the minds and character of the citizens. Is the great proprietor more interested than others in so constructing all its machinery as to encourage probity, industry, and self-denial, and to discountenance fraud, rapacity, and improvidence? In this, as in the other cases, he will be found to have little or no interest in that salutary moral teaching which would be the first of all blessings to every other man in the community.

To him the prevalence of such habits would be a loss of consequence, of ascendancy, of admiration. His position commands him to cherish far more unworthy and immoral dispositions among the community : to spread abroad that overweening and prostrate veneration of wealth, which not only softens all scruples as to the mode of acquisition, but effaces true dignity of character, and renders men the pliant instruments of any one who can help them on in life : to plant in every one's bosom a passion for that show and ostentation, which none indeed can successfully exhibit except the rich themselves, but which every one may pant after and affect, until he loses both the relish for simple and accessible enjoyments, and the feeling of sympathy and brotherhood with men of inferior style. How lamentably such defects eat up the happiness and taint the springs of beneficence among the middling and the poor, is abundantly manifest : how they have been fostered in England under the baneful ascendency of wealth in large masses, is matter of remark to all who compare it with the Continent.

It is then demoustrable, that the great proprietors are the precise persons in the nation to whom good government in all its branches is the least essential. And, if so, what pretence remains for arming them with any peculiar influence in the choice of members of Parliament ? Loose language, assisted by rooted habits of deference and idolatry, have cast a dense cloud in men's minds over this important subject. Our terminology rudely bisects the community into rich and poor—men of property and men of no property : and hence an association grows up in our thoughts between *men of property* and the *institution of property.* The deep respect, which deservedly belongs and has always been paid to that inestimable institution, is transferred mechanically to those who are surnamed after it : they come to be considered as its guardian angels and natural protectors : while such as refuse submission to them are vilified as if destitute of the just feelings towards *property.* But the truth is, that these men of property have no other interest in the institution of

C

property than that which they possess in common with the
mass of smaller proprietors, whom we so vaguely huddle
together as men of no property. To become an instrument
of benefit to his country, a great proprietor ought to act, not
upon that narrow interest which connects him with other
great proprietors, but upon that more extended interest
which binds him to all proprietors whatever. He must condescend to confound himself with their ranks, to join in the
prosecution of objects by which he benefits only in common
with them, and to catch a portion of the modesty, the
assiduous habits, and the demand for unbought sympathy
appertaining to their station. In place of that curse of
English society—small proprietors apeing the imperfections
of the great—true benevolence would teach the great proprietors to imbibe the virtues of the small. But never will
they do this so long as a peculiar and privileged interference
in elections is reserved for them: so long as peculiar electoral rights fence them off conspicuously from the remaining community, and thus both entice and enable them to
conspire for their separate interest ; and so long as unprincipled expectants are tempted to look to them for
promotion, apart from the approving voice of public opinion.

But if there be no ground for privileging great proprietors
on pretence of superior interest in good government, as little
reason is there for doing so on the score of superior knowledge and intelligence. Admitting it for the present to be
true, that without such aids as can only be procured by
persons possessing a certain moderate income, such as 100*l.*
per annum, no one can acquire sufficient instruction to perform the functions of elector—admitting that moderate income affords a just presumption of capacity as compared
with very low income—yet to rate the understandings of
men throughout the whole scale in proportion to their
wealth, would be a measurement altogether perverse and un-
warrantable. Superior income is not only an inaccurate test
in individual cases, but it affords no ground for guessing at
the capacities of men, even as a general rule. A man of

100*l*. or 200*l*. a-year, who lives in a considerable city, enjoys opportunities for mental improvement, not perhaps equalling those which richer men might command, but far exceeding those which the majority of them ever turn to account. Individuals who will labour to instruct themselves are indeed rare in this class: but they are also rare amongst the classes who possess 1000*l*., 2000*l*., or 5000*l*. per annum; and the ordinary literature and periodicals form the stock reading of the one as well as of the other. In comparing men of middling incomes, from 100*l*. per annum upwards, there is no presumption of superior capacity on either side: but when we reach the very high figures in the scale, it will be found that not only is there no presumption in favour of mental eminence, but there is a probability not easy to be rebutted against it. The position and circumstances of a very rich man cut off all motive to mental labour: he is caressed and deified by his circle without any of those toils whereby others purchase an attentive hearing; and the purple, the fine linen, and the sumptuous fare every day, of Dives, are impediments to solid improvement, hardly less fatal than the sores and wretchedness of Lazarus.

I trust that I have now shown that neither on the ground of special interest in favour of good government nor on that of presumed mental superiority, are the great proprietors entitled to privilege or ascendency in the representative system. Protection they will of course receive, in common with all other proprietors: but if they seek pre-eminence, they must be content to earn it by evidences of superior worth and ability. Equalize their political position as much as you will, the prejudices of mankind are sure to turn the scale more or less in their favour: their private munificence confounds itself with and enhances their public services; and the eyes of the unambitious many eagerly look for merit where they are predisposed to pay deference.

That property should be the basis of representation, then, in such sense as to award greater elective influence to the large proprietor than to the small, is a proposition altogether

inadmissible. No sacrifice, indeed, can be too great to protect property; but as this institution is of incalculable
benefit to the whole mass of smaller proprietors, a legislature
chosen by all of them together, great and small alike, is as
sure to protect property, as to guard personal safety. And
the great proprietors will be no less certain of enjoying
security in common with the rest, than of being debarred
from all undue usurpations beyond; for the same institutions which shut them out from the latter, guarantee to
them the former.

There is another sense in which some persons propose to
make *property the basis of representation.* They are of
opinion that no one who does not enjoy an income of a
certain given amount, ought to exercise any political rights:
to all above that minimum, they would award equal, not
graduated, elective power; all below it they would dis-
franchise without exception. Some indeed are more in-
dulgent, others more rigorous in determining the point of
actual exclusion: but the principle of exclusion is the same
with all.

The reasonings sometimes advanced on behalf of this
opinion appear to imply that no person below the appointed
minimum has any interest in preserving property: that
property is an institution beneficial indeed to a fortunate
minority, but injurious and oppressive to the remaining
multitude; and that if the interest of the latter were consulted, not only existing possessions would be divided but the
institution itself would be swept away. This theory of property, fatal as it would prove to the continuance of the institution, except in the most degraded state of the human
intelligence, is not unfrequently resorted to by aristocratical
advocates, when they wish to alarm the middling classes
into uncomplaining submission.

It is fortunate that a just comprehension of the interests
of all holds out brighter prospects. So far from being
injured by the institution of property, the multitude have a
deep and lasting interest in its continuance. No set of men,

whether all poor, or all rich, or some poor and some rich, can possibly live together in society without some rules to define what shall be enjoyed by one and what by another. One man, by virtue of these rules, may acquire a greater amount of enjoyment than another, but the fixity and observance of the rules is as much necessary to the continuous sequence of smaller acquisitions as to the safe enjoyment of the greater. One man, in like manner, may turn the air and the sun to greater account than another; but these beneficent influences are alike indispensable to all. Here and there a being may be discovered so destitute and unhappy as to be inaccessible to any additional suffering: to have no enjoyment open to him, except that which he can find unappropriated, or that which he can snatch by force: to be, in other words, in the position to which all mankind would be reduced, if no laws of property were known or respected. But such cases are rare exceptions to the ordinary lot of the many, who derive a steady subsistence from the uninterrupted exercise of their industry. Scanty as this subsistence too frequently is, it would be intercepted altogether if the safety of property became a matter even of reasonable doubt: for it arises from the outlay of capitalists, made only under assured prospect of return, and ready to be withheld the moment future acquisitions can no longer be reckoned on. Deprived of all means of recruiting his little fund, the poor labourer passes from assured subsistence into absolute and irremediable starvation.

The disfranchisement of the body of the poor, then, cannot for a moment be sustained on the pretence that they have no interest in the maintenance of property. They have at least as great an interest in its stability as the rich: for even a temporary suspension of its laws would deprive them of existence, while the rich might stand some feeble chance of defending and reserving to themselves their pre-existing hoard.

But are the poor wise enough to recognise and act upon this interest? Many reasoners contend that they are not;

and hence, in general, the reluctance to bestow on them
political rights: though there are not wanting persons who,
inconsistently enough, protest against universal suffrage,
both on one ground and on the other; insisting on the one
hand that the body of the poor have a real interest hostile
to property, and reproaching the poor on the other for their
brutish ignorance in not venerating so sacred and beneficent
an institution.

The ignorance of the body of the people is a ground for
their disfranchisement far more plausible than the former,
because, to a certain extent, the fact is undeniable. No one
can dispute that they ought to be, and might be, much
more carefully educated than they are at present. Yet I
feel well persuaded that their ignorance, comparatively to
other classes, has been greatly over-stated, and in particular that no evidence can be adduced of unfriendly feelings, in the generality of them, towards the institution of
property.

Is there any error or prejudice now current among the
poorer classes, to which a parallel cannot be produced among
the richer? If they are taunted with their hostility to
machinery, may they not recriminate on the landlords by
pointing to the Usury Laws and to the Corn Laws? If
their misapprehension of the principle of population is cited
as an evidence of stupidity, how will the squires and parsons,
and the parochial chiefs in general, stand exonerated from
the like imputation?

To me it appears that the poorer classes in general have
an understanding sufficiently just, docile, and unprejudiced,
to elect, and to submit to, the same legislators whom the
middling classes themselves, if they voted apart and voted
secretly, would single out. But assuming the contrary to
be the fact, as so many sincere reformers believe and lament
—admitting that the poor are at the present moment unprepared for the elective franchise—expedients may yet be
found for allaying the apprehensions of the middling classes,
without either degrading the lower by perpetual exclusion,

or neglecting to provide for the duties of Government towards them.

Reasoning on this admission, we should of course acquiesce, under a certain modification, in the principle that property should at present form the basis of representation,—not under the belief that men of property had any superior interest in good government, but because, under the existing difficulties in obtaining, and carelessness in diffusing, knowledge, few persons below a certain amount of income could be presumed to have yet acquired mental aptitude for the elective function. It cannot with any pretence of reason be maintained, that a man of 100*l.* annual income has not enjoyed full facilities for instructing himself up to the requisite pitch. A pecuniary qualification, therefore, if fixed at 100*l.* annual income, would embrace no one, as far as could be reasonably presumed, unworthy of. the trust.

It has been stated that a qualification of 100*l.* annual income would comprehend a million of electors: but if the conjecture were not confirmed by actual returns, I should think it requisite to lower the qualification until that number was attained. No number of voters falling much short of a million, could possibly put out of sight and out of apprehension that first of all evils, a separate interest from the community; and in order to purchase such a certainty, it would be well worth while to submit to such slight depression in the scale of instruction as might be incurred by introducing persons of an income the next degree below 100*l.* per annum. Nor could any reasonable alarmist anticipate either hostility to property, or general unsoundness of views, from the richest million in the country. They might as soon be imagined to surrender England to a foreign enemy, or to plant in it the seeds of an epidemic disease, as to invade or unsettle the sanctity of property.

A representative system including one million of voters, properly distributed and protected, would be that "*almost*

all" in Parliamentary Reform which a distinguished orator*
unworthily predicated of the proposal to admit members
from three or four great towns.

It would purify the Government, thoroughly, at once and
for ever, of that deep and inveterate oligarchical taint which
now infects it in every branch. The Old Man of the Sea
would be shaken from our backs, never more to resume his
gripe. The interest and well-being of the middling classes
would become the predominant object of solicitude, and
would be followed out with earnest and single-hearted perseverance. Economy in the state expenditure; unremitting
advance towards perfection in the law and in the administration of justice; entire abstinence from ambitious or unnecessary wars: all these great results would be ensured by
such a legislature as completely as the most ardent patriot
could desire. Nor would it fail to operate a wholesome
change in the public sentiment, and to root out or mitigate
many of our wide-spread national vices. It would suppress
that avidity for patronage which now renders so many
fathers of families petitioners at the doors of the neighbouring great: it would lower the value of the rich man's
nod, and teach men to earn advance in the world, not by
clinging to his skirts, but by their own industry and their
own frugality; and it would eradicate the proneness to
local jobbing which the imperfect constitution of parishes
and corporate bodies so fatally implants and so abundantly
remunerates. Legislators so chosen must be men of first-
rate intelligence, whose discussions would rectify and elevate
the tone of political reasoning throughout the whole
country—men in whom the accident of birth and connection
would be eclipsed by the splendour of their personal qualities
—identified in heart and spirit with the happiness of the
middling classes—and no less qualified, by laborious completion of their own mental training, to serve as an example
and an incentive to aspiring youth.

* H. Brougham, 1830.

A constituency of one million of voters would infallibly bring about these signal and beneficent results, without the slightest loss or peril to any one, except to those who are receiving undue gains or exercising a malignant influence. The very idea of peril to the middling classes is unreasonable and absurd: they would themselves form the constituent body, and the acquisition to them in every way would be incalculable. Nor would it prove injurious to the tranquil man, who enjoys his affluence apart, without seeking to club with the oligarchical confederacy. Such a person has really no interest distinct from that of the middling class; he suffers at present under their grievances, and would partake in their benefits under an improved system. To wealthy individuals of superior ability and benevolence, it would be highly gratifying and consolatory: since it would cut off the perennial source of those abuses against which they have been vainly striving in detail.

There needs but one addition to render such an electoral system every thing which the widest philanthropy could aim at. A provision should be annexed to it, gradually lowering the qualification at the end of certain fixed periods, so as to introduce successively fresh voters, and after a certain period to render the suffrage nearly co-extensive with the community. The interval might be employed in improving and extending education, so as to remove the only valid ground which is now supposed to command the disfranchisement of the poor.*

This very deficiency in the poor, on which the necessity of their present exclusion is founded, demonstrates the vast importance of impressing on the Government peculiar motives to enlighten them. What portrait shall we draw of a government, under which four-fifths of the male adults are so degraded in understanding, as to be incapable of forming any opinion on the laws to which their obedience is exacted,

---

* I owe the suggestion of this gradual enlargement of the franchise to an excellent weekly journal—the *Examiner*.

and to be destitute, therefore, of that rational attachment towards them which assists and seconds so materially the operations of justice? If their stupidity be really so deplorable, as to leave them ignorant whether they owe gratitude or execration to their laws and their legislators, it is impossible to make exertions too speedy or too strennous to amend it. Under a government faithful and energetic in the performance of all its duties, such mental darkness would be rapidly dispelled, and the reason for continued disfranchisement would disappear along with it. But inasmuch as among all the duties of Government, those which it owes to the poor are the most liable to be neglected, the determination of periods for gradually extending to them the suffrage would serve as a spur to quicken inactivity, and as an admonition to prevent forgetfulness. And it is but too possible, that a body of representatives, perfect and admirable for the middling classes, might be less keenly alive to the importance of elevating the condition and assuring the independence of the laborious many. If they seriously contemplated perpetual disfranchisement—if they considered the many, not as minors requiring farther tuition, but as half-witted by nature and smitten with inherent incapacity—they would be slow in communicating to them acquirements not deemed available to any ultimate end, and only sharpening the sense of an humiliating exclusion.

A constituency of a million of voters, however, even taken apart and without any such gradual enlargement, would effect a change so great and desirable, that I should deeply regret to abate the demand for it by thus showing that it would not accomplish every thing. The poor, though not permitted to vote, would partake in its benefits: not merely by the diminution of taxes, and by such amendments in the law as would open to them the avenues of justice, but also by the improved character of the wealthy and middling class, and by the more frequent prevalence of sober and useful virtues in the place of ostentatious frivolity.

If it be once determined that the constituency shall include a million of voters, it is better to select them by an uniform income qualification than by any other. No just excuse can be given for preference on such an occasion, except presumed mental superiority: and though the inference derived from income is by no means free from objection, I know not any better which can be obtained. If the aggregate of voters were smaller, certain professions and occupations might be resorted to, as affording adequate evidence of mental capacity: but it will be found that the richest million will embrace all those whose occupation or profession could have been thus singled out as presumptive testimony.

The endless varieties of qualification in different English boroughs appear more like an olio of anomalous customs, than like the methodical workings of a reasonable Legislature. But the principle of uniform qualification has been impugned, and that of multiform qualification maintained, by some reasoners of note, who have insisted on the propriety of rendering the representative system a representation of classes, not of individuals. That theory I shall now examine.

In combating the principle of strengthening the great proprietors at elections, I have supposed it to be acted upon openly and avowedly, by allotting a number of votes to each man proportioned to the amount of his property. Such a regulation, however, is repugnant to the general habits of English elections. Immense as the influence of great proprietors is at present, it is still exercised under a thin disguise, which enables men to quibble about its amount, and sometimes, when it suits their purpose, even to contest its reality. The conditions under which it is exercised, unhappily, aggravate its inherent mischief: for while they nowise serve to restrain or purify the oligarchical influence, they render its *modus operandi* such as to keep the minds of the people venal, open to intrigue in all shapes, athirst for irregular patronage, and insensible to any public principle. But English thinkers have become familiar with this practice of attaining by stealth ends obnoxious to avow: and those who, in their plans of reform, leave the oligarchical preponderance still unabated, usually seek for some new contrivance to screen its working, and to mystify its real character. What is called the class system of representation, advocated in the 'Edinburgh Review,' as well as in other places, is a contrivance of this description.

The plan of the class system is to divide the citizens into various classes; each consisting of individuals bound together by some interest common to them all, but separate from the rest of the citizens. Thus we are to have one class of merchants, and another of landholders: and each of these is to elect representatives, intended to watch specially over the interests of their several classes, and to see that those interests are adequately protected in parliament. Each representative is supposed peculiarly cognizant of the interests of his own class, and under special obligation to promote and prefer them. No uniform qualification for voters (we are told), either founded on property or on any other principle, could ensure the election of members either acquainted with the interests of these various classes, or animated with competent zeal to watch over them. The interests of the class of merchants will not be protected unless that class elects representatives: the same with the class of landholders, and with the rest. Whoever would see this theory explained and vindicated at length, should consult the article on Reform in No. 61 of the 'Edinburgh Review.'

Let us consider the simplest particular case which can be imagined to answer the conditions of the theory. Suppose three classes, landholders, merchants, and lawyers, each returning one member, or each an equal number of members, to form a governing body. Each member comes exclusively devoted to the service of his own class: but as no measure can be adopted without a majority, two out of the triumvirate must combine: and that combination can only take place by mutual concessions on the part of the two allies, each consenting to drop such part of his respective class interest as may interfere with the class interest of the other. Those two out of the three will combine whose alliance can be accomplished with the smallest sacrifice of their respective class interests. But when two out of the three have combined, the concurrence of the third becomes a matter of no importance. His interest, therefore, and the interest of his class, is completely disregarded. The two allies, who, as a majority, are in possession of the governing power, would be unfaithful deputies of their respective classes, were they to concede anything in favour of a colleague with whose co-operation they can dispense.

How then is the end answered of affording protection to each of the separate class interests? It is so far from being attained, that each and every one of them remains unprotected. The moment that the members begin discussion, it must become apparent that each class interest excludes the rest: and that to ensure protection to one of them is to deny it to the others. Either the assembly has a majority of its members returned by one particular class, or it has not. If the former, then the dominant class interest is indeed sedulously provided for, but all the classes in the minority are neglected and trampled upon. If the latter, then it is not the separate interest of any class whatever which is protected, but the common interest of those two or more classes who combine to form a majority; all the classes in the minority being neglected as in the previous case.

Perhaps the partisans of this system may reply, that they never imagine a deputy to seek protection for his class interest at the expense of other classes, but only so far as the interest of other classes can be made to coincide with it. But on this supposition the cardinal principle of the system is infringed, and the deputy ceases at once to be a class deputy. He does no more for the class by whom he is returned than for the other classes by whom he is not returned. He becomes, what he ought assuredly under every good system to be, a deputy devoted to the service of the country;

for the interest which all classes have in common *is* the interest of the country.

The fundamental error of the class system consists in a wrong conception of what constitutes the interest of the country. " We must divide the people into classes (observes the Edinburgh Reviewer) and examine *the variety of local and professional interests of which the general interest is composed.*" Now the general interest, far from being composed of various local and professional interests, is not only distinct from, but exclusive of, every one of them. The interest of an individual by himself apart—the interest of the same man jointly with any given fraction of his fellow-citizens—and his interest jointly with the whole body of his fellow-citizens—all these are distinct objects, abhorrent and irreconcileable in general, coinciding occasionally by mere accident. To promote the joint interest of any given class, you do not set about first to promote the separate interest of one member of it, then the separate interest of another member, and so on. You neglect all these, to fix your eyes on an independent end, the joint interest of all the members of the class one with another. Just so it is with that grand aggregate of classes, the community. The general interest is not to be attained by pursuing first the separate interest of one class, then the separate interest of another, but must be studied as an object apart from all these. Individuals compose the class, but the interest of the class is not the sum total of the separate interests of all its members : classes compose the community, but the interest of the community is not the sum total of the separate interests of all its classes. And a governing body which would promote the universal interest, must discard all inclination to the separate interest of any class whatever.

What would be the result of the class representation, as its partisans apply their principles, it is not difficult to trace. The great body of the community—the multitude—are considered to be *one class*, and are as such empowered to return certain representatives. The remaining minority are then subdivided into a great number of different classes, each of which is to elect members of its own and for its own benefit. From this nice subdivision many of the electing classes become of course numerically small. And is it not manifest that these numerically small classes will combine to form a majority in the assembly? and that the classes not included in the majority — the multitude among the number — will receive no more protection than if their deputies had never been elected? The oligarchical Proteus thus reappears, in another of his ever-varying shapes: and the result of the system may be described in the words used by Livy (i. 43) when he is explaining the Roman class system ascribed to Servius Tullius—" Gradus facti, ut neque exclusus quisquam suffragio videretur, et vis omnis penes primores civitatis esset." Votes are given to the people, not as a security for good government, but as a sop to delude and quiet them: the real power remains, where it would be if they had no votes, vested in the few of rank and property.

It may be urged, indeed, that this result arises, not from the inherent principles of the class system, but from a vicious distribution of the people into disproportionate classes: that if the separate classes framed were more equal, and each numerically large, no majority in the assembly could combine without including a number so large as to coincide in interest with the whole community. Such an arrangement is indeed conceivable: but if, in the last result, the deputies are neither able nor inclined to follow out any other interest than that of the community, what is gained by the peculiarity of the system—that of calling the electors together in classes—and what would be lost by abandoning it? Would not the same result be equally assured if the same number of electors voted in sections not coinciding with each man's class or profession, and not suggesting the idea of any distinct principle of union among themselves?

Not merely would the result be equally assured: it would be far more infallible and far more complete. The general interest will be most certain of receiving paramount and undeviating attention, when it stands forth prominently and conspicuously as the single purpose of delegation—when it enters into every man's feelings of duty—and when it is least traversed and overlaid by other objects of pursuit. All these essential requisites are frustrated by summoning the electors to vote in groups, each animated by a peculiar interest distinct from the community. Each class, convoked apart, will dwell upon and magnify its own separate interests, which it will treat as at least co-ordinate in importance with the general interest; the minds of individuals will be engrossed by the feelings of their rights and obligations as fellow-classmen; and the sentiment of a common interest with the whole nation will be to a great degree obliterated. A member thus elected will carry to Parliament the sentiments of his constituents respecting the treatment which their class ought to receive: the interest of the class will be his first duty, that of the country his second: at any rate, the two conflicting obligations will divide his soul, and drive him to perpetual trimming and evasion. No sincere or single-hearted patriot can be seen in the assembly. Instead of an union of wise and incorruptible legislators, agreeing in one common end, and only differing as to the means of promoting it—Parliament would become an arena for rival conspirators or opposing counsel, each engaged in serving a separate client; each seeking to twist a grant or to qualify a restriction, in his own peculiar sense; and no two concurring in devotion to the same ultimate objects.

Such would be the tendency of a representative system, under which each member should be chosen by a peculiar class, and should be recognised as the special guardian of the interest of his class. The more strongly and intimately the members of each choosing body are knit together, tho more perniciously would this anti-social taint infect the legislative assembly.

I grant indeed that vestiges of it may still remain—that it will not be entirely extirpated—under the best electoral system conceivable. For as each member must be chosen by a particular body of electors, and those too voting in one neighbourhood, their own separate interest may occasionally pervert their judgment, and lead them to elect with little reference to their obligations as citizens of the community. But under good electoral arrangements this cannot happen often, nor in many places at once ; and the more its mischievous tendency is denounced, the less likely it will be to occur at all.

Instead of trying to guard against such a tendency, and only submitting to it where precautions prove ineffectual, the class system actually recognises it as a sound and beneficial principle of action, and is built upon it as upon a corner-stone. Independent of all other objections, the monstrous immorality of the system cannot be too earnestly exposed. It treads out and extinguishes every spark of a general interest: it disavows all idea of the rights and obligations attached to citizenship: and those feelings which bind us to our community, the source of so many exalted virtues, become obsolete and unknown. In place of an united and harmonious nation, what does the system present to us ? A mere congeries of unfriendly confederacies, each combating for its own separate ends : the strong classes combining to prey upon the weak, and grasping at the Legislature as an engine of usurpation : the weak submitting from inability to resist, and hating a Legislature from whence they derive no protection : the members of each class deeming the others legitimate plunder, and treating them in effect as aliens under the cheat of a common country. All these consequences are infallible, if Parliament is to be corrupted into a congress of class deputies, instead of an assembly of citizen legislators.

A salutary Reform ought to proceed on principles the very reverse of the class system. Far from encouraging the exercise of the elective franchise by local bodies and corporations, every such union ought to be studiously dissevered, so that an electoral section which returns one member may seldom or never consist of individuals already united by any partial

D

tie. It is the individual judgment of each voter which is required: a certain number of voters must concur to return the same candidate, in order to answer the purpose of attesting his competence; but it is neither necessary nor desirable that all of them should vote in the same place. By proper distribution of the electoral bodies and places of voting, each elector might vote with little personal inconvenience, and disengaged from any corporate bias.

In speaking thus respecting local and partial associations, I would by no means be understood to dispute their great utility when limited to their proper sphere. For local purposes, they are excellent and indispensable: and their organization ought to be revised and purified with much greater solicitude than has ever been hitherto manifested. In England the old institutions have lingered on from generation to generation untouched by the hand of philosophy: salutary in their first commencement, they have not only outlived their period of utility, but have passed into instruments of jobbing and abuse. The history of a corporation is the history of the English Parliament. The rise and progress of these bodies in the twelfth and thirteenth centuries forms an epoch in the history of society: without them the blessings of security would have been unknown; and the European countries might still have been groaning under the tyranny of local barons, contentious indeed as against each other, but animated with a common spirit of insolence and rapacity towards the people. Against such enemies, every individual in the nascent town had a joint interest: and very imperfect corporate institutions sufficed, while the idea of danger to all from the same quarter was predominant and overpowering. But when the enemy without ceased to be formidable, the leading men in a town found themselves possessed of established ascendency over their fellow townsmen, which it was tempting to convert to their own account. The once useful corporation gradually degenerated into a field of disunion and intrigue: freemen remaining distinguished by an indefensible line, and by still more indefensible privileges, from non-freemen; and a select junto mal-administering over them all. The subject of good municipal institutions and assemblies, which is now attracting so much attention in France, deserves no less serious consideration in England: but however these bodies may be constituted, whether well or ill, it will still be essential to exclude their interference as much as possible in elections for the general legislature.

The use and abuse of corporate bodies, and the pernicious tendency of the class system in general, is a topic deserving of the deeper attention, as the existing English representative system is in effect a class government, of which the landholders form the preponderating partners. Hence such plans of Reform, as retain the class system unchanged, and profess merely to vary and remodel its component parts, come recommended by the imposing assertion, that the principle on which they proceed has already been tried, and is familiar to the Constitution.

It has, indeed, been abundantly tried, and its baneful workings are easy to be detected; not merely in the details of misgovernment, but also in the perverted tone of the current politics. What more common than to hear the country described as composed of so many "interests"— some more or less great and valuable than others — the landed interest and the manufacturing interest—the East Indian and the West Indian interest—the Ship interest, and the Wool interest! Some persons even speak as if they imagined that Parliament met for no other purpose than to watch over these great interests; each of which is constantly complaining that it does not receive adequate protection, and that "rival interests" return so many members to Parliament as to stifle its just claims. Such pretensions involve the fundamental fallacy of the class system. Landlords or manufacturers have sacred claims on the Legislature in common with the general body of citizens, but they acquire no new and peculiar claims by the fact of their sharing in the same occupation or in the same descrip-

tion of revenue. Protection to themselves, as individuals, is
their indisputable right : protection to their "interest" as
a separate interest, is a privilege over their fellow citizens —
a monstrous injustice and usurpation. Because a hundred
or a thousand men choose to band together, to give themselves a common name, and to talk of themselves as an
interest, is the Legislature to make separate terms with them,
and to grant them concessions at the expense of the modest
citizen, who seeks only a citizen's share in the benefits of
good government ? Yet such concessions, teeming as. they
do with evil, are in the ordinary spirit and track of the
English Parliament. Its constitution, tainted with the
inherent vice of the class system, has caused it to be pulled
hither and thither by the great rival "interests : " it has
been a theatre for their selfish struggles among themselves,
as well as for their common encroachments on the body of
the people, who, as they bear not the name and the banners
of any particular "interest," have been treated as if they
needed no "protection" at all. No man can have attentively studied the English Government without learning,
that the path of advancement and honour has been mono-
polized by these potent fraternities, and that the character
of a private citizen was of little account. Hence the fatal
temptation, so prevalent wherever we look, to join some one
of them in intriguing for privilege or undue gain, and to
renounce all sense of obligation towards the people as a
body. Even virtuous men, who would shudder at injustices
for their own individual benefit, become perverted with the
class-morality, and act agreeably to the memorable declaration of Lord Grey, when he set *his order* against and above
his country.

I abstain from touching, as I might well do, on the encouragement which such a state of the representation affords
to the most mischievous tenets of the mercantile system.
Though not chargeable with having given birth to them, it
has assuredly retarded their extirpation. The body of con-
sumers—the general public,—who are interested in low

and steady prices, especially of necessaries—constitute no
" interest," and are never seen in battle array. It is in vain
that political economy advocates their cause against the
sellers, not only forward in associating and loud in complaint,
but favoured by the erroneous disposition of ordinary men to
sympathise only with a special and recognised class.

Having established the necessity of a total number of
voters, so great as not to be capable of having a separate
interest from the country, and of taking their votes, not in
classes, but as individuals, I come to the important question
of open or secret voting. There is every possible reason for
taking the votes by Ballot : not one single reason, so far as I
can discern, for taking them openly. This question has
been so admirably handled in the 'Westminster Review' of
last July, that I might be satisfied with referring to the
demonstration there given : but it is impossible to pass over
a subject of such incalculable moment without a few additional words to elucidate and enforce it.

Without ballot, the most extensive provisions of Reform
in other respects would be nullified : for the creation of new
open votes would be only an empty multiplication of names,
leaving the band of real choosers scarcely larger than it was
before. Under secret suffrage, every man who has a vote is
a real chooser : he votes from genuine, intrinsic, preference,
well or ill founded, for his candidate. His vote can neither
oblige nor offend : it is an act purely public, and counts as a
separate grain of evidence to attest the competency of the
person whom he supports. Under open voting, the reverse
is true in all points. The number of nominal voters does
not afford any test of the number of real choosers : out of
a thousand voters there may not be fifty who have any
genuine preference for their candidate, or any sincere persuasion of his fitness for the trust. Provided only he be
exempt from notorious disgrace or indisputable imbecility,
the grades of superiority above that low minimum are never

scrutinised. And the election of a candidate, even by a considerable number of open votes, far from furnishing presumption of his competency, proves only that he has either many dependents, or an unusual number of influential private friends, who are willing to make his cause their own.

If reasons were needed against open voting, the disgusting details of an English election would. abundantly supply them. The candidate convenes an active committee of private friends, who look over the list of voters, and set about to consider by what weapons or baits each of them is assailable. Some of them are known to be openly venal: others are dependent tenants on the estate of Lord A. or Mr. B.: a third class are tradesmen, and supply the families of Lord C. and Mr. D.: of the remainder, several are comfortable in their incomes, but are fond of shooting, and prize highly the permission of going upon a neighbouring manor, or are anxiously seeking intimacy with some families wealthier than themselves. To track out all these ramifications of each voter's peculiar interest—to penetrate the hidden sources of his hopes and fears—and to hook his vote through the medium of one or the other—is the business of an election committee. It is futile to prohibit any part of their proceedings, while the means and the motive to practise them are left open: and however the number of open voters may be multiplied, it will only become more troublesome, but by no means less practicable, to govern the majority of them by private hopes and fears. At certain grand periods of excitement numerous voters may break loose, and give open utterance to their faith with the exalted constancy of martyrs; in ordinary times, they are tame and sequacious, and a thousand of them are marshalled with hardly less facility than a hundred.

In spite of the crooked manœuvres so universal in electioneering, there are persons who dwell much on the empty and fallacious distinction between dependent and independent voters. A poor voter, they affirm, is by his station depen-

dent, and this is urged as one reason for withholding votes from the poor : while a person of greater affluence is spoken of as if his position afforded security for his independence. But the test here assumed, for measuring dependence and independence, is equivocal to a high degree. That man is the most dependent who is liable to suffer the greatest and most irreparable evil at the hands of some one or some few others ; and many who enjoy a most eligible position are, for that very reason, exposed to far more alarming liability of evil than simple poverty ever entails. A poor artisan or labourer may be displaced, but the number of equally good situations open to him is so considerable, that he may speedily hope to repair his loss. But the higher and better paid officers have more to lose by dismissal, while the number of such places is so limited as to afford them little chance of an equivalent elsewhere. It seems evident, therefore, that shopmen, clerks, and highly paid functionaries of every description, being greater sufferers by arbitrary displacement, are really more dependent than artisans or servants, and consequently that poverty is no measure of the degree of dependence.

But it is superfluous to verify the graduation of the scale, if we can satisfy ourselves that he who is called thoroughly independent is exposed to powerful private influence, more than sufficient to pervert any open vote. I would fain ask whose position is so fortunate as to enable him to deny this ? Look at the tradesman who is making 500*l.* or 1000*l.* per annum, and the manufacturer or merchant who is making 2000*l.* or 3000*l.* Each of them acquires his income out of fractions, some large, some small, arising from connections profitable in various degrees ; and the best of these connections think themselves fully entitled to ask for his vote, whenever they take interest in an election. If the request be refused merely on public grounds, displeasure and provocation are infallible: and the refuser incurs the chance of pecuniary loss, of seeing himself supplanted by rivals, and of being stigmatised as ungrateful. How is this

consistent with the pretended independence of his position?
Even the man whose income is already treasured up, finds
many individuals around him whom it is exquisitely pleasing
to oblige and highly distressing to offend, though their
political views may be such as he entirely disapproves. Is
it not true, then, that the man most independent by position
and circumstances is yet so fettered and so vulnerable, as
to lay him under temptations far too strong for average
political integrity?

So long as voting is open, therefore, the votes of the
middling and of the affluent will be determined, in the
majority of cases, by some one of the innumerable varieties
of private influence: nor is the Ballot less essential to purify
their votes than to liberate those of the poor. I duly appreciate the beneficial effects of the private sympathies, and
of that readiness to oblige and to requite, without which life
would be a desert: but if the business of voting is to be
subservient to a public end, it ought to be abstracted altogether from the sphere of their interference. Is it at all
less detrimental to the main purpose of voting—the advancement of the wisest and best men in the community into the
Legislative Assembly—that I should vote to please a friend,
to return an obligation, or to conciliate a customer, than
that I should sell my vote for ten pounds, or for a place in
the Excise? It is melancholy to confess that on this important topic the morality both of rich and poor has yet to
be formed, nor can we hope ever to see it formed except by
means of the Ballot. Most men consider their vote merely
as a means of rendering service to a friend; and dispose of
it exactly on the same principles as they would bestow any
other favour. How abominable would be the course of
justice, if they forgot their trust as jurors in the same cool
and systematic manner: if one man thought himself au-
thorized to solicit, and another to grant, a verdict in favour
of plaintiff or defendant! Yet the function of voter is no
less a public trust than that of juror: nor would the mischief
of corrupt juries, prodigious as it is, surpass that of corrupt

voting. It is fruitless to admonish men on the pernicious tendency of what is daily before their eyes, so long as the misleading influence is left in full vigour and application : but if the door· be once shut against such influence, there is nothing· to prevent voting from being assimilated to other public trusts, and from becoming really conducive to its peculiar and all-important purpose.*

---

* The duty of a voter to the public has been banished, not only out of fact and society, but also out of political reasonings and conceptions. Hence the extraordinary difference in the public sentiment between the promise made by a voter to support a particular candidate, and the promise made by a juror to deliver a particular verdict. To be known to have made such a promise as juror, would suffice to brand a man with infamy. But assuming that he has been guilty enough to make it, and that he repents prior to the verdict, will it not be generally considered that he commits less evil by breaking his promise than by consummating an injustice? The indignation of mankind is directed, not against the violation of such a promise, but against the making it and the asking it.

Were voting considered as a public trust, the like feeling would prevail with respect to a voter. But it is considered as a matter purely private and optional ;. so that all which the public exacts of a voter is that he-shall keep a promise when he has once made it ; and strenuous opposition has been raised to the Ballot, on the ground that it would permit him to violate his promise without detection. Objectors on this ground forget that no promise, interfering with the due execution of a public trust, can be innocently made ; and that with respect to culpable promises, the desirable object is to prevent them from being over asked or over made, not to ensure their strict observance after they are made—to preserve men from ever entangling themselves in that trying position, wherein they can only choose between violating a promise or forfeiting a trust. Now it is obvious that electors are much less likely to be called upon to promise when they vote secretly, than when they vote openly : and where few promises are asked, few promises can be broken : so that the fact which the objection assumes, that promises will be habitually broken, is really untrue ; while the end is also attained, of removing one great temptation to an undue species of promise.

I had the opportunity of being present, a little before the French elections of June, 1830, at a private preliminary meeting of French electors in one of the arrondissements not far from Paris. About thirty electors met, to estimate the chances and to concert measures for the success of their candidate in the approaching contest. They called over the electoral list, and each person present pronounced respecting those whom he knew or those who lived near him, whether they were likely to be supporters or opponents. For such as were not thoroughly known, attempts were made to guess at their political sentiments or at their private partialities. But never was the slightest hint started of winning over a questionable voter by solicitation and intrigue, or of approaching his bosom by those invisible bye-paths which an English electioneerer so skilfully explores. Such artifices appear to have been considered in France too degrading for any one except the agents of Charles X., who did indeed employ them as much as was practicable, and who of course spared no pains to nullify and elude the Ballot.

Among the several objections urged against the Ballot, there is one which not only admits, but is even founded upon, the marvellous debasement produced by the English system of open voting. Some persons allege that under secret voting scarcely any elector would go to the poll: that when his vote could neither gratify a friend nor repay a benefactor, he could not be induced by a "cold sense of duty" to undertake the inconsiderable labour of going occasionally to a neighbouring voting place. So low is their estimate of the strength of the public affections amongst a community whom yet they describe as pre-eminently virtuous, and under a Government which they extol as little short of perfection! To me such eulogies either on the people or on the Government seem little better than a childish self-adulation: yet I never could have supposed an average Englishman so dead to all public feeling, as to think a good member too dearly purchased at the cost of a short walk or ride—(for the labour of voting need be no greater)—once every year, or every two or three years. Assuming the fact, however, to be true, the expediency of a secret suffrage is not impeached by it. Though few votes be actually given, yet as every vote denotes a genuine preference and esteem, some rational ground is really acquired for believing the person chosen to be a superior man : whereas a hundred times the number of privately-determined votes proves literally nothing in favour of his competency as a Legislator. Better take the evidence of ten sincere truth-tellers, than that of a thousand suborned witnesses, who speak without caring whether what they attest is true or false.

Others object that the Ballot will be found in practice not to produce secrecy, inasmuch as a man may tell and will tell how he has voted. They omit to indicate at the same time the test whereby they mean to determine whether he speaks truth or falsehood. Of what value is a man's statement, when he may violate truth without any chance of detection, and when he has a direct interest in repelling tyrannical inquisition by justifiable deceit? His vote may perhaps be guessed: but that is not enough; it must be actually and positively known, before a patron can make his displeasure or his satisfaction contingent on the direction of it. And, indeed, the virulent opposition of the vote-commanders to the Ballot, plainly demonstrates how little faith they themselves repose in this miserable quibble.

There are others who exclaim loudly against the mischiefs of secrecy, and against the lying and hypocrisy of the Ballot, forgetting that they are themselves habitually employing it in their clubs, and that they can therefore scarcely be treated as serious when they brand it with such contumelious epithets elsewhere. Secrecy is good or bad according as it conduces to a good or a bad end : and in the case of voting, it may be proved to be essential to the most beneficent of all ends. And as a vote given by Ballot quickly comes to be ranged among matters unbecoming to pry into—just as no man ever thinks himself entitled to ask about the tenor of his friend's will, or the amount of his property—so there really would be neither lying nor hypocrisy, except where a shameful intrusion had been employed to wring from the voter his secret, and where the lie was a pardonable shelter against the greater evil of oppression. "In order that all men (observes Dr. Johnson)* may be taught to speak the truth, it is necessary that all likewise should learn to hear it." When gentleness, sympathy, and tolerance of dissent shall have become habits of action in the superior, evasion and concealment in the inferior will disappear of themselves. But until the former has thrown away his spear, it is monstrous to call upon the latter to perform his duty without a shield.

But there is one argument against the Ballot which I never hear advanced without indignation. It is to be withheld because it would cut down the influence of the great proprietors. Wheresoever we turn in Reform, these tremendous giants are posted to bar our progress—

> " Apparent dirœ facies, inimicaque Trojœ
> Numina magna Deûm."

It is indeed true that the Ballot would materially abridge their influence: and any reform which did not effect that end would be hollow and delusive. Far from denying or disguising such a result, the advocates of the Ballot avow and exult in it. And they ask at the same time what peril would ensue if the influence of the great proprietors were so far cut down as to be proportioned to their individual wisdom and merit, not to the size of their rent-rolls? In order that this class, against whom mankind have never yet provided adequate safeguards—insolent bullies and ravishers in the Grecian States; cruel ejectors of neighbouring poor proprietors in the Roman Republic; sticklers for the Fist-right,† in the middle ages, against the growing

* *Rambler*, No. 96.

† I take the liberty of translating literally the significant German compound *Faust-recht.*

ideas of law and order in the cities; spoilers of the church property, for their own benefit, in the sixteenth century; auxiliaries of Charles Stuart against English liberty in the seventeenth; authors, in the eighteenth and nineteenth, of the devouring war and the Corn Laws; in an age of crime, the most high-handed criminals; in an enlightened time, the most obstinate foes of improvement. In order that this class may outbid friendless merit and ride down conscientious opposition, are we to dupe the people with the spurious forms instead of the essence and virtue of an electoral security? To cheat them with the outward and visible sign, while we rob them of the inward and spiritual grace? To invest them with an important public trust, designing beforehand that they should barter it away each to his patron-aristocrat, and thus to efface in their minds, by Legislative authority, the idea of obligation to the community? The influence of these elevated beings must indeed be as the dew from Heaven, if it be worth purchasing at the cost of all the evils of a simulated suffrage. If they must have more votes than one—for the influence which they claim means nothing else—let them become three-star, four-star, or twenty-star men, leaving to the humbler citizen his one poor vote secret and free. It will be bad enough to exalt them thus into a privileged few: they may spare us the bitterness of making them, besides, extorters and corrupters of other men's votes.

The importance of the Ballot, on every ground, as well in its direct and immediate as in its remote and indirect effects, appears to me vast and overwhelming. But it cannot, undoubtedly, be rendered efficacious, if the number of voters who concur to return a single member is permitted to be small. In that case, an opulent man might bribe them in the mass, covenanting to pay to each a certain sum after his election. But if the number be large, it will become too expensive thus to pay all in order to purchase a majority. In my opinion, no section or district which returns a member ought ever to consist of less than 2000 voters: every section ought to include an equal or nearly an equal number; and if the necessity of obtaining a certain aggregate of returns out of a certain aggregate of voters permitted, it would be an improvement to make the number of voters in each electoral section even greater than 2000. Every increase in the number of secret votes, whereby a candidate is chosen, furnishes increased presumption of his superior qualifications.

In this point of view, the number of members in the House of Commons becomes an important subject of discussion, because the smaller its total, the greater the number of voters who can be allotted to each separate returning body. The present House would be found far too numerous for the dispatch of business, if all the members were constant at their posts. The real working persons in it are notoriously a very small proportion: two hundred members constitute a large, three hundred a very large, attendance; and questions which draw together a greater number than three hundred are rare and unusual indeed. Three hundred really assiduous members appear to me amply sufficient to prosecute the business of legislation: and the surplus above that number, if any there were, would be found rather to impede than to forward the ends for which they are assembled. To lessen the total number of members, too, as much as can be done without delaying the public business, is advantageous in other ways: it renders the post itself more conspicuous and honourable: it fastens public attention more steadily upon each member's parliamentary conduct; and it will of course be easier to find three hundred highly qualified persons in the country than five hundred, so as to avoid the necessity of resorting to a lower scale of intellect.

If the aggregate of voters were a million, and the members returned to Parliament 300, no returning body need include less than 3300 voters: if the members of

Parliament were 500 in number, each returning body might then have 2000 voters allotted to it. A body of 2000 electors, voting secretly, and voting so as to occasion no expense, could not be tampered with by the most expert electioneerer. The member whom a majority of these return, must be a person of some public reputation; a person believed to possess talent and worth, not merely equal, but much superior, to the average of his fellow-citizens.

In looking over the manifold enormities of our present system of representation, it will generally be found that any one defect, if left uncorrected, suffices to neutralize the remedies applied to the rest. If voters are habitually called upon to vote at a distance, one of two consequences will ensue: either they will not vote at all, or they will find means to shift upon some one else the expense of their journey. In the first case, the benefit of their judgment is lost: in the second, solicitation, intrigue, and preponderance of the half-qualified rich man, are revived and rendered available. It is essential to any good system of voting, that an elector should vote at or near the place of his habitual residence. Any parish, any fraction of a parish, or any cluster of parishes, which comprised 200 voters, might have a separate polling-place, with proper apparatus: ten such being combined to form one returning body. Less than 200 (or such a proportion of them as chose to come) ought not to make use of the same ballotting-box: with a number smaller than this, secrecy could not be effectually guaranteed. All the votes might thus be taken on the same day, with little inconvenience to any one, and hardly any necessary expense.

The existing distinction into Town and County Elections, without any reference to the number of voters contained in each county or in each town, appears to me indefensible and injurious in every way. The grand circumstance to be considered in the electoral sub-divisions is the number of voters included in each returning body, so as to ensure that no Member enters the House of Commons who has not obtained a certain minimum of votes, and so as to equalize, besides, the value of each man's vote, or the elective force vested in each voter. For, if one man votes in a returning body of 200, and another in a returning body of 2000,—the vote of the first is worth ten times as much as the vote of the second: and comparing the elective force assigned to each, or the total effect which each is allowed to produce upon the representative body, the result is, as if the first man had ten votes and the second only one. It is obvious that such inequality, if pushed to a certain extent, would of itself be enough to corrupt a system of representation involving all the other requisite conditions; nor can any reason be given why even a small inequality should be allowed.

When the voters are polled in small fractions, at different places, and all on the same day, the enormous evils attending populous elections as now transacted would altogether disappear. The saturnalia of our present elections are enough to shock any reasonable man, and to alienate him, not only from the external show of popular control, but even from the people themselves. The riot, drunkenness, and fighting in the streets, form an appropriate parallel and accompaniment to the low manœuvres of electioneering leaders behind the scenes. Yet there are those who contend that these disgraceful and noxious tumults are essential to the existence of public spirit, and that they serve to nurture both the sublime emotions and the sense of mutual right and duty which connect a man with his fellow-citizens. To me they appear no less inconsistent with genuine patriotism than with private decency. A great public question is discredited and rolled in the dirt by being converted into the war-whoop of a hired mob, in whom the fiction of a public concern serves only to supersede the restraints of private life, without substituting any better feeling than that of devotion to their temporary employer. The band of *sicarii* organised by Clodius against his enemies at Rome could not be more destitute of attachment to the public welfare. Indeed, the whole transaction is more akin to a pugilistic contest or a horse race, than to a selection between two opponents, each professing to be qualified for the grandest function which society has to fill up. The resemblance would be complete in almost all points, if the backers of pugilists were to carry into the ring banners inscribed with some popular question or high sounding abstract word :—Dutch Sam and the Revolution of 1688! Neal and Purity of Election! When the knuckles and wind of Dutch Sam had achieved a triumph, his friends would retire, confirmed in their attachment to the Revolution of 1688, and exulting in the idea that the victory just gained would do much to imprint its benefits on the public mind.

There are some few cases of exception, even as matters are at present, where the population really take a sincere interest in the event of the election. But the evil of fixing one single place of voting, and of congregating men in large numbers about it, is still very great, though of a different character. Inflamed by one common sentiment, the crowd cannot be restrained from venting, either by words or by action, their antipathy against opposite voters, who are abused or pelted, so as to drive away the timid, and to furnish a pretence to the indolent for remaining at home. Such bursts of wrath, where no effective and tranquil system of control has as yet been organised on behalf of the people, may perhaps be pardonable against a flagitious statesman : against a private citizen, they are altogether vicious and inexcusable, and they fatally counteract the salutary lesson, so hardly learnt by any one, of tolerance towards disinterested dissent. Nor does an election, so taken, exhibit a fair result of the judgment of all the voters nominally appealed to.

Every evil incidental to elections would be done away with, and the efficacy of the system as a means to good government greatly strengthened, if voters polled secretly, in small bodies, and in different places at the same time.

E

One more addition remains to be made to the essentials of Parliamentary Reform:—increased frequency of election. A peaceful citizen, accustomed to elections as they are now, may well feel repugnant to such invasions of his comfort at shorter periods; but when it has been shown that voting may be so conducted as to molest no man's tranquillity, a most injurious prepossession will be dispelled, on this truly important part of the field.

Election for seven years certain has almost the same effect as election for life. So faintly is the imagination affected by a contingency seven years removed, that if a man can be trusted to do well for that long period, he might also be trusted to do well, though chosen for life. What would be said of the prudence of any one, who, having selected a particular attorney or physician, should enter into a contract binding himself to resort to no other for the same space of seven years? Would he not be universally considered to have taken the most effectual measure for making them remiss and indifferent?

On the other hand we find, in the actual course of affairs, that although a man may change his lawyer or physician any day, he very rarely does change: because these practitioners, knowing that if they do not give satisfaction, they will immediately lose business, take care to be attentive and zealous in their duty.

I think it may be stated, as a general fact, that when a trust is revocable at pleasure, the person entrusted acts so as not to deserve displacement, and in general is not displaced.

This is precisely what we desire to see happen with respect to Members of Parliament: and the mode of ensuring it will be, as in other cases, by conferring on them their trust for very short fixed periods. One year, in my opinion, would be quite sufficient, and better than any longer period: two years would be tolerable; three years seriously objectionable on account of its length; and any period longer than three years not to be entertained for a moment.

Many persons are alarmed at the idea of annual elections,

as if they imported actual change of members every year. This would, indeed, be a very formidable evil,—an evil only less than that of retaining dishonest or incompetent members. I feel persuaded that their real operation would be directly the reverse: that a member would retain his seat longer under annual elections than under any other, because the security for his good conduct would be so much more complete. The ideas of accountability and obligation, and the necessity of maintaining a high reputation with the public, could never be absent from his mind: the shortness of the period would leave him little hope of making up the negligence of one month by increased diligence during the remainder; and as he would indulge a reasonable hope of re-election, if he only avoided occasioning painful disappointment to his constituents, the motives to zeal and good conduct would be really at their maximum. If a man possesses the confidence of an electoral body in 1831, and is under such paramount and continuous motives to do his very best, can he be supposed likely to lose it in 1832, except by some most rare and unusual occurrence? On the other hand, if the certain duration of his trust be lengthened, the motives to the best possible discharge of it are proportionally enfeebled, and he is more likely to do or to omit something whereby he would deserve to forfeit, and would really forfeit, the confidence of his constituents. It is only under the shorter duration that the desirable result will be ensured, of members being continued, simply because they deserve to be continued, in possession of their trust.

Some persons apprehend that annual elections would make a member too attentive to the approaching end of his trust, and that they would subjugate the independence of his private judgment too much to the voters by whom he was to be re-chosen or displaced. But it is to be recollected that a voting section constituted as I have supposed—voting by ballot, in small divisions, and without any separate local tie—would be nothing more than a fraction of the general public, and that, consequently, the same behaviour which

E 2

sustained his reputation with the general public, would
also sustain it with his own peculiar voters. The only
prejudices, therefore, to which he will be called upon
to bend, are those of the general public. To these
every man must bend, more or less: and the only person
who can hope to combat them effectually and beneficially,
will be he who has established a high reputation on other
grounds for wisdom and virtue. The motive to establish and
sustain such a reputation will be highest in the bosom of
the member chosen for a year, whose authority will therefore
will be the greater when he stands up against any special
prejudice. Nor do I imagine that he would be backward in
such an opposition, so far as prudence will permit. For if
he timidly chimes in with the prejudice, and if some bolder
rival takes out of his hands the task of enlightening the
public, comparative discredit is sure to await him. The
path of evasion will be found hardly less dangerous, and far
less elevating and satisfactory, than that of sincerity.

Perhaps it may be contended, that according to the
principles on which I have reasoned, annual elections would
not be sufficiently frequent, and that monthly elections
ought to be regarded as still better. To this I reply, first,
that monthly elections would be a vast additional trouble to
voters, without any adequate benefit. Secondly, that there
are reasons which make a year preferable for this purpose
to any shorter period. For it is desirable that the voters,
when they exercise their privilege of re-choosing a member,
should fix their eyes on his general reputation for worth and
ability, more than on his conduct with reference to any
particular question. This general estimate is the resulting
impression, formed by surveying and laying to heart successively a series of his acts and speeches, assisted by the
criticisms which each of them may provoke from the organs
of public discussion. The seat of the member ought, therefore, to be assured for a period sufficiently long to include a
certain number of various acts and speeches, so as to serve as
a basis for that general estimate on which the voters ought

to proceed, and so as to prevent their judgment from being unduly absorbed by any one particular question. A year, in my opinion, is long enough to answer this condition perfectly, and short enough to keep alive the most earnest sense of obligation in the bosom of the member.

Though I regard a year as the best period, and any period longer than two years as seriously objectionable, yet I am far from denying that even triennial parliaments would be a prodigious improvement, in comparison with septennial, which are, as I have before observed, scarcely less pernicious than nominations for life.

The conditions, then, of an effectual Parliamentary Reform, without alarming the middling classes by multiplying very poor voters in their present state of intelligence, are the following :—

1. An aggregate of voters not less than one million, formed of all persons enjoying the largest income. It has been stated that a pecuniary qualification of £100 annual income would embrace one million of voters: whether this be the fact or not, can only be verified by actual returns : but I think the qualification ought to be so adjusted as to be sure of embracing such an aggregate.

2. This aggregate of one million distributed into electoral divisions of equal or nearly equal numbers, coinciding as little as possible with separate class interests, or local interests, and each voting for one member.

3. Electors to vote by ballot: in small bodies and at separate polling places, yet so that no body smaller than 200 shall be assigned to the same ballotting-box. Each election to be concluded in one day.

4. Parliaments on no consideration longer than triennial : better far, if biennial : better still, if annual.

By these provisions alone, an enormous and incalculable gain would be assured : but, to render them quite complete, they ought to be accompanied with a farther provision for gradually lowering the suffrage at the end of some fixed period, say five years, so as to introduce successively new voters at the end of every five years, and to render the suffrage at the end of twenty or twenty-five years, nearly co-extensive with the community. The interval would be more than sufficient so to educate and prepare the minds of the poorer voters, as to obviate all ground for alarm on the part of the richer.

It is but too certain, however, that we shall not at the present moment acquire even our million of voters with the requisite accompanying precautions: so that it becomes a matter important to determine, since all of the first four provisions cannot be obtained, which of them can be least injuriously postponed, and which of them ought to be most strenuously insisted on.

Whatever else may be postponed, let no man for a moment think of laying aside the Ballot. This is the vast and grand amendment, in the absence of which every other concession would be unavailing and nugatory. Without secret voting there cannot be public-minded voting: and without public-minded voting, men worthy to be legislators can neither be singled out nor preferred—scarcely even created. Under a numerous and equally distributed open suffrage, it is possible that the mutes and idlers in the present House might be replaced by active and stirring gentlemen, and that what Mr. Tennyson calls "the inert physical mass" of the House might thus be lightened. But the voters, though increased in number, would still persist in their rooted habit of voting from desire to oblige, from fear to offend, or from personal sympathy or kindness of one description or another: the election committee and the canvass would still be the grand instruments of success; and the most promising candidate would be he who, steering his political course midway between truth and falsehood, so as to offend no one, could create the most favourable impression by seducing manners, by overflowing politeness, and by officious attentions. It is not from such a school that the men are to be drawn, under whose guardianship we may lay down our heads in peace, and to whose mandates or exactions we should cheerfully submit, under the conviction that they emanated from tried wisdom and benevolence. It is only when the vote, secured by secrecy, stands upon grounds quite distinct from the ordinary track of private affections and sympathies, that the elector will look out for that assemblage of public qualities which the magnitude of the trust really calls for. Then only will such qualities be sought, and then only will they be found.

To gain the Ballot, it would be amply worth while to make concessions as to the number of voters, if we were compelled to take our choice between the two. Though I could not place full confidence in an aggregate of voters much smaller than a million, I should greatly prefer 500,000 voters, qualified by superiority of income, along with the Ballot, to 2,000,000 of voters without it. If the House of Commons were reduced in number to 300, an aggregate of 500,000 voters would allow of 1660 voters for each electoral division. A suffrage, narrowed even to this nearly oligarchical limit, but accompanied by the Ballot and by triennial parliaments, would afford a great and salutary opening to superior minds and to men of public reputation, and a comfortable foretaste of better things to come.

NOTICE

OF

SIR WILLIAM MOLESWORTH'S EDITION

OF THE

WORKS OF HOBBES.

(*The 'Spectator' Newspaper*, 1839.)

THE philosophical public are much indebted to Sir William Molesworth for this new edition of the works of Hobbes,[*] which he is in course of publishing, and of which two volumes, one English and one Latin, are now lying on our table.

A complete body of the works of this eminent man has become almost unattainable. No full and authorised collection of them was ever published: and the only two partial collections that appeared—the two Latin volumes in quarto, printed at Amsterdam in 1668, and the English volume in folio, printed in London in 1750—are each very scarce and extravagantly dear. There are, besides, many other tractates, which exist only in their separate state, and cannot be procured at all without much difficulty. No new edition, even of the best and most instructive of Hobbes's treatises, has ever been presented to the public for the last century and a half, with the single exception of the English folio in 1750. This neglect is not very creditable to the intellectual character of the nation; and the causes of it, when we trace them out

---

[*] *Thomæ Hobbes Malmesburiensis Opera Philosophica quæ Latine scripsit Omnia,* in unum corpus nunc primum collecta studio et labore Gulielmi Molesworth. Vol. I.

The English Works of Thomas Hobbes of Malmesbury; now first collected and edited by Sir William Molesworth, Bart. Vol. I.

in detail, suggest very discouraging conclusions as to the spirit infused into the English reading classes by our systems of education.

It is indeed true, that, in regard to physical and mathematical researches, Hobbes and all his contemporaries (if we except only Newton) have been so much outstripped and left behind by succeeding inquirers, as to leave to their works no other interest than that of historical curiosity. There is, moreover, interspersed throughout the works of Hobbes, a good deal of the theological polemics so fashionable in his time—controversies respecting the interpretation of Scriptural passages, and attempts to show that his conclusions in morals and politics are sustained by the authority of the sacred writings, or at least are perfectly reconcileable with that authority. In the same age, and in a similar spirit, Algernon Sydney, throughout his 'Treatise on Government,' seeks to demonstrate at length that Democracy is the form of polity which the Scriptures especially sanction. Such references to the facts and sayings of the Bible, although they have now passed out of date and are no longer regarded as relevant to political discussions, were almost universal in the controversies of the seventeenth century.

These considerations in part explain the little attention which has been paid to Hobbes's writings by the ages which have succeeded him. But let it be observed, that both the imperfection in the mode of physical reasoning and the intermixture of Scriptural polemics, is more predominant in the writings of Lord Bacon than in those of Hobbes; yet the former nevertheless occupies a prominent place in the library of reading men, and is constantly cited with a kind of superstitious reverence as the "Master of Wisdom," to use an expression of the late Sir James Mackintosh, in his Preliminary Dissertation to the Encyclopædia. There is doubtless much of striking remark, of enlarged anticipation and of aphoristic and illustrative expression, scattered throughout Lord Bacon's works; but we venture to affirm, that in all those qualities which go to make up the philosophical investigator—in the clear apprehension and searching analysis of intellectual difficulties, in systematic following out of deductions from his premises, in perspicuous exposition of the most perplexed subjects, and in earnest application of his mind to the discovery of the truth, whether the truth when attained be of a welcome or of an unwelcome character—in all these great mental endowments, the superiority of Hobbes to Bacon is most decisive and unquestionable. If we look even for short and pithy sentences, fit to be quoted with effect, we shall find at least as many in the works of the former as in those of the latter.

To what causes, then, are the marked neglect and the comparative discredit of Hobbes to be attributed ? Had the tendency of English education been such as to inspire the reading public with any sincere love of truth, or with any serious anxiety to verify their own conclusions on the most important topics connected with human society—had it not been unfortunately the fact, as Bishop Butler has remarked, that even amongst the number of persons who desire to know *what has been said,* not one in a hundred cares to find out *what is true*—we are persuaded that the moral, the metaphysical, and the political works of Hobbes would have been considered as entitled to a very distinguished place in the esteem of every instructed man. For, in order to peruse them with interest and advantage, it is by no means necessary that the reader should sit down with the submissive faith of a disciple, or that he should acquiesce implicitly in the conclusions which he finds laid out for him. No frame of mind can be less suitable for the perusal of Hobbes, who addresses himself exclusively to the rational convictions of every man, and who disdains, more perhaps than any other philosopher ancient or modern, all indirect and underhand methods of procuring mere passive adhesion. There is a fearless simplicity and straightforwardness in his manner, which, while it conveys his own meaning without reserve, operates at the same time most powerfully to awaken a train of original reflection in the reader ; and this fruit of his writings, rare and valuable to the last degree, is admitted even by the least friendly critics. "Hobbes is a writer," says Dugald Stewart, "who redeems his wildest paradoxes by the new lights which he strikes out in defending them." Mr. Stewart's eulogy is qualified by a censure which is altogether undeserved ; for there is nothing in Hobbes's opinions which can with any justice be called *wild paradox.* There are some conclusions which are untrue, and others which are only partially true; there are also some which appear to be paradoxical because the qualifications necessary to be annexed to them are not carefully stated. The most unsound of all his opinions is the fiction of an original covenant as the proximate basis of government and of its obligations ; but this is neither a discovery of his own nor does he stand at all alone in the support of it.

The remark just cited from Dugald Stewart, less unjust, indeed, than the greater number of the criticisms levelled at Hobbes, exhibits one of the many impediments which have circumscribed the reputation and the influence of this eminent thinker amongst those who succeeded him. He dared to depart from received opinions ; and not only from those opinions which were current among the Aristotelians of his own day (for that would have been considered by Mr. Stewart as a title to admiration), but also from the opinions prevalent among the greater number of metaphysical writers of the present day, and which the Scotch school, the least analytical of all writers who ever meddled with philosophy, have taken under their especial protection.

But it is not simply to his deviation from received and popular methods of thinking, that the subsequent discredit of Hobbes as a philosopher is to be attributed. He not only questioned customary prejudices, but he also exasperated powerful classes of men, and especially that class which is rarely offended with impunity—the priests. It was essential to his principles of government to prove that there could be only one supreme power in the state, and that the ecclesiastical power both must be and ought to be subordinate to

the civil. Such a doctrine was well calculated to rouse the
antipathies both of the Roman Catholic and of the Pres-
byterian clergy; but we might have expected that the clergy
of the Church of England would have listened to it with
patience since they could not well forget that their brethren,
from the time of Henry the Eighth down to Elizabeth, had
altered more than once both their faith and their discipline
in obedience to the secular authority. Yet so it happened,
that the clergy of the Church of England were no less
irritated than the Roman Catholics with this doctrine of the
inherent supremacy of the civil power; and Hobbes became
the object of fierce hatred from ecclesiastics of all denominations. He tells us, in his own curious autobiography,
written in Latin verse, which appears in the first volume of
Sir William Molesworth's edition, page xciv—

> " *Leviathan* clerum at totum mihi fecerat hostem ;
> Hostis Theologûm nidus uterque fuit.
> Nam dum Papalis Regni contrecto tumorem,
> Hos, licet abscissos, lædere visus eram.
> Contra Leviathan, primo, convicia scribunt,
> Et causa, ut tantò plus legeretur, erant."

Whatever effect the clergy may have unintentionally produced in promoting the circulation of the ' Leviathan ' during
Hobbes's life, has been effectually reversed since his death.
Their unanimous outcry has branded him with the stigma of
impiety and atheism, and placed his writings on the index
of prohibited books. Nevertheless, there is not, so far as
we are aware, a single sentence in his writings which either
discloses such sentiments in himself, or is calculated to inspire them in others: the tone in which he speaks both of
religion and of the Divine Being is uniformly reverential.
But the denunciations of the clergy, however unfounded,
have not been the less successful: the works of Hobbes have
been decried as irreligious, and this is one powerful reason
why they have been comparatively so little studied. We
may add, that Hobbes incurred the enmity of the clergy, not

simply by overthrowing their pretensions to a jurisdiction independent of the civil power, but also by exposing their glaring defects as teachers of youth and administrators of the Universities. The passages in which this exposure is performed are among the most striking and emphatic of all his writings.

It might have been anticipated that the man who incurred so much obloquy by his protest against sacerdotal ascendency, would at least have been signally extolled by that civil power the importance of which he took so much pains to magnify. But no such countenance was shown to him. And it is a remarkable testimony to the single-minded purpose and really philanthropic spirit which pervade his works, that they have never found favour with the commonplace rulers of mankind. A sovereign like Frederick the Second of Prussia, both animated with beneficent intentions towards his subjects and possessing sufficient force of personal character to conceive and work out his designs, might perhaps take delight in the relation of subject and government as depicted by Hobbes. But the monarchical form, as it has commonly existed, and still continues to exist, in most countries of Europe, has been a government not of the monarch alone, but of the monarch in confederacy with various powerful classes and fraternities, which have aided him in keeping down the people, and whose interest has been much more at variance with the public good than the interest of the monarch himself.

Now the doctrine of Hobbes, despotic as it may be, is at any rate an equalizing doctrine; not sanctioning the enthronement of any favoured or predominant class to intercept for themselves the rays emanating from the governing power, but enforcing a like claim on the part of every subject to partake in this common benefit. Such recognition of a supreme power nakedly and simply, apart from its accompanying congeries of auxiliary sinister interests, and exerting itself without favour or preference for the protection of the entire people, might have found favour at court had it been published under the vigorous and self-directing Queen Elizabeth; but it was not likely to be of much avail to its author, either during the precarious tenure of the Commonwealth or amidst the intrigues and personal helplessness of Charles the Second.* In truth, it is this repudiation of all

* The *Leviathan* was published in London in 1652, during the time of the Commonwealth, while Charles the Second was an exile at Paris, and while Hobbes was at Paris also. The expatriated Royalists who surrounded Charles, many of them zealous Churchmen and scholars of the Universities, read it with the strongest repugnance, and denounced it as an apology for Cromwell. Hobbes became the object of their bitter enmity, and was even forbidden to appear in presence of the young king, though he had previously officiated as his mathematical teacher. So violent was the enmity of the Royalists, that Hobbes was actually afraid that they would assassinate him; and he called to mind the fate of Dr. Dorislaus and Mr. Ascham, ambassadors of the English Commonwealth at the Hague and Madrid, who had both been murdered by Royalist assassins in those capitals. Such was his apprehension, that he, the loyal tutor of Charles the Second, found himself compelled to leave Paris immediately, and to seek protection under the Commonwealth of England. It was mid-winter, and the snow was on the ground: he had to undertake the journey at this inclement season, though he was then sixty-four years of age, with bad roads and upon a tumbledown horse. On arriving in London he reported himself to the Council of State; who did not in any way molest him: every man in England (he says) might study or write what he chose, provided he would be content to live "more loci." His own account of these events—his estimate of the morality of the Royalists, and his idea of the character of those councillors by whom both Charles the First and Charles the Second were guided —is eminently curious:—

> " Lutetiam ad regem multis venit inde scholaris
>   Expulsus patriâ, tristis, egenus, onus.
> Huc fuit usque meis studiis pax, multiplicata
>   Dum facerent annos octo per octo meos :
> Sed meus ille liber [*i. e.* Leviathan] simul atque scholaribus illis
>   Lectus erat, Jani dissiluêre fores.
> Nam Regi accusor falsò, quasi facta probarem
>   Impia Cromwelli, jus scelerique darem.

F

idea of privileged classes—falsely calling themselves checks upon the supreme power, but in reality fraternising with it and perverting it to their own purposes—which has contributed to render the political theories of Hobbes odious in England, quite as much as his denial of constitutional securities to the people at large. He has paid the forfeit of his anti-oligarchical as much as of his anti-popular tendencies.

Again, it is a standing reproach against his political writings, that they degrade the dignity of mankind: and this imputation may be well founded, if we compare them with the best and most liberal theories of government. But if we compare them with any political doctrines which have ever been generally recognised or practically acted upon in England, we shall find them the very reverse of degrading. The system of Hobbes is based wholly upon the willing and deliberate submission of the people to their existing rulers; which he professes to obtain simply by appealing to their reason, and by demonstrating that submission is essential to their safety as well as to their comfort. Such a doctrine both supposes and favours the widest diffusion of intelligence among the body of the people; and the French Economists, who reproduced a similar system in the last half of the eighteenth century, laid greater stress upon this necessary basis of universal instruction, than upon any other part of their reasonings. Contrast the state of passive and animal subservience to which the non-voting multitude have always been held bound in the theories most current among English

Creditur; adversis in partibus esse videbar;
Perpetuò jubeor Regis abesse domo.
Tunc *venit in mentem mihi Dorislaus, et Ascham
Tanquam proscripto terror ubique aderat.*
Nec do rege queri licuit. *Nam tunc adolescens
Credidit ille, quibus credidit antè pater.*
In patriam redeo tutelæ non benè certus,
Sed nullo potui tutior esse loco:
Frigus erat, nix alta, senex ego, ventus acerbus;
Vexat equus sternax et salebrosa via."—(P. xciii.)

politicians, with the rational obedience and exercised understanding supposed by Hobbes and the French Economists,
and we are very sure that it is not the latter who will
appear chargeable with inculcating principles debasing to the
human race. The persons most interested in these writings,
within our own observation, have usually been men of Radical
principles, who entertained the loftiest ideas both of the
functions of government and of the possible training of
the people—men who agreed with Hobbes in his antipathy
to those class-interests which constitute the working forces
of modern pseudo-representative monarchy—but who differed
from him by thinking that their best chance for combining
rational submission on the part of the governed with enlarged
and beneficent views on the part of the governors, was to be
found in a well-organised representative system.

The moral and metaphysical doctrines of Hobbes have not
escaped similar charges to those which have been advanced
against his politics. He deduced all the passions, appetites,
and sympathies of man from the simple feelings of pleasure
and pain; he derived moral obligation from the rational
desire entertained by every man of his own conservation and
happiness; he judged of moral right and wrong by the test
of utility. These doctrines are disagreeable to a large proportion of readers and writers, as giving a degrading representation of the human race; and the censure which they
have drawn upon the author has been another of the causes
which have operated to restrict the circle of his readers.
Woe to the philosopher who will not condescend to flatter in
his picture of man! Divines in the pulpit may depict the
incorrigible wickedness of man in the darkest and most overcharged colours, and their sermons are extolled by every
religious person; but let any moralist so conduct his analysis
of the human heart, as to bring out a result not congenial
to the sympathies of sentimentalists, and he sets the reading
public against him; he is refuted beforehand, or worse than
refuted, for he is laid aside unread. It seems to us that this
disposition—to test metaphysical tenets by examining, not

whether they are true and can be substantiated by sufficient
evidence, but whether the admission of them as truths would
tend to exhibit man as a better and more admirable being—
has become more fashionable of late years than ever it was
before ; at least it has been largely adopted by the Scotch
metaphysicians, as well as by the modern French school (an
emanation from the Scotch), in their multiplied attacks on
the French philosophy of the eighteenth century. And
the frequency of such attacks is to us a proof that, however
much physical science, which has no adverse predispositions
to conquer, may have been enlarged and perfected in its
details, there is very little of reverence among us for the
purity of philosophical truth. For the argument really involved in this mode of handling the question is, that the
truth or falsehood of any position in morals is a matter of
small moment; that although it be true, it ought to be
stifled and put down, if the belief of it would tend to lower
our estimate of human nature ; and that although it be false,
it ought to be held sacred and unquestioned, if it would lead
us to entertain a higher notion of our species. This is not
indeed expressly stated, perhaps it is not deliberately intended, by those who run down Hobbes as preaching tenets
debasing to human nature; but unless it be assumed as a
postulate, the cry against him on such a ground can have
neither force nor meaning.

To admit or reject particular doctrines, not on account of
the weight of affirmative or negative evidence, but on account
of the inferences to which they may give rise respecting the
excellence or turpitude of human nature, is in effect to sub-
vert the whole scientific edifice of moral and metaphysical
philosophy—to degrade the science into a mere assemblage
of conventional fictions, which it is dangerous to scrutinise
and criminal to overthrow. The less analytical philosophers
have been generally but too ready to employ this method
of discrediting those who pushed the process of analysis
further than themselves, unconscious that they were at the
same time undermining the fabric and destroying the trust-

worthiness even of such doctrines as were common to both. If Hobbes had spoken of human nature in terms of the most stinging Cynicism, or with the sternness of an Antinomian divine, it would still have been unworthy of sound philosophy to employ this method of refuting him ; but, in reality, he has dealt in no such unmeasured censure. He speaks of mankind like a shrewd and penetrating observer, applying his remarkable powers of analysis to the phenomena which he saw before him. Sir James Mackintosh complains that Hobbes "strikes the affections out of his map of human nature:" and others have alleged in like manner that he denies the existence of any benevolence in man, because he treats the benevolent as well as the other affections as being not inherent or original, but as derivative, and resolvable into the primary sentiments of pleasure and pain. It is common with metaphysicians of the Scotch school to represent such a doctrine as tantamount to a denial of the existence and efficacy of the benevolent affections: but this is a great injustice; for our compound and derivative feelings are just as real, and just as much a part of human nature, as our simple and original feelings. And it would be full as reasonable to say that Bishop Berkeley, when he showed that the perception of distance by the eye was not original, but acquired, denied the reality of the visual power in human nature—as to accuse Hobbes of disputing the fact that there *were* benevolent affections, because he disputes their title to originality.

Undeserved as the accusations against Hobbes are, they have been repeated by so many mouths, and echoed so loudly by the many powerful classes whose hostility he provoked, that he has been condemned to comparative oblivion and discredit with posterity: a memorable contrast to the incessant controversial attack of which he was the object throughout the greater part of his life. He followed the impulse of his own fearless and original intellect, without taking any pains to conciliate the distributors of fame ; and assuredly he has found no mercy at their hands. The injustice of which they have been guilty towards him, however, may even yet be partially repaired; at least the chance of such reparation will be increased by this new and convenient edition of his works.

The long life of Hobbes, from 1588 to 1679, covered most remarkable changes both in politics and in philosophy. He was the son of a clergyman at Malmesbury; was sent early to Oxford; and was recommended on leaving Magdalen College to be the fellow-student and companion of the Earl of Devonshire, with whom he passed no less than twenty years, until the Earl's decease,—years, as he himself says, by far the happiest of his whole life, which often afforded him grateful dreams in his old age; for he had ample leisure, a large command of books, and the opportunity of travelling with his patron and friend over a large portion of the Continent. On the death of this nobleman, after a short interval spent at Paris, he officiated as tutor to the young Earl; in which capacity he remained seven years, partly occupied in travelling with his pupil. His studies during this early part of his life seem to have been chiefly classical and literary; and it was during this period that he executed his translation of Thucydides, in whom he delighted more than in any other Grecian author, and who confirmed him in that aversion · to democracy and civil broils to which his constitutional timidity naturally predisposed him. It was not before the age of forty that he began to addict himself to mathematical or philosophical studies. When about that age, according to Aubrey, in the library of a friend he accidentally opened a copy of Euclid at the 47th Proposition of the 1st Book; and on reading the Theorem, he was so astonished that he exclaimed —" By God, this is impossible!" nor was he satisfied until he had studied the preceding demonstrations back to the commencement. From henceforward his meditations were largely turned towards mathematics and physics; a disposition which was much encouraged by the conversation of Father Mersenne at Paris. Father Mersenne formed the centre of a philosophical society in that capital; and Hobbes dwells with delight and gratitude both on his devotion to science, and on the disinterested zeal with which he bent himself to promote the studies of his friends. The physical and mathematical reasonings of Hobbes were embodied in the treatise 'De Corpore;' the completion of which, however, was long postponed and much interrupted, first by the treatise 'De Cive,' next by the 'Leviathan,' lastly by the essays 'On Human Nature' and 'De Corpore Politico.' The last two, together with the 'Discourse on Liberty and Necessity,' constitute what is called the 'Tripos.'

In 1640, he quitted England for Paris, in consequence of the menacing aspect of politics and the approach of the civil war. In 1652, the offence caused to the Royalists at Paris by the publication of the 'Leviathan' compelled him, as we have already mentioned, to return to England; which he never afterwards quitted. His declining years, to the time of his death, were passed at Chatsworth. The former Earl of Devonshire, with whom he had passed twenty years as a companion, had bequeathed to him an annuity, which sufficed for his very modest wants, and even enabled him to make over his small landed patrimony to his nephew.

We have left ourselves no space for any detailed account of the contents of the two volumes which Sir William Molesworth has already published. The treatise 'De Corpore' is contained in both, the Latin in one, the English in the other: to the first is prefixed his Latin biography, together with the 'Vitæ Hobbianæ Aucturium,' which had already appeared in the previous folio edition. We will only remark, that the first two sections of the treatise 'De Corpore,' entitled 'Computatio, sive Logica,' and 'Philosophia Prima,' appear to us among the most instructive and valuable of his works; exhibiting a rare combination of analytical sagacity with condensed and perspicuous expression, and assisting most powerfully to unravel those extreme abstractions, without the comprehension of which no man can successfully cope with the difficulties of mental philosophy.

We trust it will enter into the scheme of Sir William

Molesworth to annex to his edition of this distinguished man
a critical biography and a coherent exposition of the sequence
and modifications of his philosophical tenets. The great lines
which connect them with each other are indeed sufficiently
marked out by Hobbes—De Corpore, De Homine, De Cive :
but much might be done by an able biographer in furnishing
the requisite illustrations and elucidations ; and a more
stirring period, either in politics or in philosophy, is scarcely
to be found throughout the range of history. It seems
highly probable, that if the English political troubles had
not broken out in 1640, the whole intellectual career of
Hobbes would have been greatly altered : he would have
been much more eminent as a mathematician and physical
philosopher, and much less known as a writer on politics.
Both the treatise 'De Cive' and the 'Leviathan' were the
direct offspring of the English civil war ; and he himself tells
us that they broke very unseasonably the continuity of his
mathematical and physical studies.

GRECIAN LEGENDS AND EARLY HISTORY.

(*Westminster Review*, 1843.)

THE short volume* which we here introduce to the notice of our readers derives its principal value from the great name of its author—a name which no man who takes interest in historical studies can pronounce without veneration and gratitude. If we regard Niebuhr with reference to erudition alone—copious, accurate, and available erudition—he occupies a place in the foremost rank, and few indeed are the authors entitled to a station along with him. But when we consider, besides, his wonderful ingenuity in combining scattered facts, his piercing eye for the detection of latent analogies, and for the separation of leading points of evidence from that crowd of accessories under which they often lie concealed, his power of recomposing the ancient world by just deduction from small fragments of history, like the inferences of Cuvier from the bones of fossil animals—when we take these rare mental attributes, operating upon the vast mass of materials which his erudition supplied to them, he seems to us to stand alone, even among so many distinguished countrymen and contemporaries. Moreover, the moral nature of Niebuhr was distinguished not only by a fearless love of truth, but by a quality yet more remarkable among literary men—by a hearty sympathy with the mass of the people—a disposition not simply to compassionate them as sentients, which is sufficiently common, but to ap-

---

* *Griechische Heroen Geschichten.* Von B. G. Niebuhr an seinen Sohn erzählt. Hamburg, 1842. *Grecian Heroic Stories;* related by B. G. Niebuhr to his Son.

preciate them candidly as agents,—to treat their sentiments
and motives with respect, and even their mistakes with
charitable censure. We are not disposed to maintain that
Niebuhr is always right in his judgments; far from it: but
even the errors of so original a mind are constantly suggestive; and we feel assured, that to every person who has
studied his writings with attention, the evidences respecting
the ancient world of Greece, as well as of Rome, will appear
in a point of view totally different to that in which they had
presented themselves before.

Like our own lamented Dr. Arnold, a worthy second both
in historiographic intellect and in moral candour, Niebuhr
was snatched from the world in the full maturity of his
career, before he had had time to bring his great work to
completion. To these two capital losses we have to add that
of K. O. Müller, best known to the English world by his
history of the Dorians—an author of great performance and
still greater promise, cut off in the prime of life, a victim to
his zeal for the prosecution of personal researches in Greece.
Fatally have the arrows of Apollo told, during the last few
years, among the chiefs of the classical camp!

The volume before us contains portions of the early heroic
legends of Greece, prepared by Niebuhr himself for the
special purpose of being recounted to his son Marcus, then a
very young boy. From a short preface by the son, who has
now published them, we learn the vivid and ineffaceable
impression which they made upon his youthful feelings;
enforced as the narratives were by the earnest interest both
of the father and of the philologer, and illustrated by those
references to the visible remains of antiquity which a residence in Rome abundantly furnished. Marcus Niebuhr
dwells emphatically on the delight which he recollects to
have felt when he discovered, or thought that he discovered,
the cave of Cacus on the Aventine Mount; and the endless
comparisons, suggested by his father's stories about Hercules, with the bas-reliefs and sarcophagi in the Vatican.

Niebuhr has prepared, for the object here described, three

separate narratives :—1. The expedition of the Argonauts.—
2. The various legends of Hercules.—3. The Heracleids and
Orestes :—but the narratives do, in point of fact, run over a
much wider field of Grecian heroology, comprising more or
less reference to the hunting of the Calydonian boar, the
two sieges of Thebes, and the second siege of Troy by
Agamemnon, as well as the first by Hercules. The recital
is simple, neat, and we may even say, touching ; displaying
great address in presenting the stories so as to be clearly
apprehended by a very young boy, and forming a remarkable
contrast to the difficulty which we often lament to find in
the style of his elaborate work. More interesting narratives,
for boy as well as man, no book of fairy tales can supply :
nor do we know where a father or a preceptor can find them
so fitly arrayed as in this affectionate memento of the
illustrious historian of Rome.

One farther merit they have, which we may call peculiarly
Niebuhrian. They are given in their literal integrity as
legends, instead of being squeezed and tortured into authentic history ; they preserve all the fanciful sequences,
the supernatural meddling, and the predominance of individual personality, which characterise the former, and are
no way tamed down into the measured march, the constant
laws of nature, and the political aim and agency, which
prevail throughout the latter. We call this distinction
between legend and history Niebuhrian, because we believe
that the first volume of the history of Rome originally
enforced it with fulness and efficiency on the literary world,
though it has now been adopted by various eminent names,
and has become at least extensively understood, though not
universally admitted. Dr. Arnold has carried it thoroughly
out in the early part of his Roman history, and Mr.
Macaulay, in the preface to his beautiful ‘ Lays of Ancient
Rome,’ has illustrated it by many striking observations, to
which we rejoice to think that his book will give extensive
currency.

Dr. Thirlwall's ‘ History of Greece,’ in which the primitive

ages are most correctly appreciated, and the translation of
K. O. Müller's 'History of the Dorians,' ought to have
familiarised the English reader with the distinction between
legend and history in regard to Greece, no less than in
regard to Rome. But we suspect that the result produced
in this direction has hardly been commensurate with the
merit of these two excellent works. The idea of a basis of
authentic matter of fact, pervading the Grecian heroology,
and only transformed into the shape in which we read it by
amplification, or poetical ornament, or mistake,—is so deeply
rooted in the English mind, that reasonings on the opposite
side require to be often repeated before they work conviction. Certain it is that every youth who goes through a
classical education repeats the date of the sieges of Troy
and Thebes with as much confidence in the reality of those
events as in that of the siege of Syracuse by Nicias. Moreover, the recent work on Grecian chronology by Mr. Fynes
Clinton,—so full both of condensed learning and of valuable
reasoning in respect to the historical ages,—retains to a
great degree what we think ancient errors in regard to the
heroic ages; it carries up the series of real personages to a
period 800 years earlier than the first Olympiad, and it
recites even Hercules, the hero of these tales of Niebuhr,
and Phoroneus, the Argeian Adam, as if they were certified
flesh and blood, the genuine predecessors of those who lived
and moved during the Peloponnesian war; while the partial
concessions which the author makes to the opposite opinion
serve only to render his remaining positions inconsistent as
well as untenable. Considering the well-earned authority
of Mr. Clinton's Chronology, we think it not altogether
superfluous to employ a few pages in illustrating the true character of early Grecian history; and the Heroen Geschichten
of Niebuhr forms a suitable text to awaken such reflections.

Obvious as the remark seems, it still requires to be repeated, we are sorry to say, in regard to Grecian history—
that the *onus probandi* as to every alleged matter of fact
rests upon the historian.

Now, when any statement is brought before the public as alleged matter of fact, there is a disposition almost universal to believe, that, though the whole be not deserving of credit, a part of it at least must be true—that, though allowance is to be made, more or less as the case may be, for exaggeration or perversion, there must be some foundation of reality upon which the narrative has been raised. The maxim, "Fortiter calumniare, semper aliquid restat," is founded upon a just estimate of human impressibility : and the most mendacious and discredited newspaper exercises on the long run more influence over men's belief than they are at all willing to admit.

Taking this as a mere general presumption, we allow that it is more frequently correct than erroneous—at least with reference to contemporary matters, and in an age of copious historical investigation and criticism like the present. But though, under such limitations, we concede the reasonableness of the general presumption, we think that it is even now carried much farther than it ought to be. Distributing all the accredited narratives which float in society into three classes—accurate matter of fact, exaggerated matter of fact, and entire, though plausible, fiction—the last class will be found to embrace a very considerable proportion of the whole. They are tales which grow out of, and are accommodated to, the prevalent *emotions* of the public among whom they circulate : they exemplify and illustrate the partialities or antipathies, the hopes or fears, the religious or political sentiments of a given audience. There is no other evidence to certify them, indeed, except their plausibility : but that title is amply sufficient; the man who recounts what seems to fill up gaps or solve pre-existing difficulties in the minds of his hearers, runs little risk of being cal!ed upon to name an *auctor secundus* for his story. The love of new plausibility is as common as the love of genuine and ascertained truth is rare; questions of positive evidence are irksome to almost every one : and the historian, who desires general circulation, casts all such discussions into an appendix, of which he knows that the leaves will remain uncut. What is worse still—when one of these *verisimilia* has once been comfortably domiciled in a man's mind, if you proceed to apply to it the test of positive evidence, in all probability he will refuse to listen to you; but should you unhappily succeed in showing, that the story includes some chronological or geographical inconsistencies which no subtlety can evade, be assured that he will look upon you with emotions not very different from those with which he contemplates the dentist—if he be not ready "to bite you outright" (to use the homely phrase of Socrates in Plato's Theaetetus, c. 22), he will at least alter his course the next time he sees you afar off in the street.

To illustrate what we have just laid down—the genesis of this specious and plausible fiction, so radically distinct from exaggerated or misreported reality—we will cite an example having reference to a celebrated genius, not very long deceased. In the works of Lord Byron, published by Mr. Moore (vol. xi, p. 72), we find the 'Manfred' of the great English poet criticised by one greater than himself—by a person no less than Goethe. A portion of that criticism runs as follows:

" We find thus, in this tragedy, the quintessence of the most astonishing talent born to be its own tormentor. The character of Lord Byron's life and poetry hardly permits a just and equitable appreciation. He has often enough confessed what it is that torments him.——There are, properly speaking, two females whose phantoms for ever haunt him, and *which* [we cite the translation as we find it] in this piece also, perform principal parts—one under the name of Astarté,—the other without form or presence, and merely a voice. Of the horrid occurrence which took place with the former, the following is related:— *When a bold and enterprising young man, he won the affections of a Florentine lady. Her husband discovered the amour, and murdered his wife; but the murderer was the same night found dead in the street, and there was no one on whom suspicion could be attached. Lord Byron removed from Florence, and these spirits haunted him all his life after.* This romantic incident is rendered highly probable by innumerable allusions to it in his poems."

Such is Goethe's criticism; now come the remarks of Mr. Moore, the biographer and personal friend of Lord Byron.

" The grave confidence with which the venerable critic [Goethe] traces the fancies of his brother poet to real persons and events, making no difficulty even of a double murder at Florence to furnish grounds for his theory, affords an amusing instance of the disposition so prevalent throughout Europe to picture Byron as a man of marvels and mysteries, as well in his life as in his poetry. To these exaggerated, or wholly false, notions of him, *the numerous fictions palmed upon the world of his romantic tours and wonderful adventures in places he never saw, and with persons that never existed,* have no doubt considerably contributed ; and the consequence is, so *utterly out of truth and nature* are the representations of his life and character *long current on the Continent,* that it may be questioned whether the real 'flesh and blood' hero of these pages — the social, practical-minded, and, with all his faults and eccentricities, *English* Lord Byron—may not, to the over-exalted imaginations of most of his foreign admirers, appear but an ordinary, unromantic, and prosaic personage."

Here we have specimens of genuine legend or *mythus,* such as Hekatæus, Herodotus, and Thucydides, found so largely in possession of the Grecian mind, and such as even now, in the age of Blue Books and Statistical Societies, holds divided empire with reality—pullulating anew and in unexpected corners, as fast as the old plants are stifled by the legitimate seeds of history. It is not often that we have the opportunity of confronting thus nakedly the mythographer with the autoptic historian : and of demonstrating by so clear an example, that even where the mythical subject is indisputably real, the mythical predicates bear no resemblance to reality, but have their root in something generically different from actual matters of fact. Even with regard to places and persons in these narratives, the places were such as Byron had never seen, the persons such as had never existed.

Our readers, however, will not require to be told that the mythus differs essentially from accurate and well-ascertained

G

history. What we wish to enforce upon them is, that it differs not less essentially from *inaccurate* and *ill-ascertained* history; and the case just cited brings out the distinction forcibly. The story which Goethe relates of the intrigue and double murder at Florence, is not a mis-reported fact: it is a pure and absolute fiction. It is not a story of which one part is true and another part false, nor in which you can hope, by removing ever so much of superficial exaggeration, to reach at last a subsoil of reality. All is alike untrue, the basis as well as the details. In the mind of the original inventor, the legend derived its birth, not from any erroneous description which had reached his ears respecting adventures of the real Lord Byron, but from the profound and vehement impression which Lord Byron's poetry had made both upon him and upon all others around him. The poet appeared to be breathing out his own soul and sufferings in the character of his heroes—we ought rather to say of his hero, πολλῶν ὀνομάτων μορφὴ μία—he seemed like one struck down, as well as inspired, by some strange visitation of destiny. In what manner, and from what cause, had the Eumenides been induced thus to single him out as their victim? A large circle of deeply-moved readers, and amongst them the greatest of all German authors, cannot rest until this problem be solved: either a fact must be discovered, or a fiction invented, for the solution. The minds of all being perplexed by the same mystery and athirst for the same explanation, nothing is wanted except a *prima vox:* some one, more forward or more felicitous than the rest, imagines and proclaims the tragical narrative of the Florentine married couple. So happily does the story fit in, that the inventor seems only to have given clear utterance to that which others were dimly shadowing out in their minds: the lacerated feelings of the poet are no longer an enigma; the die which has stamped upon his verses their peculiar impress, has been discovered and exhibited to view. If, indeed, we ask what is the authority for the tale—to speak in the Homeric language, it has been suggested by some God, or by the airy-tongued Ossa, the bearer of encouragement and intelligence from Omniloquent Zeus;* to express the same idea in

---

* Homer, Odyss. i. 280 : Mentor advises Telemachus (also ii. 216)—

'Ερχεο πευσόμενος πατρὸς δὴν οἰχομένοιο·
'Ην τίς τοι εἴπῃσι βροτῶν, ἢ 'Οσσαν ἀκούσῃς
'Εκ Διὸς, ἥ τε μάλιστα φέρει κλέος ἀνθρώποισι.

So in the Iliad, ii. 95, when the heralds by Agamemnon's direction have proclaimed a public meeting, the Grecian soldiers crowd like bees to the agora :

'Ως τῶν ἔθνεα πολλὰ νεῶν ἄπο καὶ κλισιάων
'Ηϊόνος προπάροιθε βαθείης ἐστιχόωντο
'Ιλαδὸν εἰς ἀγορήν· μετὰ δέ σφισιν 'Οσσα δεδήει
'Οτρύνουσ' ἰέναι, Διὸς ἄγγελος.

'Οσσα ἄγγελος appears also in Odyss. xxiv. 413.

And Iliad, viii. 251—Omniloquent Zeus—

'Ενθα πανομφαίῳ Ζηνὶ ῥέζεσκον 'Αχαιοί.

Buttman (Lexilogus, sect. 9 ; compare also the Venetian Scholia ad Iliad. i. 105) is certainly right in distinguishing 'Οσσα in the Iliad and Odyssey, from φήμη or sometimes κληδών in the Homeric sense, which means a dictum, accidentally significant to the hearer of something which the speaker did not intend or think of, and therefore ominous. (Odyss. xviii. 117, xx. 100.) But we cannot admit that he is right in distinguishing 'Οσσα from θεοῦ ὀμφὴ (Il. xx. 129 ; Odyss. iii. 215), nor can we agree with him in thinking that 'Οσσα means "the general talk of men, the clamour of a multitude, as distinguished from the statement of some known individual." 'Οσσα in Homer is the voice proceeding from Zeus, heard only by some special person or persons for whom it is destined : the verb ὄσσομαι seems to denote the impression made upon the internal man by this divine agent, without any present or material cause, wherein sight is not clearly distinguished from hearing (Odyss. i. 115; xx. 81): a parallel to

" I hear a voice thou canst not hear,
That says I must not stay :
I see a form thou canst not see,
That beckons me away."

homely and infantine English, it has been whispered by a
little bird. But we may be pretty well assured that few of
the audience will raise questions about authority; the story

From hence the word ὄσσομαι passes to signify any vague, in-
distinct presentiment.

The φήμη of Hesiod (Opp. et D. 761) is different, and really
bears the meaning which Buttman assigns to the Homeric Ὄσσα—

Φήμη δ᾽ οὔτις πάμπαν ἀπόλλυται ἥντινα πολλοὶ
Λαοὶ φημίζουσι· θεός νύ τις ἐστὶ καὶ αὐτή.

Here the heavenly origin is struck off: the vox populi is exalted
into the vox Dei. Æschines, in a very curious passage too long to
be here cited, rather reverts to the old idea of Φήμη (cont. Timarch.
c. 27).

And in the account which Herodotus gives of the battle of
Mycalé, we have the Homeric Ὄσσα, the messenger of Zeus,
decidedly reproduced. The battle of Mycalé on the coast of Asia
Minor, and that of Platæa in Bœotia, were fought on the same
day: the former in the afternoon—the latter in the morning.
Previous to the onset at Mycalé, the Greeks were in much apprehension respecting their countrymen in Bœotia, who were exposed
to the very superior force under Mardonius. But just as the
Mycalean Greeks were preparing to attack, "there flew into the
whole camp a voice, and a herald's staff appeared lying on the
beach: and the voice went through them to this effect, that the
Greeks in Bœotia were then conquering the army of Mardonius.
Many indeed are the evidences by which divine phenomena
manifest themselves; since on this occasion, the defeats of Mycalé
and Platæa happening on the same day, the voice came over to the
Greeks in Asia so as to inspire new courage into their army."—
Herod. ix. 100: ἰοῦσι δέ σφι φήμη τε ἐσέπτατο ἐς τὸ στρατόπεδον
πᾶν—φήμη τοῖσι Ἕλλησιν ἐσαπίκετο. Ἦν δὲ ἀρρωδίη σφι πρὶν
τὴν φήμην ἐσαπικέσθαι—ὡς μέντοι ἡ κληδὼν αὕτη σφι ἐσέπτατο—
ix. 101.

The Φήμη or κληδὼν of Herodotus, is a voice sent by the Gods
across the Ægeian sea, to make known to the Asiatic Greeks the
victory then just accomplished by their brethren in Bœotia. The
difference between Herodotus and Homer is chiefly this: that
Homer gives Ossa directly, simply, and familiarly, as the messenger
of Zeus; whereas Herodotus introduces the Gods as a pious in-

drops into its place like the key-stone of an arch, and exactly fills the painful vacancy in their minds; it seems to carry with it the same sort of evidence as the key which imparts meaning to a manuscript in cypher, and they are too well pleased with the acquisition to be very nice as to the title. Nay, we may go further and say, that the man who demonstrates its falsehood will be the most unwelcome of all instructors; so that we trust, for the comfort of Goethe's last years, that he was spared the pain of seeing his interesting mythus about Lord Byron contemptuously blotted out by Mr. Moore.

It argues no great discernment in Mr. Moore's criticism, that he passes with disdain from these German legends to some majestic sentences extracted from Lord Jeffrey and the 'Edinburgh Review,' as the more worthy encomiasts of Byron. Now, the legends themselves shall be rational or absurd as you will; but the glory of the poet consists in his having planted in so many intellectual minds, Goethe included, the *œstrus* for creating and the appetite for believing them. In our view, this is a more unequivocal proof of his potent influence over the emotions, and a far higher compliment to his genius, than the most splendid article ever turned out in the blue and yellow clothing.

Father Malebranche, in discussing the theory of morals, has observed, that our passions all justify themselves; that is, they suggest to us reasons for justifying them. He might with equal justice have remarked, and it is the point which we have sought to illustrate by the preceding remarks on the Byronian legends, that all our strong emotions, when shared in common by a circle of individuals or a community,

---

ference, with some degree of circumlocution, as if their intervention required proof.

In analysing the sources of fabulous narrative, it is quite essential to take account of these ideas of superhuman communications and authority, prevalent in the ancient world, and superseding so constantly the necessity for positive testimony as a condition of belief.

will not only sanctify fallacious reasonings, but also call into being, and stamp with credibility, abundance of narratives purely fictitious. Whether the feeling be religious, or political, or æsthetic—love, hatred, terror, gratitude, or admiration—it will find or break a way to expand and particularise itself in appropriate anecdotes; it serves at once both as demand and supply; it both emboldens the speaker to invent, and disposes the hearers to believe him without any further warrant. Such anecdotes are fictions from beginning to end, but they are specious and impressive fictions; they boast no acknowledged parentage, but they are the adopted children of the whole community; they are embraced with an intensity of conviction quite equivalent to the best authenticated facts. And let it be always recollected—we once more repeat—that they are radically distinct from half-truths or mis-reported matters of fact; for upon this distinction will depend the different mode which we shall presently propose of dealing with them in reference to Grecian history.

In no point is the superiority of modern times over ancient so remarkable—we may add the superiority of the present time over all preceding—as in the multiplication and improvement of exact means of information as to matters of fact, physical as well as social. In former days the Florentine intrigue, and the other stories noticed by Mr. Moore, would have obtained undisputed currency as authentic materials for the life of Lord Byron; then would have succeeded rationalizing historians, who, treating the stories as true at the bottom, would have proceeded to discriminate the basis of truth from the accessories of fiction. One man would have disbelieved the supposed murder of the wife, another that of the husband; a third would have said that, the intrigue having been discovered, the husband and wife had both retired into convents, the one under feelings of deep distress, the other in bitter repentance, and that, the fleshly lusts having been thus killed, it was hence erroneously stated that the husband and wife had themselves been killed.

If the reader be not familiar with the Greek Scholiasts, we are compelled to assure him that the last explanation would have found much favour in their eyes, inasmuch as it saves the necessity of giving the direct lie to any one, or of saying that any portion of the narrative is absolutely unfounded. The misfortune is, that though the story would thus be divested of all its salient features and softened down into something very sober and colourless, perhaps even edifying, —yet it would not be one whit nearer to actual matter of fact. Something very like what we have been describing, however, would infallibly have taken place, had we not been protected by a well-informed biographer, and by the copious memoranda of a positive age.

Taking the age as it now stands, and with reference to contemporary matters, we have already said that we consider the judgment of the public, which presumes some foundation in fact for every current statement, to be in the majority of cases a just one. Fiction, though still powerful and active, is in a minority—on the whole, in a declining minority. In her old time-honoured castles, she does indeed preserve unshaken authority; but her new conquests, if not difficult to be made, are at least difficult to be maintained.

So much with reference to the present age. But when we transport ourselves back to ancient times—to the early dawn of Grecian history—the above presumption becomes directly and violently reversed.

Here we find mythus omnipotent; positive knowledge and recorded matter of fact scarcely exist, even in the dreams of the wisest individuals. With what consistency can you require that a community which either does not command the means, or has not learned the necessity, of registering the phenomena of its present, should possess any *knowledge* of the phenomena of its past? We say advisedly *knowledge*, traceable to some competent and trustworthy source, and deducible by some reasonable chain of collated evidence. The mental processes, upon which the verification of positive matter of fact depends, are of slow growth and painful acqui-

sition : men only apply them to the past after having previously applied them to the present ; and at the dawn of
Grecian history, say at the commencement of the Olympiads
in 776 B.C., they were as much untrodden ground as the
propositions of geometry.

Knowledge with respect to the past, we have said, a community so circumstanced will neither possess nor desire ; but
feelings with respect to the past they doubtless will possess
—feelings both fervent and unanimous. And these feelings
will provide abundant substitutes for knowledge ; they will
pour themselves out in legends or mythi requiring no
evidence beyond their own intrinsic beauty and plausibility ;
so that the mythopœic propensity thus exhibits a past time
of its own, suitably coloured and peopled, and thoroughly
satisfactory to the popular religious and patriotic faith,
though the actual past with its commonplace realities be
altogether buried and forgotten. Such tales are embraced
and welcomed from their entire harmony with all the general
sentiments and belief : if there be no positive evidence to
sustain them, there is none to contradict them ; they work
upon the convictions of an unrecording age with the irresistible force of authenticated truth. Add to this the presence of
individual bards or poets, endowed with a genius adequate to
the occasion, and nothing more is wanting to bring into existence a body of historical mythus or mythical history, something which is not degenerated matter of fact, but legitimate
and genuine fiction, though accepted and believed as history.

The personages who alone stand conspicuous in this supposed mythical past, are such as we should expect from the
feelings out of which the tales grew. They are the Gods
and Heroes reverenced among the present community, acknowledged in their prayers, invoked as their protectors in
the hour of danger, and presiding in spirit at their festivals and scenes of public enjoyment.* The people in the

---

* Hesiod represents the men who carried on the sieges of
Troy and Thebes as belonging to a special race, totally different

ancient epic are introduced merely as a nameless crowd to fill the scene; they serve as instruments to execute the orders, or as subject-matter to bring out the potent personality, of their divine or heroic commanders. The Æolic or Ionic colonists, to whom the Iliad was addressed, neither saw nor wished to see, in the past, men of their own stature and proportions: if you could have produced to them a history of their own real fathers, framed with all the care of Thucydides, distributed according to summers and winters, and embodying nothing but strictly human agency and positive motives, they would have turned from it with indifference, even though it had been animated by all that graphic power with which Thucydides has described the last combat of the Athenian fleet in the harbour of Syracuse. Such narratives presuppose a certain thirst of rational curiosity—a sentiment which had not yet been aroused among the hearers of the ancient epic. To captivate their emotions as well as to win their belief, you must address to them legends, of which the foundation is already laid in their religious feelings; legends exhibiting both the agents and the mode of agency, superhuman; legends cast back into an undefined past, the interval between which and the present no one then cares to fathom, when the heroes whose consecrated groves they now see before them were treading the same earth, and aided by the same Gods as themselves. To treat Grecian history without Grecian religion, is to render it essentially acephalous: when we follow the stream upwards until it becomes thoroughly scanty and unrefreshing, we find that it loses itself amidst a sea of fiction, even then both

----

from his own degenerate contemporaries, and extinct before his time.

   'Ανδρῶν ἡρώων θεῖον γένος, οἱ καλέονται

   'Ημίθεοι προτέρῃ γενέῃ κατ' ἀπείρονα γαῖαν—Opp. et D. 146–156.

   The words ἡμιθέων γένος ἀνδρῶν—Homer, Iliad xii. 23, express the same idea; the Homeric phrase—οἷοι νῦν βροτοί εἰσι—significant of present degeneracy, is of familiar occurrence.

abundant and relishing to the taste. First, we have pure
fiction passing under the name and colours of past reality:
next, we have reality clouded and perverted by fiction:
lastly, we have reality by itself—not indeed unmingled with
fiction, but under such forms that we can tolerably well
discriminate the one from the other.

Our first glimpse of the Grecian world begins with the Iliad
and Odyssey. Of these glorious and imperishable productions
we know scarcely anything, except such information as the
poems themselves furnish: nor shall we now discuss the
various hypotheses which have been proposed respecting
their authorship and promulgation. It is certain that they
suppose a pre-existing epical literature, now lost—songs or
poems of a similar character, but of what merit we cannot
judge. Both the Ante-Homeric and the Post-Homeric epical
compositions have been withheld from us by the envious
hand of fate: of the latter we have the names and a few
scanty fragments—the Cypria, the Lesser Iliad, the Destruction of Troy, the Æthiopis, the Return of the Grecian
Heroes, the Thebais, the Epigoni, the Titanomachia, the
Capture of Œchalia, the Telegonia, the Œdipodia, the Hera-
cleia, the Minyas, &c.

Of these compositions several passed under the venerated
name of Homer, and all appear to have been put together,
more or less successfully, with a view to a certain poetical
integrity, like the Iliad and the Odyssey. But there was
also another class of poems, more nakedly narrative and
genealogical, without any pretensions to poetical unity—
pedigrees given in verse of the divine and heroic personages belonging to the various Grecian communities, connecting the contemporaries of the poet with those Gods in
whom their retrospective vision always terminated. The
Catalogue of Women, and the Great Eœæ, seem to have
been two long and desultory poems, ascribed to Hesiod,
the author of the Theogonia and the Shield of Hercules,
and containing a variety of heroic genealogies: the Ægi-
mius and the marriage of Ceyx are alluded to also as

productions of Hesiod, but it is difficult to identify the many scattered allusions made by later Greek authors to the name of that poet. The Naupaktian verses, and the poems of Eumelus, Cinæthon, and Asius, bore the same genealogising character: none of them have been preserved to modern times.

Of the lyric, iambic, and elegiac poetry, once so abundant and so celebrated, a considerable portion was devoted to events of the time, and would thus have carried with it a certain historical evidence, if it had been preserved. Archilochus, Alcman, Tyrtæus, Alcæus, Sappho, all handled contemporary subjects, commemorating their affections as well as their antipathies, and blending, like Pindar, the persons and circumstances of the moment with suitable comparisons out of the ancient legends. The remains of Solon and Theognis seem like moral discourses in verse, conceived in a spirit not much exalted above the level of ordinary prose : in fact, the elaborate prose of Isocrates probably cost more care in the preparation than the elegiac or iambic verse of the Gnomic poets.

The various poets here alluded to, and others of similar genius and character, filled up the interval of two centuries and a half between the first authenticated chronological epoch (B.C. 776), and the first commencement of prose writing. So much new imagination having thus been applied to the ancient legends, the number of them became considerably multiplied, and the confusion and divergence among them proportionally augmented. And in estimating this number and confusion—a fact which bore materially upon the continuance of the ancient faith, we are not to forget that the legends which passed through the hands of the poets formed but a small proportion of the total number of analogous legends current in Greece. In each of the many autonomous communities into which that country was divided, a distinct and peculiar crop of local mythus was be found. There were presiding Heroes, like Patron Saints, not merely for each state apart from the rest, but for each separate sub-

division of the same state distinct from the other subdivisions : every *Demus* in Attica,—and every *Gens* or
extended family union,—every fraternity of men allied for a
common purpose and bearing a common name,—recognised
some divine or semi-divine Eponymus, who was supposed to
have originally bestowed the name, and to extend a watchful
protection towards his special flock. All the numerous
temples, consecrated groves, and festivals, were rich in explanatory mythi : the exegetes had always a suitable tale at
hand to show you why it was peculiarly proper to carry a
branch of laurel or to offer a honeyed cake : some adventure
of the God or the Hero was perpetually forthcoming to
justify every detail of the practised ritual. The periegesis
of Pausanias is especially valuable, as it gives us some insight
into these more obscure mythi, accredited and reverenced
each in its own peculiar corner, but prevented from circu-
lating through the general Grecian world by the want of
some " sacred poet " to give it currency : if the many similar
works, prepared at earlier periods by others, had been preserved to us, we should have acquired a fuller conception of
the exuberance of the aggregate stock.

Now, these legends, though infinitely diversified in their
details, were all cast in moulds to a great degree analogous;
all had their root in the public feeling and were consecrated
by the public faith ; they cleared up, or seemed to clear up,
those *incognita* respecting which real curiosity was entertained ; and they composed, when taken together, the political and religious antiquities of the people— a pseudo-
historical past suited to the non-historical mind. They were
the spontaneous, indigenous growth of the earliest Grecian
thought and feeling, antecedent to all record of actual fact
or consecutive exercise of reason. This last was a gradual
progress, emanating from the superior minds of the community : a new and artificial influence, whereby the mythus
was partially dispossessed of its hold on the people : but had
we been able to obtain a periegesis of Greece for the year
776 B.C., we should have discovered from one end of the

country to the other nothing but legends, preached by the men of genius, received both with earnest emotion and with sincere faith by the hearers.

Transporting ourselves back to this early period, near to the time when the Iliad and Odyssey seem to have been first promulgated, there is every reason to presume that these poems were then listened to as something much greater and more sacred than poems in the modern sense of the word. They were accepted as inspired legends, describing events which had really taken place in a distant past; and they were believed quite as literally as the history of Herodotus 400 years afterwards, when he recited it at the Olympic games. To a modern reader, this idea may seem extravagant: much as he may admire these productions as poems, as real histories they will appear to him absurd: the line between fact and fiction is clearly drawn in his mind, and the inspiration of the poet has long ceased to be anything beyond an unmeaning phrase. But with the early hearers of the Iliad, both the point of view and the preliminary state of mind were essentially different. What was there to induce them to treat descriptions conveyed to them in the most vivid narrative poetry ever poured into human ears, as a pure invention? or to draw the distinction between a basis of truth and a superstructure of poetical ornament? One or other of these they must do—if we reject the supposition of entire faith in what they heard; both of them are at variance as well with the capacities as with the inclinations of an age neither able nor willing to discriminate between authenticated truth and plausible fiction. Inspiration from the Gods or from the Muse, coming upon the poet so as to reveal to him either the past or the future, is with them a belief both sincere and familiar:* the course of nature, as they conceive

* The Muses, says Hesiod, Theogon. 33,

ἐνέπνευσαν δέ μοι αὐδὴν
Θείην, ὡς κλείοιμι τά τ' ἐσσόμενα πρό τ' ἐόντα
Καί με κέλονθ' ὑμνεῖν μακάρων γένος αἰὲν ἐόντων, &c.

it, is something not positive and regular, but subject to
perpetual jerks and breaks, and modified incessantly by the
special intervention of a God or a Hero. And those portions of the Iliad which, to our view, divest it so much of
the semblance of matter of fact—the repetition of superhuman agency and miracles—these phenomena were not only
thoroughly consonant to their general belief as to the past,
but were by far the most impressive and predominant of the
whole, sinking deeper into the mind and raising emotions
more powerful than the rest: insomuch that the subtraction
of such phenomena, far from procuring for the narrative a
more unhesitating assent, would have rendered it at once
less plausible to their reason, and less affecting to their
feelings. So great is the contrast between the tone of
mind of a primitive Homeric audience, and the preface of
Thucydides.

The feelings of the Jews, in reference to the miracles of
their early history, present a fair standard of comparison to
illustrate the sentiments here ascribed to the early Greeks:
and these feelings we can perfectly measure, since the idea of

---

Again, line 38, about the Muses—

Εἰρεῦσαι τά τ' ἐόντα, τά τ' ἐσσόμενα, πρό τ' ἐόντα.

The Homeric Muses are omniscient—

Ὑμεῖς γὰρ θεαί ἐστε, πάρεστέ τε, ἴστε τε πάντα.—*Iliad*, ii. 484.

Their inspiration imparts to the poet, and enables him to communicate to his hearers, both what is past and what is to come.
His statements are not merely agreeable fiction, they are borrowed
from this inspired source, like those of the prophet or the soothsayer. The inspiration of Calchas the prophet is described in the
Iliad almost in the same words as those employed by the poet
Hesiod with regard to himself. Iliad, i. 70.

Ὃς ἤδη τά τ' ἐόντα, τά τ' ἐσσόμενα, πρό τ' ἐόντα,
Ἣν διὰ μαντοσύνην, τήν οἱ πόρε Φοῖβος Ἀπόλλων.

The bard and the prophet are privileged co-recipients of communication from the Gods.

past historical facts, not known upon human authority, but revealed by Divine inspiration, as well as that of constant miraculous interference—is familiar and admitted amongst us as it was amongst the ancient Jews, in reference to the Jewish history. We need not employ many words to explain in what light any proposition to write the Jewish history without miracles would now appear to us, or would have appeared of old to the Jews. The whole vitality of the history would have seemed to them to have been removed : the narrative would lose its hold upon their feelings, and the explanations substituted in place of the miracles would appear more incredible than the miracles themselves. Nay, the mere suggestion that in this or that particular case it is not necessary to suppose a miracle, and that some natural solution of the phenomena recited may be practicable, is even at present not a little offensive, and is often sharply censured as a "lowering tone of explanation." Mr. Milman's 'History of the Jews,' written in a perfectly religious spirit, but exhibiting some disposition to economise the supernatural energy, has, by that single circumstance, been deprived of much of its legitimate success. Miracles, where the mind is animated by a living religious faith, appear quite as credible as ordinary facts, and far more impressive : and the multitude of them which occur in the Iliad forms not the smallest reason for doubting that the primitive Homeric audience literally and faithfully believed the events recited to them.

If there be one miracle more than another, throughout the Iliad, which would appear to a modern critic unlikely to be accepted as a real fact by the audience, it is the speech of the horse Xanthus, one of the immortal pair who draw the chariot of Achilles. Every reader of Homer will appreciate the epical interest and beauty of this incident. Xanthus and Balius, offspring of Zephyrus and the Harpy Podargé, fleet as the wind, unmanageable by ordinary hands, and exempt from old age as well as from death—have been presented by the special favour of Zeus to Peleus, though almost too precious

to partake in the sorrowful existence of miserable man : *
they have been lent by Achilles to carry Patroclus to the
field, and have manifested, even by tears, a vehement afflic-
tion and sympathy for his death.   The fierce Achilles, when
mounting his chariot for the purpose of re-entering the war,
under all the stimulus of furious grief and unsatisfied re-
venge, discharges his anger partly upon the horses—" Now
take better care to bring me safe back out of the battle, and
do not leave *me* dead on the field, as you left Patroclus."   So
poignant and unmerited an insult is intolerable: and the
kindness of the Goddess Heré lends to Xanthus a voice for
the purpose of replying to it, which he does in terms full of
dignity and emphasis.   The moment the reply is finished,
the Erinnyes repress his voice.   (Iliad, xix, 407–418.)

If there could have been introduced among the primitive
hearers of the Iliad, at the festivals of Smyrna or Chios, in
the eighth century before the Christian era, a critic of the
temper of Thucydides, who would have said—" This incident
is very good as a poetical incident, but no one can believe it
to have really occurred "—what would have been the reply
made to him ?   It would have been made in terms such
as the reproof by which Athené dispels the scepticism of
Telemachus (Odyss. iii, 230), and substantially similar to
the observation of the learned and pious Le Clerc, when he
comments upon that narrative of the Old Testament where-

---

* Homer, Iliad xvii. 442, shortly after the death of Patroclus—

Μυρομένω δ' ἄρα τώγε (the horses) ἰδὼν ἐλέησε Κρονίων,
Κινήσας δὲ κάρη, προτὶ ὃν μυθήσατο θυμόν·
᾿Α δειλὼ, τί σφῶϊ δόμεν Πηλῆϊ ἄνακτι
Θνητῷ, ὑμεῖς δ' ἐστον ἀγήρω τ' ἀθανάτω τε.
῍Η ἵνα δυστήνοισι μετ' ἀνδράσιν ἄλγε' ἔχητον ;
Οὐ μὲν γάρ τί πού ἐστιν ὀϊζυρώτερον ἀνδρὸς
Πάντων, ὅσσα τε γαῖαν ἔπι πνείει τε καὶ ἕρπει.

So Thetis complains bitterly that she has been constrained by the
decree of Zeus to a reluctant wedlock with the mortal man Peleus
(Iliad, xviii. 431).

in the ass of Balaam is miraculously empowered to make a speech—a narrative which the Rabbi Maimonides had presumed to resolve into a vision of Balaam himself; Le Clerc observes—

"God, either by himself or by His angel, produced the same effect in the mouth of the ass, as the organist produces in the organ, when, by certain motions in the instrument, he brings out various modulations. It is not more incredible that God should have been able to do this, than that he should have created men, and endowed them with speech from the beginning. Really, the thing in itself presents no difficulty at all; and the only objection which can be made to the story is, that it appears surprising that a miracle, to which there is no parallel, should have been worked for so inconsiderable a purpose. For this reason Maimonides and others have supposed that the events were only seeming events presented in a vision to Balaam : but there is nothing in the narrative which can create the smallest suspicion that it is a dream which is here described. For, although we can discover no reason which should have induced God to work so great a miracle, who shall dare to conclude from hence that it was not worked in reality? Who shall pretend to so thorough a comprehension of the designs and purposes of God? No objection can be raised to render the credibility of this miracle dubious."—(Le Clerc, *On Numbers*, c. xxii. 28.)

The passage here given from Le Clerc is a faithful expression of the sentiment which would have been found prevalent among the ancient Jews, the hearers of Jeremiah or Ezekiel, though Philo, yielding in part to the influences of Greek philosophy, omitted all mention of the incident. Nor can there be any doubt that the benevolent miracle described in the Iliad as having been wrought by Heré to relieve the overcharged feelings of Xanthus, was believed with equal sincerity, and would have been vindicated on similar grounds, by the contemporary Greeks.

But, though the legendary productions of Greece during her earliest ages, acted not only upon the emotions of the people as works of art, but upon their belief as supposed histories, this point of view was by no means continuously maintained. Three distinct causes were in operation to alter it, during the 300 years which separate the first re-corded Olympiad from the century of Hecatæus, Herodotus and Thucydides.

First, the mere multiplication, diffusion, and modification, of the legends themselves, had a tendency to lessen the hold of the ancient epic and heroic legends on the national faith. The same subject came to be handled in many different ways, comformably to the taste of particular subdivisions of the Grecian world : contradictory attributes and conflicting adventures were ascribed to the same person ; and it was im-possible to believe them all. Moreover, the increase of com-munication between these various subdivisions familiarised the travelled man with legends for which he had acquired no early reverence, and taught him to distinguish some as true, others as false ; some as impressive, others as displeas-ing. Mystic rites, and expiatory ceremonies, religious asso-ciations, such as the Orphic and Pythagorean, acquired foot-ing : Egypt, with its ancient civilization and its many wonders and peculiarities, first became largely visited by curious Greeks in the sixth century before the Christian era, and the effect which it produced upon their religious belief was evi-dently considerable ; it not only displaced old legends and superadded new, but it seems also to have degraded their native antiquities in their own eyes, and to have brought the Egyptian priests into higher estimation than their own old poets. An influence of this kind pervades especially a large portion of the narrative of Herodotus. At last, the legends passed from the hands of poets into those of the prose my-thographers, who recounted them in a bald and naked style, and thus deprived them of all that auxiliary genius and fer-vour, which had previously kept up in the hearers a tone of mental exaltation highly favourable to uninquiring faith. The mere act of uniting the mythi in one collection, tended as well to reveal their inherent discrepancies, as to discredit the worse by immediate juxtaposition of the better ; and it seems to have been an aggregate view of this sort which drew forth the pointed declaration of Hecatæus of Miletus (500 B.C., not more than one generation after the first commencement of prose writing): "Thus saith Hecatæus the Milesian—The "fables of the Greeks are many and ridiculous," &c. This brief passage is preserved among the few fragments of his writings. Yet Hecatæus was not deeply tainted with scepticism; he still continued to recount the story, how the golden-fleeced ram, who carried Phrixus and Hellé across the Hellespont, addressed words of encouragement to the terrified Phrixus, after Hellé had fallen off into the water.—(Hecat. ap. Schol. Apollon. Rhod. i, 256.)

Secondly, during the interval now under consideration, the internal governments of the Greeks experienced violent change and considerable ultimate improvement; the inter-political law pervading the members of the Hellenic world became better settled; and the moral and social ideas assumed a gentler as well as a juster cast, suited to a progressive community. Many of the ancient legends came to be entirely at variance with this altered tone of public feeling. The exploits ascribed to the Gods and Heroes were often tarnished with violence, thievishness, treachery, and licentiousness—qualities which appeared unworthy and revolting, when tried by a higher standard of morality. The rudiments of moral as well as of physical philosophy, began to be shadowed out in the minds of intellectual men; and the Colophonian Xenophanes—one of the most conspicuous men of his time, and father of the Eleatic school of philosophy—expressed both his disbelief and his disapprobation of the ancient poets with a boldness truly astonishing (B.C. 567–475). "Homer and Hesiod (he said) had imputed to the Gods everything disgraceful and blameable in man: theft, adultery, and mutual deceit,"*—and Homer was then the universal schoolmaster (Ἐξ ἀρχῆς καθ' Ὅμηρον ἐπεὶ μεμαθήκασι πάντες—Xenophanes ap. Dracon. de Metris, p. 33): the reader will bear in mind that in those days the name of Homer comprehended not merely the Iliad and

---

* Xenophan. ap. Sext. Empiric. adv. Mathemat., ix. 193.

Odyssey, but also many other epic poems as well as hymns;
and the name of Hesiod was applied hardly less extensively
to poems of the genealogising class.   The hymns to God
which preceded the banquet (according to Xenophanes)
ought to comprise nothing but pure ideas and acceptable
narratives, "excluding as well the battles of the Titans, the
Giants, and the Centaurs, which were fictions of their predecessors—as those violent wranglings in which no good
moral was to be found."*   Respecting the Gods, or the constitution of the universe, he said, "no one had ever seen or
known anything clear and certain: for though a man might
by chance speak ever so rightly about them, he could have
no means of knowing that he was right: the semblance of
truth was to be found everywhere"†   Nor let us leave un-
noticed the imposing confidence with which this remarkable
man proclaimed—"Good wisdom, such as mine, is of more
value to you than the boxing or the wrestling,—the victories
with the chariot and in the foot-race, on which you now
bestow such extravagant honours and donations: for these
will do nothing to procure for you a well-regulated community, or to fatten the interior of your city."‡

These citations afford striking evidence of the altered state
of mind with which the old legends had now to deal, and
indicate how much the idea of an inspired authority was
passing away from the superior minds.   Thucydides, in his
preface, justly criticises the cool simplicity with which the
Homeric heroes both put and answer questions implying
habitual and licensed piracy—"What has brought you here?
Are you come on a piratical excursion?"   We may be pretty

* Xenophan. Fragm. 1, Poetæ Græc. ed. Schneidewin, p. 41.
† Καὶ τὸ μὲν οὖν σαφὲς οὔτις ἀνὴρ ἴδεν, οὔτε τίς ἐστιν
Εἰδὼς ἀμφὶ θεῶν τε καὶ ἄσσα λέγω περὶ πάντων.
Εἰ γὰρ καὶ τὰ μάλιστα τύχοι τετελεσμένον εἰπών,
Αὐτὸς ὅμως οὐκ οἶδε, δόκος δ' ἐπὶ πᾶσι τέτυκται.
             —Xenophanes ap. Sext., adv. Mathem. Empiric.,
                                    vii. 50, viii. 326.
‡ Fragm. 3 Schneidewin.

sure that this observation, marking as it does a complete
revolution in the received public morality, had been made
long before Thucydides, and that, in particular, it did not
escape the clear-sighted and eminently regulative genius of
Solon.

A third cause there was, of not less importance in the
present examination : between the century of Homer and
that of Thucydides, the habit grew up of recording and
connecting positive and present facts, and of determining
authentic chronology. There was thus gradually created,
among the superior minds, what may be called an *historical
sense*—a habit of requiring positive evidence, and of distinguishing the certified truth from the uncertified, though
plausible, supposition—of acknowledging a regular course
of nature, and not looking beyond or above it for the explanation of particular phenomena. The intellectual dispositions suitable to an historiographer, in regard to present or
recent events, exist to the utmost perfection in Thucydides :
nothing greater or better of its kind has been produced, even
to this day, than his history. What Thucydides was in
historical evidence, his contemporary Hippocrates was in
pathological : we shall transcribe, from the latter, one out of
many passages, which illustrates the altered modes of judgment now introduced amongst instructed Greeks. Discussing the habits of the Scythians, in his treatise *De Aere, Locis,
et Aquis,* Hippocrates specifies certain disorders and peculiar
debilities to which they were subject, and adds—

" The Scythians themselves ascribe the cause of this to God, and
reverence and bow down to such sufferers ; *each man fearing that he
may suffer the like.* But to me, in my judgment, both those affections, and all others besides, appear to be divine : no one amongst
them is either more divine, or more human, than another, but all are
alike and all divine : nevertheless each of them has its own physical
cause, and not one supervenes without such physical cause." *

---

* Hipp. *De Aere, Loc. et Aq.* c. 22. Οἱ μὲν ἐπιχώριοι τὴν αἰτίην
προστιθέασι θεῷ, καὶ σέβονται τουτέους τοὺς ἀνθρώπους καὶ προσκυ-

The belief here ascribed to the Scythians would have found perfect sympathy, as well in the bosom of the untaught contemporaries of Hippocrates, as in that of the Homeric man, the primitive hearer of ancient Grecian mythus : while to all men imbued with the Hippocratic or Thucydidean order of thought, the mythus might serve as a stimulus to the fancy and emotions, but it could no longer be retained as a genuine, serious, and literal faith.

We have thus briefly explained how the ancient legends, during the interval between Homer and Thucydides, came to lose that easy sway and unsuspecting assent upon which their original authors had counted, and which appears to us (we may say it in passing) to be one of the causes of the unaffected and inimitable beauties of the Iliad and Odyssey. Yet to reject these legends avowedly and as a whole, would have disconnected a man from the religion of his country in a manner highly painful to his feelings ; not to mention that the reverence for Homer, implanted by the education of every intellectual Greek, amounted in itself almost to a religion, so as to render it imperiously necessary that the honour of the poet should be preserved. The result was, a new impulse, partaking of both the discordant forces—one of those thousand unconscious compromises between the rational convictions of the mature man, and the indelible illusions of early faith, religious as well as patriotic—which human affairs are so often destined to exhibit—γιγνόμενα μὲν, καὶ ἀεὶ ἐσόμενα, ἕως ἂν ἡ αὐτὴ φύσις τῶν ἀνθρώπων ᾖ. The mode of compromise was not the same in all cases : but one of two processes was commonly resorted to.

The philosophical men distinguished between the literal meaning, and the concealed or symbolical meaning, of the

---

νέουσι, δεδοικότες περὶ ἑωυτέων ἕκαστοι. Ἐμοὶ δὲ καὶ αὐτέῳ δοκέει ταῦτα τὰ πάθεα θεῖα εἶναι, καὶ τἆλλα πάντα, καὶ οὐδὲν ἕτερον ἑτέρου θειότερον οὐδὲ ἀνθρωπινώτερον, ἀλλὰ πάντα ὅμοια καὶ πάντα θεῖα· ἕκαστον δὲ ἔχει φύσιν τῶν τοίουτων, καὶ οὐδὲν ἄνευ φύσιος γίγνεται.

ancient legends. They professed to detect in them physical or moral truths under the veil of allegory, which had been forced upon the poet, as they pretended, only by the imperfect apprehensions and childish fancies of his hearers. They thus continued to believe and respect the ancient legends, but it was in a new sense of their own, totally different from the primitive and ordinary sense. They believed in Homer the philosopher, as contrasted with Homer the poet—a distinction completely foreign to the apprehensions of the original hearers of the Iliad. It forms no part of our present task, though the subject is one highly interesting, to follow out in detail the various eccentricities of this exegetical system, pushed to excess by Anaxagoras and Metrodorus, but adopted more or less by almost all the philosophers, and especially prevalent during the Orientalised state of the Pagan mind in the third and fourth centuries after the Christian era.

Those men who, without devoting themselves much to pure speculation, were yet essentially positive-minded, of whom Thucydides, Polybius, and Strabo may be taken as the types, were not averse, on special occasions, to recognise the preceding theory: but for the most part they took another course; they distinguished between Homer the historian or relating witness, and Homer the poet—between a basis of truth and matter of fact, and a superstructure of ornament and exaggeration. The statements of the Iliad and Odyssey were alleged to be, in the main, both historically and geographically correct, but coloured, enlarged, and varied, for purposes of poetical effect: and Strabo maintains, in the most emphatic language, that it was quite unworthy of Homer to start from any other point of commencement than that of actual matter of fact.* We have here again to remark, that this distinction between historian and poet is

---

* See Strabo, i. p. 20, Casaub. The same opinion is advocated throughout the larger portion of his first book, in continued controversy with Eratosthenes.

the idea of a subsequent age, and would have been thoroughly
incomprehensible to the original hearers of the Iliad: positive history was then unknown.

How or where to draw the line between the supposed basis
of fact and the superstructure of fiction, was the grand difficulty inherent in this hypothesis—not a tittle of evidence
being available for its solution. There was one point, however, in which they pretty generally agreed: they dismissed
the special interferences of the gods, together with all supernatural motives and agency, and they degraded the Heroes
into ordinary men. Such a change was alone sufficient to
suck the life-blood out of the ancient legend, and to reduce
it to an emaciated skeleton, as any one may see who tries to
apply the process to the Iliad: along with the gods and
heroes disappear all the actual motives and determining
forces which the poem offers. To supply the place of all
these, Thucydides, in his preface, furnishes us with a brief
sketch of what he calls the Trojan war, conducted according
to approved political views, and appreciated according to the
same reasonings which he applies in criticising the siege of
Syracuse by Nicias. The Agamemnon of Thucydides takes
the command, "*not so much* because the suitors of Helen
had been previously bound by an oath (we see here that
Thucydides had to displace the purely personal motives
assigned by the old legend, but did not dare to reject them
altogether), as because he was the most powerful prince in
Peloponnesus:" * the Homeric catalogue is treated as an

---

* Thucyd. i. 9. Ἀγαμέμνων δέ μοι δοκεῖ τῶν τότε δυνάμει προύχων,
καὶ οὐ τοσοῦτον τοῖς Τινδάρεω ὅρκοις κατειλημμένους τοὺς μνηστῆρας
παραλαβὼν, τὸν στόλον ἀγεῖραι.

Thucydides then proceeds to show how Agamemnon acquired
this great power, which he traces back to Pelops. Pelops was, he
states, an Asiatic, who came with great wealth among the poor
population of Peloponnesus, and by means of his wealth acquired
both great power, and the privilege of giving his name to the
country. Here the great historian silently obliterates the legendary Pelops—the Πέλοψ πλήξιππος of the Iliad, who receives his

authentic muster-roll, and is supposed to afford evidence, that the power of Greece in those early days had been much smaller than it was in the Peloponnesian war: the Greeks were detained ten years in the prosecution of the siege, because they could not employ their whole force at once, but were compelled, from poverty and want of provisions, to send one detachment to cultivate the Chersonese, and others to plunder the neighbouring towns: this necessity of dispersing their force was the only reason which induced them, immediately after a successful battle with the Trojans, to build a wall and rampart round their camp (Thuc. i. 8-12). Now such remarks all proceed upon the supposition that the statements in the Iliad are to be taken as trustworthy, subtracting only what is divine, heroic, miraculous or otherwise incredible: but the misfortune is, that these latter elements are so interwoven with the constitution of the poem, from the first book to the last, that you cannot pluck them out without tearing the poem to tatters. And this, in point of fact, Thucydides does: he gives an entirely new view of the Trojan war, preserving the statistics, chronology, and topography of the Iliad, but introducing actors and agencies of his own, such as the Homeric hearer would neither have understood nor cared for. The result is a sort of palimpsest, not unlike those of the monks in the middle ages, when they rashly obliterated a manuscript of the Æneid, in order to fill the same parchment with their own chronicles. It is without the smallest aid from extrinsic evidence (we again repeat) that Thucydides thus cuts down and mutilates the old legend, to suit his own historical ideas. Our profound reverence for his character as an historian, must not restrain

sceptre from Hermes and Zeus, and bears no trace of Lydian origin —and the Πέλοψ of Pindar, who is suitor of Hippodamia, and victorious, by the aid of Poseidon, over her father Œnomaus in the chariot-race—a competition in which thirteen suitors have already failed and perished. These legendary creations are dismissed to make room for an historical phantom, framed on the model of Crœsus and Gyges.

us from entering an emphatic protest against this proceeding, alike unauthorised and unfortunate.

The pretended matter of fact, which Thucydides gives as the basis of the Trojan epic, is open to little remark, because it is so exceedingly vague and general. But other authors —adopting the same theory as Thucydides, that the epic was a superstructure of fiction raised upon a basis of fact—pushed the element of fact much farther, even to the specialties and particular incidents of the Homeric poems. Some truth (they thought) was to be found at the bottom of all of them. To revert to the same example upon which we before touched —the horses of Achilles. The chariot of Achilles is made ready to carry Patroclus into the field, and the immortal horses Xanthus and Balius are placed under the yoke: alongside of them is attached, as an outrigger, the mortal horse Pedasus. The epical importance of this distinction is forcibly felt when the combat between Patroclus and Sarpedon comes to be described: the spear of the latter misses Patroclus, but pierces the horse Pedasus, who falls and expires: the two remaining horses start asunder, the yoke is strained and crackles, and the chariot becomes unmanageable, until Automedon, the charioteer, draws his sword and severs the rein of the expiring animal. But the Scholiasts were not satisfied with a simple illustration of the epical narrative: they sought to determine the real matter of fact from which the poet had started when he called Xanthus and Balius immortal, and Pedasus mortal: and the following is one of their solutions, as given by Eustathius (ad Iliad. xvi. 147). Xanthus and Balius were entire horses, possessing the power of propagating their species: they were, therefore, *quasi-immortal*. But Pedasus was a gelding, and unable to immortalise himself in his offspring: he was for this reason called mortal. Accordingly, the Homeric statement that Patroclus set forth with two immortal horses, and one mortal horse, attached to his chariot, was merely a poetical way of describing the matter of fact historically true—that he had two stallions and one gelding.

Our readers will deem this nothing better than an ingenious absurdity; but we assure them that the Scholia on Homer will furnish copious parallels to it. Nay, we can point out explanations, hardly less unfortunate, sanctioned by the name of the judicious and estimable Polybius, when he steps aside from his career of positive history to dig for matter of fact in the ancient legends. The Homeric Æolus in the Odyssey is familiar to every one. He dwells in a floating island, surrounded by a brazen wall; he has six sons and six daughters, and he marries the one to the other; he is, by appointment of Zeus, dispenser of the winds, which he imprisons or sets free at his discretion. Odysseus, driven by storms to the island, and being hospitably entertained for a month, solicits a course homeward; and Æolus not only grants to him a special Zephyrus to impel him in the right direction, but puts into his hands a closed leather bag containing all the other unfavourable winds in strict confinement. Unfortunately Odysseus falls asleep when within sight of Ithaca; his companions, from guilty curiosity, untie the bag, and immediately all the winds, having obtained their liberty, raise a furious storm, which drives the vessel back to the island of Æolus; who now repels Odysseus with abhorrence, as one under the special displeasure of the immortal Gods.— (Odyss. x. 1–75.)

We briefly recite the various characteristics of the Homeric Æolus, in order that the reader may see how essentially gaseous the conception is, and how completely it defies all possible compression into the solidity which our judgments require in matter of fact. Much, indeed, are we astonished to observe that Mr. Fynes Clinton (Introd., p. vii.) treats Æolus as a man of flesh and blood, belonging to some given year before the Christian era; he retains the Homeric subject without any of the Homeric predicates, and, therefore, without ascertained predicates of any kind. But Polybius goes farther, and draws up a new set of predicates for Æolus, who was a person (he tells us) possessing unrivalled skill in navigation, and unerring in his anticipations of coming

weather; this was a real matter of fact, of which the Homeric
description is a mere colouring and exaggeration. (Polyb.
xxxiv. 2; also ap. Strab. i. p. 21–24.) In like manner
Polybius described the Cyclopes and Læstrygones of the
Odyssey as having been, in point of fact, savage and inhos-
pitable men, resident in Sicily; and the Scylla and Charybdis,
by whom Odysseus so narrowly escapes being swallowed up,
as poetical representations of the real dangers arising from
numerous pirates in the Straits of Messina. Strabo, too,
speaks of the amazing expeditions ascribed to Dionysus and
Hercules in the same category with the extended voyages
of the Phœnicians; he explains the story of the descent of
Theseus and Peirithous into Hades, by referring it to the
length and celebrity of their real earthly marches; and he
derives the prayers addressed to the Dioskuri, as guardians
and preservers of mariners in danger at sea, from the
celebrity which they had acquired as real men and navigators.
(Strab. i. p. 48.) Such hypotheses may, perhaps, be less
fantastic than the explanation cited above from the Homeric
Scholiast respecting the horses of Achilles; but assuredly
they are neither less erroneous nor less arbitrary.

Eratosthenes seems to have stood almost alone in contending that Homer was to be considered as a poet, "ad-
dressing himself to the emotions, not seeking to impart
instruction." (στοχάζεσθαι ψυχαγωγίας, καὶ οὐ διδασκα-
λίας.) With regard to the localities described in the
Odyssey as visited by Odysseus, he said that it would be
time enough to look for them in reality, when the name of
the currier had been ascertained who sewed the leathern bag
wherein Æolus imprisoned the winds. (Eratosthenes, ap.
Strabo i. p. 15–24.) This doctrine was strenuously combated
not less by Polybius and Strabo, than by the great astronomer Hipparchus, who all of them treated Homer as the
grandfather of geographical science, of social philosophy,
and of the habit of transmitting to posterity historical facts.
They admitted, indeed, that his means of information had
been imperfect, and that he had indulged in poetical license

and exaggeration; but they still professed to detect everywhere traces of geographical reality, and vehemently contended that all his fictions were ornaments superinduced
upon a basis of truth. It is not uninstructive to contrast
ancient criticism with modern; Mr. Payne Knight treats all
who *believe* in the local reality of the voyage of Odysseus in
the Odyssey, and all who *disbelieve* the historical basis of the
Iliad, as men alike silly and out of their senses. (Pro-
legomen. ad Homer. c. 49–52, 53.)

It would be easy to multiply examples out of ancient
writers, of this transfusion of legend into history; but we
can only find room for one more, out of Pausanias. This
writer is a conscientious observer, a profoundly pious man,
and a believer in miracles not merely past but present; he
retains much of the old reverential faith towards Grecian
legend, cites Cinæthon, Asius, and other genealogical poets
with unqualified confidence, and Homer with a feeling even
stronger than simple confidence. Yet there are cases in
which even Pausanias cannot literally believe, and one of
them is the story of the well-known Trojan horse. But, to
escape the necessity of rejecting the statement point-blank,
he transforms it into accordance with his own taste. The
Trojan horse (he says) was in reality an engine for battering
down the walls of Troy, employed by the Greeks: "whoever
thinks otherwise, must impute to the Trojans inconceivable
silliness." (Paus. i. 23–8.) Nothing can be more just than
the criticism of Pausanias, if we treat the siege of Troy as an
historical event. But when we view it as a legend, it will be
seen that the incident of the literal Trojan horse "pregnant
with armed men," is, in the highest degree, consistent and
suitable. It saves the honour of the impregnable walls,
built by Poseidon and Apollo—for the Trojans themselves
make the breach; it taints with fraud the ultimate success
of the Greeks, and thus prepares us for the signal calamities
which the anger of the Gods is about to inflict upon them
both in and after their return; moreover, the very point
upon which Pausanias grounds his unbelief, the extreme

childishness implied in the Trojans, is thoroughly consonant to the general body of sentiment on which the ancient legend rested. *Quos Deus vult perdere, prius dementat*—the man marked out for destruction is abandoned by the Gods and deprived of his foresight and powers of self-defence.*

---

* In proof of what is here said about the Trojan horse, we need only refer the reader to the second book of the Æneid, where the incident is presented in its genuine character, and with the most striking effect. The Gods have doomed Troy to destruction; the Trojans are blinded and rendered the willing agents of their own ruin; the horse, constructed by Epeius, with the divine aid of Pallas, is the instrument; Laocoon, whose undisturbed reason stands in the way of the purpose of the Gods, perishes by a cruel death—" Et si fata Deûm, si mens non læva fuisset," &c. (ver. 55.)
Again, ver. 234--it is Æneas who speaks—

" Dividimus muros, et mœnia pandimus urbis ;
   Accingunt omnes operi ——
                  Pueri circum innuptæque puellæ
   Sacra canunt, funemque manu contingere gaudent :
   Illa subit ——
                  quater ipso in limine portæ
   Substitit, atque utero sonitum quater arma dedere.
   Instamus tamen *immemores, cæcique furore*
   Et monstrum infelix sacrata sistimus arce."

The suitors in the Odyssey, shortly before their destruction, are plunged by Pallas into a fit of insanity ; they talk, laugh, weep, and perform other acts, like senseless men, without knowing why ; they despise the warnings of Theoclymenus (Odyss. xv. 345-370). The Gods sometimes take away a man's reason and infuse foolish counsels into him (Iliad, xvii. 469—xviii. 311).

This " inconceivable folly " of the Trojans, upon which Pausanias dwells in reference to the Trojan horse, is in like manner argued upon by Herodotus, when he cites the story told to him by the Egyptian priests about Helen. According to them, Paris, when he eloped with Helen from Sparta, was driven by storms to Egypt, where Proteus, king of the country, detained both her and the stolen property, in trust for Menelaus ; sending Paris away by himself with sharp rebukes and menaces. When the Greeks arrived before Troy, and re-demanded Helen, the Trojans affirmed

But the most elaborate example of this method of historicising ancient legend, is to be found in the narrative of

---

that she was not nor ever had been there : they persisted in that answer until the city was taken, and it was then found that they had spoken truly, for Menelaus did not discover Helen thoro, nor did he regain possession of her until he came to Egypt (Herod. ii. 115-120).

"Now I (says Herodotus—we give the substance) believe this tale of the Egyptian priests. If Helen had been in Troy, she would have been given up to the Greeks whether Paris consented to it or not. For Priam and his relatives were not so *utterly insane* (οὕτω φρενοβλαβής) as to encounter the extremity of peril for themselves, their children, and their city, in order to preserve Helen for Paris : even if Helen *had lived with Priam himself*, he would have given her up, as a means of escape from such terrible calamities. Besides, Paris was not the eldest son and successor of Priam : there was Hector, his elder brother, and more of a man than he (ἀνὴρ ἐκείνου μᾶλλον ἐών), who cannot be reasonably supposed to have abetted his brother in an act of injustice so destructive to himself and his country. No :—they did not give Helen up, only because they could not : the Greeks did not believe them, even when they spoke the truth—in my judgment, by the special provision of God—in order that they might be destroyed root and branch, and might thus become a warning to mankind, that ' upon great crimes the Gods inflict great punishments.' "

Mr. Payne Knight, also, is amazed and incredulous about the "folly" of the Trojans : he (*Prolegom.* c. 53) tells us that the Greeks and the Trojans can *hardly* have been such fools as to take so much trouble and suffer so many calamities "*for one little woman.*" "Nam Helena, si prætexta, *vix vera causa* tanti belli esse potuit : nunquam enim homines usque adeò *fatui et stulti* fuerunt, ut *pro una muliercula*, aut illi tot labores suscipere voluissent, aut isti tot mala sustinuerint." And then Mr. Knight gives us a sketch of the *true causes* of the Trojan war—repeating the political fancies of Thucydides, amplified by some other fancies of his own.

"*For one little woman !*" We can hardly bring ourselves to transcribe the words as applied to Helen! And this from a scholar who must have had present to his mind not only the third book of the *Iliad*, but the fourth book of the *Odyssey*, and especially that passage in which we are informed that the possession of Helen, as

the Trojan war given in prose by Dictys Cretensis. Any one who is disposed to treat the siege of Troy, not as a legend but as an historical event, cannot do better than take this narrative as it stands. He will find in it everything reduced to a consistent and credible historical march—decent and well-behaved historical personages from beginning to end—the freaks and abnormities of the original tale are made to give place to a series of consecutive proceedings, conducted according to the received rules of diplomacy and political genius. One thing alone is wanting to give to Dictys Cretensis a high place among historians—unfortunately this one thing is the very soul of history—a slight infusion of evidence either positive or presumptive. Evidence it has none, either in the general features or in the details: it is fiction, without the charms of fiction, clothed only in the stolen and unsuitable habiliments of truth.

We have briefly indicated these various interpretations of the Grecian mythi by various historical and geographical

a wife, procures for Menelaus, not merely the exalted rank of son-in-law of Zeus, but also immortality, and a residence in the Elysian plain along with Rhadamanthus, in the most delicious climate conceivable (*Odyss.* iv. 564)! It is some relief to us that Mr. Knight employed the word *vix* instead of *non*, in rejecting the received belief that Helen was the cause of the Trojan war: had he *peremptorily* denied this, the shock to our faith would have been intolerable. Would he have ventured even to intimate a doubt, in the presence of an Æolic audience in festival, 800 years before the Christian era, fresh from the hearing of the third book of the Iliad?

Now all these objections of Pausanias, Herodotus, and Mr. Knight, against the received narrative of the Trojan war, granting their fundamental supposition, are quite unanswerable. If you once admit that war to be an historical fact, Helen descends into "a little woman," and the Greeks as well as the Trojans become the silliest of mankind: you cannot vindicate them from that imputation except by cutting out and transforming events, and adding new matter, to such a degree that you end by producing a new war of Troy, as Dio Chrysostom has done in his eleventh oration. This is, in our view, a *reductio ad absurdum* of the fundamental supposition.

authors from Thucydides downwards, considering them all
as different applications of one and the same theory: and
we have considered the Homeric poems as the type of the
mythus both in its greatest beauty and in its most complete
peculiarity as distinguished from positive history. Whether
we consult Thucydides, who tells us that the siege of Troy
was prolonged for ten years because the Greeks were too
poor to procure provisions, and were therefore compelled to
fortify their camp and send away detachments to cultivate
the Chersonese — or the presumptuous Scholiast who de-
grades Xanthus and Balius into ordinary stallions—or Pausanias, who transforms the Trojan horse into a battering
engine — or Mr. Knight, when he terms Helen "a little
woman," for whom none but fools would take trouble or
endure calamity—in all, the assumption is involved, tacitly
and as a thing of course, that the Grecian epic is at bottom
matter of fact, only disguised, magnified, and inaccurately
expressed: and that the pure matter of fact may by analysis
be separated from its alloy of fiction.

This assumption we hold to be incorrect—not less incorrect than the opinion of those philosophers who saw in the
epic only an allegorical veil concealing various positions in
physics and morals. It passed naturally to the modern
world from the historians of antiquity, and we have endeavoured to point out that in their minds it was a sort of compromise with the ancient literal faith—a semi-belief, which
seemed to reconcile inherited sentiments and emotions with
the personal rights of reason, and which spared them the
painful necessity of renouncing altogether the prescriptive
tales interwoven both with the patriotism and the piety of
all around them.

With an ancient Pagan, to pronounce the legends of his
country altogether fiction would have been most repulsive to
his feelings, and not very promising for his comfort; because
it would have placed him in direct conflict with the religion
of his fellow-citizens. With a modern writer, we might
imagine that the step would be easy and natural, because

I

he begins by disbelieving all the Gods and the Heroes of Paganism, as well as the legends connected with them ; unless, indeed, he adopts the theory of Euemerus, that all the ancient Gods as well as Heroes were originally real men, deified in consequence of services rendered to mankind or from some other special cause. But this theory, though countenanced by Polybius and some other eminent individuals, was regarded as a disguised atheism, and never obtained extensive currency among the Pagans : it received support chiefly from the subsequent Christian writers, such as Lactantius and St. Augustin, who found it a convenient way of dispeopling the Pagan Olympus. St. Augustin willingly adopted the tale of an historical Zeus, of human parentage, and born in the time and place specified by Euemerus, because it strengthened his argument against the worshippers of the God Zeus. But modern writers, not being engaged in controversy with living Pagans, do not follow him in this facility of historical belief.*

---

* Euemerus was generally considered among the Pagans as an Atheist—Εὐήμερος, ὁ ἐπικληθεὶς ἄθεος—Sext. Empiric. adv. *Physicos*, ix. §§ 17 and 51 ; Cicero, *De Naturâ Deorum*, i. 42. His doctrine is sharply denounced by Plutarch on this ground. De Isid. et Osirid. c. 23, t. ii. p. 475, Wyttenb.

For the sentiments of the Christian writers, we may cite Minucius Felix (*Octav.* 20–21): " Euemerus exequitur Deorum natales ; patrias, sepulcra, dinumerat, et per provincias monstrat ; Dictæi Jovis, et Apollinis Delphici, et Phariæ Isidis, et Cereris Eleusiniæ." And St. Augustin (*De Civitate Dei*, vi. 7): " Quid de ipso Jove senserunt, qui nutricem ejus in Capitolio posuerunt ? Nonne adtestati sunt omnes Euemero, qui omnes tales Deos, non fabulosa garrulitate, *sed historicâ diligentiâ*, homines fuisse mortalesque conscripsit ?" We may add, also, xviii. 8-14 of the same work ; Lactant. *De Ira Dei*; and Clemens Alexandr. *Admonit. ad Gentes*, pp. 15–18, ed. Sylb.

As Lactantius and St. Augustin adopt the views of Euemerus respecting the originally human position of Jupiter and Apollo, so Bede, William of Malmesbury, Saxo Grammaticus, &c., treat Woden and the ancient Teutonic gods and heroes as having been mere men

Euemerism has, in our eyes, the merit of consistency: it applies the same scheme of explanation to the divine and the heroic legends, nor is it possible to assign any tenable distinction between the one and the other. We adopt an explanation the reverse of Euemerism: instead of assuming an historical basis for both, we contend that it is fruitless to look for such a basis in either, and that both alike grew and developed themselves out of the feelings and emotions of the people.

We endeavoured to show, in the earlier part of this article, that in classifying the stories currently believed amongst a community, though a large portion of them consisted of matters of fact misreported or exaggerated, yet another large portion had no foundation in fact at all, but were generated by, and illustrative of, certain feelings, commonly both earnest and wide-spread: We pointed out the fundamental mistake of confounding pure legend or mythus with inaccurate history, inasmuch as the mode of treatment suitable to the one was totally misapplied with regard to the other: We showed that mere plausibility—*i.s.* consonance with pre-existing feelings common to speakers and hearers —was amply sufficient, without any positive evidence, both to call forth and extensively to accredit such fictions: We illustrated, by the case of Lord Byron's life, the material fact, that even in our present age, when muniments of evidence are multiplied and accessible, and when historical research is effectively prosecuted, still the mythopœic propensity was fruitful and unsubdued; and that the minds of the nineteenth century — "sine ullis Conjugiis, vento

---

falsely deified.   See Grimm, *Deutsche Mythologie*, art. ' Holden,' cap. xi., and the curious citations in that instructive article.   One from Alboricus we transcribe (p. 201): " In hâc generatione decimâ ab incarnatione Domini (*i. e.* before) regnasse invenitur quidam Mercurius in Gottlandia insulâ : a quo Mercurio, quo *Wodan* dictus est, descendit genealogia Anglorum et multorum aliorum," &c. This is to the full as authentic as Mr. Clinton's *Phoroneus.*

gravidæ"—were ready to pour forth, and still more ready
to welcome, impressive legends calculated to satisfy any
earnest feeling which animated them. Finally, we added,
that transporting ourselves back to Greece in the seventh
and eighth centuries before the Christian era, when recorded
matter of fact was unknown, we should find the empire of
mythus all but omnipotent, and the necessity of requiring
some positive evidence as a condition of belief, neither
recognised nor thought of, even among the superior minds
of the community; plausible fiction in exclusive vogue,
authenticated truth not yet risen above the horizon.

The countless divine legends engendered during these
ealry ages by the religious feelings of the Greeks, both attest
and elucidate what has been here advanced. Such tales are
found possessing the firmest hold on the public mind and
belief, yet confessedly without any foundation in fact;
emanating originally from the poets or other productive
minds of the community, but adapted by them to the state
of feeling which they shared in common with the rest, and
requiring no stronger certificate to procure for them both
a cordial welcome, and a sincere belief.

> Αὐτοδίδακτος δ' εἰμί, θεὸς δέ μοι ἐν φρεσὶν οἴμας
> Παντοίας ἐνέφυσεν,

says Phemius in the Odyssey (xxii. 347). The self-taught
bard, whose nature is penetrated in all directions by the
heavenly inspiration, is in this state of the public mind
the most irresistible of all witnesses; his information, like
that of the prophet and the soothsayer, is eagerly caught
at by the auditors as proceeding from that source in which
they most implicitly and unhesitatingly confide.

But the religious feeling, though at that time stronger,
more pervading, and more prolific than any other, has yet
no exclusive privilege to create accredited fiction. Other
feelings, when earnest and diffused, will produce the same
result, though religion blends itself and coalesces more or
less with them all. An abundant growth of mythi, semi-

divine and semi-human, is the spontaneous produce of such
a soil—mythi quite as much independent of matter of fact
as the legend of Zeus and Heré—mythi which spring out
of, and are sustained by, some prevailing hopes, fears, sympathies, admiration, antipathy,—any sentiment whatever,
provided only it be fervent and shared by a considerable
number of persons.

To this latter class the early poetical legends of Greece
seem to us to belong — the Trojan war, the Argonautic
voyage, the hunt of the Calydonian boar, the labours and
sufferings of Hercules, the tales of Cadmus and Œdipus, the
invasion of Attica by the Amazons, with several others. It
is from the aggregate of mythi such as these, that what is
called the history of Greece prior to the commencement of
the Olympiads has been made out. In respect of beauty
of incident and genius of combination, there are very great
differences between these various legends: in respect of
evidence, homogeneous origin, and common influence over
Grecian sentiment, they are all in the main alike. They
constitute the heroic antiquities of Greece, a world completely distinct from the world of historical fact, and connected with it only by that thread of genealogy which the
great families in every Grecian community prided themselves
in tracing up to the heroes and the gods.

Of the particular circumstances which originally determined these legendary creations of the Grecian mind, our
means of knowledge do not enable us to speak; but the
Trojan war, the most memorable of them all, belongs to a
class of which several parallels can be produced. To the
Æolic and Ionic colonists, a cluster of men from various
Grecian tribes who had migrated to Asia Minor and acquired
for themselves settlements by extruding the prior occupants,
it was pleasing to imagine a supposed expedition of their
gods and their heroes to the same shores in some distant
period of the unknown past: the victory so obtained by
these superhuman persons gave to their descendants what
may be called a mythical title to the territory which they

occupied. The gods and heroes, those who were worshipped in the festivals of the Asiatic Grecian islands and towns, as well as in the gentile sacrifices of the illustrious families, constituted the prime agents in this supposed past expedition; the conductors of the Æolic emigration were considered as the personal descendants of Agamemnon (Strabo, xiii. p. 582), and the rights acquired by the conquest of the latter were believed to have been transmitted to his progeny. This seems to have been the basis of a legend, afterwards expanded and adorned to so prodigious an extent by the splendour of the Grecian epic. The idea of a right to the soil, deduced from such legendary events, occurs not unfrequently in Grecian proceedings. The Athenians contended that their right to Sigeium was as good as that of the Mitylenæans, because their progenitors had taken part in the Trojan war (Herodot. v. 94). According to the Cyrenian legends, Apollo had carried off the nymph Cyrene from Pelion, in Thessaly, taken her into Africa, and established her as mistress of the soil on which the city stood (Pindar, Pyth. ix. 5). When Dorieus, the younger brother of Cleomenes, king of Sparta (and of course of Heracleidan descent), was about to lead out a colony, he was apprised by persons familiar with current oracular dicta or prophecies, that the territory round Mount Eryx, in Sicily, belonged of right to the descendants of Hercules, because Hercules himself had acquired it by his victory over the indigenous Eryx; and he was determined by this announcement to conduct his colonists to the spot (Herodot. v. 43). But perhaps the most curious example of the application of a legend to sustain pretended right to territory, is to be found in the case of the Athenians in regard to Amphipolis. The first attempt made by the Athenians to establish this important settlement, on the river Strymon, in the territory then belonging to the Edonian Thracians, dates in the year B.C. 465, fifteen years after the battle of Plutæa and the expulsion of the Persians from Greece; the first settlers perished, but a second body under Agnon permanently maintained the post

and built the city, which became both powerful and populous. In the eighth year of the Peloponnesian war, it was
surprised and taken by the Lacedæmonian general Brasidas;
conformably to the stipulations of the peace of Nicias, it
ought to have been restored to Athens, but the restitution
was never consummated. It continued for the next half-
century as an independent city, in spite of various unavailing attempts on the part of Athens, until at length it fell
into the hands of Philip of Macedon among his early conquests; but the Athenians did not even then abandon their
pretensions to it, and their ambassadors were instructed
to acquaint him that he had taken a town which of right
belonged to them. Æschines, one of the ambassadors, recounts to the Athenian public assembly the arguments by
which he had tried to convince the conqueror, and amongst
them he says—(Περὶ παραπρεσβείας, c. 14)—

"Respecting our original acquisition of the territory, and respecting the sons of Theseus—one of whom, Acamas, is stated to
have received this territory as a dowry with his wife—it was then
a suitable occasion to speak, and I enlarged upon the matter as
accurately as I could; now, however, I must compress my discourse,
and I will mention only those evidences (of our rights) derived, not
from the ancient mythi, but from the events of our own day."

Here are two remarkable points to be noticed. First, we
find a narrative, purely legendary or mythical, placed at
the head of a territorial abstract of title; and that too in
a thoroughly business-like discussion between the Athenian
ambassadors and Philip. Next, it is certain that this narrative must either have been originally invented, or at least
applied to the territory in question, posterior to the time
when the Athenians established themselves at Amphipolis,
since B.C. 465; for before that time there was nothing whatever to connect Athenian legends with a spot both remote
and barbarous. And this illustrates forcibly the point
maintained by C. O. Müller, in his learned 'Prolegomena
zu einer wissenschaftlichen Mythologie '—that genuine and
original legendary inventions continued to be made through-

out the historical ages—new matter added to the ancient mythi (though Müller has not included it amongst his citations, Prolegg., cap. 6, p. 132). If we were in possession of the reply of Philip, which Æschines compliments for its pertinence and completeness, we should probably find that he too was provided with a counter-legend, justifying his acquisition of Amphipolis by some ancient mythical grant—perhaps from his ancestor Hercules.

In canvassing the historical value of Grecian legend, we have confined our attention chiefly to the early ante-historical class; those of which the scene is laid in the remote past, anterior to the first Olympiad, or 776 B.C.; such as the siege of Troy, the Argonautic expedition, the Calydonian boar-hunt, the legends of Hercules, Cadmus, Œdipus, Theseus, &c. But new original mythi continued to be invented throughout the subsequent ages of positive history; and the example which we have cited, in reference to Lord Byron, proves that the earth out of which such plants spring is far from being yet effete. Of these new creations, some were aggregated on to the old ante-historical stock, as in the case of the Amphipolitan legend connected with the son of Theseus; but others were interpolated into the positive history, and fastened on to the ascertained historical persons of the succeeding age. Take, as an example, the story of Arion, the celebrated harper and dithyrambic poet, recounted by Herodotus (i. 21). Arion had gone from Corinth, where he was much protected and favoured by the despot Periander, on an excursion to the Grecian cities in Italy; having made large gains in the exercise of his profession, he was carrying them back to Corinth in a Corinthian ship; the seamen, eager to possess themselves of his gold, compel him to leap overboard in mid-sea on pain of being killed, but first grant him permission to clothe himself in his solemn costume, to stand upon the rowers' bench, and sing the Orthian nome. Having done this Arion jumped into the sea; but a dolphin, attracted by his strains, took him on his back and landed him safely at Cape Tænarus in the south of Laconia, from whence he made his way back, clothed in his full costume, to Corinth. There stood at Tœnarus, in the days of Herodotus, a small brazen statue, the offering of Arion, representing a man sitting on a dolphin.

Such was the legend respecting the great dithyrambic composer Arion. When we add that it was recounted and believed, both by the Lesbians and by the Corinthians, in the time of Herodotus—two communities, certainly, among the most wealthy and intelligent of Greece, our readers will not think it wonderful that the primitive Homeric audience should have accepted the Iliad as a literal history of the past.

Now this story is a precise counterpart of the various legends to which we have alluded concerning Lord Byron. It contains a basis of authentic fact—perhaps a superstructure of exaggerated or misreported fact—and certainly a portion of genuine mythus. Arion, like Byron, is an unquestionably historical person—a friend of the Corinthian Periander, and a great and original dithyrambic poet. Perhaps the story of his voyage from Tarentum may be misreported fact—of this we do not speak with confidence—yet, probably a vessel returning from Tarentum to Corinth would enter by the Gulf of Corinth, instead of going round Peloponnesus, and braving the proverbial dangers of Cape Malein. But it would be a great mistake to treat the story of the danger of Arion, and his salvation by the dolphin, as a mere exaggeration and mis-report of fact; it is a mythus quite as marked and unequivocal as the Florentine intrigue and murders associated with Lord Byron, and traceable to a very analogous source. It is composed mainly to illustrate the prodigious and superhuman effect of the dithyrambs of Arion, and especially of the nomus Orthius, upon men's hearts and imaginations; it is calculated to satisfy the feelings, and win the belief, of Greeks who were not less profoundly impressed with these lyric efforts, than the German legend-makers were with the poems of Lord Byron; it brings out, in a secondary way, the fancy entertained in antiquity, that the dolphin was of an affectionate temper and fond of music ($\H{i}\nu'$ ὁ φίλαυλος

ἔπαλλε δέλφις—Eurip. Electr., 435; see also the Fragment
of Pindar ap. Plutarch. Terrestria et Aquatilia Animal. c. 36,
p. 984. c.) We have here, then, a perfect mythus, but tacked
on to an historical fact and an historical person—a mythico-
historical incident.

Now it appears to us that the mistake so commonly made,
in regard to the Grecian early legends, consists in dealing
with the Trojan war and the Argonautic expedition, in the
same way as we deal with this story of Arion—in seeking a
basis of fact for the two former, as we successfully do for the
latter.   There is this essential difference between the two.
In regard to the Trojan war and the Argonautic expedition,
the legend stands alone, professing only to refer to an undefined past time: there is no collateral evidence of any
kind to corroborate either its incidents or the reality of its
personal characters.   But in the case of Arion, we know the
existence, the celebrity, and the date of the poet, upon
evidence quite independent of the legend, just as we know
the existence of Lord Byron: if we affirm that the legend
has an historical basis, we do not ground our affirmation on
the single certificate of the legend itself.   When any similar
independent evidence can be produced to certify the main
fact of an expedition of confederated Greece against Troy in
1183 B.C., or the outfit of a commonplace vessel, Argo, from
Jolcos to Colchis in the preceding generation, we shall then
readily yield our assent: until this is done, it is unreasonable
to call for any such historical assent.   A certain number of
the plays of Shakspeare have an historical basis.   How do
we know this?   Not upon the testimony of Shakspeare
himself, or of these particular plays themselves, but upon
positive testimony, independent both of the one and the
other.   Any play for which you cannot, by some independent
evidence, demonstrate an historical basis, passes *ipso facto*
as non-historical.   Apply the same test to the early Grecian
poems, and we exact no more.

And this brings us back to the principle which we laid
down some time ago, that the *onus probandi* always lies upon

the historian, and the simple absence of evidence is sufficient to put him out of court. Obvious as such a position will seem, it places us at issue with an inquirer no less eminent than Mr. Fynes Clinton.

In speaking of the personages of the old Grecian poems, belonging to a supposed date anterior to all recorded chronology, and long before all positive history, Mr. Clinton says (Introduction, p. vi.) :—

" Wo may acknowledge as real persons all those whom there is no reason for rejecting. The presumption is in favour of the early tradition, if no argument can be brought to overthrow it. The persons may be considered real, when the description of them is consistent with the state of the country at that time : when no national prejudice or vanity could be concerned in inventing them : when the tradition is consistent and general : when rival or hostile tribes concur in the leading facts : when the acts ascribed (divested of their poetical ornament) enter into the political system of the age, or form the basis of other transactions which fall within known historical times."

Such are Mr. Clinton's rules for appreciating historical evidence : we think them every way inadmissible.

First,—Mr. Clinton practically annuls the obligation of positive proof, as incumbent on the historian ; for the obligation comes to nothing, if he can satisfy it by producing simply " an early tradition," and then calling upon his opponents for arguments to overthrow it. Admit this position, and Brute, the Trojan, may still remain at the apex of English history. According to Mr. Clinton's rule, the assertions of the early tradition, in respect to times long anterior to positive history, will be admitted upon easier terms than the assertion of a contemporary witness in regard to his own times. For as you know nothing at all of the remote past, you cannot produce any evidence to contradict events alleged to have then taken place. Mr. Clinton not only lightens his own shoulders of all the burden of proving, but casts upon those of his adversary a burden of disproving, altogether intolerable and unheard of.

Secondly,—the word *tradition* is not merely vague, but thoroughly misleading: it acts upon the mind by means of an assumption, which being tacitly implied and not openly expressed, escapes direct confutation. The plain meaning of the word is, a narrative handed down from generation to generation; and fiction may be handed down in this way quite as well as fact, as we see by the Grecian religious legends. But the assumption whereby this word is made to carry evidentiary force, is that the narrative originally arose contemporaneously with, and was derived from, the incident which it professes to recount. As soon as this assumption is clearly stated, we perceive it to be often untrue, always gratuitous. The birth and parentage of tradition is essentially unsearchable—"caput inter nubila condit"—you hear the voice, but cannot tell from whence it proceeds.

Thirdly,—No greater privilege can be required in favour of a known and good contemporary witness, than that which Mr. Clinton here claims for mere impersonal hearsay. If you put into the box a veracious witness who has had means of knowing the facts to which he deposes, we are bound either to believe him, or to overthrow his testimony by argument or counter-testimony. In placing "early tradition" on this very same footing, Mr. Clinton effaces all the graduating lines by which the value of positive evidence is to be determined.

Fourthly,—Mr. Clinton overlooks the very existence of *plausible fiction,* and its generic difference from historical matter of fact. Plausible fiction will satisfy all the conditions which he lays down, to determine what persons are "real" in the old legends, just as well as authenticated truth; the plausibility of the fiction consists in its satisfying such conditions. One of the tests, indeed, furnished by Mr. Clinton is to be excepted—" Persons are to be considered as real, when no national prejudice or vanity could be concerned in inventing them." But, in the first place, we are far too little acquainted with the range of sentiment prevalent among the early Greeks to allow of our applying this negative test in practice: and in the second place, we again repeat, that the burden of proof rests with those who claim for a narrative or for a person the privilege of being inscribed on the tablet of history; not upon those who treat it as uncertified, and for that reason as presumptively fictitious.

It is by no means our purpose to maintain that there is no historical matter in the ancient Grecian legends. Amongst the varied and interesting agglomerate which they compose, we doubt not that there are fragments of historical matter of fact imbedded : and we shall rejoice much when any one will furnish some assured criterion by which to verify them and detach them from the rest. How unsuccessful have been the attempts hitherto made to accomplish such discrimination, we desire no better proof than this recent work on Chronology by Mr. Clinton, wherein he professes to compute the number of generations occupied by Grecian legendary personages anterior to the first Olympiad—to strike out such as are fictitious, and to retain only those which are real.

To seek a fixed chronological arrangement in this antemundane chaos, appears to us much the same as if any one were to take the flat round plate, constituting the surface of the earth as conceived by Homer,—with the deep and gentle river Oceanus flowing round it and returning into itself,—and distribute it into regular parallels of latitude, one passing through the island of Calypso, and another through the territory of the Cyclopes. And when we follow Mr. Clinton through the details of his scheme, we remark a curious alternation of cautious doubt with extreme licence of positive assertion ; enough of doubt is admitted to invalidate the whole series, yet numerous statements are made which imply that no such doubts ought to have application.

Thus Mr. Clinton tells us (p. 123) " that the Olympiad of Corœbus, B.C. 776, is the first date in Grecian chronology which can be fixed upon authentic evidence "—and that " in proceeding *upward*, this date is our highest point." The chronology for the anterior period he professes to reckon *downwards*, starting from Phoroneus, 977 years before the first Olympiad. But, let us ask, where is the value, and what is the credibility, of chronology, reckoned downwards? All chronological reckonings in the past must first be made upwards: you start from the present, and you then reckon upwards to some fixed point in the past, from which you may make a fresh start in either direction. If, for example, we are to reckon downwards from Phoroneus, we must first have performed the reckoning upwards from the present time to Phoroneus: if we are compelled, from want of "authentic evidence," to suspend our upward reckoning at the year B.C. 776, as Mr. Clinton allows, then any reckoning downwards to the year B.C. 776, from some undetermined point in anterior time such as the supposed epoch of Phoroneus, must be completely illusory. Having informed us —most correctly, as we think—that there is no authentic chronology higher than B.C. 776, Mr. Clinton might have spared himself the trouble of tracing imaginary chronological parallels for the earlier time.

Again, Mr. Clinton for the most part treats as fictitious the general class of eponymous persons—those whose names coincide with, and are produced as having given origin to, the name of a tribe, a city, a demus, a mountain, a river, a spring, &c. This class is very numerous throughout the legendary genealogies, and would appear to be still more so if we were better acquainted with the nomenclature of places and communities throughout Greece. Thus Hellen, Caucon, Pelasgus, and others, are, in Mr. Clinton's opinion, fictitious persons; such names and genealogies are not to be understood in their literal meaning, but as symbolical of certain circumstances in the history of the tribe—" the genealogical expression may be false (he tells us, p. 3), but the connexion which it describes is real." This, in our judgment, is a just remark, and points at the true value of the legendary genealogies: but we must observe, in the first place, that Mr. Clinton flinches from the application of his own principle when he recognizes as real persons, Cadmus, Danaus, Hyllus, and others, the eponymous heroes of the Cadmeians, the Danaans, and the Doric tribe Hylleis, just as Kruse (Hellas, vol. i., cap. v., sec. i., p. 414) distinguishes between Hellen and Pelasgus, affirming the former to be real, and the latter fabulous: and, in the second place, that whoever adopts such a view, subverts altogether the general authority of the genealogies, considered as attesting personal and chronological reality. For when it is conceded that so large a proportion of the story, told by the same witnesses, and depending upon the same authority, is fiction, we cannot with any reason be called upon to admit the remainder as so much authentic history.

The genealogical tables of Mr. Clinton, conformably to this method of partial scepticism inlaid with general faith, present a singular medley of mythical and real personages; a real father preceding a mythical son; or a real son following a mythical father; or real personality intermarrying with mythical, under the name either of husband or wife. It appears to us quite as easy, and we will add, not less philosophical, to credit the heroic genealogies entire, than to accept the mangled limbs of them as they appear in Mr. Clinton's pages, distinguished by common and italic type.

Mr. Clinton contends vehemently for the humanity and historical personality of Hercules; and we understand why he is so easy of faith upon this point, seeing that the genealogy of the Spartan kings, upon which the computations of Eratosthenes as to the date of the Trojan war were founded, assumes an unbroken series of real persons from Leonidas or Cleombrotus up to Hercules. If Mr. Clinton can bring himself to believe that Hercules was an historical man, we cannot understand why he should have any scruple in adopting the entire theory of Euemerus, and in humanising not only all the Pagan heroes but all the Pagan gods: for there is not a single personage to be found amongst them, who, from the mother's womb to the funeral pile, is more pointedly distinguished from ordinary humanity than

Hercules. We read with amazement the reasoning by which Mr. Clinton professes to demonstrate that Hercules was a real man who lived so many hundred years before the Christian era. If we had not already prolonged this article too much, we would analyse them and exhibit their futility : upon grounds equally good we would engage to degrade and humanise all the divine tenants of Olympus. Nothing can be more thoroughly un-Hellenic than to believe in Hercules as a man. If we had been born in Greece in the fifth century before the Christian era, we should have imbibed a faith which would have led us to carry offerings to his Herakleion ; we should have invoked his aid during peril, and should have listened with veneration to the epic poems which commemorated his marvellous exploits, his journeys, and his sufferings. Perhaps we might have believed, with Pindar and the Sicyonians (Pindar, Nem. iii. 21 — Pausan. ii., 10, 1), that he combined in mysterious unity the attributes of a Hero and a God : or we might have adopted the conviction of Herodotus, that there were two different beings named Hercules : the one a God, the other a Hero (Herod. ii. 44). But to conceive Hercules as a real ordinary historical man, begotten by some father of our own contemptible stature and infirmities, and no nearer to the Gods than ourselves, is a tenet which we must have regarded as impious and inadmissible.

In reverence for this ancient faith—now extinct, but once so fruitful in productions of lasting beauty—we ought at least to suffer its magnificent and essentially superhuman creations to set, like the tropical sun, with unabated splendour, without passing through the "pale gradation" and inglorious commonplace of physical humanity.

One other observation we will cite from Mr. Clinton. "It is necessary (he says, p. 3), for the right understanding of antiquity, that the opinions of the Greeks concerning their own origin should be set before us, even if these are erroneous opinions: and that their story should be told as they have told it themselves."

This is just and important: and, if Mr. Clinton had laid the remark to heart, he would have spared the heroic personality of Hercules, instead of dealing with it upon the same principle as the Homeric scholiast applies to the immortal horses Xanthus and Balius. It is not indeed too much to say, that if he had laid this remark to heart, he would have re-written his whole early chronology. For he constantly abandons the views of the Greeks, without any scruple; he admits distinctions between real and fictitious persons, such as they would never have dreamt of; he casts away, as fictions, personages more frequently thought of, and more reverentially believed in, than the rest, viz., the eponymous heroes of cities, tribes, and demi. No bribe would have induced us to read aloud Mr. Clinton's work in the presence of Herodotus.

We agree, then, with Mr. Clinton, that the antiquities of the Greeks should be told as they themselves have told them. And the very first condition for accomplishing this object is, that we should rightly appreciate the creative and unrecording age, of inspired bards and believing listeners, in which the early legends originally sprung up—as distinguished from the after-growth of positive and historical criticism, to which they were no way adapted, and by which they were disintegrated and recast into a seeming chronological sequence; above all, that we should place ourselves at the point of view of Grecian religious faith. The antiquities of every Grecian state are merged in and identified with its religion: without it they become utterly incomprehensible. At the opening of the Grecian world, Gods and Heroes, beings super-human and extra-human, occupy the canvas: realities in the eye of faith—fictions in that of modern criticism; but in no case human realities, nor fit subjects for history and chronology. The ancients did indeed introduce a sort of chronology even among their Gods and Heroes, for it was noway offensive to their belief to speak of a God being born, or of one God being more ancient than another. But when we once keep in view the light in which the

K

ancients regarded these initial personages in their history,
it will appear preposterous to expect an adherence to human
scale or measurement, either in their exploits, their suc-
cessions, or their duration. " Datur hæc venia (says Livy),
antiquitati, ut miscendo humana divinis, primordia urbium
augustiora faciat." Livy here tells us that the history of
the past is to be accommodated, by a proper mixture of
things human and divine, to the sentiments, in the minds
of the present, of what is august and holy. In other words,
it is to be *mythus*, which the sentiment of the present can
both abundantly supply and profoundly appreciate; not
positive matter of fact, which is insufficient for the purpose
as well as inaccessible to the view.

Hekatæus, of Miletus, the historian, boasted of a pedigree,
for himself and his gens or phratry, commencing with a God
and descending through fifteen successive links to himself
(Herod. ii. 143). In like manner the gens to which Thucydides, the historian, belonged, was traced up to Æacus the
son of Zeus (Marcellin. Vit. Thuc. init.) : these may serve as
a specimen of similar genealogies which every noble family
in the Grecian cities could boast of and commemorate in its
gentile sacrifices. According to the ancient point of view,
the God at the top was quite as firmly believed to be a
reality as any of the members of the series, and was far more
deeply cherished than the rest : nay, the principal value of
the whole genealogy was derived from the circumstance, that
it connected the living members with the God whom
they worshipped as their progenitor as well as their pro-
tector. According to the modern point of view, the God
at least is struck off as a fiction, and the genealogy thus
becomes essentially acephalous. We have a continuous
pedigree, of which the last member is indisputably real, the
first member as indisputably fictitious. At some point or
other between the two, the line separating fiction from truth
must be drawn : but we know not where to find that point,
and Mr. Clinton's rules, which were intended to solve this
problem, are altogether insufficient and illusory. Whether

the undetermined point is to be taken a little higher or a little lower in the series, let this be recollected—that to us who reject the Grecian religious faith, the earlier phenomena and the earlier persons of Grecian history are pure fable, not exaggerations or mis-reports of matter of fact.*

Agreeing then as we do with Mr. Clinton in the opinion that all authentic evidence of Grecian chronology—all chronological reckoning upwards—ceases with B.C. 776; we are compelled to treat the period earlier than B.C. 776, more in accordance with this fundamental supposition than he has treated it himself. We regard it as an—

" Illimitable ocean, without bound,·
Without dimension, where length, breadth, and height,
And time and space, are lost"—

the empire of mythus or legend, purely and simply; rich in plausible incidents adapted to the sentiment and accredited

---

* As an illustration of the inseparable connexion between early genealogies and religious belief, we cite an analogous fact respecting the Anglo-Saxon genealogies, from Grimm, ' *Deutsche Mythologie*,' Anhang, pp. 1–11, art. " Angel Sächsische Stammtafeln." " In the fifth and sixth centuries," he says, " the Anglo-Saxons at their transit into Britain brought with them out of Germany the tale of the descent of their noblest families. All of them carry themselves back to Woden; but they sometimes ascend even higher, and enumerate a series of gods or deified heroes as ancestors of Woden. After their conversion to Christianity, the attempt was made to connect the family stem of these gods and heroes with the Hebraic tradition of the first human family—to bring their heathen forefathers into harmony with the Noah and Adam of Scripture." (Anhang, p. 11.) Here we see that the change of religion brought about an entire change of the earlier genealogies.

Grimm thinks that similar genealogies were received among the other Teutonic tribes—the Frisians, Westphalians, Franks, &c. He treats them as quite worthless in respect to chronological matter of fact. " These catalogues of names," he says, " possess not the smallest chronological value for the oldest times: they first become historical with the lines of the Anglo-Saxon kings. But this detracts nothing from the importance of the legend."

K 2

by the religion of the auditors, but neither entitled to the authority, nor amenable to the laws, of historical reality. The scenes which it presents may be looked at, either with the eye of pious faith, as they were by the original recipients, or with that of æsthetic and poetical faith, by those who are unbelievers in the Homeric Paganism. But in either case they must be contemplated from a given and distant point of view, which the spectator is not at liberty to alter: like the beautiful feminine image which fascinates the gaze of Faust whilst in the witch's cell, they vanish into untraceable mist, the moment he approaches either to touch or to scrutinise.

That there is more or less of matter of fact among these ancient legends, we do not at all doubt. But if it be there, it is there by accident, because it happened to fall in with the purpose of the mythopœic narrator, who will take fact, as he takes fiction, when it is suggested by the impulse in his own mind, or germane to the sentiment of his hearers. To discriminate the fact from the fiction, is a problem which we ourselves know not how to solve, in the absence of some positive evidence independent of the legend itself. We shall gratefully listen, if any one will teach us: but sure we are that some road must be discovered very far removed from that hitherto trodden by historical critics. For we cannot too strongly protest against the process of picking out pretended matter of fact, by simply decomposing the legend and eliminating all which is high-coloured, or impressive, or miraculous; it condemns us to all the tameness and insipidity of prose, but we remain as far as ever from the certainty and solid nourishment of truth.

For the period after B.C. 776, we conceive that a different manner of dealing with evidence becomes both necessary and admissible. We then come to tread a beaten chronological track, and to deal with assured historical personages: our positive information, though scanty, is yet sufficient to afford us holding ground when we try to discriminate matter of fact either from exaggeration or from fiction. Mythus has ceased to be predominant, but it still continues to spring up as an element of itself out of its own soil of emotion and sentiment; attached, indeed, to positive facts, yet in many cases clearly distinguishable from inaccuracy or mis-report of facts. We tried to illustrate this point by the legend of Arion quoted from Herodotus.

The German poet Schiller, in his beautiful ode, 'Die Goetter Griechenlands,' describes the physical world as it was conceived in antiquity, replete with personifications, and animated in all its localities by unseen beings who mingled their sympathies and interests with the chequered lot of short-lived man. And he presents, as a repulsive contrast, the physical world as it is now studied and understood—a lifeless and impersonal aggregate, slavishly obedient to rules of which it has no consciousness, and destitute of all sympathy with the men who suffer or profit by it. Estimated by a poetical standard, the loss has been serious indeed: but it has been far more than compensated by the acquisition of lasting and substantial benefits. We have obtained in exchange an ascertained, methodical, and constantly increasing body of authentic truth: and we have obtained it, let us remark, not by transforming and refining the imperfect ancient physics themselves, but by following cautiously the track, and respecting the limits, of positive evidence. There were, however, in antiquity, as we have already stated, a body of allegorising philosophers, who could neither accept literally the interesting personifications of the old world, nor strike out for themselves a means of reaching the assured results of the new. These men extracted from the ancient mythi a string of pretended physical sequences, resolving the embraces of Zeus and Heré into the descent of the pure ether from on high upon the lower strata of the atmosphere, and dissipating all the charm of the original conception under pretence of banishing exaggeration and poetical ornament. The allegorised physics of Heraclides and Porphyry form a suitable counterpart to the historicised legend.

There is music in the high-pitched voice and irregular

rhythm of childhood, and there is something better than
music in the grave tone and discriminating emphasis of the
mature man.   But between the two lies an awkward interval,
of intolerable harshness and dissonance—the broken voice of
the youth just bursting into puberty : and this seems to us
the only fit accent for the reading of the historical war of
Troy, as it is sketched by Thucydides and Mr. Payne Knight,
and as it is detailed by Dictys the Cretan.

ANCIENT WEIGHTS, COINS, AND MEASURES.

(*Classical Museum*, 1844.)

ANCIENT WEIGHTS, COINS, AND MEASURES.

M. Boeckh has so long been celebrated in the philological world for profound erudition—for method, as well as ingenuity, in the combination of scattered facts, and for the quality, somewhat rare among eminent scholars, of sobriety in the field of conjecture—that no preface is necessary when I proceed to offer a few remarks upon one of his recent and most elaborate productions.[*]

The *Metrologie* is a work not unworthy of its distinguished author. The dispersed fragments of evidence, respecting the weights, measures, and monetary systems of the ancient world—one of the most perplexing subjects in the whole range of philology,—are patiently collected, and perspicuously discussed: and the thirty chapters, of which the book consists, are so closely packed with matter, as to forbid the possibility of any condensed abstract of the entire contents. The views of M. Boeckh are, in several respects, original, differing even from opinions stated by himself in former publications: he has, moreover, imparted to the subject a new interest, by considering the metrological systems of the various countries in antiquity in continual comparison with each other, so as to elicit valuable proofs of

[*] *Metrologische Untersuchungen über Gewichte, Münzfüsse, und Masse des Alterthums in ihrem Zusammenhange,* Von August. Boeckh. Berlin, 1838. 1 vol. 8vo.

early communion and transition of ideas between them. His book ' embraces the weights and measures prevalent throughout all the countries known to us in the ancient world,—Babylon, Syria, Phenicia, Judæa, Egypt, Sicily, Italy, and Rome: and the comparative metrology of these nations is presented to us in a way analogous to the *Vergleichende Grammatik* of Bopp, in regard to the extensive family of the Indo-Germanic languages; it exhibits the diffusion of institutions, originating in the very ancient civilization of Babylon, to the neighbouring countries whose period of settled ordinances and commerce was more recent.

Though this transition must have taken place anterior to recorded history, and, therefore, in a manner which we cannot now fathom, yet the reality of the fact is sufficiently proved by its lasting and ascertained results. In cases where the weights and measures of two different nations are found to be in a precise and definite ratio one to the other—either exactly equal, or exact multiples and parts of each other— we may fairly presume, either that the one has borrowed from the other, or that each has borrowed from some common source (*Metrol.* c. ii. § 3). Where the ratio is inaccurate, or simply approximative, it is to be treated as accidental and undesigned.

I request particular attention to this distinction between a precise ratio, and a ratio merely approximative, which M. Boeckh lays down very clearly, and which he justly announces as the cardinal principle of his metrological reasonings. To a great extent, he has succeeded in exhibiting an analogy, both interesting and hitherto unknown, between the metrical and statical systems of the various countries to which his work relates. But I must at the same time add, that there are several of his conclusions which appear to me very imperfectly supported, and some even which are not to be reconciled with the evidence. In a subject so obscure and perplexed from beginning to end, this is by no means wonderful.

In investigating the subject of the ancient weights and

measures, in so far as they afford evidence of communion or analogous proceeding between the different nations of antiquity, the great point to be attended to is the normal system as it was fixed by law, abstracting from those imperfections which attended the execution of it in detail. All mechanical processes in antiquity were carried on far more loosely and inaccurately than they are at present: pieces of money, as well as weights and measures, were both less durable and less exact, in spite of the solicitude of the ancient governments. We know by the evidence of inscriptions, with respect to Athens, that normal weights and measures were preserved under custody of a public officer in the chapel of the Hero Stephanephorus; that copies of these were made and distributed for private use; and that strict watch was directed to be kept for the purpose of excluding fraudulent or incorrect weights and measures in the shops and market.[*] The case was similar at Rome, and seemingly also at Jerusalem (*Metrol.* c. ii. § 3). In this manner the theoretical perfection of the standard was maintained in the minds of the people as it was when originally adopted, in spite of imperfect execution in practice.

M. Boeckh enters upon his subject, in the third chapter of the work, by an investigation of the Roman liquid measure, quadrantal or amphora, in its relation to the Roman pound weight. According to the Silian plebiscite, as reported by Festus, the legal definition of a quadrantal was, a vessel containing eighty pounds weight of wine or water: the congius being one-eighth part of it, and containing ten pounds weight of the same. By this regulation the dimensions of the vessels containing liquids were made dependent, not upon cubical measurement, but upon weight, like the imperial gallon in England. Now the Attic liquid measure called χοῦς, was the exact equivalent of the Roman congius; and the Attic μετρήτης, the largest unity of liquid measures at Athens, contained twelve χόες, and was equivalent to one

---

[*] Boeckh, *Corpus Inscript. Græcar.* No. 123-150.

and a half amphoræ, or quadrantalia. Such a definite ratio does undoubtedly indicate either some common original from which both systems must have been deduced, or an imitation of one of them by the other. M. Boeckh seeks to deduce both one and the other from the East, where it will be presently shewn that the Chaldæans at Babylon had adopted in very early times a system of determining their cubic measures by ultimate reference to a given weight.

" If," (he says, iii. 4. p. 26) " we regard this relation of the weights and measures, based upon a given weight of water, which is the keystone of the Roman system, and if we carry the application of this water-weight backwards to the chief measures of the ancient world, we shall find a connection really and truly organic between the systems of the different people of antiquity, and we shall arrive at last at the fundamental unity of weight and measure in the Babylonian system; so that this supposition is found to be verified in all its consequences and details. To give some preliminary intimation of this, I shall shew that the Grecian (or more accurately, the Æginæan) and the Roman pound are in the ratio 10 : 9; the Æginæan pound is half the Æginæan mina; but the cubical measures stood normally in the ratio of the weights; and therefore the Grecian cubic foot was to the Roman as 10 : 9 ; and as the Roman cubic foot weighs eighty pounds of rain-water, so also the Grecian cubic foot weighs eighty Grecian or Æginæan pounds, equal to forty Æginæan minæ. The unity of weight (in Greece) however is, not forty minæ, but sixty minæ, or a talent. In the original institutions of the people of antiquity every thing has its reason, and we find scarcely any thing purely arbitrary : nevertheless, this unity of weight, the talent, does not coincide with the unity of measure—neither with the cubic foot, nor with any other specific cubical denomination. But the coincidence reveals itself at once, as soon as we discover that the Babylonian cubic foot, standing as it does in the ratio of 3 : 2 to the Grecian cubic foot, weighs sixty Æginæan minæ (= 60 Babylonian minæ = 1 Babylonian talent) of rain-water."

M. Boeckh here promises more than his volume will be found to realise. He does, indeed, satisfactorily shew that the Babylonian talent was identical with, and was the original prototype of, the Æginæan talent, and that the standard and scale of *weight* was strikingly and curiously similar in Asia, in Egypt, and in Greece. But he has not, I think, made out the like with regard to the Grecian *measures*, either of length or capacity, and his proof of the ratio of 3 : 2 between the Babylonian and the Grecian foot will be found altogether defective. Nor has he produced adequate evidence to demonstrate, either the ratio of 10 : 9 between the Grecian or Æginæan pound and the Roman pound, or that of 1 : 2 between the Æginæan pound and the Æginæan mina ; the ratio between the Grecian cubic foot and the Roman cubic foot, too, as also that between the Grecian cubic foot and any given Grecian weight, is, as he proposes it, inadmissible. In fact, there is no such thing (properly speaking) as an Æginæan pound weight : nor is there any fixed normal relation between Grecian weight and Grecian measures, either of length or of capacity, though there is a fixed normal relation between Babylonian weight and Babylonian measures, as also between Roman weight and Roman measures.

The Greek scale of weight consisted of the talent, the mina, the drachma, and the obolus : the talent consisting of 60 minæ—the mina of 100 drachmæ—the drachma of 6 obols. The scale of weight in Sicily and Italy was essentially and originally different, having for its unit the pound —always divided into twelve ounces, except in central Italy, north of the Apennines, where it contained only ten ounces. These denominations were universal throughout Sicily and Italy, though the pound, in one part of Italy and another, was not the same absolute weight, any more than the talent in Greece. M. Boeckh, as well as all other writers on the subject, recognises this radical distinction between the Hellenic population on the one hand, and the earliest inhabitants, both of Italy and Sicily, on the other, in respect,

both to the denomination and divisions, of the statical and
monetary scale. And I may here remark, that the supposition of identity of Pelasgian race between the original
population of Epirus, and that of the south-eastern regions
of Italy, announced with confidence by Niebuhr, and adopted
by K. O. Müller, becomes open to doubt from our finding
no mention of pound weight or ounce weights among the
Epirots. The Corinthian colonies on the coast of Epirus—
Leukas, Anaktorium, and Ambrakia, as well as the island
of Korkyra—pursued a system of coinage purely Hellenic,
consisting of talents, minæ, and drachmæ. But the Corinthian colony of Syrakuse, as well as every other Hellenic
establishment, either in Sicily or Italy, adopted a mixed
system, in which talents, minæ, and drachmæ, were blended
together with pounds and ounces, not according to any
one uniform principle, but varying from town to town both
in Italy and Sicily. The statical denominations prevalent
among the Italian and Sicilian Greeks, arising as they do
out of a compound of two systems originally distinct, present
questions full of perplexity, and such as can hardly be solved
with our existing stock of information.

The words talent, drachma, and obolus, are genuine Greek,
and of Grecian origin: the first of the three even occurs in
Homer, though in a sense quite different from that which
it subsequently bore in Greece; denoting, seemingly, a
definite, but small, weight.[*]   But the systematic graduation

---

[*] Aristotle had said (*Schol. Ven. ad Iliad.* xxiii. 269) that the
talent in Homer was a weight altogether undefined. M. Boeckh
agrees with him (*Metrol.* iv. 1. p. 33). But surely this opinion
cannot be reconciled with the assertion that "Odysseus weighed
out ten talents of gold" (*Iliad* xix. 247: Χρύσου δὲ στήσας 'Οδυσσεὺς
δέκα πάντα τάλαντα); or even with the specification of a definite
number of talents of gold—*ten* talents, *two* talents, &c. (*Odyss.* iv.
526, and other passages cited in Damm's *Lexicon*). The word
τάλαντον originally means a *scale*, as is well known, and is often so
used by Homer.

In the *Iliad* and *Odyssey*, as well as in the Hesiodic *Works and*

of weights in Greece seems of a date later than the Odyssey;
and the word mna, or mina, which forms the central point
of the scale, has no root in the Greek language. It is of
Chaldaic origin, and has also been discovered by Cham-
pollion among the ancient hieroglyphic writing of Egypt
(*Metrol.* iv. 2. p. 39). The etymology of this word points
to the quarter from whence the Greeks received their scale
of weight: and it will be found that there is sufficient
analogy between the scales adopted in Greece, Judæa, Phenicia, and Egypt, to warrant a belief that all of them were
derived from one common origin—the Chaldaic priesthood
at Babylon. We are told by Herodotus, that the Greeks
adopted from the Babylonians the sun-dial, the gnomon,
and the division of the day into twelve hours: and M.
Boeckh, in one of the most learned sections of the *Metrologie*
(iv. 4), has traced the diffusion of the worship of Mylitta, or
Aphrodité Urania, original in Assyria, through the inter-
me-liation of the Phenicians, to Greece, Asia Minor, and
Sicily.

In the fifth chapter of his work, M. Boeckh investigates
the value of the Babylonian talent-weight as compared with
the Grecian. Herodotus, in his enumeration of the tribute-
money paid by the various regions subject to the kings of

Days, reference occurs to the chief measures of length and of area;
ὄργυια, πῆχυς, πούς, σπιθαμή, δῶρον, πλέθρον, γῆ; but no precise or
definite measure of capacity is noticed in them; μέτρον and ἀμφι-
φορεύς are of unknown bulk. But the scale of dry measure is at
least as old as the Hesiodic poem called *The Catalogue of Women,*
as we may ascertain by the occurrence of the word μέδιμνος, which
only belongs to the language as a technical denomination of
measure. See the story of Mopsus and Kalchas, *Hesiod ap. Strab.*
xiv. p. 921; *Fragm.* ed. Gaisf. xiv.

Μύριοί εἰσιν ἀριθμὸν· ἀτὰρ μέτρον γε μέδιμνος.

The word μέδιμνος seems to belong to the same family as μέτρον,
metior, which is said to be traceable to a Sanskrit root. (Curtius,
*De Nominum Græcorum Formatione, Linguarum Cognatarum Ratione
habitâ,* p. 48. Berlin, 1842.)

Persia, states that the greater number of them were directed to pay in silver, a given number of Babylonian talents; while the Indians were required to pay in gold, a certain number of Euboic talents: and he then adds that the Babylonian talent was equivalent to 70 Euboic minæ (Herod. iii. 89). The total sums however, as Herodotus states them, do not precisely coincide with the items of his estimate; but there is a confusion either in the calculations of the historian, or in the text, which cannot be rectified by the aid of our present MSS., and we are only enabled to see that the estimate of 70 Euboic minæ is lower than the real value of the Babylonian talent.

Two other statements are found, of the value of the latter : Pollux gives it at 70 Attic talents, Ælian at 72 Attic talents. That the number 72 is more exact than 70, is a reasonable presumption : but if we attach to Attic talents the value of the Attic money talent as established by Solon, the three statements of Herodotus, Pollux, and Ælian, will become absolutely irreconcileable : for the Euboic talent was a weight decidedly and considerably larger than the Solonian Attic talent. But the three statements come into complete harmony when we interpret the Attic talents, as stated by Pollux and Ælian, to mean "great Attic talents," as they are called by Dardanus the ancient Metrologue; that is, Attic talents as they stood before the reduction of Solon. It is ascertained not merely by the evidence of Dardanus, but by the still more incontrovertible testimony of a published Athenian inscription, that the "great Athenian talent and mina" continued in exclusive use at Athens, *as weights*, for several centuries after Solon—that the debasement introduced by that legislator applied only to the coins, drachmæ, obols and their multiples, together with the mina and talent considered as pecuniary denominations apart from actual weight. The Attic mina and talent underwent, by the enactment of Solon, a change similar to that of the English pound during successive centuries. Our pound originally contained a full pound weight of standard silver, and its signification both as

money and as weight was identical; but in process of time
the standard was lowered, and its pecuniary meaning was
greatly changed, while its meaning as weight remained unaltered. We know by the evidence of the inscription above
alluded to, that the mina as weight—the *commercial mina*,
as it was formally denominated—was required to weigh
138 Solonian standard drachmæ: and it will be shewn presently that its exact weight had originally been 138⅔ of
such drachmæ.

Construed in this very rational and admissible sense, the
three accounts of Herodotus, Pollux, and Ælian, respecting
the value of the Babylonian talent will be found concurrent.
It is divided according to the common scale, viz. 60 minæ,
and 6000 drachmæ of its own: and it is equivalent to 72
Euboic minæ each weighing 138⅔ Solonian standard drachmæ.
In other words, it is equivalent to 10,000 of these Solonian
drachmæ; the precise value of the Æginæan talent, according to the express announcement of Pollux, being in the
proportion of 5 : 3 to the Solonian standard. Calculating
by this proportion, the standard weight of a Babylonian or
Æginæan drachma (the 6000th part of a Babylonian or
Æginæan talent) ought to be 112.295 English grains Troy.
We are hardly entitled to expect any remaining actual coins
to be of full standard weight, since almost every state in
antiquity coined below its own standard, even when the
standard continued legally unchanged; and we must allow
besides for loss arising from wear and tear. But it is remarkable that the Persian silver darics, now in the British
Museum, adjusted as they doubtless were to the Babylonian
scale by which the silver tribute was measured, do exhibit a
weight of 224 English grains troy, or a little above—nearly
the exact weight which they ought to have as Babylonian
or Æginæan didrachms.

In the sixth chapter of his work, M. Boeckh enters into
an elaborate examination of the Hebraic, Phenician, and
Syrian system of weight and money: and he establishes on
probable grounds, that the scale followed in these countries

L

even from very early times, agreed with and was borrowed
from the Babylonian. The Hebraic talent had 60 minæ,
and 3000 holy shekels or didrachms : of the latter, the best
and heaviest specimens now remaining approach so very
near to the normal weight of the Babylonian or Æginæan
didrachm, that we may confidently reckon them as having
been originally the same (c. vi. § 3). It appears however,
that the subordinate divisions of the Hebraic scale were not
coincident with those of the Æginæan, which portioned the
drachma into 6 obols : the Hebraic holy shekel or didrachm
was divided into 20 gera, and the common shekel or drachma
(the half of the holy shekel) into 10 gera : thus rendering a
gera the equivalent of an Attic obolus (vi. 3 and vi. 5).
M. Boeckh gives, in c. vi. § 7, the weight of a number of
different coins, some of various Syrian kings, others of the
Phenician cities. The heaviest and least worn amongst them
come so near to the normal weight of the Æginæan didrachm
as to authorise the conclusion that they were intended to
conform to it : and there are several conformable coins,
belonging to the Sicilian city of Panormus, which raise an
inference that the same standard of weight and money had
passed from Tyre to its colony Carthage.

That both the Euboic talent with its subdivisions, and the
Babylonian talent with its subdivisions, were in use throughout the Persian empire, is proved by the fact that the
tributes to government were required to be paid in them.
I may remark however, that it is very doubtful whether the
Persian tribute was paid in coined money. Herodotus tells
us, that it was the practice of the great king's officers to
melt the silver and gold which they received in payment of
tribute, and to pour it into large earthenware jars : as soon
as the metal cooled, the jars were broken : portions were
then detached from the mass when there was occasion to
make disbursements. * We know farther from the same his-

---

* Herod. iii. 96. Τοῦτον τὸν φόρον θησαυρίζει ὁ βασιλεὺς τρόπῳ
τοιῷδε. Ἐς πίθους κεραμίνους τήξας κατεγχέει· πλήσας δὲ τὸ ἄγγος,
περιαιρέει τὸν κέραμον· ἐπεὰν δὲ δεηθῇ χρημάτων, κατακόπτει τοσοῦτο
ὅσον ἂν ἑκάστοτε δέηται.

torian, that the gold and silver in the treasury of Kroesus was principally, if not entirely uncoined.[*] There could be no advantage in receiving coin when it was destined to be melted : moreover, the coins, which the great king might receive at one extremity of his large empire, would be unsuitable for payments at the other extremity, or even at the centre. The object of the requisition was a given weight of fine metal ; weighed according to the Euboic, or smaller talent, for the gold ; according to the Babylonian, or larger talent, for the silver. I shall have occasion to revert to this point, which I do not find noticed by M. Boeckh, when I come to speak of the conventions between Antiochus and the Romans.

Both the Babylonian and the Euboic scale of weight passed from Asia, probably through the medium of Phenicians, into Greece : the former being adopted principally in Peloponnesus and the Dorian states, in Boeotia, Phokis, Thessaly, Makedonia, and Krete. M. Boeckh adds Achaia to the list : but the passage of Hesychius, on which he relies, is obscure and unsatisfactory.[†] The conventions between Athens, Argos, Elis, and Mantineia, in the Peloponnesian war, respecting the pay of troops, were stipulated in Æginæan drachmæ and trioboli ; and the reckoning of the assembled Amphiktyonic council was carried on in Æginæan staters or didrachms.[‡] There may possibly have been other scales in some Grecian cities not coinciding either with the Æginæan, the Euboic, or the Attic : but we have no distinct information concerning any such. The coins now remaining, of those Grecian states which followed the Æginæan standard,

---

* Herod. vi. 125.

† Hesych. παχείη δραχμῇ· τὸ δίδραχμον· Ἀχαιοί. When the Achæan confederacy first established itself extensively in Peloponnesus, the cities composing it were bound by a special resolution to use the same weights and measures and coins. Polyb. ii. 37.

‡ Thukyd. v. 47 ; also Xenoph. *Hellen.* v. 2, 21. Boeckh, *Corp. Inscrip. Græcarum,* No. 1688.

do not exhibit a full proportion of 5 : 3 between the Æginæan and the Attic drachma; their actual weight falls decidedly below it. On the ground of this inferior weight, Mr. Hussey, in his instructive *Treatise on the Ancient Weights and Measures*, disputes the correctness of Pollux, in giving the proportion of 5 : 3, a statement hitherto universally admitted, and which M. Boeckh successfully vindicates. That states which professed to follow the Æginæan scale, should nevertheless coin a degraded money, is by no means astonishing, nor does the fact furnish any reason 'for questioning the proportions announced to us as normally belonging to the scale. Of the various Greek states which professed to follow the same standard, some coined better money, others worse, according to circumstances : the general tendency amongst them, as it has been in modern no less than in ancient times, was to lower continually the value of their coins, and never again to raise it. The Athenian mint maintained the integrity of its coinage, from Solon downward, longer than the rest; but we may perfectly well admit—as it is stated by K. O. Müller, no less than by Mr. Hussey, that the Æginæan didrachm, as it was actually coined in Peloponnesus during the Peloponnesian war, had become so lowered as only to be worth 1½ Attic didrachm—without discarding the belief, that the Æginæan scale, as first introduced and applied, placed these two coins in the ratio of 5 : 3. M. Boeckh produces positive evidence that such was actually the fact, from the still remaining coins of Melos and Byzantium ; both of them Dorian settlements, and one a colony of Sparta. Very ancient coins are found of both these cities, exhibiting the full weight of the Æginæan standard, with a deduction altogether insignificant ; and there is every reason to conclude that these states must have derived their scale of coinage from their mother cities in Greece Proper, maintaining it faithfully in practice even after the latter had silently receded from it. The coins of the Makedonian kings, anterior to Alexander the Great—those of the Bisaltæ and those of the Chalkideans in Thraké—exhibit in like manner very

nearly the full Æginæan standard weight. Either these are
to be taken as examples of the genuine, undegraded Æginæan
standard, and as authenticating the proportion which Pollux
gives us, of 5 : 3 between that standard and the Solonian
Attic: or else they must be taken as instances of some
other monetary scale heavier than the Æginæan; which is
unsupported by any evidence, and contrary to all probability.

Respecting the Euboic talent, the opinion which M.
Boeckh now maintains, that it is identical with the ante-
Solonian Attic talent, is supported by the approximative
weight of many actual coins, as well as by strong indirect
evidence; the adoption of it introducing a high degree of
symmetry into the systems of Grecian coinage. In his
Public Economy of Athens, our author had treated the Euboic
talent as closely approximating to the Attic talent introduced
by Solon, but he has since seen reason to alter his judgment.

We know the value of the Solonian Attic talent, as well
as the extent of depreciation which Solon introduced : we
know, therefore, that the talent, as it stood before his depreciation, was considerably less than the Æginæan talent.
Apart from the Solonian Attic, the Æginæan and the Euboic
are the only scales of which we find any mention throughout
Greece Proper, in the earlier periods of Grecian history : the
scale prevalent at Athens was not the Æginæan ; and there
is presumption, both negative and positive, that the Euboic,
which derived its name from the Ionic cities of Eubœa, and
which we know to have lasted for many centuries afterwards in the Ionic city of Priené* in Asia Minor, was also
adopted in the metropolis of the Ionic race, just as the
chief seat of the Æginæan scale was among the cities of
Dorian race.

---

* Boeckh, *Corp. Inscript. Græcar.* No. 2906. Dioskurides promises, to each of the persons going through their training in the
gymnasium, an Euboic mina of beef: βοιωῦ κρέως μνᾶν Εὐβοϊκήν.
I do not perceive that M. Boeckh has referred to this in his
Metrologie.

Admitting the Euboic talent to have been that which existed at Athens down to the legislation of Solon, it stood to the Æginæan talent in the ratio of 5 : 6, and to the Solonian talent in the ratio of 25 : 18 : the drachma belonging to it being of the weight of 93.5 English grains. And this weight is, to a considerable degree, borne out by the remaining coins of various cities in Eubœa, as well as by those of the Chalkidic cities of Rhegium in Italy, and Naxos in Sicily (*Metrol.* viii. 3, 4).

In the ninth chapter of the *Metrologie*, M. Boeckh investigates the proceeding of Solon in respect to the Athenian moneys, and establishes upon grounds, very sufficient and satisfactory, the extent of depreciation which he introduced. He supposes, with much probability, that the precise point to which Solon carried his depreciation was determined by the definite and simple ratio which he desired to establish with the Æginæan talent. At that early time, in all probability, the latter was really adhered to in practice by the Peloponnesian and other states around, which it ceased to be afterwards. The ratio of the Æginæan to the Euboic or ante-Solonian talent was as 6 : 5 ; to the Attic talent established by Solon, as 5 : 3. The ratio of the Euboic to the Attic talent was as 25 : 18.

The Attic monetary standard as established by Solon was the lowest then known in Greece, but it was at the same time faithfully adhered to by the Athenian mint, to a degree at that time very unusual. Partly from the general tendency to substitute a low standard in place of a high one, partly from the ascendency subsequently acquired by Athens, the Attic standard became extensively diffused throughout Greece as well as Sicily and Asia Minor. M. Boeckh seems to be of opinion, that the Solonian Attic talent was originally co-existent in Asia along with the Æginæan and Euboic talent: but for this there seems little evidence.

Respecting the Egyptian scale of weight and money, of which M. Boeckh treats in his tenth chapter, there is no

information anterior to the time of the Ptolemies; no coins
have been found of an earlier date, nor does it appear that
any earlier Egyptian coins were ever struck. The coins of
the Ptolemies now remaining conform very nearly to the
Æginæan or Babylonian scale of weight: they are principally tetradrachms and didrachms adapted to the weight
of the Æginæan talent: and the reason why they were so
was, in all probability, that the first Ptolemy adopted that
scale of weight which he found already current in Egypt.
For the tendency throughout Greece during the preceding
century had been to discontinue the Æginæan scale in
coinage, and to adopt the Attic; and Alexander the Great
had recently introduced this change into the Makedonian
coinage.   There is therefore a strong presumption that
the scale of weight current in Egypt in the earlier times
was the Babylonian or Æginæan. Gradually this standard
became degraded in practice and abandoned, in Egypt as
well as elsewhere: the name drachma at the time when
that country passed from its native kings to the formal
dominion of the Romans, was given to a coin equivalent
only to the Roman denarius and the Attic drachma of the
same period: but the time and manner in which this change
was brought about, cannot be clearly made out.

Such is the extensive and interesting analogy which M.
Boeckh has established between the units and scale of
weight, and the monetary scales founded upon them,
throughout the various portions of the Hellenic and Oriental
world : and such is the relation, which he has been the first
to set forth clearly, between the three principal monetary
scales prevalent in Greece—the Æginæan, the Euboic, and
the Attic. Of the copious collection of particular facts,
and the luminous reasonings by which his conclusions are
sustained, I cannot, in the present short paper, pretend to
give any adequate idea. I now pass to other points on which
he has not been equally successful.

He lays it down (*Metrol.* ix. 2. p. 122) as a ratio both
certain and precise, that the Roman pound was ¾ of the

Attic mina of 100 Solonian standard drachmœ: and this ratio he cites frequently in the course of his work, appealing to it as a means of establishing numerous ulterior conclusions. But the proof upon which it rests is neither adequate nor convincing. First, he refers to the stipulation in the treaty between the Romans and the Asiatic king, Antiochus. During the first negociations carried on by the Romans with that defeated prince, they required that he should pay them 15,000 Euboic talents, by stated instalments (Polyb. xxi. 14): but in the second negociations, or final and amended treaty, the conditions stood as follows—
'Αργυρίου δὲ δότω 'Αντίοχος 'Αττικοῦ 'Ρωμαίοις ἀρίστου τάλαντα 12,000, ἐν ἔτεσι 12, διδοὺς καθ' ἕκαστον ἔτος χίλια· μὴ ἔλαττον δὲ ἑλκέτω τὸ τάλαντον λιτρῶν 'Ρωμαϊκῶν 80. (Polyb. xxii. 26). Antiochus engages to pay to the Romans 12,000 talents of *the finest Attic silver*, each talent to weigh not less than 80 Roman pounds. Because Attic silver is here specified, M. Boeckh contends that no other can be meant than Attic talents: but this is an unfounded inference, as we may see by examining the treaty concluded a short time before, between the Romans and Ætolians, wherein the latter thus covenant—Δότωσαν δὲ Αἰτωλοὶ ἀργυρίου μὴ χείρονος 'Αττικοῦ, παραχρῆμα μὲν τάλαντα Εὐβοϊκὰ 200 τῷ στρατηγῷ τῷ ἐν τῇ 'Ελλάδι· ἀντὶ τρίτου μέρους τοῦ ἀργυρίου χρύσιον, ἐὰν βούλωνται, διδόντες, τῶν δέκα μνῶν ἀργυρίου, χρυσίου μνᾶν διδόντες. (Polyb. xxii. 15). Here we find an engagement to pay 200 Euboic talents of fair Attic silver: thus evincing that the mention of " *the best Attic silver*," in the treaty with Antiochus, neither implies any reference to Attic talents, nor sustains the inference which M. Boeckh builds upon it, viz., the normal ratio 60 : 80 between the Roman pound and the Solonian Attic talent.*

---

* Livy, in reciting the treaty between the Romans and Antiochus, gives the sum—"Argenti probi 12,000 Attica talenta—talentum no minus pondo octoginta Romanis ponderibus pendat " (xxxviii. 38).

To me there appears something anomalous in defining a recognised Grecian metallic standard by a given weight in Roman pounds: and, accordingly, we find in the other treaties that when the Euboic standard is specified, no mention is made of Roman pounds, nor of any foreign weight. The fact, that in this final treaty with Antiochus, all specification of a Grecian standard is omitted, and a standard composed of Roman pounds substituted in its place, seems to me to indicate that the talent, so defined, was a mere denomination of weight, chosen for the occasion —not identified with any known Grecian system, though approximating to the Attic talent. It is to be remembered, that what the Romans wanted, was, not Grecian coins, but Grecian silver of a given weight and fineness: this is shown by the stress laid upon the quality of the silver—"*fair Attic silver*"—"*the best Attic silver.*" When, in their first negociations, they required Antiochus to pay 15,000 Euboic talents, or, when they demanded from Carthage 10,000 Euboic talents (Polyb. xv. 7), they could not have meant to insist upon receiving that enormous sum in didrachms and tetradrachms of the Euboic scale: such coins, if brought to Rome, must be melted and re-coined before they could be made available. The essential object with them, was to define the weight of silver to be paid to them, and a definition by Roman pounds would be most easily acted upon by Roman commissioners. The word *talent* was received in many different senses, in Sicily, Italy, and Greece: a special meaning was put upon it for this particular occasion: just as, in any payment required to be made from

---

But this, I conceive, is not to be attended to, when we have before us the far higher authority as well as the much more specific statement of Polybius. When Livy recites the former treaty with the Ætolians, he describes the sum to be paid simply as *Euboica talenta*, without any regard to the additional words of Polybius, ἀργυρίου μὴ χείρονος Ἀττικοῦ; which words, nevertheless, are essential to the comprehension of the mode and form in which the payment was to be made (xxxviii. 9).

England to America, an arbitrary rate of exchange, not widely removed from the ordinary rate, might be determined beforehand between the pound sterling and the dollar.

The only other testimony adduced by M. Boeckh, of the alleged exact ratio of the Roman pound and the Attic Solonian mina (3 : 4), is contained in a sentence of the *Metrologus* of the Benedictine *Analekta*; in the interpretation of which he assumes as certain, what is at best doubtful, that 'Αττικὰς δραχμὰς, in the language of so very late a writer, means standard Solonian drachmæ. But even if we grant this assumption, the evidentiary force of the passage will still remain very disputable. For there are several statements in the other metrological writers (see Galen, Dioskorides and Kleopatra, as printed in Stephens's *Thesaurus*, besides Priscian *de Ponderibus*, v. 33), distinctly contradicting it, and announcing other proportions; and M. Boeckh has shewn no reason why they should all be set aside, and the authority of the Benedictine *Analekta* exclusively trusted. It is true that there is much contradiction and discrepancy in their various statements of the ratio between mina, drachma, libra, and uncia (*Metrol.* p. 116–120); but the reasonable inference, even from this irreconcileable confusion, is, that the two scales of weight were in the beginning radically distinct, having no point of actual contact, and no exact or normal ratio between them. If, as M. Boeckh supposes, there had been a normal and original correspondence between the two scales, in the proportion of 60 minæ, or 1 Solonian talent to 80 Roman pounds, would not this fact have been intimated by Pliny or by Celsus? Both of these authors treat the Attic drachma as the equivalent of the denarius, 84 to the Roman pound: they consider the Attic mina as 100 : 84, in reference to the Roman pound. Now this was nothing more than an approximative ratio first derived from the comparison of the degraded coinage of both states; and if M. Boeckh's supposition be correct, it must have superseded the ancient, precise normal ratio of 100 : 75, which must have been as well known as

the ratio of the Attic χοῦς and μετρήτης to the Roman
congius and amphora. The silence of Pliny and Celsus is to
me a strong reason for believing that no such exact proportion between the Attic mina and the Roman pound originally
existed. And this contradictory evidence, positive as well
as negative, of which M. Boeckh takes little notice, appears
to me to outweigh the unsupported testimony of the Benedictine *Metrologus.*

Wurm in his treatise (*De Ponderum, Nummorum, &c.
Rationibus ap. Romanos et Græcos:* Stuttgard, 1821) adopts
the same view as M. Boeckh in regard to the treaty between
the Romans and Antiochus: he considers it certain that
exact Attic talents and nothing else, must be meant: and
he says, "Sequitur in his pressè Livius Polybium:" which
is not correct, since in the very cardinal point of the question, in the specification of "Attica talenta," Livy departs
from Polybius. Wurm also agrees with M. Boeckh in setting
aside the dissentient testimonies of the later metrological
writers. But the general scope of Wurm's book is not the
same with that of M. Boeckh: the former professes only to
exhibit the actual relative weight, as nearly as it can be
found, of Attic talents, and Roman pounds: and for this purpose we have evidence enough in the coins, without any appeal
to the treaty above mentioned. The number of Attic coins
still remaining is quite sufficient to enable us to determine
approximatively, with sufficient accuracy for practical purposes, the standard weight of the Solonian drachma: the
result of very numerous particular trials brings it to 67.37
grains Troy, according to M. Boeckh: to 66.6, according to
Mr. Hussey. One Attic talent, or 6000 of these drachmæ,
is nearly equal in weight to 80 Roman pounds: and therefore the ratio of 3 : 4 between the Roman pound and the
Attic mina, if stated simply as a tolerably near approach
to the truth, is one which I am by no means disposed to
question.

But this is not sufficient for M. Boeckh's argument, which
requires a rigid distinction between precise ratios and ap-

proximative ratios. For the latter, as he himself justly lays it down, are to be regarded as merely accidental and undesigned: while the former carry with them evidence of systematic and intentional harmony between the two scales compared—of original relationship either in the way of filiation or in that of fraternity. M. Boeckh is thus compelled to maintain a position much more difficult than that of Wurm: he undertakes to demonstrate that the ratio of 3 : 4 between the Roman pound and the Attic mina is mathematically exact, being involved in the normal schemes of the two systems; and he dwells upon it as a capital point of original and intentional contact between them. It is in this light that he considers it, in very many passages of his book, when he treats it as a matter proved, and appeals to it confidently as a ground for farther inferences: it is in this light that I consider it also, when I maintain that he has produced no sufficient evidence to entitle him to do so.

To point out an instance of his employment of this very problematical ratio as an ascertained premise in ulterior reasoning, we need only pass to the 17th chapter, in which he proposes to establish "the deduction of the Roman cubic foot and foot of length, from the Æginæan weight and the Grecian cubic measure, and the *intentional* ratio of the Roman foot to the Grecian foot, as the cube root of 9 to the cube root of 10; $\sqrt[3]{9} : \sqrt[3]{10}$" (p. 284). He first seeks to prove that "the Grecian (or more properly speaking, the Æginæan) pound is to the Roman pound as 10 : 9:" next, that the Grecian cubic foot is to the Roman cubic foot in the same ratio—10 : 9; and his argument proceeds as follows (p. 285):

"It is a matter of fact that the Roman pound is to the half of the Æginæan mina as 9 : 10; for *it* (viz. the Roman pound) is to the Attic mina as 3 : 4; and the Attic mina is to the Æginæan mina as 3 : 5, consequently the Roman pound is to the Æginæan mina as 9 : 20, or to the half of the Æginæan mina as 9 : 10. But this half Æginæan mina was a pound, as will be shewn hereafter: it is therefore demonstrated, that the Æginæan and the Roman pound were in the ratio of 10 : 9. It remains still to demonstrate, that the Olympic cubic foot, and the Roman quadrantal, stood in the same relation; but this cannot be done with equal strictness." Unable to offer a strict proof of this ratio of 10 : 9 between the Grecian cubic foot and the Roman quadrantal, M. Boeckh gives some general considerations in the way of indirect evidence, and he here again puts in the front rank the precise ratio between the Grecian and Roman pound which he supposes himself to have just before demonstrated. " We acknowledge a complete coincidence of the Grecian and Roman pound in the ratio of 10 : 9, which implies that the latter was originally adapted to the standard of the former" (p. 286). Here we see that he is dealing not with simple approximations, leaving a certain amount of practical error, but with exact coincidences, involved in the normal schemes of the two systems, and shewing that the framers of the one have adjusted their arrangements with a view to the other. And the whole of his proof of systematic analogy between the Roman and Grecian scales of weight, rests upon the admission of an exact ratio of 3 : 4 between the Roman pound and the Solonian mina; which I have already shewn to be uncertain and unattested.

Another point which M. Boeckh includes as established, in the demonstration which I have cited just above, is, that the Æginæan mina contained two Æginæan litræ or pounds. When we turn to the chapters in which he assigns his evidence for this, it will appear very inconclusive (xix. 1. p. 303; xxiv. 2. p. 343). The Æginæan scale of weight consisted of talents, minæ, drachmæ, and oboli: it had no pounds nor ounces. When the Greek colonies settled in Sicily, they found a copper currency among the Sikel population, and an independent scale of weight consisting of pounds and ounces, with which their own became blended. The result is highly perplexing, and in many points not intelligible, for want of evidence: but we know, and M. Boeckh has very clearly shewn in opposition to the opinion of Bentley and others, that the Sicilian talent contained 120 litræ in money value, and therefore that one Sicilian mina contained two litræ in money value. We know also from Aristotle that the Sicilian litra was equal in value to an Æginæan obolus of silver, which was therefore in Sicily called a silver litra. But it is nowhere shewn that the Sicilian talent containing 120 litræ in value was of the *weight* of an Æginæan talent: nor that the *weight* called a litra in Sicily was $\frac{1}{120}$th part of the *weight* called a Sicilian talent; much less, of an Æginæan talent. At the time when the identity of meaning between litra and obolus first took its rise, the litra contained a quantity of copper such as could be purchased in the market for an Æginæan obolus: that this quantity of copper was in weight precisely the $\frac{1}{120}$th part of an Æginæan talent weight, is certainly not very probable, and not to be admitted without some positive proof. And M. Boeckh himself appears only to contend that the ratio was something originally not very far from the truth (see xxiv. 2 p. 343); so that it is altogether impossible to rely upon it as evidence of original and intrinsic relationship between the Roman and the Æginæan pound, even if we consider the expression *Æginæan pound* as admissible.

I now come to the ratio which M. Boeckh alleges to have subsisted between the Olympic cubic foot, and the Roman cubic foot or quadrantal—as 10 : 9. Of this he has himself stated (see the passage already cited from p. 285) that he is unable to offer sufficient direct proof: and the general considerations into which he enters (pp. 286, 287) will not be found to compensate for the absence of such proof. Yet he introduces in other places this unproved ratio for the purpose of establishing ulterior conclusions: for example in p. 277 (xv. 2) he says: "The Attic metretes contains 72 Roman sextarii: but the Greek cubic foot is, as will be hereafter shewn, $\frac{10}{9}$ of the Roman quadrantal, which contains 48 sextarii: the Greek cubic foot is therefore 53$\frac{1}{3}$ sextarii, and the Attic metretes $\frac{9}{40}$ of the Greek cubic foot." Here are two new conclusions, the authority of which rests entirely upon the admission of the ratio of 10 : 9 between the Greek cubic foot and the Roman quadrantal, which M. Boeckh believes himself to have proved, but has not proved: and again these two new conclusions—the equality of the Greek cubic foot to 53½ Roman sextarii, and the ratio of the same to the Attic metretes, as 20 : 27—appear in other parts of his volume as if they too were matters ascertained (see xiii. 7. p. 242; xiv. 3. p. 263; xvi. 2. p. 282). In researches such as these of M. Boeckh, unless the fundamental positions are placed beyond all doubt, the subsequent deductions become illusory, and are but too well calculated to illustrate the impressive warning, which he has himself delivered in his preface, against fine-spun metrological hypotheses.

The well-known correspondence between the Attic measures of capacity, both liquid and dry, and the Roman measures of capacity — both as to positive quantities and scale of division—is a fact very striking and remarkable. Now the Roman measures of capacity exhibit an exact proportion with the Roman weights : an amphora or quadrantal weighing precisely 80 Roman pounds, and a congius (the parallel both in quantity and denomination of the Attic χοῦς) weighing precisely 10 pounds. This correspondence, a fact certain but hitherto unexplained, M. Boeckh wishes to trace to a supposed original correspondence of the scale of weight, transmitted from Babylon first to Greece and then to Rome: the cubical unit being in all the three cases (he asserts) determined by a given weight of rain-water (see pp. 286, 287). I have already said that his deduction of the Æginæan scale of weight from the Babylonian appears to me sufficiently sustained, and the light which he has thereby thrown upon the statical systems, both of Greece and the East, is new and valuable. But in extending the same deduction to Rome—in tracing the acknowledged correspondence of Roman and Attic cubical measures to a primitive correspondence of Roman and Attic weights,—he has, in my judgment, altogether failed. I am the more anxious to point this out, because his copious erudition may perhaps

enable him either to strengthen his proof, or to discover
some better mode of explanation: and I am very sure that
there is no man in Europe more capable of solving a
problem at once so difficult and so interesting to philological
enquirers.

I pass over M. Boeckh's remarks on the relation of the
Grecian and Roman foot of length: his eleventh chapter
contains ample particulars as to the actual length both of
one and the other, but his attempt to connect them in
theory, as if the Roman foot had been originally adapted to
the Grecian in the ratio of 24 : 25, is an hypothesis resting
upon unsupported analogies (compare xi. 8. p. 199; and xvii.
2, 3, 4. pp. 288–292). I come to the positions which he
lays down, respecting the relation of Grecian weights and
measures one with another: wherein I discover much which
appears to me erroneous and illusory.

It has been already mentioned that there exists in the
Roman system, a precise, determinate connection between
the weights and the cubic measures: the amphora or quadrantal weighing by legal standard 80 pounds; and the
congius (= Attic χοῦς) weighing 10 pounds. Now M. Boeckh
thinks that he can establish the like precise and determinate
connection between the Grecian weights and Grecian cubic
measures. The Roman amphora contains 48 sextarii, the
Attic metretes 72 sextarii: the former weighs 80 Roman
pounds, therefore the latter weighs 120 Roman pounds: but
the Roman pound is ¾ of the Attic mina: therefore the Attic
metretes weighs 90 Attic minæ or 1½ Attic talent: or in
other words, the Solonian talent is equal to a weight of
water ⅔ of the Attic metretes (xv. 2. p. 278).

Such is M. Boeckh's proof of the exact and determinate
connection between the Grecian weights and Grecian cubic
measures. And here again we see that the whole cogency
of the proof depends upon the admission, that the Roman
pound is ¾ of the Solonian mina; and that the ratio between
them is rigorous, numerical, and essentially belonging to
the two systems; not simply approximative. In such pre-

liminary admissions no inquirer can acquiesce, as I have already endeavoured to shew, until ampler evidence is produced than that which is contained in the *Metrologie*. ,

Nor is this the only defective point in the book respecting the Grecian cubic measures. It is a recognised fact, that in the Solonian Attic scale the monetary talent, mina, and drachma, are each ⅗ of the respective denominations in the Æginæan scale: M. Boeckh has attempted to shew that the same ratio prevails between the cubic measures of the two scales; that the Solonian Attic metretes and medimnus are each ⅗ of the Æginæan. The evidence in support of this position is really so feeble that I cannot explain to myself how it should have appeared to him satisfactory. First (*Metrol.* xv. 1. p. 275), he cites a passage from Lucian, which proves only, at the very most, that the Æginæan medimnus was larger than other measures of the same denomination; if indeed it proves anything to the point, of which reasonable doubt may be entertained (Lucian, *Timon*, c. 57). Next, he quotes a passage out of the *Etymologikon Magnum*, v. Αἰγιναῖα, Ἐλέγετο δὲ τὰ μέγαλα, Αἰγιναῖα, ἀπὸ τοῦ νομίσματος· καὶ γὰρ τὸ Αἰγιναῖον τάλαντον πλεῖον ἠδύνατο τοῦ Ἀττικοῦ; a citation which not only does not assist M. Boeckh's conclusion, but operates powerfully to contradict it; and so sensible is he of this, that he permits himself to discredit his own witness, by annexing as a criticism of his own—" Since the Æginæan money was more notorious than the Æginæan measures, the incorrect limitation is added, ἀπὸ τοῦ νομίσματος, &c." Accepting the statement of the witness, I must reject M. Boeckh's unfounded semi-negation of it. Thirdly, he produces in juxtaposition two distinct testimonies with regard to the contributions to the public meals at Sparta. Plutarch says, that every partaker of these public meals contributed monthly a medimnus of barley-meal, eight choes of wine, five minæ of cheese, and two and a half minæ of figs (Plutarch. *Lykurg.* 12). But Dikæarchus (*ap. Athen.* iv. p. 141) states that each person contributed to these same meals near upon one Attic me-

M

dimnus and a half, and some eleven or twelve choes of wine, besides a certain weight of cheese and figs : moreover, for the purchase of condiment, about ten Æginæan oboli (ἀλφίτων μὲν ὡς τρία μάλιστα ἡμιμέδιμνα ᾿Αττικὰ, οἴνου δὲ χόας ἔνδεκά τινα ἢ δώδεκα, &c.). Now, before we can combine these two passages, to draw any inference from them as to the relative value of Æginæan and Attic measures, we must adopt several assumptions, each of which is liable to more or less of doubt. First, we must assume that Plutarch and Dikæarchus both speak of the same period, and had in their minds the same actual quantities of meal and wine. Secondly, that Plutarch *meant* an *Æginæan* medimnus, and *Æginæan* choes ; for he *says* no such thing. Thirdly, that Dikæarchus speaks of a *monthly* contribution, and not of any different period : for he specifies no time, whereas, Plutarch specifies a month. And fourthly, that Dikæarchus had heard of and intended to designate some known and definite quantity ; for his words, in their obvious meaning, imply that he did not himself accurately know, or that no precise weight was even fixed by law. And when we have taken all these matters for granted, what is the inference which the two passages combined present ? Something quite foreign to M. Boeckh's purpose ; I will state it in his own words :—" Dikæarchus therefore (he says *Theophrastus*, by an oversight) estimated the Lakonian measure as something less than 1⅓ of the Attic. This doubtless coincides in some measure with that value of the Æginæan talent which Hussey had elicited from the coins, something above 1⅓ of the Attic : but that was merely a value of coins which no longer corresponded with their original standard ; and I have sufficiently proved that the Æginæan talent, as weight, stood to the Attic in the ratio of 5 : 3. Even without any closer historical testimony, there *is an internal probability* that the Æginæan and the Solonian Attic measures stood to each other in the same ratio as the two scales of weights, namely, as 5 : 3 ; possibly the Spartan measure, even if it conformed to that proportion, might be viewed roundly as about half as much again as the Attic, and by mistake *it might then be treated* as something *less than half* as much again, instead of something *more* than half as much again."—This is all the positive evidence produced.

Surely, so distinguished a critic as M. Boeckh cannot think that the definite ratio of 5 : 3, between Æginæan and Attic measures, can be admitted upon evidence such as this; passages not only amplified by so many gratuitous postulates, but even distorted from their true and plain meaning. The misfortune is, that he goes on to treat the ratio here spoken of as a matter perfectly ascertained, and to deduce ulterior consequences from it.

But M. Boeckh farther contends, that independent of positive testimony, there is "an *internal probability* that the Æginæan cubic measures stood to the Solonian Attic in the same ratio as the two scales of weight, namely, as 5 : 3." Admitting for a moment this very questionable position— that identity of ratio between the measures and weights of the two systems is a fact to be presumed, and not to be proved—it amounts to a decisive negation of the ratio of 5 : 3, for which M. Boeckh is contending. When he says that "he has sufficiently proved the Æginæan talent *as weight* to have been in the ratio of 5 : 3 to the Attic," he cannot have had present to his memory the earlier parts of his own book: for he has distinctly shewn the reverse. He has shewn, and the inscription to which he appeals places the fact beyond a doubt, that Solon, while he altered the value of the talent *as money*, so as to establish a ratio of 3 : 5 with the Æginæan talent, left the talent *as weight* un-changed; or, to use the words of our author himself, p. 115 (ix. 1), "the ante-Solonian mina had disappeared in the money-weight, but still continued in use as commercial weight" (down to the period at least to which the inscription refers). A mina of money, or 100 drachmæ of silver, came by the depreciation of Solon to weigh $\frac{4}{5}$ of an Æginæan mina: but a mina weight of tin, iron, or any other com-modity, remained as it was before, not $\frac{4}{5}$ of an Æginæan

mina, but $\frac{3}{4}$ of it. Consequently, the appeal which M.
Boeckh makes to the original ratio of the Æginæan and
Attic weights, distinctly contradicts his position—that the
Attic cubic measures were in the ratio of 3 : 5 to the
Æginæan.

In order to maintain the doctrine here alluded to, M.
Boeckh is driven to the inadmissible hypothesis that Solon,
when he created the ratio of 3 : 5 between the Attic money-
talent and the Æginæan talent, altered at the same time the
Attic metretes and medimnus, so as to introduce the same
ratio to the corresponding Æginæan denominations. " When
Solon," (he says) " diminished the Attic money-weight to
$\frac{3}{4}$ of the Æginæan, he at the same time *enlarged* the
measures, as we are told by Plutarch on the authority of
Androtion. This enlargement once appeared to me a doubtful point: but if the Attic measure had been before purely
accidental and local, *without any* correspondence with the
weight, it may, doubtless, have been smaller than the new
Solonian measure : at any rate, we learn from this statement
that Solon established *a new* metrical scale." (ix. 2. p. 276).
Here M. Boeckh overthrows the fundamental assumption on
which his previous argument had rested. He had before
told us that we might safely presume the Attic and Æginæan
measures to be in the same ratio as the respective weights :
now he intimates, that the primitive Attic measures may
have been " purely local and accidental, without any correspondence with the weights." The argument derived from
internal probability, on which he before dwelt, is here formally discarded ; and we are left, not only without any
positive testimony, but without any rational ground for
presuming à *priori*, that the Attic medimnus and metretes
were to the Æginæan in the ratio of 3 : 5.

I believe that the statement of Androtion, as quoted by
Plutarch (*Solon*, c. 15), has no reference to the medimnus
and metretes, and that we cannot even deduce from it the
vague inference last intimated by M. Boeckh—viz., that
Solon made *some* new arrangement of the measures. The

words of Plutarch are—καὶ τὴν ἅμα τούτῳ γενομένην τῶν τε μέτρων ἐπαύξησιν καὶ τοῦ νομίσματος ἐς τιμήν; (so it stands in Reiske's edition: Coray leaves out ἐς). Ἕκατον γὰρ ἐποίησε δραχμῶν τὴν μνᾶν, πρότερον ἐβδομήκοντα τρίων οὖσαν. Now I think that the words, τῶν μέτρων ἐπαύξησιν, apply simply to the statement which immediately follows—to the increase of the mina as a *monetary measure*, from 73 drachmæ to 100; of course too, the increase of the talent in the same proportion. I agree with the remark made by M. Boeckh, p. 114, that this is an incorrect way of describing the real monetary change introduced by Solon, inasmuch as the mina before that change, as well as after it, was divided into 100 drachmæ, and not into 73: the difference consisting in the diminished size and weight of the drachmæ. But still it is the mode of description adopted by Androtion: and we may fairly suppose that the words "*increase of the measures*," refer to nothing beyond the increased number of drachmæ, which every mina and every talent were now made to contain, as particularised in the succeeding sentence.

Moreover, it will appear that the strongest considerations of "internal probability"—something very little short of an internal certainty, conduct us to the conclusion that Solon left the Attic measures generally undisturbed—the reverse of that which M. Boeckh lays down. For we know positively that Solon did not meddle with the weights: he created a double meaning for the words *mina* and *talent*: he introduced the anomaly, that the mina—which had hitherto meant a known weight of silver, iron, tin, or any other merchandise—received a special and exceptional sense when applied to silver coin. However men may, in time, become accustomed to this, the first moment of divorce between the scale of weight and that of money, must present to them a perplexing anomaly and repugnance: and there could be but one motive for Solon to permit it. All interference with customary weights and measures is well known to produce so much vexation and discontent, that even the most popular and powerful governments experience prodigious difficulty in carrying it into effect. For the express purpose of affording relief to debtors, Solon degraded the monetary standard: but the anomaly, which his new arrangement introduced, is an evident proof of his reluctance to disturb the general system of weights. And it affords a proof, no less evident, that he would not choose such a moment for re-arranging the liquid and dry measures. For the fragments preserved of his poems, impressively attest his painful sense of the difficulties and dangers against which he had to contend, in the midst of angry mutiny on the part of the degraded and enslaved poor, and murmuring acquiescence on the part of the rich, in whom all political power had hitherto been vested. To add, to the many prevalent elements of discontent, a new one of his own creating, would be, least of all, consistent with the cautious and compromising spirit, which is conspicuous throughout all his enactments.

These arguments, I think, will suffice to shew that the position laid down by M. Boeckh, in regard to the ratio between Attic measures and Æginæan measures, is not only unsupported, but incorrect. We have no ground whatever for believing that the Attic metretes or medimnus was $\frac{4}{3}$ of the Æginæan. We do not at all know what was the ratio between the two; if indeed it be certain that they were not the same.

Along with this position, we are compelled to dismiss all the series of imaginary ratios comprised in the following sentences of the *Metrologie* (xvi. 1. p. 281).

"If it be true that the Olympic cubic foot is $\frac{10}{9}$ of the Roman quadrantal (N.B. this is altogether unproved), it then contains $53\frac{1}{3}$ Roman sextarii, since the quadrantal contains 48 sextarii. But the Æginæan metretes contains 120 sextarii (N.B. this is incorrect, depending only on the supposed ratio of the Æginæan metretes to the Attic): therefore its ratio to the Olympic cubic foot is as 120 : $53\frac{1}{3}$ = 9 : 4—or it is $2\frac{1}{4}$ Olympic cubic feet. But the cubic foot has 64 cubic palms: if then the Æginæan metretes was divided like the Attic, as it unquestionably was, into 144 kotylœ, the Æginæan kotylé contained exactly one cubic palm, because 4 : 9 :: 64 : 144. This beautiful coincidence resulted necessarily from the fact, that the Olympic cubic foot stood to the great Babylonian cubic foot as 2 : 3, and that the Æginæan metretes contained 1½ Babylonian cubic feet."

I sincerely wish that this *coincidence* had been sustained by such evidence as to render its trustworthiness commensurate with its beauty.

In the last sentence quoted from M. Boeckh, an alleged ratio is noticed between the Olympic cubic foot and the great Babylonian cubic foot, as 2 : 3—a subject to the investigation of which he devotes the twelfth chapter of his volume. And here again I am compelled to lament the feebleness of the positive testimony, in the midst of a series of suppositions and possibilities, all of which end only in an approximative result: whereas the author professes to detect determinate numerical ratios, and to deduce from them evidence of original correspondence and derivative adjustment between the two systems.

He cites distinct passages from Hero and Didymus, which attest an exact ratio (as 5 : 6) of the Roman foot, to the Philetærian foot employed by the kings of Pergamus in Asia Minor, as well as to the Ptolemaic foot in Egypt: and this Philetærian foot is probably the same with the royal Persian or Babylonian foot, employed under the Persian empire. But the ratio alleged of $\sqrt[3]{2} : \sqrt[3]{3}$ between the Grecian foot and the Babylonian foot rests only upon two passages; of the sufficiency of which the reader shall judge. Herodotus gives the height and thickness of the walls of Babylon in *royal cubits:* he then adds—'Ο δὲ βασιληἴος πῆχυς τοῦ μετρίου ἐστὶ πήχεος μέζων τρίσι δακτυλίοισι (i. 178). Again, the Scholiast on Lucian's *Kataplus*, evidently copying from Herodotus, comments (c. 16) upon the expression of Lucian, ὅλῳ πήχει βασιλικῷ, as follows—'Ο γὰρ βασιλικὸς πῆχυς ἔχει ὑπὲρ τὸν ἰδιωτικὸν καὶ κοινὸν τρεῖς δακτύλους. Upon which M. Boeckh remarks, p. 214: "By the expression μέτριος πῆχυς, as Ideler and others have already observed, *nothing can be meant* except the well-known common cubit *of the Greeks*, of 1½ Olympic feet:" and he adds that Ideler's view is in this respect confirmed by the Scholiast on Lucian (*Metrol.* xii. 2. p. 214). Wurm (*de Ponderibus,* § 56) adopts the same construction of the passage: but in spite of the concurrence of so many able expositors, I venture to contend that they all put upon Herodotus a meaning which his words do not bear. Herodotus contrasts the royal cubit with the moderate or ordinary cubit: he is speaking purely and simply of Babylonian measures; he intimates nothing whatever respecting the identity of the ordinary Babylonian cubit with the Grecian cubit.

M. Boeckh has shewn very instructively, in the 13th and 14th chapters of the *Metrologie,* that there were in Assyria, in Palestine, and in Egypt, two distinct scales of length—a royal cubit or sacred cubit, and a common cubit: the former longer by a definite quantity than the latter, and employed principally for solemn or public purposes. Now it is plain, when Herodotus calls the royal cubit "longer by three finger-breadths or daktyls than the *moderate cubit*," that the direct comparison is between two distinct Babylonian measures. On what ground are we to presume an implied identity between the smaller Babylonian measure and a Grecian measure of the same denomination?

I say, designedly, *identity,* or *precise equality:* the point which M. Boeckh's argument requires him to make out. For if nothing more be meant than approximative equality, this is a matter which I willingly concede. It is to be recollected that the cubit and the foot, having a natural standard, cannot differ very much from each other in any two countries, though they will always differ to a certain extent, unless we suppose an intentional derivation or adjustment. Any English traveller visiting France during the last century, and describing the length of a room or a building, would probably mention the number of feet as reported to him, without noticing the minute difference between the French foot and the English foot. But if he found that the French government, in measuring farms for the assessment of the land-tax, employed a special foot measure, called the royal foot, three inches longer than the ordinary foot of France, he would be struck with this fact, and would insert in his journal—" The royal foot is three inches longer than the ordinary foot." But he would not mean thereby to assert, nor would any reader be authorised to infer, that the ordinary foot of France was equal to the ordinary foot of England.

Just such is the declaration of Herodotus. All that we can legitimately deduce from it, is, that the " moderate cubit " of Babylon differed from the Grecian cubit no more than the ordinary cubit of one nation might naturally differ from the ordinary cubit of another.

. Nor is it indeed certain that there was one common cubit in Greece: meaning always a measure adapted to one precise standard. That the Samians had a cubit of their own, we know from Herodotus (ii. 168), who says that the Egyptian cubit was equal to the Samian. M. Boeckh admits that the Samian cubit was completely different from the common Grecian cubit (xiii. 2. p. 221): of course therefore the Samian foot measure must have differed in the same proportion : a fact not easy to be reconciled with the statement of M. Boeckh in another place (xvi. 1. p. 281) " that no other Grecian foot than the Olympic foot, or the foot of the Olympic stadium, existed." What evidence is there to prove that the Olympic standard of the foot-measure was adopted by all the countless autonomous communities of Greece? Why are we to regard Samos as the solitary case of exception? Long measures differ in this respect from cubic measures or weights—they have a natural standard : but the unit of weight or of capacity must be determined by the special dictum of law. An autonomous community, on first establishing a scale of weight, being under the necessity of making some arbitrary selection, might naturally borrow the Euboic or the Æginæan scale, prevalent amongst its neighbours: but many distinct standards of the foot-measure, all proceeding from the natural standard of the human foot, but each minutely differing from the rest, might co-exist in Greece without any serious inconvenience. We are not to presume here any precise identity, or universal adoption of one common standard, unless we can prove the fact by some positive evidence.

Until the abundant erudition of M. Boeckh can supply such evidence, I must contend that he is not entitled to treat the Olympic foot as an universally adopted Grecian foot: still less is he entitled to consider Herodotus as having alluded to this Olympic foot, and the cubit founded upon it, when he said that "the Babylonian cubit was three daktyls longer than the moderate cubit." Unfortunately, these two unauthorized assumptions. lie at the bottom of all the elaborate calculations in the *Métrologie* respecting the Grecian and Babylonian long measures—calculations leading after all only to an approximative result, which M. Boeckh is obliged to excuse by appealing to the inaccurate mechanical proceedings of. the ancients. Such mechanical inaccuracy I freely admit; and if sufficient positive testimony were produced, of intentional correspondence between two distinct metrical systems in the ancient world, I should not reject the testimony on the ground that details of the proceeding had not precisely conformed to the attested designs of the framers. But here we are without positive testimony: we are called upon to infer intentional adaptation, or relationship between two systems, merely from harmony in the results; and for such an inference nothing short of exact harmony—no approximative analogies—will suffice. More especially is this true with respect to the foot and the cubit: measures which always have been and always will be nearly equal, even in countries the most widely separated.

The most remarkable circumstance which characterizes

the long measures as well as the weights, of Greece, Asia,
and Egypt, is the prevalence of the same scale of division
—the cubit, the foot, the span, the palm, and the dactyl.
Thoroughout all the wide extent of territory here spoken of,
this same scale of division prevailed, pointedly distinguished
from the uncial or duodecimal division of the foot which we
find in Italy and Sicily.

That so precise a conformity in the metrical scale argues
one common origin, and that Greece was in this respect a
borrower from the East, I see no reason to doubt. But that
the actual standard of the lengths measured was identical
and derivative, I cannot believe until I see it proved. M.
Boeckh nevertheless permits himself to assert positively—
"As the Grecian long measure has been already shewn to
have existed in the earliest times in Egypt, which had a
community of system with the Chaldæans, the derivation of
the Grecian measure either from the East or from Egypt
no longer admits of a doubt" (xvi. 1. p. 281). I trust that
the complete conviction which this sentence breathes will
induce M. Boeckh to re-examine and improve the very
precarious evidence on which alone it now reposes.

As I have felt myself compelled to call in question many
references upon which M. Boeckh seems implicitly to rely, I
will notice one case in which he seems to me to impugn
without reason the testimony of one of his own best authorities. In treating of the royal or Philetærian foot, applied
in the measurements of Asia Minor under the kings of Pergamus, he cites a passage from Hero, in which the ratio of
the Philetærian foot to the Roman foot is given as 6 : 5—
given in plain language and with precise fractions (*Metrol.*
xii. 2; p. 215). But M. Boeckh finds that this ratio does
not exactly comport with that which he imagines himself
to have discovered as the original determining ratio of the
Babylonian foot to the Grecian foot, viz. $\sqrt[4]{3}$ $\sqrt[4]{2}$. Accordingly, he denies the rigid accuracy of the valuation given by
Hero : he says—"Assuredly the estimate of the Philetærian
foot in reference to the Roman foot as 6 : 5, is not precise,

because it is certain that neither of them was determined
with any view to the other" (p. 218). Now there is not
throughout the whole of M. Boeckh's metrological investigations, a more direct, precise, or unimpeached testimony
than this of Hero, which he treats as merely approximative:
and that too because it does not coincide with a long tissue
of calculations of his own, based upon assumptions as yet
unsupported. If a statement such as this of Hero is not
to be trusted, the class of researches to which the *Metrologie*
is devoted will become utterly impracticable: for no better
evidence can be procured.

The last four chapters of M. Boeckh's volume are devoted
to an account of the various pound weights and scales of
weight throughout Italy; of the perplexing variations in
the Roman silver and copper money; and of the monetary
estimates in the census of Servius Tullius. They are chapters
highly instructive: in respect to the Roman silver money,
the clearest and most complete that I know. He rejects
and refutes the opinion of Niebuhr, that the debasement of
the Roman standard was caused or accompanied by an extraordinary rise in the value of copper, so that the diminished
coins possessed as great a purchasing power as the full-sized
coins had possessed before. Whether the value of the metal
copper underwent any serious or continued reduction in reference to silver, may be a matter of reasonable doubt: certain
it is, that no such adventitious cause need be invoked to
account for the degradation of the standard. Such a proceeding has been so nearly universal with governments both
ancient and modern, that the contrary may be looked upon
as a remarkable exception.

The limits to which this article has already extended will
not permit me to furnish any detailed remarks upon M.
Boeckh's account of the Italian and Roman scales of weight
and money. I will only mention, that since the publication
of the *Metrologie*, another work of singular importance on
the same subject has appeared in Italy, by the learned
fathers Marchi and Tessieri: ' L'æs grave del Museo Kirche-

riano, ovvero le Monete primitive de' Popoli dell' Italia
Media ordinate e descritte. Roma 1839.' The collection
of the Kircherian Museum at Rome, unrivalled in the
number and completeness of its specimens of the ancient
Italian *æs grave*, and enriched by many recent discoveries,
has here, for the first time, been explained and reduced
to order, and connected with the inferences legitimately
deducible from it.

Two of these inferences I will briefly glance at, inasmuch
as they bear directly upon the positions maintained in M.
Boeckh's *Metrologie*; in one case, in the way of confirmation,
in the other, of contradiction.

M. Boeckh advances two positions; first, that the duodecimal division of the pound prevailed all over Italy; next,
that the absolute weight called by the name of a *pound* was
not the same throughout that country—heavier in some parts,
lighter in others.

The second of these two positions has been placed beyond
a doubt by the new facts set forth in the work of the two
learned fathers. They have produced ancient cast copper-
money of the Latins and Volscians, which belong to an as, or
pound weighing 13 Roman ounces, and coins of Hadria in
Picenum, which indicate an as, reaching even to 16 Roman
ounces. The ancient Etruscan pound, as far as we can judge
by the coins published and authenticated, appears to have
been the lightest in Italy.

But, on the other hand, the opinion of M. Boeckh, that
the duodecimal division of the pound was universal throughout Italy, has been shewn to be erroneous. Amongst the
people of middle Italy, north of the Apennines, a decimal
division of the pound prevailed, distinguishing them from the
people south of the same chain, who employed the duodecimal scale. Of the numerous coins belonging to the people
south of the Apennines, not a single quincunx, or coin of five
ounces, has yet been discovered: the complete series runs
from the semis or six ounces downwards, omitting the quincunx—triens, quadrans, sextans, and uncia. On the other

hand, for the coins north of the Apennines, comprising those of seven different townships, no semis has ever been found ; the highest denomination below the as is the quincunx, below which the other coins appear just as in the duodecimal series. There is no way of explaining this very marked and uniform contrast, except by admitting a decimal division of the pound north of the Apennines.* In Sicily, where the coalescence of the Grecian and Italian systems produced a complication almost inextricable, a silver quincunx as well as a semis appears to have prevailed : at least we find in the fragments of Epicharmus mention both of πεντώγκιον and ἡμίλιτρον (Pollux, ix. 82). This double scale of weight, prevalent in different regions of Italy, is a remarkable phenomenon ; only recently verified, and as yet unexplained.

---

* See the valuable dissertation of Dr. Lepsius, *Ueber die Verbreitung des Italischen Münzsystems von Etrurien aus*, p. 74. (Leipzig, 1842.)

PRESIDENTIAL ADDRESS,

IN COMMEMORATION OF THE TWENTY-FIRST ANNIVERSARY OF THE LONDON SCIENTIFIC INSTITUTION.

(In the London Tavern, 1st June, 1846.)

PRESIDENTIAL ADDRESS,

THE usual loyal toasts having been drunk, the CHAIRMAN then said:—I now have to propose to you, gentlemen, the toast which forms the immediate subject of our present meeting. It will need no eloquence to recommend it to your cordial reception; nevertheless, I should be doing little justice, either to my own feelings or to yours, if I did not preface the introduction of it with a few words of allusion to the past as well as to present circumstances. I propose to you the toast, "Prosperity to the City of London Literary and Scientific Institution."

Twenty-one years have now elapsed, gentlemen, since this Institution was first projected and brought into existence, intended for the special use and benefit of persons engaged in professional and commercial pursuits. Twenty-one years forms a large fraction of every man's life; a space of time in which much may be achieved, and much ought to be achieved, by individuals as well as by communities; a space long enough to take measure of the practical benefits and efficiency of any association, and to judge how far it may boast of good fruit in the past, or carry the promise of still better fruit for the future. I am happy in the knowledge that the twenty-one years of collective life which this Institution has enjoyed, have more than justified the largest expectations of its original projectors. I am still more happy in the conviction that, while a fair allowance is to be made for

N

human infirmity of temper, and while occasional mistakes in dealing with untried contingencies have been inevitable, there has been throughout the management of our Institution nothing in the nature of extravagance, or destructive party spirit, or delusive conceptions of its legitimate scope and purposes—much less any reproach of graver character—to sully the honourable recollections of our earliest and most difficult period.

In the month of June, 1825, at the time when our first meeting for the establishment of the Institution took place, I believe that no Institution of this precise character, and intended for the same description of persons, yet existed in the United Kingdom. We had, indeed, before us the encouraging example of the Mechanics' Institution, then recently brought into working, and producing, as now, admirable results; and Dr. Birkbeck, the founder of that Institution, to whose indefatigable and creative genius the cause of popular instruction owes more than to any man that ever lived, was still in the full vigour of his career, to show how much could be done by single-hearted energy and talent in bringing together isolated individuals for the common purpose of improvement. But there existed no analogous scheme for the large and important class by whom our city is chiefly occupied; and it was to fill up in part this gap that the present Institution was projected. I know, indeed, and I rejoice to know, that there are now several Institutions analogous to our own; some in other parts of London — some in the other great towns of this country. I am sure that every gentleman who hears me will wish them success and prosperity. I pretend not to raise invidious comparisons between those societies and our own; I hope, in all good and useful results, they will fully rival us, and that they will leave to us nothing but that which is indisputably our due—the honour of historical precedence—the honour of having been the first to originate a Literary Institution for commercial and professional persons.

To an audience like you, gentlemen—and I would fain hope,

to any intelligent audience of the present day—arguments to demonstrate the value of institutions such as ours would be trite and superfluous. But such was not the case when this Institution first began. In 1825 the idea was novel, and the scheme untried; it required a degree of openness and liberality of mind, then by no means common, to appreciate its usefulness; it required a certain degree of penetration, and, I will add, a certain measure of that valuable attribute called a hopeful temperament, to believe that, if useful, it was also practicable. There were many who doubted whether, when the banner of instruction and improvement was unfurled, there would be found any considerable body of volunteers from the commercial and professional classes to flock to it: there were still more who doubted whether those volunteers who came would stay to uphold it, would accept a systematic organization, or would furnish out of their own number a body of managers willing and able to undertake laborious functions of detail. A new member, who now for the first time visits our premises in Aldersgate Street, sees at once that his subscription purchases for him something substantive, tangible, full of interest and convenience, to say the least of it; but in June, 1825, all these conveniences were yet only in promise, and it might reasonably be held uncertain whether a sufficient number of members would have faith in that promise being realized, to induce them to come forward with subscriptions, at that time necessarily confided to the employment of gentlemen not personally known. To those among the friends and gentlemen around me who have present to their minds (as I have present to mine) the debates and calculations of the spring of 1825, when we were engaged in ushering this Institution into existence, it will be well known that we had a thousand uncertainties of this character to contend with. They will recollect how much we owe to the high public character, and the forward and generous zeal of my late lamented friend, Mr. John Smith, the first president of our nascent Institution—a gentleman whose name cannot be mentioned without esteem and honour, and who stood always among the foremost in the promotion of public instruction. Besides Mr. John Smith, the new Institution was fortunate enough to find other liberal and high-minded commercial men to support and encourage its early efforts: what was better than any supporters, it obtained earnest, discreet, and laborious committee-men among its own members, several of whom I am happy to see at this table, who undertook the troublesome and unrewarded task of overcoming all the difficulties of its first organization, and accomplished that task with skill and success. Moreover—a point no less essential than good committee-men—the Institution was also fortunate enough to find an exemplary secretary, Mr. Stacy, whose last twenty-one years have been devoted to the service of the Institution with a diligence as unwearied as it has been well-directed, and whose remarkable talent, both for business and for conciliation, was of the most special necessity during the first years of difficulty with which the Institution had to struggle. Through these valuable and meritorious agencies our Institution was enabled to take an honourable start even from the first, to work itself gradually into efficient operation, even when it had everything to create and provide, and to realize fully that which its sponsors had promised and vowed when the name was first bestowed.

I glance, briefly, gentlemen, at these topics, connected with the infancy of our Institution, not less in the way of congratulation as to the past than in that of contrast and encouragement as to the present. It was then in its season of probation; it had to win its way to confidence, and to establish a character with the commercial and professional public. It has now earned that confidence, and needs no testimonial of character, except its own past conduct. Our course has been one of progressive increase, with interruption only rare and occasional. Distributing our past life of twenty-one years into three periods of seven years each, our average number of members was, during the first of these periods, 728; during the second, 903;

during the third, 974; and we now number a total of
1073 members. We possess a library, for reference and
circulation, of between 9000 and 10,000 volumes;
we have spacious and convenient premises, enlarged and
remodelled—I might almost say rebuilt—by ourselves,
though, in spite of the most careful economy, at a very
heavy cost; we can show a Museum with various scientific
accompaniments and instructive specimens, and a sufficient
number of class-rooms for those classes which are formed
among the members to prosecute some continuous branch
of study. We can boast, also, an excellent and com-
modious lecture-room, built by ourselves, and paid for by
our own money. This lecture-room was opened in 1829,
in the fifth year of our existence, by an inaugural address,
which the present Lord Chief Justice of England, then
Mr. Common-Sergeant Denman, did us the honour to deliver.
The room holds, with perfect convenience, between 500 and
600 persons, and when first opened was amply sufficient
for all our wants; but the increase in our numbers has
now rendered it inadequate to its purpose, and the just
complaint of our members respecting the insufficiency of
room and comfort on evenings of crowded attendance, is
one of the most pressing difficulties with which our Institution has now to contend, and which I hope it will be
soon in a position to remove. Independent of the lecture-
room, the large outlay upon our premises generally has
of course driven us to contract a considerable debt; and
the interest upon this debt, as well as the setting apart of
instalments for its gradual liquidation, constrains us to the
painful necessity of circumscribing both our usefulness to
the members and our furtherance to science and literature.
But, gentlemen, this necessity, painful as it is, is not beyond
our means. Our Institution, though a debtor, is not an
embarrassed debtor: that which it has promised it has
performed faithfully, and is competent as well as willing
still to perform. I dwell upon this fact with emphasis,
and I should deeply regret if it were not true to the

letter. It is not for us, who rest altogether upon the support
of a commercial and professional public, to set the example
of disregarding that which, among such a public especially,
is as the staff and guardian of life—pecuniary good faith
and probity. No, gentlemen; if our Institution invokes,
as it does invoke, an augmentation of funds, we do not
come forward as suppliant insolvents, to solicit relief or
extrication from past imprudences or present embarrassments; we take higher ground. We come forward as
stewards in the cause of literature and science in this city,
feeling that we have established a fair and honourable
claim to the confidence of all who have that holy cause
at heart. We come prepared to show that our Institution,
as it stands, both is now, and has been throughout its
twenty-one years' life, good and useful; and we ground
upon that fact a wish to acquire means of extending our usefulness yet further. We know that we have done far more
than could reasonably have been expected, or than any
one actually did expect, in 1825; and that, assuming only
the same degree of generous zeal for literature and science
which prevailed then, the man who desires to deepen their
roots and promote their development in the city of London
will find no better hands to aid him than our Institution.
Feeling a pride, gentlemen, in what we have done for these
objects during the past, we are in no way ashamed of saying
that we desire to be armed with still ampler and more unfettered powers of serving the same purposes during the future.

Gentlemen, the twenty-one years' biography of our Institution stands permanently on record in the two thick manuscript volumes in the hands of our secretary, containing the
minutes of forty-two regular half-yearly meetings of the
members of the Institution, and of various special general
meetings held by public notice. I need not remind you that,
at each of these half-yearly meetings, it is both the duty and
the practice of the managing committee to present a report
on the general and financial condition of the Institution; so
that the series of those reports forms a continuous narrative,

not less instructive than authentic. At several of those meetings I had myself the honour to preside : and I can personally testify to the good feeling and propriety with which they were conducted, to the due admixture of a free spirit of criticism with a reasonable confidence in the board of management, and with cheerful acquiescence in the concluding vote of the majority.   I have recently refreshed my memory, and renewed my acquaintance with these forty-two half-yearly reports, and with the facts set forth in them from time to time by the committee ; and I find in them ample evidences of an intellectual movement at once well sustained and well directed.   I find in them, besides, proofs of an assiduous cultivation of those arts and tastes which, if they lie apart from the intellect properly so called, are yet of a character most in harmony with the intellectual man, and tend to awaken and develop the imaginative impulses of our nature.   First, I trace with satisfaction the gradual growth of the library of the Institution from its first modest poverty in 1825—not more than 89 volumes—to its present comparative abundance, of more than 9000 volumes.   I content myself with calling this comparative abundance, for I trust that it is destined to still further increase, and still wider usefulness.   Nor is it only the catalogue of the library which has become more bulky, or the shelves which have become fuller ; there is ample proof that the members make good use of the library, and desire to read the books as well as to possess them.   There is ample proof of this, even for those to whom the fact is not familiar by personal experience, in the difficulty which the committee have had in so framing their library regulations as to satisfy the impatience of members for procuring books to read.

From the library I pass to the lectures, many paid, some gratuitous ; and when I go through the list of these various lectures, I find that there is scarcely any subject—scientific, literary, philosophical, economical, historical, or connected with poetry and the arts—which has not been presented, more or less extensively, to the minds of the members of our Insti-

tution. The list would be far too long to read, and it is of
course diversified so as to meet great varieties of taste and
tendencies on the part of different members: there may be
some subjects too dry, others too frivolous, according to the
judgment of the person criticising; but I, for my part, should
be sorry to see any of them left out. The Institution only
lives and thrives by the alliance of these diversities of pursuit;
the co-operation of both is indispensable to the gratification
of every one singly. Of these numerous lectures—whether
on astronomy and geography, on the productions and attributes of distant countries, on experimental chemistry, physics,
or physiology, on mental philosophy and political economy,
on history, the drama, poetry, or painting—of all these lectures, the least impressive will not have been without its echo
and response in the minds of those who heard it, while the
richest and most emphatic will have proved eminently stirring and suggestive. And, gentlemen, the number of these
lectures which have been gratuitous is a fact highly deserving
of notice on the part of those who are interested in the prosperity of the Institution, just as it well merits the continued
expressions of thanks which have been passed at every half-
yearly meeting. It proves the valuable influence of such
institutions as ours in calling forth disinterested exertions
on the part of instructed men; and it is the more gratifying,
inasmuch as several of these lecturers have themselves been
members of the Institution.

But, gentlemen, the lectures, though beneficial and indispensable, are not the department of our Institution which I
look at with the greatest interest. The classes for special and
continuous instruction on particular subjects, formed among
the members themselves, under the auspices of the managing
committee, are, in my mind, a circumstance yet more impressive and encouraging. In the lecture-room, let the talents
of the lecturer be what they may, the minds of the hearers
are more passive than active: they hear and they feel, they
receive wholesome nutriment, a part of which will doubtless
remain with them; but they are, after all, only recipients—

recipients of an impulse which comes upon them from without, and is to a great degree transient. It is otherwise with the classes meeting continuously for special, persevering, and laborious instruction: whether assisted and superintended, as many of them have been, by a paid master, provided by the committee, or formed without that assistance, where the committee have not been able, with a due regard to the finances of the Institution, to grant assistance, by the members themselves on the principle of mutual instruction. It is in these class-rooms, gentlemen, that you see our Institution in active and living function. The library and the lecture-room do, indeed, furnish the previous helps; but it is in these class-rooms that you see the nutriment assimilate, the blood circulate, the muscle move. It is here that you witness that most gratifying phenomenon— the adult man again putting himself to school; undergoing that self-imposed labour and training which, with reference to individuals, has in all ages been the great cause of eminence to those whom the world has ennobled, but which, with reference to more numerous bodies, stands as the imposing distinction of our nineteenth century. For the French and Latin languages, I observe that classes have been constantly going on and well attended, with little interruption. For the German, less constantly, yet still frequently. For the Italian and Spanish, also frequently. Nor have languages alone formed the subjects of this class study. I notice also other pursuits, usually less popular, which have been approached with the same persevering and earnest devotion of time and trouble. I observe records of classes on natural and experimental physics, on mathematics, on political economy, on logic, on phrenology, and various other subjects; which I state, gentlemen, not at all with a view of pretending to set forth a list of all that has been done, but only as specimens of what I may call the intellectual vitality of our Institution, calculated to make our tendencies and purposes better understood. There is, however, one class which I cannot omit specially to notice, because it both is now, and has long been, well sustained and popular; and because it is, in my judgment, eminently useful, as exercising a powerful stimulus to activity on the minds of the members, I mean the class for historical and philological discussion. Standing, as the Institution does, apart from all party political excitement and controversial religion, and deeply interested as it is in maintaining internal harmony among its members, the discussion class has been kept free from the two great perils which might have impaired its usefulness. The questions, announced beforehand, have been found to provoke a serious preliminary study, and to cultivate among the members both the faculties of thought and expression, in a manner very different from that empty fluency about nothing, which the habits of a mere debating society too often generate. The listening members have been disposed to enforce, and the speakers to observe, a degree of good feeling, as well as an intelligent handling of the subject, which renders this class a valuable instrument of improvement. And here again we meet with a new provocative to that mental labour on the value of which I have so much insisted.

I shall not forget to notice, also, the music and drawing classes, conducted by members of the Institution; partly because the former especially is found to be one of the most attractive and popular classes within its walls; partly because those musical exercises which Milton did not disdain to comprehend in his lofty sketch of the curriculum of a gentleman's education, may well be numbered among the allurements of our premises in Aldersgate Street, once the actual site of that illustrious man's house and abode. They form a necessary part of that character of universality to which the Institution aspires, and which it must maintain undiminished, if it would be at once self-supporting and permanent. Complexity and variety of pursuit is essential to its usefulness not less than to its stability; it must be competent to meet the demands both of the intellect and the imagination in their principal branches; it must represent, if I may so

speak, a little mental world, wherein all the manifold workings of the vast mental world without, are seen in abridgment and in miniature. Much credit is due to its managers
for having steadily kept in view this comprehensive mission,
neither disdaining the light and recreative subjects, nor
shrinking from the dry and serious; the fuller audiences of
the former both sustain, and are sustained by, the more
select and laborious students who devote themselves to the
latter.

I am happy further to know that the advantages of
the lectures and of the library are open to ladies, and
that this privilege is actually employed to a considerable extent, producing unmixed benefit. For, certainly,
literary and intellectual culture is not less advantageous to
one sex than to the other; and our Institution ought to be
the last to sanction that narrow view which would deprive
our female relatives of access to the means of improvement,
while we are labouring hard to disseminate them among ourselves.

Now, gentlemen, it is the essential principle of our Institution to be voluntary and self-supporting. We have no other
permanent fund of reliance than the subscriptions of our
members; and if ever the time shall come when they shall
deem the advantages of the Institution an insufficient
equivalent for what they are called upon to pay, we shall
not survive, nor shall we deserve to survive, any longer.
I am one of those who number self-reliance among the cardinal virtues of the human bosom, second in rank only to
honesty and integrity; and it is one of the circumstances
of which I feel proud in the history of this Institution,
that it has been self-relying and self-supporting. Its
members have proved this, as by their other conduct, so also
by raising the large sum of money required for the repair
and enlargement of their premises, through loans derived
chiefly from individuals of their own number. But, gentlemen, the man that helps himself is the man that best deserves the help of others; and I will not scruple to maintain

that this Institution renders a service to the commercial and professional public of London, which entitles it to call for such help, even from those who may not feel induced to join it as members. I believe it to have a powerful claim on the approbation, countenance, and aid of the merchants and bankers generally of this great city. To say nothing of that disinterested sympathy which ought to prevail, and which doubtless in most cases will prevail, between the principal of an establishment and the younger men who serve as his auxiliaries, I do not hesitate to affirm that he has a positive interest in upholding their morality, in enlarging their intelligence, in opening the most favourable avenues (as far as he can do so without obtrusive interference) for the employment and direction of their leisure hours. Speaking as one, the best years of whose life have been passed as principal of a banking house, I contend, emphatically, that merchants and bankers will obey the call of interest, as well as the call of duty, in seconding the voluntary efforts of our members, and in strengthening the self-acquired position which our Institution now occupies. Though useful for men of all ages, its beneficial influence will, of course, be found most efficient in regard to younger men—to that age when the character is ductile and the tastes undetermined— when much depends, for good or evil, on the associates with whom a youth may be thrown into connection. In those early, and, to a certain extent, doubtful years, the admission of a young man into our Institution, whether you look at it as keeping him out of the reach of expense, as guaranteeing him against dissipated company, or as opening to him the largest measure of elevating and refined pursuits which in his position is attainable,—in all these points of view, I say, the admission to our Institution will prove to him at once tutelary and attractive. He has his bread to get, doubtless; his industrious habits must not be impaired. Certainly, if I supposed for a moment that our Institution would impair them, I should not be here to uphold it. I should consider that any other service which the Institution might do him would be a poor compensation for the loss of his independent industry. But, gentlemen, the young man who enters our Institution, having his bread to get, finds every other member of it in the same situation as himself; every member of it is also commercial and professional, having his leisure to bestow upon the Institution, but having no free time besides. It is not among a body of men such as this that any sentiment unfavourable to industry—any sentiment tending to excuse negligence or distraction of mind—can ever for a moment have a chance of succeeding.

Well, gentlemen, I shall grant most fully, that with a commercial and professional public, habits of steady industry are the first thing needful; but I shall contend, with equal strenuousness, that they are not the only thing needful. There are, in the life of every commercial and professional man, hours of leisure, as well as hours of work—I wish, indeed, from the bottom of my heart, that the circumstances were such as to enable him to command still longer hours of leisure—but that which he now enjoys is enough to make a considerable difference, according as it is well or ill bestowed. Now, gentlemen, there are many innocent and agreeable ways of passing leisure; and I am the last person to obtrude the literary, the scientific, the recreative pursuits of our Institution upon any unwilling partaker. If a young man has tastes of another kind, I wish him happy in his own way. But I do say, that if he chance to have a taste for literary or scientific pursuits, or for mental recreations, it is of very great moment that the taste should not be stifled for want of nourishment, nor die out from the mere impossibility of gratification. Suppose him to come from that valuable and economical place of education now flourishing among us —the City of London School—or from any other good school elsewhere, and to pass from thence into a counting-house; he will doubtless have treasured up a certain stock of acquired knowledge, and will perhaps have brought away a treasure hardly less valuable—the wish to acquire more knowledge.

This is the exact case with many a young man when he first enters upon the threshold of his commercial career; for the fatal supposition, that what has been learnt at school has been learnt only to be thrown aside or buried like the talent in a napkin, is a mistake, committed, indeed, by too many persons in every rank of life, but not committed by all. I do not hesitate to affirm, gentlemen, that to a young man with these dispositions our Institution holds out the most effective support, and the most propitious allurement, which his situation admits. It brings into play those principles of sociability which are so predominant in the youthful character, and which, if they do not find good objects to fasten upon, are but too likely to be seduced towards frivolities, perhaps even towards what is positively bad—it brings into play, I say, those principles of sociability, and allies them with pursuits at once improving to the intellect and elevating to the imagination. Gentlemen, this is a great and a noble end—to blend the extension of human sociability with the improvement of human intellect, and with the expansion of our imaginative pleasures; to bring men together, not merely as partakers of the same meat and drink, not merely as partners in the same scheme of commercial gain, but also as fellow-proprietors of the same rational nature, and as mutual agents each in the improvement of others. Under one form or another, this is one of the capital problems of modern society, and our Institution may well be proud of helping to accomplish it. Humble, indeed, our efforts are, and on a small scale, as compared with what we can all wish and conceive: but even the undistinguished soldier in the ranks derives some dignity from the consciousness of a grand cause upheld in part by his arm.

A young man of the commercial or professional class, who enlists in our regiment, finds himself in a companionship calculated to develop all the improving tendencies of his nature, and, I venture boldly to assert, not calculated to develop any others; certainly none for which himself, or his relatives, might have reason to feel after-repentance. He finds encouragement and sympathy in keeping alive the acquisitions of his school period, or in extending the same habits to new subjects of study; the dead volumes on the library shelves, and the living voice in the lecture-room, are alike calculated to enlarge the range of his ideas; whatever be his vein of taste, or line of study, he will enjoy greater facilities for prosecuting it than would be open to him in any other quarter. He will learn to respect and value the intellectual tendencies of others, even though they happen to be different from his own, and to regard human improvement as one great whole, towards which many different streams converge. If his mind be strung no higher than the pitch of passive curiosity, it will, at least, find an apt and abundant nutriment, often invigorating, always pleasing and harmless: if it be more self-working and inquisitive, there will be ample materials of thought, and definite objects of acquisition, placed within his reach, together with a little community quite sufficiently extensive to sustain within him the wholesome fire of emulation. In those years which precede the age when he will think it prudent to take upon him the charge of a family, our Institution offers to him a harbour for his leisure hours, a diversion from his daily toil, and a stimulus for all the seeds of intellectual life that are dormant within him. It holds out opportunities such as Daniel Defoe, or other men of genius, who knew the city of London in its earlier and grosser days, must have sighed for in vain in their own solitary parlours.

And, gentlemen, let me again say it, he will find everything in our Institution arranged with a view to the prior and imperious exigencies of a life of industry. We look to the commercial and professional classes, and we look to none besides: we offer them mental occupation for their leisure hours only, with the full knowledge, and with the sincere regret, that they have no room for more. We know both the moderate means, and the moderate leisure, of those for whom we work; we shall seek to engraft upon their habits of business as much of literature and science as the case admits, but we shall not encourage them to convert the necessary occupation into the principal. Upon the individual industry, prudence, and success of our members, each in his own separate walk of life, depends, not merely the prosperity, but even the continued existence, of the collective Institution. We have this important truth present to our minds as intimately as if it were engraven on the walls of our building; and could we by possibility forget it, we should find it thrust upon our attention by the manner in which occasional depressions, in the general state of London commerce, operate in diminishing the number of our members. The unfavourable state of commerce in London, during the years between 1841 and 1844, caused a temporary falling-off in our numbers, which, for a moment, disturbed the calculation of our managers. From this I rejoice to say that we have now completely recovered; but we have not forgotten its past occurrence, and it serves as a salutary admonition to prudence and watchfulness.

Gentlemen,—I shall again remind you that this is our twenty-first birthday. Our season of youth is over, and we now pass into the period of maturity. We have taken rank, and are identified with the mind and intelligence of this great city; be it ours to act in a manner worthy of our age and our calling. To those—whether they be many or few, I know not—who may still hold the ungenial prejudice that there is an inherent incompatibility between a day of industry in the counting-house, and an evening of study in the lecture-room, the class-room, or the library—we must continue to present the best of all refutations, in the lives and behaviour of our members. To those, on the other hand, whose sentiments are more generous and exalted, who esteem an enlightened population a greater glory than splendid edifices, and immeasurable capital, and who account it an honour to London to interweave the threads of literature and science with the staple of a commercial and professional life; to these minds, we offer ourselves with confidence as auxiliaries and instruments, prepared to justify our claim upon their fraternal sympathy. There always have been minds of this enlarged and kindly stamp: witness, among other things, the great amount of property bequeathed for educational purposes; of which bequests some, indeed, have been ill-considered and capricious; but many too have been dictated by the purest and most earnest solicitude for the diffusion of human knowledge. It is but too well known how many of these bequests have become misemployed or useless by negligence or fraud on the part of trustees; how many of them too, even where the original purpose has been faithfully adhered to, have turned to nullity or mischief, because that purpose itself is no longer in harmony with the exigencies of a modern age. Let it be our task to prove to minds such as these, and to all who really have at heart the diffusion of literature and science in the City of London, that they can in no way better assist this inestimable object than by employing our ministration, and by seconding the voluntary efforts of our members. That which is given or bequeathed to us can neither lie useless nor become unemployed, for our financial proceedings are both well known and diligently watched by the members; our purposes are of endless necessity, and can never grow obsolete, while a due flexibility as to the means of accomplishing them is inseparable from our management. To-morrow, as well as to-day—in the times of our descendants as in our own—the life of the commercial and professional man will consist of a day of labour and an evening of leisure, which may be well or ill appropriated; to-morrow, as well as to-day, the sociability of his nature may be enlisted in favour of the better employment instead of the worse—in favour of mental progress and elevating recreations, and against both seductions and lassitude; provided there be a brotherhood ready organized, commanding as well as deserving his confidence, with whom he can mingle and fraternise. This organization, gentlemen, it is our pride to have created; we shall bequeath it to our successors, together with an unfinished but noble task, which will never cease to require the exertions of an enlightened benevolence, and never cease to bless them with the requiting consciousness of well doing. That which we have begun will be matured and perfected by others; and our Institution, destined for enduring mental wants, fed by the energies of a concentrated population, and sustained by the silent stream of human improvement, will pass from well-spent youth to vigorous manhood, without being fated to reach the age of superannuation or decrepitude.

[This Institution, on which Mr. Grote had lavished his support, in every form, during twenty years, declined in its prosperity from this date, owing to the altered habits of the class for whose benefit it had existed. The introduction of the "Omnibus," or cheap conveyance system, induced the young men engaged in business in the city to lodge in the suburbs, and the purposes of the London Scientific Institution ceased to offer the same inducements to become members.]

ADDRESS

ON

DELIVERING THE PRIZES AT UNIVERSITY COLLEGE.

(1st *July*, 1846.)

o 2

ADDRESS

DELIVERING THE PRIZES AT UNIVERSITY COLLEGE.

LADIES AND GENTLEMEN,—I should depart from the precedents of former years, and I should do little justice either
to your feelings or to my own, if I permitted this meeting to
separate without saying a few words on the business which
has just been auspiciously concluded. In regard to myself
personally, I feel that the Council of University College
have done me great honour by inviting me to preside at a
ceremony so interesting in its character, and so beneficial in
its tendencies. To be the instrument of placing in the
hands of those students most distinguished for their ability
and diligence that meed of honour which they have so fairly
won, is a duty which no man can perform unmoved, and
which the first men among us for position and intellect might
well be proud to perform.

In the success of University College I have always felt
a sincere and lively interest, having taken a part, though a
humble part, in its first foundation, and having had my name
honoured by being commemorated with the foundation stone
as a member of its earliest Council. I rejoice to find, from
the Report read by Professor De Morgan, that the hold which
the College had in former years acquired on the public
mind, as a good and efficient place of instruction, has been
fully sustained, that the number of pupils has increased,
and that their conduct has been so creditable and exemplary.
There was, indeed, one portion of the Report which occa-

sioned me the deepest regret—I mean that portion which announced the retirement of Professor Long from the Chair of Latin, a gentleman whose extensive erudition, discriminating criticism, and remarkable power of illustrating ancient literature and history, are so well known and so highly appreciated by every classical scholar amongst us.

If it should appear to the more zealous friends of the College that its students are not so numerous as might have been expected from the number of affluent families in and near the metropolis, to whose children it offers facilities for an elevated range of education such as they never before possessed, we must consider, on the other hand, that the College at its first formation had to encounter much un-candid hostility, which has only of late become discredited and forgotten; that it had nothing but the force of truth and its own intrinsic merit to rely upon, without any extraneous support from powerful and organised parties, either in Church or State.

According to the temper and character of our population, the greatest amount of real merit will not dispense with this necessary advantage, of being known as an establishment fixed and settled—not dating from yesterday, but having a past to look back upon, traditional or historical. But this season of disadvantage and hostility is now overpast; the College has outlived the stigma of novelty, as well as the more unjust stigma of irreligion. It has now taken its rank as one of the great and permanent institutions of the metropolis, and may fairly calculate on that steady increase, which real good management, distinguished teachers, and educational efficiency, when they find a clear stage and no prejudice, are sure to bring about. It can already appeal to the 'Calendar of the University of London,' and to the award of scholarships and other prizes by the senate of that body, as an evidence of the proficiency of its students and the success of its professors; and the proportion of prizes, obtained by its students from the award of the University of London, will be found not merely to satisfy, but greatly to surpass, all reasonable expectation. It will confide in the same results, and will require only the same fair and impartial trial, to ensure its future increase and extension.

You, Gentlemen, the successful students whom the Examiners have this day pronounced worthy to receive from my hands prizes and certificates of honour, you will require no words of mine to enhance the well-earned gratification which now fills your bosom. Your triumph has been one honestly achieved, which all will envy you, but which none can either impeach or disparage. Any man who reads over the questions of the different professors in the examination papers, will see at once that the test of proficiency applied is not merely strict, but exceedingly trying and severe; that the student who has answered such queries even fairly and tolerably, has profited much by the lessons of his professor; but that he, whose answers merit a prize or a certificate of honour, has displayed that rare mastery of his subject, and that happy combination of laborious study beforehand with spontaneous and productive association at the moment of trial, which mark the rich and well-endowed mind, and give the amplest promise of future success and improvement. It will enhance in your view, Gentlemen, the value of your prizes, that your parents and near relatives will feel hardly less of satisfaction than yourselves, and that you are thus enabled to commence the task of discharging that debt of gratitude which parental affection has been so long imposing upon you. You will exult, and you have good reason to exult, in that which has just been achieved; but let the achievement of this day serve but as a prelude and an incentive to yet further progress, and yet larger acquisitions, beyond. Let the prize which you now hold demonstrate to you the efficacy of steady, single-minded, well-directed application; but let it at the same time prove to you that without a continuance of that application, no fresh rewards will await you. The triumphs of the youth are most valuable, as they presage and assist the future eminence of the adult man; but in the one competition as well as in the other, it is the same sterling quality of mind, the same devotion and concentration of purpose, the same docility to good teaching and to a good system, which wins the race.

But it is not to those students alone, into whose hands I have had the gratification of delivering prizes and certificates of honour—it is not to them alone that I would address my observations. There are other students present whom personally I am not permitted to know, but whose efforts have been less fortunate in the competition just terminated. To them, I fear, the acclamations which have welcomed the prizemen of this day will speak only of disappointed attempt; yet I venture to remind them, that the auguries for the future are not merely consoling, but full of hope and promise. Though the prize can be only for one, and special notice only for a few, yet all those competitors who have diligently and seriously put forth their best efforts, may be well assured that every particle of that diligence will reap its due fruit and reward. They have dug the field carefully, without obtaining the pot of golden treasure there concealed; but still, the field *has* been dug, and has been placed in condition to throw up a rich future harvest; and in the fulness of time that harvest will be reaped. It is on this common ground that all the assiduous and earnest competitors for the prize, the defeated as well as the successful, may meet, with equal pride and confidence. In the great field of mental improvement there is room for all, without monopoly or exclusive possession to any one; all, without exception, have advanced themselves to a higher grade of knowledge and capacity, and have qualified themselves for greater achievements and for ruder labours in future years.

I have already remarked, that in estimating the difficulties with which the student has had to grapple, and the degree of proficiency which has been rewarded by the prize of this day, we are not confined simply to the declaration of the Examiner; we have before us also the list of questions which have been propounded for answer, and we are thus as it were introduced into the class-room, so as to measure the range of instruction embraced by the Professor. I venture to assert that no man can read those papers without feeling satisfied that a competent answer, given on the spot, to such queries, involves no common amount of intellectual resources and requirements. And when we go through the long series of these various lists, as they stand here printed in the successive pages of the little volume annually set forth by the College, we are presented with an aggregate idea, both encouraging and impressive, of the wide mental field which its entire course covers. To suffice for the intellectual necessities of the present day, theoretical as well as practical, enlarged and diversified as they now are, is no easy task. In former centuries, when the great universities now existing in Europe were founded, the range of science and literature open to be studied was very narrow ; but now, each separate branch has been widened, and several new branches have been put forth ; the mathematical and physical sciences have come to comprise an immeasurable heap of theorems and general facts, such as could not have been imagined even in the time of Lord Bacon : the true requirements of scientific method, the process of logic and induction, and the phenomena of psychology generally, have been revived and analysed anew by minds trained in these positive investigations ; the languages and literature of the ancient world, though not more extensive in respect of original documents than they were a century ago, have yet been examined by more piercing eyes, and have been found to suggest inferences which reproduce Rome and Athens under new points of view ; comparative grammar and philology have brought languages, ancient and modern, distant and near, under one common analytical survey. Moreover, in addition to that which constitutes the stock of the scientific and literary man, there are the ministers of applied science, the practical chemist and the civil engineer, who have acquired, in the present industrial development of society, an importance such as those professions never before enjoyed ; and though last mentioned, not least in importance, the school-

master of the present day has come to have his dignified
mission correctly appreciated. Here are large intellectual
exigencies, belonging to our age, and tending even to yet
farther increase and expansion for the future.

It has been the honourable aim of University College to
adapt itself to that large measure of pure science and
literature, as well as to that combination of science with
practice, which the forward minds of our generation have
marked out—to make provision for the legal and medical
student, as well as for the classical and mathematical—to
furnish appropriate aid and training to the schoolmaster,
the civil engineer, and the practical chemist. The scheme
includes classes which had not before been made the subjects
of special professorship; and the largest, as well as the
cheapest, range of instruction accessible in London, has thus
been opened to the willing student, embracing both theory
and practice. If, in providing so comprehensive a scheme
of education, the administrators of the College have presumed upon a wider extension of demand than is yet found
to exist among the opulent and middling community of
London—if they have anticipated intellectual appetites
which have not as yet spread beyond chosen minds, and
if some of their classes are therefore for the present scantily
attended—I shall not affect to extenuate what they have
done as an error or an imprudence. I shall rather glory in
it as redounding to their honour, that they have set up an
elevated standard of educational requirement, and that they
have endeavoured to attract others to the eminence thus
selected. While supplying to the full all the recognised
subjects of instruction, they have tried to guide and to
enlarge the public sentiment on this important matter,
instead of contracting their own views so as to court only
the maximum of immediate resort. I hope, and I believe,
that they will succeed in diffusing among the public of
London larger ideas on the proper measure of a citizen's
education—in correcting that mistaken impatience with
which parents, often under no pressure of necessity, abridge

those years requisite for their son's complete education, and hurry him into professional life a half-educated man: above all, I hope they will succeed in extending and deepening that love of knowledge, without which every man, let his station or prosperity in life be what they may, remains essentially mutilated in one of the most essential features of the human character. To bind men together by this common love of knowledge, the primitive meaning of the word *philosophy*—a tie more ample and comprehensive than either political or theological party, to concentrate in the same establishment an array of distinguished teachers, with wide diversities of intellectual aptitude, yet organised and acting in concert towards the grand purpose of an all-sided education, to eliminate at the same time those seeds of discord which cause what is meant for mankind, to be given up to sect or party,—this has been the animating scheme of University College, in which every exalted and patriotic mind will wish to it the fullest success.

Upon you, Gentlemen, the students of the College, whom I now see around me, that success will mainly depend—upon every one of you more or less—but most of all upon those meritorious and conspicuous students to whom I have this day had the pleasure of delivering prizes and certificates of honour, as well as those for whom the like distinctions may be in reserve on future occasions similar to the present. It is from your conduct and character that the place in which you have received your education will be judged; and among the tutelary motives which will be required, to guard you through the various trials of life, this consideration will doubtless have its fair and prominent place. I trust that the maxims which you have imbibed in University College —the distinguished men from whom you have received instruction, and the companions with whom you have received it—perhaps also the scene of this day and the few, but deep-felt, words which you now hear from this chair— may form recollections of no mean force in assisting all your best and most virtuous resolutions. That you will be estimable and honourable citizens, I shall not permit myself for a moment to doubt; but I am farther sanguine enough to hope, not less for your own sakes than for that of the College in which you have been educated, that you will also be something more. The knowledge which your residence in University College has implanted in you, the literary and scientific associations which are now grouped in your minds, the habits of reading and application · of which you have shown such conspicuous proof, are not mere artificial enforcements applied to your youth, destined to be thrown aside when you take up the active duties of a profession; they are to be preserved and cultivated side by side with those duties, as the recreation, the treasure, the interior mental life, of the professional man. The man of regulated habits will suffice for both exigencies; he will indeed account pecuniary independence and self-reliance to be an obligation not less imperative than pecuniary integrity, but the largest construction of this obligation will still leave him leisure enough to preserve him from the misfortune—I had almost said, the disgrace—of an unlettered life—that unlettered life which has been characterised by more than one eminent man, as a life no better than death, "Vita sine literis mors est." I trust that the studies and intellectual associations of your College period will pass by unbroken tradition into your mature life, enlarged and improved, but never relinquished; and while you thus procure for yourselves personally a dignified existence and a source of perennial satisfaction, you will at the same time repay the care and labours of your teachers, you will confer an honour on University College, and you will second in the most effective manner the noble purposes of its Founders, to raise the level, as well as to enlarge the spread of public education.

REVIEW OF SIR G. C. LEWIS

ON THE

CREDIBILITY OF EARLY ROMAN HISTORY.

(*Edinburgh Review*, 1856.)

REVIEW OF SIR G. C. LEWIS

CREDIBILITY OF EARLY ROMAN HISTORY.*

AMONG the wide circle of historical readers, there are few who follow with satisfaction, and some who even repudiate with impatience, investigations into the evidence on which the narrative before them rests. Such investigations they regard as the special duty of the author. They desire only to know the results, set forth in a luminous and attractive manner, with suitable reflections. If they are perusing an animated narrative—adjusted to their notions of probability in respect to the succession of events, and accommodated to their ethical and æsthetical sentiments in its appreciation of characters and situations—they willingly hail the matter as so much added to their previous knowledge. A moderate show of references suffices to make them presume that the author has collated the necessary evidence and elicited from it a true or credible history. No such presumption indeed will arise, if he contradicts their notions of probability, or adopts canons of ethical and æsthetical appreciation departing from theirs—if he describes sequences to them unexpected, or introduces supernatural forces on occasions which they deem inappropriate—if he disparages persons and institutions admirable in their eyes. The shock to their feelings

---

* *Inquiry into the Credibility of the Early Roman History.* By Sir George Cornewall Lewis, Bart. 2 vols. 8vo. 1855.

will then certainly raise doubts, and may perhaps provoke to
examination of the original authorities. But except under
such a stimulus, the idea of mistrusting the sufficiency of the
author's proofs is one which neither suggests itself spon-
taneously to them, nor finds ready admission when suggested
by others. The degree to which an historian can count
upon easy faith, depends upon the pre-established harmony of
sentiment between him and his readers, enforced by his own
powers of style and exposition.

Both the appreciating sentiments, and the received measure of internal credibility, vary materially from age to age,
and from nation to nation : but subject to this condition, the
description above given applies to historical readers generally. For the large majority of them, indeed, the fact
cannot be otherwise. They have no time—to pass over other
disqualifications—even for hearing all the distinct matters of
proof; much less for weighing and comparing them, for
hunting out what may have been overlooked, or for studying
the process of combination and elimination which the historian's task requires from him. Such labour must be performed by one or a few for the benefit of many. And the
security which the many possess for its being faithfully performed, arises not so much from their own demand, as from
the emulation and competition of historical students themselves. The probability of eventual animadversion, from a
few censors themselves conversant with the original sources,
is a motive almost indispensable to keep the historian up
to the proper pitch, throughout his long and often irksome
preparations. By such censorship the comparison of his
narrative with the sum total of attainable evidence becomes
forced upon general readers, little disposed of themselves to
originate the question. The analytical or dissecting process
of criticism serves as a valuable control on the synthetical
and constructive effort of the historian ; who, however conscientious, is under temptation to aim too exclusively at
those charms of pictorial execution without which large
popularity is hardly attainable.

Of this analytical process, the work of Sir George Lewis, now before us, affords an admirable specimen. It exhibits a complete and intelligent mastery of the original authorities, a full knowledge of what has been done by former critics, with an equitable spirit of appreciation towards them, and a familiarity with historical research, modern as well as ancient. It is full of copious illustration from the kindred subject of Grecian antiquity. While rich in premises, it is sparing in conclusions, and strictly exigent as to sufficiency of proof—the work of one who, though seeking earnestly for truth, is not ashamed to confess that he cannot find it, and to rest in such acknowledgment of ignorance, where there is no evidence, at once literal and cogent, to enforce some positive affirmation. We recognise in Sir George Lewis the precise antithesis of that vehement impulse of divination, confident alike both in belief and in disbelief, which so often carried away the vigorous intellect of Niebuhr. If indeed there be any single purpose, prominent and peculiar, in a work of so much breadth and learning as this 'Enquiry,' it is to protest against the Niebuhrian licence of substitution and reconstruction. The book is not, and does not profess to be, a history of Rome; but we are mistaken if it does not tend to influence materially the composition of future Roman histories. Like the critical philosophy of Kant, as contrasted with the antecedent dogmatic philosophy of Leibnitz and Wolf, it is a magazine of arms on the negative side of the question. The historian will find brought before him, more fully than in any previous work, the problems with which he has to grapple, the means of solving them, and the amount of success hitherto attained by employing those means; lastly, the contradictions and inconsistencies which the original authorities, scanty as they are, present in abundance.

Sir George Lewis reviews the Roman history from its earliest times down to the fall of the Republic, about forty years before the Christian era. Upon the subsequent events during the Empire, he does not touch. Counting upwards

P

from the fall of the Republic to the received date of the capture of Troy and the migration of Æneas, there was a space of about 1140 years. Through this long antiquity Augustus and his contemporaries looked up to Æneas and the exiles from Troy, mythical ancestors of the Julian and other great Roman families. The series of years is here distributed into several periods, with the evidences, primary or secondary, discordant or harmonious, indicated and appreciated.

In writing a history of Rome, the historian must necessarily begin from the beginning; and the difficulty is, in this as well as in other inquiries, to find a beginning. He must grope his way for some time nearly in the dark, until at length he emerges into twilight, and into a slowly improving daylight. In the process of criticism this order is reversed. Sir George Lewis takes his point of departure from the latest period. Proceeding backward from the fall of the Republic to the invasion of Italy by Pyrrhus in 281 B.C., he exhibits a full catalogue of the historical productions of the Roman world during the last two centuries before the Christian era.

The catalogue is a very respectable one; and though nearly all the works are lost, we have notices remaining which inform us of their general contents and style of execution. Julius Cæsar and Sallust, comparatively recent as they are, must be named as the oldest Roman writers from whom any entire historical compositions remain. Livy was born B.C. 59, and died at the age of seventy-six. His history extended from the earliest times of Rome to the death of Drusus, nine years before the Christian era. Between him and Cato the Censor (the earliest Roman historian who composed in his own language, about 150 B.C.) the following historians are known to us by name and by a few fragments:—Calpurnius Piso Frugi, Cassius Hemina, Caius Fannius, L. Attius, Caius Sempronius Tuditanus, Lucius Cœlius Antipater, Cnæus Gellius, Sextus Gellius, Aulus Gellius, Clodius Licinus, Publius Sempronius Asellio, Marcus Æmilius Scaurus, Publius Ru-

tilius Rufus, Quintus Lutatius Catulus, Caius Licinius Macer
Quintus Claudius Quadrigarius, Quintus Valerius Antias,
Lucius Otacilius Pilitus, Lucius Cornelius Sylla, Lucius Cor-
nelius Sisenna, Quintus Ælius Tubero, &c.

Besides these and other historians in the Latin language,
there were several Romans, some of illustrious position, who
composed historical works in Greek. Among them there
were the two earliest of all Roman historians—Quintus
Fabius Pictor and Lucius Cincius Alimentus, both of them in
high public position and active service throughout the Second
Punic War. Cincius was even taken prisoner by Hannibal,
from whom he learnt various facts afterwards reported in
his history.

Ennius (B.C. 239–169) and Nævius, a generation older,
though poets, are also historical witnesses. Ennius, the
first composer of hexameter verses in Latin, wrote a sort of
metrical chronicle, called 'Annales,' of the affairs of Rome
from Romulus and Remus down to his own time. Nævius
wrote a similar chronicle of the First Punic War (in which
he had himself served), employing the native Latin metre,
Saturnian verse.

Passing to Greeks: the life of Polybius is comprised between B.C. 210–120, and his forty books of universal history
(of which only five remain entire) included the period from
B.C. 220 down to B.C. 146, the date of the capture of Carthage
and Corinth, which events Polybius witnessed. Sosilus and
Silenus, contemporary with and companions of Hannibal,
wrote histories of the Second Punic War. Philinus of Agrigentum described the First Punic War, with which he was
contemporary, in a spirit blamed by Polybius as unfair
towards the Romans. Lastly, both Hieronymus of Cardia
and Timaeus of Tauromenium, contemporaries of Pyrrhus,
described his war against the Romans. Indeed Pyrrhus himself seems to have composed memoirs of his own operations.

These are the earliest portions of Roman affairs, described
by historians either actually or nearly contemporaneous.
Besides these histories, there existed in the last two cen-

turies of the Republic, many orations spoken on various public occasions by magistrates and senators, and preserved as well as edited by the speakers themselves. Among the orations, the oldest was that of Appius the Blind, who being conducted in his old age into the Senate when the question of peace or war with Pyrrhus was under discussion, determined his countrymen to reject the propositions of peace (B.C. 280). In the time of Cicero, a large collection of these miscellaneous public harangues existed. He had read no less than a hundred and fifty from the elder Cato alone, and he indicates Cornelius Cethegus (who died in B. C. 196, shortly after the Second Punic War) as the earliest Roman distinguished for eloquence.

It is to this later period of the Republic that Sir George Lewis devotes his first two chapters—among the most instructive in the work. He sets before us the really historical age of Rome—the assemblage of all the authors from whom we derive (mediately or immediately) our knowledge of Roman events; and he appreciates, as far as is practicable under the loss of their works, their scope, manner, and point of view.

The following summary deserves attention both in itself and as furnishing a standard of comparison for the evidences of the earlier age of Rome :—

" If we trace the Roman history back from the dictatorship of Julius Cæsar, we find that its events were fully recorded by intelligent, trustworthy, and well-informed contemporary writers, up to the beginning of the Gallic war of 225 B.C. Up to that period, the majority of these historians were native Romans, though some of them, and particularly those of the earlier time, wrote in Greek. For the period of thirty-nine years between the beginning of the first Punic War and the Gallic War (264-225, B.C.) there were no native historians who were personal witnesses of the events of the day: but they lived with the generation who were actors in them, and were able to obtain their information from sources of unquestionable authenticity. The First Punic War was narrated by one Greek at least who lived during its progress ; and probably other Sicilians at the time wrote its history.

" It is true that the native historians of Rome from Fabius Pictor down to Claudius Quadrigarius and Valerius Antias, did not hold a high rank as artists; that their manner was in general dry, stiff, and jejune; that they were deficient in philosophical spirit; and that their historical style resembled rather that of a mediæval chronicle, or of such writers as Holinshed or Stow, than the work of Thucydides, which they might have imitated; or the works of Sallust, Livy, and Tacitus, which their own literature afterwards produced. Cicero will not even allow them the name of historians. So inferior were they to the Greek writers in that line of composition, that he regards them as mere annalists or memoir-writers—as mere mechanical registrars of facts, without any claim to the higher merits of the historian. According to the Roman standard of history (he says), the only requisite is, that the writer should tell the truth: the style of his composition is immaterial. They studied only to express their meaning in the smallest number of words consistent with being understood. Their model was, the official annals of the year, kept by the Pontifex Maximus. Cicero himself wished to produce a history which should equal those of the Greek writers; as Virgil attempted to rival Homer, and Horace the Greek lyric poets. He looks upon history chiefly as a work of art, and as a composition fitted for an orator." (Vol. i. p. 40.)

After noticing criticisms from Sallust, Velleius Paterculus, and Dionysius of Halicarnassus, coinciding in spirit with those of Cicero, Sir George Lewis proceeds :—

" But though the series of historical writers who have been enumerated, from Fabius and Cincius down to Sylla and Macer, were not distinguished for any literary or philosophical excellence —though they were not artists in history—yet they were trustworthy witnesses respecting the events of their own time. They were most of them men conversant with public affairs both civil and military—who had filled high offices and sat in the senate—who had in some cases been actors in the events which they narrated—and who by their social position, had access to good information and enlightened opinions respecting the political events of their time." (Vol. i. p. 43.)

The loss, almost total, of these later historians—combined with the preservation of so many details respecting the early

Roman history in the extant books of Livy and Dionysius
—fostesr an involuntary illusion in the reader's mind, that
the earlier periods were both better known and more interesting to the Romans themselves, than the later.   This is a
mistake pointed out by Sir George Lewis :—

> " They (Fabius, Cincius, and the other historians) were concise
> in the early periods, and full in the times of which they had per-
> sonal experience.   Their main purpose was to write recent and
> contemporary history.   Even Livy, whom, on account of the acci-
> dental preservation of the earlier books and loss of the later books,
> of his history, we are accustomed to regard as an antiquarian com-
> piler, was in truth regarded in quite a different light, when his
> entire work was extant.   The principal object of Livy was to relate
> the events of the period immediately preceding his own life, and
> partly contemporary with it.   The books of his history beginning
> with 103, and extending to 142, being nearly a third part of the
> entire work, were coincident with his own lifetime.   He himself,
> in his preface, supposes his readers to be more solicitous to read
> the history of the civil wars, than to dwell on the early period."
> (VoL i. p. 44.)

The superior interest felt by Livy and others in the events
of the later Republic is not difficult to explain.   Those events
surpassed prodigiously, in magnitude and in awe-striking
accompaniments, the wars and internal disputes of Rome in
her earlier days of comparative feebleness,—

> " Vincere cum Voios posse, laboris erat."

It is these antecedent events, recorded in the first ' Decad '
of Livy*, which form the special subject of Sir George
Lewis's ' Enquiry into the Credibility of the Early Roman
History.'   We have approached them, as he has done, by
an upward march through the later events ; because we con-

---

* The first Decad of Livy ends with the Consulship of Fabius
Maximus Gurges and Junius Brutus Scæva, in B.C. 292.   His
eleventh book (now lost) brought the third Samnite War to a
conclusion.   His twelfth book (also lost) described the beginning
of the war of Pyrrhus against the Romans (B.C. 280).

sider it an important feature in his method, to pass from
the more known to the less known, and to appreciate the
reporting historians before he begins to weigh and measure
the evidences open to their inspection.

We find in Livy and other writers a history of Rome for
472 years earlier than Pyrrhus; from B.C. 753, the period
assigned for the foundation of the city. This narrative which
we read,—or something like it, though with many differences
of detail,—was received during the literary ages of Rome,
and appealed to as matter of popular belief by poets and
orators. Now the question is, what authorities had Fabius
and Cincius, the earliest Roman historians (who flourished
during the Second Punic War), and those who came after
them, for composing the history of five centuries anterior to
themselves?

Sir George Lewis sets forth the various hypotheses which
have been advanced as answers to this question. He examines with much care (Vol. i. 155, seq.), the real comprehension and evidentiary value of what were called the
Pontifical Annals—'Annales Maximi,'—kept by the Chief
Pontiff from an early period down to the Pontificate of P.
Mucius in B.C. 121. The pontiff caused various notable
incidents to be inscribed on a whitened board and publicly
posted up. What these incidents were, we are very imperfectly informed; but as far as we can make out, they were
events susceptible of a religious interpretation, which called
upon the pontiff to prescribe some expiatory ceremony for
appeasing the wrath of the gods,—events such as dearth,
pestilence, earthquakes, eclipses, prodigies of various kinds.[*]
Livy, who occasionally mentions incidents of this character,
is likely to have derived them, directly or indirectly, from
the Pontifical Annals. The prodigies, such as divine voices,

---

[*] A fragment of Cato says (ap. Aul. Gell. ii. 28), "Non lubet
scribere, quod in tabulâ apud Pontificem Maximum est, quoties
annona cara est, quoties lunæ aut solis lumini caligo aut quid
obstiterit," &c.

speaking oxen, rain of blood or of flesh, &c., are more distinctly traceable to contemporary record than any other events in the early Roman history. That these pontifical annals were meagre, and destitute of all information on public matters, there is every reason to believe. At what precise date they commenced, and even whether there was matter registered in every successive year, we are ignorant. But it seems certain that there can have been no continuous preservation of them for the time anterior to the capture of Rome by the Gauls (B.C. 390).

These pontifical tablets were all that early Rome possessed in the nature of annals prior to Fabius Pictor and Cincius. Sir George Lewis justly censures the laxity with which Niebuhr, Arnold, and other historians, appeal to certain invisible witnesses, called *The Old Annals, The Ancient Annalists, some Old Annalist,* &c., as authorities for facts between B.C. 500-300 (see numerous examples cited, vol. i. p. 93, *seq.*). Nothing can be more misleading than this language. There existed no such annals (except the pontifical tablets) of an earlier date than B.C. 210. And when Livy says, as we sometimes find, "Invenio in quibusdam annalibus," &c., he must mean authors of this date, or later. To him these authors were ancient, very ancient—at the distance of 150 years. Nay, we even find Cicero a generation earlier than Livy, speaking of Cato as extremely ancient (*perveterem*).[*] But the vague allusions of Niebuhr and Arnold suggest to readers the erroneous belief that there were Roman annalists, contemporary with the seige of Veii or the Decemvirate, from whom Livy's statements, or a modified version of them at least, are borrowed.

Though there existed no continuous history or annals during the first two centuries of the Republic, yet there were undoubtedly throughout all that period detached memorials : contemporary registrations of notable isolated facts

---

[*] Cicero, Brutus, 15. 61. " Eum nos ut perveterem habemus," &c. (*i. e.* Cato).

— treaties with foreign states — laws (such as the Twelve Tables)—decrees of the senate—inscriptions on brazen plates, or on linen cloth—commemoration of the magistracies of particular men, and even partial lists of their succession— precedents kept by the scribes or secretaries who carried on the routine of business in the magisterial offices of the consuls, censors, and prætors. The earliest known inscription, commemorating any public event—the treaty between Rome and Carthage, seen by Polybius—dated very shortly after the expulsion of the kings. Even the earliest times of the Republic were thus not destitute of documents; but none such can be traced during the regal period. Sir George Lewis, in his fifth chapter, reviews and estimates these sources of Roman history. They were (to cite his words in another place, vol. ii. p. 361.) "detached notices and fragments of evidence, but not a continuous narrative; they were not the work of an historian, and they did not of themselves form a history of the period : there was a *substratum of notation*, but not an authentic narrative of events."

This "substratum of notation" can be traced distinctly to the earliest times of the Republic; but no history was erected upon it by any Roman until Fabius Pictor, three centuries afterwards. Nevertheless, the history of Rome, as we read it in Dionysius and Livy (both of them much later than Fabius), contains, not merely a string of naked facts, such as might be noted on brazen plates, or on whitened boards, but also abundance of incidents related with minute details, animated descriptions, precise relation of the words and thoughts of the principal actors. It was in the same copious and circumstantial manner that Fabius and succeeding annalists recounted the family tragedies of the Roman kings, as well as many of the wars and internal political contests which marked the first two centuries of the Republic. From whence then did Fabius and his successors obtain the knowledge of these details, so long anterior to their own time? Not certainly from the "substratum of notation:" which, even if it had been systematic and continuous, instead of being merely disjointed and occasional, could have supplied nothing beyond bare and brief facts. We must here look for sources of information distinct from contemporary brass, wood, or linen.

To find a source for these detailed incidents, many of them highly poetical and interesting, Niebuhr contended for the existence of early ballad-poems, or epic lays, anterior to Nævius and Ennius. Dr. Arnold and Mr. Macaulay have adopted the same hypothesis: and the beautiful 'Lays of Ancient Rome,' composed by the latter, will imprint it on the recollection of every English reader. Sir George Lewis examines the point at considerable length (Vol. i. pp. 212–38). Niebuhr distributes large portions of the Roman history, from Romulus down to the Gallic conflagration, into various epic lays; which, however, he supposes to have been composed long after the events to which they referred, chiefly about B.C. 320–300; and to have been once extremely popular, though they were discredited and lost after Ennius had introduced Greek metres, and after the Latin poetry became assimilated to the Greek.

That ballads were sung among the early Romans, we may readily presume. The fact is common to almost all countries. But that there existed poems of considerable bulk, embodying a large proportion of that which we now read as Livy's prose, is by no means to be presumed without proof; though, if the fact could be proved, it would be an interesting accession to our knowledge. Now no such poems were known to the Romans of the historical age. It is true that the incidents themselves are often of a cast highly romantic and poetical; and upon this ground chiefly the inference is founded, that they must have been derived from poems. But such inference is shown by Sir George Lewis to be unwarranted. Incidents of a romantic character may be real, and are accepted as such if properly attested. The career of Alexander the Great is as full of romance as that of Coriolanus: the suicide of Cleopatra is intrinsically not less poetical than that of Lucretia; while that of the Emperor

Otho is more sublime and impressive than either. Moreover, the early Roman history, though partly poetical in its incidents, is in still larger measure wholly unpoetical: the ballad-theory, even if admitted, accounts for the smaller portion only; not for the larger, nor yet for the mixture of the two. Lastly, Niebuhr supposes that the incidents of these ballad-poems were generally fictitious: but if this be granted, the hypothesis of poems becomes unnecessary: the origin of fictitious stories may be sufficiently explained by oral tradition alone, without any poems, written or un-written :—

"There is nothing in the fictitious part of the early Roman history which may not be accounted for, by supposing that it consists of legends floating in the popular memory, composed of elements partly real but chiefly unreal, and moulded into a connected form as they passed from mouth to mouth; the picturesque, interesting, or touching incidents being selected, and the whole grouped and coloured by the free pencil of tradition. Even those legends would be improved and polished by the successive historians through whose hands they passed, after they had been once reduced to writing. Such an origin would account for their poetical features without supposing them derived from a metrical original —from a poem in the proper sense of the word." (Vol. i. p. 221.)

. . . . . "The theory of Niebuhr is unsupported by evidence sufficient to prove its truth; and, even if it were proved, would afford little or no assistance towards solving the most difficult and important problem of this history. That there were poems of some sort composed in the Latin language, before the time of Livius, Nævius, and Ennius, cannot be doubted : the prohibition of defamatory verses, in the laws of the Twelve Tables, is an undoubted proof of the practice of the poetic art among the Romans in the year B.C. 450. But all positive evidence and all arguments from analogy and probability conspire to prove, that the Latin language at this time was in a rude, uncultivated state, unsuited to poetical treatment; that the old native Saturnian metre, which Horace stigmatises as unfit for the contact of civilised life, was rough, inharmonious, and scarcely distinguishable from prose; and that the early Romans, however poetical may have been the ideas in which they conceived their ancient annals and the exploits of their forefathers, were principally occupied with military pursuits, and bestowed little thought on poetry or the fine arts." (Vol. i. p. 235.)

Niebuhr's ' Theory of Epic Lays,' therefore, cannot be accepted as the source of any considerable portion of the details of early Roman history. For these details no source can be assigned except oral statements and traditions ; many of them, doubtless, current in the great families, respecting their distinguished ancestors (whose waxen images were preserved, and carried in funeral processions), and first embodied in a written continuous history by Fabius and his successors. Upon " the substratum of notation " was thus at length erected a fabric of history.

" There was a continuous list of magistrates, more or less com-. plete and authentic, ascending to the commencement of the consular government; from the burning of the city, there was a series of meagre official annals, kept by the chief pontiff; many ancient treaties and texts of laws, including the Twelve Tables, were preserved, together with notes of ancient usages and rules of customary law, civil and religious, recorded in the books of the pontiffs and some of the civil magistrates ; and these documentary sources of history, which furnished merely the dry skeleton of a narrative, were clothed with flesh and muscle by the addition of various stories handed down from preceding times by oral tradition. Some assistance may have been derived from popular songs, and still more from family memoirs ; but there is nothing to make it probable that private families began to record the deeds of their distinguished members before any chronicler had arisen for the events which interested the commonwealth as a whole." (Vol. i. p. 243.)

We think that this is a correct statement of the means of information possessed by the Roman annalists of B.C. 210, and later, when they undertook to draw up a history of Rome, beginning with B.C. 753, and even earlier; 472 years before the war with Pyrrhus, and 540 years before their own times. It is to be remarked that the "notation" ascends only to the commencement of the Republic ; but the details are carried 244 years higher, throughout the kingly period, and even more. The whole of the kingly period is an assemblage of oral details, uncontrolled by any ascertainable notation.

Having laid down these principles as to the sources of early Roman history, Sir George Lewis illustrates them by analysing the received narrative, from the earliest times to the landing of Pyrrhus in Italy. He distributes it into six portions:—1. The primitive history and ethnology of Italy. 2. The settlement of Æneas in Italy. 3. The Alban kingdom and the foundation of Rome. 4. The period of the seven kings of Rome. 5. The period from the expulsion of the kings to the capture of the city by the Gauls. 6. The period from the capture of the city by the Gauls to the war with Pyrrhus.

"These six periods (observes Sir G. Lewis, p. 266) it will be convenient to investigate separately; as their historical character, and the proportion in which fact and fiction are mixed, differ considerably." The distinction here drawn, as to proportions of fact and fiction, appears to us true only respecting the last three of the six periods,—hardly true respecting the first three.

It is to the two last periods, comprising together the early history of the Republic, that we must devote all the remarks which our space will allow: but we cannot pass over the four first without stating generally, that Sir G. Lewis has consecrated to them two chapters of abundant erudition with an excellent running commentary. In perusing the multifarious discrepancies, the fanciful adventures, and the licence of detailed assertion, which these chapters set forth, we see what Fabius, Cincius, Cato, &c., with their full religious and patriotic faith, were content to accept as their national history. We can take measure of their critical judgment and canon of credibility. There was, however, a considerable difference in this point between Fabius and Cato on the one hand, and writers a century or a century and a half later (such as Cicero, Atticus, Varro, Livy, &c.) on the other. The latter not only censure the chronological ignorance of their predecessors (e.g. the description of Numa as a disciple of Pythagoras), but also seek to rationalise (much to the displeasure of Dionysius of Halicarnassus), the miraculous stories and divine interventions—such as the suckling of Romulus and Remus by a she-wolf, and the interviews of Numa with the nymph Egeria (Vol. i. pp. 402–48).*

In Chapter xii., occupying about the first half of Sir George Lewis's second volume, the Roman history is analysed, from the expulsion of the kings to the burning of the city: an interval of about 120 years (B.C. 510–390). Its earliest portion includes the wars carried on by the nascent Republic against the Tarquinian exiles; who were aided, first by the Etruscan Porsena, next by the Latins mustered in arms at Regillus, and there totally defeated. These incidents are given with many details, often highly picturesque and interesting. They are supposed by Niebuhr to have formed the subject of one of the epic lays: but even if this were granted, we must suppose something like them to have floated probably in the form of oral narrative or legend. Yet Pliny had seen a treaty between Porsena and the Romans, whereby the

---

* It appears that Varro and his immediate predecessors and contemporaries were the first to bring into historical notice many memorials then existing of Roman registered antiquity which had been unknown to, or overlooked by, preceding annalists, such as Fabius and Cato. The "substratum of notation," composed as it was of unconnected fragments, became thus more fully explored and better understood in B.C. 50, than it had been a century before, in B.C. 150. Hence arise in part the discrepancies recited by Livy and Dionysius. The writers of the Varronian age differed from their predecessors because they had consulted new matters of evidence.

This comparison of the age of Varro with that of Fabius is much insisted on in a recent work of learning and research published last year at Basle, L. O. Bröcker, *Untersuchungen über die Glaubwürdigkeit der alt-Römischen Geschichte.* Bröcker notes especially that the Varronians treated the Regal period more briefly, and the Republican period far more copiously, than Fabius and Cato, the new matters of evidence relating apparently to the Republic only. See the second of Bröcker's *Abhandlungen*, pp. 41–82.

latter became bound to the humiliating condition of not
using iron for any other purposes than those of agriculture.
This treaty cannot be reconciled with the accounts which we
read of the wars between the Romans and Porsena. The
oral details and the "notation" are here at variance.

While setting forth the ancient statements respecting
these wars, with his usual fulness of reference, Sir George
Lewis touches on the first nomination of a dictator at Rome.
That Titus Lartius was the first dictator, and that he was
appointed during one of the years not long preceding the
battle of Regillus, is affirmed both by Livy and by Dionysius.
As to the precise year they do not agree: nor does Livy
give many antecedent particulars—not knowing which to
prefer among the dissentient accounts before him. Dionysius, however,—to whom, as a Greek, the dictatorial office
seemed probably more striking and peculiar than it did to
Livy,—works up one of these narratives at great length :—

"Dionysius gives the detailed account of the dictatorship, and
of the appointment of the first dictator, as if it was as well ascertained as the history of the creation of the first presidency of the
India Board, and the appointment of the first president, under the
administration of Mr. Pitt. He knows not only the causes which
led to the creation of the office, but also the various stages of the
proceedings, the debates in the senate, the speeches of the senators,
the motives of their policy, the mutual feelings of delicacy, and all
the other material circumstances of the transaction.

. . . . . "The long and detailed account of the creation of the
office of dictator appears to belong to a class of fictions, of which we
meet with many examples in the early Roman history, and which we
may call *institutional legends*. The whole narrative of Dionysius
is plainly a political drama, invented to explain the very peculiar
institution of the Roman dictatorship: the officer being supreme
and absolute, although for a limited time; the senate being judges
of the necessity of the appointment, and the appointment being
made by one of the consuls." (Vol. ii. pp. 27-46.)

Among the Roman "institutional legends"—which, let it
be observed, even if Niebuhr's epic lays existed, can hardly
have been embodied in them, and can be referred to no other

source than oral narrative—one of the most curious is, the
first secession of the Plebs, and the first appointment of tribunes of the people (B. C. 492), about seven years after the
earliest dictator. The recital is set forth and examined by
Sir George Lewis pp. 62–88. It is given in minute detail
and with long harangues intermixed, by Dionysius. Livy
tells the story more briefly. Cicero and other authors touch
on it incidentally.

The Roman annalists, in recounting the circumstances
of this event (more than 250 years prior to the earliest
of them) can have had no other authority than oral in-
formants. In analysing the narrative, Sir George Lewis
further seeks to show that the internal discrepancies and
inconsistencies are so serious as to exclude the possibility of
any better authority. Now we cannot think that this latter
part of his case is fully made out. It seems to us that
he overrates the magnitude of the discrepancies; that they
are neither inexplicable, nor greater than might well have
occurred between witnesses all contemporaneous.

It is true that Dionysius and Livy differ as to the nature
of the treaty which the senate were obliged to conclude with
the exasperated plebeians, after the latter had seceded to the
Mons Sacer.

" According to Dionysius, the main subject of the negotiation
was a Seisachtheia, for the relief of the plebeian debtors. When
this measure had been conceded, the institution of the tribunes was
suggested by Lucius Junius Brutus, as an additional guarantee;
and this after-thought was made the subject of a separate negotiation. Livy is entirely silent as to any arrangement about a
remission of debts, and describes the compact as limited to the
institution of tribunes. Cicero agrees with Livy, and considers
the tribunate as the sole result of the first secession." (Vol. ii.
p. 77.)

We admit that Livy says nothing about a remission of
debts. But we contend that this is an omission on his part:
that his own narrative implies virtually the fact of such
remission having been granted, so as to be hardly consistent

with itself, unless upon that hypothesis. He had told us explicitly that the cause which drove the plebeians to the desperate measure of secession,* was, the cruel suffering inflicted upon the great multitude of them by debt, and by the law which made the insolvent debtor the slave of his creditor: that the liberal patricians had been doing their utmost, though in vain, to procure for them relief from such suffering: and that the very last act which precipitated the secession was, the abdication of the popular dictator (Valerius) in disgust, because he could not prevail on the senate to grant any relief. Assuming this state of things, how can it be believed that the plebeians, when they became masters of the situation and forced the senate to offer terms, demanded no redress of this severe and present grievance; and that they were satisfied with the prospective benefit to be derived from appointing two tribunes, about whom before not a word had been said? To confirm our view—that Livy's own account requires us to assume a remission of debts as having been granted—we may add, that after having dwelt so much upon the pressure of debt before the secession, he says nothing more about it after the secession: the grievance disappears for a long series of years.

Turning to Dionysius, we find that his account is consistent, complete, and natural. The plebeians had seceded on account of debt: the first concession whereby the intimidated senate try to pacify them is a promise of relief from debt: and with this the plebeians are so overjoyed that they are not disposed of themselves to demand more. But their long-sighted leader, L. Junius, reminds them that their only guarantee for the observance of the promise is, that they should have tribunes of their own appointment, and with powers adequate to their protection. The tribunes are thus (to use the phrase of Sir George Lewis) "an afterthought;" they are not a substitute for debt-relief, but a guarantee for its accomplishment.

* Livy, vol. ii. pp. 23, 27, 31.—" Totam plebem ære alieno demersam esse," &c.

In regard to the passage of Cicero, we agree rather with the interpretation of Niebuhr than with that of Sir George Lewis. We think that Cicero (like Livy) says what implies that a remission of debts must have been granted.* And it appears to us that an historian who finds himself in the presence of three such accounts as those of Dionysius, Livy, and Cicero, is warranted in supplying out of the first that fact which, though not expressly mentioned by the other two, is required to make each of them consistent with himself.

Sir George Lewis pursues his minute analysis of the contradictions and incoherences which pervade the immediately succeeding period of Roman history—the story of Coriolanus—that of Spurius Cassius, the proposer of the first agrarian law—the expedition and death of the three hundred Fabii, &c. All these are details which must have been derived by the annalist from oral communication. Yet in the midst of them the "substratum of notation" occasionally crops

---

* The passage of Cicero is in the Fragment *De Republicá*, ii. 33, 34. Cicero states, as explicitly as Dionysius and Livy, that the cause which brought about the suffering and secession of the plebeians, was the pressure of their private debts. The senate (he adds) might have applied a measure of relief to this grievance of debt, but they let slip the opportunity of doing so. Accordingly, they were constrained at last to submit to a concession much more formidable to their own power — the creation of the tribunate. " Quo tum consilio prætermisso, causa populo nata est, duobus tribunis plebis per seditionem creatis, ut potentia senatus atque auctoritas minueretur." If the Senate were forced ultimately to make a more serious concession, this proves that the mutinous debtors had acquired increased strength. How then is it credible that they should become willing to bear the pressure of debt, which they had mutinied in order to escape? The tribunate in itself could not mitigate this grievance. Cicero means (in our judgment) that the Senate, having refused to grant a measure of debt-relief in time, when it would have given satisfaction, were forced, when the discontent ripened into irresistible mutiny, to grant, not only this debt-relief, but something much greater besides.

out, thus (B.C. 462), we have:—" Many of the notices are of
a character which seem to betoken contemporaneous regis-
tration, such for instance, as the consecration of the temple
of Dius Fidius on the nones of June, on the Quirinal hill, by
the Consul Spurius Posthumius, in the year 466 B.C." (Vol.
ii. p. 162)—and the punishment of two Vestal Virgins,
Opimia and Orbinia (Vol. ii. pp. 141, 152, 183), who were
buried alive for unchastity. This punishment was probably
registered in the Pontifical Annals, since it had a salutary
effect, as we learn from Livy and Dionysius, in appeasing
the anger of the Gods, recently manifested in alarming
prodigies.

To the Decemviral Government an elaborate section is
devoted (Vol. ii. pp. 161, 252). These Decemvirs were named,
after eleven years of plebeian importunity, to prepare written
laws for rendering the administration of the Consuls both
determinate in its principles and equal in its operation on
patricians as well as plebeians. They composed the Twelve
Tables—the earliest authentic monument of Roman law.
The history of the Decemvirate—given in detail by Livy,
and in still greater detail by Dionysius—is " the institutional
legend" respecting the origin, promulgation, and authors of
these memorable and much admired tables.

We agree with Sir George Lewis that this narrative must
have been first put together by annalists long posterior,
mainly from oral report; and that its credibility must be
estimated accordingly. But we cannot think that the proof
of this point is strengthened by his analysis of the texture of
the narrative, nor that the internal difficulties and discrepancies are so grave as he represents. That which he conceives
as a tissue of improbabilities is so far from appearing in the
same light to Dionysius, that the latter (x. 1) expressly takes
credit for furnishing on this occasion a philosophical and instructive recital. The character and proceedings of the chief
Decemvir Appius do not appear to us unnatural, nor do we
feel the embarrassments started by Sir George Lewis. Why
did Appius (it is asked) resign his place in the decemvirate

after the first year, and thus expose himself to the chance of
not being re-elected? (Vol. ii. p. 229.) We may surely
answer—Because those who had been his colleagues during
the meritorious proceedings of the first year, would not have
been suitable for the atrocities of the second. Then by
what force were Appius and his second colleagues enabled
to tyrannise with temporary impunity? "We hear (says Sir
George Lewis) of no instruments of their power, except a *few*
clubs or associations of young patricians, who are paid for
their services by confiscated property." These *were* the
instruments of the decemviral tyranny ; and they appear to
us, as they appeared to Dionysius and Livy, sufficient for the
purpose. These historians do not recognise the attenuating
numerical adjective, a *few:* Dionysius even mentions (x. 60)
bands of poor and reckless satellites enlisted by the decemvirs, in addition to the patrician youth. Moreover Livy
expressly states that the only sufferers by the decemviral
tyranny were the plebeians ; that among the patrician order,
the younger men, who formed the real force, were gainers
in every way ; and that even the elder or senatorial patricians,
who disliked the decemvirs, disliked the suffering plebeians
as much or more, were pleased to see them humbled, and
even aggravated their humiliation by insult.* With such
antipathy and mistrust between the two orders, and with
such an amount of positive support from the more powerful of the two, the Decemvirs possessed ample means of
maintaining their tyranny during eighteen months, not to
say longer.

---

* Livy, iii. 36, 37. "Aliquamdiu æquatus inter omnes terror
fuit ; paulatim *totus vertere in plebem cœpit. Abstinebatur à Patribus :*
in humiliores libidinose crudeliterque consulebatur ; hominum, non
causarum, toti erant : ut apud quos gratia vim æqui haberet."

. . . . . "Primores Patrum odisse Decemviros, odisse plebem :
nec probare, quæ fierent ; et credere, haud indignis accidere. Avidè
ruendo in libertatem lapsos juvare nolle : *cumulare quoque injurias,*
ut tædio præsentium consules duo tandem et status pristinus rerum
in desiderium venirent."

Again " We might have expected " (says Sir George Lewis, p. 238), "judging by the other atrocities ascribed to Appius, that he would have caused Virginia to be seized without the formalities of a public trial, and that he would have imprisoned or killed her relatives and protectors." It might have been safer for him if he had done so. But Dionysius describes it as the ordinary practice of the Decemvirs in their tyranny, to suborn accusers and pronounce iniquitous judgments: when this had been done in a long series of cases without resistance, Appius did not sufficiently calculate the chances of resistance in a new case. Nor can we wonder that he did not anticipate the tragical event of a father publicly stabbing his own daughter in the forum.

These and other embarrassments which a critical inquirer brings to view in the Decemviral history, are all very proper for notice. But we think that they are by no means incapable of solution: that the author himself, if he had been writing a work of history instead of criticism, would easily have found solutions: and that they are no greater than an historian, who has the advantage of contemporary authorities, must often be prepared to solve. Though poorly furnished as to external attestation, the story in its internal texture appears to us more plausible and coherent than his book exhibits it.

During the sixty years between the fall of the Decemvirs and the Gallic capture, the internal history of Rome betokens a forward movement on the part of the plebeians. The demand made by the latter for equal admissibility to the consulship, is refused by the patricians; who are, however, obliged to make the concession of substituting, in place of consuls, new magistrates entitled military tribunes (with powers nearly approaching to those of the consuls), among whom plebeians were eligible. These consular tribunes, with many alternating years of patrician consulship, continued for seventy-seven years, when the Licinian laws re-established the consulship, with the peremptory en-

actment that one of the two consuls must be a plebeian.
Respecting the historical character of this period, our author
observes,—

" After the year B.C. 367, we hear no more of consular tribunes,
and the office disappears from the Fasti. With the exception of
the account of the first election of consular tribunes, the history
of this magistracy during the seventy-seven years of its existence
is consistent, coherent, and intelligible; and the historical narrative supports and explains the lists of names in the tables of
magistrates. So far, therefore, as the internal evidence goes, it
confirms the authenticity of the traditionary accounts of the period
in question." (Vol. ii. p. 396.)

Here we have "the substratum of notation" and the
traditionary details in a state of admitted harmony. Sir
George Lewis pursues his analysis of the history through
the 110 years between the Gallic capture and the landing
of Pyrrhus. Though he still detects many contradictions
and inconsistencies, they do not appear to him so glaring as
those of the former period. As to the foreign wars with the
Gauls, indeed, there are discrepancies impossible to reconcile
between Polybius and Livy; as to those with the Latins and
Samnites, there are no such grave contradictions, though
much is obscure and uncertain. Among the internal affairs
of Rome, we commend to particular attention what is said
about the Agrarian Laws, which are handled in a manner
extremely perspicuous and instructive. (Vol. ii. p. 137, 183,
384.) Some proofs are also adduced (which might probably
be multiplied) of the continuance of the contemporary regis-
tration for various isolated facts. (Vol. ii. p. 483–6.) On
the whole, the facts and narratives indicate that we are
approaching towards that clearer sunlight of history which
begins to prevail for the times after Pyrrhus.

Having performed this dissection of the evidences, with
many most profitable comments upon Niebuhr, Arnold, and
other previous expositors, Sir George Lewis adds a concluding chapter, summing up the general results of his
inquiry, and illustrating his reasonings by comparisons with

Grecian history. We have no space to dwell upon these pertinent and well-chosen analogies, and can only advert to the general conclusion. Remarking that as the different schools of historical criticism agree in considering attestation by contemporary witnesses as the essential condition for justifying belief in an alleged fact, he thus proceeds :—

" The main difference between the divergent schools is as to the extent to which contemporary attestation may be presumed without direct and positive proof. Both assume the same mode of proving an historical fact : but the former refuse to infer the proof from the existence of an oral tradition ; the latter consider that inference legitimate. The former deny that the existence of a popular belief with respect to the past, derived from oral reports, raises a presumption that the events narrated were at the time of their supposed occurrence observed by credible witnesses, and by them handed down to posterity. The latter, on the other hand, hold that the existence of such a popular belief (combined perhaps with some accessory circumstances) authorises the conclusion that the current story was derived from credible contemporary witnesses, and has descended from them in a substantially unfalsified state." . . . . " The difference between the opposite opinions on this subject is therefore a difference of degree rather than of principle. Nobody asserts that all history must be taken directly from the reports of percipient witnesses. No historian applies the strict rule of judicial evidence, that all hearsay reports are to be discarded. In treating of the period which precedes contemporary history, all persons admit traditionary, secondary, or hearsay evidence, up to a certain point. The question is, where that point ought to be fixed?" (Vol. ii. p. 490.)

After a few words (p. 494) upon the " difficulties which beset the application of rules of evidence to *the semi-historical or crepuscular period*,—a period of which some knowledge has been preserved, though by imperfect means, and in a deteriorated state,"—the last result is thus given :—

" All the historical labour bestowed upon the early centuries of Rome will, in general, be wasted. The history of this period, viewed as a series of picturesque narratives, will be read to the greatest advantage in the original writers, and will be deteriorated by reproduction in a modern dress. If we regard a historical painting merely as a work of art, the accounts of the ancients can only suffer from being retouched by the pencil of the modern restorer.   On the other hand, all attempts to reduce them to a purely historical form, by conjectural omissions, additions, alterations, and transpositions, must be nugatory."

" Those who are disposed to labour in the field of Roman history will find a worthier reward for their toils, if they employ themselves upon the time subsequent to the Italian expedition of Pyrrhus." . . . . " In this history, much must remain incomplete, uncertain, and unknown : but the great outlines are as firmly marked as in a modern history, composed with brighter lights and from ampler materials : and the historical inquirer will meet with · a richer return for his labours, than if he bewildered himself with vain attempts to distinguish between fact and fiction, in the accounts of the foundation of Rome, the constitution of Servius, the expulsion of Tarquin, the war with Porsena, the creation of the dictatorship and tribunate, the decemviral legislation, the siege of Veii and the capture of Rome by the Gauls ; or even the Licinian rogations, and the Samnite Wars." (Vol. ii. p. 556.)

We subscribe to these conclusions fully, so far as regards Roman history under the kings and prior to the Republic. As to the period of the Republic, we cannot adopt them without some qualification. Sir George Lewis fairly states the question : It being admitted, that there is a certain point antecedent to the beginning of contemporary history, up to which point historical research is legitimate and reasonable—where is this terminus to be fixed in regard to Rome?   He would fix it at the landing of Pyrrhus in Italy. But we submit that this is within the actual limits of contemporary Grecian authorship, and, in a certain sense, even of Roman authorship—through the speech of Appius in the Senate, which was preserved to later times. This terminus is therefore too low to correspond with the principles laid down.   The Licinian laws can hardly be thrown into the category of the unsearchable—along with the foundation of Rome.

In fixing the upward terminus, we perceive no index so appropriate as the beginning of *contemporary notation ;* which is, in truth, contemporary history in fragment and rudiment.

Wherever matters of fact and of public import were recorded, even though detached and without coherence, historical research becomes admissible.

Now in Rome, "the substratum of notation" can be traced up to the commencement of the Republic, but not higher. No similar notation belongs to the regal period: at least, if any such existed, it never crops out, but is irrevocably submerged and undiscernible. Accordingly, the suitable upward terminus for historical research is, in our view, the commencement of the Republic. We consider the kingly period as lying above the limit of historical research, and as "a series of picturesque narratives" in which no matter of fact had ever any recorded existence apart from fiction. Comparing Roman with Grecian history, we regard (conformably to Sir George Lewis's view) all that precedes the Roman Republic as corresponding to heroic or legendary Greece; we consider the first two centuries of the Republic as corresponding to Greece between the first recorded Olympiad (776 B.C.) and the year 500 B.C. To the first of the two, the microscope of the historian is inapplicable. Respecting the second, we cannot say the same; for there are, or were, some recorded realities which an attentive contemplation may hope to magnify and bring into fuller day-light, both in themselves and in the consequences deducible from them.

This is the only line of demarcation which we see any theoretical reason for drawing. Whether the researches into the history of the early Republic will turn out very fruitful, or will yield much of new certainty and new probability, is a different question. We are not sanguine in hoping that they will: but neither are we sanguine respecting those investigations, recommended by Sir George Lewis as preferable, into the later history of the Roman Republic; where there was once much contemporary information, now entirely lost, and represented by little except the Epitomes of Livy. What we expect from farther study of the early Republic, is, not so much a corrected version of the facts of detail, as better and clearer views of the institutional practice and development, gathered by combination, inference, and cautious hypothesis, from a variety of distinct sources. Books on Roman antiquities (especially the excellent work of Becker and Marquardt) already teach us much respecting the magistracies and constitutional growth of the Republic: but we acquire no knowledge (beyond the literal statements as they stand) respecting the period of the Kings. And though there is much fanciful conjecture in Niebuhr, it is indisputable that many portions of Roman republican antiquity (the Agrarian Laws especially) are far better understood than they were before his writings.

Discountenancing as Sir George Lewis does all historical inquiry into Roman history anterior to Pyrrhus, it is natural that he should pronounce, as to that period, "All attempts to reduce the accounts of the ancients to an historical form by conjectural omissions, additions, alterations, and transpositions, must be nugatory." This is perfectly true respecting the period of the Kings, but we are not prepared to pronounce the like peremptory verdict (must) about the first two centuries of the Republic. The former (as we have above remarked) contains none of the genuine materials of history; the latter contains some, in greater or less proportion. In our view, wherever the genuine materials of history exist, all the processes above indicated are frequently indispensable, to bring out of them either continuous narrative or determinate results. It is by going through such elaboration that history is distinguished from a mere collection of depositions.

The manner in which Sir George Lewis sets forth the discrepancies between Livy and Dionysius, and the tone of his criticisms on Niebuhr, tend to suggest two impressions, which we are by no means sure that he would sanction, but from which we certainly dissent. 1. That discrepancies, as many and as great, are not to be found between contemporary witnesses. 2. That the Niebuhrian spirit of hypothesis and recombination is illegitimate in principle,—not simply objectionable from abusive excess in Niebuhr's hands.

Now we think that contemporary witnesses often form a multitude with every variety of dissonance and contradiction:* and that if, out of such perplexities, an historian is to construct a narrative setting forth the true or the probable, he cannot proceed without a large latitude of preference and hypothesis. Even with the most unexceptionable historians—with Gibbon or Mr. Hallam—the narrative supplied to the reader is a result put together in their own minds, founded upon an attentive study of all the evidences, yet not without many inferences, comparisons, and eliminations of their own. Neither of these authors could have performed his task, if "conjectural omission, addition, alteration, and transposition," had been forbidden. We know that these liberties are liable to much abuse, and that they have been abused by Niebuhr.

---

* As a parallel to the discrepancies between Livy and Dionysius, we transcribe the following account of the original authorities respecting the wars in La Vendée, from the beginning of 1793 downwards. We have here contemporary witnesses, under the full publicity of modern times, described by M. Michelet, eminent both as an historian and as a laborious examiner of original archives. (*Histoire de la Révolution Française*, vol. vii. p. 78.)

"Le livre le plus instructif sur l'histoire de la Vendée (j'allais dire, le seul) est celui de Savary, père du membre de l'Académie des Sciences : *Guerres des Vendéens, par un officier*, 1824. Dans les autres, il y a peu à prendre. Ce sont des romans, qui ne soutiennent pas l'examen : les noms, les dates, les faits, presque tout y est inexact, faux, impudemment surchargé de fictions. Je le sais maintenant à mes dépens, après avoir perdu des années dans la critique inutile de ces déplorables livres. Savary donne les vraies dates, et un nombre immense de pièces : les notes de Canclaux, de Kléber, d'Oppenheim, y ajoutent un prix inestimable."

We know the work of Savary, and can certify that it fully merits the encomiums bestowed upon it by M. Michelet. But to compose such a work, requires a combination of ability, diligence, and opportunity, such as are rarely brought together in the same person. How many periods are there of human affairs, in which there are contemporary authors approximating to the dark side of Michelet's picture, without any such witness to control them as Savary !

But in commending a salutary vigilance of criticism on this
eminent man, in so many instances of his arbitrary dealing
with evidence, we must at the same time guard against
what appears to us an opposite extreme. We cannot disallow the constructive imagination of the historian, nor
lighten his responsibility by tying him down to a literal
sequence.

While claiming for historians this freedom of judgment,
in their laborious task of eliciting probability out of conflicting statements and analogies, we should be glad if it
could always be exercised subject to such a censorship as
that of Sir George Lewis. No man interested either in
ancient history or in the general theory of historical study,
can read his book without profit; but none will profit by it
so much as those who, adopting his conclusions only in part,
account the first two centuries of the Roman Republic a
subject still open to historical research and philosophical
explanation.

PLATO'S DOCTRINE

RESPECTING THE

ROTATION OF THE EARTH,

AND

ARISTOTLE'S COMMENT UPON THAT DOCTRINE.

1860.

Examination of the three following Questions :—

1. WHETHER THE DOCTRINE OF THE EARTH'S ROTATION IS AFFIRMED OR IMPLIED IN THE PLATONIC TIMÆUS?

2. IF AFFIRMED OR IMPLIED, IN WHAT SENSE?

3. WHAT IS THE COSMICAL FUNCTION WHICH PLATO ASSIGNS TO THE EARTH IN THE TIMÆUS?

THE following paper was originally intended as an explanatory note on the Platonic Timœus, in the work which I am
now preparing on Plato and Aristotle. Interpreting, differently from others, the much debated passage in which Plato
describes the cosmical function of the Earth, I found it
indispensable to give my reasons for this new view. But
I soon discovered that those reasons could not be comprised
within the limits of a note. Accordingly I here publish
them in a separate Dissertation. The manner in which the
Earth's rotation was conceived, illustrates the scientific character of the Platonic and Aristotelian age, as contrasted
with the subsequent development and improvement of astronomy.

In Plato, Timœus, p. 40 B, we read the following words—
Γῆν δὲ τροφὸν μὲν ἡμετέραν, εἰλλομένην δὲ περὶ τὸν διὰ παντὸς
πόλον τεταμένον φύλακα καὶ δημιουργὸν νυκτός τε καὶ ἡμέρας
ἐμηχανήσατο, πρώτην καὶ πρεσβυτάτην θεῶν, ὅσοι ἐντὸς οὐρανοῦ γεγόνασι. I give the text as it stands in Stallbaum's
edition.

The obscurity of this passage is amply attested by the
numerous differences of opinion to which it has given rise,
both in ancient and in modern times. Various contemporaries of Plato (ἔνιοι—Aristot. De Cœlo, II. 13, p. 293 b. 30)
understood it as asserting or implying the rotatory movement
of the earth in the centre of the Kosmos, and adhered to
this doctrine as their own. Aristotle himself alludes to these

contemporaries without naming them, and adopts their interpretation of the passage ; but dissents from the doctrine, and proceeds to impugn it by arguments. Cicero mentions (Academic. II. 39) that there were persons who believed Plato to have indicated the same doctrine obscurely, in his Timæus : this passage must undoubtedly be meant. Plutarch devotes a critical chapter to the enquiry, what was Plato's real doctrine as to the cosmical function of the earth —its movement or rest (Quæstion. Platonic. VII. 3, p. 1006).

There exists a treatise, in Doric dialect, entitled Τιμαίω τῶ Λόκρω Περὶ Ψυχᾶς Κόσμω καὶ φύσιος,—which is usually published along with the works of Plato. This treatise was supposed in ancient times to be a genuine production of the Lokrian Timæus, whom Plato introduces as his spokesman in the dialogue so called. As such, it was considered to be of much authority in settling questions of interpretation as to the Platonic Timæus. But modern critics hold, I believe unanimously, that it is the work of some later Pythagorean or Platonist, excerpted or copied from the Platonic Timæus. This treatise represents the earth as being in the centre and at rest. But its language, besides being dark and metaphorical, departs widely from the phraseology of the Platonic Timæus : especially in this—that it makes no mention of the cosmical axis, nor of the word ἰλλομένην or εἰλουμένην.

Alexander of Aphrodisias (as we learn from Simplikius ad Aristot. De Cœlo, fol. 126) followed the construction of Plato given by Aristotle. " It was improbable (he said) that Aristotle could be ignorant either what the word signified, or what was Plato's purpose " (ἀλλὰ τῷ Ἀριστοτέλει, φησὶν, οὕτω λέγοντι ἴλλεσθαι, οὐκ εὔλογον ἀντιλέγειν· ὡς ἀληθῶς γὰρ οὔτε τῆς λέξεως τὸ σημαινόμενον εἰκὸς ἦν ἀγνοεῖν αὐτὸν, οὔτε τὸν Πλάτωνος σκοπόν. This passage is not given in the Scholia of Brandis). Alexander therefore construed ἰλλομένην as meaning or implying rotatory movement, though in so doing he perverted (so Simplikius says) the true meaning to make it consonant with his own suppositions.

Proklus maintains that Aristotle has interpreted the passage erroneously,—that ἰλλομένην is equivalent to σφιγγομένην or ξυνεχομένην—and that Plato intends by it to affirm the earth as at rest in the centre of the Kosmos (ad Timœum, Book iv., p. 681 ed. Schneider). Simplikius himself is greatly perplexed, and scarcely ventures to give a positive opinion of his own. On the whole, he inclines to believe that ἰλλομένην might possibly be understood, by superficial readers, so as to signify rotation, though such is not its proper and natural sense: that some Platonists did so misunderstand it: and that Aristotle accepted their sense for the sake of the argument, without intending himself to countenance it (ad Aristot. De Cœlo, p. 126).

Both Proklus and Simplikius, we must recollect, believed in the genuineness of the Doric treatise ascribed to Timæus Locrus. Reasoning upon this basis, they of course saw, that if Aristotle had correctly interpreted Plato, Plato himself must have interpreted *incorrectly* the doctrine of Timæus. They had to ascribe wrong construction either to Plato or to Aristotle: and they could not bear to ascribe it to Plato.

Alkinous, in his Eisagôge (c. 15) gives the same interpretation as Proklus. But it is remarkable that in his paraphrase of the Platonic words, he calls the earth ἡμέρας φύλαξ καὶ νυκτός: omitting the significant epithet δημιουργός.

In regard to modern comments upon the same disputed point, I need only mention (besides those of M. Cousin, in the notes upon his translation of the ‘Timæus,’ and of Martin in his ‘Études sur le Timée ’) the elaborate discussion which it has received in the two recent Dissertations ‘ Ueber die kosmischen Systeme der Griechen,’ by Gruppe and Boeckh. Gruppe has endeavoured, upon the evidence of this passage, supported by other collateral proofs, to show that Plato, towards the close of his life, arrived at a belief, first, in the rotation of the earth round its own axis, next, at the double movement of the earth, both rotation and translation, round the sun as a centre (that is, the heliocentric or Copernican system): that Plato was the first to make this discovery, but

R

that he was compelled to announce it in terms intentionally
equivocal and obscure, for fear of offending the religious
sentiments of his contemporaries (' Die kosmischen Systeme
der Griechen,' by O. F. Gruppe, Berlin, 1851). To this dissertation M. Boeckh—the oldest as well as the ablest of all
living philologists—has composed an elaborate reply, with
his usual fulness of illustrative matter and sobriety of inference. Opinions previously delivered by him (in his early
treatises on the Platonic and Pythagorean philosophy)
had been called in question by Gruppe: he has now re-
asserted them and defended them at length, maintaining
that Plato always held the earth to be stationary and the
sidereal sphere rotatory ; and answering or extenuating the
arguments which point to an opposite conclusion (' Untersuchungen über das kosmische System des Platon,' by August
Boeckh, Berlin, 1852).

Gruppe has failed in his purpose of proving that Plato
adopted either of the two above-mentioned doctrines—either
the rotation of the earth round its own axis, or the translation of the earth round the sun as a centre. On both
these points I concur with Boeckh in the negative view.
But though I go along with his reply as to its negative
results, I cannot think it satisfactory in its positive aspect
as an exposition of the doctrine proclaimed in the Platonic
Timæus: nor can I admit that the main argument of M.
Boeckh's treatise is sufficient to support the inference which
he rests upon it. Moreover, he appears to me to set aside or
explain away too lightly the authority of Aristotle. I agree
with Alexander of Aphrodisias and with Gruppe who follows
him, in pronouncing Aristotle to be a good witness, when
he declares what were the doctrines proclaimed in the Platonic Timæus ; though I think that Gruppe has not accurately interpreted either Timæus or Aristotle.

The capital argument of Boeckh is as follows: " The Platonic Timæus affirms, in express and unequivocal terms, the
rotation of the outer celestial sphere (the sidereal sphere or
Aplanes) in twenty-four hours, as bringing about and deter-

mining the succession of day and night. Whoever believes this cannot at the same time believe that the earth revolves round its own axis in twenty-four hours, and that the succession of day and night is determined thereby. The one of these two affirmations excludes the other; and, as the first of the two is proclaimed, beyond all possibility of doubt, in the Platonic Timæus, so we may be sure that the second of the two cannot be proclaimed in that same discourse. If any passage therein seems to countenance it, we must look for some other mode of interpreting the passage."

This is the main argument of M. Boeckh, and also of Messrs. Cousin and Martin. The latter protests against the idea of imputing to Plato "un mélange monstrueux de deux systèmes incompatibles" ('Études sur le Timée,' vol. ii. p. 86–88).

As applied to any person educated in the modern astronomy, the argument is irresistible. But is it equally irresistible when applied to Plato and to Plato's time? I think not. The incompatibility which appears so glaring at present, did not suggest itself to him or to his contemporaries. To prove this we have only to look at the reasoning of Aristotle, who (in the treatise De Cœlo, ii. 13–14, p. 293. b. 30, 296. a. 25) notices and controverts the doctrine of the rotation of the earth, with express reference to the followers of the Platonic Timæus, and who (if we follow the view of Martin) imputes this doctrine with wilful falsehood to Plato, for the purpose of contemptuously refuting it, "pour se donner le plaisir de la réfuter avec dédain." Granting the view of M. Boeckh (still more that of Martin) to be correct, we should find Aristotle arguing thus:—" Plato affirms the diurnal rotation of the earth round the centre of the cosmical axis. This is both incredible, and incompatible with his own distinct affirmation that the sidereal sphere revolves in twenty-four hours. It is a glaring inconsistency that the same author should affirm both the one and the other." Such would have been Aristotle's reasoning, on the hypothesis which I am considering; but when we turn to his

R 2

treatise we find that he does not employ this argument at
all. He contests the alleged rotation of the earth upon
totally different arguments — chiefly on the ground that
rotatory motion is not natural to the earth, that the kind
of motion natural to the earth is rectilineal, towards the
centre; and he adds various corollaries flowing from this
doctrine which I shall not now consider. At the close of his
refutation, he states in general terms that the celestial appearances, as observed by scientific men, coincided with his
doctrine.

Hence we may plainly see that Aristotle probably did
not see the incompatibility, supposed to be so glaring, upon
which M. Boeckh's argument is founded. To say the least,
even if he saw it, he did not consider it as glaring and
decisive. He would have put it in the foreground of his
refutation, if he had detected the gross contradiction upon
which M. Boeckh insists. But Aristotle does not stand
alone in this dulness of vision. Among the various commentators, ancient and modern, who follow him, discussing
the question now before us, not one takes notice of M.
Boeckh's argument. He himself certifies to us this fact,
claiming the argument as his own, and expressing his astonishment that all the previous critics had passed it over,
though employing other reasons much weaker to prove the
same point. We read in M. Boeckh's second 'Commentatio
de Platonico Systemate Cœlestium Globorum et de Verâ
Indole Astronomiæ Philolaicæ,' Heidelberg, 1810, p. 9, the
following words : —

"Non moveri tellurem, Proclus et Simplicius ostendunt
ex Phædone. Parum firmum tamen argumentum est ex
Phædone ductum ad interpretandum Timæi locum : nec
melius alterum, quod Locrus Timæus, quem Plato sequi
putabatur, terram stare affirmat : quia, ut nuper explicuimus,
non Plato ex Locro, sed personatus Locrus ex Platone, sua
compilavit. At omnium firmissimum et certissimum argumentum ex ipso nostro dialogo sumptum, *adhuc, quod jure
mirere, nemo reperit.* Etenim, quum, paulo supra, orbem

stellarum fixarum, quem Græci ἀπλανῆ appellant, dextrorsum
ferri quotidiano motu Plato statuebat, non poterat ullum
terræ motum admittere; quia, *qui hunc admittit, illum non
tollere non potest.*" (This passage appears again cited by
M. Boeckh himself in his more recent dissertation ' Untersuchungen über das kosmische System des Platon,' p. 11). The
writers named (p. 7) as having discussed the question, omitting or disregarding this most cogent argument, are names
extending from Aristotle down to Ruhnken and Ideler.

It is honourable to the penetration of M. Boeckh that he
should have pointed out, what so many previous critics had
overlooked, that these two opinions are scientifically incompatible. He wonders, and there may be good ground for
wondering, how it happened that none of these previous
writers were aware of the incompatibility. But the fact
that it did not occur to them, is not the less certain, and
is of the greatest moment in reference to the question now
under debate; for we are not now inquiring what is or is not
scientifically true or consistent, but what were the opinions
of Plato. M. Boeckh has called our attention to the fact,
that these two opinions are incompatible; but can we safely
assume that Plato must have perceived such incompatibility between them? Surely not. The Pythagoreans of his
day did not perceive it; their cosmical system included both
the revolution of the earth and the revolution of the sidereal
sphere round the central fire, ten revolving bodies in all
(Aristotel. Metaphysic. i. 35, p. 96 a. 10. De Cœlo, ii. 13,
p. 293 b. 21). They were not aware that the revolutions
of the one annulled those of the other as to effect, and that
their system must involve the two contradictory articles, or
" mélange monstrueux," of which Martin speaks so disdain-
fully. Nay, more, their opponent, Aristotle, while producing
other arguments against them, never points out the contradiction. Since it did not occur to them, we can have no
greater difficulty in believing that neither did it occur to
Plato. Indeed, the wonder would rather be if Plato *had*
seen an astronomical incompatibility which escaped the

notice both of Aristotle and of many subsequent writers who wrote at a time when astronomical theories had been developed and compared with greater fulness. Even Ideler, a good astronomer as well as a good scholar, though he must surely have known that Plato asserted the rotation of the sidereal sphere (for no man can read the 'Timæus' without knowing it), ascribed to him also the other doctrine inconsistent with it, not noticing such inconsistency until M. Boeckh pointed it out.

It appears to me, therefore, that M. Boeckh has not satisfactorily made good his point—"Plato cannot have believed in the diurnal rotation of the earth, because he unquestionably believed in the rotation of the sidereal sphere as causing the succession of night and day." For, though the two doctrines really are incompatible, yet the critics antecedent to M. Boeckh took no notice of such incompatibility. We cannot presume that Plato saw what Aristotle and other authors, many even writing under a more highly developed astronomy, did not see. We ought rather, I think, to presume the contrary, unless Plato's words distinctly attest that he did see farther than his successors.

Now let us examine what Plato's words do attest :—γῆν δὲ τροφὸν μὲν ἡμετέραν εἰλλομένην (al. εἰλομένην, ἰλλομένην) δὲ περὶ τὸν διὰ παντὸς πόλον τεταμένον φύλακα καὶ δημιουργὸν νυκτός τε καὶ ἡμέρας ἐμηχανήσατο, πρώτην καὶ πρεσβυτάτην θεῶν, ὅσοι ἐντὸς οὐρανοῦ γεγόνασι.

I explain these words as follows :—

In the passage immediately preceding, Plato had described the uniform and unchanging rotation of the outer sidereal sphere, or Circle of The Same, and the erratic movements of the sun, moon, and planets, in the interior Circles of the Diverse. He now explains the situation and functions of the earth. Being the first and most venerable of the intrakosmic deities, the earth has the most important place in the interior of the kosmos—the centre. It is packed, fastened, or rolled, close round the axis which traverses the entire kosmos; and its function is to watch over and bring about the succession of night and day. *Plato conceives the kosmic axis itself as a solid cylinder revolving or turning round, and causing thereby the revolution of the circumference or the sidereal sphere.* The outer circumference of the kosmos not only revolves round its axis, but obeys a rotatory impulse emanating from its axis, like the spinning of a teetotum or the turning of a spindle. Plato in the Republic illustrates the cosmical axis by comparison with a spindle turned by Necessity, and describes it as causing by its own rotation the rotation of all the heavenly bodies (Republ. x. p. 616, c. 617 A). *ἐκ δὲ τῶν ἄκρων τεταμένον Ἀνάγκης ἄτρακτον, δι' οὗ πάσας ἐπιστρέφεσθαι τὰς περίφορας . . . . κυκλεῖσθαι δὲ δὴ στρεφόμενον τὸν ἄτρακτον ὅλον μὲν τὴν αὐτὴν φορὰν . . . . στρέφεσθαι δὲ αὐτὸν ἐν τοῖς Ἀνάγκης γόνασιν.**

Now the function which Plato ascribes to the earth in the passage of the Timæus before us is very analogous to that which in the Republic he ascribes to Necessity—the active guardianship of the axis of the kosmos and the maintenance of its regular rotation. With a view to the exercise of this function, the earth is planted in the centre of the axis, the

---

* Proklus in his Commentary on the Platonic *Timæus* (p. 682, Schn.) notes this passage of the *Republic* as the proper comparison from which to interpret how Plato conceived the cosmical axis. In many points he explains this correctly; but he omits to remark that the axis is expressly described as revolving, and as causing the revolution of the peripheral substance :—

—— τὸν δὲ ἄξονα μίαν θεότητα συναγωγὸν μὲν τῶν κέντρων τοῦ παντός, συνεκτικὴν δὲ τοῦ ὅλου κόσμου, κινητικὴν δὲ τῶν θείων περιφορῶν, περὶ ἣν ἡ χορεία τῶν ὅλων, περὶ ἣν αἱ ἀνακυκλήσεις, ἀνέχουσαν τὸν ὅλον οὐρανόν, ἣν καὶ Ἄτλαντα διὰ τοῦτο προσειρήκασιν, ὡς ἄτρεπτον καὶ ἄτριτον ἐνέργειαν ἔχουσαν. καὶ μέντοι καὶ τὸ τεταμένον ἐνδείκνυται τιτήνιον εἶναι τὴν μίαν ταύτην δύναμιν, τὴν φρουρη- τικὴν τῆς ἀνακυκλήσεως τῶν ὅλων.

Here Proklus recognizes the efficacy of the axis in producing and maintaining the revolution of the Kosmos, but he does not remark that it initiates this movement by revolving itself. The Θεότης, which Proklus ascribes to the axis, is invested in the earth packed round it, by the Platonic *Timæus.*

very root of the kosmic soul (Plato, Timæus, p. 34 B). It is even "packed close round the axis," in order to make sure that the axis shall not be displaced from its proper situation and direction. The earth is thus not merely active and influential, but is really the chief regulator of the march of the kosmos, being the immediate neighbour and auxiliary of the kosmic soul. Such a function is worthy of "the first and eldest of intra-kosmic deities," as Plato calls the earth. With perfect propriety he may say that the earth, in the exercise of such a function, "is guardian and artificer of day and night." This is noway inconsistent with that which he says in another passage, that the revolutions of the outer sidereal sphere determine day and night. For these revolutions of the outer sidereal sphere depend upon the revolutions of the axis, which latter is kept in uniform position and movement by the earth grasping it round its centre and revolving with it. The earth does not determine days and nights by means of its own rotations, but by its continued influence upon the rotations of the kosmic axis, and (through this latter) upon those of the outer sidereal sphere.

It is important to attend to the circumstance last mentioned, and to understand in what sense Plato admitted a rotatory movement of the earth. In my judgment, the conception respecting the earth and its functions, as developed in the Platonic Timæus, has not been considered with all its points taken together. One point among several, and that too the least important point, has been discussed as if it were the whole, because it falls in with the discussions of subsequent astronomy. Thus Plato admits the rotation of the earth, but he does not admit it as producing any effects, or as the primary function of the earth: it is only an indirect consequence of the position which the earth occupies in the discharge of its primary function—of keeping the cosmical axis steady, and maintaining the uniformity of its rotations. If the cosmical axis is to revolve, the earth, being closely packed and fastened round it, must revolve along with it. If the earth stood still, and resisted all rotation of its own, it would at the same time arrest the rotations of the cosmical axis, and of course those of the entire kosmos besides.

The above is the interpretation which I propose of the passage in the Platonic Timæus, and which I shall show to coincide with Aristotle's comment upon it. Messrs. Boeckh and Martin interpret differently. They do not advert to the sense in which Plato conceives the axis of the kosmos—not as an imaginary line, but as a solid revolving cylinder; and moreover they understand the function assigned by the Platonic Timæus to the earth in a way which I cannot admit. They suppose that the function assigned to the earth is not to keep up and regularize, but to withstand and countervail, the rotation of the kosmos. M. Boeckh comments upon Gruppe, who had said (after Ideler) that when the earth is called φύλακα καὶ δημιουργὸν νυκτὸς καὶ ἡμέρας, Plato must have meant to designate some active function ascribed to it, and not any function merely passive or negative. I agree with Gruppe in this remark, and I have endeavoured to point out what this active function of the earth is, in the Platonic theory. But M. Boeckh (Untersuchungen, &c., p. 69-70) controverts Gruppe's remark, observing, first, that it is enough if the earth is in any way necessary to the production of the given effect; secondly, that if active force be required, the earth (in the Platonic theory) does exercise such, by its purely passive resistance, which is in itself an energetic putting forth of power.

M. Boeckh's words are:—" Es kommt nur darauf an, dass er ein Werk, eine Wirkung, hervorbringt oder zu einer Wirkung beiträgt, die ohne ihn nicht wäre: dann ist er durch seine Wirksamkeit ein Werkmeister der Sache, sei es auch ohne active Thätigkeit, durch bloss passiven Widerstand, der auch eine mächtige Kraftäusserung ist. Die Erde ist Werkmeisterin der Nacht und des Tages, wie Martin (b. ii. p. 88) sehr treffend sagt, 'par son énergique existence, c'est à dire, par son immobilité même:' denn sie setzt der täglichen Bewegung des Himmels beständig eine gleiche Kraft in entgegengesetzter Richtung entgegen. So *muss* nach dem

Zusammenhange ausgelegt werden: so meint es Platon klar und ohne Verhüllungen: denn wenige Zeilen vorher hat er gesagt, Nacht und Tag, das heisst, ein Sterntag oder Zeittag, sei ein Umlauf des Kreises des Selbigen — *das ist, eine tägliche Umkreisung des Himmels von Osten nach Westen, wodurch also die Erde in Stillstand versetzt ist*: und diese tägliche Bewegung des Himmels hat er im vorhergehenden immer und immer gelehrt.". . . . . "Indem Platon die Erde nennt εἱλομένην, nicht περὶ τὸν ἑαυτῆς πόλον, sondern περὶ τὸν διὰ παντὸς πόλον τεταμένον, setzt er also die tägliche Bewegung des Himmles voraus" (p. 70–71).*

I not only admit but put it in front of my own case, that Plato in the Timæus assumes the diurnal movement of the celestial sphere; but I contend that he also assumes the diurnal rotation of the earth. M. Boeckh founds his contrary interpretation upon the unquestionable truth that these two assumptions are inconsistent; and upon the inference that because the two cannot stand together in fact, therefore they cannot have stood together in the mind of Plato.

---

* "We are only required to show, that the Earth produces a work or an effect,—or contributes to an effect which would not exist without such help: the Earth is then, through such operation, an *Artificer* of what is produced, even without any positive activity, by its simply passive resistance, which indeed is in itself a powerful exercise of force. The Earth is Artificer of night and day, according to the striking expression of Martin, ' par son énergique existence, c'est-à-dire, par son immobilité même:' for the Earth opposes, to the diurnal movement of the Heavens, a constant and equal force in the opposite direction. This explanation *must* be the true one required by the context: this is Plato's meaning, plainly and without disguise: for he has said, a few lines before, that Night and Day (that is, a sidereal day, or day of time) is a diurnal revolution of the Heaven from East to West, whereby accordingly the Earth is assumed as at rest: And this diurnal movement of the Heaven he has taught over and over again in the preceding part of his discourse."—"Since therefore Plato calls the Earth εἱλομένην, not περὶ τὸν ἑαυτῆς πόλον, but περὶ τὸν διὰ παντὸς πόλον τεταμένον, he implies thereby the diurnal movement of the Heaven."

In that inference I have already stated that I cannot acquiesce.

But while M. Boeckh takes so much pains to vindicate Plato from one contradiction, he unconsciously involves Plato in another contradiction, for which, in my judgment, there is no foundation whatever. M. Boeckh affirms that the function of the earth (in the Platonic Timæus) is to put forth a great force of passive resistance—"to oppose constantly, against the diurnal movement of the heavens, an equal force in an opposite direction." Is it not plain, upon this supposition, that the kosmos would come to a standstill, and that its rotation would cease altogether? As the earth is packed close or fastened round the cosmical axis, so, if the axis endeavours to revolve with a given force, and the earth resists with equal force, the effect will be that the two forces will destroy one another, and that neither the earth nor the axis will move at all. There would be the same nullifying antagonism as if,—reverting to the analogous case of the spindle and the verticilli (already alluded to) in the tenth book of the Republic,—as if, while Ananké turned the spindle with a given force in one direction, Klotho (instead of lending assistance) were to apply her hand to the outermost verticillus with equal force of resista..ce in the opposite direction (see Reipubl. x. p. 617 D). It is plain that the spindle would never turn at all.

Here, then, is a grave contradiction attaching to the view of Boeckh and Martin as to the function of the earth. They have not, in my judgment, sufficiently investigated the manner in which Plato represents to himself the cosmical axis: nor have they fully appreciated what is affirmed or implied in the debated word εἰλόμενον—εἰλούμενον—ἰλλόμενον. · That word has been explained partly by Ruhnken in his notes on Timæi Lexicon, but still more by Buttmann in his Lexilogus, so accurately and copiously as to leave nothing further wanting. I accept fully the explanation given by Buttmann, and have followed it throughout this article. After going over many other examples, Buttmann comes to consider this

passage of the Platonic Timœus; and he explains the word
εἰλομένην, or ἰλλόμενην, as meaning— " *sich drängen* oder
gedrängt werden um die Axe: d. h. von allen Seiten her an
die Axe. Auch lasse man sich das Praesens nicht irren: die
Kräfte, welche den Weltbau machen und zusammenhalten,
sind als fortdauernd thätig gedacht. Die Erde dräng sich
(ununterbrochen) an den Pol, *macht, bildet eine Kugel um ihn.*
Welcher Gebrauch völlig entspricht dem, wonach dasselbe
Verbum ein *einwickeln, einhüllen,* bedeutet. Auch hier mengt
sich in der Vorstellung einiges hinzu, was auf ein *biegen,
winden* und mitunter auf ein *drehen* führt: was aber *überall
nur ein durch die Sache selbst hinzutretender Begriff ist,*"
p. 151. And again, p. 154, he gives the result—that the
word has only " die Bedeutung *drängen, befestigen,* nebst den
davon ausgehenden—die von *drehen, winden,* aber ihm *gänz-
lich fremd* sind *und nur aus der Natur der Gegenstände in
einigen Fällen als Nebengedanken hinzutreten.*" *

In these last words Buttmann has exactly distinguished
the true, constant, and essential meaning of the word, from
the casual accessories which become conjoined with it by the
special circumstances of some peculiar cases. The constant
and true meaning of the word is, *being packed or fastened close
round, squeezing or grasping around.* The idea of *rotating* or

----

* To *pack itself,* or to *be packed,* round the axis; that is, upon the
axis from all sides. We must not be misled by the present tense:
for the forces, which compose and hold together the structure of the
universe, are conceived as continuously in active operation. The
Earth *packs itself,* or *is packed,* on to the axis — *makes or forms a ball
round the axis;* which corresponds fully to that other usage of the
word, in the sense of *wrapping up* or *swathing round.* Here too
there is a superadded something blended with the idea, which con-
ducts us to *turning, winding,* and thus to *revolving:* but this is everywhere nothing more than an accessory notion, suggested by the
circumstances of the case. The word has only the meaning, to *pack,*
to *fasten*—the senses, to *wind,* to *revolve,* are altogether foreign to it,
and can only be superadded as accessory ideas, in certain particular
instances, by the special nature of the case."

revolving is quite foreign to this meaning, but may nevertheless become conjoined with it, in certain particular cases,
by accidental circumstances.

Let us illustrate this. When I say that a body *A* is
εἰλόμενον, or ἰλλόμενον (packed or fastened close round,
squeezing or grasping around), another body *B*, I affirm
nothing about revolution or rotation. This is an idea foreign
to the proposition *per se*, yet capable of being annexed or
implicated with it under some accidental circumstances.
Whether in any particular case it be so implicated or not
depends on the question " What is the nature of the body *B*,
round which I affirm *A* to be fastened?" 1. It may be an
oak tree or a pillar, firmly planted and stationary. 2. It
may be some other body, moving, but moving in a rectilinear direction. 3. Lastly, it may be a body rotating or
intended to rotate, like a spindle, a spit, or the rolling
cylinder of a machine. In the first supposition, all motion
is excluded : in the second, rectilinear motion is implied, but
rotatory motion is excluded : in the third, rotatory motion
is implied as a certain adjunct. The body which is fastened
round another, must share the motion or the rest of that
other. If the body *B* is a revolving cylinder, and if I affirm
that *A* is packed or fastened close round it, I introduce the
idea of rotation ; though only as an accessory and implied
fact, in addition to that which the proposition affirms. The
body *A*, being fastened round the cylinder *B*, must either
revolve along with it and round it, or it must arrest the
rotation of *B*. If the one revolves, so must the other ;
both must either revolve together, or. stand still together.
This is a new fact, distinct from what is affirmed in the proposition, yet implied in it or capable of being inferred from
it through induction and experience.

Here we see exactly the position of Plato in regard to the
rotation of the earth. He does not affirm it in express terms,
but he affirms what implies it. For when he says that the
earth is packed or fastened close round the cosmical axis, he
conveys to us by implication the knowledge of another and

distinct fact—that the earth and the cosmical axis must
either revolve together or remain stationary together—that
the earth must either revolve along with the axis or arrest
the revolutions of the axis.　It is manifest that Plato does
not mean the revolutions of the axis of the kosmos to be
arrested : they are absolutely essential to the scheme of the
Timæus—they are the grand motive-agency of the kosmos.
He must, therefore, mean to imply that the earth revolves
along with and around the cosmical axis.　And thus the
word εἰλόμενον or ἰλλόμενόν, according to Buttmann's doctrine, becomes accidentally conjoined, through the specialities
of this case, with an accessory idea of rotation or revolution ; though that idea is foreign to its constant and natural
meaning.

Now if we turn to Aristotle, we shall find that he understood the word εἰλόμενον or ἰλλόμενον, and the proposition of
Plato, exactly in this sense.　Here I am compelled to depart
from Buttmann, who affirms (p. 152), with an expression of
astonishment, that Aristotle misunderstood the proposition of
Plato, and interpreted εἰλόμενον or ἰλλόμενον as if it meant
directly as well as incontestably, *rotating* or *revolving*.
Proklus, in his Commentary on the Timæus, had before
raised the same controversy with Aristotle—ἰλλομένην δὲ,
τὴν σφιγγομένην δηλοῖ καὶ συνεχομένην οὐ γὰρ ὡς 'Αριστο-
τέλης οἴεται, τὴν κινουμένην (Procl. p. 681).　Let us, therefore, examine the passages of Aristotle out of which this
difficulty arises.

The passages are two, both of them in the second book
De Cœlo ; one in cap. 13, the other in cap. 14 (p. 293 b. 30
296 a. 25).

1. The first stands—ἔνιοι δὲ καὶ κειμένην (τὴν γῆν) ἐπὶ τοῦ
κέντρου φασὶν αὐτὴν ἰλλεσθαι περὶ τὸν διὰ παντὸς τεταμένον
πόλον, ὥσπερ ἐν τῷ Τιμαίῳ γέγραπται.　Such is the reading
of Bekker in the Berlin edition: but he gives various readings
of two different MSS.—the one having ἰλλεσθαι καὶ κινεῖσθαι
—the other εἰλεῖσθαι καὶ κινεῖσθαι.

2. The second stands, beginning chap. 14— ἡμεῖς δὲ λέγωμεν

πρῶτον πότερον (the earth) ἔχει κίνησιν ἢ μένει· καθάπερ γὰρ
εἴπομεν, οἱ μὲν αὐτὴν ἐν τῶν ἄστρων ποιοῦσιν, οἱ δ' ἐπὶ τοῦ
μέσου θέντες ἴλλεσθαι καὶ κινεῖσθαί φασι περὶ τὸν πόλον μέσον.

Now in the first of these two passages, where Aristotle
simply brings the doctrine to view without any comment, he
expressly refers to the Timæus, and therefore quotes the
expression of that dialogue without any enlargement. He
undoubtedly understands the affirmation of Plato—that the
earth was fastened round the cosmical axis—as implying that
it rotated along with the rotations of that axis. Aristotle
thus construes ἴλλεσθαι, *in that particular proposition* of the
Timæus, as implying rotation. But he plainly did not construe ἴλλεσθαι as naturally and constantly either denoting or
implying rotation. This is proved by his language in the
second passage, where he reproduces the very same doctrine
with a view to discuss and confute it, and without special
reference to the Platonic Timæus. Here we find that he
is not satisfied to express the doctrine by the single word
ἴλλεσθαι. He subjoins another verb—ἴλλεσθαι καὶ κινεῖσθαι:
thus bringing into explicit enunciation the fact of rotatory
movement, which, while ἴλλεσθαι stood alone, was only
known by implication and inference from the circumstances
of the particular case. If he had supposed ἴλλεσθαι by
itself to signify *revolving*, the addition of κινεῖσθαι would
have been useless, unmeaning, and even impertinent. Aristotle, as Boeckh remarks, is not given to multiply words
unnecessarily.

It thus appears, when we examine the passage of Aristotle,
that he understood ἴλλεσθαι quite in conformity with Buttmann's explanation. Rotatory movement forms no part of
the meaning of the word; yet it may accidentally, in a
particular case, be implied as an adjunct of the meaning, by
virtue of the special circumstances of that case. Aristotle
describes the doctrine as held by *some persons*. He doubtless has in view various Platonists of his time, who adopted
and defended what had been originally advanced by Plato in
the Timæus.

M. Boeckh, in a discussion of some length (Untersuch. p. 76-84), maintains the opinion that the reading in the first passage of Aristotle is incorrect; that the two words ἴλλεσθαι καὶ κινεῖσθαι ought to stand in the first as they do in the second,—as he thinks that they stood in the copy of Simplikius: that Aristotle only made reference to Plato with a view to the peculiar word ἴλλεσθαι, and not to the general doctrine of the rotation of the earth: that he comments upon this doctrine as held by others, but not by Plato, who (according to Boeckh) was known by everyone not to hold it. M. Boeckh gives this only as a conjecture, and I cannot regard his arguments in support of it as convincing. But even if he had convinced me that ἴλλεσθαι καὶ κινεῖσθαι were the true reading in the first passage, as well as in the second, I should merely say that Aristotle had not thought himself precluded by the reference to the Timæus from bringing out into explicit enunciation what the Platonists whom he had in view knew to be implied and intended by the passage. This indeed is a loose mode of citation, which I shall not ascribe to Aristotle without good evidence. In the present case such evidence appears to me wanting. *

M. Martin attributes to Aristotle something more than improper citation. He says (Études sur le Timée, vol. ii. p. 87), "Si Aristote citait l'opinion de la rotation de la terre comme un titre de gloire pour Platon, je dirais—il est probable que la vérité l'y a forcé. Mais Aristote, qui admettait l'immobilité complète de la terre, attribue à Platon l'opinion contraire, *pour se donner le plaisir de la réfuter avec dédain.*" A few lines before, M. Martin had said that the arguments whereby Aristotle combated this opinion ascribed to Plato were "very feeble." I am at a loss to imagine in which of Aristotle's

---

* Exactness of citation is not always to be relied on among ancient commentators. Simplikius cites this very passage of the *Timæus* with more than one inaccuracy.—(Ad Aristot. *De Cœlo,* fol. 125.)

phrases M. Martin finds any trace of disdain or contempt, either for the doctrine or for those who held it. For my part, I find none. The arguments of Aristotle against the doctrine, whatever be their probative force, are delivered in that brief, calm, dry manner which is usual with him, without a word of sentiment or rhetoric, or anything ἔξω τοῦ πράγματος. Indeed, among all philosophers who have written much, I know none who is less open to the reproach of mingling personal sentiment with argumentative debate than Aristotle. Plato indulges frequently in irony, or sneering, or rhetorical invective; Aristotle very rarely. Moreover, even apart from the question of contempt, the part which M. Martin here assumes Aristotle to be playing, is among the strangest anomalies in the history of philosophy. Aristotle holds, and is anxious to demonstrate, the doctrine of the earth's immobility; he knows (so we are required to believe) that Plato not only holds the same doctrine, but has expressly affirmed it in the Timæus: he might have produced Plato as an authority in his favour, and the passage of the Timæus as an express declaration; yet he prefers to pervert, knowingly and deliberately, the meaning of this passage, and to cite Plato as a hostile instead of a friendly authority—simply " to give himself the pleasure of contemptuously refuting Plato's opinion !" But this is not all. M. Martin tells us that the arguments which Aristotle produces against the doctrine are, after all, very feeble. But he farther tells us that there was one argument which might have been produced, and which, if Aristotle had produced it, would have convicted Plato of " an enormous contradiction " (p. 88) in affirming that the earth revolved round the cosmical axis. Aristotle might have said to Plato—" You have affirmed, and you assume perpetually throughout the Timæus, the diurnal revolution of the outer sidereal sphere ; you now assert the diurnal revolution of the earth at the centre. Here is an enormous contradiction ; the two cannot stand together."—Yet Aristotle, having this triumphant argument in his hands, says not a word about it, but contents

S

himself with various other arguments which M. Martin pronoúnces to be very feeble.

Perhaps M. Martin might say—"The contradiction exists; but Aristotle was not sharpsighted enough to perceive it; otherwise he would have advanced it." I am quite of this opinion. If Aristotle had perceived the contradiction, he would have brought it forward as the strongest point in his controversy. His silence is to me a proof that he did not perceive it. But this is a part of my case against M. Martin. I believe that Plato admitted both the two contradictory doctrines without perceiving the contradiction; and it is a strong presumption in favour of this view that Aristotle equally failed to perceive it—though in a case where, according to M. Martin, he did not scruple to resort to dishonest artifice.

It appears to me that the difficulties and anomalies, in which we are involved from supposing that Aristotle either misunderstood or perverted the meaning of Plato, are far graver than those which would arise from admitting that Plato advanced a complicated theory involving two contradictory propositions, in the same dialogue, without perceiving the contradiction; more especially when the like failure of perception is indisputably ascribable to Aristotle, upon every view of the case.

M. Cousin maintains the same interpretation of the Platonic passage as Boeckh and Martin, and defends it by a note on his translation of the Timæus (p. 339). The five arguments which he produces are considered both by himself and by Martin to be unanswerable. As he puts them with great neatness and terseness, I here bestow upon them a separate examination.

1. "Platon a toujours été considéré dans l'antiquité comme partisan de l'immobilité absolue de la terre." M. Cousin had before said, "Aristote se fonde sur ce passage pour établir que Platon a fait tourner la terre sur elle-même : mais Aristote est, dans l'antiquité, le seul qui soutienne cette opinion."

My reply is, that Aristotle is himself a portion and member of antiquity, and that the various Platonists, whom he undertakes to refute, are portions of it also.   If M. Cousin appeals to the authority of antiquity, it must be to antiquity, not merely *minus* Aristotle and these contemporary Platonists, but *against* them.   Now these are just the witnesses who had the best means of knowledge.   Besides which, Aristotle himself, adopting and anxious to demonstrate the immobility of the earth, had every motive to cite Plato as a supporter, if Plato was such, and every motive to avoid citing Plato as an opponent, unless the truth of the case compelled him to do so.   I must here add, that M. Cousin represents Aristotle as ascribing to Plato the doctrine that "la terre tourne sur elle-même."   This is not strictly exact.   Aristotle understands the Platonic Timæus as saying "That the earth is packed and moved *round the axis of the kosmos*"—a different proposition.

2. " Dans plusieurs endroits de ses ouvrages où Platon parle de l'équilibre de la terre, il ne dit pas un mot de sa rotation."

I know of only *one* such passage—Phædon, p. 108—where undoubtedly Plato does not speak of the rotation of the earth; but neither does he speak of the rotation of the sidereal sphere and of the kosmos, nor of the axis of the kosmos. It is the figure and properties of the earth, considered in reference to mankind who inhabit it, that Plato sketches in the Phædon; he takes little notice of its cosmical relations, and gives no general theory about the kosmos.   M. Cousin has not adverted to the tenth Book of the Republic, where Plato does propound a cosmical theory, expressly symbolising the axis of the kosmos with its rotatory functions.

3. "Si la *terre suit le mouvement de l'axe du monde*, le mouvement de la huitième sphère, qui est Le Même, devient nul par rapport à elle, et les étoiles fixes, qui appartiennent à elle, demeurent en apparence dans une immobilité absolue : ce qui est contraire à *l'expérience et au sens*

commun, et à l'opinion de Platon, exprimée dans ce même passage."

This third argument of M. Cousin is the same as that which I have already examined in remarking upon M. Boeckh. The diurnal rotation of the earth cannot stand in the same astronomical system with the diurnal rotation of the sidereal sphere. Incontestably true (I have already said) as a point of science. But the question here is, not what opinions are scientifically consistent, but what opinions were held by Plato, and whether he detected the inconsistency between the two. I have shown grounds for believing that he did not, and not he alone, but many others along with him, Aristotle among the number. How, indeed, can this be denied, when we find M. Boeckh announcing that he is the *first* among all the critics on the Timæus, who has brought forward the inconsistency as a special ground for determining what Plato's opinion was—that no other critic before him had noticed it?

· The first words of this argument deserve particular attention, "Si la terre suit le mouvement de l'axe du monde." Here we have an exact recital of the doctrine proclaimed by the Platonic Timæus, and ascribed to him by Aristotle (quite different from the doctrine " que la terre tourne sur elle-même "). M. Cousin here speaks very distinctly about the cosmical axis, and about its movement; thus implying that Plato conceived it as a solid revolving cylinder. This, in my judgment, is the most essential point for clearing up the question in debate. The cosmical axis being of this character, when Plato affirms that the earth is *packed or fastened round it* (se roule—Cousin: *se serre et s'enroule*—Martin: *drängt sich, macht eine Kugel um ihn*—Buttmann), I maintain that, in the plainest construction of the word, the earth does and must follow the movement of the axis, or else arrest the movement of the axis. The word εἰλομένην or ἰλλομένην has no distinct meaning at all, if it does not mean this. The very synonyms (σφιγγομένην, περιδεδεμένην, &c.), which the commentators produce to prove that Plato describes

the earth as at rest, do really prove that he describes it
as rotating round and with the cosmical axis. We ought
not to be driven from this plain meaning of the word, by
the assurance of M. Cousin and others that Plato *cannot* have
meant so, because it would involve him in an astronomical
inconsistency.

4. "Les divers mouvemens des huit sphères expliquent
toutes les apparences célestes; il n'y a donc aucune raison
pour donner un mouvement à la terre."

The terms of this fourth argument, if literally construed,
would imply that Plato had devised a complete and satisfactory astronomical theory. I pass over this point, and
construe them as M. Cousin probably intended: his argument will then stand thus—"The movement of the earth
does not add anything to Plato's power of explaining astronomical appearances; therefore Plato had no motive to
suggest a movement of the earth."

I have already specified the sense in which I understand
the Platonic Timæus to affirm, or rather to imply, the
rotation of the earth; and that sense is not open to the
objections raised in M. Cousin's fourth and fifth arguments.
The rotation of the earth, as it appears in the Platonic
Timæus, explains nothing, and is not intended to explain
anything. It is a consequence, not a cause: it is a consequence arising from the position of the earth, as packed or
fastened round the centre of the cosmical axis, whereby the
earth participates, of necessity and as a matter of course, in
the movements of that axis. The *function* of the earth, thus
planted in the centre of the kosmos, is to uphold and regulate
the revolutions of the cosmical axis; and this function explains, in the scheme of the Platonic Timæus, why the axis
revolves uniformly and constantly without change or displacement. Now upon these revolutions of the cosmical
axis all the revolutions of the exterior sphere depend. This
is admitted by M. Cousin himself in argument 3. There is
therefore every reason why Plato should assign such regulating function to the earth, the "first and oldest of intra-

kosmic deities." The movement of the earth (as I before
observed) is only an incidental consequence of the position
necessary for the earth to occupy in performing such
function.

5. "Enfin Platon assigne un mouvement aux étoiles fixes,
et deux mouvemens aux planètes; puisqu'il ne range la
terre ni avec les unes ni avec les autres, il y a lieu de croire
qu'elle ne participe à aucun de leurs mouvemens."

In so far as this argument is well-founded, it strengthens
my case more than that of M. Cousin. The earth does not
participate in the movements either of the fixed stars or
of the planets; but it does participate in the revolutions of
the cosmical axis, upon which these movements depend—
the movements of the outer sphere, wholly and exclusively
—the movements of the planets, to a very great degree, but
not exclusively. The earth is not ranked either among
the fixed stars or among the planets; it is a body or deity
sui generis, having a special central function of its own, to
regulate that cosmical axis which impels the whole system.
The earth has a motion of its own, round and along with
the cosmical axis to which it is attached; but this motion
of the earth (I will again repeat, to prevent misapprehension)
is a fact not important by itself, nor explaining anything.
The grand and capital fact is the central position and
regulating function of the earth, whereby all the cosmical
motions, first those of the axis, next those of the exterior
kosmos, are upheld and kept uniform.

M. Cousin adds, as a sixth argument:—

"On peut ajouter à ces raisons que Platon aurait néces-
sairement insisté sur le mouvement de la terre, s'il l'avait
admis; et que ce point étoit trop controversé de son temps
et trop important en lui-même, pour qu'il ne fît que l'indi-
quer en se servant d'une expression équivoque."

In the first place, granting Plato to have believed in the
motion of the earth, can we also assume that he would necessarily have asserted it with distinctness and emphasis, as
M. Cousin contends? I think not. Gruppe maintains exactly

the contrary; telling us that Plato's language was intentionally obscure and equivocal—from fear of putting himself
in open conflict with the pious and orthodox sentiment prevalent around him.   I do not carry this part of the case so
far as Gruppe, but I admit that it rests upon a foundation of
reality.   When we read (Plutarch, De Facie in Orbe Lunæ,
p. 923) how the motion of the earth, as affirmed by Aristarchus of Samos (doubtless in a far larger sense than Plato
ever imagined, including both rotation and translation), was
afterwards denounced as glaring impiety, we understand the
atmosphere of religious opinion with which Plato was surrounded.   And we also perceive that he might have reasons
for preferring to indicate an astronomical heresy in terms
suitable for philosophical hearers, rather than to proclaim
it in such emphatic unequivocal words, as might be quoted
by some future Melêtus in case of an indictment before the
Dikasts.

We must remember that Plato had been actually present
at the trial of Sokrates.   He had heard the stress laid by
the accusers on astronomical heresies, analogous to those
of Anaxagoras, which they imputed to Sokrates, and the
pains taken by the latter to deny that he held such opinions
(see the Platonic Apology).   The impression left by such
a scene on Plato's mind was not likely to pass away: nor
can we be surprised that he preferred to use propositions
which involved and implied, rather than those which directly
and undisguisedly asserted, the heretical doctrine of the
earth's rotation.   That his phraseology, however indirect,
was perfectly understood by contemporary philosophers, both
assentient and dissentient, as embodying his belief in the
doctrine—is attested by the two passages of Aristotle.

Upon these reasons alone I should dissent from M. Cousin's
sixth argument.   But I have other reasons besides.   He rests
it upon the two allegations that the doctrine of the earth's
motion was the subject of much controversial debate in
Plato's time, and of great importance in itself.   Now the
first of these two allegations can hardly be proved, as to

the time of Plato ; for Aristotle, when he is maintaining the earth's immobility, does not specify any other opponents than the Pythagoreians and the followers of the Platonic Timæus. And the second allegation I believe to be unfounded, speaking with reference to the Platonic Timæus. In the cosmical system therein embodied, the rotation of the earth round the cosmical axis, though a real part of the system, was in itself a fact of no importance, and determining no results. The capital fact of the system was the position and function of the earth, packed close round the centre of the cosmical axis, and regulating the revolutions of that axis. Plato had no motive to bring prominently forward the circumstance that the earth revolved itself along with the cosmical axis, which circumstance was only an incidental accompaniment.

I have thus examined all the arguments adduced by M. Cousin, and have endeavoured to show that they fail in establishing his conclusion. There is, however, one point of the controversy in which I concur with him more than with Boeckh and Martin. This point is the proper conception of what Plato means by *the cosmical axis*. Boeckh and Martin seem to assume this upon the analogy of what is now spoken of as the axis of the earth : M. Boeckh (p. 13) declares the axis of the kosmos to be a prolongation of that axis. But it appears to me (and M. Cousin's language indicates the same) that Plato's conception was something very different. The axis of the earth (what astronomers speak of as such) is an imaginary line traversing the centre of the earth ; a line round which the earth revolves. Now the cosmical axis, as Plato conceives it, is a solid material cylinder, which not only itself revolves, but causes by this revolution the revolution of the exterior circumference of the kosmos. This is a conception entirely different from that which *we* mean when we speak of the axis of the earth. It is, however, a conception symbolically enunciated in the tenth book of the Republic, where the spindle of Necessity is said to be composed of adamant, hard and solid material, and to cause by its own rotation the rotation of all the *verticilli* packed and fastened around it. What is thus enunciated in the Republic is implied in the Timæus. For when we read therein that the earth is packed or fastened round the cosmical axis, how can we understand it to be packed or fastened round an imaginary line? I will add that the very same meaning is brought out in the translation of Cicero—" *trajecto axe sustinetur* " (terra). The axis, round which the earth is fastened, and which sustains the earth, must be conceived, not as an imaginary line, but as a solid cylinder, itself revolving; while the earth, being fastened round it, revolves round and along with it. The axis, in the sense of an imaginary line, cannot be found in the conception of Plato.

Those contemporaries of Plato and Aristotle, who all agreed in asserting the revolution of the celestial sphere, did not all agree in their idea of the force whereby such revolution was brought about. Some thought that the poles of the celestial sphere exercised a determining force: others symbolised the mythical Atlas, as an axis traversing the sphere from pole to pole and turning it round. (Aristotel. De Motu Animal. 3. p. 699 a. 15-30.) Aristotle himself advocated the theory of a *primum movens immobile* acting upon the sphere from without the sphere. Even in the succeeding centuries, when astronomy was more developed, Aratus, Eratosthenes, and their commentators, differed in their way of conceiving the cosmical axis. Most of them considered it as solid: but of these, some thought it was stationary, with the sphere revolving round it, others that it revolved itself: again, among these latter, some believed that the revolutions of the axis determined those of the surrounding sphere, others, that the revolutions of the sphere caused those of the axis within it. Again, there were some physical philosophers who looked at the axis as airy or spiritual—τὸ διὰ μέσου τῆς σφαίρας διῆκον πνεῦμα. Then there were geometers who conceived it only as an imaginary line. (See the Phænomena of Aratus 20-25—with the Scholia thereon; Achilles Tatius ad Arati Phænom. apud Petavium—Ura-

nolog. p. 88; also Hipparchus ad Arat. ib. p. 144.) I do not
go into these dissentient opinions farther than to show, how
indispensable it is, when we construe the passage in the
Platonic Timæus, περὶ τὸν διὰ παντὸς πόλον τεταμένον, to
enquire in what sense Plato understood the cosmical axis:
and how unsafe it is to assume at once that he must have
conceived it as an imaginary line.

Proklus argues that because the earth is mentioned by
Plato in the Phædon as stationary in the centre of the
heaven, we cannot imagine Plato to affirm its rotation in
the Timæus. I agree with M. Boeckh in thinking this argument inconclusive; all the more, because, in the Phædon,
not a word is said either about the axis of the kosmos, or
about the rotation of the kosmos; all that Sokrates professes to give is τὴν ἰδέαν τῆς γῆς καὶ τοὺς τόπους αὐτῆς
(p. 108 E). No cosmical system or theory is propounded in
that dialogue.

When we turn to the Phædrus, we find that, in its highly
poetical description, the rotation of the heaven occupies a
prominent place. The internal circumference of the heavenly
sphere, as well as its external circumference or back (νῶτον),
are mentioned; also its periodical rotations, during which
the Gods are carried round on the back of the heaven,
and contemplate the eternal Ideas occupying the super-
celestial space (p. 247, 248), or the plain of truth.* But
the purpose of this poetical representation appears to be
metaphysical and intellectual, to illustrate the antithesis
presented by the world of Ideas and Truth on one side,
against that of sense and appearances on the other. Astro-
nomically and cosmically considered, no intelligible meaning
is conveyed. Nor can we even determine whether the
rotations of the heaven, alluded to in the Phædrus, are intended to be diurnal or not; I incline to believe not (μέχρι

---

* Whether Ἑστία in the Phædrus, which is said " to remain alone
stationary in the house of the Gods," can be held to mean the Earth,
is considered by Proklus to be uncertain (p. 681).

τῆς ἑτέρας περιόδου—p. 248—which can hardly be understood of so short a time as one day). Lastly, nothing is said
in the Phædrus about the cosmical axis; and it is upon this
that the rotations of the earth intimated in the Timæus
depend.

Among the different illustrations, given by Plato in his
different dialogues respecting the terrestrial and celestial
bodies, I select the tenth book of the Republic as that which
is most suitable for comparison with the Timæus, because it
is only therein that we learn how Plato conceived the axis of
the kosmos. M. Boeckh (Untersuchungen, p. 86) wishes us
to regard the difference between the view taken in the
Phædon, and that in the Republic, as no way important; he
affirms that the adamantine spindle in the Republic is altogether mythical or poetical, and that Plato conceives the
axis as not being material. On this point I dissent from M.
Boeckh. The mythical illustrations in the tenth book of the
Republic appear to me quite unsuitable to the theory of an
imaginary, stationary, and immaterial axis. Here I much
more agree with Gruppe (p. 15, 26–29), who recognises the
solid material axis as an essential feature of the cosmical
theory in the Republic; and recognises also the marked
difference between that theory and what we read in the
Phædon. Yet, though Gruppe is aware of this important
difference between the Republic and the Phædon, he still
wishes to illustrate the Timæus by the latter and not by the
former. He affirms that the earth in the Timæus is conceived as unattached, and freely suspended, the same as in
the Phædon; but that in the Timæus it is conceived, besides,
as revolving on its own axis, which we do not find in the
Phædon (p. 28, 29). Here I think Gruppe is mistaken. In
construing the words of Timæus, εἰλομένην (ἰλλομένην) περὶ
τὸν διὰ παντὸς πόλον τεταμένον, as designating "the unattached earth revolving round its own axis," he does violence not less to the text of Plato than to the expository
comment of Aristotle. Neither in the one nor the other is
anything said about *an axis of the earth;* in both, the cos-

mical axis is expressly designated; and, if Gruppe is right
in his interpretation of εἰλομένην, we must take Plato as
affirming, not that the earth is fastened round the cosmical
axis, but that it revolves, though unattached, around that
axis, which is a proposition both difficult to understand,
and leading to none of those astronomical consequences with
which Gruppe would connect it. Again, when Gruppe says
that εἰλομένην περὶ does *not* mean *packed or fastened round*,
but that it *does* mean *revolving round*, he has both the
analogies of the word and the other commentators against
him. The main proof, if not the only proof, which he
brings, is that Aristotle so construed it. Upon this point
I join issue with him. I maintain that Aristotle does *not*
understand εἰλομένην or ἰλλομένην περὶ as naturally meaning
revolving round, and that he does understand the phrase as
meaning *fastened round*. When we find him, in the second
passage of the treatise De Cœlo, not satisfied with the verb
ἴλλεσθαι alone, but adding to it the second verb καὶ κινεῖσθαι, we may be sure that he did not consider ἴλλεσθαι as
naturally and properly denoting *to revolve* or *move round*.

Agreeing as I do with Gruppe in his view, that the interpretation put by Aristotle is the best evidence which we can
follow in determining the meaning of this passage in the
Timæus, I contend that the authority of Aristotle contradicts
instead of justifying the conclusion at which he arrives.
Aristotle understands ἰλλομένην as meaning *packed or fastened round;* he does not understand it as meaning, when
taken by itself, *revolving round*.

The two meanings here indicated are undoubtedly distinct
and independent. But they are not for that reason contradictory and incompatible. It has been the mistake of critics
to conceive them as thus incompatible; so that if one of the
two were admitted, the other must be rejected. I have endeavoured to show that this is not universally true, and that
there are certain circumstances in which the two meanings
not only may come together, but must come together. Such
is the case when we revert to Plato's conception of the

cosmical axis as a solid revolving cylinder. That which is packed or fastened around the cylinder must revolve around it, and along with it.

Both M. Boeckh and Gruppe assume the incompatibility of the two meanings; and we find the same assumption in Plutarch's criticisms on the Timœus (Plutarch. Quæst. Platon. p. 1006 C), where he discusses what Plato means by ὄργανα χρόνου; and in what sense the earth as well as the moon can be reckoned as ὄργανον χρόνου (Timœus, p. 41 E, 42 D). Plutarch inquires how it is possible that the earth, if stationary and at rest, can be characterised as "among the instruments of time;" and he explains it by saying that this is true in the same sense as we call a gnomon or sun-dial an instrument of time, because, though itself never moves, it marks the successive movements of the shadow. This explanation might be admissible for the phrase ὄργανον χρόνου; but I cannot think that the immobility of the earth can be made compatible with the attribute which Plato bestows upon it of being φύλαξ καὶ δημιουργὸς νυκτός τε καὶ ἡμέρας.

The difficulty, however, vanishes when we understand the function ascribed by Plato to the earth as I have endeavoured to elucidate it. The earth not only is not at rest, but cannot be at rest, precisely because it is packed round the solid revolving cosmical axis, and must revolve along with it. The function of the earth, as the first and oldest of intra-kosmic deities, is to uphold and regulate the revolutions of this axis, upon which depend the revolutions of the sidereal sphere or outer shell of the kosmos. It is by virtue of this regulating function (and not by virtue of its rotation) that the earth is the guardian and artificer of night and day. It is not only "an instrument of time," but the most potent and commanding among all instruments of time.

What has just been stated is, in my belief, the theory of the Platonic Timæus, signified in the words of that dialogue, and embodied in the comment of Aristotle. The commentators, subsequent to Aristotle, so far as we know them, understood the theory in a sense different from what Plato intended. I think we may see how this misconception arose. It arose from the great development and elaboration of astronomical theory during the two or three generations immediately succeeding Plato. Much was added by Eudoxus and others, in their theory of concentric spheres: more still by others of whom we read in Cicero (Academ. II. 39.) "Hicetas Syracusius, ut ait Theophrastus, coelum, solem, lunam, stellas, supera denique omnia, stare censet, neque præter terram rem ullam in mundo moveri: quæ cum circum axem se summâ celeritate convertat et torqueat, eadem effici omnia, quæ si stante terrâ coelum moveretur. Atque hoc etiam Platonem in Timæo dicere quidam arbitrantur, sed paullo obscurius." The same doctrine is said to have been held by Herakleides of Pontus, the contemporary of Aristotle, and by others along with him. (Simplikius ad Aristot. Physic. p. 64—De Coelo, p. 132—Plutarch. Plac. Phil. III. 13.) The doctrine of the rotation of the earth here appears along with another doctrine—the immobility of the sidereal sphere and of the celestial bodies. The two are presented together, as correlative portions of one and the same astronomical theory. There are no celestial revolutions, and therefore there is no solid celestial axis. Moreover, even Aristarchus of Samos (who attained to a theory substantially the same as the Copernican, with the double movement of the earth, rotation round its own axis, and translation round the sun as a centre) comes within less than a century after Plato's death.

Though the *quidam* alluded to by Cicero looked upon the obscure sentence in Plato's Timæus as a dim indication of the theory of Hicetas, yet the two agree only in the supposition of a rotation of the earth, and differ essentially in the pervading cosmical conceptions. Hicetas states distinctly that which his theory denies, as well as that which it affirms. The negation of the celestial rotations, is in his theory a point of capital and co-ordinate importance, on which he contradicts both Plato and Aristotle as well as the apparent evidence of sense. I cannot suppose that this theory can have been proclaimed or known to Aristotle when his works were composed : for the celestial revolutions are the keystone of his system, and he could hardly have abstained from combating a doctrine which denied them altogether.   In the hands of Hicetas (perhaps in those of Herakleides, if we may believe what is said about him) astronomy appears treated as a science by itself, with a view "to provide such hypotheses as may save the phenomena" (σώζειν τὰ φαινόμενα, Simpl. ad Aristot. De Cœlo, p. 498, Schol. Brandis).   It becomes detached from those religious, ethical, poetical, teleological, arithmetical decrees or fancies, in which we see it immersed in the Platonic Timæus, and even (though somewhat less) in the Aristotelian Treatise De Cœlo.   Hence the meaning of Plato, obscurely announced from the beginning, ceased to be understood ; the solid revolving axis of the Kosmos, assumed without being expressly affirmed in his Timæus, dropped out of sight : the doctrine of the rotation of the earth was presented in a new point of view, as a substitute for the celestial revolutions.   But no proper note was taken of this transition.   The doctrine of Plato was assumed to be the same as that of Hicetas.

When we read Plutarch's criticism (Quæst. Plat. p. 1006 C) upon the word ἰλλομένην, we see that he puts to himself the question thus—" Does Plato in the Timæus conceive the earth as kept together and stationary—or as turning round and revolving, agreeably to the subsequent theory of Aristarchus and Seleukus ? " Here we find that Plutarch conceives the alternative thus—Either the earth does not revolve at all, or it revolves as Aristarchus understood it.   One or other of these two positions must have been laid down by Plato in the Timæus.   So we read in Plutarch.   But the fact is, that Plato meant neither the one nor the other.   The rotation of the earth round the solid cosmical axis, which he affirms in the Timæus, is a phenomenon utterly different from the rotation of the earth as a free body round the imaginary line called its own axis, which was the doctrine of Aristarchus.

When expositors in Plutarch's day, and since his day,

enquired whether or not the Platonic Timæus affirmed the
rotation of the earth, they meant to designate the rotation
of the earth in the sense of Aristarchus, and in the sense
in which modern astronomy understands that capital fact.
Now speaking the language of modern astronomy, I think
it certain that the rotation of the earth is *not* to be found
affirmed in the Platonic Timæus; and I agree with M.
Boeckh when he says (Untersuch. p. 77), "Granting that
Aristotle ascribed to Plato the doctrine of the rotation of
the earth, he at least did not ascribe to him the doctrine
as Gruppe assumes, and as now understood." · As between
Gruppe—who holds that the Platonic Timæus affirms the
rotation of the earth, and that Aristotle ascribes it to him,
in our sense of the words—and M. Boeckh, who denies this
—I stand with the latter for the negative. But when M.
Boeckh assumes that the only alternative doctrine is the
immobility of the earth, and tries to show that this doctrine
is proclaimed in the Platonic Timæus—nay, that no opposite
doctrine *can* be proclaimed, because the discourse expressly
announces the rotation of the sidereal heaven in twenty-four
hours—I am compelled to dissent from him as to the conclusion, and to deny the cogency of his proof. M. Boeckh
has hardly asked himself the question, whether there was
not some other sense in which Plato might have affirmed it
in the Timæus. I have endeavoured to show that there was
another sense; that there are good analogies in Plato to justify
the belief that he intended to arm the doctrine in that
other sense; and that the comments of Aristotle—while
thoroughly pertinent, if we thus understand the passage in
the Timæus—become either irrelevant, dishonest, or absurd, if
we construe the passage as signifying either what is maintained by M. Boeckh or what is maintained by Gruppe.

The eminent critics, whose opinions I here controvert,
have been apparently misled by the superior astronomical
acquirements of the present age, and have too hastily made
the intellectual exigencies of their own minds a standard for
all other minds, in different ages as well as in different states

of cultivation. The question before us is, not what doctrines are scientifically true or scientifically compatible with each other, but what doctrines were affirmed or implied by Plato. In interpreting him, we are required to keep our minds independent of subsequent astronomical theories. We must look, first and chiefly, to what is said by Plato himself; next, if that be obscure, to the construction and comments of his contemporaries so far as they are before us. In no case is this more essential than in the doctrine of the rotation of the earth, which in the modern mind has risen to its proper rank in scientific importance, and has become connected with collateral consequences and associations foreign to the ideas of the ancient Pythagoreans, or Plato, or Aristotle. Unless we disengage ourselves from these more recent associations, we cannot properly understand the doctrine as it stands in the Platonic Timæus.

This doctrine, as I have endeavoured to explain it, leads to an instructive contrast between the cosmical theories of Plato (in the Timæus) and Aristotle.

Plato conceives the kosmos as one animated and intelligent being or god, composed of body and soul. Its body is moved and governed by its soul, which is fixed or rooted in the centre, but stretches to the circumference on all sides, as well as all round the exterior. It has a perpetual movement of circular rotation in the same unchanged place, which is the sort of movement most worthy of a rational and intelligent being. The revolutions of the exterior or sidereal sphere (Circle of the Same) depend on and are determined by the revolutions of the solid cylinder or axis, which traverses the kosmos in its whole diameter. Besides these, there are various interior spheres or circles (Circles of the Different) which rotate by distinct and variable impulses in a direction opposite to the sidereal sphere. This latter is so much more powerful than they, that it carries them all round with it; yet they make good, to a certain extent, their own special opposite movement, which causes their positions to be ever changing, and the whole system to be complicated. But

T

the grand capital, uniform, overpowering, movement of the kosmos, consists in the revolution of the solid axis, which determines that of the exterior sidereal sphere. The impulse or stimulus to this movement comes from the cosmical soul, which has its root in the centre. Just at this point is situated the earth, "the oldest and most venerable of intra-kosmic deities," packed round the centre of the axis, and having for its function—to guard and regulate those revolutions of the axis, and through them those of the outer sphere, on which the succession of day and night depends—as well as to nurse mankind.

In all this we see that the ruling principle and force of the kosmos (τὸ ἡγεμονικὸν τοῦ κόσμου) is made to dwell in and emanate from *its centre*.

When we come to Aristotle, we find that the ruling principle or force of the kosmos is placed, not in its centre, but in its circumference. He recognises no solid revolving axis traversing the whole diameter of the kosmos. The interior of the kosmos is occupied by the four elements—earth, water, air, fire—no one of which can revolve except by violence or under the pressure of extraneous force. To each of them rectilinear motion is *natural;* earth moves naturally towards the centre—fire moves naturally towards the circumference, away from the centre. But the peripheral substance of the kosmos is radically distinct from the four elements : rotatory motion in a circle is *natural* to it, and is the only variety of motion natural to it. That it is moved at all, it owes to a *primum movens immobile* impelling it : but the two are coeternal, and the motion has neither beginning nor end. That when moved, its motion is rotatory and not rectilinear, it owes to its own nature. It rotates perpetually, through its own nature and inherent virtue, not by constraining pressure communicated from a centre or from a soul. If constraint were required—if there were any contrary tendency to be overcome—the revolving periphery would become fatigued, and would require periods of repose; but, since in revolving it only obeys its own peculiar nature, it persists for ever without knowing fatigue. This peripheral or fifth essence, perpetually revolving, is the divine, venerable, and commanding portion of the kosmos, more grand and honourable than the interior parts or the centre. Aristotle lays this down (De Cœlo, ii. 13, p. 293, b. 10) in express antithesis to the Pythagoreans, who, (like Plato) considered the centre as the point of grandeur and command, placing fire in the centre for that reason. The earth has no positive cosmical function in Aristotle; it occupies the centre because all its parts have a natural movement towards the centre: and it is unmoved because there *must be* something in the centre which is always stationary, as a contrary or antithesis to the fifth essence or peripheral substance of the kosmos, which is in perpetual rotation by its own immutable nature.

I do not here go farther into the exposition of these ancient cosmical theories. I have adverted to Aristotle's doctrine only so far as was necessary to elucidate, by contrast, that which I believe to be the meaning of the Platonic Timæus about the rotation of the earth.

REVIEW OF JOHN STUART MILL

ON THE

PHILOSOPHY OF SIR WM. HAMILTON.

(*Westminster Review*, 1866.)

PHILOSOPHY OF SIR WM. HAMILTON.

THE work* bearing the above title is an octavo volume, consisting of twenty-eight chapters, and five hundred and sixty pages. This is no great amount of print; but the amount of matter contained in it is prodigious, and the quality of that matter such as to require a full stretch of attention. Mr. Mill gives his readers no superfluous sentences, scarcely even a superfluous word, above what is necessary to express his meaning briefly and clearly. Of such a book no complete abstract can be given in the space to which we are confined.

To students of philosophy—doubtless but a minority among the general circle of English readers—this work comes recommended by the strongest claims both of interest and instruction. It presents in direct antithesis two most conspicuous representatives of the modern speculative mind of England—Sir W. Hamilton and Mr. John Stuart Mill.

Sir W. Hamilton has exercised powerful influence over the stream of thought during the present generation. The lectures on Logic and Metaphysics delivered by him at Edinburgh, for twenty years, determined the view taken of those subjects by a large number of aspiring young students,

---

* *An Examination of Sir William Hamilton's Philosophy, and of the Principal Philosophical Questions discussed in his Writings.* By John Stuart Mill. London : Longmans. 1865.

and determined that view for many of them permanently
and irrevocably.[*] Several eminent teachers and writers of
the present day are proud of considering themselves his
disciples, enunciate his doctrines in greater or less proportion,
and seldom contradict him without letting it be seen that
they depart unwillingly from such a leader. Various new
phrases and psychological illustrations have obtained footing
in treatises of philosophy, chiefly from his authority. We
do not number ourselves among his followers ; but we think
his influence on philosophy was in many ways beneficial.
He kept up the idea of philosophy as a subject to be studied
from its own points of view : a dignity which in earlier times
it enjoyed, perhaps, to mischievous excess, but from which
in recent times it has far too much receded—especially in
England. He performed the great service of labouring
strenuously to piece together the past traditions of philosophy, to re-discover those which had been allowed to drop

---

[*] Mr. Mansel and Mr. Veitch, the editors of Sir W. Hamilton's
Lectures on Metaphysics, posthumously published, say in their preface (p. xiii.)—

" For twenty years—from 1836 to 1856—the courses of logic
and metaphysics were the means through which Sir William
Hamilton sought to discipline and imbue with his philosophical
opinions the numerous youth who gathered from Scotland and
other countries to his class-room ; and while, by these prelections,
the author supplemented, developed, and moulded the national
philosophy, leaving thereon the ineffaceable impress of his genius
and learning, he, at the same time and by the same means, exercised
over the intellects and feelings of his pupils an influence which, for
depth, feeling and elevation, was certainly never surpassed by that
of any philosophical instructor. Among his pupils there are not a
few who, having lived for a season under the constraining power
of his intellect, and been led to reflect on those great questions
regarding the character, origin, and bounds of human knowledge,
which his teaching stirred and quickened, bear the memory of their
beloved and revered instructor inseparably blended with what is
highest in their present intellectual life, as well as in their practical
aims and aspirations."

into oblivion, and to make out the genealogy of opinions as far as negligent predecessors had still left the possibility of doing so.

The forty-six lectures on Metaphysics, and the thirty-five lectures on Logic, published by Messrs. Mansel and Veitch, constitute the biennial course actually delivered by Sir W. Hamilton in the Professorial Chair. They ought therefore to be looked at chiefly with reference to the minds of youthful hearers, as preservatives against that mischief forcibly described by Rousseau—"L'inhabitude de penser dans la jeunesse en ôte la capacité pendant le reste de la vie."

Now, in a subject so abstract, obscure, and generally unpalatable, as Logic and Metaphysics, the difficulty which the teacher finds in inspiring interest is extreme. That Sir W. Hamilton overcame such difficulty with remarkable success, is the affirmation of his two editors; and our impression, as readers of his lectures, disposes us to credit them. That Sir W. Hamilton should have done this effectively is in itself sufficient to stamp him as a meritorious professor—as a worthy successor to the chair of Dugald Stewart, whose unrivalled perfection in that department is attested by every one. Many a man who ultimately adopted speculative opinions opposed to Dugald Stewart, received his first impulse and guidance in the path of speculation from the lasting impression made by Stewart's instructions.

But though we look at these lectures, as they ought to be looked at, chiefly with a view to the special purpose for which they were destined, we are far from insinuating that they have no other merits, or that they are useless for readers who have already a metaphysical creed of their own. We have found them both instructive and interesting: they go over a large portion of the field of speculative philosophy, partly from the point of view (not always the same) belonging to the author, partly from that of numerous predecessors whom he cites. We recognise also in Sir W. Hamilton an amount of intellectual independence which seldom

accompanies such vast erudition. He recites many different
opinions, but he judges them all for himself; and, what is of
still greater moment, he constantly gives the reasons for his
judgments. To us these reasons are always of more or less
value, whether we admit them to be valid or not. Many
philosophers present their own doctrine as if it were so much
ascertained and acknowledged truth, either intimating, or leading you to suppose, that though erroneous beliefs to the contrary formerly prevailed, these have now become discredited
with every one. We do not censure this way of proceeding,
but we prefer the manner of Sir W. Hamilton. He always
keeps before us divergence and discrepancy of view as the
normal condition of reasoned truth or philosophy; the characteristic postulate of which is, that every affirmative and
every negative shall have its appropriate reasons clearly and
fully enunciated.

In this point of view, the appendix annexed to the lectures
is also valuable; and the four copious appendixes or dissertations following the edition of Reid's works, are more
valuable still. How far Sir W. Hamilton has there furnished
good proof of his own doctrines on External Perception,
and on the Primary Qualities of Matter, we shall not now
determine; but to those who dissent from him, as well as
to those who agree with him, his reasonings on these subjects
are highly instructive : while the full citations from so many
other writers contribute materially not only to elucidate the
points directly approached, but also to enlarge our knowledge of philosophy generally. We set particular value
upon this preservation of the traditions of philosophy, and
upon this maintenance of a known perpetual succession
among the speculative minds of humanity, with proper
comparisons and contrasts. We have found among the
names quoted by Sir W. Hamilton—thanks to his care—
several authors hardly at all known to us, and opinions
cited from them not less instructing than curious. He
deserves the more gratitude, because he departs herein from
received usage since Bacon and Descartes. The example

set by these great men was admirable, so far as it went
to throw off the authority of predecessors; but pernicious
so far as it banished those predecessors out of knowledge,
like mere magazines of immaturity and error. Throughout
the eighteenth century, all study of the earlier modes of
philosophizing was, for the most part, neglected. Of such
neglect, remarkable instances are pointed out by Sir W.
Hamilton.

While speaking about the general merits and philosophical
position of Sir William Hamilton, we have hitherto said
nothing about those of Mr. Mill. But before we proceed to
analyse the separate chapters of his volume, we must devote
a few words to the fulfilment of another obligation.

Mr. John Stuart Mill has not been the first to bestow
honour on the surname which he bears. His father, Mr.
James Mill, had already ennobled the name. An ampler
title to distinction in history and philosophy can seldom be
produced than that which Mr. James Mill left behind him.
We know no work which surpasses his ' History of British
India ' in the main excellences attainable by historical
writers: industrious accumulation, continued for many years,
of original authorities; careful and conscientious criticism of
their statements; and a large command of psychological
analysis, enabling the author to interpret phenomena of
society, both extremely complicated, and far removed from
his own personal experience. Again, Mr. James Mill's
' Elements of Political Economy' were, at the time when
they appeared, the most logical and condensed exposition of
the entire science then existing. Lastly, his latest avowed
production, the ' Analysis of the Phenomena of the Human
Mind,' is a model of perspicuous exposition of complex states
of consciousness, carried farther than by any other author
before him; and illustrating the fulness which such exposition may be made to attain, by one who has faith in the
comprehensive principle of association, and has learnt the
secret of tracing out its innumerable windings. It is moreover, the first work in which the great fact of Indissoluble

Association is brought into its due theoretical prominence. These are high merits, of which lasting evidence is before the public; but there were other merits in Mr. James Mill, less publicly authenticated, yet not less real. His unpremeditated oral exposition was hardly less effective than his prepared work with the pen; his colloquial fertility on philosophical subjects, his power of discussing himself, and of stimulating others to discuss, his ready responsive inspirations through all the shifts and windings of a sort of Platonic dialogue,—all these accomplishments were, to those who knew him, even more impressive than what he composed for the press. Conversation with him was not merely instructive, but provocative to the dormant intelligence. Of all persons whom we have known, Mr. James Mill was the one who stood least remote from the lofty Platonic ideal of Dialectic—Τοῦ διδόναι καὶ δέχεσθαι λόγον—(the giving and receiving of reasons) competent alike to examine others, or to be examined by them on philosophy. When to this we add a strenuous character, earnest convictions, and single-minded devotion to truth, with an utter disdain of mere paradox, it may be conceived that such a man exercised powerful intellectual ascendency over younger minds. Several of those who enjoyed his society—men now at or past the maturity of life, and some of them in distinguished positions—remember and attest with gratitude such ascendancy in their own cases : among them the writer of the present article, who owes to the historian of British India an amount of intellectual stimulus and guidance such as he can never forget.

When a father, such as we have described, declining to send his son either to school or college, constituted himself schoolmaster from the beginning, and performed that duty with laborious solicitude—when, besides full infusion of modern knowledge, the forcing process applied by the Platonic Socrates to the youthful Theætêtus, was administered by Mr. James Mill, continuously and from an earlier age, to a youthful mind not less pregnant than that of

Theætêtus—it would be surprising if the son thus trained had not reached even a higher eminence than his father. The fruit borne by Mr. John Stuart Mill has been worthy of the culture bestowed, and the volume before us is at once his latest and his ripest product.

The 'Examination of Sir William Hamilton's Philosophy' is intended by Mr. Mill (so he tells us in the preface to the sixth published edition of his 'System of Logic, Ratiocinative and Inductive') as a sequel and complement to that system. We are happy to welcome so valuable an addition; but with or without that addition, the 'System of Logic' appears to us to present the most important advance in speculative theory which the present century has witnessed. Either half of it, the Ratiocinative or the Inductive, would have surpassed any previous work on the same subject. The Inductive half discriminates and brings into clear view, for the first time, those virtues of method which have insensibly grown into habits among consummate scientific enquirers of the post-Baconian age, as well as the fallacies by which some of these authors have been misled; the Ratiocinative half, dealing with matters which had already been well handled by Dutrieu and other scholastic logicians, invests their dead though precise formalism with a real life and application to the actual process of finding and proving truth. But besides thus working each half up to perfection, Mr. Mill has performed the still more difficult task of overcoming the repugnance, apparently an inveterate repugnance, between them, so as chemically to combine the two into one homogeneous compound; thus presenting the problem of Reasoned Truth, Inference, Proof, and Disproof, as one connected whole. For ourselves, we still recollect the mist which was cleared from our minds when we first read the 'System of Logic,' very soon after it was published. We were familiar with the Syllogistic Logic in Burgersdicius and Dutrieu; we were also familiar with examples of the best procedure in modern inductive science; but the two streams flowed altogether apart in our minds, like two parallel lines never

joining nor approaching. The irreconcileability of the two
was at once removed, when we had read and mastered the
second and third chapters of the Second Book of the 'System
of Logic;' in which Mr. Mill explains the functions and
value of the syllogism, and the real import of its major
premiss. This explanation struck us at the time as one
the most profound and original efforts of metaphysical
thought that we had ever perused, and we see no reason to
retract that opinion now.* It appears all the more valuable
when we contrast it with what is said by Mr. Mill's two
contemporaries—Hamilton and Whately: the first of whom
retains the ancient theory of Reasoning, as being only a
methodised transition from a whole to its parts, and from the
parts up to the whole—Induction being only this ascending
part of the process, whereby, after having given a complete
enumeration of all the compound parts, you conclude to
the sum total described in one word as a whole ;† while

* We are happy to find such high authorities as Dr. Whewell,
Mr. Samuel Bailey, and Sir John Herschel concurring in this estimation of the new logical point of view thus opened by Mr. Mill.
We will not call it a *discovery*, since Sir John Herschel thinks the
expression unsuitable.—See the recent sixth edition of the *System
of Logic*, vol. i. p. 229.

† See Sir William Hamilton's *Lectures on Logic* (Lect. xvii. pp.
320–321; also Appendix to those Lectures, p. 361). He here distinguishes also formal induction from material induction, which
latter he brings under the grasp of syllogism, by an hypothesis
in substance similar to that of Whately. There is, however, in
Lecture xix. (p. 380), a passage in a very different spirit, which
one might almost imagine to have been written by Mr. Mill :—
" In regard to simple syllogisms, it was an original dogma of the
Platonic school, and an early dogma of the Peripatetic, that science,
strictly so called, was only conversant with, and was exclusively
contained in, universals ; and the doctrine of Aristotle, which taught
that all our general knowledge is only an induction from an observation of particulars, was too easily forgotten or perverted by his
followers. It thus obtained almost the force of an acknowledged
principle, that everything to be known must be known under some

the second (Whately) agrees in subordinating Induction to Syllogism, but does so in a different way—by representing inductive reasoning as a syllogism, with its major premiss suppressed, from which major premiss it derived its authority. The explanation of Mr. Mill attacks the problem from the opposite side. It subordinates syllogism to induction, the technical to the real; it divests the major premiss of its illusory pretence to be itself the proving authority, or even any real and essential part of the proof; and acknowledges it merely as a valuable precautionary test and security for avoiding mistake in the process of proving. Taking Mr. Mill's 'System of Logic' as a whole, it is one of the books by which we believe ourselves to have most profited. The principles of it are constantly present to our mind when engaged in investigations of evidence, whether scientific or historical.

Concerned as we are here with Mr. Mill only as a logician and philosopher, we feel precluded from adverting to his

---

general form or notion. Hence the exaggerated importance attributed to definition and deduction; it not being considered that we only take out of a general notion what we had previously placed therein, and that the amplification of our knowledge is not to be sought for from above but from below—not from speculation about abstract generalities, but from the observation of concrete particulars. But however erroneous and irrational, the persuasion had its day and influence, and it perhaps determined, as one of its effects, the total neglect of one half, and that not the least important half, of the reasoning process."

These very just observations are suggested to Sir William Hamilton by a train of thought which has little natural tendency to suggest them, viz., by the distinction upon which he so much insists, between the logic of comprehension and the logic of extension, and by his anxiety to explain why the former had been exclusively cultivated, and the latter neglected.

That which Sir William Hamilton calls here truly the doctrine of Aristotle (at least, in one place at the close of the *Analyt. Post.*), and which he states to have been forgotten by Aristotle's followers, was hardly less forgotten or neglected by Aristotle himself.

works on other topics—even to his 'Elements of Political Economy,' by which he is probably more widely known than by anything else. Of the many obligations which Political Economy owes to him, one only can be noticed consistent with the scope of the present article: the care which he has taken—he alone, or at least, he more explicitly and formally than any other expositor—to set forth the general position of that science in the aggregate field of scientific research; its relation to sociology as a whole, or to other fractions thereof, how far derivative or co-ordinate; what are its fundamental postulates or hypotheses, with what limits the logical methods of induction and deduction are applicable to it, and how far its conclusions may be relied on as approximations to truth. All these points will be found instructively handled in the Sixth Book of Mr. Mill's 'System of Logic,' as well as in his smaller and less known work, 'Essays on Some Unsettled Questions in Political Economy.' We find him, while methodizing and illustrating the data of the special science, uniformly keeping in view its relation to philosophy as a whole.

But there is yet another work in which the interests of philosophy, as a whole, come into the foreground and become the special object of vindication in their largest compass and most vital requirements. We mean Mr. Mill's 'Essay on Liberty,' one half of which takes for its thesis the *libertas philosophandi*. He maintains, emphatically, in this book the full dignity of reasoned truth against all the jealous exigencies of traditional dogma and self-justifying sentiment. He claims the most unreserved liberty of utterance for negative and affirmative on all questions—not merely for the purpose of discriminating truth from falsehood, but also to keep up in individual minds the full sense and understanding of the matters controverted, in place of a mere partial and one-sided adhesion. At first sight, indeed, it might seem as if Mr. Mill was fighting with a shadow; for liberty of philosophizing is a postulate which, in general terms, every one concedes. But when you come to fathom the real feelings which underlie this concession, you discover that almost every man makes it under reserves which, though acting in silence, are not the less efficacious. Every one has some dogmas which he cannot bear to hear advocated, and others which he will not allow to be controverted in his presence. A writer has to consider not merely by what reasons any novelty of belief or disbelief may be justified, but also how much it will be safe for him to publish, having regard to the irritable sore places of the public judgment. In July, 1864, we were present at the annual meeting of the French Academy at Paris, where the prizes for essays sent in, pursuant to subjects announced for study beforehand, are awarded. We heard the titles of various compositions announced by the President (M. Villemain), with a brief critical estimate of each. Their comparative merits were appreciated, and the prize awarded to one of the competitors. Among the compositions sent to compete for the prize, one was a work by M. Taine, upon which the President bestowed the most remarkable encomiums, in every different point of view : extent of knowledge, force of thought, style, arrangement, all were praised in a manner which we have rarely heard exceeded. Nevertheless, the prize was not awarded to this work, but to another which the President praised in a manner decidedly less marked and emphatic. What was here the *ratio decidendi ?* The reason was, and the President declared it in the most explicit language, that the work of M. Taine *was deeply tainted with materialism.* "Sans doute," said the esteemed veteran of French literature in pronouncing his award, "sans doute les opinions sont libres, *mais.*"—It is precisely against this *mais*—ushering in the special anathematised or consecrated conclusion which it is intended to except from the general liberty of enforcing or impugning—in matters of philosophical discussion, that Mr. Mill, in the 'Essay on Liberty,' declares war as champion of Reasoned Truth.

He handles this grand theme—ἐλευθέρους ἐλευθέρως φιλοσοφεῖν—involving as it does the best interests of philosophy, as an instructress to men's judgments, and a stimulus to their intelligence—with great depth of psychological analysis sustained by abundant historical illustration. And he in the same volume discusses most profitably another question akin to it—To what extent and by what principles the interference of others is justifiable, in restraining the liberty of taste and action for each individual? A question at once grave and neglected, but the discussion of which does not belong to our present article.

A new work from one who has already manifested such mastery of philosophy, both in principle and in detail, and a work exhibiting the analysis and appreciation of the philosophical views of an eminent contemporary, must raise the highest expectation. We think no reader will be disappointed who peruses Mr. Mill's 'Examination,' and we shall now endeavour to give some account of the manner in which he performs it. Upon topics so abstract and subtle as the contents of this volume, the antithesis between two rival theories is the best way, and often the only way, for bringing truth into clear view; and the 'Examination' here before us is professedly controversy. But of controversy in its objectionable sense—of captious or acrimonious personality—not a trace will here be found. A dignified, judicial equanimity of tone is preserved from first to last. Moreover, though the title and direct purpose of the volume is negative and critical, yet the destructive criticism is pervaded by many copious veins of constructive exposition, embodying Mr. Mill's own views upon some of the most intricate problems of metaphysics.

Mr. Mill begins his work by analysing and explaining the doctrine called the Relativity of Human Knowledge:—

" The doctrine (chap. ii. p. 5) which is thought to belong in the most especial manner to Sir W. Hamilton, and which was the ground of his opposition to the transcendentalism of the later French and German metaphysicians, is that which he and others have called the Relativity of Human Knowledge. It is the subject of the most generally known and impressive of all his writings—the one which first revealed to the English metaphysical reader that a new power had arisen in philosophy. Together with its developments, it composes the Philosophy of the Conditioned, which he opposed to the French and German philosophies of the Absolute, and which is regarded by most of his admirers as the greatest of his titles to a permanent place in the history of metaphysical thought. But ' the relativity of human knowledge,' like most other phrases into which the words *relative* or *relation* enter, is vague, and admits of a great variety of meanings," &c.

Mr. Mill then proceeds to distinguish these various meanings, and to determine in which of them the phrase is understood by Sir W. Hamilton.

One meaning is, that we only know anything by knowing it as distinguished from something else—that all consciousness is of difference. It is not, however, in this sense that the expression is ordinarily or intentionally used by Sir W. Hamilton, though he fully recognises the truth which, when thus used, it serves to express. In general, when he says that all our knowledge is relative, the relation he has in view is not between the thing known and other objects compared with it, but between the thing known and the mind knowing—(p. 6).

The doctrine in this last meaning is held by different philosophers in two different forms. Some (*e.g.*, Berkeley, Hume, Ferrier, &c.), usually called Idealists, maintain not merely that all we can possibly know of anything is the manner in which it affects the human faculties, but that there is nothing else to be known ; that affections of human or of other minds are all that we can know to exist—that the difference between the ego and the non-ego is only a formal distinction between two aspects of the same reality. Other philosophers (Brown, Mr. Herbert Spencer, Auguste Comte, with many others) believe that the ego and the non-ego denote two realities, each self-existent, and neither dependent on the other ; that the Noumenon, or "thing *per se*," is in itself a different thing from the Phenomenon, and equally or more real, but that, though we know its existence,

u 2

we have no means of knowing what it is. All that we can know is, relatively to ourselves, the modes in which it affects us, or the phenomena which it produces—(pp. 9–11).

The doctrine of Relativity, as held by Kant and his many followers, is next distinguished from the same doctrine as held by Hartley, James Mill, Professor Bain, &c., compatible with either acceptance or rejection of the Berkeleian theory. Kant maintains that the attributes which we ascribe to outward things, or which are inseparable from them in thought, contain additional elements, over and above sensations *plus* an unknowable cause—additional elements added by the mind itself, and therefore still only relative, but constituting the original furniture of the mind itself—inherent laws, partly of our sensitive, partly of our intellectual faculty. It is on this latter point that Hartley and those going along with him diverge. Admitting the same additional elements, these philosophers do not ascribe to the mind any innate forms to account for them, but hold that Place, Extension, Substance, Cause, and the rest, &c., are conceptions put together out of ideas of sensation, by the known laws of Association—(pp. 12–14.)

Partial Relativity is the opinion professed by most philosophers (and by most persons who do not philosophise). They hold that we know things partly as they are in themselves, partly as they are merely in relation to us.

This discrimination of the various schools of philosophers is highly instructive, and is given with the full perspicuity belonging to Mr. Mill's style. He proceeds to examine in what sense Sir W. Hamilton maintained the Relativity of Human Knowledge. He cites passages both from the 'Discussions on Philosophy' and from the Lectures, in which that doctrine is both affirmed in its greatest amplitude, and enunciated in the most emphatic language—(pp. 17, 88, 22, 23.) But he also produces extracts from the most elaborate of Sir W. Hamilton's 'Dissertations on Reid,' in which a doctrine quite different and inconsistent is proclaimed—that our knowledge is only partially, not wholly, relative; that the secondary qualities of matter, indeed, are known to us only relatively, but that the primary qualities are known to us as they are in themselves, or as they exist objectively, and that they may be even evolved by demonstration *à priori*—(pp. 19–26, 30). The inconsistency between the two doctrines, professed at different times and in different works by Sir W. Hamilton, is certainly manifest. Mr. Mill is of opinion that one of the two must be taken " in a non-natural sense," and that Sir W. Hamilton either did not hold, or had ceased to hold, the doctrine of the full relativity of knowledge, (pp. 20–28)—the hypothesis of a flat contradiction being in his view inadmissible. But we think it at least equally possible that Sir W. Hamilton held both the two opinions in their natural sense, and enforced both of them *at different times* by argument; his attention never having been called to the contradiction between them. That such forgetfulness was quite possible, will appear clearly in many parts of the present article. His argument in support of both is equally characterised by that peculiar energy of style which is frequent with him, and which no way resembles the qualifying refinements of one struggling to keep clear of a perceived contradiction.

From hence Mr. Mill (chap. iv.) proceeds to criticise at considerable length what he justly denominates the celebrated and striking review of Cousin's philosophy, which forms the first paper in Sir W. Hamilton's ' Discussions on Philosophy.' According to Mr. Mill—

" The question really at issue is this : Have we or have we not an immediate intuition of God ?   The name of God is veiled under two extremely abstract phrases, ' The Infinite and the Absolute,' perhaps from a reverential feeling; such, at least, is the reason given by Sir W. Hamilton's disciple, Mr. Mansel, for preferring the more vague expressions; but it is one of the most unquestionable of all logical maxims, that the meaning of the abstract must be sought for in the concrete, and not conversely : and we shall see, both in the case of Sir William Hamilton and of Mr. Mansel, that the process cannot be reversed with impunity."—p. 32.

Upon this we must remark, that though the "logical maxim" here laid down by Mr. Mill may be generally sound, we think the application of it inconvenient in the present case. Discussions on points of philosophy are best conducted without either invoking or offending religious feeling. M. Cousin maintains that we have a direct intuition of the Infinite and the Absolute: Sir W. Hamilton denies that we have. Upon this point Mr. Mill sides entirely with Sir W. Hamilton, and considers "that the latter has rendered good service to philosophy by refuting M. Cousin," though much of the reasoning employed in such refutation seems to Mr. Mill unsound. But Sir W. Hamilton goes further, and affirms that we have no faculties capable of apprehending the Infinite and the Absolute—that both of them are inconceivable to us, and by consequence unknowable. Herein Mr. Mill is opposed to him, and controverts his doctrine in an elaborate argument.

Of this argument, able and ingenious, like all those in the present volume, our limits only enable us to give a brief appreciation. In so far as Mr. Mill controverts Sir W. Hamilton, we think him perfectly successful, though there are some points of his reasoning in which we do not fully concur.

In our opinion, as in his, the Absolute alone (in its sense as opposed to relative) can be declared necessarily unknowable, inconceivable, incogitable. Nothing which falls under the condition of relativity can be declared to be so. The structure of our minds renders us capable of knowing everything which is relative, though there are many such things which we have no evidence, nor shall ever get evidence, to enable us to know. Now the Infinite falls within the conditions of relativity, as indeed Sir W. Hamilton himself admits, when he intimates (p. 58) that though it cannot be known, it is, must be, and ought to be, *believed* by us, according to the marked distinction which he draws between belief and knowledge. We agree with Mr. Mill in the opinion that it is thinkable, conceivable, knowable. Doubtless we do not conceive it adequately, but we conceive it sufficiently to discuss and reason upon it intelligibly to ourselves and others. That we conceive the Infinite inadequately, is not to be held as proof that we do not conceive it at all; for in regard to finite things also, we conceive the greater number of them only inadequately.

We cannot construe to the imagination a polygon with an infinite number of sides (*i.e.*, with a number of sides greater than any given number), but neither can we construe to the imagination a polygon with a million of sides; nevertheless, we understand what is meant by the first description as well as by the second, and can reason upon both. There is, indeed, this difference between the two: That the terms used in describing the first proclaim at once in their direct meaning that we should in vain attempt to construe it to the imagination; whereas the terms used in describing the second do not intimate that fact. We know the fact only by trial, or by an estimate of our own mental force which is the result of many past trials. If the difference here noted were all which Sir W. Hamilton has in view when he declares the Infinite to be unknowable and incogitable, we should accede to his opinion; but we apprehend that he means much more, and he certainly requires more to justify the marked antithesis in which he places himself against M. Cousin and Hegel. Indeed, the facility with which he declares matters to be incogitable, which these two and other philosophers not only cogitate but maintain as truth, is to us truly surprising. The only question which appears to us important is, whether we can understand and reason upon the meaning of the terms and propositions addressed to us. If we can, the subjects propounded must be cogitable and conceivable, whether we admit the propositions affirmed concerning them or not; if we cannot, then these subjects are indeed incogitable by ourselves in the present state of our knowledge, but they may not be so to our opponent who employs the terms.

In criticising the arguments of Sir W. Hamilton against

M. Cousin, Mr. Mill insists much on a distinction between
(1) the Infinite, and (2) the Infinite in any one or more
positive attributes, such as infinite wisdom, goodness, redness,
hardness, &c.* He thinks that Sir W. Hamilton has made
out his case against the first, but not against the last; that
the first is really "an unmeaning and senseless abstraction,"
a fasciculus of negations, unknowable and inconceivable, but
not the last. We think that Mr. Mill makes more of this
distinction than the case warrants; that the first is not unmeaning, but an intelligible abstraction, only a higher reach
of abstraction, than the last; that it is knowable inadequately,
in the same way as the last, though more inadequately, because of its higher abstraction.

As the Finite is intelligible, so also is its negation—the
Infinite: we do not say (with M. Cousin) that the two are
conjointly given in consciousness, but the two are understood and partially apprehended by the mind, conjointly and
in contrast. Though the Infinite is doubtless negative as
to degree, it is not wholly or exclusively negative, since it
includes a necessary reference to some positive attribute,
to which the degree belongs; the positive element is not
eliminated, but merely left undetermined. The Infinite
(like the Finite, τὸ πεπερασμένον—τὸ ἄπειρον) is a genus;
it comprehends under it the Infinitely Hard and the Infinitely Soft, the Infinitely Swift and the Infinitely Slow
—the infinite, in short, of any or all positive attributes.
It includes, doubtless, "a farrago of contradictions;" but
so, also, does the Finite; and so, also, do the actual manifestations of the real, concrete universe, which manifestations constitute a portion of the Finite. Whoever
attempts to give any philosophical account of the generation of the universe, tracing its phenomena as an aggregate, to some ultra-phenomenal origin, must include

---

* The distinction is given by Stier and other logicians. 1. Infinitum simpliciter. 2. Infinitum secundum quid, sive in certo
genere.

in his scheme a *fundamentum* for all those opposite and contradictory manifestations which experience discloses in the universe. There always have been, and still are, many philosophers who consider the Abstract and General to be prior both in nature and time to the Concrete and Particular; and who hold further that these two last are explained, when presented as determinate and successive manifestations of the two first, which they conceive as indeterminate and sempiternal. Now the Infinite (ens Infinitum or entia Infinita, according to the point of view in which we look at it) is a generic word, including all these supposed indeterminate antecedents; and including therefore, of course, many contradictory agencies. But this does not make it senseless or unmeaning; nor can we distinguish it from "the Infinite in some one or more given attributes," by any other character than by greater reach of abstraction. We cannot admit the marked distinction which Mr. Mill contends for—that the one is unknowable and the other knowable.

It may be proper to add, that the mode of philosophising which we have just described is not ours. We do not agree in this way either of conceiving, or of solving, the problem of philosophy. But it is a mode so prevalent that Trendelenberg speaks of it, justly enough, as "the ancient Hysteron-Proteron of Abstraction." The doctrine of these philosophers appears to us unfounded, but we cannot call it unmeaning.

In another point, also, we differ from Mr. Mill respecting that inferior abstraction which he calls "the Infinite in some particular attribute." He speaks as if this could be known not only as an abstraction, a conceivable, an ideal, but also as a concrete reality; as if " we could know a concrete reality as infinite or as absolute" (p. 45); as if there really existed in actual nature "concrete persons or things possessing infinitely or absolutely certain specific attributes"—(pp. 55–93). To this doctrine we cannot subscribe. As we understand concrete reality, we find no evidence to believe that there exist in nature any real concrete persons or things,

possessing to an infinite degree such attributes as they do
possess : *e. g.*, any men infinitely wise or infinitely strong,
any horses infinitely swift, any stones infinitely hard.   Such
concrete real objects appear to us not admissible, because
experience not only has not certified their existence in any
single case, but goes as far to disprove their existence as it
can do to disprove anything.   All the real objects in nature
known to us by observation are finite, and possess only
in a finite measure their respective attributes.   Upon this is
founded the process of Science, so comprehensively laid out
by Mr. Mill in his ' System of Logic'—Induction, Deduction
from general facts attested by Induction, Verification by experience of the results obtained by Deduction.   The attributes, whiteness or hardness, in the abstract, are doubtless
infinite ; that is, the term will designate, alike and equally,
any degree of whiteness or hardness which you may think
of, and any unknown degree even whiter and harder than
what you think of.   But when perceived as invested in a
given mass of snow or granite before us, they are divested
of that indeterminateness, and become restricted to a determinate measure and degree.

Having thus indicated the points on which we are compelled to dissent from Mr. Mill's refutation of Sir W.
Hamilton in the pleading against M. Cousin, we shall pass
to the seventh chapter, in which occurs his first controversy
with Mr. Mansel.   This passage has excited more interest,
and will probably be remembered by a larger number of
readers, than any portion of the book.   We shall give it in
his own words (pp. 99–103), since the energetic phraseology
is quite as remarkable as the thought:—

" There is but one way for Mr. Mansel out of this difficulty, and
he adopts it.   He must maintain not merely that an Absolute Being
is unknowable in himself, but that the Relative attributes of an
Absolute Being are unknowable also.*   He must say that we do

---

* This doctrine has been affirmed (so far as reason is concerned,
apart from revelation) not merely by Mr. Mansel, but also by Pascal,

not know what Wisdom, Justice, Benevolence, Mercy, &c., are, as they exist in God. Accordingly, he does say so. 'It is a fact,' says Mr. Mansel, 'which experience forces upon us, and which it is useless, were it possible, to disguise, that the representation of God after the model of the highest human morality which we are capable of conceiving, is not sufficient to account for all the phenomena exhibited by the course of His natural Providence. The infliction of physical suffering, the permission of moral evil, the adversity of the good, the prosperity of the wicked, the crimes of the guilty involving the misery of the innocent, the tardy appearance and partial distribution of moral and religious knowledge in the world—these are facts which no doubt are reconcileable, we know not how, with the Infinite Goodness of God, but which certainly are not to be explained on the supposition that its sole and sufficient type is to be found in the finite goodness of man.'

"In other words," continues Mr. Mill, commenting, "it is necessary to suppose that the infinite goodness ascribed to God is not the goodness which we know and love in our fellow-creatures, distinguished only as infinite in degree; but is different in kind, and another quality altogether. Accordingly Mr. Mansel combats as a heresy of his opponents, the opinion that infinite goodness differs only in degree from finite goodness.—Here, then, I take my stand upon the acknowledged principle of logic and of morality; that when we mean different things we have no right to call them by the same name, and to apply to them the same predicates, moral and intellectual. If instead of the glad tidings that there exists a Being in whom all the excellencies which the highest human mind can conceive, exist in a degree inconceivable to us, I am informed that the world is ruled by a Being whose attributes are infinite, but what they are we cannot learn, except that the highest human morality does not sanction them—convince me of this, and I will bear my fate as I may. But when I am told that I must believe this, and at the same time call this Being by the names which

---

one of the most religious philosophers of the seventeenth century, in the *Pensées* :—

"Parlons selon les lumières naturelles. S'il y a un Dieu, il est infiniment incompréhensible ; puisque, n'ayant ni principes ni bornes, il n'a nul rapport à nous ; nous sommes donc incapables de connaître ni ce qu'il est, ni s'il est." (See Arago, *Biographie de Condorcet*, p. lxxxiv., prefixed to his edition of Condorcet's works).

express and affirm the highest human morality, I say, in plain terms, that I will not. Whatever power such a Being may have over me, there is one thing which he shall not do; he shall not compel me to worship him. I will call no being good, who is not what I mean when I apply that epithet to my fellow-creatures; and if such a being can sentence me to hell for not so calling him, to hell I will go."

This concluding declaration is memorable in many ways. Mr. Mill announces his resolution to determine for himself, and according to his own reason and conscience, what God he will worship, and what God he will not worship. For ourselves, we cordially sympathize with his resolution. But Mr. Mill must be aware that this is a point on which society is equally resolved that no individual shall determine for himself, if they can help it.* Each new-born child finds his religious creed ready prepared for him. In his earliest days

---

* The indictment under which Socrates was condemned at Athens, as reported by Xenophon at the commencement of the *Memorabilia*, ran thus :—" Socrates is guilty of crime, inasmuch as he does not believe in those Gods in whom the City believes, but introduces other novelties in regard to the Gods ; he is guilty also, inasmuch as he corrupts the youth."

These words express clearly a sentiment entertained, not merely by the Athenian people, but generally by other societies also. They all agree in antipathy to free, individual, dissenting reason, though that antipathy manifests itself by acts, more harsh in one place, less harsh in another. The Hindoo who declares himself a convert to Christianity, becomes at the same time an outcast (ἀφρήτωρ, ἀθέμιστος, ἀνέστιος) among those whose Gods he has deserted. As a general fact, the man who dissents from his fellows upon fundamentals of religion, purchases an undisturbed life only by being content with that " semi-liberty under silence and concealment," for which Cicero was thankful under the dictatorship of Julius Cæsar. " Obsecro—abjiciamus ista, et semi-liberi saltem simus ; quod assequemur *et tacendo et latendo*" (*Epist. ad Attic.* xiii. 31). Contrast with this the memorable declaration of Socrates, in the Platonic *Apology*, that silence and abstinence from cross-examination were intolerable to him ; that life would not be worth having under such conditions.

of unconscious infancy, the stamp of the national, gentile, phratric, God, or Gods, is imprinted upon him by his elders ; and if the future man, in the exercise of his own independent reason, acquires such convictions as compel him to renounce those Gods, proclaiming openly that he does so—he must count upon such treatment as will go far to spoil the value of the present life to him, even before he passes to those ulterior liabilities which Mr. Mill indicates in the distance. We are not surprised that a declaration so unusual and so impressive should have been often cited in critical notices of this volume; that during the month preceding the last Westminster election, it was studiously brought forward by some opponents of Mr. Mill, and more or less regretted by his friends, as likely to offend many electors, and damage his chance of success; and that a conspicuous and noble minded ecclesiastic, the Dean of Westminster, thought the occasion so grave as to come forward with his characteristic generosity for the purpose of shielding a distinguished man suspected of heresy.

The sublime self-assertion, addressed by Prometheus to Zeus, under whose sentence he was groaning, has never before been put into such plain English.* Mr. Mill's declaration reminds us also of Hippolytus, the chaste and pure youth, whose tragic fate is so beautifully described by Euripides. Hippolytus is exemplary in his devotions to the Goddess

---

* *Æschyl. Prometh.* 996–1006 :—

πρὸς ταῦτα, ῥιπτέσθω μὲν αἰθαλοῦσσα φλόξ,
λευκοπτέρῳ δὲ νιφάδι καὶ βροντήμασιν
χθονίοις κυκάτω πάντα καὶ ταρασσέτω·
γνάμψει γὰρ οὐδὲν τῶνδέ μ'——
εἰσελθέτω σε μήποθ', ὡς ἐγὼ, Διὸς
γνώμην φοβηθεὶς, θηλύνους γενήσομαι,
καὶ λιπαρήσω τὸν μέγα στυγούμενον
γυναικομίμοις ὑπτιάσμασιν χερῶν,
λῦσαί με δεσμῶν τῶνδε· τοῦ παντὸς δέω.

Also v. 1047, et seq. The memorable ode of Goethe, entitled *Prometheus*, embodies a similar vein of sentiment in the finest poetry.

Artemis; but he dissents from all his countrymen, and determines for himself, in refusing to bestow the smallest mark of honour or worship upon Aphrodite, because he considers her to be a very bad Goddess.* In this refusal he persists with inflexible principle (even after having received, from an anxious attendant, warning of the certain ruin which it will bring upon him), until the insulted Aphrodite involves him along with the unhappy Phædra and Theseus himself, in one common abyss of misery. In like manner, Mr. Mill's declaration stands in marked contrast with the more cautious proceeding of men like Herodotus. That historian, alike pious and prudent, is quite aware that all the Gods are envious and mischief-making, and expressly declares them to be so.† Yet, far from refusing to worship them on that account, he is assiduous in prayer and sacrifice—perhaps, indeed, all the more assiduous from what he believes about their attributes ;‡ being persuaded (like the attendant who warned Hippolytus) that his only chance of mollifying their ungentle dispositions in regard to himself is, by honorific tribute in words and offerings.

When, however, after appreciating as we are bound to do, Mr. Mill's declaration of subjective sentiment, we pass to its

---

* Euripid. *Hippol.* 10 :—

> Aph. ὁ γάρ με Θησέως ταῖς, 'Αμάζονος τόκος,
> μόνος πολιτῶν τῆσδε γῆς Τροιζηνίας
> λέγει κακίστην δαιμόνων πεφυκέναι·
> Φοίβου δ' ἀδελφὴν "Αρτεμιν . . . . .
> τιμᾷ, μεγίστην δαιμόνων ἡγούμενος·

Hipp. τὴν σὴν δὲ Κύπριν πόλλ' ἐγὼ χαίρειν λέγω.—(112.) See also v. 1328–1402.

† Herodot. i. 32. 'Ω Κροῖσε, ἐπιστάμενον με τὸ θεῖον πᾶν ἐὸν φθονερόν τε καὶ ταραχῶδες, ἐπειρωτᾷς ἀνθρωπηΐων πρηγμάτων πέρι; also iii. 40.

‡ See Eurip. *Hipp.* 6–96–140. The language of the attendant, after his affectionate remonstrance to Hippolytus had been disregarded, supplicating Aphrodite to pardon the recalcitrancy of that virtuous but obstinate youth, is characteristic and touching (114–120).

logical bearing on the controversy between him and Mr. Mansel, we are obliged to confess that in this point of view it has little objective relevancy. The problem was, how to reconcile the actual evil and suffering in the universe (which is recited as a fact by Mr. Mansel, though in terms conveying a most inadequate idea of its real magnitude) with the goodness of God. Mr. Mill repudiates the explanatory hypothesis tendered by Mr. Mansel as a solution, but without suggesting any better hypothesis of his own. For ourselves, we are far from endorsing Mr. Mansel's solution as satisfactory; yet we can hardly be surprised if he considers it less unsatisfactory than no solution at all. And when we reflect how frequently and familiarly predicates applicable to man are applied to the Supreme Being, when they cannot possibly be understood about Him in the same sense, we see no ground for treating the proceeding as disingenuous, which Mr. Mill is disposed to do. Indeed, it cannot easily be avoided: and Mr. Mill himself furnishes us with some examples in the present volume. At page 491, he says :—

" It would be difficult to find a stronger argument in favour of Theism, than that the eye must have been made by one who sees, and the ear by one who hears."

In the words here employed, *seeing* and *hearing* are predicated of God.

Now when we predicate of men, that they *see* or *hear*, we affirm facts of extreme complexity, especially in the case of *seeing*; facts partly physical, partly mental, involving multifarious movements and agencies of nerves, muscles, and other parts of the organism, together with direct sensational impressions, and mental reconstruction of the past, inseparably associated therewith; all which, so far as they are known, are perspicuously enumerated in the work of Professor Bain * on the 'Senses and the Intellect.' Again, Mr.

---

* See especially his chapter ii. 'On the Sensations of Sight,' pp. 222, 241-247, in the second edition of this work.

conducting such interpretation; for the number of different modes in which Consciousness has been interpreted is astonishing. Mr. Mill begins by citing from Sir W. Hamilton's lectures a passage of some length, upon which he bestows considerable praise, regarding it as—

" One of the proofs that, whatever may be the positive value of his (Sir W. Hamilton's) achievements in metaphysics, he had a greater capacity for the subject than many metaphysicians of high reputation; and particularly than his two distinguished predecessors in the same school of thought—' Reid and Stewart.' "—p. 131.

This is one of the greatest compliments to Sir W. Hamilton that the book contains, and as such we are glad to cite it.

On the subject of Consciousness, Mr. Mill has cited from Sir W. Hamilton other good observations besides the one last alluded to; but, unfortunately, these are often neutralised by opposite or inconsistent opinions also cited from other parts of his works. The number of such inconsistencies produced is indeed one remarkable feature in Sir W. Hamilton's philosophical character. He seems to follow out energetically (as Plato in his various dialogues) the vein of thought pervading his mind at each particular moment, without troubling himself to look back upon his own prior speculations. Even compared with the best views of Sir W. Hamilton, however, Mr. Mill's mode of handling the subject of Consciousness exhibits signal improvement. To some of his observations we shall call particular attention.

All philosophers agree that what Consciousness testifies is to be believed; but they differ much on the question—To what points Consciousness does testify? and even on the still deeper question—How shall we proceed to ascertain what *are* these attested points? What is the proper method of studying or interrogating Consciousness? Upon this, Mr. Mill remarks (pp. 145–147) :—

" Here emerges the distinction between two different methods of studying the problems of metaphysics; forming the radical dif-

X

" ' The proof that any of the alleged Universal Beliefs, or Principles of Common Sense, are affirmations of Consciousness, supposes two things : that the beliefs exist, and that they cannot possibly have been acquired. The first is, in most cases, undisputed ; but the second is a subject of enquiry which often taxes the utmost resources of psychologists. Locke was therefore right in believing that ' the origin of our ideas ' is the main stress of the problem of mental science, and the subject which must be first considered in forming the theory of the Mind.' "

This citation from Mr. Mill's book is already almost too long, yet we could have wished to prolong it still more, from the importance of some of the succeeding paragraphs. It presents, in clear discrimination and contrast, two opposite points of view according to which the phenomena of mind are regarded by different philosophers, and the method of studying them determined: the *introspective* method, adopted by M. Cousin and others—the *psychological* or analytical method, pursued by Locke and by many other eminent men since Locke—"the known and approved method of physical science, adapted to the necessities of psychology "—(p. 148.)

There are passages of Sir W. Hamilton's writings in which he appears to feel that the *introspective* method alone is insufficient for the interpretation of Consciousness, and that the analytical method must be employed to reinforce it. But on this as on other points, he is not always consistent with himself. For in laying down the principle upon which the primary truths of Consciousness, the original data of intelligence, are to be ascertained and distinguished from generalizations out of experience and custom, he declares that the one single and certain mark is Necessity; they must be beliefs which we are under the necessity of believing —of which we cannot get rid by any mental effort. He decides this, of course, for himself, by the *introspective* method alone. He (with M. Cousin and other philosophers who take the same view) does not apply the analytical method to enquire whether his necessity of belief may not be a purely acquired necessity, and nowise congenital. It is, indeed, remarkable that these philosophers do not even seek to apply the introspective method as far as that method will really go. They are satisfied with introspection of their own present minds, without obtaining results of the like process, as applied to other minds, in different times and places. They declare various beliefs to be necessary to the human mind universally, merely because such is the actual fact with their own minds and with those immediately around them; sometimes even in defiance of proof that there are (or have been) persons not sharing such beliefs, and occasionally even believing the contrary; therefore, when even the introspective method really disallows their affirmative instead of sustaining it. This is, in truth, an abuse of the introspective method; yet, even if that method were employed in its fullest extent—if the same incapability of believing otherwise could be shown as common to all mankind—it might still be only the effect of a strong association. The analytical method must still be called in to ascertain whether we are forced to suppose such incapability to be an original fact of consciousness, or whether it may not have been generated in the mind by circumstances, under the natural working of the laws of association. It is certain that these laws not only may, but must, give birth to artificial inconceivabilities in the mind; and that some of these may be equal in strength to such, if any, as are natural.

" The History of Science," says Mr. Mill, following out the same train of reasoning which we read in the third book of his *System of Logic*, " teems with inconceivabilities which have been conquered; and with supposed necessary truths, which have first ceased to be thought necessary, then to be thought true, and have finally come to be deemed impossible."—p. 150.

After various observations, chiefly exhibiting the rashness of many censures bestowed by Sir W. Hamilton on Brown, Mr. Mill gives us three valuable chapters (xi., xii., xiii.), wherein he analyses the Belief in an External World, the Belief in Mind as a separate Substance or Noumenon, and the Primary Qualities of Matter. To each of these topics he applies what he calls the *psychological* method, as contrasted with the simply *introspective* method of Sir W. Hamilton (the Ego and Non-Ego affirmed to be given together in the primary deliverance of Consciousness) and so many other philosophers. He proves that these beliefs are noway intuitive, but acquired products; and that the known laws of Association are sufficient to explain how they are acquired; especially the Law of Inseparable Association, together with that of *Obliviscence*—a very useful, discriminating phrase, which we first find employed in this volume (p. 259 et passim). He defines Matter to be a *permanent possibility of Sensation;* he maintains that this is really all which (apart from philosophical theories) mankind in general mean by it; he shows that mere possibilities of sensation not only may, but must, according to the known Laws of Association, come to present " to our artificialized Consciousness " a character of objectivity—(pp. 198, 199). The correlating subject, though present in fact and indispensable, is eliminated out of conscious notice, according to the Law of Obliviscence.

These chapters will well repay the most careful perusal. We can only find room for one passage (pp. 214, 215):—

" Throughout the whole of our sensitive life, except its first beginnings, we unquestionably refer our sensations to a *me* and a *not-me.* As soon as I have formed, on the one hand, the notion of Permanent Possibilities of Sensation, and on the other, of that continued series of feelings which I call my life—both these notions are, by an irresistible association, recalled by every sensation I have. They represent two things, with both of which the sensation of the moment, be it what it may, stands in relation; and I cannot be conscious of the sensation without being conscious of it, as related to these two things. They have accordingly received relative names, expressive of the double relation in question. The thread of consciousness which I apprehend the relation as a part of, is called the *Subject;* the group of Permanent Possibilities of Sensation to which I refer it, and which is partially realised and actualised in it, is called the *Object* of the sensation. The sensation itself ought to have a correlative name, or rather ought to have two such names — one denoting the sensation as opposed to its Subject, the other denoting it as opposed to its Object; but it is a remarkable fact that this necessity has not been felt, and that the need of a correlative name to every relative one has been considered to be satisfied by the terms Object and Subject themselves. It is true that these two are related to one another, but only through the sensation. We have no conception of either Subject or Object, either Mind or Matter, except as something to which we refer our sensations, and whatever other feelings we are conscious of. *The very existence of them both, so far as cognisable by us, consists only in the relation they respectively bear to our states of feeling.* Their relation to each other is only the relation between those two relations. The immediate correlatives are, not the pair, *Object, Subject,* but the two pairs, Object, *Sensation objectively considered* — Subject, *Sensation subjectively considered.* The reason why this is overlooked might easily be shewn, and would furnish a good illustration of that important part of the Laws of Association, which may be termed the Laws of Obliviscence."

This chapter, on the Primary Qualities of Matter, controverts the opinion of Sir W. Hamilton, that extension, as consisting of coexistent *partes extra partes*, is immediately and necessarily apprehended by our consciousness. It cites, as well as confirms, the copious proof given by Professor Bain (in his work on the Senses and the Intellect) that our conception of extension is derived from our muscular sensibility: that our sensation of *muscular motion unimpeded* constitutes our notion of empty space, as our sensation of *muscular motion impeded* constitutes that of filled space: 'that our conception of extension, as an aggregate of coexistent parts, arises from the sense of sight, which comprehends a great number of parts in a succession so raipd as to be confounded with simultaneity; and which not only becomes the symbol of muscular and tactile succession, but even acquires such ascendency as to supersede both of them in our consciousness. Confirmation is here given to this important doctrine, not merely by observations from Mr. Mill himself, but also from the very curious narrative, discovered and produced by Sir W. Hamilton, out of a work of the German philosopher, Platner. Platner instituted a careful examination of a man born blind, and ascertained that this man did not conceive extension as an aggregate of simultaneous parts, but as a series of sensations experienced or to be experienced in succession—(pp. 232, 233). The case reported from Platner both corroborates the theory of Professor Bain, and receives its proper interpretation from that theory; while it is altogether adverse to the doctrine of Sir W. Hamilton—as is also another case, which he cites from Maine de Biran:—

" It gives a very favourable idea of Sir W. Hamilton's sincerity and devotion to truth," remarks Mr. Mill, p. 247, " that he should have drawn from obscurity, and made generally known, two cases so unfavourable to his own opinions."

We think this remark perfectly just; and we would point out besides, in appreciating Sir W. Hamilton's merits, that his appetite for facts was useful to philosophy, as well as his appetite for speculation. But the person whose usefulness to philosophy we prefer to bring into the foreground, is Platner himself. He spent three weeks in patient examination of this blind man, and the tenor of his report proves that his sagacity in interpreting facts was equal to his patience in collecting them. The rarity of all such careful and premeditated observation of the facts of mind, appears to us one main reason why (what Mr. Mill calls) the *psychological* theory finds so little acceptance; and why those who maintain that what now seems a mental integer was once a multiplicity of separate mental fragments, can describe the antecedent steps of the change only as a *latens processus*, which the reader never fully understands, and often will not admit. Every man's mind is gradually built up from infancy to maturity; the process is always going on before our eyes, yet the stages of it—especially the earliest stages, the most pregnant with instruction—are never studied and put on record by observers trained in inductive logic knowing beforehand what they ought to look for as the *sine quâ non* for proving or disproving any proposed theory. Such cases as that cited by Platner—cases of one marked congenital defect of sense, enabling us to apply the Method of Difference —are always within reach; but few Platners are found to scrutinise and record them. Historians of science describe to us the laborious and multiplied observations, and the elaborate precautions for ensuring accuracy of observation, which recent chemical and physical enquirers have found indispensable for the establishing of their results. We cannot, therefore, be surprised that mental philosophers, dealing with facts even more obscure, and careless about enlarging, varying, authenticating their records of particular facts, should have had little success in establishing any results at all.

But if even those, who adopt the psychological theory, have been remiss in the observation of particular mental facts, those who deny the theory have been far more than remiss; they have been blind to obvious facts contradicting the principles which they lay down. Mr. Mill, in chap. xiv., deals with this denial, common to Mr. Mansel with Sir W. Hamilton. That philosophers so eminent as both of them should declare confidently—" what I cannot but think, must be *à priori*, or original to thought; it cannot be engendered by experience upon custom " (p. 264)—appears to us as extraordinary as it does to Mr. Mill. Though no one ever surpassed Sir W. Hamilton in large acquaintance with the actual diversities of human belief, and human incapacities of believing—yet he never seems to have thought of bringing this acquaintance into account, when he assured the students in his lecture-room that custom, experience, indissoluble association, were altogether insufficient to engender a felt necessity of believing. Such forgetfulness of well-known mental facts cannot be reproached to the advocates of the psychological theory.

In chap. xv., Mr. Mill examines Sir W. Hamilton's doctrine on unconscious mental modifications. He points out the confused manner in which Sir W. Hamilton has conceived

mental latency, as well as the inconclusive character of the reasoning whereby he refutes the following doctrine of Dugald Stewart—That in the most rapid trains of association, each separate item must have been successively present to consciousness, though for a time too short to leave any memory. Sir W. Hamilton thinks that the separate items may pass, and often do pass, unconsciously; which opinion Mr. Mill also, though not approving his reasons, is inclined to adopt.

" I am myself inclined (p. 285) to admit unconscious mental modifications, in the only sense in which I can attach any very distinct meaning to them, namely, unconscious modifications of the nerves. It may well be believed that the apparently suppressed links in a chain of association, those which Sir W. Hamilton considers as latent, really are so : that they are not even momentarily felt, the chain of causation being continued only physically — by one organic state of the nerves succeeding another so rapidly that the state of mental consciousness appropriate to each is not produced."

Mr. Mill gives various illustrations in support of this doctrine. He at the same time calls attention to a valuable lecture of Sir W. Hamilton's, the thirty-second lecture on Metaphysics; especially to the instructive citation from Cardaillac contained therein, noting the important fact, which descriptions of the Law of Association often keep out of sight—that the suggestive agency of Association is carried on, not by single antecedents raising up single consequents, but by a mass of antecedents raising up simultaneously a mass of consequents, among which attention is very unequally distributed.

We shall say little upon Mr. Mill's remarks on Sir W. Hamilton's Theory of Causation—(chap. xvi.). This theory appears to Mr. Mill absurd; while the theory of Mr. Mill (continued from Hume, Brown, and James Mill) on the same subject appears to Sir W. Hamilton insufficient and unsatisfactory—" professing to explain the phenomenon of causality, but previously to explanation, evacuating the phenomenon

of all that desiderates explanation "—(p. 295). For ourselves, we embrace the theory of Mr. Mill:* yet we are
aware that the remark just cited from Sir W. Hamilton represents the dissatisfaction entertained towards it by many
objectors. The unscientific and antiscientific yearnings prevalent among mankind lead them to put questions which
no sound theory of Causation will answer; and they
are ready to visit and trust any oracle which professes
to deliver a confident affirmative solution of such questions. Among all the terms employed by metaphysicians,

---

* At the same time we cannot go along with Mr. Mill in the
following affirmation (p. 201) :—

" This natural probability is converted into certainty when we
take into consideration that universal law of our experience which
is termed the Law of Causation, and which makes us *unable to
conceive the beginning of anything without* an antecedent condition
or cause."

Such " inability to conceive " appears to us not in correspondence
with facts. First, it cannot be properly either affirmed or denied,
until agreement is obtained what the word *cause* means. If
three persons, A, B, and C, agree in affirming it—A adopting the
meaning of Aristotle, B that of Sir William Hamilton, and C that
of Mr. Mill—the agreement is purely verbal; or rather, all three
concur in having a mental exigency pressing for satisfaction, but
differ as to the hypothesis which satisfies it.

Next, if we reason upon Mr. Mill's theory as to Cause, certainly
those who deny his theory can have no difficulty in conceiving
events without any cause (in that sense); nor have those who adopt
his theory any greater difficulty. These last *believe* that there are,
throughout, constant and uniform conditions on which the occurrence of every event depends; but they can perfectly *conceive* events
as occurring without any such uniform sequence. In truth, the
belief in such causation, as pervading *all nature,* is an acquired
result of scientific training. The greater part of mankind believe
that some events occur in regular, others in irregular, succession.
Moreover, a full half of the metaphysical world espouse the doctrine
of free-will, and consider that all volitions occur without any cause
at all.

none is used in a greater variety of meanings than the term Cause.

In Mr. Mill's next chapter (xvi.), he comments on Sir W. Hamilton's doctrine of Concepts or General Notions. There are portions of this chapter with which we agree less than with most other parts of the volume; especially with his marked hostility to the term *Concept*, and the reasons given for it; which reasons appear to us not very consistent with what he has himself said in the 'System of Logic,' Book IV. ch. ii. § 1–3. The term *Concept* has no necessary connexion with the theory called Conceptualism. It is equally available to designate the idea called up by a general name, as understood either by Mr. Bailey or by James Mill. We think it useful as an equivalent to the German word *Begriff*, which sense Sir W. Hamilton has in view when he introduces it, though he does not always adhere to his profession. And when Mr. Mill says (p. 331)—

" I consider it nothing less than a misfortune, that the words Concept, General Notion, or any other phrase to express the supposed mental modification corresponding to a general name, should ever have been invented,"

we dissent from his opinion. To talk of "the Concept of an individual," however, as Mr. Mansel does (pp. 338, 339), is improper and inconsistent with the purpose for which the name is given.

We are more fully in harmony with Mr. Mill in his two next chapters (xviii. et seq.) on Judgment and Reasoning; which are among the best chapters in the volume. He there combats and overthrows the theory of Reasoning laid down by Sir W. Hamilton; but we doubt the propriety of his calling this "the Conceptualist theory" (pp. 367, 368): since it has nothing to do with Conceptualism, in the special sense of antithesis to Realism and Nominalism,—but is, in fact, the theory of the Syllogism as given in the Analytics of Aristotle, and generally admitted since. Not merely Conceptualists, but (to use Mr Mill's own language, p. 366) "nearly all the writers on logic, taught a theory of the science too small and narrow to contain their own facts." Such, indeed, was the theory constantly taught until the publication of Mr. Mill's 'System of Logic;' the first two books of which corrected it, by arguments which are reinforced and amplified in these two chapters on Judgment and Reasoning, as well as in the two chapters next following —chaps. xx. and xxi.—("Is Logic the Science of the Forms of Thought—On the Fundamental Laws of Thought"). The contrast which is there presented, in many different ways, between the limited theory of logic taught by Sir W. Hamilton and Mr. Mansel, and the enlarged theory of Mr. Mill, is instructive in a high degree. We consider Mr. Mill as the real preserver of all that is valuable in Formal Logic from the unfortunate consequences of an erroneous estimate, brought upon it through the exaggerated pretensions of logicians. When Sir W. Hamilton contrasts it pointedly with physical science (of which he talks with a sort of supercilious condescension, in one of the worst passages of his writings, p. 401)—when all its apparent fruits were produced in the shape of ingenious but barren verbal technicalities—what hope could be entertained that Formal Logic could hold its ground in the estimation of the recent generation of scientific men? Mr. Mill has divested it of that assumed demonstrative authority which Bacon called "regere res per syllogismum," but he has at the same time given to it a firm root amidst the generalities of objective science. He has shown that in the great problem of Evidence or Proof, the Laws of Formal Logic, though bearing only on one part of the entire procedure, yet bear upon one essential part, proper to be studied separately: and that the maintenance of consistency between our affirmations (which is the only special province of Formal Logic) has great importance and value as a part of the process necessary for ascertaining and vindicating their truth, or exposing their character when false or uncertified—but no importance and value except as a part of that larger exigency.

While Mr. Mill was amending the Syllogistic theory so as to ensure for Formal Logic its legitimate place among the essentials of scientific procedure, Sir W. Hamilton was at the same time enlarging it on its technical side, in two modes which are highly esteemed both by himself and by others: 1. The recognition of two kinds of Syllogisms; one in Extension, the other in Comprehension; 2. The doctrine of the Quantification of the Predicate. Both these novelties are here criticised by Mr. Mill in chapter xxii., which we recommend the reader to peruse conjointly with Lectures 15 and 16 of Sir W. Hamilton on Logic.

Now whereas the main objection, by which the study of the syllogistic logic has been weighed down and discredited in modern times, is this, that it encumbers the memory with formal distinctions, having no useful application to the real process and purposes of reasoning—the procedure of Sir W. Hamilton might almost lead us to imagine that he himself was trying to aggravate that objection to the uttermost. He introduces a variety of new canons (classifying Syllogisms as Extensive and Intensive, by a distinction founded on the double quantity of notions, in Extension and in Comprehension) which he intimates that all former logicians have neglected—while it plainly appears, even on his own showing, that the difference between syllogisms, in respect to these two sorts of quantity, is of no practical value; and that "we can always change a categorical syllogism of the one quantity into a categorical syllogism of the other by reversing the order of the two premises, and by reversing the meaning of the copula" (Lect. xvi. p. 296); nay, that every syllogism is already a syllogism in both quantities (Mill, p. 431). Against these useless ceremonial reforms of Sir W. Hamilton, we may set the truly philosophical explanation here given by Mr. Mill of the meaning of propositions.

" All judgments (he says, p. 423), except where both the terms are proper names, are really judgments in Comprehension; though it is customary, and the natural tendency of the mind, to express most of them in terms of Extension. In other words, we never really predicate anything but attributes; though, in the usage of language, we commonly predicate them by means of words which are names of concrete objects, because (p. 426) we have no other convenient and compact mode of speaking. Most attributes, and nearly all large bundles of attributes, have no names of their own. We can only name them by a circumlocution. We are accustomed to speak of attributes, not by names given to themselves, but by means of the names which they give to the objects they are attributes of."

" All our ordinary judgments (p. 428) are in Comprehension only; Extension not being thought of. But we may, if we please, make the Extension of our general terms an express object of thought. When I judge that all oxen ruminate, I have nothing in my thoughts but the attributes and their co-existence. But when by reflection I perceive what the proposition implies, I remark that other things may ruminate besides oxen, and that the unknown multitude of things which ruminate form a mass, with which the unknown multitude of things having the attributes of oxen is either identical or is wholly comprised in it. Which of these two is the truth I may not know, and if I did, took no notice of it when I assented to the proposition, all oxen ruminate; but I perceive, on consideration, that one or other of them must be true. Though I had not this in my mind when I affirmed that all oxen ruminate, I can have it now; I can make the concrete objects denoted by each of the two names an object of thought, as a collective though indefinite aggregate; in other words, I can make the Extension of the names (or notions) an object of direct consciousness. When I do this, I perceive that this operation introduces no new fact, but is only a different mode of contemplating the very fact which I had previously expressed by the words, all oxen ruminate. The fact is the same, but the mode of contemplating it is different. There is thus in all Propositions a judgment concerning attributes (called by Sir W. Hamilton a Judgment in Comprehension) which we make as a matter of course; and a possible judgment in or concerning Extension, which we *may* make, and which will be true if the former is true."

From the lucid explanation here cited (and from a following paragraph too long to transcribe, p. 433), we see that there is no real distinction between Judgments in Comprehension and Judgments in Extension; that the *appearance* of distinction between them arises from the customary mode of enunciation, which custom is here accounted for; that the addition to the theory of the Syllogism, for which Sir W. Hamilton takes credit, is alike troublesome and unprofitable.

The like may also be said about his other innovation, the Quantification of the Predicate. Still more extensive are the changes (as stated by himself) which this innovation would introduce in the canons of Syllogism. Indeed, when we read his language (Appendix to 'Lectures on Logic,' pp. 291-297) censuring generally the prior logicians from Aristotle downwards, and contending that "more than half the value of logic had been lost" by their manner of handling it—we may appreciate the magnitude of the reform which he believed himself to be introducing. The larger the reform, the more it behoved him to be sure of the ground on which he was proceeding. But on this point we remark a serious deficiency. After laying down, with appropriate emphasis, the valuable logical postulate, *to state explicitly what is thought implicitly*, on which, Sir W. Hamilton says,

" Logic ever insists, but which logicians have never fairly obeyed—it follows that logically we ought to take into account the quantity, *always understood in thought*, but usually, and for manifest reasons, elided in expression, not only of the *subject*, but also of the *predicate* of a judgment."—*Discussions on Philos.*, p. 614.

Here Sir W. Hamilton assumes that the quantity of the predicate is always understood in thought; and the same assumption is often repeated, in the Appendix to his 'Lectures on Logic,' p. 291 and elsewhere, as it was alike obvious and incontestable. Now it is precisely on this point that issue is here taken with Sir W. Hamilton. Mr. Mill denies altogether (p. 437) that the quantity of the predicate is always understood or present in thought, and appeals to every reader's consciousness for an answer:—

" Does he, when he judges that all oxen ruminate, advert even in the minutest degree to the question, whether there is anything else that ruminates ? Is this consideration at all in his thoughts, any more than any other consideration foreign to the immediate subject? One person may know that there are other ruminating animals, another may think that there are none, a third may be without any opinion on the subject; but if they all know what is meant by ruminating, they all, when they judge that every ox ruminates, mean precisely the same thing. The mental process they go through, *as far as that one judgment is concerned*, is precisely identical; though some of them may go on farther, and *add other judgments to it*."

The last sentence cited from Mr. Mill indicates the vice of Sir W. Hamilton's proceeding in quantifying the predicate, and explains why it was that logicians before him declined to do so. Sir W. Hamilton, in this proceeding, insists on stating explicitly, not merely all that is thought implicitly, but a great deal more;* adding to it something else, which

---

* Among the various authorities (upon this question of quantifying the predicate) collected by Sir W. Hamilton in the valuable Appendix to his *Lectures on Logic*, we find one (p. 311) which takes the same ground of objection as Mr. Mill, in these words:—
' The cause why the quantitative note is not usually joined with the predicate, is, that there would thus be two *quæsita* at once; to wit, whether the predicate were affirmed of the subject, and whether it were denied of everything beside. For when we say, *all man is all rational*, we judge that *all man is rational*, and judge likewise *that rational is denied of everything but man*. But these are, in reality, two different *quæsita;* and therefore it has become usual to state them, not in one, but in two several propositions. And this is self-evident, seeing that a *quæsitum*, in itself, asks only,—*Does or does not this inhere in that?* and *not*, Does or does not this inhere in that, *and at the same time inhere in nothing else?*"

The author of this just and sagacious remark—much surpassing what the other writers quoted in the Appendix say—was a Jew who died at Perpignan in or near 1370, named Levi Ben Gerson or Gersonides. An interesting account of this man, eminent as a writer and thinker in his age, will be found in a biography by Dr. Joel, published at Breslau in 1862, *Levi Ben Gerson als Religions philosoph*. He distinguished himself as a writer on theology, philosophy, and astronomy; he was one of the successors to the free

may, indeed, be thought conjointly, but which more frequently *is not* thought at all. He requires us to pack two distinct judgments into one and the same proposition: he interpolates the meaning of the Propositio Conversa *simpliciter* into the form of the Propositio Convertenda (when an universal Affirmative), and then claims it as a great advantage, that the proposition thus interpolated admits of being converted *simpliciter*, and not merely *per accidens.* Mr. Mill is, nevertheless, of opinion (pp. 439–443) that though "the quantified syllogism is not a true expression of what is in thought, yet writing the predicate with a quantification may be sometimes a real help to the Art of Logic." We see little advantage in providing a new complicated form, for the purpose of expressing in one proposition what naturally throws itself into two, and may easily be expressed in two. If a man is prepared to give us information on one Quæsitum, why should he be constrained to use a mode of speech which forces on his attention at the same time a second and distinct Quæsitum—so that he must either give us information about the two at once, or confess himself ignorant respecting the second?

The two next chapters of Mr. Mill, noticing some other minor peculiarities (all of them unfortunate, and one, p. 447, really unaccountable) of Sir W. Hamilton's Formal Logic; and some Fallacious Modes of Thought countenanced by Sir W. Hamilton (chs. xxiii., xxiv.—pp. 446, 478), we are compelled to pass over. We must find space, however, for a few words on the Freedom of the Will (ch. xxv.), which (in Mr. Mill's language, pp. 488–549), "was so fundamental with Sir W. Hamilton, that it may be regarded as the central idea of his system—the determining cause of most of his philosophical opinions." Prior to Sir W. Hamilton, we find

---

speculative vein of Maimonides, and one of the continuators of the Arabic Aristotelian philosophy. He both commented on and combated the doctrines of Averroes. Dr. Joel thinks that he died earlier than 1370.

some writers who maintain the doctrine of Free-will, others who maintain that of Necessity: each supporting their respective conclusions by reasons which they deem sufficient. Sir W. Hamilton declares that both the one doctrine and the other are inconceivable and incomprehensible; yet that, by the law of Excluded Middle, one or other of them must be true: and he decides in favour of Free-will, of which he believes himself to be distinctly conscious; moreover, Free-will is essential (he thinks) to moral responsibility, of which also he feels himself conscious. He confesses himself, however, unable to explain the possibility of Free-will; but he maintains that the same may be said about Necessity also. " The champions of both the two opposite doctrines are at once resistless in attack, and impotent in defence"—(Hamilton's ' Footnotes on Reid,' p. 602).   Mr. Mansel also asserts, even more confidently than Sir W. Hamilton, that we are directly conscious of Free-will—(p. 503).

Sir W. Hamilton has himself given some of the best arguments against the doctrine of Free-will, in refutation of Reid : arguments, some of which are here cited by Mr. Mill with praise which they well deserve—(pp. 497, 498).   But Mr. Mill's own reasoning on the same side is of a still higher order, enlarging the grounds previously urged in the last book of his 'System of Logic.'   He protests against the term *Necessity;* and discards the idea of Necessity, if it be understood to imply anything more than invariability of antecedence and consequence.   If it mean *that,* experience proves thus much about antecedents in the world of mind, as in the world of matter: if it mean more, experience does not prove more, either in the world of matter or in the world of mind : nor have we any grounds for affirming it in either—(p. 501).   If it were true, therefore, that consciousness attested Free-will, we should find the testimony of consciousness opposed to a full proof from experience and induction.   But does consciousness really attest what is called Free-will?   Mr. Mill analyses the case, and declares in the negative.

" To be conscious of Free-will, must mean to be conscious, before I have decided, that I am able to decide either way; exception may be taken *in limine* to the use of the word *consciousness* in such an application. Consciousness tells me what I do or feel. But what I am *able* to do, is not a subject of consciousness. Consciousness is not prophetic; we are conscious of what is, not of what will or can be. We never know that we are able to do a thing, except from having done it, or something similar to it. Having acted, we know, as far as that experience reaches, how we are able to act; *and this knowledge, when it has become familiar, is often confounded with, and called by, the name of consciousness.* But it does not derive any increase of authority from being misnamed: its truth is not supreme over, but depends upon, experience. If our so-called consciousness is not borne out by experience, it is a delusion. It has no title to credence, but as an interpretation of experience; and if it is a false interpretation it must give way."
—pp. 503, 504.

After this salutary and much-needed warning against the confusion between consciousness as an infallible authority, and belief upon experience, of which we are conscious as a belief—Mr. Mill proceeds to sift the alleged self-evident connexion between Free-will and Accountability. He shows, not merely that there is no connexion, but that there is a positive repugnance between the two. By Free-will is meant that a volition is not determined by motives, but is a spontaneous mental fact, neither having a cause, nor admitting of being predicted. Now, the very reason for giving notice that we intend to punish certain acts, and for inflicting punishment if the acts be committed, is, that we trust in the efficacy of the threat and the punishment as deterring motives. If the volition of agents be not influenced by motives, the whole machinery of law becomes unavailing, and punishment a purposeless infliction of pain. In fact, it is on that very ground that the madman is exempted from punishment; his volition being presumed to be not capable of being acted upon by the deterring motive of legal sanction. The *free* agent, thus understood, is one who can neither feel himself accountable, nor be rendered accountable, to or by others. It is only the *necessary* agent (the person whose volitions are determined by motives, and, in case of conflict, by the strongest desire or the strongest apprehension) that can be held really accountable, or can feel himself to be so.

" The true doctrine of the Causation of human actions," says Mr. Mill, p. 516, " maintains, in opposition both to pure and to modified Fatalism, that not only our conduct, but our character is in part amenable to our will : that we can, by employing the proper means, improve our character : and that if our character is such that, while it remains what it is, it necessitates us to do wrong— it will be just to apply motives which will necessitate us to strive for its improvement. We shall not indeed do so unless we desire our improvement, and desire it more than we dislike the means which must be employed for the purpose."

It thus appears that of the two propositions, 1, volitions are necessary, or depend on causes; 2, volitions are free, or do not depend on causes—neither the one nor the other is inconceivable or incomprehensible, as Sir W. Hamilton supposed them to be. That the first is true, and the second false, we learn by experience, and by that alone; just as we learn the like in regard to the phenomena of the material world. Indeed, the fact that human volitions are both predictable and modifiable, quite as much as all those physical phenomena that depend upon a complication of causes— which is only a corollary from what has just been said—is so universally recognised and acted upon by all men, that there would probably be little difference of opinion about this question, if the antithesis were not obscured and mystified by the familiar, but equivocal, phrases of Free-will and Necessity.

Passing over chapter xxvii., in which Mr. Mill refutes Sir W. Hamilton's opinion that the study of mathematics is worthless, or nearly so, as an intellectual discipline—we shall now call attention to the concluding remarks which sum up the results of the volume. After saying that he " differs from almost everything in Sir W. Hamilton's philosophy, on which ho particularly valued himself, or which is specially his own," Mr. Mill describes Sir W. Hamiliton's general merits as follows :—

" They chiefly consist in his clear and distinct mode of bringing before the reader many of the fundamental questions of metaphysics : some good specimens of psychological analysis on a small scale : and the many detached logical and psychological truths which he has separately seized, and which are scattered through his writings, mostly applied to resolve some special difficulty, and again lost sight of. I can hardly point to anything he has done towards helping the more thorough understanding of the greater mental phenomena, unless it be his theory of Attention (including Abstraction), which seems to me the most perfect we have; but the subject, though a highly important, is comparatively a simple one."—p. 547.

Agreeing in this general view of Sir W. Hamilton's merits, we should be disposed to describe them in language stronger and more emphatic as to degree, than that which has just been cited. But what is stated in the pages immediately following (pp. 550, 551)—That Sir W. Hamilton's doctrines appear to be usually taken up under the stimulus of some special dispute and often afterwards forgotten ; That he did not think out subjects until they were thoroughly mastered, or until consistency was attained between the different views which the author took from different points of observation ; That, accordingly, his philosophy seems made up of scraps from several conflicting metaphysical systems—All this is literally and amply borne out by the many inconsistencies and contradictions which Mr. Mill has brought to view in the preceding chapters. It would appear that the controversial disposition was powerful with Sir W. Hamilton, and that a present impulse of that sort (as has been said respecting Bayle, Burke, and others) not only served to provoke new intellectual combinations in his mind, but also exercised a Lethæan influence in causing obliviscence of the old. But we can hardly follow Mr. Mill in ascribing the defect to " excessive absorption of time and energy by the study of old writers "

(p. 551). If this study did no other good, it at least kept the memory in exercise. Now, what surprises us most in Sir W. Hamilton's inconsistencies, is the amount of self-forgetfulness which they imply.

While the laborious erudition of Sir W. Hamilton cannot be fairly regarded as having produced any of his intellectual defects, it undoubtedly stamped upon him his special title of excellence as a philosopher. This is fully recognised by Mr. Mill; though he treats it as belonging not so much to a philosopher as to an historian of philosophy. He concludes (pp. 552—554):—

" It is much to be regretted that Sir W. Hamilton did not write the history of philosophy, instead of choosing, as the direct object of his intellectual exertions, philosophy itself. He possessed a knowledge of the materials such as no one, probably for many generations, will take the trouble of acquiring again. Independently of the great interest and value attaching to a knowledge of the historical development of speculation, there is much in the old writers on philosophy, even those of the middle ages, really worth preserving for its scientific value. But this should be extracted, and rendered into the phraseology of modern thought, by persons as familiar with that as with the ancient, and possessing a command of its language : a combination never yet so perfectly realised as in Sir W. Hamilton. This, which no one but himself could have done, he has left undone, and has given us instead a contribution to mental philosophy, which has been more than equalled by many not superior to him in powers, and wholly destitute of erudition. Of all persons in modern times entitled to the name of philosophers, the two, probably, whose reading on the subject was the scantiest, in proportion to their intellectual capacity, were Archbishop Whately and Dr. Brown. Accordingly they are the only two of whom Sir W. Hamilton, though acknowledging their abilities, speaks with some tinge of superciliousness. It cannot be denied that both Dr. Brown and Whately would have thought and written better than they did, if they had been better read in the writings of previous thinkers ; but I am not afraid that posterity will contradict me when I say, that either of them has done far greater service to the world in the origination and diffusion of important thought than Sir W. Hamilton with all his learning;

because, though indolent readers, they were both of them active and fertile thinkers.

" It is not that Sir W. Hamilton's erudition is not frequently of real use to him on particular questions of philosophy. It does him one valuable service : it enables him to know all the various opinions which can be held on the questions he discusses, and to conceive and express them clearly, leaving none of them out. This it does, though even this not always; but it does little else, even of what might be expected from erudition when enlightened by philosophy. He knew, with extraordinary accuracy, the ὅτι of each philosopher's opinions, but gave himself little trouble about the διότι. With one exception, I find no remark bearing upon that point in any part of his writings. I imagine he would have been much at a loss if he had been required to draw up a philosophical estimate of the mind of any great thinker. He never seems to look at any opinion of a philosopher in connection with the same philosopher's other opinions. Accordingly he is weak as to the mutual relations of philosophical doctrines. One of the most striking examples of this inability is in the case of Leibnitz," &c.

Here we find in a few sentences the conclusion which Mr. Mill conceives to be established by his book. We shall state how far we are able to concur with it. He has brought the matter to a direct issue, by weighing Sir W. Hamilton in the balance against two other actual contemporaries ; instead of comparing him with some unrealised ideal found only in the fancy of critics and reviewers.

Comparing Sir W. Hamilton with Dr. Brown, we cordially subscribe to the opinion of Mr. Mill. We think that Dr. Brown has "done far greater service to the world than Sir W. Hamilton, in the origination and diffusion of important thought." To speak only of two chief subjects in the field of important thought—Causality and the Freedom of the Will—we not only adopt the conclusions of Dr. Brown, but we admire both his acuteness and his originality in vindicating and illustrating the first of the two, while we dissent entirely from the views of Sir W. Hamilton. This alone would be sufficient to make us approve the superiority assigned by Mr. Mill to Dr. Brown. We discover no compensating item to be placed to the credit of Sir W. Hamilton :

for the great doctrine of the Relativity of Knowledge, which is our chief point of philosophical brotherhood with him, was maintained by Brown also.

But in regard to Dr. Whately, our judgment is altogether different. We cannot consent to admit him as a superior, or even as an equal, to Sir W. Hamilton, "in the origination and diffusion of important thought." He did much service by reviving an inclination and respect for Logic, and by clearing up a part of the technical obscurity which surrounded it: but we look upon him as an acute and liberal-minded English theologian, enlarging usefully, though timidly, the intellectual prison in which many orthodox minds are confined—rather than as a fit aspirant to the cosmopolitan honours of philosophy. "An active and fertile thinker," Mr. Mill calls Whately; and such he undoubtedly was. But such also we consider Sir W. Hamilton to have been, in a degree at least equal. If the sentence which we have quoted above be intended to deny the predicate, "active and fertile thinker," of Sir W. Hamilton, we cannot acquiesce in it. His intellect appears to us thoroughly active and fertile, even when we dissent from his reasonings—nay, even in the midst of his inconsistencies, when a new growth of opinions is unexpectedly pushed up, on ground which we supposed to be already pre-occupied by another both older and different. And we find this same judgment implied in the discriminating remarks upon his philosophical procedure made by Mr. Mill himself—(pp. 271, 272). For example, respecting Causality and the Freedom of the Will, we detect no want of activity and fertility, though marked evidence of other defects—especially the unconditional surrender of a powerful mind to certain privileged inspirations, worshipped as "necessities of thought."

While thus declaring how far we concur in the parallel here drawn of Sir W. Hamilton with Brown and Whately, we must at the same time add that the comparison is taken under circumstances unduly favourable to these two last. There has been no exposure of *their* errors and inconsistencies, equal in penetration and completeness to the crushing volume which Mr. Mill has devoted to Sir W. Hamilton. To make the odds fair, he ought to furnish a similar systematic examination to Brown and Whately; enabling us to read their works (as we now do those of Sir W. Hamilton) with the advantage of his unrivalled microscope, which detects the minutest breach or incoherence in the tissue of reasoning, and of his large command of philosophical premisses, which brings into full notice what the author had overlooked. Thus alone could the competition between the three be rendered perfectly fair.

We regret, as Mr. Mill does, that Sir W. Hamilton did not undertake the composition of a history of philosophy. Nevertheless we must confess that we should hardly feel such regret, if we could see evidence to warrant Mr. Mill's judgment (p. 554) that Sir W. Hamilton was "indifferent to the διότι of a man's opinions, and that he was incompetent to draw up an estimate of the opinions of any great thinker," &c. Such incompetence, if proved to be frequent and considerable, would deprive an author of all chance of success in writing a history of philosophy. But the study of Sir W. Hamilton's works does not prove it to us, though Mr. Mill has convicted him of an erroneous estimate of Leibnitz. We say *frequent* and *considerable*, because no historian of philosophy is exempt from the defect more or less; or rather (to pass out of the self-confidence of the Absolute into the modesty of the Relative) we seldom find any historian whose estimate of great philosophical thinkers does not often differ from our own. Hence we are glad when ample and original extracts are produced, enabling us to test the historian, and judge for ourselves—a practice which Sir W. Hamilton would have required no stimulus to enforce upon him. There ought, indeed, to be various histories of philosophy, composed from different points of view; for the ablest historian cannot get clear of a certain exclusiveness belonging to himself. But so far as we can conjecture what Sir W. Hamilton *would* or *could* have done, we think that a history of philosophy composed by him would have surpassed any work of the kind in our language.

We trust that Sir W. Hamilton's works will long continue to be read, along with Mr. Mill's examination of them ; and we should be glad if the works of other philosophers could be read along with a comment of equal acuteness and impartiality. Any point of view which could command the adherence of such a mind as Sir W. Hamilton's, deserves to be fully considered. Moreover, the living force of philosophy, as directress of human intelligence, depends upon keeping up in each of her devotees a full mastery of many divergent and opposite veins of reasoning—a knowledge, negative and affirmative, of the full case of opponents as well as of his own.

It is to Philosophy alone that *our* allegiance is sworn, and while we concur mostly with Mr. Mill's opinions, we number both him and Sir W. Hamilton as a noble pair of brethren, serving alike in her train.

Amicus Hamilton ; magis amicus Mill ; amica ante omnes Philosophia.

PAPERS ON PHILOSOPHY.

(From the Author's MSS.)

UNDER the date 1822, Mrs. Grote has preserved a fasciculus of very interesting essays on Metaphysics, Mr. Grote's earliest productions in that walk. They prove both the extent of his reading, and the subtlety and the depth of his own reflections.

The longest and best essay is entitled " Object and Extent of Metaphysics." It not only raises the most difficult questions in the philosophy of mind, but shows that he had already made up his mind, and taken his side, on the controversies that divide the schools. Five years before, he represented himself as half-convinced by Berkeley; he is now a Berkleian, and something more.

He comes at once to the point—What is the meaning of 'External body'? and answers it according to Berkeley, although with a more advanced psychology. He expands in his own way the Berkleian motto—*esse est percipi*—and does not shirk any of the difficulties. The following extracts are a specimen :—

When the word Carlton-house is pronounced, a certain set of visible and tangible sensations is re-kindled in my mind—that is, I fancy myself again seeing or touching Carlton-house. When the word is pronounced, I myself supply unconsciously the act of seeing or touching, by virtue of which such a sound excites the idea habitually associated with it. And when I say, *"Carlton-house exists"*—the full and accurate description of my state of mind is, *"I fancy that*

I see Carlton-house—I remember to have lately seen it—or I now see it, &c."

But it will doubtless be asked, " Does not Carlton-house exist when I am not thinking of it ? Would it not exist though I were annihilated ?"

This question, if strictly analysed, will appear to be an utter sophism—involving conditions which preclude the possibility of replying to it either in the affirmative or negative. How can I frame any kind of affirmation or denial on a subject, on which I am interdicted from employing my thoughts ? I am forbidden to think upon Carlton-house—yet I am desired, notwithstanding, to say whether it exists or not. I am to suppose my mind and powers of judging annihilated—yet I am required to deliver a judgment on a subject placed before me. Now surely when these self-contradicting conditions are exposed, this question, which is usually the experimentum crucis of the Materialist, shrinks into an unmeaning puzzle. In order to reply to a question regarding Carlton-house, it is obvious that I must employ my thoughts about it. My decision, therefore, whether affirmative or negative, implies uniformly two things—first, that my mind is in action, *i.e.*, not annihilated, secondly, that it is employed upon that particular subject and upon nothing else. In other words, any conceivable answer which I may return must imply two conditions the direct reverse of that which the question demands.

If indeed I am asked, " whether Carlton-house cannot exist *except when I am looking at it,*" I readily answer, that it may exist just as much when I do not see it, as when I do. But when I say this, the whole amount of my affirmation is, that I remember distinctly to have seen it, and expect fully that I may see it again—and that without at present looking upon it. The states of mind which I call remembrance and expectation may doubtless occur separately from what is usually termed perception, and may kindle a lively belief in the existence of the thing so remembered and expected.

But this feeling of remembrance, expectation, and belief, is precisely as strong in the case of other sensations, when constant, as it is in those of sight and touch. My remembrance and belief that the noise of a cataract, which I have visited formerly, now exists, is just as strong as my remembrance and belief that the water or the rocks exist. I have as full a conviction that I may again hear the one, as that I may again see the other. Should it be asked, whether there is any noise when I am not near to hear it, I should answer, that there unquestionably was. It matters not whether I actually hear it or not. I remember to have heard it and expect to hear it again. There is not a shade of difference in my feelings with regard to the sound, and with regard to the rocks.

I have already remarked that partly from their permanence, partly from their urgency, the visual and tactile sensations come to exercise prodigious ascendency over our minds. All our other states of mind are viewed with reference to these others, as antecedents or concomitants or consequents, and the visual and tactile sensations thus appropriate and enslave all the rest. But these two predominant classes of sensations acquire, as I have endeavoured to explain, a seeming independence of our mental modifications, and appear to have an existence distinct from and without our minds. Hence, since a powerful interest continually impels us to consider all our sensations with reference to the visual and tactile, and since these appear to exist distinct from the mind—we contract an habitual desire of tracing our states of mind up to something distinct from and independent of ourselves. We search about for an external something to which we may attribute any mental affection of which we are conscious; and when the latter has once been fastened and domiciliated with any external something, the process of the mind appears to be performed, its dissatisfaction is appeased, and it is set at rest.

The early growth of this tendency is of infinite and melancholy importance. It thrusts itself upon us upon all occasions, as an operation of primary necessity ; it perverts our views of what is desirable or practicable to know, and distorts altogether the application of the power of thought ; and it casts so deep a mist over all the proceedings of the understanding, as no subsequent reflexion can entirely dissipate. When a state of mind occurs which is not familiar to us, and which we desire to explain, we are drawn away from that path of observation and comparison which alone can conduct us to a solid result ; we do not think of comparing the different trains of which it forms a member, in order to separate its casual from its constant companions. We instantly look for an external something on which we may hitch it, and if none such presents itself, we slide easily into the process of creation, and fasten that which is to be accounted for upon some fictitious and imaginary entity. Of these numberless mistakes the source is to be sought in that early habit which bestows upon the visual and tactile sensations so complete an ascendency over the mind, and which leads us to father all our other mental modifications upon them alone.

I cannot depart from this topic without offering a few remarks on the controversy between Berkeley and Reid, with regard to which much misconception appears to have arisen. The merits of the latter have been blazoned forth, and his refutation paraded far and wide as victorious and irresistible, by his disciple and expositor, Mr. Stewart, whereas the treatise of the former has been left an orphan (to use a beautiful expression of Plato) and defenceless, and seems to have met with few who could comprehend its bearings, or disengage the truth which its author so successfully struck out, from the errors which particular prejudices led him to array by its side. Few treatises ever stood more in need of such a commentator ; for the mixture which it presents is indeed singular. It is remarkable, that both Berkeley and Reid (as each has left upon record) were led into their different and contradictory trains of thought by the very same motive—an aversion to Atheism, and a zeal for the maintenance of religious belief.

To place religion on a firm and unassailable foundation, the Bishop thought it requisite to refute the supposition that there was any unthinking substance existing without the perceiving mind, and to prove that only spiritual or thinking substances could be thus independently existent. While, in pursuance of these views, he adheres to the former track, his reasonings are strikingly ingenious and original. He insists forcibly on the impossibility of seeing anything unseen, hearing anything unheard, conceiving anything unconceived, &c., which is what is meant by affirming that the objects of sight, of touch, of conception, or of any other mental feeling whatever, exist independent of the mind. I shall not dwell any longer upon this part of his writings, because I have endeavoured to enforce the same line of argument in various parts of these Essays, and because perhaps the very best statement of the doctrine, which Berkeley's book affords, is a passage already cited.

But when, in furtherance of his original plan, the Bishop sought to evade the application of these reasonings to the case of Spirit, it is melancholy to observe the confusion which begins to overcloud his mind, and the unreal distinctions which appear to satisfy his once piercing and irresistible scrutiny. "A spirit (said he) cannot be known by way of idea; it is a simple, undivided, active Being, percipient of ideas, but not itself perceived, like an Idea. We know a Spirit immediately by way of notion. Now though it is impossible that an Idea, whose *esse* is *percipi*, should exist without being perceived; yet it is not impossible that a Spirit, whose *esse* is *percipere*, should exist without being perceived."

Such was the distinction by which Berkeley strove to shelter Spirit from the arguments by which he had attacked matter. A very cursory inspection will discover its insufficiency. For either the word *Spirit* means nothing, or

z

else it means something conceived, believed, imagined, supposed, &c., call the state of mind · what you will. To say, that my ideas may be perceived by another percipient, is merely to say, that I may conceive, or believe, or know, or suppose, &c., that they are perceived by another percipient. Another percipient is, in other words, something known or conceived as perceiving. And it is impossible that anything known or conceived can have an existence independent of the knowing or conceiving mind. At any rate, it makes no difference whether the thing known be thinking or unthinking. If the independent existence of the latter is impossible, that of the former is equally so; if that of the former be possible, so is that of the latter.

Now as this line of distinction could not be maintained, it was obvious that Berkeley's doctrine was self-contradictory. The question was, which half of it should destroy the other.

Viewing the controversy simply as it stood between Reid and Berkeley, it must be owned that the inconsistency, which so glaringly pervades the doctrine of the latter, placed his adversary upon a ground of attack singularly advantageous. The admissions, in which the Bishop had so liberally indulged towards Spirit, were perfectly sufficient to vindicate the existence of Matter, if they could be shewn to apply equally to it—that is, if the distinction which Berkeley had drawn between the two could be removed. But this distinction consisted in the hypothesis, that we knew matter by way of ideas, or of an intervening something immediately perceived by the mind—while we knew spirit immediately, or without any such intervention. This was the ideal theory, and Dr. Reid directed the whole force of his reasonings against it. "We are admitted (said he) to know Spirit immediately; what reason is there for supposing that we know Matter in any other way? Why should not our apprehension of the one be as direct and immediate as that of the other? Can any evidence be adduced of the intervention of an idea, in the case of material substance?"

It was perfectly true that no such evidence could be adduced. And as far as regards Berkeley, or any one who coincides with Berkeley's admissions concerning Spirit, I think the arguments of Reid are decisive and invincible. But his advantage over the Bishop merely arose from his consistency in vindicating two errors, which must stand or fall together; while his adversary, in dismissing one, clung with increased vehemence and pertinacity to the other. By the removal, therefore, of the ideal theory, it must be allowed that the repugnance and self-contradiction of Berkeley's system was demonstrated, and the controversy decided in favour of Reid.

Not so the controversy about the independent existence of material substance. The real value of Berkeley's arguments on the negative side of this question is not at all impaired, because they happened in his mind to be closely knit together with certain errors, which rendered it inconsistent in him to maintain them. And the actual force of these arguments is so far from depending on the ideal theory (on the destruction of which Mr. Stewart rests the celebrity of Reid), that they must, if received, exclude and nullify that theory altogether. For the ideal theory is nothing but a supposition framed to explain the mode in which we perceive external objects. Now if there exist no objects independent of the mind, the ideal theory becomes altogether useless and unmeaning, inasmuch as the difficulty, which it was destined to explain, is terminated. When I affirm that I am conscious of nothing but my own states of mind or mental modifications—whether called sensations, conceptions, acts of belief, or by any other name, this general statement of fact is certainly no theory at all; but least of all is it the ideal theory, which is of a nature and purpose altogether inconsistent with this statement of fact. The truth is, that if the ideal theory is an unsupported hypothesis, so also is the supposition of external independent objects. If the ideas, of which I am conscious, are really nothing, distinct from and independent of the conscious

z 2

mind—then neither are the external objects, which I perceive, anything distinct from and independent of the perceiving mind. To say that there may exist objects without my mind, distinct from its perceptions; but that there cannot possibly exist any objects within my mind, distinct from its consciousness, is· an assumption destitute of all evidence, and virtually predetermining the very question in dispute, by introducing the expressions, *without* and *within the mind;* a phraseology altogether unmeaning, if the hypothesis of external objects be rejected.

[In 1860, there occurred an interesting correspondence on the same subject, which is here reproduced in full. The ostensible start was from the concluding chapter of Professor Bain's work, 'The Emotions and the Will,' where a criticism was made on Ferrier's 'Institutes,' from the point of view of the Relativity of all Knowledge; the Subject-and-Object Relativity being only one example, although possessing an altogether exceptional importance. In point of fact, however, Mr. Grote had of his own motion been meditating intently on the correlation of the Subject and Object in perception, and took this opportunity to put down his thoughts in writing.]

SUBJECT AND OBJECT.

THERE are portions of your section on this subject which do not quite satisfy me. I coincide more fully with your treatment of the same matter (or the branch of the same matter which relates to the material world), in your first volume ['The Senses and the Intellect '], pp. 366–376.

The relativeness of Subject to Object, as I conceive it, stands singly and by itself, apart from all relativeness between two or more diverse objects of cognition. Whether cognition be only possible under the assumption of a known contrast between two different objects, as you imagine—or whether it be also possible with only one object, not consciously contrasted with any foil, as I incline to believe—in either case the cognizant subject is the same, equally present and incorporated in the fact of cognition. An act of cognition has no meaning without a cognizing subject and a cognitum object: the former always the same, the latter variable: both being opposite points of view (or poles) of the same indivisible fact of mind. If, in addition to this, it be true that there must be *two distinct objects*, known in antithesis to each other by the cognizant subject, let the position be proved: but it seems to me distinct from, and independent of, the position above laid down respecting *subject and object*. The two positions ought to be affirmed and reasoned upon apart from each other: not thrown together under one general head. You say truly (vol. i. p. 376) that to speak of a cognitum apart from a cognoscens is " *self-contradiction :*" but it is surely no *self-contradiction* (whether exact or not) to say that we can know red without green, or light without darkness.

You seem to consider the antithesis of subject and object, as coinciding with that of ideal and real—mind and matter— internal and external. I cannot but think that subject and object is more general and fundamental than this. The distinction Subject—Object belongs to the ideal world, as well as to the sensational. John Mill says in his ' Logic' (Book i. c. iii. p. 55)—" Even imaginary objects, which are said to exist only in our ideas, are to be distinguished from our ideas of them. The hobgoblin which never existed is not the same thing with my idea of a hobgoblin. They are all, not thoughts, but objects of thought, though all the objects are alike non-existent." Plato's archetypal Ideas were Objects, though neither material nor extended.

The act of Conception, as well as the act of Perception, is in itself indivisible: but both the one and the other may be looked at either in the subjective or in the objective point of view. The Subject is that which either one or the other has in common with all the other acts of our mind or consciousness—the *indeterminate Ego*. The Object is that which either one or the other has either peculiar to itself, or common only to a select fraction of our acts of consciousness: it is the varying Ego, or the principle of variation and specialisation in Ego. We cannot properly speak of it as *Non*-Ego: it involves, not a negation, but a simple modification and determination, of the Subject. The antithesis of Ego and Non-Ego, which some writers adopt, involves an illusion : the real antithesis is between Ego determinate and Ego indeterminate: the determinate Ego being the complete mental fact, from which the indeterminate Ego is the highest abstraction.

There seem to be various sources of confusion in reference to this antithesis of Subject—Object.

1. Our own bodies. I apprehend that the earliest conception of *Subject*, that which prevails in unreflecting minds, is the distinction between each man's body and matter external to his body. He considers his body to be *Subject*— that is, *himself*. What is external to his body is Object, or *not himself*. This distinction gets early and powerful hold upon the mind. But it is evidently an objective distinction, between two different objects: for each man's body is *object* to himself as Subject: it is seen and felt, and the boundary between it and what is beyond it can be traced by sensation and movement. The body partakes of the nature both of Subject and Object. Considered as object, the distinction between our body and matter extraneous to our body, is not only clear and marked but highly important: it is the most familiar and indispensable of all distinctions. What is extraneous to our own body, is extraneous to ourselves as Subject: for the Subject is identical with the body, or at least co-extensive with it. What is really an antithesis between two objects, is converted into antithesis or divorce between object and subject.

2. The second source of confusion is, that we look back upon our own *past* sensations, perceptions, and mental acts generally. When I recollect or conceive an object which I

saw or touched an hour ago, I know that I am not *now*
seeing or touching it. My *percipient* Subject forms no
part of the recollection: and it appears as if that which
I recollect or conceive was Object pure and simple, without
a Subject. But there is here an illusion : because my
Subject, though not interfering as *percipient*, interferes as
reminiscent or *concipient*, and forms an equally essential part
of the real fact. To our memory, or conception, is present
only the *objective* point of view of the past sensation; but
the memory or conception itself forms the subjective to
correlate with it.

3. A third source of confusion relates to the distinction
between myself and *other subjects*. I believe that other
subjects are often affected in the same manner as I am—
often not so. But in making this comparison, it is plain
that I regard my own subject as an object. Other persons
can be only *objects* to me: and when I compare myself to
them, I become an *object* to myself: that is my past sensations and mental acts pass under my review, or become
objects to my reminiscent or reflecting subject. I, the
Subject, am in this way, as it were, counted twice over:
once as reflecting, once again as object reflected upon; and
it is in the latter capacity alone that I am compared with
other subjects. The distinction, or resemblance, which I
note between my sensations and those of other men, is in
reality an objective distinction, noted by myself as *comparing subject* between myself and others as *compared objects*.
But the fact that I am the comparing subject passes un-
noticed and out of sight: all that is usually noticed is, the
two compared *objects*, myself and others. It is forgotten
that this comparison cannot be made without myself as
subject to make it. The subject, as such, is overlooked : it
cannot come into separate consciousness: it can only be
understood by comparing together some or all of our
past mental acts and attending to that which they all
have in common. But in this process, *my past self*
becomes an *Object*, to my *present self* as *Subject*: my

present self being of necessity implied, but not consciously present.

James Mill ('Analysis', vol. i. pp. 244, 245, 249) adverts to this distinction between *past self* and *present self*. He seems however to think that *present self* can come into separate consciousness as well as *past self*. If he means this, I cannot agree with him. I think that self only comes into consciousness as an *object—past or future self*: as *subject*, or *present self*, it is implied, but never revealed or discernible.

The distinction between *past self*, or object, and present self, or subject, enables us to criticise Ferrier's position, that "every cognition must involve a cognition of self." If he had said, that "every cognition must involve self as the cognizant," I think he would have been perfectly correct. The self, present self or subject, is constant and indispensable as the cognoscens, but cannot become the cognitum. The *present self* forms one constant and unalterable pole of the indivisible act of cognition. Our *past self*, on the contrary, belongs to the other or objective pole. But even in this sense of the objective self, Ferrier's position is not exact. It is not true that every cognition must involve a cognition of self. In many cognitions, the objective self is not at all included. I know many things, which I do not at all recollect to have seen, or heard, or discovered, or reasoned out, by my *past or objective self*. Of some cognitions, this past self makes a part; but not of all. But the present self belongs to all.

The distinction between these two sorts of cognitions is important to bear in mind, because it contributes materially to generate the illusion of an Objective Absolute. Because many of my cognitions include no reference to a (past or objective) self, and are in this respect distinguishable from those which do include such reference—it is imagined that the first class are wholly divorced from *self*; that they are complete and independent absolutes. It is forgotten that the present or subjective self is implicated alike in both the two classes.

In explaining this abstruse point of psychological theory, the first great problem is, to find means of bringing the *forgotten present or subjective self* into notice. It cannot be known by direct and immediate consciousness, in reference to any present sensation or cognition. It can only be known by inference from the sum total of our past mental states, and by appeal to the fact of cognition as the radical or primordial element from which psychology takes its start. Instead of pretending to explain this primordial fact by the hypothesis of an Absolute Object acting upon an Absolute Subject to generate cognition, we have to take the cognition itself as an indivisible act capable of being looked at from two sides—either from the side common to all cognitions, or from that which varies from time to time in each particular case.

The second problem is, while rescuing the subjective self from oblivion, to bring it into notice as not isolated but always incorporated with some particular object, with which it is fused in one and the same mental act. Every mental act or condition—be it sensation, perception, conception, emotion, volition, belief, intuition, ratiocination—includes the subject determined by its object, and may be looked at from one or from the other point of view. If I speak of an Object of perception, of belief, of intuition, of ratiocination —I myself am present, in the mental state which dictates the speech, as percipient, credent, intuent, ratiocinant: the Object is relative to me, in one or other of these capacities; and I am relative to that as to other objects. The Noumena require a Nous to apprehend them, and reciprocally the Nous requires Noumena to enable it to come into act: so also the Percepta and Percipiens mutually imply each other, and are two modes of looking at the same real fact.

The distinction between the Real and the Ideal is doubtless very important to be maintained : but it does not turn upon the distinction between Object and Subject. It turns on the distinction between Sentient Subject and Concipient or Cogitant Subject, or (which is equivalent) between

Objectum Sensum and Objectum Cogitatum or Conception—between the act of Sensation and the act of Ideation. Subject and Object are each common to both: but in the one class, I am sentient subject, in the other class, cogitant subject: in the one class the object is an object of perception, in the other an object of conception or an Ens Rationis. I am myself the true and fundamental subject of all my propositions: every proposition announces by implication—*I* feel, *I* think, *I* believe, and so and so. There are many propositions in which this is not directly included in the formal enunciation: but it is not the less really understood in all, without exception. In explaining the nature of propositions, this ineffaceable subjective basis ought to be formally and emphatically laid down. In practice men lose sight of it, because of its universality: but these forgotten but constant elements are the very matters which the analysing philosopher should take the most pains to bring clearly into view.

[The foregoing was transmitted to Professor Ferrier, who made to it the reply published in his Remains, vol. 1. The interest of that reply will be greatly enhanced by its being read in connection with Mr. Grote's paper.]

" The point at issue between Mr. G. and me is this :—He
" holds that the *present* self is never the object, or any part
" of the object, of our consciousness. I venture to hold the
" opposite opinion, and have given expression to it in my
" opening proposition, in which it is maintained that the self
" and the not-self are always apprehended *simultaneously,*
" although I admit that the self is usually no prominent or
" explicit portion of the cognition.
" In Mr. G.'s paper there is a certain ambiguity (as I dare-
" say there are plenty on my side of the question), something
" at least about which I am in doubt, and which must be
" cleared up before any progress can be made in the discus-
" sion; in fact, before there can be either any disagreement

" or any agreement between us. I shall endeavour, at the
" outset, to explain what this ambiguity or inconsistency is.

" In every case of cognition more is *implied* than is
" *expressly* known. For instance, when I look at a tree, all
" that I am expressly cognisant of is the tree. This at least
" is usually the whole—the whole that is explicit. But
" much more is implied. *I* am implied, *seeing* is implied, a
" *retina* is implied, a *brain* is implied. All these are impli-
" cated in the process. They are present and instrumental,
" but the tree alone is expressly known. So far, I think,
" Mr. G. and I will agree ; so far there is no ambiguity.

" But a question here arises. Are these implicated ele-
" ments not known *at all*, or are they only not known *ex-*
" *pressly ?* In other words, may not that which is not known
" expressly or explicitly be nevertheless known—known
" implicitly ?

" This is an important question. In reference to the
" present discussion it is all-important, and it must be an-
" swered unambiguously. For myself, I answer the question
" in the affirmative. I argue for implicit, as well as for
" explicit cognition. And I maintain that some of the ele-
" ments above referred to, as implicated in my cognition of
" the tree, are known implicitly, and that others of them are
" not known at all. 'I' and 'seeing' are known implicitly
" in and along with my explicit knowledge of the tree ;
" 'retina' and 'brain' are not known *at all*. And the
" ground of the distinction is this, that reflection enables me
" to recover and render explicit ' me ' and 'seeing'—a cir-
" cumstance which to my mind proves that these were
" already known implicitly, although overlooked at the time ;
" whereas no power of reflection can reveal to me a retina or
" brain as having been concerned in the operation. To dis-
" cover these I must have recourse to renewed observation
" and anatomy.

" But what I am at a loss about is the answer which Mr. G.
" gives to this important question. This is the article in
" regard to which I venture to think that he is ambiguous.

" From the general purport of the remarks in which he con-
" troverts my position, I would conclude that he is opposed
" to the doctrine of ' implicit cognitions.' But there are
" expressions in his note which seem to point to the opposite
" conclusion. He says that the ego 'is *understood* in all
" propositions,' understood, of course, by itself and to itself;
" that is to say, known implicitly and in the present time.
" And in his last sentence he says, 'In practice men lose
" sight of it (the ego) because of its universality; but these
" forgotten but distinct elements are the very matters which
" the analysing philosopher should take the most pains to
" bring clearly into view.' On this I would remark that it is
" not possible for the analysing philosopher to bring· clearly
" into view any element of consciousness which was not
" known obscurely beforehand. Reflection is his only instru-
" ment; and reflection cannot originate knowledge : it can
" only make us know clearly and explicitly what we already
" know confusedly and implicitly.

" The result is, that I am in doubt as to the ground occu-
" pied by Mr. G. in reference to implicit cognitions. Does
" he deny them altogether? Must all cognition be either
" express or null? In that case, he will find it very difficult,
" or rather impossible, to explain how a reflective analysis
" can go to work upon its materials, these being, on this
" supposition, the absolutely unknown. On the other hand,
" does he admit implicit cognition? In that case, I think
" that there cannot be any very great difference between us;
" and that, with a little explanatory coaxing, he might be
" brought round to my side of the question : for if a man
" admits any implicit cognitions, or, I should rather say,
" implicit *elements* of cognition, he may surely accept the *ego*
" as among the number. But until I know whether, and to
" what extent, Mr. G. accepts or rejects the doctrine of im-
" plied cognitions, I do not see how he and I can properly
" join issue, either in the way of agreement or disagreement.
" So much in reference to the ambiguity of which I com-
" plain.

" For the reason given I shall not go much into argument
"on the point more particularly in dispute. Let me just
" say that Mr. G.'s doctrine, that we have no cognisance of
" our *present*, but only of our *past* self, is, in my opinion,
" untenable, for these among other reasons :—

" *First*, I cannot have any cognisance of my past self
" without distinguishing myself as past from myself as pre-
" sent. But I cannot make this distinction without being
" cognisant of my present self. Therefore, in being cognisant
" of my past self, I must always be cognisant (implicitly it
" may be) of my present self. *Secondly*, would the words 'I
" am' have any meaning, except in reference to a self cog-
" nised in the present ? *Thirdly*, it would not be possible for
" a man to *be* cognisant of his past self unless he *had been*
" cognisant of his present self. What a man remembers is,
" that certain sensations were *his*, that certain events befell
" *him* ; that is, he remembers both himself and those events,
" and the connection between him and them. If he had not
" been cognisant of himself in the present (which is now
" past), he either would remember only the events, and their
" having happened to nobody, at least not to him (which is
" absurd), or he would not have remembered them at all,
" which is the more probable alternative. But he does re-
" member them ; and he remembers, moreover, that they
" happened to *him*, which seems to me to prove that he was
" cognisant (however inexplicitly) of himself at the time.
" But I have exhausted my paper, and I daresay your
" patience, so I shall say no more at present, except that I
" cannot think that Mr. G.'s position is not blasted, or that
" mine is shaken, by anything that has been as yet advanced.
" Perhaps he thinks that a contradiction is involved in sup-
" posing that the *cognoscens* can be in the same instant the
" *cognition*. But that is precisely the idea and definition of
" the ego, that it is at once its own subject and its own
" object — not, however, without a contrasting element, the
" non-ego."

[To this Mr. Grote rejoined.]

I have read with much interest the paper of Professor Ferrier. He has handled this abstruse subject with great acuteness, and in a manner which, if it does not bring about agreement between two dissentients, enables both of them to understand better both the grounds and the measure of their dissent.

The point at issue between us is brought to view more distinctly in the concluding sentence of his letter than in the preceding parts. He there says—

" Perhaps he (G.) thinks, that a contradiction is involved in supposing that the *cognoscens* can be in the same instant the *cognitum*. But that is precisely the idea and definition of the *Ego*—that it is at once its own subject and its own object—not however without a contrasting element, the *non-Ego*."

The question between Mr. F. and myself, as I conceive it, is, whether this "idea and definition of the Ego" be a correct one: whether there be really any such duplication or double function of the Ego, in the same instant or in the same act of present cognition. In my judgment, such duplication or double function belongs, not to present cognition, but to reflex cognition only.

On two points, I think, we are both agreed.

First, there is in every act of cognition an essential implication of Cognoscens and Cognitum—Subject and Object.

Secondly, there is in every act of *reflex* cognition a duplication of the Ego. Here it is at once Cognoscens and Cognitum. The case which Mr. F. states, about "seeing the tree," illustrates this perfectly; and I quite agree with the manner in which he states it. In reflection, I *disimplicate* that which in the act itself had been implicated. My *reflecting Ego* is the *cognoscens*: the *Ego* of my previous act of vision is the *cognitum*.

On these points Mr. F. and I concur: but our difference lies in the manner of conceiving and stating the elements really implicated in the original, present, act of cognition (or vision). He maintains that the duplication or double function of the Ego occurs in the original act of cognition as well as in the reflex act: and he argues that it could not occur in the reflex unless it had previously occurred in the original. I submit that this argument is not satisfactory. That which in the original cognition had been simply *Ego cognoscens*, would present itself as *Ego cognitus* to the new *Ego cognoscens* acting in the work of reflection. It is by no means necessary to assume, that in the original act of cognition, the Ego must have been at once *cognoscens* and *cognitus*. In Mr. F.'s theory, the Ego is counted twice over in the original act of cognition—where, as I think, it really occurs only once: while no account is taken of the new *Ego cognoscens* which appears in the act of reflection. The intervention of this new *Ego cognoscens* makes an important difference between the act of reflection and the act of present cognition. It is an additional element, blending itself with the revived elements of the previous cognition, and generally with other cognitions brought into comparison with this latter. And it is moreover an essential condition, enabling us to disimplicate elements which had been essentially implicated in the act of cognition itself.

I will not go so far as to affirm "that a *contradiction* is involved in supposing that the *cognoscens* can be in the same instant the *cognitum*." But it appears to me, that this hypothesis assumes more in the act of cognition than really belongs to it. The implication, in that act, of the *cognoscens* with the *cognitum*, is indisputable: not so, when we come to assume the triple implicate—*cognoscens, cognoscens cognitum,* and *cognitum*. Here we count the *cognoscens* twice over: not upon any evidence of direct consciousness (which is inapplicable to the case), but as an inference from what occurs in the act of reflection. The grounds upon which Mr. F. rests this inference appear to me insufficient, and it is upon this point that I join issue with him. What occurs in the act of reflection would, in my judgment, occur equally, if we admit in the primary act of cognition nothing more than an implication of the *cognoscens* with some *cognitum—subject with object*. I do not use the terms *Ego* and *Non-Ego*, because they appear to me less appropriate. The last is as much positive as the first, though it is variable, while the first is constant.

If I am right, this implication of subject with object is the simplest and most universal statement of what is common to all acts of cognition: whether in its ruder form, as among children and animals—or in its more complicated form, as among reflecting and analysing students. We cannot abolish either of the two without dismissing mind altogether: though we may look at cognitions from either of the two points of view, leaving out for the time the consideration of the other. In such processes of abstraction, comparison, reflection, we disimplicate the two elements of those cognitions which we compare and reflect upon. But we do not even here disimplicate the *process* of cognition: for our reflecting or comparing *Ego* becomes itself implicated in the act of reflexion or comparison.

With reference to the reasoning in Mr. F.'s fourth page (p. 349), I would say, that the *present self* is present as cognizing, not as cognized : and that the words *I am*, though they include the present self, include a great deal more besides. Mr. F. says : " Thirdly, it would not be possible for a man to be cognizant of his *past* self, unless he had been cognizant of his *present self.*" I incline to believe that the reverse of the proposition is more accurate, and that we are cognizant of our present self only through inferences from our past self. I see the books in my study now before me—I hear the noise of carriages in the street—I meditate on Mr. F.'s paper now on my table—but all this while my present self never shews himself as a part of the scene, or as an object of cognition or consciousness. In fact, it seems to me that *self* is a complicated word, which requires many comparisons before its meaning can be understood, and which cannot be understood except as including more than the present moment. I cannot conceive my present self except as the continuance of an unbroken line from the past. I am conscious of my present act of cognition: but that which is present to my consciousness is, simply the object cognized: by reflection on past acts, I know that the cognizing subject must be present and implicated—but I know it in no other way.

On looking over again Mr. F.'s letter (Mr. Grote continues), before sending off my reply, I perceive that I have dwelt rather too exclusively on the fourth page. I will therefore add a few words, answering more directly the question in page 2.

I admit that there *are* implicit cognitions: that is, as I understand it, cognitions of which we have no consciousness distinct at the time or capable of being remembered afterwards—but which nevertheless may be proved, by evidence *aliundè*, to have been objects of consciousness and to have left their effects behind. You give in your first volume ('Senses and Intellect,' p. 390) an interesting example of this kind, in reference to the intellectual discrimination between different sensations of touch, such sensations being undistinguishable both emotionally and volitionally.

But while I admit this as a fact of frequent occurrence in the human mind, and therefore as a legitimate explanation in various obscurities of mental philosophy, I must at the same time add, that the *onus probandi* lies upon him who advances the explanation. He must produce evidence to prove that these implicit cognitions have really been in the mind as cognitions. Now the evidence produced by Mr. F. does not appear to me sufficient to prove the point, in his particular case.

Again, he remarks upon a phrase of mine in my first paper —" G. says that the Ego is *understood* in all propositions— understood (F. remarks) of course by itself and to itself— that is to say, known implicitly " (bottom of page 2). In regard to this, I would say, that I do not clearly remember

2 A

the phrases in my first paper, but I presume that I meant *understood* in the sense of the Latin word *subauditum*, not *intellectum*: as the knowing element tacitly implied, and essentially as a condition, in all present knowledge, but not knowable itself except through reflex view upon past acts of knowledge.

Pray read the above remarks, and forward them to Mr. F., if you think they deserve it. I am much obliged to him for the trouble he has taken in drawing up the paper of criticism on my former remarks. I hope he will accept the present communication as a mark both of gratitude and respect.

[In the months of February and March, 1871, when the fatal malady was making progress, Mr. Grote read with avidity and with much admiration the work of M. Taine, 'De l'Intelligence.' He still kept up undiminished his life-long interest in Logical and Psychological discussions, and could give forth his thoughts with clearness and vigour, as will be seen from the following observations, being the text of letters written on such parts of Mr. Taine's work as related to the fundamental notions and the axioms of science. These were the last rays of the setting sun.]

Taine seeks to rehabilitate the Absolute, or an external self-existent, under the attenuated form of Motion reduced to its lowest terms of Order and Number, and divested of everything which distinguishes one case of Motion from another. His argument appears to me very inconclusive in these thirteen pages: for while he in several passages admits (to all appearance) the fundamental reference to ourselves and our own sensations—he in other passages professes to point out other characteristics which lie apart from this reference: the truth being, that these latter characteristics involve the same reference, just as much as the former, only that it lies behind, and requires rather more attention to see it: which attention Taine does not bestow. Thus (*e.g.*) look at p. 54, where he professes to discriminate the characteristics *relative to us* from those which are *absolute* and have no reference to us. For example, he says:—"Le *moi* est un réactif entre cent millions d'autres.—A ses notations, nous substituons d'autres notations équivalentes, et nous définissons les propriétés des corps, *non plus par nos événemens,* mais par certains de *leurs* événemens. Au lieu de *notre sensation* de température, nous prenons pour indice l'élévation ou l'abaissement de l'alcohol dans le thermomètre." Taine here overlooks the fact that the rise or fall of alcohol in the thermomètre is only another variety of our sensations: an application of our sense of vision appealed to in place of our sense of temperature, and certifying comparison of temperature inferentially instead of directly. The case is the same with the other example cited by Taine —the rise or fall in one of the scales of a balance, informing us of comparative weights, much better than could be done by our own muscular sensations when we support the two bodies with our hands. Here again appeal is made to another variety of *our* sensations: what Taine says—"nous définissons les propriétés des corps, *non plus* par *nos* événemens, mais par leurs événemens,"—is not true. We do not, and cannot, leave out *nos événemens.*

It appears as if Taine thought, that whenever we had recourse to an indirect and inferential measure respecting the properties of a body, we thereby departed from the principle of Relativity. In this I think he is quite mistaken: and moreover inconsistent with himself. For we read, p. 57, the following passage—"Entre les diverses classes d'événemens par lesquels on peut définir les choses, l'homme en choisit une, y ramène la plupart des autres, suppose qu'il pourra un jour y ramener le reste. Mais, si l'on analyse celui qu'il à choisi, on découvre que tous les élémens originels et constitutifs de sa définition, comme de la définition de tous les autres, ne sont jamais que des sensations, ou des extraits plus ou moins élaborés de sensations." Surely it is impossible to declare *universal Relativity* —the universal implication of us the sentients, and of our sensations, in every definition—in *plainer* language than this.

Again, I cannot but question the manner in which Taine conceives and defines Motion (p. 55)—"une série de sensations successives interposées entre les momens de départ et d'arrivée—une série d'états successifs interposés entre les momens de départ et d'arrivée." Surely Motion is *continuous* between departure and arrival: there is *no* series or succession of states in Motion. There is a series or order in the *places* through which the Motum passes—but in the fact of Motion itself, there is no series or succession. Motion is essentially *continuous,* from departure to stoppage: it is the very type of continuity: in order that you may have *succession* of states or of sensations, you must have stoppage and recommencement of motion. I consider it a *contradictio in adjecto* when Taine (p. 63) talks of "la *série continue* des *événemens successifs* qui constituent le mouvement d'une pierre transportée par notre main—cette *série continue* de sensations *musculaires successives* qui constituent pour nous le mouvement de notre main." When I affirm continuity, I virtually deny succession—and *vice versâ.* We are all moving along with the Earth in its two uniform motions of rotation and translation : but we have no consciousness of successive sensations constituting this motion. The terms *series* and *succession* belong, not to the motion itself, but to the places through which the Motum passes, or to the collateral sensations which attach to those places respectively : as when we move from light to dark, from cold to hot, &c. *Number* and *Order,* to which Taine professes to reduce the fact of Motion when pared down by abstraction, do not (in my opinion) belong to Motion at all, unless you include along with it certain concomitant sensations which are not of the essence of Motion, and which may be absent as well as present.

In regard to Taine's reasoning, from p. 57 to p. 65, where

he attempts to erect an Absolute on the back of Mill's theory and yours, I consider it altogether fallacious. I admit indeed that it holds good as an *argumentum ad hominem*. If I granted the absolute and independent existence of minds other than my own, I should be prepared also to grant the absolute and independent existence of rocks and trees. Indeed I think the reasons for granting it in the latter case are stronger than those applying to the former. For I have no direct knowledge or commerce with another man's mind, but only with his body: before I can infer the absolute existence of his mind, I must begin by recognizing the absolute existence of his body: and when once I have done that, I cannot refuse absolute existence to rocks and trees.

Taine takes for granted this recognition of absolute existence of *other minds*, by all the followers of Berkeley. This is really his one and only argument, which he puts forward with easy confidence — "légitimement (pp. 58, 59) sur preuves valables," p. 62. He certainly is right in supposing that Berkeley recognises this doctrine, and I think (without being quite sure) that John Mill recognises it: but *I* dissent from it entirely. Indeed I think that the common, unphilosophical, opinion of the absolute existence of the material world generally, is *more* consistent and tenable than the opinion which restricts absolute existence to minds only, our own and all others besides. No one has done more than Taine to illustrate the frequent illusions of the mind in assuming, as external and independent, what is merely subjective. But in this particular case, he cannot bear to admit "une illusion de l'esprit humain" (p. 58), which he has shown to be omnipotent in so many other cases. Yet many of his sentences appear to be written as if he held the same opinion as we do. For example (p. 68)—"Il essaye de considérer à part et en soi ce quelque chose indépendant et permanent qu'il n'a isolé que *par un oubli*. Il crée ainsi la substance vide: sur cette entité la metaphysique travaille et bâtit ainsi ses châteaux de cartes: pour les faire

2 B

tomber, ce n'est pas trop de l'analyse la plus rigoureuse." This sentence expresses my opinion, and I think very well: the *oubli* of which he speaks, is intended by him to express only the objective attributes from which *la substance vide* is detached: but I should extend the meaning so as to include also the judging and believing *Subject*; which, though omnipresent and inseparable, is just as much forgotten and put out of sight as if it had no existence.

Taine's highly abstract *attenuation* of Motion is a fetch of Realism. It is on a par with *la substance vide* in the passage last cited. How few philosophers are there who carry out consistently the doctrine which Aristotle took so much pains to inculcate—that reality is to be sought in the concrete and particular, not in the abstract and universal!

In the attempt made by Taine to bring the geometrical and arithmetical Axioms under the head of Analytic Propositions instead of Synthetic, he reasons in direct opposition to John Mill's argument in the second chapter of his second book: Taine adopts what Mill there calls "the *ultra-Nominalism* of Hobbes and Condillac" (p. 199): Taine considers "that the process of arriving at new truths by reasoning consists in the mere substitution of one set of arbitrary signs for another" and a *substitution*, in fact, is Taine's favourite phrase for the function of general words in carrying on reasonings.

I do not admit the justice of Taine's reasoning (p. 341) upon the Maxim of Contradiction: he forgets that many philosophers in the time of Aristotle, together with Hegel and others in recent years, disallowed and denied this maxim: and that they would have equally disallowed Taine's proof of it: they would not have admitted his assertion that *present* meant *not absent*—and that *absent* meant *not present*. You can only prove the maxim by uncontradicted repetition of appeals to particular facts of sense; and if your opponent will not admit these facts of sense, you cannot prove it at all. The aggregate effect on the memory and belief of these multiplied repetitions constitutes what Taine calls (p. 342)

" *l'efficacité des idées latentes* ": a phrase not psychologically correct, nor at all proper for a work on *reasoned truth*, seeing that he puts the grounds of belief in axiomatic truths on a level with emotional fancies and prejudices. That these *idées latentes* (p. 342-343) do as a matter of fact very often determine our belief, he tells us very truly : but the characteristic feature of *reasoned truth* is that those secret grounds of belief shall be brought out into distinct consciousness and critically appreciated : seeing that in their latent state, they are available alike for support either of true or false belief, and carry no authority.

In p. 344, Taine says (in proceeding to discuss the Axiom that ' the sums of equals are equal ' and the differences of equals also equal)—" Certainement, nous pouvons former ces deux propositions par l'induction ordinaire : et très probablement, c'est de cette manière qu'elles s'établissent d'abord dans notre esprit.—Toutes les fois que j'ai pratiqué dans des conditions semblables des opérations semblables, j'ai verifié que l'issue était semblable " (344, bottom).— There cannot be a clearer admission that these Axioms both may be and are of inductive origin. But in the next page, he tells us that they may also be formed *without induction* (346-347). The very supposition that there are truths proveable by Induction, (including, as Taine justly says *verification*) but which are also proveable *without* Induction —appears to me a strange one, and most unnecessary. His attempt to shew it is by resolving Equality into *Sameness*, and Inequality into Difference : and by saying that two lines which are capable of exactly coinciding " ne font plus qu'une seule et même ligne (350)—sont les mêmes—" while, if not so capable, they are *different*. It appears to me that this is a new definition of equality, which goes far to abolish it as a real attribute, and which is at the same time incorrect. Two lines capable of coinciding are equal : this is a conception essentially different from, and opposed to, the conception of two lines merged and confounded into one and the same line : the first of the two conceptions involves duality of the objects compared, the second abolishes it. You may say that twelve is *the same as* twelve, or as *duodecim, douze, zwölf*, &c. : here is one and the same thing either described twice over by different names, or the same name repeated both in subject and predicate—a mere tautology. But you cannot with propriety say—twelve is *equal* to *twelve, duodecim* : here are no two objects to compare : the proposition *twelve is equal to itself*—is either unmeaning, or metaphorical. In framing any equation of which twelve forms one side, you must find some different number to place on the other side :

$$12 = \frac{24}{2} = \frac{48}{4} = 4 \times 3 = 6 \times 2 = \sqrt{144}\text{—and so forth.}$$

Here you predicate of 12, that it is equal to the result of a certain operation performed upon some other number : that it is equal to a function of that other number, arising in a certain way. Here are always two different real terms compared ; and the number as well as variety of such comparisons might be infinitely multiplied.

Taine says (p. 353)—"Sous le mot *égal*, réside le mot *même* : voilà le mot essentiel : telle est *l'idée* latente incluse dans l'idée d'égalite. Dégagée et suivie à travers plusieurs propositions intermédiaires, elle ramène l'axiome à une proposition analytique. Par elle nous relions l'attribut au sujet : nous la voyons présente dans les deux : mais avant de l'y voir, nous l'y pressentions : elle y était et témoignait de sa présence par la contrainte qu'elle exerçait sur notre affirmation : quoique non démêlée, elle faisait son office.—Nous devinions avec certitude, mais sans pouvoir préciser les choses, que dans les deux données et dans les deux opérations, il y avait *du même* : l'analyse n'a fait qu'isoler *ce même*, et nous montrer à l'état distinct la vertu qu'il y avait en nous à l'état latent."

This paragraph seems to me incorrect : Equality seems to me to exclude *sameness*, instead of implying it : moreover we see here what an arbitrary proceeding it is to invoke these *idées latentes*, and to ascribe to their influence " *la contrainte exercée sur notre affirmation.*"

It is here formally announced that these axioms are nothing more than analytical propositions.

Taine ought to have tried his hand upon the Axiom— "Things which are equal to the same are equal to one another "—before he meddled with the more advanced proposition—The sums of equals are equal.

Suppose that a person puts before you two propositions thus framed :—

1. If there be two magnitudes A and B, both of them equal to a third magnitude C, one of those two magnitudes will be equal to the other.

2. If there be two magnitudes A and B, both of them greater than a third magnitude C, one of those two magnitudes will be greater than the other.

On hearing these two propositions for the first time, who can tell that the first is true, and the second not true, except by trying both one and the other in application to a string of particular cases ? What *idées latentes* are there in each, to enable him to make this distinction? Taine's appeal (p. 347), that we should shut our eyes and reflect upon the meaning of the terms will certainly not enable us to do this, unless we employ the interval of closed eyes in imagining a variety of triplets conforming to Propositions 1 and 2, and, examining mentally what the results would be in each case. Proposition 1, though true, is not an analytic Proposition, but synthetic. Its contradictory includes no contradiction in terms. Proposition 2 is alike synthetic, and can only be shewn to be false generally, by the production of some particular case in which observation attests it as false.

Taine's exposition and criticism of the definition of *parallels* (355—363) are also unsatisfactory to me: there is the same gratuitous substitution of *same distance* between the parallels of *equal distance.*

Also about *straight line,* (356) I agree with what he says (355) about Legendre's definition (*shortest* distance between two points). His own exposition however (356) implies the very same antithesis ("en remarquant la ligne que trace le

premier point lorsqu'il se meut vers le second et vers le
second seulement, *par opposition* à la ligne qu'il trace lorsqu'-
avant de se mouvoir vers le second, il se meut soit vers un
autre, &c.").

In this exposition, the idea of *direction* is assumed as
already acquired and familiar. In fact, it is the *idée latente*
which Taine is fond of assuming arbitrarily in other cases,
but which really exists in our minds in this case as the true
constituent of the straight line. Taine cannot resolve *direction* into anything more simple and fundamental : but he
ought to have brought it out into clearer light by varied
exposition and illustration. *Sameness* (of direction) is here
in its right place : while employed as an exponent of equality,
it is quite out of place and misleading. Direction and
Distance are both of them distinct aspects of the fact of
motion ; but both of them are fundamental and universal ;
neither of them can be resolved into the other. Legendre's
definition of *the straight line* (above noticed) attempts to
resolve direction into *distance* ; and is for that reason inadmissible as a definition, though true as an affirmation. *One
and the same* direction is known by immediate consciousness,
farther illustrated by contrast with a different immediate
consciousness—*varying direction—from and towards.* All
that can be done towards defining a straight line is, to state
and illustrate this consciousness and contrast in the most
perspicuous manner.

As to Taine's demonstration (p. 371 seq.) that several or
all of the principles of mechanics are not merely truths of
experience or inductively established, but also *analytical propositions*, I think it quite unsatisfactory : indeed I consider it
as among the worst parts of his book. The demonstration
is founded upon the same abusive appeal to "*la même*"
(p. 373) which he had reasoned upon before. It is no better
than the presumption of Aristotle, that the celestial bodies
moved in perfect circles, because it was their nature so to
move. To say that because a moving body has moved two
inches in the same direction, we are entitled to presume,

and even required to believe, that it will continue to move
onward in the same uniform direction and velocity, unless
some disturbing cause intervene—to say that this is an axiom
of which we can neither conceive nor believe the contrary
(p. 386), when he had before said (p. 370) that Aristotle and
the philosophers prior to Galileo all *did believe* the *contrary*
—seems to me an exaggeration of bold and unwarranted
assertion. It is indeed well calculated "to increase in an
infinite measure the powers of our minds" (la portée de notre
esprit s'accroit à l'infini—p. 392), and to give us knowledge
not relative, but absolute, without doubts or conditions ("ne
souffrent ni doutes, ni limites, ni conditions, ni restrictions"
—p. 393). Now that, after truths have been for a long time
unknown or disallowed, and only built up in the face of able
opponents by laborious induction, a philosopher should come
forward and say that the induction was altogether superfluous, and that the conclusion was really contained in, and
inseparable from, the premisses—appear to me assertions no
less incredible than anything which we read in Aristotle 'De
Cœlo.'

In all your remarks about the Postulate of the Uniformity
of Nature I perfectly concur. But we must remember that
Aristotle and the Peripatetics not only did not allow this Postulate, but affirmed another Postulate distinctly contradicting
it, viz.: That there were some sequences essentially regular,
others essentially irregular and unpredictable. The Postulate
of Uniform Nature has been ascertained and verified by a large
and ever increasing sweep of Induction, and is *now* well
entitled to overbear the counter-presumption which Aristotle
in his day admitted as dividing with it the empire of phenomena. But it derives its certainty and authority entirely
from Induction: and the last Chapter of Taine's book appears to me extremely misleading, inasmuch as it is a hazy
maze of words tending to make you believe that there is
a distinct authority co-operating with and even superior to
Induction—viz.: "la raison explicative, *la soudure*," between
the separate links of the Inductive process. This extra-

physical authority is alleged by Taine to do what Induction cannot do: that is, it gives us knowledge absolute and unconditional, which we can never obtain by Induction. Taine cites (with praise) Mill's Chapter on the Explanation of Laws of Nature: but he either misunderstands, or deliberately departs from, the main doctrines of that valuable Chapter: which presents in the clearest manner the true relation between the more comprehensive and the less comprehensive theorems in science. Taine speaks as if he thought that whenever we study one particular property of objects apart from the rest, we desert the path of Induction, and enable ourselves to discover and handle extra-physical entities such as *le même, la soudure*, &c., thus putting ourselves on a platform above the inductive process.

This last chapter of Taine appears to me a surrender of Mill's Logic to the *à priori* of Leibnitz. It really contains some things which surprise me. "Nos yeux ne peuvent percevoir l'étendue que comme colorée: de même, notre intelligence ne peut concevoir des faits que comme explicables. Il n'y a de concevable pour nous que ce qui est explicable; comme il n'y a de visible pour nous que ce qui est colorée" (p. 481). He forgets that Aristotle and the Peripatetics distinctly held the contrary, and treated this position as itself incredible.

The last page of Taine's book (491, 492) I do not clearly understand, but it seems to invest *à priori* procedure with a degree of power which enables it to dispense with experience altogether, and to determine beforehand, among the entire catalogue of possible existences, which of them (or how many among them) admit of becoming real. Taine then suggests that the enterprise of Hegel should be re-attempted with greater precautions. I can hardly think that he has studied Mill's Logic with any hearty and serious grasp of its spirit and contents.

LONDON: PRINTED BY WILLIAM CLOWES AND SONS, STAMFORD STREET
AND CHARING CROSS.

ALBEMARLE STREET, LONDON,
February, 1873.

MR. MURRAY'S

GENERAL LIST OF WORKS.

ALBERT (THE) MEMORIAL. The National Monument erected
to the PRINCE CONSORT at Kensington. Illustrated by Engravings
of its Architecture, Decorations; Sculptured Groups, Statues, Mosaics,
Metalwork, &c. With Descriptive Text. With 24 Plates. Folio. 12*l*. 12*s*.
Large Paper. 15*l*. 15*s*. Published by Authority.

. A POPULAR HANDBOOK to the above Monument. Woodcuts.
16mo. 1*s*.

———— (PRINCE) SPEECHES AND ADDRESSES ON PUBLIC
Occasions; with an Introduction, giving some outline of his Character.
With Portrait. 8vo. 10*s*. 6*d*.; or *Popular Edition*, fcap. 8vo. 1*s*.

ABBOTT'S (REV. J.) Memoirs of a Church of England Missionary
in the North American Colonies. Post 8vo. 2*s*.

ABERCROMBIE'S (JOHN) Enquiries concerning the Intellectual
Powers and the Investigation of Truth. 19*th Edition*. Fcap. 8vo. 3*s*. 6*d*.

———————— Philosophy of the Moral Feelings. 14*th
Edition*. Fcap. 8vo. 2*s*. 6*d*.

ACLAND'S (REV. CHARLES) Popular Account of the Manners and
Customs of India. Post 8vo. 2*s*.

ÆSOP'S FABLES. A New Version. With Historical Preface.
By Rev. THOMAS JAMES. With 100 Woodcuts, by TENNIEL and WOLF.
64*th Thousand*. Post 8vo. 2*s*. 6*d*.

AGRICULTURAL (ROYAL) JOURNAL. 8vo. 6*s*. (*Half yearly*.)

AIDS TO FAITH : a Series of Theological Essays. 8vo. 9*s*.

CONTENTS.

Miracles	DEAN MANSEL.
Evidences of Christianity	BISHOP OF KILLALOE.
Prophecy & Mosaic Record of Creation	Rev. Dr McCAUL.
Ideology and Subscription	Canon COOK.
The Pentateuch	Canon RAWLINSON.
Inspiration	BISHOP OF ELY.
Death of Christ	ARCHBISHOP OF YORK.
Scripture and its Interpretation	BISHOP OF GLOUCESTER AND BRISTOL.

AMBER-WITCH (THE). A most interesting Trial for Witchcraft. Translated by LADY DUFF GORDON. Post 8vo. 2*s*.

ARMY LIST (THE). *Published Monthly by Authority*. 18mo. 2*s*.

ARTHUR'S (LITTLE) History of England. By LADY CALLCOTT.
New Edition, continued to 1872. Woodcuts. Fcap. 8vo. 2*s*. 6*d*.

AUSTIN'S (JOHN) LECTURES ON GENERAL JURISPRUDENCE ; or, the
Philosophy of Positive Law. 5*th Edition*. Edited by ROBERT CAMP-
BELL. 2 Vols. 8vo. 32*s*.

———————— (SARAH) Fragments from German Prose Writers.
With Biographical Notes. Post 8vo. 10*s*.

B

ADMIRALTY PUBLICATIONS; Issued by direction of the Lords Commissioners of the Admiralty:—

A MANUAL OF SCIENTIFIC ENQUIRY, for the Use of Travellers. Edited by Sir JOHN F. HERSCHEL and ROBERT MAIN, M.A. *Fourth Edition*. Woodcuts. Post 8vo. 3s. 6d.

AIRY'S ASTRONOMICAL OBSERVATIONS MADE AT GREENWICH. 1836 to 1847. Royal 4to. 50s. each.

——— MAGNETICAL AND METEOROLOGICAL OBSERVA-TIONS. 1840 to 1847. Royal 4to. 50s. each.

——— ASTRONOMICAL, MAGNETICAL, AND METEOROLO-GICAL OBSERVATIONS, 1848 to 1870. Royal 4to. 50s. each.

——— APPENDICES TO THE ASTRONOMICAL OBSERVA-TIONS.

1836.—I. Bessel's Refraction Tables.
II. Tables for converting Errors of R.A. and N.P.D. into Errors of Longitude and Ecliptic P.D. } 8s.

1837.—I. Logarithms of Sines and Cosines to every Ten Seconds of Time.
II. Table for converting Sidereal into Mean Solar Time. } 8s.

1842.—Catalogue of 1439 Stars. 8s.

1845.—Longitude of Valentia. 8s.

1847.—Description of Altazimuth. (*Reprint.*) 5s.

1851.—Maskelyne's Ledger of Stars. 6s.

1852.—I. Description of the Transit Circle. (*Reprint.*) 5s.
II. Regulations of the Royal Observatory. 2s.

1853.—Bessel's Refraction Tables. 3s.

1854.—I. Description of the Zenith Tube. 3s.
II. Six Years' Catalogue of Stars. 10s.

1856.—Description of the Galvanic Apparatus at Greenwich Observatory. 8s.

1862.—I. Seven Years' Catalogue of Stars. 10s.
II. Plan of the Building and Ground of the Royal Observatory, Greenwich.
III. Longitude of Valentia. } 3s.

1864.—I. Moon's Semidiameter.
II. Planetary Observations, 1831 to 1835.

1868.—I. Corrections of Bouvard's Elements of Jupiter and Saturn. 4s.
II. Seven Years' Catalogue of 2760 Stars for 1864. 10s.
III. Description of the Great Equatoreal. 5s.

——— ASTRONOMICAL RESULTS. 1848 to 1870. 4to. 8s.

——— MAGNETICAL AND METEOROLOGICAL RESULTS. 1848 to 1870. 4to. 8s. each.

——— REDUCTION OF THE OBSERVATIONS OF PLANETS. 1750 to 1830. Royal 4to. 50s.

——— LUNAR OBSERVATIONS. 1750 to 1830. 2 Vols. Royal 4to. 50s. each.
——— 1831 to 1851. 4to. 20s.

BERNOULLI'S SEXCENTENARY TABLE. *London*, 1779. 4to. 5s.

BESSEL'S AUXILIARY TABLES FOR HIS METHOD OF CLEAR-ING LUNAR DISTANCES. 8vo. 2s.

ADMIRALTY PUBLICATIONS—*continued.*

COOK, KING, AND BAYLY'S ASTRONOMICAL OBSERVATIONS. *London,* 1782. 4to. 21*s.*

ENCKE'S BERLINER JAHRBUCH, for 1830. *Berlin,* 1828. 8vo. 9*s.*

HANSEN'S TABLES DE LA LUNE. 4to. 20*s.*

HARRISON'S PRINCIPLES OF HIS TIME-KEEPER. PLATES. 1797. 4to. 5*s.*

LAX'S TABLES FOR FINDING THE LATITUDE AND LONGI- TUDE. 1821. 8vo. 10*s.*

LUNAR OBSERVATIONS at GREENWICH. 1783 to 1819. Compared with the Tables, 1821. 4to. 7*s.* 6*d.*

MACLEAR ON LACAILLE'S ARC OF MERIDIAN. 2 Vols. 20*s.*

MASKELYNE'S ACCOUNT OF THE GOING OF HARRISON'S WATCH. 1767. 4to. 2*s.* 6*d.*

MAYER'S DISTANCES of the MOON'S CENTRE from the PLANETS. 1822, 3*s.*; 1823, 4*s.* 6*d.* 1824 to 1835. 8vo. 4*s.* each.

—— TABULÆ MOTUUM SOLIS ET LUNÆ. 1770. 5*s.*

—— ASTRONOMICAL OBSERVATIONS MADE AT GOT- TINGEN, from 1756 to 1761. 1826. Folio. 7*s.* 6*d.*

NAUTICAL ALMANACS, from 1767 to 1876. 8vo. 2*s.* 6*d.* each.

—— SELECTIONS FROM THE ADDITIONS up to 1812. 8vo. 5*s.* 1834-54. 8vo. 5*s.*

—— SUPPLEMENTS, 1828 to 1833, 1837 and 1838. 8vo. 2*s.* each.

—— TABLE requisite to be used with the N.A. 1781. 8vo. 5*s.*

POND'S ASTRONOMICAL OBSERVATIONS. 1811 to 1835. 4to. 21*s.* each.

SABINE'S PENDULUM EXPERIMENTS to DETERMINE THE FIGURE OF THE EARTH. 1825. 4to. 40*s.*

SHEPHERD'S TABLES for CORRECTING LUNAR DISTANCES. 1772. Royal 4to. 21*s.*

—— TABLES, GENERAL, of the MOON'S DISTANCE from the SUN, and 10 STARS. 1787. Folio. 5*s.* 6*d.*

TAYLOR'S SEXAGESIMAL TABLE. 1780. 4to. 15*s.*

—— TABLES OF LOGARITHMS. 4to. 3*l.*

TIARK'S ASTRONOMICAL OBSERVATIONS for the LONGITUDE of MADEIRA. 1822. 4to. 5*s.*

—— CHRONOMETRICAL OBSERVATIONS for DIFFERENCES of LONGITUDE between DOVER, PORTSMOUTH, and FALMOUTH. 1823. 4to. 5*s.*

VENUS and JUPITER: OBSERVATIONS of, compared with the TABLES. *London,* 1822. 4to. 2*s.*

WALES' AND BAYLY'S ASTRONOMICAL OBSERVATIONS. 1777. 4to. 21*s.*

WALES' REDUCTION OF ASTRONOMICAL OBSERVATIONS MADE IN THE SOUTHERN HEMISPHERE. 1764—1771. 1788. 4to. 10*s.* 6*d.*

BARBAULD'S (MRS.) Hymns in Prose for Children. With 112 Illustrations. Small 4to. 5*s.* ; or *Fine Paper,* 7*s.* 6*d.*

BARROW'S (SIR JOHN) Autobiographical Memoir, from Early Life to Advanced Age. Portrait. 8vo. 16*s.*

—— (JOHN) Life, Exploits, and Voyages of Sir Francis Drake. Post 8vo. 2*s.*

B 2

BARRY'S (Sir Charles) Life and Works. By Canon Barry, D.D.
Second Edition. With Portrait and Illustrations. Medium 8vo. 15s.

BATES' (H. W.) Records of a Naturalist on the River Amazon
during eleven years of Adventure and Travel. *Third Edition.* Illustrations. Post 8vo.

BEAUCLERK'S (Lady Diana) Summer and Winter in Norway.
Third Edition. With Illustrations. Small 8vo. 6s.

BEES AND FLOWERS. Two Essays. By Rev. Thomas James.
Reprinted from the "Quarterly Review." Fcap. 8vo. 1s. each.

BELCHER'S (Lady) Account of the Mutineers of the 'Bounty,'
and their Descendants; with their Settlements in Pitcairn and Norfolk
Islands. With Illustrations. Post 8vo. 12s.

BELL'S (Sir Chas.) Familiar Letters. Portrait. Post 8vo. 12s.

BERTRAM'S (Jas. G.) Harvest of the Sea: a Contribution to the
Natural and Economic History of British Food Fishes. *Second Edition.*
With 50 Illustrations. 8vo. 12s.

BIBLE COMMENTARY. Explanatory and Critical. With
a Revision of the Translation. By BISHOPS and CLERGY of the
ANGLICAN CHURCH. Edited by F.C. Cook, M.A., Canon of Exeter.
Medium 8vo. Vol. I. 30s. Vol. II. 20s.

Vol. I.	Genesis	Bishop of Ely.
	Exodus	Canon Cook & Rev. Sam. Clark.
	Leviticus	Rev. Samuel Clark.
	Numbers	Canon Espin & Rev. J. F. Thrupp.
	Deuteronomy	Canon Espin.
Vol. II.	Joshua	Canon Espin.
	Judges, Ruth, Samuel.	Bishop of Bath and Wells,
	I. Kings	Canon Rawlinson.

BICKMORE'S (A. S.) Travels in the Eastern Archipelago,
1865-6; a Popular Description of the Islands, with their Natural History, Geography, Manners and Customs of the People, &c. With Maps
and Illustrations. 8vo. 21s.

BIRCH'S (Samuel) History of Ancient Pottery and Porcelain:
Egyptian, Assyrian, Greek, Roman, and Etruscan. *Second Edition.*
With 200 Illustrations. Medium 8vo. 42s.

BISSET'S (Andrew) History of the Commonwealth of England,
from the Death of Charles I. to the Expulsion of the Long Parliament
by Cromwell. Chiefly from the MSS. in the State Paper Office. 2 vols.
8vo. 30s.

BLUNT'S (Rev. J. J.) Undesigned Coincidences in the Writings of
the Old and New Testament, an Argument of their Veracity: containing
the Books of Moses, Historical and Prophetical Scriptures, and the
Gospels and Acts. *Eleventh Edition.* Post 8vo. 6s.

———— History of the Church in the First Three Centuries.
Fifth Edition. Post 8vo. 6s.

———— Parish Priest; His Duties, Acquirements and Obligations. *Fifth Edition.* Post 8vo. 6s.

———— Lectures on the Right Use of the Early Fathers.
Third Edition. 8vo. 9s.

———— Plain Sermons Preached to a Country Congregation.
Sixth Edition. 2 Vols. Post 8vo. 12s.

———— Essays on various subjects. 8vo. 12s.

BLOMFIELD'S (Bishop) Memoir, with Selections from his Correspondence. By his Son. *Second Edition.* Portrait, post 8vo. 12s.

BOSWELL'S (James) Life of Samuel Johnson, LL.D. Including the Tour to the Hebrides. Edited by Mr. Croker. Portraits. Royal 8vo. 10s.

BRACE'S (C. L.) Manual of Ethnology; or the Races of the Old World. Post 8vo. 6s.

BOOK OF COMMON PRAYER. Illustrated with Coloured Borders, Initial Letters, and Woodcuts. 8vo. 18s.

BORROW'S (George) Bible in Spain; or the Journeys, Adventures, and Imprisonments of an Englishman in an Attempt to circulate the Scriptures in the Peninsula. Post 8vo. 3s. 6d.

———— Zincali, or the Gipsies of Spain; their Manners, Customs, Religion, and Language. Post 8vo. 3s. 6d.

———— Lavengro; The Scholar—The Gipsy—and the Priest. Post 8vo. 5s.

———— Romany Rye—a Sequel to "Lavengro." Post 8vo. 5s.

———— Wild Wales: its People, Language, and Scenery. Post 8vo. 5s.

BRAY'S (Mrs.) Life of Thomas Stothard, R.A. With Portrait and 60 Woodcuts. 4to. 21s.

———— Revolt of the Protestants in the Cevennes. With some Account of the Huguenots in the Seventeenth Century. Post 8vo. 10s. 6d.

BRITISH ASSOCIATION REPORTS. 8vo.

York and Oxford, 1831-32, 13s. 6d.	Belfast, 1852, 15s.
Cambridge, 1833, 12s.	Hull, 1853, 10s. 6d.
Edinburgh, 1834, 15s.	Liverpool, 1854, 18s.
Dublin, 1835, 13s. 6d.	Glasgow, 1855, 15s.
Bristol, 1836, 12s.	Cheltenham, 1856, 18s.
Liverpool, 1837, 16s. 6d.	Dublin, 1857, 15s.
Newcastle, 1838, 15s.	Leeds, 1858, 20s.
Birmingham, 1839, 13s. 6d	Aberdeen, 1859, 15s.
Glasgow, 1840, 15s.	Oxford, 1860, 25s.
Plymouth, 1841, 13s. 6d.	Manchester, 1861, 15s.
Manchester, 1842, 10s. 6d.	Cambridge, 1862, 20s.
Cork, 1843, 12s.	Newcastle, 1863, 25s.
York, 1844, 20s.	Bath, 1864, 18s.
Cambridge, 1845, 12s.	Birmingham, 1865, 25s
Southampton, 1846, 15s.	Nottingham, 1866, 24s.
Oxford, 1847, 18s.	Dundee, 1867, 26s.
Swansea, 1848, 9s.	Norwich, 1868, 25s.
Birmingham, 1849, 10s.	Exeter, 1869, 22s.
Edinburgh, 1850, 15s.	Liverpool, 1870, 18s.
Ipswich, 1851, 16s. 6d.	Edinburgh, 1871, 18s.

BROUGHTON'S (Lord) Journey through Albania, Turkey in Europe and Asia, to Constantinople. Illustrations. 2 Vols. 8vo. 30s.

———— Visits to Italy. 2 Vols. Post 8vo. 18s.

BROWNLOW'S (Lady) Reminiscences of a Septuagenarian. From the year 1802 to 1815. *Third Edition.* Post 8vo. 7s. 6d.

BUBBLES FROM THE BRUNNEN OF NASSAU. By Sir Francis B. Head, Bart. *7th Edition.* Illustrations. Post 8vo. 7s. 6d.

BUNYAN (John) and Oliver Cromwell. By Robert Southey. Post 8vo. 2s.

BURGON'S (Rev. J. W.) Christian Gentleman; or, Memoir of Patrick Fraser Tytler. *Second Edition.* Post 8vo. 9s.

———— Letters from Rome. Post 8vo. 12s.

BURN'S (Col.) Dictionary of Naval and Military Technical Terms, English and French—French and English. *Fourth Edition*. Crown 8vo. 15*s*.

BURROW'S (Montagu) Constitutional Progress. A Series of Lectures delivered before the University of Oxford. *2nd Edition*. Post 8vo. 5*s*.

BUXTON'S (Charles) Memoirs of Sir Thomas Fowell Buxton, Bart. With Selections from his Correspondence. Portrait. 8vo. 16*s*. *Popular Edition*. Fcap. 8vo. 5*s*.

———— Notes of Thought. With Biographical Sketch. By Rev. Llewellyn Davies. With Portrait. Crown 8vo. 10*s*. 6*d*.

———— Ideas of the Day on Policy. *3rd Edition*. 8vo. 6*s*.

BURCKHARDT'S (Dr. Jacob) Cicerone; or Art Guide to Painting in Italy. Edited by Rev. Dr. A. Von Zahn, and Translated from the German by Mrs. A. Clough. Post 8vo.

BYRON'S (Lord) Letters and Journals. By Thomas Moore. *Cabinet Edition*. Plates. 6 Vols. Fcap. 8vo. 18*s*.

———— *Popular Edition*. Portraits. Royal 8vo.

———— Poetical Works. *Library Edition*. Portrait. 6 Vols. Demy 8vo. 45*s*.

———— *Cabinet Edition*. Plates. 10 Vols. Fcap. 8vo. 30*s*.

———— Pocket Edition. 8 Vols. 24mo. 21*s*. *Bound, and in a Case*.

———— *Popular Edition*. Plates. Royal 8vo.

———— *Pearl Edition*. Crown 8vo. 2*s*. 6*d*.

———— Childe Harold. With 80 Engravings. 8vo. 12*s*.

———— 16mo. 2*s*. 6*d*.

———— Vignettes. 16mo. 1*s*.

———— Portrait. 16mo. 6*d*.

———— Tales and Poems. 24mo. 2*s*. 6*d*.

———— Miscellaneous. 2 Vols. 24mo. 5*s*.

———— Dramas and Plays. 2 Vols. 24mo. 5*s*.

———— Don Juan and Beppo. 2 Vols. 24mo. 5*s*.

———— Beauties. Portrait. Fcap. 8vo. 3*s*. 6*d*.

BURR'S (G. D.) Instructions in Practical Surveying, Topographical Plan Drawing, and on sketching ground without Instruments. *Fourth Edition*. Woodcuts. Post 8vo. 6*s*.

BUTTMAN'S LEXILOGUS; a Critical Examination of the Meaning of numerous Greek Words, chiefly in Homer and Hesiod. Translated by Rev. J. R. Fishlake. *Fifth Edition*. 8vo. 12*s*.

———— CATALOGUE OF IRREGULAR GREEK VERBS. With all the Tenses extant—their Formation, Meaning, and Usage, accompanied by an Index. Translated, with Notes, by Rev. J. R. Fishlake. *Fifth Edition*. Revised by Rev. E. Venables. Post 8vo. 6*s*.

CALLCOTT'S (Lady) Little Arthur's History of England. *New Edition, brought down to* 1872. With Woodcuts. Fcap. 8vo. 2*s*. 6*d*.

CAMPBELL'S (LORD) **Lives of the Lord Chancellors and Keepers** of the Great Seal of England. From the Earliest Times to the Death of Lord Eldon in 1838. *Fourth Edition.* 10 Vols. Crown 8vo. 6s. each.

———— **Lords Lyndhurst and Brougham.** 8vo. 16s.

———— **Chief Justices of England.** From the Norman Conquest to the Death of Lord Tenterden. *Second Edition.* 3 Vols. 8vo. 42s.

———— **Shakspeare's Legal Acquirements.** 8vo. 5s. 6d.

———— **Life of Lord Bacon.** Fcap. 8vo. 2s. 6d.

———— (SIR NEIL) **Account of Napoleon at Fontainebleau** and Elba. Being a Journal of Occurrences and Notes of his Conversations, &c. Portrait. 8vo. 15s.

———— (GEORGE) **Modern India. A Sketch of the System** of Civil Government. With some Account of the Natives and Native Institutions. *Second Edition.* 8vo. 16s.

———— (THOS.) **Essay on English Poetry.** With Short Lives of the British Poets. Post 8vo. 3s. 6d.

CARNARVON'S (LORD) **Portugal, Gallicia, and the Basque Provinces.** *Third Edition.* Post 8vo. 3s. 6d.

———— **Reminiscences of Athens and the Morea.** With Map. Crown 8vo. 7s. 6d.

———— **Recollections of the Druses of Lebanon.** With Notes on their Religion. *Third Edition.* Post 8vo. 5s. 6d.

CASTLEREAGH (THE) **DESPATCHES, from the commencement** of the official career of Viscount Castlereagh to the close of his life. 12 Vols. 8vo. 14s. each.

CATHCART'S (SIR GEORGE) **Commentaries on the War in Russia** and Germany, 1812-13. Plans. 8vo. 14s.

CAVALCASELLE AND **CROWE'S History of Painting in** Italy, from the 2nd to the 16th Century. With Illustrations. 5 Vols. 8vo. 21s. each.

———— **Early Flemish Painters, their Lives and** Works. Illustrations. Post 8vo. 10s. 6d.; or Large Paper, 8vo. 15s.

CHILD (G. CHAPLIN, M.D.) **Benedicite; or, the Song of the Three** Children; being Illustrations of the Power, Beneficence, and Design manifested by the Creator in his works. *10th Thousand.* Post 8vo. 6s.

CHURTON'S (ARCHDEACON) **Gongora. An Historical Essay on the** Age of Philip III. and IV. of Spain. With Translations. Portrait. 2 Vols. Small 8vo. 12s.

———— **New Testament.** Edited with a Plain Practical Commentary for the use of Families and General Readers. With 100 Panoramic and other Views, from Sketches and Photographs made on the Spot. 2 vols. 8vo. 21s.

CICERO'S LIFE AND TIMES. His Character as a Statesman, Orator, and Friend, with a Selection from his Correspondence and Orations. By WILLIAM FORSYTH, LL.D. *Third Edition.* With Illustrations. 8vo. 10s. 6d.

CLARK'S (SIR JAMES) **Memoir of Dr. John Conolly.** Comprising a Sketch of the Treatment of the Insane in Europe and America. With Portrait. Post 8vo. 10s. 6d.

CHURCH (The) & THE AGE. Essays on the Principles and
Present Position of the Anglican Church. 8vo. 14s. Contents:—

Anglican Principles —Dean Hook.
Modern Religious Thought.—Bishop of
Gloucester and Bristol.
State, Church, and Synods.—Rev. Dr.
Irons.
Religious Use of Taste.—Rev. R. St.
John Tyrwhitt.
Place of the Laity.— Professor Burrows.
Parish Priest.—Rev. Walsham How.

Divines of 16th and 17th Centuries.
—Rev. A. W Haddan.
Liturgies and Ritual, Rev. M. F.
Sadler.
Church & Education.—Canon Barry.
Indian Missions.—Sir Bartle Frere.
Church and the People.—Rev. W. D.
Maclagan.
Conciliation and Comprehension.—
Rev. Dr. Weir.

———————— SECOND SERIES. 8vo. 12s. Contents:—

Church and Pauperism —Earl Nelson.
American Church.—Bishop of Western
New York.
Church and Science. — Prebendary
Clark.
Ecclesiastical Law.—Isambard Brunel.
Church & National Education.—
Canon Norris.
Church and Universities.—John G.
Talbot.

Toleration.—Dean Cowie.
Eastern Church and Anglican Com-
munion.—Rev. Geo. Williams.
A Disestablished Church.—Dean of
Cashel.
Christian Tradition.—Rev. Dr. Irons.
Dogma.—Rev. Dr. Weir.
Parochial Councils. — Archdeacon
Chapman.

CLIVE'S (Lord) Life. By Rev. G. R. Gleig. Post 8vo. 3s. 6d.

CLODE'S (C. M.) Military Forces of the Crown ; their Administration and Government. 2 Vols. 8vo. 21s. each.

———————— Administration of Justice under Military and Martial
Law. 8vo. 12s.

COLCHESTER (The) PAPERS. The Diary and Correspondence
of Charles Abbott, Lord Colchester, Speaker of the House of Commons,
1802–1817. Portrait. 3 Vols. 8vo. 42s.

COLERIDGE'S (Samuel Taylor) Table-Talk. Sixth Edition.
Portrait. Fcap. 8vo. 3s. 6d.

COLLINGWOOD'S (Cuthbert) Rambles of a Naturalist on the
Shores and Waters of the China Sea. Being Observations in Natural
History during a Voyage to China, &c. With Illustrations. 8vo. 16s.

COLONIAL LIBRARY. [See Home and Colonial Library.]

COOK'S (Canon) Sermons Preached at Lincoln's Inn Chapel,
and on Special Occasions. 8vo. 9s.

COOKERY (Modern Domestic). Founded on Principles of Economy
and Practical Knowledge, and adapted for Private Families. By a
Lady. New Edition. Woodcuts. Fcap. 8vo. 5s.

COOPER'S (T. T.) Travels of a Pioneer of Commerce on an
Overland Journey from China towards India. Illustrations. 8vo. 16s.

CORNWALLIS (The) Papers and Correspondence during the
American War,—Administrations in India,—Union with Ireland, and
Peace of Amiens. Second Edition. 3 Vols. 8vo. 63s.

COWPER'S (Countess) Diary while Lady of the Bedchamber
to Caroline Princess of Wales, 1714–20. Edited by Hon. Spencer
Cowper. Second Edition. Portrait. 8vo. 10s. 6d.

CRABBE'S (Rev. George) Life and Poetical Works. With Illustrations. Royal 8vo. 7s.

CROKER'S (J. W.) Progressive Geography for Children.
Fifth Edition. 18mo. 1s. 6d.
——— Stories for Children, Selected from the History of England. *Fifteenth Edition.* Woodcuts. 16mo. 2s. 6d.
— Boswell's Life of Johnson. Including the Tour to the Hebrides. Portraits. Royal 8vo. 10s.
——— Essays on the Early Period of the French Revolution. 8vo. 15s.
——— Historical Essay on the Guillotine. Fcap. 8vo. 1s.

CROMWELL (Oliver) and JOHN BUNYAN. Essays. By Robert Southey. Post 8vo. 2s.

CUMMING'S (R. Gordon) Five Years of a Hunter's Life in the Far Interior of South Africa; with Anecdotes of the Chace, and Notices of the Native Tribes. *Sixth Edition.* Woodcuts. Post 8vo. 6s.

CROWE'S and CAVALCASELLE'S Lives of the Early Flemish Painters. Woodcuts. Post 8vo, 10s. 6d.; or Large Paper, 8vo, 15s.

——— History of Painting in Italy, from 2nd to 16th Century. Derived from Historical Researches as well as Inspection of the Works of Art in that Country. With more than 100 Illustrations. 5 Vols. 8vo. 21s. each.

CUNYNGHAME'S (Sir Arthur) Travels in the Eastern Caucasus, on the Caspian, and Black Seas, in Daghestan and the Frontiers of Persia and Turkey. With Map and Illustrations. 8vo. 18s.

CURTIUS' (Professor) Student's Greek Grammar, for the Upper Forms. Edited by Dr. Wm. Smith. *Third Edition.* Post 8vo. 6s.
——— Elucidations of the above Grammar. Translated by Evelyn Abbot. Post 8vo. 7s. 6d.
——— Smaller Greek Grammar for the Middle and Lower Forms. Abridged from the above. 12mo. 3s 6d.
——— Accidence of the Greek Language. Extracted from the above work. 12mo. 2s. 6d.
——— Principles of Greek Etymology. Translated by A. S. Wilkins, M.A, and E. B. England, B.A. Post 8vo.

CURZON'S (Hon. Robert) Armenia and Erzeroum. A Year on the Frontiers of Russia, Turkey, and Persia. *Third Edition.* Woodcuts. Post 8vo. 7s. 6d.
——— Visits to the Monasteries of the Levant. *Fifth Edition.* Illustrations. Post 8vo. 7s. 6d.

CUST'S (General) Lives of the Warriors of the 17th Century—The Thirty Years' War. 2 Vols. 16s. Civil Wars of France and England.- 2 Vols. 16s. Commanders of Fleets and Armies before the Enemy. 2 Vols. 18s.
——— Annals of the Wars—18th & 19th Century, 1700—1815. Compiled from the most Authentic Sources. With Maps. 9 Vols. Post 8vo. 5s. each.

DAVIS'S (Nathan) Visit to the Ruined Cities of Numidia and Carthaginia. Illustrations. 8vo. 16s.

DAVY'S (Sir Humphry) Consolations in Travel; or, Last Days of a Philosopher. *Seventh Edition.* Woodcuts. Fcap. 8vo. 3s. 6d.
——— Salmonia; or, Days of Fly Fishing. *Fifth Edition.* Woodcuts. Fcap. 8vo. 3s. 6d.

DE BEAUVOIR'S (Marquis) Voyage Round the World : touching at Australia, Java, Siam, Canton, Pekin, Jeddo, and San Francisco. 3 vols. Post 8vo.

DARWIN'S (CHARLES) Journal of Researches into the Natural
History of the Countries visited during the Voyage of H.M.S. "Beagle"
round the World. *Eleventh Thousand.* Post 8vo. 9s.

—   Origin of Species by Means of Natural Selection ;
or, the Preservation of Favoured Races in the Struggle for Life. *Sixth
Edition.* Post 8vo. 7s. 6d.

—   Variation of Animals and Plants under Domestication.
With Illustrations. 2 Vols. 8vo. 28s.

—   Descent of Man, and on Selection in Relation to Sex.
With Illustrations. 2 Vols. Crown 8vo. 24s.

—   Expressions of the Emotions in Man and Animals.
With Illustrations. Crown 8vo. 12s.

—   Fertilization of Orchids through Insect Agency, and
as to the good of Intercrossing. Woodcuts. Post 8vo. 9s.

—   Fact and Argument for Darwin. By FRITZ MULLER.
With numerous Illustrations and Additions by the Author. Translated
from the German by W. S. DALLAS. Woodcuts. Post 8vo. 6s.

DELEPIERRE'S (OCTAVE) History of Flemish Literature. 8vo. 9s.

—   Historical Difficulties and Contested Events.
Being Notes on some Doubtful Points of History. Post 8vo. 6s.

DENISON'S (E. B.) Life of Bishop Lonsdale. With Selections
from his Writings. With Portrait. Crown 8vo. 10s. 6d.

DERBY'S (EARL OF) Iliad of Homer rendered into English
Blank Verse. *7th Edition.* 2 Vols. Post 8vo. 10s.

DE ROS'S (LORD) Memorials of the Tower of London. *Second
Edition.* With Illustrations. Crown 8vo. 12s.

—   Young Officer's Companion ; or, Essays on Military
Duties and Qualities : with Examples and Illustrations from History.
Post 8vo. 9s.

DOG-BREAKING ; the Most Expeditious, Certain, and Easy
Method, whether great excellence or only mediocrity be required. With
a Few Hints for those who Love the Dog and the Gun. By LIEUT.-
GEN. HUTCHINSON. *Fifth Edition.* With 40 Woodcuts. Crown 8vo. 9s.

DOMESTIC MODERN COOKERY. Founded on Principles of
Economy and Practical Knowledge, and adapted for Private Families.
New Edition. Woodcuts. Fcap. 8vo. 5s.

DOUGLAS'S (SIR HOWARD) Life and Adventures. Portrait. 8vo. 15s.

—   Theory and Practice of Gunnery. *Fifth Edition.* Plates.
8vo. 21s.

—   Constructions of Bridges and the Passage of Rivers,
in Military Operations. *Third Edition.* Plates. 8vo. 21s.

DRAKE'S (SIR FRANCIS) Life, Voyages, and Exploits, by Sea and
Land. By JOHN BARROW. *Third Edition.* Post 8vo. 2s.

DRINKWATER'S (JOHN) History of the Siege of Gibraltar,
1779-1783. With a Description and Account of that Garrison from the
Earliest Periods. Post 8vo. 2s.

DUCANGE'S MEDIÆVAL LATIN-ENGLISH DICTIONARY.
Translated by Rev. E. A. DAYMAN, M.A. Small 4to.
                                        (*In preparation.*)

DU CHAILLU'S (PAUL B.) EQUATORIAL AFRICA, with
Accounts of the Gorilla, the Nest-building Ape, Chimpanzee, Croco-
dile, &c. Illustrations. 8vo. 21s.

—   Journey to Ashango Land ; and Further Penetration into Equatorial Africa. Illustrations. 8vo. 21s.

DUFFERIN'S (LORD) Letters from High Latitudes; an Account of a Yacht Voyage to Iceland, Jan Mayen, and Spitzbergen. *Fifth Edition*. Woodcuts. Post 8vo. 7s. 6d.

DUNCAN'S (CAPTAIN) History of the Royal Artillery. Compiled from the Original Records. Vol. 1 to the Peace of 1783. With Portrait. 8vo. 15s.

DYER'S (THOS. H.) History of Modern Europe, from the taking of Constantinople by the Turks to the close of the War in the Crimea. With Index. 4 Vols. 8vo. 42s.

EASTLAKE'S (SIR CHARLES) Italian Schools of Painting. From the German of KUGLER. Edited, with Notes. *Third Edition*. Illustrated from the Old Masters. 2 Vols. Post 8vo. 30s.

——— Contributions to the Literature of the Fine Arts. With Memoir of the Author, and Selections from his Correspondence. By LADY EASTLAKE. 2 Vols. 8vo. 24s.

EDWARDS' (W. H.) Voyage up the River Amazon, including a Visit to Para. Post 8vo. 2s.

ELDON'S (LORD) Public and Private Life, with Selections from his Correspondence and Diaries. By HORACE TWISS. *Third Edition*. Portrait. 2 Vols. Post 8vo. 21s.

ELGIN'S (LORD) Letters and Journals. Edited by THEODORE WALROND. *Second Edition*. 8vo. 14s.

ELLESMERE'S (LORD) Two Sieges of Vienna by the Turks. Translated from the German. Post 8vo. 2s.

ELLIS'S (W.) Madagascar, including a Journey to the Capital, with notices of Natural History and the People. Woodcuts. 8vo. 16s.

——— Revisited. Setting forth the Persecutions and Heroic Sufferings of the Native Christians. Illustrations. 8vo. 16s.

ELPHINSTONE'S (HON. MOUNTSTUART) History of India—the Hindoo and Mahomedan Periods. *Fifth Edition*. Map. 8vo. 18s.

——— ——— (H. W.) Patterns for Turning; Comprising Elliptical and other Figures cut on the Lathe without the use of any Ornamental Chuck. With 70 Illustrations. Small 4to. 15s.

ENGEL'S (CARL) Music of the Most Ancient Nations; particularly of the Assyrians, Egyptians, and Hebrews; with Special Reference to the Discoveries in Western Asia and in Egypt. *Second Edition*. With 100 Illustrations. 8vo. 10s. 6d.

ENGLAND (HISTORY OF) See CALLCOTT, CROKER, HUME, MARKHAM, SMITH, and STANHOPE.

ENGLISHWOMAN IN AMERICA. Post 8vo. 10s. 6d.

ESSAYS ON CATHEDRALS. With an Introduction. By DEAN HOWSON. 8vo. 12s.

CONTENTS.

Recollections of a Dean.—Bishop of Carlisle.

Cathedral Canons and their Work.—Canon Norris.

Cathedrals in Ireland, Past and Future.—Dean of Cashel.

Cathedrals in their Missionary Aspect. A. J. B. Beresford Hope.

Cathedral Foundations in Relation to Religious Thought.—Canon Westcott.

Cathedral Churches of the Old Foundation.—Edward A. Freeman.

Welsh Cathedrals.—Canon Perowne.

Education of Choristers.—Sir F. Gore Ouseley.

Cathedral Schools.—Canon Durham.

Cathedral Reform.—Chancellor Massingberd.

Relation of the Chapter to the Bishop. Chancellor Benson.

Architecture of the Cathedral Churches.—Canon Venables.

ETHNOLOGICAL SOCIETY'S TRANSACTIONS. Vols. I. to VI. 8vo.

ELZE'S (KARL) Life of Lord Byron. With a Critical Essay on his Place in Literature. Translated from the German, and Edited with Notes. With Original Portrait and Facsimile. 8vo. 16s.

FAMILY RECEIPT-BOOK. A Collection of a Thousand Valuable and Useful Receipts. Fcap. 8vo. 5s. 6d.

FARRAR'S (A. S.) Critical History of Free Thought in reference to the Christian Religion. 8vo. 16s.

———— (F. W.) Origin of Language, based on Modern Researches. Fcap. 8vo. 5s.

FERGUSSON'S (JAMES) History of Architecture in all Countries from the Earliest Times. Vols. I. and II. With 1200 Illustrations. 8vo. 42s. each.

———————— Rude Stone Monuments in all Countries; their Age and Uses. With 230 Illustrations. Medium 8vo. 24s.

———————— Holy Sepulchre and the Temple at Jerusalem; being the Substance of Two Lectures delivered at the Royal Institution, 1862 and '65. Woodcuts. 8vo. 7s. 6d.

FLEMING'S (PROF.) Manual of Moral Philosophy. Post 8vo. 7s. 6d.

FLOWER GARDEN (THE). By REV. THOS. JAMES. Fcap. 8vo. 1s.

FONNEREAU'S (T. G.) Diary of a Dutiful Son. Fcap. 8vo. 4s. 6d.

FORSTER'S (JOHN) Arrest of the Five Members by Charles the First. A Chapter of English History re-written. Post 8vo.

———————— Grand Remonstrance, 1641. With an Essay on English freedom under the Plantagenet and Tudor Sovereigns. Second Edition. Post 8vo. 12s.

———————— Oliver Cromwell, Daniel De Foe, Sir Richard Steele, Charles Churchill, Samuel Foote. Third Edition. Post 8vo. 12s.

FORD'S (RICHARD) Gatherings from Spain. Post 8vo. 3s. 6d.

FORSYTH'S (WILLIAM) Life and Times of Cicero. With Selections from his Correspondence and Orations. Third Edition. Illustrations. 8vo. 10s. 6d.

———————— History of Ancient Manuscripts. Post 8vo. 2s. 6d.

FORTUNE'S (ROBERT) Narrative of Two Visits to the Tea Countries of China, 1843-52. Third Edition. Woodcuts. 2 Vols. Post 8vo. 18s.

FOSS' (Edward) Judges of England. With Sketches of their Lives, and Notices of the Courts at Westminster, from the Conquest to the Present Time. 9 Vols. 8vo. 126s.

———————— Biographia Juridica, or Biographical Dictionary of the Judges of England, from the Conquest to the Present Time, 1066-1870. (820 pp.) Medium 8vo. 21s.

———————— Tabulæ Curiales; or, Tables of the Superior Courts of Westminster Hall. Showing the Judges who sat in them from 1066 to 1864. 8vo. 10s. 6d.

FRANCE (HISTORY OF). See MARKHAM, SMITH, Students.

FRENCH (THE) in Algiers; The Soldier of the Foreign Legion— and the Prisoners of Abd-el-Kadir. Translated by Lady DUFF GORDON. Post 8vo. 2s.

FRERE'S (Sir Bartle) Results of Indian Missions. Small 8vo. 2s. 6d.

———— (M.) Old Deccan Days; or Fairy Legends Current in Southern India. Collected from Oral Tradition. With Notes, by Sir Bartle Frere. *Second Edition.* With Illustrations. Fcap. 8vo. 6s.

GALTON'S (Francis) Art of Travel; or, Hints on the Shifts and Contrivances available in Wild Countries. *Fifth Edition.* Woodcuts. Post 8vo. 7s. 6d.

GEOGRAPHY. *** See Student's Manual.

GEOGRAPHICAL SOCIETY (Journal of). 8vo. 20s. (*Yearly.*)

GERMANY (History of). See Markham.

GIBBON'S (Edward) History of the Decline and Fall of the Roman Empire. Edited by Milman and Guizot. *A New Edition.* Preceded by his Autobiography. And Edited, with Notes, by Dr. Wm. Smith. Maps. 8 Vols. 8vo. 60s.

———— (The Student's Gibbon); Being an Epitome of the above work, Incorporating the Researches of Recent Commentators. By Dr. Wm. Smith. Woodcuts. Post 8vo. 7s. 6d.

GIFFARD'S (Edward) Deeds of Naval Daring; or, Anecdotes of the British Navy. Fcap. 8vo. 3s. 6d.

GLADSTONE'S (W. E.) Financial Statements of 1853, 60, 63–65, and with Speeches on Tax-Bills and Charities. 8vo. 12s.

GLEIG'S (G. R.) Campaigns of the British Army at Washington and New Orleans. Post 8vo. 2s.

———— Story of the Battle of Waterloo. Post 8vo. 3s. 6d.

———— Narrative of Sale's Brigade in Affghanistan. Post 8vo. 2s.

———— Life of Robert Lord Clive. Post 8vo. 3s. 6d.

———— Sir Thomas Munro. Post 8vo. 3s. 6d.

GOLDSMITH'S (Oliver) Works. A New Edition. Edited with Notes by Peter Cunningham. Vignettes. 4 Vols. 8vo. 30s.

GORDON'S (Sir Alex.) Sketches of German Life, and Scenes from the War of Liberation. Post 8vo. 3s. 6d.

———— (Lady Duff) Amber-Witch: A Trial for Witchcraft. Post 8vo. 2s.

———— French in Algiers. 1. The Soldier of the Foreign Legion.' 2. The Prisoners of Abd-el-Kadir. Post 8vo. 2s.

GRAMMARS (English, Latin, and Greek). See Curtius; Hutton; Matthiæ; Smith; King Edward, &c.

GREECE (History of). *See* Grote—Smith—Student.

GREY'S (Earl) Correspondence with King William IVth and Sir Herbert Taylor, from 1830 to 1832. 2 Vols. 8vo. 30s.

———— Parliamentary Government and Reform; with Suggestions for the Improvement of our Representative System. *Second Edition.* 8vo. 9s.

GRUNER'S (Lewis) Terra-Cotta Architecture of North Italy, from careful Drawings and Restorations. With Illustrations, engraved and printed in Colours. Small folio. 5l. 5s.

GUIZOT'S (M.) Meditations on Christianity, and on the Religious Questions of the Day. Part I. The Essence. Part II. Present State. Part III. Relation to Society and Opinion. 3 Vols. Post 8vo. 30s.

GROTE'S (George) History of Greece. From the Earliest Times to the close of the generation contemporary with the death of Alexander the Great. *Fourth Edition.* Portrait, Maps, and Plans. 10 Vols. 8vo. 120s. Or, *Popular Edition.* Portrait and Plans. 12 Vols. Post 8vo. 6s. each.

———— Plato, and the other Companions of Socrates. *Second Edition.* 3 Vols. 8vo. 45s.

———— Aristotle. Edited by Alexander Bain and G. Croom Robertson. 2 Vols. 8vo. 32s.

———— (Mrs.) Personal Life of George Grote. Illustrated by numerous Letters. Portrait. 8vo.

     - Memoir of Ary Scheffer. *Second Edition.* With Portrait. 8vo. 8s. 6d.

HALLAM'S (Henry) Constitutional History of England, from the Accession of Henry the Seventh to the Death of George the Second. *Seventh Edition.* 3 Vols. 8vo. 30s., or 3 Vols. Post 8vo. 12s.

———— Student's Constitutional History of England. Edited by Wm. Smith, D.C.L. Post 8vo. 7s. 6d.

———— History of Europe during the Middle Ages. *Tenth Edition.* 3 Vols. 8vo. 30s., or 3 Vols. Post 8vo. 12s.

———— Student's History of the Middle Ages. With Author's Supplemental Notes. Edited by Wm. Smith, D.C.L. Post 8vo. 7s. 6d.

———— Literary History of Europe, during the 15th, 16th and 17th Centuries. *Fourth Edition.* 3 Vols. 8vo. 36s., or 4 Vols. Post 8vo. 10s.

———— (Arthur) Remains; in Verse and Prose. Portrait. Fcap. 8vo. 3s. 6d.

HANNAH'S (Rev. Dr.) Divine and Human Elements in Holy Scripture. 8vo. 10s. 6d.

HART'S ARMY LIST. (*Quarterly and Annually.*) 8vo.

HAY'S (Sir J. H. Drummond) Western Barbary, its Wild Tribes and Savage Animals. Post 8vo. 2s.

HEAD'S (Sir Francis) Royal Engineer. Illustrations. 8vo. 12s.

———— Life of Sir John Burgoyne. Post 8vo. 1s.

———— Rapid Journeys across the Pampas. Post 8vo. 2s.

———— Bubbles from the Brunnen of Nassau. *Seventh Edition.* Illustrations. Post 8vo. 7s. 6d.

———— Emigrant. Fcap. 8vo. 2s. 6d.

———— Stokers and Pokers; or, the London and North Western Railway. Post 8vo. 2s.

———— (Sir Edmund) Shall and Will; or, Future Auxiliary Verbs. Fcap. 8vo. 4s.

HEBER'S (Bishop) Journey through India from Calcutta to Bom- bay, Madras, &c. 2 Vols. Post 8vo. 7s.

———— Poetical Works. Portrait. Fcap. 8vo. 3s. 6d.

———— Hymns adapted to the Church Service. 16mo. 1s. 6d.

HERODOTUS. A New English Version. Edited, with Notes and Essays, historical, ethnographical, and geographical, by Rev. G. Rawlinson, assisted by Sir Henry Rawlinson and Sir J. G. Wilkinson. *Second Edition.* Maps and Woodcuts. 4 Vols. 8vo. 48s.

FOREIGN HANDBOOKS.

HAND-BOOK—TRAVEL-TALK. English, French, German, and Italian. 18mo. 3s. 6d.

.... - NORTH GERMANY,—HOLLAND, BELGIUM, PRUSSIA, and the Rhine from Holland to Switzerland. Map. Post 8vo | 12s.

——— SOUTH GERMANY, Bavaria, Austria, Styria, Salzburg, the Austrian and Bavarian Alps, the Tyrol, Hungary, and the Danube, from Ulm to the Black Sea. Map. Post 8vo. 12s.

——— KNAPSACK GUIDE TO THE TYROL. 16mo. 6s.

——— PAINTING. German, Flemish, and Dutch Schools. Illustrations. 2 Vols. Post 8vo. 24s.

——— LIVES OF EARLY FLEMISH PAINTERS. By CROWE and CAVALCASELLE. Illustrations. Post 8vo. 10s. 6d.

——— SWITZERLAND, Alps of Savoy, and Piedmont. Maps. Post 8vo. 10s. (on thin paper).

——— KNAPSACK GUIDE TO SWITZERLAND. 16mo, 5s.

——— FRANCE, Normandy, Brittany, the French Alps, the Rivers Loire, Seine, Rhone, and Garonne, Dauphiné, Provence, and the Pyrenees. Maps. Post 8vo.

CORSICA and SARDINIA. Maps. Post 8vo. 4s.

——— PARIS, and its Environs. Map and Plans. 16mo. 3s. 6d.

. MURRAY'S PLAN OF PARIS, mounted on canvas. 3s. 6d.

——— SPAIN, Madrid, The Castiles, The Basque Provinces, Leon, The Asturias, Galicia, Estremadura, Andalusia, Ronda, Granada, Murcia, Valencia, Catalouia, Arragon, Navarre, The Balearic Islands, &c. &c. Maps. 2 Vols. Post 8vo. 24s.

——— PORTUGAL, LISBON, Porto, Cintra, Mafra, &c. Map. Post 8vo. 9s.

——— NORTH ITALY, Piedmont, Liguria, Venetia, Lombardy, Parma, Modena, and Romagna. Map. Post 8vo. 12s. (on thin paper).

——— CENTRAL ITALY, Lucca, Tuscany, Florence, The Marches, Umbria, and the Patrimony of St. Peter's. Map. Post 8vo. 10s.

ROME AND ITS ENVIRONS. Map. Post 8vo. 10s.

——— SOUTH ITALY, Two Sicilies, Naples, Pompeii, Herculaneum, and Vesuvius. Map. Post 8vo. 10s.

KNAPSACK GUIDE TO ITALY. 16mo. 6s.

——— SICILY, Palermo, Messina, Catania, Syracuse, Etna, and the Ruins of the Greek Temples. Map. Post 8vo. 12s.

——— PAINTING. The Italian Schools. Edited by Sir CHARLES EASTLAKE, R.A. Illustrations. 2 Vols. Post 8vo. 30s.

——— LIVES OF ITALIAN PAINTERS, FROM CIMABUE to BASSANO. By Mrs. JAMESON. Portraits. Post 8vo. 12s.

——— RUSSIA, ST. PETERSBURGH, Moscow, POLAND, and FINLAND. Maps. Post 8vo. 15s.

HAND-BOOK—DENMARK, Sweden, and Norway. Maps. Post
8vo. 15s.
——————— KNAPSACK GUIDE TO NORWAY. Map.
12mo. 6s.
——————— GREECE, the Ionian Islands, Continental Greece,
Athens, the Peloponnesus, the Islands of the Ægean Sea, Albania,
Thessaly, and Macedonia. Maps. Post 8vo. 15s.
——————— TURKEY IN ASIA—Constantinople, the Bos-
phorus, Dardanelles, Broussa, Plain of Troy, Crete, Cyprus, Smyrna,
Ephesus, the Seven Churches, Coasts of the Black Sea, Armenia,
Mesopotamia, &c. Maps. Post 8vo. 15s.
——————— EGYPT, including Descriptions of the Course of
the Nile through Egypt and Nubia, Alexandria, Cairo, and Thebes, the
Suez Canal, the Pyramids, the Peninsula of Sinai, the Oases, the
Fyoom, &c. Map. Post 8vo. 15s.
——————— HOLY LAND—Syria and Palestine, Peninsula
of Sinai, Edom, and Syrian Desert. Maps. 2 Vols. Post 8vo. 24s.
——————— INDIA — Bombay and Madras. Map. 2 Vols.
Post 8vo. 12s. each.

ENGLISH HANDBOOKS.

HAND-BOOK—MODERN LONDON. Map. 16mo. 3s. 6d.
——————— ESSEX, CAMBRIDGE, SUFFOLK, AND NOR-
FOLK, Chelmsford, Colchester, Maldon, Cambridge, Ely, Newmarket,
Bury, Ipswich, Woodbridge, Felixstowe, Lowestoft, Norwich, Yarmouth,
Cromer, &c. Map and Plans. Post 8vo. 17s.
——————— CATHEDRALS of Oxford, Peterborough, Norwich,
Ely, and Lincoln. With 90 Illustrations. Crown 8vo. 18s.
——————— KENT AND SUSSEX, Canterbury, Dover, Rams-
gate, Sheerness, Rochester, Chatham, Woolwich, Brighton, Chichester,
Worthing, Hastings, Lewes, Arundel, &c. Map. Post 8vo. 10s.
——————— SURREY AND HANTS, Kingston, Croydon, Rei-
gate, Guildford, Dorking, Boxhill, Winchester, Southampton, New
Forest, Portsmouth, and Isle of Wight. Maps. Post 8vo. 10s.
——————— BERKS, BUCKS, AND OXON, Windsor, Eton,
Reading, Aylesbury, Uxbridge, Wycombe, Henley, the City and Uni-
versity of Oxford, Blenheim, and the Descent of the Thames. Map.
Post 8vo. 7s. 6d.
——————— WILTS, DORSET, AND SOMERSET, Salisbury,
Chippenham, Weymouth, Sherborne, Wells, Bath, Bristol, Taunton,
&c. Map. Post 8vo. 10s.
——————— DEVON AND CORNWALL, Exeter, Ilfracombe,
Linton, Sidmouth, Dawlish, Teignmouth, Plymouth, Devonport, Tor-
quay, Launceston, Truro, Penzance, Falmouth, the Lizard, Land's End,
&c. Maps. Post 8vo. 12s.
——————— CATHEDRALS of Winchester, Salisbury, Exeter,
Wells, Chichester, Rochester, Canterbury. With 110 Illustrations.
2 Vols. Crown 8vo. 24s.
——————— GLOUCESTER, HEREFORD, and WORCESTER,
Cirencester, Cheltenham, Stroud, Tewkesbury, Leominster, Ross, Mal-
vern, Kidderminster, Dudley, Bromsgrove, Evesham. Map. Post 8vo.
9s.
——————— CATHEDRALS of Bristol, Gloucester, Hereford,
Worcester, and Lichfield. With 50 Illustrations. Crown 8vo. 16s.
——————— NORTH WALES, Bangor, Carnarvon, Beaumaris,
Snowdon, Llanberis, Dolgelly, Cader Idris, Conway, &c. Map. Post
8vo. 6s. 6d.

HAND-BOOK—SOUTH WALES, Monmouth, Llandaff, Merthyr, Vale of Neath, Pembroke, Carmarthen, Tenby, Swansea, and The Wye, &c. Map. Post 8vo. 7s.

———— CATHEDRALS OF BANGOR, ST. ASAPH, Llandaff, and St. Davids. With Illustrations. Post 8vo. 15s.

———— DERBY, NOTTS, LEICESTER, STAFFORD, Matlock, Bakewell, Chatsworth, The Peak, Buxton, Hardwick, Dove Dale, Ashborne, Southwell, Mansfield, Retford, Burton, Belvoir, Melton Mowbray, Wolverhampton, Lichfield, Walsall, Tamworth. Map. Post 8vo. 7s. 6d.

———— SHROPSHIRE, CHESHIRE AND LANCASHIRE —Shrewsbury, Ludlow, Bridgnorth, Oswestry, Chester, Crewe, Alderley, Stockport, Birkenhead, Warrington, Bury, Manchester, Liverpool, Burnley, Clitheroe, Bolton, Blackburn, Wigan, Preston, Rochdale, Lancaster, Southport, Blackpool, &c. Map. Post 8vo. 10s.

———— YORKSHIRE, Doncaster, Hull, Selby, Beverley, Scarborough, Whitby, Harrogate, Ripon, Leeds, Wakefield, Bradford, Halifax, Huddersfield. Sheffield. Map and Plans. Post 8vo. 12s.

———— CATHEDRALS of York, Ripon, Durham, Carlisle, Chester, and Manchester. With 60 Illustrations. 2 Vols. Crown 8vo. 21s.

———— DURHAM AND NORTHUMBERLAND, New-castle, Darlington, Gateshead, Bishop Auckland, Stockton, Hartlepool, Sunderland, Shields, Berwick-on-Tweed, Morpeth, Tynemouth, Cold-stream, Alnwick, &c. Map. Post 8vo.

———— WESTMORLAND AND CUMBERLAND—Lan-caster, Furness Abbey, Ambleside, Kendal, Windermere, Coniston, Keswick, Grasmere, Ulswater, Carlisle, Cockermouth, Penrith, Appleby. Map. Post 8vo. 6s.

₀ MURRAY'S MAP OF THE LAKE DISTRICT, on canvas. 3s. 6d.

———— SCOTLAND, Edinburgh, Melrose, Kelso, Glasgow, Dumfries, Ayr, Stirling, Arran, The Clyde, Oban, Inverary, Loch Lomond, Loch Katrine and Trossachs, Caledonian Canal, Inverness, Perth, Dundee, Aberdeen, Braemar, Skye, Caithness, Ross, Suther-land, &c. Maps and Plans. Post 8vo.

———— IRELAND, Dublin, Belfast, Donegal, Galway, Wexford, Cork, Limerick, Waterford, Killarney, Munster, &c. Maps. Post 8vo. 12s.

HAND-BOOK OF FAMILIAR QUOTATIONS. From English Authors. Third Edition. Fcap. 8vo. 5s.

HATHERLEY (LORD) On the Continuity of Scripture. As declared by the Testimony of our Lord and of the Evangelists and Apostles. Fourth Edition. 8vo. 6s. Or Popular Edition. Post 8vo. 2s. 6d.

HESSEY (REV. DR.). Sunday—Its Origin, History, and Present Obligations. Post 8vo. 9s.

HICKMAN'S (WM.) Treatise on the Law and Practice of Naval Courts-Martial. 8vo. 10s. 6d.

HOLLWAY'S (J. G.) Month in Norway. Fcap. 8vo. 2s.

HONEY BEE (THE). An Essay. By REV. THOMAS JAMES. Reprinted from the "Quarterly Review." Fcap. 8vo. 1s.

HOOK'S (DEAN) Church Dictionary. Tenth Edition. 8vo. 16s.

———— (THEODORE) Life. By J. G. LOCKHART. Fcap. 8vo. 1s.

HOPE'S ARCHITECTURE OF AHMEDABAD, with His-torical Sketch and Architectural Notes by T. C. HOPE, and JAMES FERGUSSON, F.R.S. With 2 Maps, 120 Photographs and 22 Woodcuts. 4to. 5l. 5s.

c

HOME AND COLONIAL LIBRARY. A Series of Works adapted for all circles and classes of Readers, having been selected for their acknowledged interest, and ability of the Authors. Post 8vo, Published at 2s. and 3s. 6d. each, and arranged under two distinctive heads as follows:—

CLASS A.

HISTORY, BIOGRAPHY, AND HISTORIC TALES.

1. SIEGE OF GIBRALTAR. By JOHN DRINKWATER. 2s.
2. THE AMBER-WITCH. By LADY DUFF GORDON. 2s.
3. CROMWELL AND BUNYAN. By ROBERT SOUTHEY. 2s.
4. LIFE OF SIR FRANCIS DRAKE. By JOHN BARROW. 2s.
5. CAMPAIGNS AT WASHINGTON. By REV. G. R. GLEIG. 2s.
6. THE FRENCH IN ALGIERS. By LADY DUFF GORDON. 2s.
7. THE FALL OF THE JESUITS. 2s.
8. LIVONIAN TALES. 2s.
9. LIFE OF CONDE. By LORD MAHON. 3s. 6d.
10. SALE'S BRIGADE. By REV. G. R. GLEIG. 2s.

11. THE SIEGES OF VIENNA. By LORD ELLESMERE. 2s.
12. THE WAYSIDE CROSS. By CAPT. MILMAN. 2s.
13. SKETCHES OF GERMAN LIFE. By SIR A. GORDON. 3s. 6d.
14. THE BATTLE OF WATERLOO. By REV. G. R. GLEIG. 3s. 6d.
15. AUTOBIOGRAPHY OF STEFFENS. 2s.
16. THE BRITISH POETS. By THOMAS CAMPBELL. 3s. 6d.
17. HISTORICAL ESSAYS. By LORD MAHON. 3s. 6d.
18. LIFE OF LORD CLIVE. By REV. G. R. GLEIG. 3s. 6d.
19. NORTH - WESTERN RAILWAY. By SIR F. B. HEAD. 2s.
20. LIFE OF MUNRO. By REV. G. R. GLEIG. 3s. 6d.

CLASS B.

VOYAGES, TRAVELS, AND ADVENTURES.

1. BIBLE IN SPAIN. By GEORGE BORROW. 3s. 6d.
2. GIPSIES OF SPAIN. By GEORGE BORROW. 3s. 6d.
3 & 4. JOURNALS IN INDIA. By BISHOP HEBER. 2 Vols. 7s.
5. TRAVELS IN THE HOLY LAND. By IRBY and MANGLES. 2s.
6. MOROCCO AND THE MOORS. By J. DRUMMOND HAY. 2s.
7. LETTERS FROM THE BALTIC. By a LADY. 2s.
8. NEW SOUTH WALES. By MRS. MEREDITH. 2s.
9. THE WEST INDIES. By M. G. LEWIS. 2s.
10. SKETCHES OF PERSIA. By SIR JOHN MALCOLM. 3s. 6d.
11. MEMOIRS OF FATHER RIPA. 2s.
12. 13. TYPEE AND OMOO. By HERMANN MELVILLE. 2 Vols. 7s.
14. MISSIONARY LIFE IN CANADA. By REV. J. ABBOTT. 2s.

15. LETTERS FROM MADRAS. By a LADY. 2s.
16. HIGHLAND SPORTS. By CHARLES ST. JOHN. 3s. 6d.
17. PAMPAS JOURNEYS. By SIR F. B. HEAD. 2s.
18. GATHERINGS FROM SPAIN. By RICHARD FORD. 3s. 6d.
19. THE RIVER AMAZON. By W. H. EDWARDS. 2s.
20. MANNERS & CUSTOMS OF INDIA. By REV. C. ACLAND. 2s.
21. ADVENTURES IN MEXICO. By G. F. RUXTON. 3s. 6d.
22. PORTUGAL AND GALLICIA. By LORD CARNARVON. 3s. 6d.
23. BUSH LIFE IN AUSTRALIA. By REV. H. W. HAYGARTH. 2s.
24. THE LIBYAN DESERT. By BAYLE ST. JOHN. 2s.
25. SIERRA LEONE. By LADY. 3s. 6d.

** Each work may be had separately.

HORACE; a New Edition of the Text. Edited by DEAN MILMAN. With 100 Woodcuts. Crown 8vo. 7s. 6d.

———— Life of. By DEAN MILMAN. Illustrations. 8vo. 9s.

HOUGHTON'S (LORD) Monographs, Personal and Social. With Portraits. Crown 8vo.

HUME'S History of England, from the Invasion of Julius Cæsar to the Revolution of 1688. Corrected and continued to 1868. Abridged for Students. Edited by DR. WM. SMITH. Woodcuts. Post 8vo. 7s. 6d.

HUTCHINSON (GEN.), on the most expeditious, certain, and easy Method of Dog-Breaking. Fifth Edition. With 40 Illustrations. Crown 8vo. 9s.

HUTTON'S (H. E.) Principia Græca; an Introduction to the Study of Greek. Comprehending Grammar, Delectus, and Exercise-book, with Vocabularies. Sixth Edition. 12mo. 3s. 6d.

IRBY AND MANGLES' Travels in Egypt, Nubia, Syria, and the Holy Land. Post 8vo. 2s.

JAMES' (REV. THOMAS) Fables of Æsop. A New Translation, with Historical Preface. With 100 Woodcuts by TENNIEL and WOLF. Sixty-fourth Thousand. Post 8vo. 2s. 6d.

JAMESON'S (MRS.) Lives of the Early Italian Painters— and the Progress of Painting in Italy—Cimabue to Bassano. New Edition. With 50 Portraits. Post 8vo. 12s.

JENNINGS' (L. J.) Eighty Years of Republican Government in the United States. Post 8vo. 10s. 6d.

JESSE'S (EDWARD) Gleanings in Natural History. Eleventh Edition. Fcp. 8vo. 3s. 6d.

JOHNS' (REV. B. G.) Blind People; their Works and Ways. With Sketches of the Lives of some famous Blind Men. With Illustrations. Post 8vo. 7s. 6d.

JOHNSON'S (DR. SAMUEL) Life. By James Boswell. Including the Tour to the Hebrides. Edited by MR. CROKER. Portraits. Royal 8vo. 10s.

———————— Lives of the most eminent English Poets. Edited with Notes by PETER CUNNINGHAM. 3 vols. 8vo. 22s. 6d.

JUNIUS' HANDWRITING Professionally investigated. By Mr. CHABOT, Expert. With Preface and Collateral Evidence, by the Hon. EDWARD TWISLETON. With Facsimiles, Woodcuts, &c. 4to. £3 3s.

KEN'S (BISHOP) Life. By a LAYMAN. Portrait. 2 Vols. 8vo. 18s.

———————— Exposition of the Apostles' Creed. 16mo. 1s. 6d.

KERR'S (ROBERT) GENTLEMAN'S HOUSE; OR, HOW TO PLAN ENGLISH RESIDENCES, FROM THE PARSONAGE TO THE PALACE. Third Edition. With Views and Plans. 8vo. 24s.

———— Ancient Lights; a Book for Architects, Surveyors, Lawyers, and Landlords. 8vo. 5s. 6d.

———— (R. MALCOLM) Student's Blackstone. A Systematic Abridgment of the entire Commentaries, adapted to the present state of the law. Post 8vo. 7s. 6d.

KING EDWARD VITH's Latin Grammar; or, an Introduction to the Latin Tongue. Seventeenth Edition. 12mo. 3s. 6d.

———————— First Latin Book; or, the Accidence, Syntax, and Prosody, with an English Translation. Fifth Edition. 12mo. 2s. 6d.

c 2

KING GEORGE THE THIRD'S CORRESPONDENCE WITH LORD NORTH, 1769-82. Edited, with Notes and Introduction, by W. BODHAM DONNE. 2 vols. 8vo. 32s.

KIRK'S (J. FOSTER) History of Charles the Bold, Duke of Burgundy. Portrait. 3 Vols. 8vo. 45s.

KIRKES' Handbook of Physiology. Edited by W. MORRANT BAKER, F.R.C.S. Eighth Edition. With 240 Illustrations. Post 8vo. 12s. 6d.

KUGLER'S Italian Schools of Painting. Edited, with Notes, by SIR CHARLES EASTLAKE. Third Edition. Woodcuts. 2 Vols. Post 8vo. 30s.

———— German, Dutch, and Flemish Schools of Painting. Edited, with Notes, by DR. WAAGEN. Second Edition. Woodcuts. 2 Vols. Post 8vo. 24s.

LANE'S (E. W.) Account of the Manners and Customs of the Modern Egyptians. New Edition. With Illustrations. 2 Vols. Post 8vo. 12s.

LAYARD'S (A. H.) Nineveh and its Remains. Being a Narrative of Researches and Discoveries amidst the Ruins of Assyria. With an Account of the Chaldean Christians of Kurdistan; the Yezedis, or Devil-worshippers; and an Enquiry into the Manners and Arts of the Ancient Assyrians. Sixth Edition. Plates and Woodcuts. 2 Vols. 8vo. 36s.
. A POPULAR EDITION of the above work. With Illustrations. Post 8vo. 7s. 6d.

———— Nineveh and Babylon; being the Narrative of Discoveries in the Ruins, with Travels in Armenia, Kurdistan and the Desert, during a Second Expedition to Assyria. With Map and Plates. 8vo. 21s.
. A POPULAR EDITION of the above work. With Illustrations. Post 8vo. 7s. 6d.

LEATHES' (STANLEY) Practical Hebrew Grammar. With an Appendix, containing the Hebrew Text of Genesis I.—vi., and Psalms I.—vi. Grammatical Analysis and Vocabulary. Post 8vo. 7s. 6d.

LENNEP'S (REV. H. J. VAN) Missionary Travels in Asia Minor. With Illustrations of Biblical History and Archæology. With Map and Woodcuts. 2 Vols. Post 8vo. 24s.

LESLIE'S (C. R.) Handbook for Young Painters. Second Edition. With Illustrations. Post 8vo. 7s. 6d.

———— Life and Works of Sir Joshua Reynolds. Portraits and Illustrations. 2 Vols. 8vo. 42s.

LETTERS FROM THE BALTIC. By a LADY. Post 8vo. 2s.

———— MADRAS. By a LADY. Post 8vo. 2s.

———— SIERRA LEONE. By a LADY. Post 8vo. 3s. 6d.

LEVI'S (LEONE) Wages and Earnings of the Working Classes. With some Facts Illustrative of their Economic Condition. 8vo. 6s.

———— History of British Commerce; and of the Economic Progress of the Nation, from 1763 to 1870. 8vo. 18s.

LEWIS'S (M. G.) Journal of a Residence among the Negroes in the West Indies. Post 8vo. 2s.

LIDDELL'S (DEAN) Student's History of Rome, from the earliest Times to the establishment of the Empire. With Woodcuts. Post 8vo. 7s. 6d.

LINDSAY'S (LORD) Lives of the Lindsays; or, a Memoir of the Houses of Crawford and Balcarres. With Extracts from Official Papers and Personal Narratives. Second Edition. 3 Vols. 8vo. 24s.

———— Etruscan Inscriptions. Analysed, Translated, and Commented upon. 8vo. 12s.

LLOYD'S (W. Watkiss) History of Sicily to the Athenian War; with Elucidations of the Sicilian Odes of Pindar. With a Map. 8vo. 14s.

LISPINGS from LOW LATITUDES; or, the Journal of the Hon. Impulsia Gushington. Edited by Lord Dufferin. With 24 Plates. 4to. 21s.

LITTLE ARTHUR'S HISTORY OF ENGLAND. By Lady Callcott. New Edition, continued to 1871. With Woodcuts. Fcap. 8vo. 2s. 6d.

LIVINGSTONE'S (Dr.) Missionary Travels in South Africa. Illustrations. Post 8vo. 6s.

———— ———— Expedition to the Zambezi and its Tributaries; and the Lakes Shirwa and Nyassa. Map and Illustrations. 8vo. 21s.

LIVONIAN TALES. By the Author of "Letters from the Baltic." Post 8vo. 2s.

LOCH'S (H. B.) Personal Narrative of Events during Lord Elgin's Second Embassy to China. Second Edition. With Illustrations. Post 8vo. 9s.

LOCKHART'S (J. G.) Ancient Spanish Ballads. Historical and Romantic. Translated, with Notes. New Edition. With Portrait and Illustrations. Crown 8vo. 5s.

———— ———— Life of Theodore Hook. Fcap. 8vo. 1s.

LONSDALE'S (Bishop) Life. With Selections from his Writings. By E. B. Denison. With Portrait. Crown 8vo. 10s. 6d.

LOUDON'S (Mrs.) Gardening for Ladies. With Directions and Calendar of Operations for Every Month. Eighth Edition. Woodcuts. Fcap. 8vo. 3s. 6d.

LUCKNOW: a Lady's Diary of the Siege. Fcap. 8vo. 4s. 6d.

LYELL'S (Sir Charles) Principles of Geology; or, the Modern Changes of the Earth and its Inhabitants considered as illustrative of Geology. Tenth Edition. With Illustrations. 2 Vols. 8vo. 32s.

———— ———— Student's Elements of Geology. With 600 Illustrations. Post 8vo. 9s.

———— ———— Geological Evidences of the Antiquity of Man. Fourth Edition. Illustrations. 8vo. (In Preparation.)

———— ———— (K. M.) Geographical Handbook of Ferns. With Tables to show their Distribution. Post 8vo. 7s. 6d.

LYTTELTON'S (Lord) Ephemera. 1st & 2nd Series. Post 8vo. 10s. 6d. each.

LYTTON'S (Lord) Poems. Post 8vo. 10s. 6d.

———— ———— Lost Tales of Miletus. Post 8vo. 7s. 6d.

———— ———— Memoir of Julian Fane. Second Edition. With Portrait. Post 8vo. 5s.

McCLINTOCK'S (Sir L.) Narrative of the Discovery of the Fate of Sir John Franklin and his Companions in the Arctic Seas. Third Edition. With Illustrations. Post 8vo. 7s. 6d.

MacDOUGALL'S (Col.) Modern Warfare as Influenced by Modern Artillery. With Plans. Post 8vo. 12s.

MACGREGOR (J.), Rob Roy on the Jordan, Nile, Red Sea, Gen- nesareth, &c. A Canoe Cruise in Palestine and Egypt and the Waters of Damascus. With Map, and 70 Illustrations. Crown 8vo. 12s.

MACPHERSON'S (Major) Services in India, while Political Agent at Gwalior during the Mutiny. Illustrations. 8vo. 12s.

MAETZNER'S COPIOUS ENGLISH GRAMMAR. A Methodical, Analytical, and Historical Treatise on the Orthography, Prosody, Inflections, and Syntax of the English Tongue. 3 Vols. 8vo. (*In preparation.*)

MAHON (Lord), see Stanhope.

MAINE'S (Sir H. Sumner) Ancient Law : its Connection with the Early History of Society, and its Relation to Modern Ideas. *Fourth Edition.* 8vo. 12s.

—— VILLAGE COMMUNITIES IN THE EAST AND WEST. *2nd Edition.* 8vo. 9s.

MALCOLM'S (Sir John) Sketches of Persia. Post 8vo. 3s. 6d.

MANSEL'S (Dean) Limits of Religious Thought Examined. *Fifth Edition.* Post 8vo. 8s. 6d.

—— Letters, Lectures, and Papers. 8vo.

MANTELL'S (Gideon A.) Thoughts on Animalcules ; or, the Invisible World, as revealed by the Microscope. Plates. 16mo. 6s.

MANUAL OF SCIENTIFIC ENQUIRY. For the Use of Travellers. Edited by Sir J. F. Herschel & Rev. R. Main. Post 8vo. 3s. 6d. (*Published by order of the Lords of the Admiralty.*)

MARCO POLO'S TRAVELS. A New English Version. With Copious Illustrative Notes. By Col. Henry Yule. With Maps and Illustrations. 2 Vols. Medium 8vo. 42s.

MARKHAM'S (Mrs.) History of England. From the First Invasion by the Romans. *New Edition, continued down to 1867.* Woodcuts. 12mo. 3s. 6d.

—— History of France. From the Conquest by the Gauls. *New Edition, continued to 1867.* Woodcuts. 12mo. 3s. 6d.

—— History of Germany. From the Invasion by Marius. *New Edition, continued to 1867.* Woodcuts. 12mo.

—— (Clements R.) Travels in Peru and India. Maps and Illustrations. 8vo. 16s.

MARRYAT'S (Joseph) History of Modern and Mediæval Pottery and Porcelain. With a Description of the Manufacture. *Third Edition.* Plates and Woodcuts. 8vo. 42s.

MARSH'S (G. P.) Manual of the English Language. Edited by Dr. Wm. Smith. Post 8vo. 7s. 6d.

MATTHIÆ'S SHORTER GREEK GRAMMAR. Abridged by Bishop Blomfield. *A New Edition, revised and enlarged* by E. S. Crooke. 12mo. 4s.

MAUREL, on the Character, Actions, and Writings of Wellington. Fcap. 8vo. 1s. 6d.

MAYNE'S (Capt.) Four Years in British Columbia and Vancouver Island. Illustrations. 8vo. 16s.

MEADE'S (Hon. Herbert) Ride through the Disturbed Districts of New Zealand to Lake Taupo, at the Time of the Rebellion ; with a Cruise among the South Sea Islands. With Illustrations. Medium 8vo. 14s.

MELVILLE'S (Hermann) Adventures amongst the Marquesas and South Sea Islands. 2 Vols. Post 8vo. 7s.

MEREDITH'S (Mrs. Charles) Notes and Sketches of New South Wales. Post 8vo. 2s.

MESSIAH (THE) : A Narrative of the Life, Travels, Death, Resurrection, and Ascension of our Blessed Lord. By A Layman. Map. 8vo. 18s.

MILLS' (Rev. John) Three Months' Residence at Nablus, with an Account of the Modern Samaritans. Illustrations. Post 8vo. 10s. 6d.

MILMAN'S (Dean) History of the Jews, from the earliest Period down to Modern Times. 3 Vols. Post 8vo. 18s.

———— History of Early Christianity, from the Birth of Christ to the Abolition of Paganism in the Roman Empire. *Fourth Edition.* 3 Vols. Post 8vo. 18s.

———— History of Latin Christianity, including that of the Popes to the Pontificate of Nicholas V. *Fourth Edition.* 9 Vols. Post 8vo. 54s.

———— Annals of St. Paul's Cathedral, from the time of the Romans to the funeral of the Duke of Wellington. *Second Edition.* Portrait and Illustrations. 8vo. 18s.

———— Character and Conduct of the Apostles considered as an Evidence of Christianity. 8vo. 10s. 6d.

———— Quinti Horatii Flacci Opera. *New Edition.* With 100 Woodcuts. Small 8vo. 7s. 6d.

———— Life of Quintus Horatius Flaccus. *Second Edition.* With Illustrations. 8vo. 9s.

———— Poetical Works. The Fall of Jerusalem—Martyr of Antioch—Belshazzar—Tamor—Anne Boleyn—Fazio, &c. With Portraits and Illustrations. 3 Vols. Fcap. 8vo. 18s.

———— Fall of Jerusalem. Fcap. 8vo. 1s.

———— (Capt. E. A.) Wayside Cross. Post 8vo. 2s.

MICHIE'S (Alexander) Siberian Overland Route from Peking to Petersburg. Maps and Illustrations. 8vo. 16s.

MODERN DOMESTIC COOKERY. Founded on Principles of Economy and Practical Knowledge. *New Edition.* Woodcuts. Fcap. 8vo. 5s.

MONGREDIEN'S (Augustus) Trees and Shrubs for English Plantation. A Selection and Description of the most Ornamental which will flourish in the open air in our climate. With Classified Lists. With 30 Illustrations. 8vo. 16s.

MOORE & JACKMAN on the Clematis as a Garden Flower. Descriptions of the Hardy Species and Varieties, with Directions for their Cultivation, and purposes for which they are adapted in Modern Gardening. Plates. 8vo. 10s. 6d.

MOORE'S (Thomas) Life and Letters of Lord Byron. *Cabinet Edition.* With Plates. 6 Vols. Fcap. 8vo. 18s.; or *Popular Edition,* with Portraits. Royal 8vo. 9s.

MOTLEY'S (J. L.) History of the United Netherlands: from the Death of William the Silent to the Twelve Years' Truce, 1609. *Library Edition.* Portraits. 4 Vols. 8vo. 60s. Or *Cabinet Edition,* 4 Vols. Post 8vo. 6s. each.

MOUHOT'S (Henri) Siam, Cambojia, and Lao; a Narrative of Travels and Discoveries. Illustrations. 2 vols. 8vo.

MOZLEY'S (Canon) Treatise on Predestination. 8vo. 14s.

———— Primitive Doctrine of Baptismal Regeneration. 8vo. 7s.6d.

MUNDY'S (General) Pen and Pencil Sketches in India. *Third Edition.* Plates. Post 8vo. 7s. 6d.

MUNRO'S (General) Life and Letters. By Rev. G. R. Gleig. Post 8vo. 3s. 6d.

MURCHISON'S (Sir Roderick) Russia in Europe and the Ural Mountains. With Coloured Maps, &c. 2 Vols. 4to. 5l. 5s.

———— Siluria; or, a History of the Oldest Rocks containing Organic Remains. *Fifth Edition.* Map and Plates. 8vo. 18s.

MURRAY'S RAILWAY READING. Containing:—

WELLINGTON. By LORD ELLESMERE. 6d.	MAHON'S JOAN OF ARC. 1s.
NIMROD ON THE CHASE. 1s.	HEAD'S EMIGRANT. 2s. 6d.
MUSIC AND DRESS. 1s.	NIMROD ON THE ROAD. 1s.
MILMAN'S FALL OF JERUSALEM. 1s.	CROKER ON THE GUILLOTINE. 1s.
MAHON'S "FORTY-FIVE." 3d.	HOLLWAY'S NORWAY. 2s.
LIFE OF THEODORE HOOK. 1s.	MAUREL'S WELLINGTON. 1s. 6d.
DEEDS OF NAVAL DARING. 2s. 6d.	CAMPBELL'S LIFE OF BACON. 2s. 6d.
THE HONEY BEE. 1s.	THE FLOWER GARDEN. 1s.
JAMES' ÆSOP'S FABLES. 2s. 6d.	TAYLOR'S NOTES FROM LIFE. 2s.
NIMROD ON THE TURF. 1s. 6d.	REJECTED ADDRESSES. 1s.
ART OF DINING. 1s. 6d.	PENN'S HINTS ON ANGLING. 1s.

MUSTERS' (CAPT.) At Home with the Patagonians; a Year's Wanderings over Untrodden Ground from the Straits of Magellan to the Rio Negro. *2nd Edition.* Illustrations. Post 8vo.

NAPIER'S (SIR CHAS.) Life, Journals, and Letters. By SIR W. NAPIER. *Second Edition.* Portraits. 4 Vols. Post 8vo. 48s.

———— **(SIR WM.)** Life and Letters. Edited by RT. HON. H. A. BRUCE. Portraits. 2 Vols. Crown 8vo. 28s.

———— English Battles and Sieges of the Peninsular War. *Fourth Edition.* Portrait. Post 8vo. 9s.

NAPOLEON AT FONTAINEBLEAU AND ELBA. A Journal of Occurrences and Notes of Conversations. By SIR NEIL CAMPBELL, C.B., British Commissioner. With a Memoir of that Officer By REV. A. N. C. MACLACHLAN, M.A. Portrait. 8vo. 15s.

NAUTICAL (THE) ALMANAC. Royal 8vo. **2s. 6d.** *(By Authority.)*

NAVY LIST. Monthly, 1s. 6d. and Quarterly, 3s. Post 8vo. *(By Authority.)*

NEW TESTAMENT. With Short Explanatory Commentary. By ARCHDEACON CHURTON, M.A., and ARCHDEACON BASIL JONES, M.A. With 110 authentic Views, &c. 2 Vols. Crown 8vo. 21s. bound.

NICHOLLS' (SIR GEORGE) History of the English, Irish and Scotch Poor Laws. 4 Vols. 8vo.

NICOLAS' (SIR HARRIS) Historic Peerage of England. Exhibiting the Origin, Descent, and Present State of every Title of Peerage which has existed in this Country since the Conquest. By WILLIAM COURTHOPE. 8vo. 30s.

NIMROD, On the Chace—Turf—and Road. With Portrait by Maclise and Plates by Alken. Crown 8vo. 5s. Or with Coloured Plates, 7s. 6d.

OLD LONDON; Papers read at the Archæological Institute. By various Authors. 8vo. 12s.

ORMATHWAITE'S (LORD) Astronomy and Geology—Darwin and Buckle—Progress and Civilisation. Crown 8vo. 6s.

OWEN'S (LIEUT.-COL.) Principles and Practice of Modern Artillery, including Artillery Material, Gunnery, and Organisation and Use of Artillery in Warfare. *Second Edition.* With Illustrations. 8vo. 15s.

OXENHAM'S (REV. W.) English Notes for Latin Elegiacs; designed for early Proficients in the Art of Latin Versification, with Prefatory Rules of Composition in Elegiac Metre. *Fourth Edition.* 12mo. 3s. 6d.

PALGRAVE'S (R. H. J.) Local Taxation of Great Britain and Ireland. 8vo. 6s.

PALLISER'S (MRS.) Brittany and its Byeways, its Inhabitants, and Antiquities. With Illustrations. Post 8vo. 12s.

———— Mottoes for Monuments, or Epitaphs selected for General Use and Study. With Illustrations. Crown 8vo. 7s. 6d.

PARIS' (Dr.) Philosophy in Sport made Science in Earnest; or, the First Principles of Natural Philosophy inculcated by aid of the Toys and Sports of Youth. *Ninth Edition.* Woodcuts. Post 8vo. 7s. 6d.

PARKMAN'S (Francis) Discovery of the Great West; or, the Valleys of the Mississippi and the Lakes of North America. An Historical Narrative. Map. 8vo. 6d.

PARKYNS' (Mansfield) Three Years' Residence in Abyssinia: with Travels in that Country. *Second Edition,* with Illustrations. Post 8vo. 7s. 6d.

PEEL'S (Sir Robert) Memoirs. Edited by Earl Stanhope and Mr. Cardwell. 2 Vols. Post 8vo. 7s. 6d. each.

PENN'S (Richard) Maxims and Hints for an Angler and Chess- player. Woodcuts. Fcap. 8vo. 1s.

PERCY'S (John, M.D.) Metallurgy. Vol. I. Fuel, Coal, Fire- Clays, Copper, Zinc, Brass, &c. *New Edition.* With Illustrations. 8vo. *(Nearly ready.)*

—— Vol. II. Iron and Steel. *New Edition.* With Illustrations. 8vo. *(In preparation.)*

—— Vol. III. Lead, including Desilverization and Cupellation. With Illustrations. 8vo. 30s.

—— Metallurgy. Vols. IV. and V. Gold, Silver, and Mercury, Platinum, Tin, Nickel, Cobalt, Antimony, Bismuth, Arsenic, and other Metals. With Illustrations. 8vo. *(In Preparation.)*

PHILLIPS' (John) Memoirs of William Smith. 8vo. 7s. 6d.

—— Geology of Yorkshire, The Coast, and Limestone District. Plates. 4to. Part I., 20s.—Part II., 30s.

—— Rivers, Mountains, and Sea Coast of Yorkshire. With Essays on the Climate, Scenery, and Ancient Inhabitants. *Second Edition,* Plates. 8vo. 15s.

PHILPOTTS' (Bishop) Letters to the late Charles Butler, on his "Book of the Roman Catholic Church." *New Edition.* Post 8vo. 6s.

PICK'S (Dr.) Popular Etymological Dictionary of the French Language. 8vo. 7s. 6d.

POPE'S (Alexander) Works. With Introductions and Notes, by Rev. Whitwell Elwin. Vols. I., II., VI., VII., VIII. With Portraits. 8vo. 10s. 6d. each.

PORTER'S (Rev. J. L.) Damascus, Palmyra and Lebanon. With Travels among the Giant Cities of Bashan and the Hauran. *New Edition.* Map and Woodcuts. Post 8vo. 7s. 6d.

PRAYER-BOOK (Illustrated), with Borders, Initials, Vig- nettes, &c. Edited, with Notes, by Rev. Thos. James. Medium 8vo. 18s. *cloth ;* 31s. 6 d. *calf ;* 36s. *morocco.*

PUSS IN BOOTS. With 12 Illustrations. By Otto Speckter. 16mo. 1s. 6d. Or coloured, 2s. 6d.

PRINCIPLES AT STAKE. Essays on Church Questions of the Day. 8vo. 12s. Contents :—

Ritualism and Uniformity.—Benjamin Shaw.

The Episcopate.—Bishop of Bath and Wells.

The Priesthood.—Dean of Canterbury.

National Education.—Rev. Alexander R. Grant.

Doctrine of the Eucharist.—Rev. G. H. Sumner.

Scripture and Ritual.—Canon Bernard.

Church in South Africa. — Arthur Mills.

Schismatical Tendency of Ritualism. — Rev. Dr. Salmon.

Revisions of the Liturgy.—Rev. W. G. Humphry.

Parties and Party Spirit.—Dean of Chester.

QUARTERLY REVIEW (The). 8vo. 6s.

RAMBLES in the Syrian Deserts. Post 8vo. 10s. 6d.

RANKE'S (Leopold) History of the Popes of Rome during the 16th and 17th Centuries. Translated from the German by Sarah Austin. Third Edition. 3 Vols. 8vo. 30s.

RASSAM'S (Hormuzd) Narrative of the British Mission to Abyssinia. With Notices of the Countries Traversed from Massowah to Magdala. Illustrations. 2 Vols. 8vo. 28s.

RAWLINSON'S (Rev. George) Herodotus. A New English Version. Edited with Notes and Essays. Second Edition. Maps and Woodcut. 4 Vols. 8vo. 48s.

———— Five Great Monarchies of Chaldæa, Assyria, Media, Babylonia, and Persia. Second Edition. With Maps and Illustrations. 3 Vols. 8vo. 42s.

REED'S (E. J.) Shipbuilding in Iron and Steel; a Practical Treatise, giving full details of Construction, Processes of Manufacture, and Building Arrangements. With 5 Plans and 250 Woodcuts. 8vo. 30s.

———— Iron-Clad Ships; their Qualities, Performances, and Cost. With Chapters on Turret Ships, Iron-Clad Rams, &c. With Illustrations. 8vo. 12s.

REJECTED ADDRESSES (The). By James and Horace Smith. New Edition. Woodcuts. Post 8vo. 3s. 6d.; or Cheap Edition, Fcap. 8vo. 1s.

RENNIE'S (D. F.) British Arms in Peking, 1860. Post 8vo. 12s.

———— Narrative of the British Embassy in China. Illustrations. 2 Vols. Post 8vo. 24s.

———— Story of Bhotan and the Dooar War. Map and Woodcut. Post 8vo. 12s.

RESIDENCE IN BULGARIA ; or, Notes on the Resources and Administration of Turkey, &c. By S. G. B. St.Clair and Charles A. Brophy. 8vo. 12s.

REYNOLDS' (Sir Joshua) Life and Times. By C. R. Leslie, R.A. and Tom Taylor. Portraits. 2 Vols. 8vo.

RICARDO'S (David) Political Works. With a Notice of his Life and Writings. By J. R. M'Culloch. New Edition. 8vo. 16s.

RIPA'S (Father) Thirteen Years' Residence at the Court of Peking. Post 8vo. 2s.

ROBERTSON'S (Canon) History of the Christian Church, from the Apostolic Age to the end of the Fifth Council of the Lateran, 1517. 4 Vols. 8vo.

The Work may be had separately.

Vol. 1.—a.d. 64-590. 8vo. 18s.

Vol. 2.—a.d. 590-1122. 8vo. 20s.

Vol. 3.—a.d. 1122-1303. 8vo. 18s.

Vol. 4.—a.d. 1303-1517. 8vo.

———— How shall we Conform to the Liturgy of the Church of England ? Third Edition. Post 8vo. 9s.

ROME. *See* Liddell and Smith.

ROWLAND'S (David) Manual of the English Constitution ; Its Rise, Growth, and Present State. Post 8vo. 10s. 6d.

———— Laws of Nature the Foundation of Morals. Post 8vo. 6s.

RUNDELL'S (MRS.) Modern Domestic Cookery. Woodcuts.
Fcap. 8vo. 5s.

RUXTON'S (GEORGE F.) Travels in Mexico; with Adventures among the Wild Tribes and Animals of the Prairies and Rocky Mountains. Post 8vo. 3s. 6d.

ROBINSON'S (REV. DR.) Biblical Researches in Palestine and the Adjacent Regions, 1838—52. *Third Edition.* Maps. 3 Vols. 8 vo. 42s.

———————— Physical Geography of the Holy Land. Post 8vo. 10s. 6d.

———————— (WM.) Alpine Flowers for English Gardens. With 70 Illustrations. Crown 8vo. 12s.

———————— Wild Garden; or, our Groves and Shrubberies made beautiful by the Naturalization of Hardy Exotic Plants. With Frontispiece. Small 8vo. 6s.

———————— Sub-Tropical Garden ; or, Beauty of Form in the Flower Garden. With Illustrations. Small 8vo. 7s. 6d.

SALE'S (SIR ROBERT) Brigade in Affghanistan. With an Account of the Defence of Jellalabad. By REV. G. R. GLEIG. Post 8vo. 2s.

SALLESBURY'S (EDWARD) "Children of the Lake." A Poem. Fcap. 8vo. 4s. 6d.

SCOTT'S (SIR G. G.) Secular and Domestic Architecture, Present and Future. 8vo. 9s.

———————— Rise and Development of Mediæval Architecture. 8vo. *(Nearly Ready.)*

———————— (DEAN) University Sermons. Post 8vo. 8s. 6d.

SCROPE'S (G. P.) Geology and Extinct Volcanoes of Central France. Illustrations. Medium 8vo. 30s.

SHAW'S (T. B.) Manual of English Literature. Edited, with Notes and Illustrations. Post 8vo. 7s. 6d.

———————— Specimens of English Literature. Selected from the Chief Writers. Post 8vo. 7s. 6d.

———————— (ROBERT) Visit to High Tartary, Yarkand, and Kashgar (formerly Chinese Tartary), and Return Journey over the Karakorum Pass. With Map and Illustrations. 8vo. 16s.

SMILES' (SAMUEL) Lives of British Engineers; from the Earliest Period. With 9 Portraits and 400 Illustrations. 4 Vols. 8vo. 21s. each.

———————— Lives of George and Robert Stephenson. With Portraits and Illustrations. Medium 8vo. 21s. Or *Popular Edition,* with Woodcuts. Post 8vo. 6s.

———————— Lives of Boulton and Watt. With Portraits and Illustrations. Medium 8vo. 21s.

———————— Self-Help. With Illustrations of Conduct and Perseverance. Post 8vo. 6s. Or in French. 5s.

———————— Character. A Companion Volume to "SELF-HELP." Post 8vo. 6s.

———————— Industrial Biography: Iron-Workers and Tool Makers. Post 8vo. 6s.

———————— Lives of Brindley and the Early Engineers. With Portrait and 50 Woodcuts. Post 8vo. 6s.

———————— Life of Thomas Telford. With a History of Roads and Travelling in England. Woodcuts. Post 8vo. 6s.

———————— Huguenots in England and Ireland : their Settlements, Churches and Industries. *Third Edition.* Post 8vo. 6s.

———————— Boy's Voyage round the World; including a Residence in Victoria, and a Journey by Rail across North America. With Illustrations. Post 8vo. 6s.

SHIRLEY (Evelyn P.) on Deer and Deer Parks, or some Account of English Parks, with Notes on the Management of Deer. Illustrations. 4to. 21s.

SIERRA LEONE; Described in Letters to Friends at Home. By A Lady. Post 8vo. 3s. 6d.

SIMMONS (Capt. T. F.) on the Constitution and Practice of Courts-Martial; with a Summary of the Law of Evidence, and some Notice of the Criminal Law of England with reference to the Trial of Civil Offences. Sixth Edition. 8vo.

STANLEY'S (Dean) Sinai and Palestine. Map. 8vo. 14s.

———— ———— Bible in the Holy Land; Extracted from the above Work. By a Lady. Woodcuts. Fcap. 8vo. 2s. 6d.

———————— St. Paul's Epistles to the Corinthians. With Dissertations and Notes. 8vo. 18s.

— · ———— History of the Eastern Church. Plans. 8vo. 12s.

———————— Jewish Church. Third Edition. 2 Vols. 8vo. 24s.

———————— Church of Scotland. 8vo. 7s. 6d.

————————— Historical Memorials of Canterbury Cathedral. Fifth Edition. Woodcuts. Post 8vo. 7s. 6d.

———————— ———— Westminster Abbey. Third Edition. With Illustrations. 8vo. 21s.

· ———— Sermons in the East, during a Tour with the Prince of Wales. 8vo. 9s.

——————— on Evangelical and Apostolical Teaching. Post 8vo. 7s. 6d.

———— - Addresses and Charges of Bishop Stanley. With Memoir. 8vo. 10s. 6d.

SMITH'S (Dr. Wm.) Dictionary of the Bible; its Antiquities, Biography, Geography, and Natural History. Illustrations. 3 Vols. 8vo. 105s.

———— Concise Dictionary of the Bible. With 300 Illustrations. Medium 8vo. 21s.

———— Smaller Dictionary of the Bible. With Illustrations. Post 8vo. 7s. 6d.

—— Historical Atlas of Ancient Geography—Biblical and Classical. (5 Parts.) Parts I. and II. Folio. 21s. each.

———— Greek and Roman Antiquities. With 500 Illustrations. Medium 8vo. 28s.

———————— —— Biography [and Mythology With 600 Illustrations. 3 Vols. Medium 8vo. 4l. 4s.

———————— Geography. 2 Vols. With 500 Illustrations. Medium 8vo. 56s.

———— Classical Dictionary of Mythology, Biography, and Geography. 1 Vol. With 750 Woodcuts. 8vo. 18s.

———— Smaller Classical Dictionary. With 200 Woodcuts. Crown 8vo. 7s. 6d.

———————— Greek and Roman Antiquities. With 200 Woodcuts. Crown 8vo. 7s. 6d.

———— Latin English Dictionary. With Tables of the Roman Calendar, Measures, Weights, and Money. Medium 8vo. 21s.

———— Smaller Latin-English Dictionary. 12mo. 7s. 6d.

———— English-Latin Dictionary. Medium 8vo. 21s.

———— Smaller English-Latin Dictionary. 12mo. 7s. 6d.

SMITH'S (Dr. Wm.) School Manual of English Grammar, with
Copious Exercises. Post 8vo. 3s. 6d.

———— Primary English Grammar. 16mo.

——————————— History of Britain. 12mo. 2s. 6d.

————— Principia Latina—Part I. A Grammar, Delectus, and
Exercise Book, with Vocabularies. With the ACCIDENCE arranged for
the "Public School Primer." 12mo. 3s. 6d.

—————————————— Part II. A Reading-book of Mythology, Geography, Roman Antiquities, and History. With Notes and
Dictionary. 12mo. 3s. 6d.

————————— Part III. A Latin Poetry Book.
Hexameters and Pentameters; Eclog. Ovidianæ; Latin Prosody.
12mo. 3s. 6d.

————————— Part IV. Latin Prose Composition.
Rules of Syntax, with Examples, Explanations of Synonyms, and
Exercises on the Syntax. 12mo. 3s. 6d.

————————— Part V. Short Tales and Anecdotes
for Translation into Latin. 12mo. 3s.

————— Latin-English Vocabulary and First Latin-English Dictionary for Phœdrus, Cornelius Nepos, and Cæsar. 12mo. 3s. 6d.

————— Student's Latin Grammar. Post 8vo. 6s.

————— Smaller Latin Grammar. 12mo. 3s. 6d.

————— Initia Græca, Part I. An Introduction to Greek;
comprehending Grammar, Delectus, and Exercise-book. With Vocabularies. 12mo. 3s. 6d.

————— Initia Græca, Part II. A Reading Book. Containing
Short Tales, Anecdotes, Fables, Mythology, and Grecian History.
12mo. 3s. 6d.

————— Initia Græca, Part III. Greek Prose Composition. Containing the Rules of Syntax, with copious Examples and Exercises.
12mo. 3s. 6d.

————— Student's Greek Grammar. By PROFESSOR CURTIUS.
Post 8vo. 6s.

————— Smaller Greek Grammar. 12mo. 3s. 6d.

————— Greek Accidence, extracted from the above work.
12mo. 2s. 6d.

————— Smaller History of England. Woodcuts. 16mo. 3s. 6d.

——————————— History of Greece. Woodcuts. 16mo. 3s. 6d.

——————————— History of Rome. Woodcuts. 16mo. 3s. 6d.

——————————— Classical Mythology. With Translations from
the Poets. Woodcuts. 16mo. 3s. 6d.

——————————— History of English Literature. 16mo. 3s. 6d.

——————————— Specimens of English Literature. 16mo. 3s. 6d.

——————————— Scripture History. Woodcuts. 16mo. 3s. 6d.

——————————— Ancient History of the East. Woodcuts. 16mo.
3s. 6d.

————————————— Geography. Woodcuts. 16mo. 3s. 6d.

————— (PHILIP) History of the Ancient World, from the
Creation to the Fall of the Roman Empire, A.D. 455. Fourth Edition.
3 Vols. 8vo. 31s. 6d.

————— (REV. A. C.) Attractions of the Nile and its Banks.
Woodcuts. 2 Vols. Post 8vo. 15s.

STUDENT'S HUME. A History of England from the Invasion of Julius Cæsar. By DAVID HUME. Continued to 1868. Woodcuts. Post 8vo. 7s. 6d.
    *** Questions on the above Work, 12mo. 2s.

————— HISTORY OF FRANCE; from the Earliest Times to the Establishment of the Second Empire, 1852. By REV. H. W. JERVIS. Woodcuts. Post 8vo. 7s. 6d.

————— HISTORY OF ROME; from the Earliest Times to the Establishment of the Empire. By DEAN LIDDELL. Woodcuts. Crown 8vo. 7s. 6d.

————— GIBBON; an Epitome of the Decline and Fall of the Roman Empire. Woodcuts. Post 8vo. 7s. 6d.

————— HISTORY OF GREECE; from the Earliest Times to the Roman Conquest. By WM. SMITH, D.C.L. Woodcuts. Crown 8vo. 7s. 6d.
    *** Questions on the above Work, 12mo. 2s.

————— ANCIENT HISTORY OF THE EAST; Egypt, Assyria, Babylonia, Media, Persia, Asia Minor, and Phœnicia. By PHILIP SMITH. Woodcuts. Post 8vo. 7s. 6d.

————— OLD TESTAMENT HISTORY; from the Creation to the Return of the Jews from Captivity. Maps and Woodcuts. Post 8vo. 7s. 6d.

————— NEW TESTAMENT HISTORY. With an Introduction connecting the History of the Old and New Testaments. Maps and Woodcuts. Post 8vo. 7s. 6d.

————— ANCIENT GEOGRAPHY. By REV. W. L. BEVAN. Woodcuts. Post 8vo. 7s. 6d.

————— MODERN GEOGRAPHY; Mathematical, Physical, and Descriptive. By REV. W. L. BEVAN. Woodcuts. Post 8vo. 7s. 6d.

————— ENGLISH LANGUAGE. By GEO. P. MARSH. Post 8vo. 7s. 6d.

————— LITERATURE. By T. B. SHAW, M.A. Post 8vo. 7s. 6d.

————— SPECIMENS of English Literature from the Chief Writers. By T. B. SHAW, Post 8vo. 7s. 6d.

————— MORAL PHILOSOPHY. By WILLIAM FLEMING, D.D. Post 8vo. 7s. 6d.

————— BLACKSTONE. By R. MALCOLM KERR, LL.D. Post 8vo. 7s. 6d.

SPALDING'S (CAPTAIN) Tale of Frithiof. Translated from the Swedish of ESIAS TEGNER. Post 8vo. 7s. 6d.

STEPHEN'S (REV. W. R.) Life and Times of St. Chrysostom. With Portrait. 8vo. 15s.

ST. CLAIR and BROPHY'S RESIDENCE IN BULGARIA; or, Notes on the Resources and Administration of Turkey. 8vo. 12s.

ST. JOHN'S (CHARLES) Wild Sports and Natural History of the Highlands. Post 8vo. 3s. 6d.

————— (BAYLE) Adventures in the Libyan Desert. Post 8vo. 2s.

STORIES FOR DARLINGS. With Illustrations. Sq. 16mo. 5s.

STOTHARD'S (THOS.) Life. With Personal Reminiscences. By Mrs. BRAY. With Portrait and 60 Woodcuts. 4to. 21s.

STREET'S (G. E.) Gothic Architecture in Spain. *Second Edition.* With Illustrations. Medium 8vo. 30s.

STANHOPE'S (Earl) Reign of Queen Anne until the Peace of Utrecht. 1701—13. *Library Edition.* 8vo. 16s. *Cabinet Edition.* With Portrait, 2 Vols. Post 8vo. 10s.

———— History of England, from the Peace of Utrecht to the Peace of Versailles, 1713-83. *Library Edition.* 7 vols. 8vo. 93s. Or, *Cabinet Edition,* 7 vols. Post 8vo. 6s. each.

———— British India, from its Origin to 1783. P. 8vo. 3s 6d.

———— History of "Forty-Five." Post 8vo. 3s.

———— Spain under Charles the Second. Post 8vo. 6s. 6d.

———— Historical and Critical Essays. Post 8vo. 3s. 6d.

———— Life of Belisarius. Post 8vo. 10s. 6d.

———— Condé. Post 8vo. 3s. 6d.

———— William Pitt. Portraits. 4 Vols. P. 8vo. 24s.

———— Miscellanies. 2 Vols. Post 8vo. 13s.

———— Story of Joan of Arc. Fcap. 8vo. 1s.

STYFFE (Knutt) On the Strength of Iron and Steel. Translated by C. P. Sandberg. With Preface by Dr. Percy. With Plates. 8vo. 12s.

SOMERVILLE'S (Mary) Physical Geography. *Sixth Edition,* *Revised.* By W. H. Bates. Portrait. Post 8vo. 9s.

———— Connexion of the Physical Sciences. *Ninth Edition.* Woodcuts. Post 8vo. 9s.

———— Molecular and Microscopic Science. Illustrations. 2 Vols. Post 8vo. 21s.

———— Personal Recollections from Early Life to Advanced Age. Crown 8vo. (*In Preparation.*)

SOUTH'S (John F.) Household Surgery; or, Hints on Emergencies. Woodcuts. Fcp. 8vo. 4s. 6d.

SOUTHEY'S (Robert) Book of the Church. Post 8vo. 7s. 6d.

———— Lives of Bunyan and Cromwell. Post 8vo. 2s.

SYBEL'S (Von) History of Europe during the French Revolution, 1789—1795. 4 Vols. 8vo. 48s.

SYMONDS' (Rev. W.) Records of the Rocks; or Notes on the Geology, Natural History, and Antiquities of North and South Wales, Siluria, Devon, and Cornwall. With Illustrations. Crown 8vo. 12s.

TAYLOR'S (Sir Henry) Notes from Life. Fcap. 8vo. 2s.

THOMS' (W. J.) Longevity of Man; its Facts and its Fiction. Including Observations on the more Remarkable Instances. Post 8vo.

THOMSON'S (Archbishop) Lincoln's Inn Sermons. 8vo. 10s. 6d.

———— Life in the Light of God's Word. Post 8vo. 5s.

TOCQUEVILLE'S (M. de) State of France before the Revolution, 1789. Translated by Henry Reeve. 2nd *Edition.* 8vo.

TOZER'S (H. F.) Highlands of Turkey, with Visits to Mounts Ida, Athos, Olympus, and Pelion. Illustrations. 2 Vols. Crown 8vo. 24s.

TRISTRAM'S (Canon) Great Sahara. Illustrations. Post 8vo. 15s.

———— Land of Moab; Travels on the East side of the Dead Sea and the Jordan. Illustrations. Crown 8vo.

TWISS' (Horace) Life of Lord Eldon. 2 Vols. Post 8vo. 21s.

TYLOR'S (E. B.) Early History of Mankind, and the Development of Civilization. *Second Edition.* 8vo. 12s.

———— Primitive Culture; the Development of Mythology Philosophy, Religion, Art, and Custom. 2 Vols. 8vo. 24s.

VAMBERY'S (ARMINIUS) Travels from Teheran across the Turkoman Desert on the Eastern Shore of the Caspian. Illustrations. 8vo. 21s.

VAN LENNEP'S (HENRY J.) Travels in Asia Minor. With Illustrations of Biblical Literature, and Archæology. With Woodcuts. 2 Vols. Post 8vo. 24s.

WELLINGTON'S Despatches; during his Campaigns in India, Denmark, Portugal, Spain, the Low Countries, and France. Compiled by COLONEL GURWOOD, C.B. 8 Vols. 8vo. 20s. each.

———————— Supplementary Despatches, relating to India, Ireland, Denmark, Spanish America, Spain, Portugal, France, Congress of Vienna, Waterloo and Paris. Edited by his SON. 14 Vols. 8vo. 20s. each.

. An Index to the Despatches. 8vo. 20s.

———————— Civil and Political Correspondence. Edited by his SON. Vols. I. to IV. 8vo. 20s. each.

———————— Selections from Despatches. 8vo. 18s.

———————— Speeches in Parliament. 2 Vols. 8vo. 42s.

WHEELER'S (G.) Choice of a Dwelling; a Practical Handbook of Useful Information on all Points connected with Hiring, Buying, or Building a House. *Third Edition.* Plans. Post 8vo. 7s. 6d.

WHITE'S (HENRY) Massacre of St. Bartholomew. Based on Documents in the Archives of France. 8vo. 16s.

WHYMPER'S (EDWARD) Scrambles among the Alps. With the First Ascent of the Matterhorn, and Notes on Glacial Phenomena. *Second Edition.* With 100 Illustrations. 8vo. 21s.

———————— (FREDERICK) Travels and Adventures in Alaska and on the River Yukon. With Illustrations. 8vo. 16s.

WILBERFORCE'S (WILLIAM) Life. By his Son, the BISHOP OF WINCHESTER. Portrait. Post 8vo. 6s.

WILKINSON'S (SIR J. G.) Popular Account of the Ancient Egyptians. With 500 Woodcuts. 2 Vols. Post 8vo. 12s.

WOOD'S (CAPTAIN) Journey to the Source of the Oxus. *New Edition.* With an Essay on the Geography of the Valley of the Oxus. By COLONEL HENRY YULE, C.C. With Map. 8vo. 12s.

WORDSWORTH'S (BISHOP OF LINCOLN) Athens and Attica. *Fourth Edition.* Plates. Post 8vo. 5s.

———————— Pictorial, Descriptive, and Historical Account of Greece. *New Edition.* With 600 Woodcuts. Royal 8vo. 21s.

YULE'S (COLONEL) Book of Marco Polo, concerning the Kingdoms and Marvels of the East. A new English Version. Illustrated by the Light of Oriental Writers and Modern Travels. With Maps and 80 Plates. 2 Vols. Medium 8vo. 42s.

ZINCKE'S (REV. F. B.) Winter in the United States. Post 8vo. 10s. 6d.

BRADBURY, AGNEW, & CO., PRINTERS, WHITEFRIARS.